KB232689

다빈출 코드

2027 수능대비

듣기

The future belongs to those who believe in the beauty of their dreams.

미래는 자신의 꿈이 아름답다고 믿는 사람들의 것이다.

- Eleanor Roosevelt

대학수학능력시험 영어 영역 절대평가의 의미와 학습 전략

01 수능 영어 절대평가의 목적

A. 지나친 경쟁을 지양하고 학습 부담을 경감시킴

B. 의사소통 중심의 수업 활성화 등 학생들의 실제 영어 능력을 향상시키는 방향으로 학교 영어교육이 정상화되는 계기를 마련

02 상대평가 vs. 절대평가

구분	상대평가	절대평가
점수 산정 방식	다른 학생들의 점수에 따라 등급이 달라짐	다른 학생들의 순위에 관계없이 본인의 점수에 따라 등급이 결정됨
시험 문항 출제	변별력을 위해 일정 수의 문항은 고난도로 출제하는 것이 불가피	학생 변별보다는 성취 수준을 달성했는지를 중점적으로 고려하여 출제
점수 제공 방식	백분위, 표준점수, 등급(9등급)	등급(9등급)

▶ 백분위와 표준점수를 활용하여 수험생들의 상대적 실력을 평가하는 상대평가 제도와 달리, 절대평가 제도에서는 학생 변별보다는 학력 성취 수준의 달성 여부가 문항 출제의 기준이 되며, 이는 곧 노력 여하에 따라 누구든 높은 등급을 받을 수 있음을 의미한다.

03 수능 영어 영역 대학별 반영 방식

모집시기	반영방법	대학 수
수시	최저학력기준	151개교
정시	최저학력기준	0개교
	비율반영	186개교
	가점부여	10개교
	감점부여	3개교

04 주요 대학 영역별 반영비율

대학명		2026학년도 수능 영역별 반영비율(%)				영어 영역 가점/감점 여부
		국어	수학	영어	탐구	
고려대	인문	35.7	35.7		28.6	등급당 2.4, 4.8, 7.2 …씩 감점 반영
	자연	35.7	35.7		28.6	등급당 3, 6, 9 …씩 감점 반영
서강대	인문	43.3	36.7		20	1등급에 100점 가점 부여 (9등급 92점)
	자연	43.3	36.7		20	

서울대		33.3	40		26.7	등급당 0.5, 2, 4 …씩 감점 반영
성균관대	인문	40	30	10	20	
		30	40	10	20	
	자연	20	40	10	30	
		20	40	10	30	
연세대	인문	33.3	33.3	16.7	16.7	1등급에 100점 부여 (등급별 감점 커짐)
	자연	33.3	33.3	16.7	16.7	
이화여대	인문	30	30	20	20	1~3 등급에 5점 4~5 등급에 4점 …
	자연	30	30	20	20	
한양대	인문	35	35	10	20	1등급에 100점 부여 (등급별 감점 커짐)
	자연	35	35	10	20	

*위 수치는 대략적인 수치이므로 전형별, 모집단위별 세부적인 내용은 각 대학 입시 요강 참고

05 요약

A. 1등급 학생 수 증가

절대평가의 등급 산정 기준이 표준점수가 아닌 원점수이므로 상위권의 척도라 할 수 있는 1등급의 학생 수가 증가할 가능성이 있다.

B. 낮은 영어 비중의 유지

주요 대학들의 2026학년도 정시모집 전형을 보면 영어 영역 반영비율이 소폭 상승한 연세대 외에는 2025학년도와 유사한 수준이다. 이들 대학 대부분이 영어 영역 반영비율을 국어, 수학 등에 비해 낮게 유지하고 있어 영어의 입시 영향력이 약한 편이다.

★ 학습 전략 ★

A. 상위권

상위권 학생들의 경우 영어 1등급을 받는 것이 중요한데, 1·2점차로 당락이 좌우되므로 실수로 문제를 틀려 등급이 내려가지 않도록 주의해야 한다. 지금까지 공부해온 방식에서 크게 벗어나지 않되 EBS 교재 이외의 지문이나 변형 방식 등에 주목하고, 실수를 줄일 수 있도록 잘 틀리는 유형은 오답노트를 작성하는 것도 좋다.

B. 중위권 ~ 하위권

중위권 학생들의 경우 1~2등급으로 성적을 끌어 올려 상위권 대학 진입을 노려볼 수 있기 때문에 영어의 중요성이 더욱 클 수 있다. 중위권 학생들은 어휘와 구문을 탄탄하게 학습하고 어려운 유형(빈칸 추론 등)보다는 쉬운 유형을 모두 맞히는 전략을 세우는 것이 효율적이다. 또한 실제 시험과 같이 70분 안에 문제를 풀어보는 연습이 필요하다. 하위권 학생들의 경우 기초적인 문법과 어휘 학습을 통해 기본을 다지고 한 문장 한 문장 지문을 꼼꼼히 해석하는 연습을 할 필요가 있다.

구성과 특징

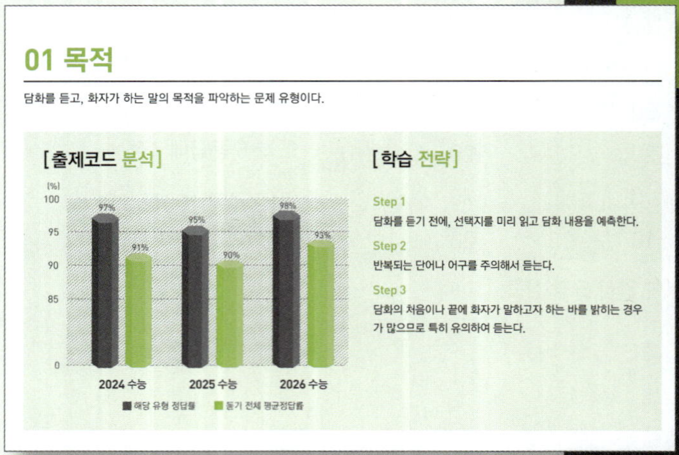

01 목적

담화를 듣고, 화자가 하는 말의 목적을 파악하는 문제 유형이다.

[출제코드 분석]

[학습 전략]

Step 1
담화를 듣기 전에, 선택지를 미리 읽고 담화 내용을 예측한다.

Step 2
반복되는 단어나 어구를 주의해서 듣는다.

Step 3
담화의 처음이나 끝에 화자가 말하고자 하는 바를 밝히는 경우가 많으므로 특히 유의하여 듣는다.

출제코드 분석과 학습 전략

출제코드 분석

최근 수능 듣기 문제의 유형별 정답률을 분석한 내용을 도표로 나타냈습니다. 학생들이 어려워하는 문제 유형을 참고하여 학습 전략에 반영할 수 있게 하였습니다.

학습 전략

시험에 대비하기 위해 출제코드별로 효과적으로 학습하는 방법을 제시했습니다.

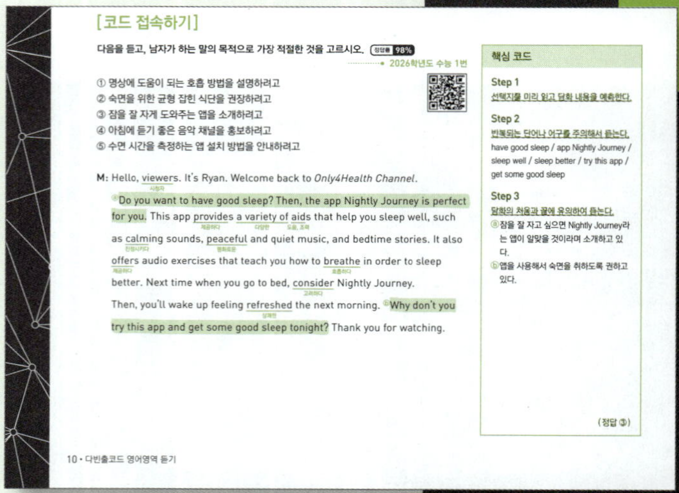

[코드 접속하기]

다음을 듣고, 남자가 하는 말의 목적으로 가장 적절한 것을 고르시오. 정답률 98%

2026학년도 수능 1번

① 명상에 도움이 되는 호흡 방법을 설명하려고
② 숙면을 위한 균형 잡힌 식단을 권장하려고
③ 잠을 잘 자게 도와주는 앱을 소개하려고
④ 아침에 듣기 좋은 음악 채널을 홍보하려고
⑤ 수면 시간을 측정하는 앱 설치 방법을 안내하려고

M: Hello, viewers. It's Ryan. Welcome back to *Only4Health Channel*. ⓐDo you want to have good sleep? Then, the app Nightly Journey is perfect for you. This app provides a variety of aids that help you sleep well, such as calming sounds, peaceful and quiet music, and bedtime stories. It also offers audio exercises that teach you how to breathe in order to sleep better. Next time when you go to bed, consider Nightly Journey. Then, you'll wake up feeling refreshed the next morning. ⓑWhy don't you try this app and get some good sleep tonight? Thank you for watching.

핵심 코드

Step 1
선택지를 미리 읽고 담화 내용을 예측한다.

Step 2
반복되는 단어나 어구를 주의해서 듣는다.
have good sleep / app Nightly Journey / sleep well / sleep better / try this app / get some good sleep

Step 3
담화의 처음과 끝에 유의하여 듣는다.
ⓐ잠을 잘 자고 싶으면 Nightly Journey라는 앱이 알맞을 것이라며 소개하고 있다.
ⓑ앱을 사용해서 숙면을 취하도록 권하고 있다.

(정답 ③)

10 • 다빈출코드 영어영역 듣기

코드 접속하기

기출 예제

출제코드의 대표 기출 예제와 대본 및 어휘 해설을 제시했습니다.

핵심 코드

출제코드에서 학습한 학습 전략을 적용하여 기출 예제를 풀어볼 수 있습니다.

코드 공략하기

출제코드가 적용된 학력평가(교육청)와 수능 기출 문제 중 우수 문제를 선별하여 제시했습니다. 코드 접속하기에서 학습하고 연습한 핵심 내용과 전략을 적용하여 문제를 풀며 실전 감각과 문제 해결 능력을 향상시킬 수 있습니다.

Pattern Practice

듣기 문제에 자주 나오는 표현을 듣고 따라 말하면서 익힐 수 있도록 했습니다.

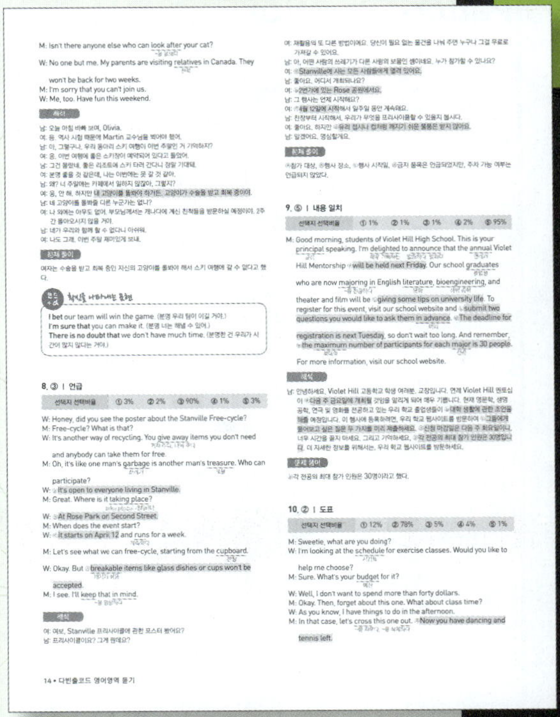

친절한 정답 해설

교재에 수록된 문제에 대해 자세하고 친절한 해설을 제공합니다. 듣기 대본의 해석과 어휘 및 문제 해설을 제공하고, 문제 해결에 단서가 되는 부분을 눈에 띄게 표시하여 문제 해결 능력을 한층 높일 수 있도록 했습니다.

코드 +α

대화에 자주 나오는 유용한 표현과 배경지식을 제시했습니다.

목차

학습 계획

하루 40분, 27일 완성 프로젝트

출제코드별 분석과 학습 전략	대표 기출 예제로 코드 접속하기	모의고사로 코드 공략하기
시험에 나오는 유형과 핵심 전략 학습하기	학습한 핵심 전략을 대표 기출 문제에 적용하는 연습하기	다양한 기출문제를 풀며 문제 해결력을 높이고 실전 감각 향상시키기

PLANS		DAYS	맞은 개수	틀린 문제 복습
유형별 출제 분석	pp.10-23	월 일	/ 18	☐
제1회 초급 모의고사	pp.26-31	월 일	/ 17	☐
제2회 초급 모의고사	pp.32-37	월 일	/ 17	☐
제3회 초급 모의고사	pp.38-43	월 일	/ 17	☐
제4회 초급 모의고사	pp.44-49	월 일	/ 17	☐
제5회 초급 모의고사	pp.50-55	월 일	/ 17	☐
제6회 초급 모의고사	pp.56-61	월 일	/ 17	☐
제7회 초급 모의고사	pp.62-67	월 일	/ 17	☐
제8회 초급 모의고사	pp.68-73	월 일	/ 17	☐
제9회 초급 모의고사	pp.74-79	월 일	/ 17	☐
제1회 중급 모의고사	pp.82-87	월 일	/ 17	☐
제2회 중급 모의고사	pp.88-93	월 일	/ 17	☐
제3회 중급 모의고사	pp.94-99	월 일	/ 17	☐
제4회 중급 모의고사	pp.100-105	월 일	/ 17	☐
제5회 중급 모의고사	pp.106-111	월 일	/ 17	☐
제6회 중급 모의고사	pp.112-117	월 일	/ 17	☐
제7회 중급 모의고사	pp.118-123	월 일	/ 17	☐
제8회 중급 모의고사	pp.124-129	월 일	/ 17	☐
제9회 중급 모의고사	pp.130-135	월 일	/ 17	☐
제1회 고급 모의고사	pp.138-145	월 일	/ 17	☐
제2회 고급 모의고사	pp.146-153	월 일	/ 17	☐
제3회 고급 모의고사	pp.154-161	월 일	/ 17	☐
제4회 고급 모의고사	pp.162-169	월 일	/ 17	☐
제5회 고급 모의고사	pp.170-177	월 일	/ 17	☐
제6회 고급 모의고사	pp.178-185	월 일	/ 17	☐
多빈출 Pattern Practice 1 ~ 3	pp.188-193	월 일	1차 ☐ 2차 ☐ 3차 ☐	
多빈출 Pattern Practice 4 ~ 5	pp.194-197	월 일	1차 ☐ 2차 ☐ 3차 ☐	

다빈출 코드

영어
듣기

PART 1

유형별 출제 분석

X

유형 01 ~ 14

코드 접속하기

01 목적

담화를 듣고, 화자가 하는 말의 목적을 파악하는 문제 유형이다.

[출제코드 분석]

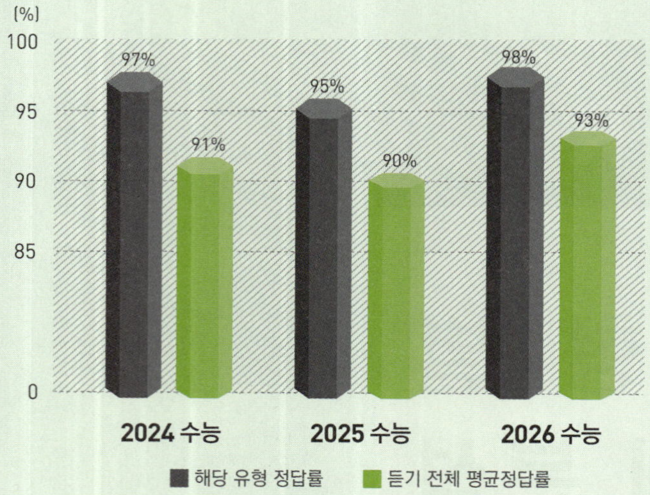

[학습 전략]

Step 1

담화를 듣기 전에, 선택지를 미리 읽고 담화 내용을 예측한다.

Step 2

반복되는 단어나 어구를 주의해서 듣는다.

Step 3

담화의 처음이나 끝에 화자가 말하고자 하는 바를 밝히는 경우가 많으므로 특히 유의하여 듣는다.

[코드 접속하기]

다음을 듣고, 남자가 하는 말의 목적으로 가장 적절한 것을 고르시오. 정답률 98%

● 2026학년도 수능 1번

① 명상에 도움이 되는 호흡 방법을 설명하려고
② 숙면을 위한 균형 잡힌 식단을 권장하려고
③ 잠을 잘 자게 도와주는 앱을 소개하려고
④ 아침에 듣기 좋은 음악 채널을 홍보하려고
⑤ 수면 시간을 측정하는 앱 설치 방법을 안내하려고

M: Hello, viewers(시청자). It's Ryan. Welcome back to *Only4Health Channel*. ⓐDo you want to have good sleep? Then, the app Nightly Journey is perfect for you. This app provides(제공하다) a variety of(다양한) aids(도움, 조력) that help you sleep well, such as calming(진정시키다) sounds, peaceful(평화로운) and quiet music, and bedtime stories. It also offers(제공하다) audio exercises that teach you how to breathe(호흡하다) in order to sleep better. Next time when you go to bed, consider(고려하다) Nightly Journey. Then, you'll wake up feeling refreshed(상쾌한) the next morning. ⓑWhy don't you try this app and get some good sleep tonight? Thank you for watching.

핵심 코드

Step 1

선택지를 미리 읽고 담화 내용을 예측한다.

Step 2

반복되는 단어나 어구를 주의해서 듣는다.

have good sleep / app Nightly Journey / sleep well / sleep better / try this app / get some good sleep

Step 3

담화의 처음과 끝에 유의하여 듣는다.

ⓐ잠을 잘 자고 싶으면 Nightly Journey라는 앱이 알맞을 것이라며 소개하고 있다.

ⓑ앱을 사용해서 숙면을 취하도록 권하고 있다.

(정답 ③)

02 요지 · 의견 · 주장 · 주제

대화나 담화를 듣고, 화자의 의견이나 주장하는 바가 무엇인지 또는 주제가 무엇인지 파악하는 문제 유형이다.

[출제코드 분석]

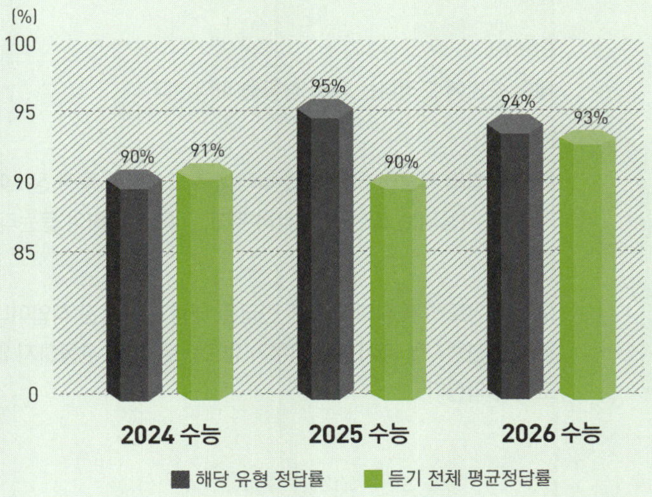

[학습 전략]

Step 1

화자 중 누구의 의견이나 주장을 묻는지 확인하고, 그 화자의 말에 집중한다.

Step 2

화자가 반복적으로 사용하는 특정 단어나 어구에 주목한다.

Step 3

대화의 후반부에 화자의 생각을 다시 한 번 집약적으로 표현하는 경우가 많으므로 이에 유의하여 듣는다.

[코드 접속하기]

대화를 듣고, 남자의 의견으로 가장 적절한 것을 고르시오. 정답률 98%

2022학년도 수능 2번

① 여행 전에 합리적으로 예산을 계획해야 한다.
② 여행 가서 할 것을 너무 많이 계획하면 안 된다.
③ 인생에서 자신의 원칙을 고수하는 것이 중요하다.
④ 여행은 사고의 폭을 확장시켜 사람을 성장하게 한다.
⑤ 보호자 없이 학생끼리 여행하는 것은 안전하지 않다.

M: Monica. Have you made plans for your trip to Busan?

W: Yes, Dad. I'm going to the beach and visiting an aquarium in the morning. Then I'll eat lunch at a fish market and go hiking.

M: Hold on! ⓐThat sounds quite demanding. (demanding: 부담이 큰, 힘든)

W: You know, it's my first trip after starting college.

M: I understand, but I think ⓑyou shouldn't plan too many things to do for a trip.

W: Well, I only have one day, and I want to experience as much as possible.

M: ⓒYou'll be worn out if you stick to your plan. Also, consider the time it takes to move to each place. (be worn out: 몹시 지치다 / stick to: ~을 고수하다 / consider: 고려하다, 감안하다)

W: I guess you're right. And there could be a long waiting line at some places.

M: Right. That's why ⓓyou shouldn't fill your trip plan with too many things.

W: Okay. I'll revise my plan. (revise: 변경하다)

핵심 코드

Step 1
화자 중 누구의 의견을 묻는지 확인하고 이에 집중한다.
남자의 말에 집중한다.

Step 2
화자의 말에서 반복되는 특정 단어나 어구에 주목한다.
ⓐ꽤 힘들어 보임
ⓑ여행에 너무 많은 할 것을 계획하면 안 됨
ⓒ계획을 고수하면 몹시 지칠 수 있음
ⓓ여행을 너무 많은 것들로 채우면 안 됨

(정답 ②)

03 관계

대화를 나누고 있는 두 사람의 관계나 대화가 이루어지고 있는 장소를 유추하는 문제 유형이다.

[출제코드 분석]

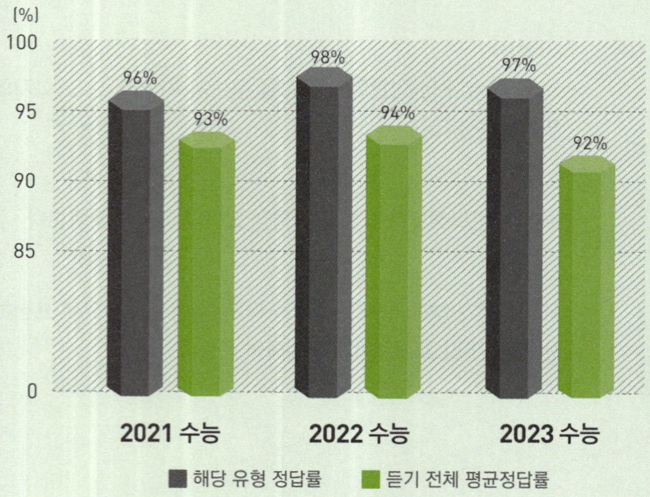

[학습 전략]

Step 1

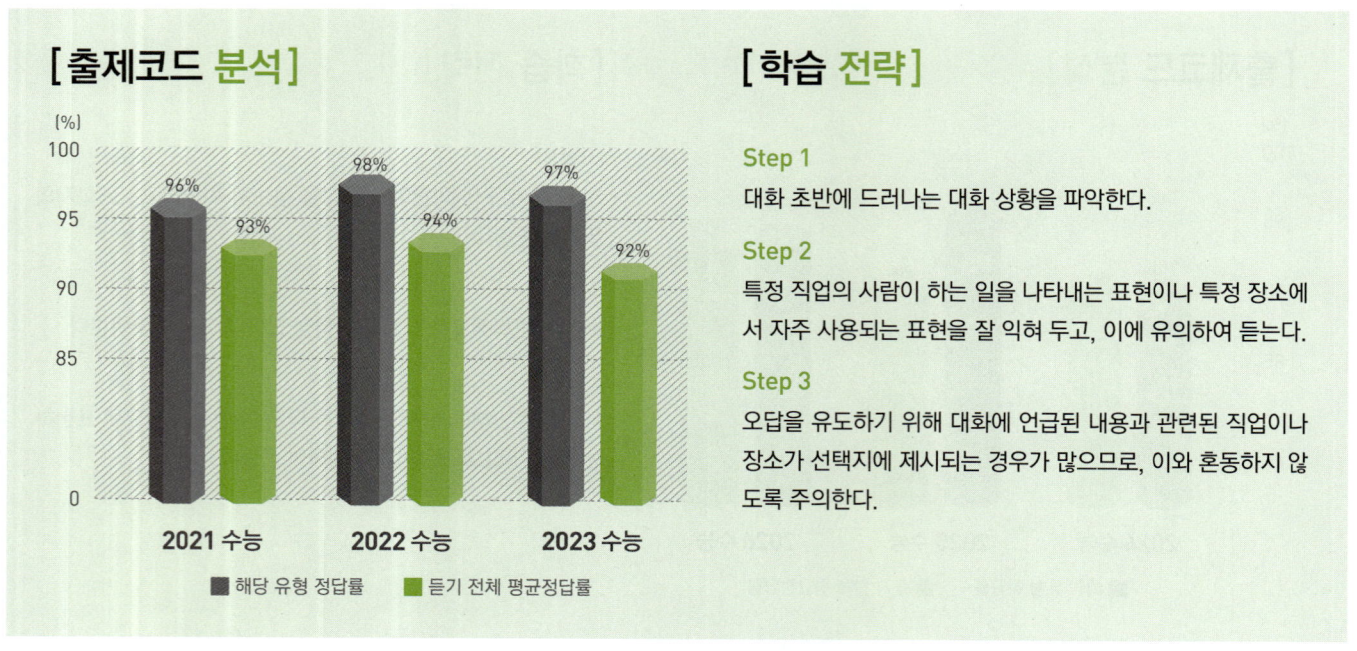

대화 초반에 드러나는 대화 상황을 파악한다.

Step 2

특정 직업의 사람이 하는 일을 나타내는 표현이나 특정 장소에서 자주 사용되는 표현을 잘 익혀 두고, 이에 유의하여 듣는다.

Step 3

오답을 유도하기 위해 대화에 언급된 내용과 관련된 직업이나 장소가 선택지에 제시되는 경우가 많으므로, 이와 혼동하지 않도록 주의한다.

[코드 접속하기]

대화를 듣고, 두 사람의 관계를 가장 잘 나타낸 것을 고르시오. 정답률 96%

• 2021학년도 수능 3번

① 학생 – 건축가　② 신문 기자 – 화가　③ 탐험가 – 환경 운동가
④ 건물 관리인 – 정원사　⑤ 교사 – 여행사 직원

M: Hello, Ms. Watson. ⓐThank you for accepting(수락하다) my interview request(요청).

W: My pleasure. You must be Michael from Windmore High School.

M: Yes. I'm honored(영광으로 생각하여) to interview ⓑthe person who designed the school I'm attending(다니다).

W: Thank you. I'm very proud of that design.

M: What was the concept behind it?

W: When ⓒplanning the design of the school building, I wanted to incorporate((일부로) 포함하다) elements(요소) of nature into it.

M: I see. Did you apply(적용하다) this concept in any other building designs?

W: Yes. Skyforest Tower. My design included(포함하다) mini gardens for each floor and a roof-top((건물) 옥상) garden, making the building look like a rising forest.

M: That's impressive(인상적인). Actually, my art teacher is taking us on a field trip(현장학습) there next week.

W: Really? Make sure to visit the observation deck(전망대) on the 32nd floor. The view is spectacular(장관을 이루는).

M: Thanks. I'll check it out with my classmates.

핵심 코드

Step 1

대화 초반에 드러나는 상황을 파악한다.

ⓐ여자가 남자의 인터뷰 요청을 수락한 상황이다.

Step 2

특정 직업을 유추할 수 있는 표현에 유의하여 듣는다.

여자는 ⓑ남자가 다니는 학교 ⓒ건물을 설계한 사람이다.

(정답 ①)

04 그림 일치

대화를 듣고, 그림에서 대화의 내용과 일치하지 않는 부분을 고르는 문제 유형이다.

[출제코드 분석]

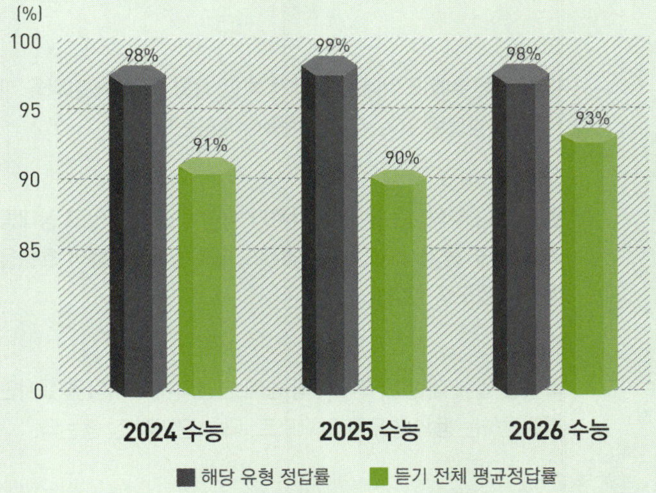

[학습 전략]

Step 1

대화를 듣기 전에, 그림 속의 인물이나 사물의 특징과 위치를 파악한다.

Step 2

모양이나 위치를 나타내는 표현을 잘 익혀 두고, 그림 속의 인물이나 사물을 묘사하는 해당 표현을 집중해서 듣는다.

[코드 접속하기]

대화를 듣고, 그림에서 대화의 내용과 일치하지 않는 것을 고르시오. 정답률 90%

2023년 6월 교육청(고1) 4번

M: Kayla, I heard you went busking on the street last weekend.

W: It was amazing! I've got a picture here. Look!

M: Oh, ⓐyou're wearing the hat I gave you.

W: Yeah, I really like it.

M: Looks great. ⓑThis boy playing the guitar next to you must be your brother Kevin.

W: You're right. He played while I sang.

M: Cool. Why did you ⓒleave the guitar case open?

W: That's for the audience(관객). If they like our performance(공연), they give us some money.

M: Oh, and ⓓyou set up two speakers!

W: I did. I recently bought them.

M: I see. And did you design ⓔthat poster on the wall?

W: Yeah. My brother and I worked on it together.

M: It sounds like you really had a lot of fun!

핵심 코드

Step 1

대화를 듣기 전에 그림 속 인물 및 사물의 특징과 위치를 파악한다.

Step 2

그림 속 인물 및 사물들을 묘사하는 표현에 집중하여 듣는다.

ⓐ모자를 쓰고 있는 여자
ⓑ여자 옆에서 기타를 연주하는 소년
ⓒ열어 둔 기타 케이스
ⓓ스피커: 스피커 두 대가 있어야 하는데 한 대만 있다.
ⓔ벽에 있는 포스터

(정답 ④)

05 할 일 · 부탁한 일

대화를 듣고, 남자나 여자 혹은 두 사람이 앞으로 할 일이나 상대방에게 부탁한 일을 고르는 문제 유형이다.

[출제코드 분석]

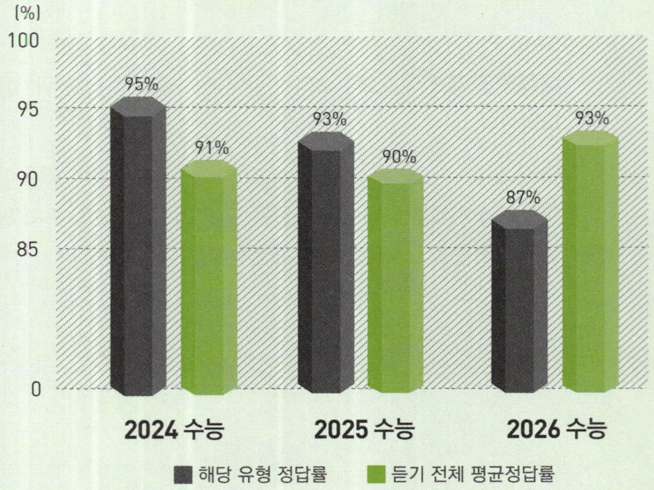

[학습 전략]

Step 1

대화 초반부에 드러나는 화자가 처한 상황 등 대화 상황을 파악하고, 앞으로 일어날 일을 예측하며 듣는다.

Step 2

할 일이나 부탁하는 일을 당사자가 직접 언급하지 않고 상대방이 의향을 묻거나 제안하는 경우도 있으므로, 대화의 흐름을 놓치지 않도록 한다.

Step 3

하려는 일에 대한 계획이 대화 중에 변경되거나 부탁을 했지만 거절당하는 등의 경우가 많으므로, 대화 끝까지 잘 듣는다.

[코드 접속하기]

대화를 듣고, 여자가 할 일로 가장 적절한 것을 고르시오. 정답률 82%

● 2024년 9월 교육청(고1) 5번

① 선물 준비하기
② 온라인 초대장 보내기
③ 음식 주문하기
④ 초대 손님 명단 확인하기
⑤ 전시 부스 설치하기

W: Tony, ⓐI'm so excited for our Go-Green event!

M: Me too. The event is almost here. ⓑWhy don't we go over(~을 점검하다) our preparations(준비) together?

W: Okay. I think the exhibition(전시) booths are very important for our event. How are they going?

M: Almost ready. I'm working on the booth setup(설치) this afternoon. What about the welcome gifts?

W: I've already prepared some eco-friendly(친환경적인) bags.

M: Perfect! What's next?

W: We need to confirm(확인하다) the list of guests for the ceremony(의식, 행사).

M: I double-checked the list. But ⓒI haven't sent the online invitation(초대(장)) cards, yet.

W: No problem. ⓓI'll deal with(~을 처리하다) it right away. How about the food and drinks?

M: I've scheduled food and drink services and I'll serve the guests with reusable(재사용할 수 있는) dishes.

W: Nice! I'm confident(자신감 있는, 확신하는) our event will be a great success.

핵심 코드

Step 1

대화 초반부를 통해 상황을 파악한다.

ⓐⓑGo-Green 행사 준비 사항을 점검하는 상황이다.

Step 2

할 일을 간접적[직접적]으로 언급한 부분을 놓치지 않고 듣는다.

ⓒ남자가 아직 온라인 초대장은 보내지 않았다고 했다.

Step 3

대화의 마지막까지 잘 들어 최종적으로 여자가 할 일을 확인한다.

남자의 말을 들은 여자가 ⓓ자신이 (온라인 초대장 보내는 일을) 바로 처리하겠다고 말했다.

(정답 ②)

06 숫자 정보

대화를 듣고, 주어진 금액, 시간, 무게 등의 숫자 정보를 활용하여 간단한 계산을 통해 답을 찾는 문제 유형이다.

[출제코드 분석]

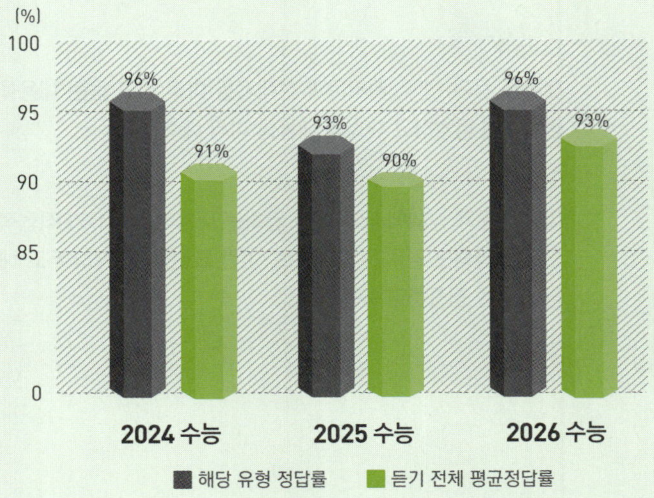

[학습 전략]

Step 1

대화를 듣기 전에, 지시문을 읽고 무엇을 묻는지 확인한다.

Step 2

대화에서 언급되는 금액, 시각 등 숫자 정보를 메모하며 듣는다. 할인율, 인원이나 수량을 명확하게 파악한다.

Step 3

대화 도중에 인원이나 수량이 변경되는 경우가 많으므로, 대화를 끝까지 잘 듣는다.

[코드 접속하기]

대화를 듣고, 여자가 지불할 금액을 고르시오. 정답률 93% ········ 2023학년도 수능 6번

① $55 ② $63 ③ $70 ④ $81 ⑤ $90

M: Hello, are you enjoying your time here at Magic Unicorn Children's Farm?

W: Yes, thank you. I'd like to buy some snacks to feed(먹이를 주다) the animals.

M: Sure. We sell two kinds of food for the animals, vegetable sticks and sliced(썰다) fruits.

W: How much do they cost?

M: It's ⓐ$5 for a pack of vegetable sticks and ⓑ$10 for a pack of sliced fruits.

W: I'll take ⓒfour packs of vegetable sticks. Are there any other activities?

M: We offer horseback riding. ⓓA ticket for a ride around the farm is $25.

W: Oh, my son and daughter will love it. ⓔTwo tickets, please.

M: So, four packs of vegetable sticks and two horseback riding(승마) tickets, correct?

W: Right. And I heard you're offering(제공하다) ⓕa 10% discount as an autumn(가을) promotional(판촉의) event.

M: I'm sorry. ⓖThat event ended last week.

W: I see. Here's my credit card.

핵심 코드

Step 1

대화를 듣기 전에 지시문에서 묻는 내용을 확인한다.

Step 2

대화에서 언급되는 숫자 정보를 메모하며 듣는다.

ⓐ채소 스틱 5달러 ⓒ네 봉지
ⓑ썰은 과일 10달러
ⓓ승마 25달러 ⓔ두 장
ⓕ10% 할인 ⓖ종료

Step 3

대화 도중에 수량 등이 변경되지 않는지 확인한다.

ⓓⓔ여자가 문의한 10% 할인 판촉 행사는 종료되어 적용되지 않음

(정답 ③)

07 이유

대화를 듣고, 특정 행동이나 감정의 이유를 추론하는 문제 유형이다.

[출제코드 분석]

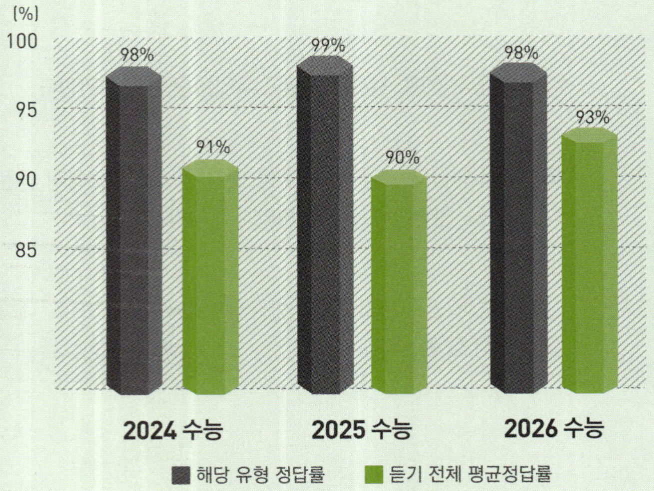

[학습 전략]

Step 1
대화를 듣기 전에, 지시문과 선택지를 미리 읽고 묻는 내용을 정확하게 파악하고 대화의 내용을 미리 예측한다.

Step 2
이유나 문제 상황에 대해 묻고 답하는 내용에서 이유가 직접적으로 언급되는 경우가 많으므로, 이런 표현을 잘 익혀 두고 해당 표현을 집중하여 듣는다.

[코드 접속하기]

대화를 듣고, 남자가 배드민턴 레슨에 갈 수 없는 이유를 고르시오. 정답률 **85%**

2020년 3월 교육청(고2) 8번

① 독감 예방 주사를 맞아서
② 발표 준비를 해야 해서
③ 수면 시간이 부족해서
④ 왼쪽 발목을 다쳐서
⑤ 진료 예약이 있어서

M: Hi, Claire. How did your chemistry (화학) presentation (발표) go?
W: It went better than I expected (예상하다).
M: Good. You look a little tired, though.
W: I didn't get enough sleep last night, but I'm okay now. You know we have a badminton lesson today, right?
M: Yes, but I don't think I can come.
W: Oh, does your left ankle (발목) still hurt?
M: No, I've fully recovered (회복하다).
W: Then, why?
M: Actually, ⓐI got a flu shot (독감 예방 주사) this morning.
W: I see. ⓑI once had a terrible muscle ache (근육통) after a flu shot.
M: Well, anyway, I'll skip (빠지다, 거르다) the lesson and get some rest today.
W: Okay, take care.

핵심 코드

Step 1
남자가 배드민턴 레슨에 갈 수 없는 이유를 파악한다.
여자가 짐작하여 묻는 이유와 혼동하지 않는다.

Step 2
남자가 배드민턴 레슨에 갈 수 없는 이유에 대해 직접적으로 이야기하는 부분을 집중하여 듣는다.
남자가 ⓐ오늘 아침에 독감 예방 주사를 맞았다고 하자, 여자도 ⓑ예전에 독감 예방 주사를 맞은 후 근육통이 심했던 적이 있다고 말하고 있다.

(정답 ①)

08 언급

대화를 듣고, 화자가 언급하지 않은 것을 고르는 문제 유형이다.

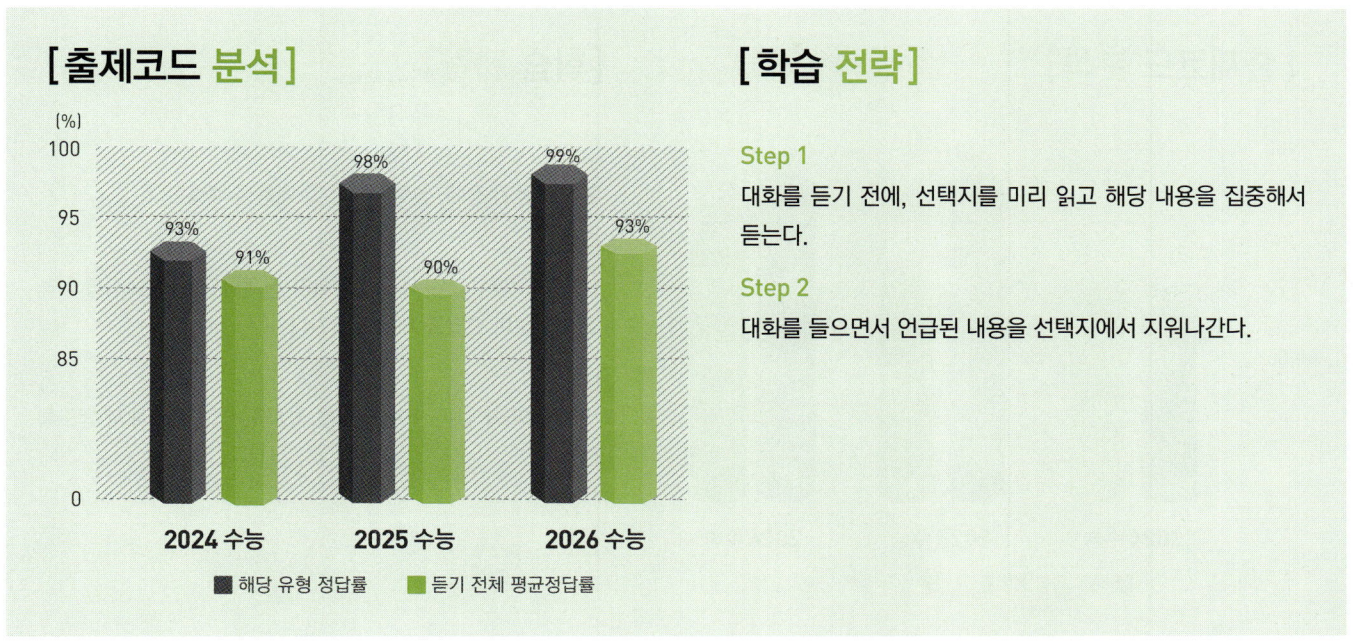

[출제코드 분석]

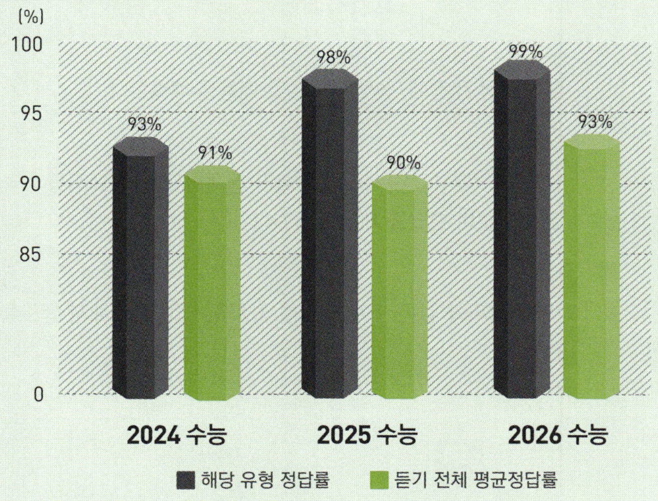

[학습 전략]

Step 1

대화를 듣기 전에, 선택지를 미리 읽고 해당 내용을 집중해서 듣는다.

Step 2

대화를 들으면서 언급된 내용을 선택지에서 지워나간다.

[코드 접속하기]

대화를 듣고, Little Readers' Class에 관해 언급되지 않은 것을 고르시오. 정답률 97%

2022학년도 수능 8번

① 장소　② 시간　③ 대상 연령
④ 모집 인원　⑤ 등록 방법

M: Christine, I heard your daughter Jennifer loves reading. Unfortunately, my daughter doesn't.

W: Actually, Jennifer didn't enjoy reading until she took the Little Readers' Class. It provides (제공하다) various fun reading activities.

M: Really? It might be good for my daughter, too. Where's it held?

W: ⓐIt's held at the Stonefield Library. I have a picture of the flyer ((광고·안내용) 전단) somewhere in my phone. *[Pause]* Here.

M: Oh. ⓑThe class is from 4 p.m. to 5 p.m. every Monday.

W: Is that time okay for her?

M: Yeah, she's free on Monday afternoons.

W: Great. ⓒThe class is for children ages seven to nine. Your daughter is eight years old, right?

M: Yes, she can take it. So, ⓓto register (등록하다), I should send an email to the address (주소) on the flyer.

W: That's right. I hope the class gets your daughter into reading.

핵심 코드

Step 1

선택지를 미리 읽고 집중해서 들어야 하는 내용을 확인한다.

Step 2

대화를 들으면서 언급된 내용을 선택지에서 하나씩 제거해 나간다.

ⓐ장소
ⓑ시간
ⓒ대상 연령
ⓓ등록 방법

(정답 ④)

09 내용 일치

담화를 듣고, 내용과 일치하지 않는 진술을 고르는 문제 유형이다.

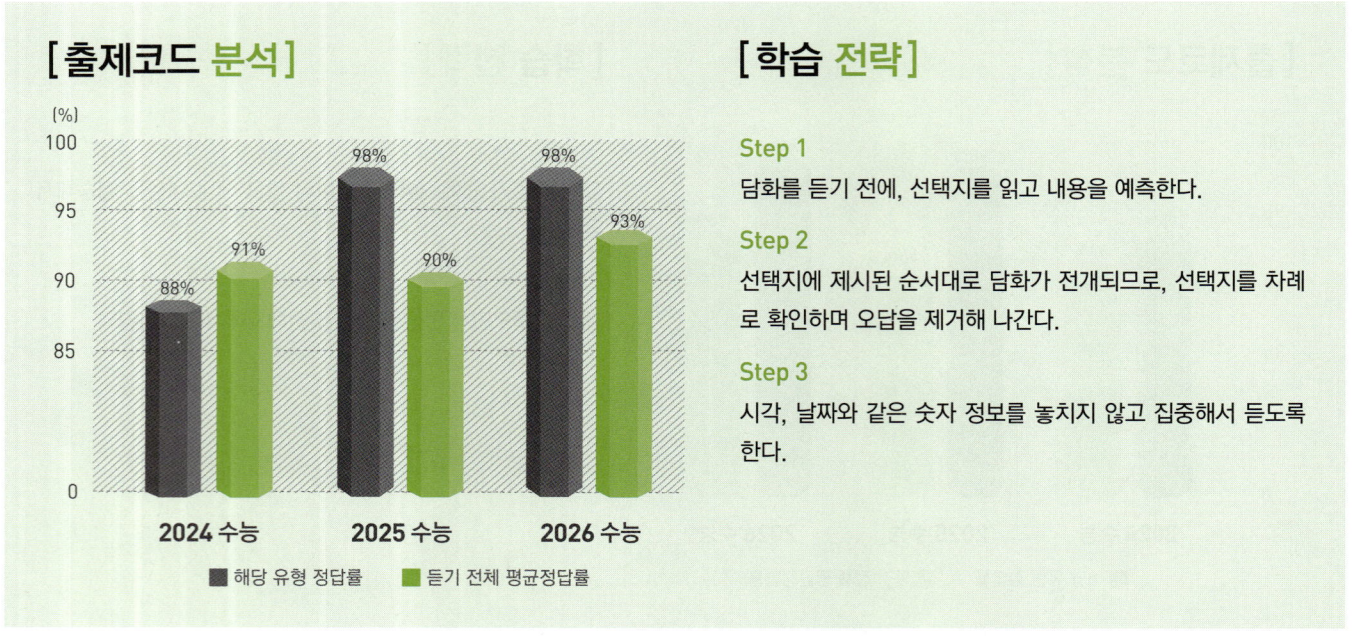

[출제코드 분석]

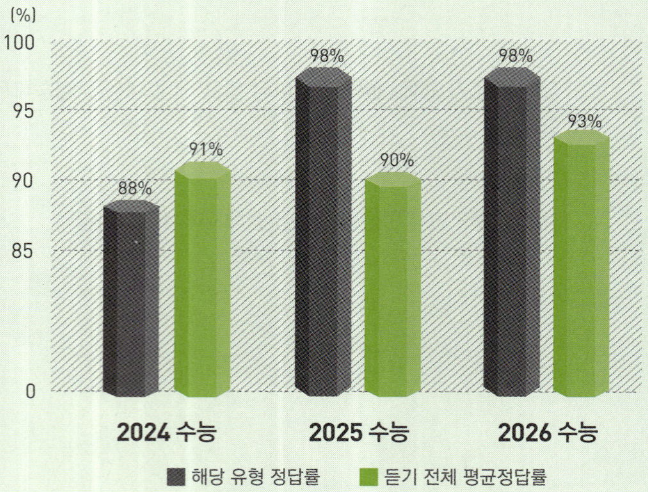

[학습 전략]

Step 1
담화를 듣기 전에, 선택지를 읽고 내용을 예측한다.

Step 2
선택지에 제시된 순서대로 담화가 전개되므로, 선택지를 차례로 확인하며 오답을 제거해 나간다.

Step 3
시각, 날짜와 같은 숫자 정보를 놓치지 않고 집중해서 듣도록 한다.

[코드 접속하기]

2021 Family Science Festival에 관한 다음 내용을 듣고, 일치하지 않는 것을 고르시오.

정답률 92% ······· 2022학년도 수능 9번

① 12월 7일부터 일주일 동안 진행된다.
② 8개의 프로그램이 제공될 것이다.
③ 어린이 과학 잡지를 판매할 것이다.
④ 11세 미만의 어린이들은 성인을 동반해야 한다.
⑤ 참가를 위해 미리 등록해야 한다.

M: Hello, WBPR listeners. Are you looking for a chance to enjoy quality(고급의, 양질의) family time? Then, we invite you to the 2021 Family Science Festival. ⓐIt starts on December 7th and runs for one week at the Bermont Science Museum located near(~에 위치한) City Hall. ⓑEight programs will be offered for parents and children to enjoy together, including(~을 포함하여) robot building and VR simulations(모의실험). ⓒWe'll also give out(~을 나눠주다) a children's science magazine for free. This event is open to anyone, but remember that ⓓall children under age 11 must be accompanied by(~을 동반하다) an adult. There's no admission fee(입장료), but ⓔto participate(참여하다, 참가하다), you must register in advance(미리). Come and learn about the exciting world of science with your family. For more information, visit our website, www.wbpr.com.

핵심 코드

Step 1
선택지를 미리 읽고 담화 내용을 예측한다.

Step 2
담화를 들으며 선택지를 하나씩 대조한다.
ⓒ어린이 과학 잡지를 판매하는 게 아니라 무료로 나눠줄 예정이다.

Step 3
숫자 정보를 놓치지 않도록 한다.
December 7th / for one week / Eight programs / under age 11

(정답 ③)

10 도표

도표를 보면서 대화를 듣고, 대화에 제시된 정보를 토대로 질문에 맞는 답을 찾는 문제 유형이다.

[출제코드 분석]

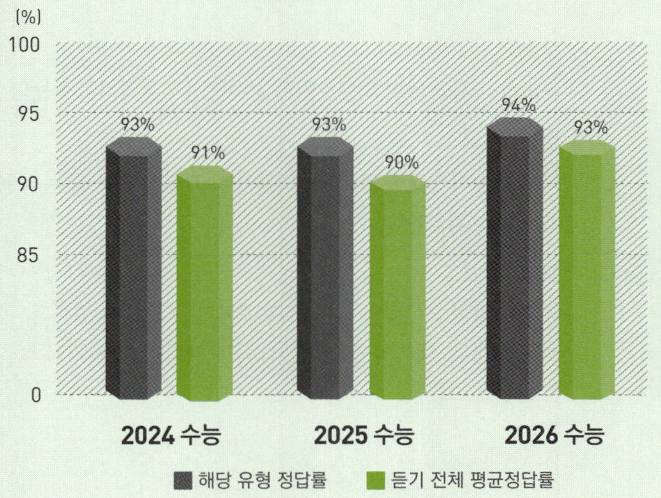

[학습 전략]

Step 1
대화를 들으면서, 대화 내용과 일치하지 않는 내용은 지우고 일치하는 내용에 표시하여 정답의 범위를 좁혀 나간다.

Step 2
시각, 날짜와 같은 숫자 정보를 놓치지 않도록 한다.

Step 3
두 화자가 제안과 거절을 반복하는 대화 흐름을 따라 최종적으로 무엇을 선택하는지 대화 마지막까지 집중해서 듣는다.

[코드 접속하기]

다음 표를 보면서 대화를 듣고, 두 사람이 구입할 미니 오븐을 고르시오. 정답률 84%

• 2022년 3월 교육청(고2) 10번

Mini Ovens

	Model	Price	Capacity (liters)	Weight (kilograms)	Baking Pan
①	A	$92	9	6.0	X
②	B	$93	10	6.5	O
③	C	$95	12	5.5	X
④	D	$98	13	5.0	O
⑤	E	$110	13	4.5	O

M: Honey, are you trying to buy a mini oven on the Internet?

W: Yes, we need it to bake cookies or biscuits. What do you think of these five models?

M: Let me have a look. *[Pause]* All of them look nice, but ⓐit seems too much to spend more than $100 for a mini oven.

W: I agree. We should eliminate(제거하다) this one then. I think ⓑthe capacity(용량) should be at least 10 liters.

M: Then let's choose one of these three. What about the weight?

W: I guess the lighter, the better. ⓒI don't want it to be more than 6 kg.

M: All right. Now we're down to these two models. ⓓShall we go for(~을 선택하다) the one with a baking pan?

W: ⓔI don't think so. We can use the pans we already have.

M: I see. Let's buy the other one then.

W: Okay.

핵심 코드

Step 1
대화 내용과 일치하는 내용에 표시하여 정답의 범위를 좁힌다.
ⓐ가격: 100달러 이하
ⓑ용량: 최소 10리터
ⓒ무게: 6kg 이하
ⓓⓔbaking pan: 불필요

Step 2
숫자 정보를 놓치지 않고 듣는다.
too much to spend more than $100 / should be at least 10 liters / don't want it to be more than 6 kg에 주목한다.

Step 3
대화 마지막까지 잘 듣고 화자의 최종 선택을 확인한다.

(정답 ③)

11 짧은 대화 응답

짧은 대화를 듣고, 남자나 여자의 마지막 말에 대한 상대방의 응답을 고르는 문제 유형이다.

[출제코드 분석]

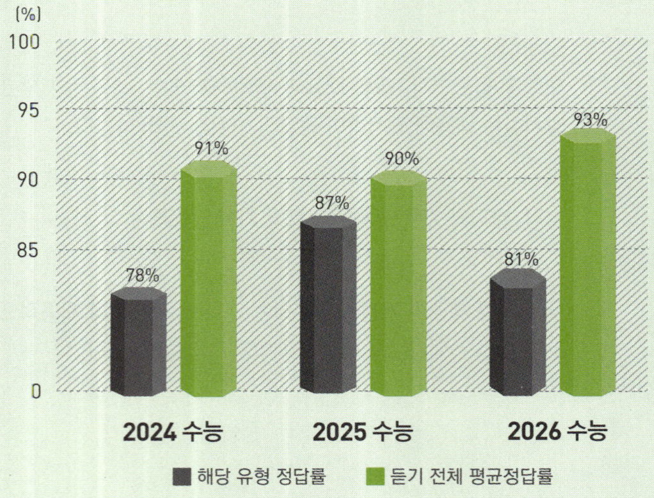

[학습 전략]

Step 1

대화의 마지막 말이 의문문인지 평서문인지 유의하여 듣는다.

Step 2

마지막 말이 의문문인 경우, 의문사 등에 유의하여 묻는 내용을 정확히 파악한다.

Step 3

마지막 말이 의문문인 경우, 질문에 적합한 응답을 고른다. 평서문인 경우, 대화의 전체적인 내용과 맥락을 통해 가장 적절한 응답을 고른다.

[코드 접속하기]

대화를 듣고, 남자의 마지막 말에 대한 여자의 응답으로 가장 적절한 것을 고르시오. 정답률 71%

2020년 9월 교육청(고1) 2번

① Good idea! I'll look for some videos online.
② Great! Teach me how to make a video clip.
③ Wow! You're good at controlling the drone.
④ Okay. Let's go buy a new drone together.
⑤ Right. I should read the instructions.

M: Jane, ⓐare you almost done setting up your drone?
(set up: ~을 설치하다)

W: Not yet. ⓑI'm having a hard time understanding the instructions.
(have a hard time v-ing: ~하는 데 어려움을 겪다 / instructions: *(pl.)* (제품 등의) 사용 설명서)

M: ⓒWatching some video clips might be helpful. I'm sure you'll find some showing you how to do it.

W: Good idea! I'll look for some videos online.

핵심 코드

Step 1

대화 초반부를 통해 상황을 파악한다.

남자가 ⓐ드론 설정을 거의 다 했는지 물었고, 여자는 ⓑ사용 설명서를 이해하기 어렵다고 답했다.

Step 2

대화의 마지막 말에 유의하며 듣는다.

남자는 사용 설명서를 이해하기 어려워하는 여자에게 ⓒ영상을 보는 게 도움이 될 것이라고 조언했다.

(정답 ①)

12 긴 대화 응답

긴 대화를 듣고, 남자나 여자의 마지막 말에 대한 상대방의 응답을 고르는 문제 유형이다.

[출제코드 분석]

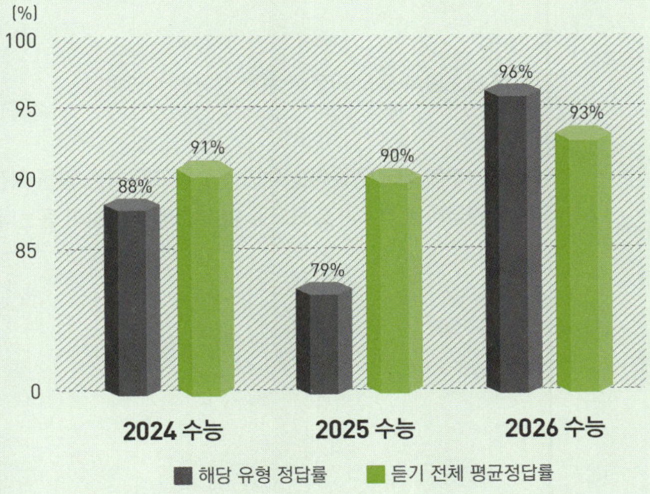

[학습 전략]

Step 1
대화의 전반적인 상황과 흐름을 파악하며, 마지막 부분에 단서가 제시되는 경우가 많으므로 끝까지 집중해서 듣는다.

Step 2
응답자가 남자인지 여자인지 확인하고 그 사람의 입장에 맞는 선택지를 고른다.

Step 3
대화 중에 나온 표현을 활용하여 제시된 오답 선택지를 고르지 않도록 유의한다.

[코드 접속하기]

대화를 듣고, 남자의 마지막 말에 대한 여자의 응답으로 가장 적절한 것을 고르시오. 정답률 78%

2025학년도 수능 13번

Woman: ____________________

① Too bad. I hope you can find your lost bike.
② Good job. You'll get used to riding a bike soon.
③ Awesome! Thank you for lending me your new bike.
④ I'm sorry. I'm afraid our auction has already finished.
⑤ Excellent! I'm sure your donation will be appreciated.

[Cell phone rings.]
M: Hi, Rachel. What's up?
W: Hi, Kevin. Do you have any plans for next weekend?
M: No, I'm free. Why do you ask?
W: The City Transportation Office is hosting (열다, 개최하다) a bike auction (경매) at their parking lot. Do you want to check it out together?
M: Sounds like fun. Are they selling new bicycles?
W: No, they're selling used bikes. People have donated (기증하다, 기부하다) them for a good cause (대의, 목적).
M: What's the cause?
W: I heard all the money they raise ((자금 등을) 모으다) will be used to support (지원하다, 후원하다) youth sports clubs.
M: Oh, really? Then, ⓐI'd like to contribute to (~에 기여하다) the auction. Actually, I have a bike that I don't ride anymore.
W: That's great. ⓑJust make sure it's in a good enough condition to be sold.
M: ⓒNot to worry. It's only been used two or three times.
W: Excellent! I'm sure your donation will be appreciated.

핵심 코드

Step 1
대화의 후반부에 제시된 단서에 집중한다.
남자는 ⓐ경매에 기여하고 싶다며 타지 않는 자전거가 있다고 했다. 이에 ⓑ판매 가능한 상태인지 확인하라는 여자의 말에 남자가 ⓒ걱정 말라며 두세 번밖에 사용하지 않았다고 했다.

Step 2
여자가 남자에게 할 말로 적절한 말을 고른다.
경매에 자전거를 기부하려는 남자에게 할 말을 생각해 본다.

Step 3
대화 중에 나온 표현을 활용한 오답 선택지를 정답으로 고르지 않도록 한다.
① 자전거가 언급되었지만, 자전거 분실과는 무관하다.
② 자전거가 언급되었지만, 자전거 타는 데 익숙해지는 것과는 무관하다.
③ 자전거가 언급되었지만, 자전거를 빌리는 것과는 무관하다.
④ 경매가 언급되었지만, 여자는 경매의 주최측이 아니다.

(정답 ⑤)

13 상황에 적절한 말

담화를 듣고, 담화의 상황에서 해당 인물이 할 적절한 말을 고르는 문제 유형이다.

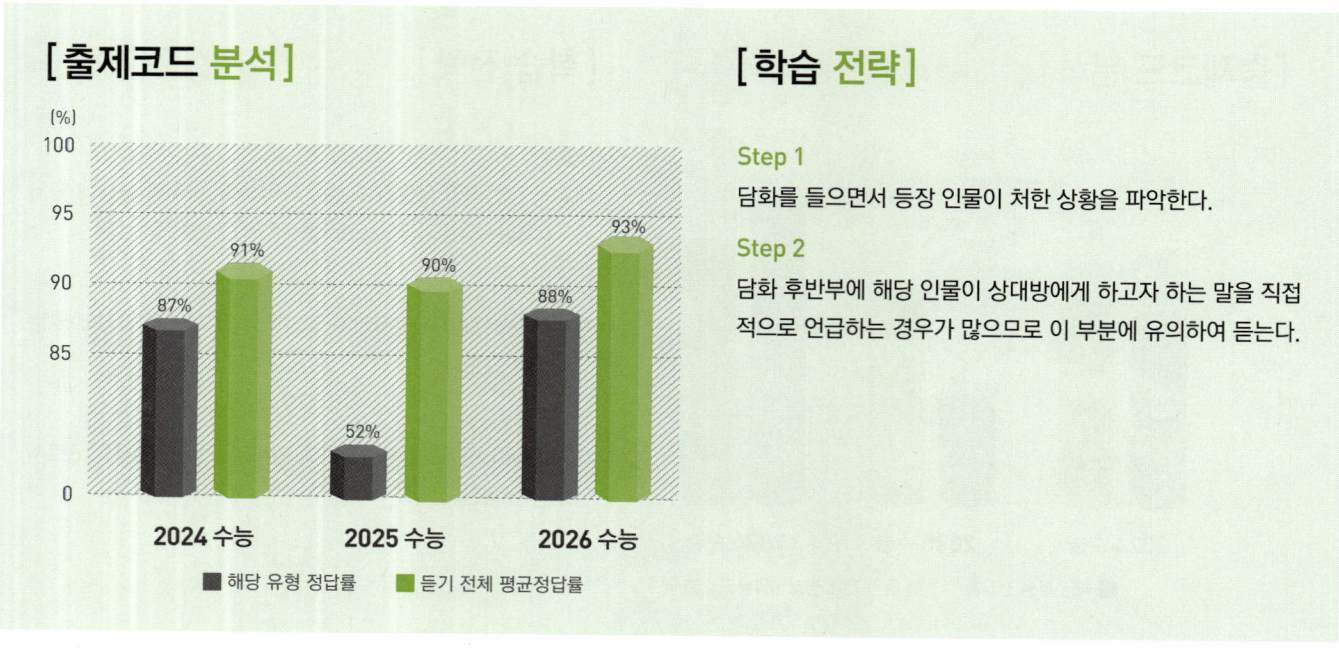

[출제코드 분석]

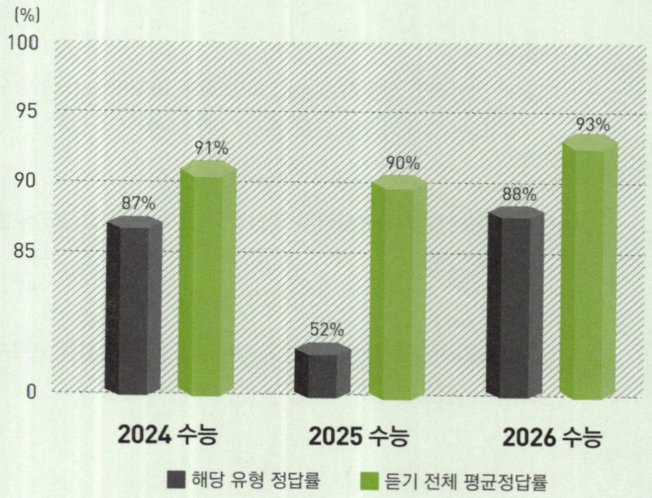

[학습 전략]

Step 1

담화를 들으면서 등장 인물이 처한 상황을 파악한다.

Step 2

담화 후반부에 해당 인물이 상대방에게 하고자 하는 말을 직접적으로 언급하는 경우가 많으므로 이 부분에 유의하여 듣는다.

[코드 접속하기]

다음 상황 설명을 듣고, Eve가 Tom에게 할 말로 가장 적절한 것을 고르시오. 정답률 76%

2019년 9월 교육청 (고2) 15번

Eve: ______________________________

① You should find a job related to your field of study.
② How about getting help from a career counselor?
③ Do some research before choosing your major.
④ If I were you, I'd focus on studying history.
⑤ Why don't you apply for an internship?

M: Eve is a college student who is majoring in(~을 전공하다) history. She has been worried about her career path(진로) because she's uncertain(불확실한) about what to do after she graduates(졸업하다). So, to learn more about her career options(선택), she regularly(정기적으로) meets a career counselor(상담가) at her college. She feels that it has helped her a lot. One day, Eve finds out(~을 알게 되다) that her classmate ⓐTom is also worried about what to do after he graduates. ⓑEve wants to suggest(제안하다) that Tom go see the career counselor for advice. In this situation, what would Eve most likely say to Tom?

핵심 코드

Step 1

담화를 들으면서 등장인물이 처한 상황을 파악한다.

ⓐTom은 졸업 후 진로를 걱정하고 있다.

Step 2

담화 후반부에 직접적으로 언급한, Eve가 Tom에게 하고 싶은 말에 주목한다.

ⓑ직업 상담가의 도움을 받으라고 제안하고 싶다고 했다.

(정답 ②)

14 세트 문항

긴 담화나 대화를 듣고, 주제나 목적 등 중심 생각을 묻는 문제와 언급 내용 등 세부 사항을 파악하는 문제 두 개를 푸는 문제 유형이다.

[출제코드 분석]

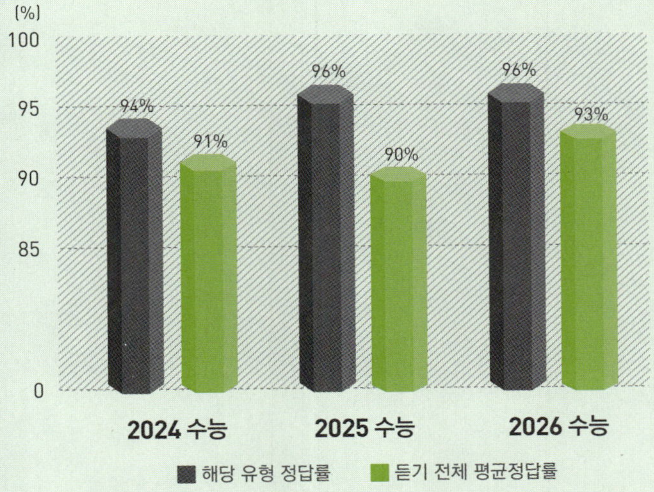

[학습 전략]

Step 1

주제나 목적을 묻는 경우, 시작이나 끝에 단서가 제시되는 경우가 많으므로, 이 부분에 주목한다.

Step 2

세부 사항을 묻는 문제의 경우, 오답을 하나씩 지워가며 듣는다.

Step 3

담화나 대화를 두 번째 들으면서 고른 답이 맞는지 점검한다.

[코드 접속하기]

다음을 듣고, 물음에 답하시오. ········• 2020년 3월 교육청(고1) 16, 17번

1. 여자가 하는 말의 주제로 가장 적절한 것은? 정답률 87%

① major exporting countries of dairy products
② health benefits of drinking milk regularly
③ unique food cultures around the world
④ suitable environments for dairy animals
⑤ various milk sources in different countries

2. 언급된 나라가 아닌 것은? 정답률 88%

① Canada ② India ③ Finland ④ Norway ⑤ Romania

W: Good morning, class. What did you have for breakfast? I guess some of you had your favorite cereal with milk. ⓐHave you ever wondered where milk comes from? Most people would say it's from cows, and they're right. Around ninety percent of milk in ⓑCanada and the U.S. comes from cows. But cows are not the only source(공급원, 출처) of milk. ⓒPeople around the world get milk from different animals. Water buffalos are the main source of milk in ⓓIndia. They produce half the milk consumed(소비하다, 섭취하다) in the country. Some people in the northern part of ⓔFinland drink reindeer(순록) milk because they are the only dairy animals(착유 동물) that can survive(살아남다, 견뎌 내다) such a cold environment. People in ⓕRomania get milk from sheep and use it to make cheese. It has twice the fat(지방) content(함량) of cow milk. Now let's watch a video about these animals.

핵심 코드

Step 1

담화의 주제를 파악하며 듣는다.

담화 시작 부분에서 ⓐ우유가 어디서 나오는지 궁금해 본 적이 있냐는 질문을 한 뒤, ⓒ전 세계의 사람들은 여러 동물들로부터 우유를 얻는다고 답하고 있다.

Step 2

선택지를 하나씩 지워가며 듣는다.

ⓑ캐나다, ⓓ인도, ⓔ핀란드, ⓕ루마니아

Step 3

담화를 두 번째 들으면서 답이 맞는지 점검한다.

(정답 1. ⑤ 2. ④)

다빈출 코드

영어 듣기

PART 2

초급 모의고사

X

1 ~ 9회

고1 교육청 학력평가
기출에서 선별한
우수 문항 모의고사

제1회 초급 모의고사

맞은 개수: 2점 문항 ___개, 3점 문항 ___개
알고 푼 문항은 ○, 찍어서 맞힌 문제는 △에 표시하고,
△와 ×는 다시 복습하세요.

1번부터 17번까지는 듣고 답하는 문제입니다. 1번부터 15번까지는 한 번만 들려주고, 16번부터 17번까지는 두 번 들려줍니다. 방송을 잘 듣고 답을 하시기 바랍니다.

1 ○△× • 2025년 3월 교육청(고1) 1번

다음을 듣고, 남자가 하는 말의 목적으로 가장 적절한 것을 고르시오. 정답률 88%

① 학교 운동장 공사 계획을 안내하려고
② 교내 드론 대회 개최 소식을 알리려고
③ 학교 홍보용 드론 촬영 일정을 공지하려고
④ 학교 드론 동아리 공연의 관람을 권하려고
⑤ 교내 드론 공연의 관람 안전 수칙을 강조하려고

2 ○△× • 2022년 9월 교육청(고1) 2번

대화를 듣고, 남자의 의견으로 가장 적절한 것을 고르시오. 정답률 94%

① 중고품은 직접 만나서 거래해야 한다.
② 물품 구매 시 여러 제품을 비교해야 한다.
③ 계획적으로 예산을 세워 물품을 구매해야 한다.
④ 온라인 거래 시 개인 정보 유출에 유의해야 한다.
⑤ 중고품 구매 시 세부 사항을 꼼꼼히 확인해야 한다.

3 ○△× • 2024년 6월 교육청(고1) 3번

다음을 듣고, 여자가 하는 말의 요지로 가장 적절한 것을 고르시오. 정답률 92%

① 소셜 미디어는 원만한 대인관계 유지에 도움이 된다.
② 온라인에서는 자아가 다양한 모습으로 표출될 수 있다.
③ 소셜 미디어는 자존감에 부정적인 영향을 줄 수 있다.
④ 친밀한 관계일수록 상대의 언행에 쉽게 영향을 받는다.
⑤ 유명인 사생활 보호의 중요성은 종종 간과된다.

4 ○△× • 2023년 3월 교육청(고1) 4번

대화를 듣고, 그림에서 대화의 내용과 일치하지 않는 것을 고르시오. 정답률 89%

5 ○△× • 2017년 6월 교육청(고1) 7번

대화를 듣고, 남자가 여자에게 부탁한 일로 가장 적절한 것을 고르시오. 정답률 89%

① 음식 만들기
② 꽃 사러 가기
③ 친구 초대하기
④ 거실 청소하기
⑤ 식료품 구입하기

6 ○△× • 2018년 6월 교육청(고1) 9번

대화를 듣고, 남자가 지불할 금액을 고르시오. [3점] 정답률 71%

① $13 ② $15 ③ $17 ④ $20 ⑤ $22

7 ○△× • 2022년 3월 교육청(고1) 7번

대화를 듣고, 두 사람이 오늘 실험을 할 수 없는 이유를 고르시오. 정답률 94%

① 실험용 키트가 배달되지 않아서
② 실험 주제를 변경해야 해서
③ 과학실을 예약하지 못해서
④ 보고서를 작성해야 해서
⑤ 남자가 감기에 걸려서

8 ○△× • 2024년 6월 교육청(고1) 8번

대화를 듣고, Victory Marathon에 관해 언급되지 않은 것을 고르시오. 정답률 92%

① 행사 날짜
② 신청 방법
③ 출발 지점
④ 참가비
⑤ 예상 참가 인원

9 ○△× • 2025년 3월 교육청(고1) 9번

Science Day 행사에 관한 다음 내용을 듣고, 일치하지 않는 것을 고르시오. 정답률 84%

① 이번 주 토요일에 진행된다.
② 학생들이 직접 로봇을 작동해 볼 수 있다.
③ 선생님들이 오전에 실험 부스를 운영한다.
④ QR 코드를 스캔하여 참가 신청을 할 수 있다.
⑤ 참가자들에게 점심을 제공한다.

10 ○△×
• 2023년 3월 교육청(고1) 10번

다음 표를 보면서 대화를 듣고, 여자가 구입할 프라이팬을 고르시오. 정답률 91%

Frying Pans

	Model	Price	Size (inches)	Material	Lid
①	A	$30	8	Aluminum	○
②	B	$32	9.5	Aluminum	○
③	C	$35	10	Stainless Steel	×
④	D	$40	11	Aluminum	×
⑤	E	$70	12.5	Stainless Steel	○

11 ○△×
• 2023년 3월 교육청(고1) 11번

대화를 듣고, 남자의 마지막 말에 대한 여자의 응답으로 가장 적절한 것을 고르시오. 정답률 88%

① I don't think I can finish editing it by then.
② I learned it by myself through books.
③ This short movie is very interesting.
④ You should make another video clip.
⑤ I got an A+ on the team project.

12 고득점 ○△×
• 2024년 9월 교육청(고1) 11번

대화를 듣고, 여자의 마지막 말에 대한 남자의 응답으로 가장 적절한 것을 고르시오. 정답률 63%

① If it's too dry inside, you can easily get a cold.
② When you cough, you should cover your mouth.
③ You need to wash your hands not to get a cold.
④ It's really important to keep yourself warm.
⑤ Drinking water can make your skin soft.

13 ○△×
• 2025년 3월 교육청(고1) 14번

대화를 듣고, 남자의 마지막 말에 대한 여자의 응답으로 가장 적절한 것을 고르시오. [3점] 정답률 93%

Woman: ____________________

① Reading books can also be a good hobby.
② You had to practice a lot to win the game.
③ How about going out with me this Saturday?
④ Just bring your racket and some comfortable clothes.
⑤ If you don't have a hobby, you can get more stressed.

14 ○△×
• 2020년 9월 교육청(고1) 13번

대화를 듣고, 여자의 마지막 말에 대한 남자의 응답으로 가장 적절한 것을 고르시오. [3점] 정답률 83%

Man: ____________________

① Your sister had difficulty booking them.
② I'm sure the construction will be done soon.
③ The community center will be available tomorrow.
④ I hope I can reserve a court to continue practicing.
⑤ I don't think they'll allow us to practice in the gym.

15 고득점 ○△×
• 2019년 6월 교육청(고1) 15번

다음 상황 설명을 듣고, Alex가 Olivia에게 할 말로 가장 적절한 것을 고르시오. 정답률 66%

Alex: ____________________

① You're very lucky to have a new job.
② I'll tell you where you should transfer to.
③ Let's keep in touch even after we part.
④ I was deeply touched by your kind words.
⑤ I hope you'll get used to your new school.

[16~17] 다음을 듣고, 물음에 답하시오.

16 ○△×
• 2023년 9월 교육청(고1) 16번

남자가 하는 말의 주제로 가장 적절한 것은? 정답률 84%

① advantages of renting houses in cities
② reasons tourists prefer visiting old cities
③ ways cities deal with overtourism problems
④ correlation between cities' sizes and overtourism
⑤ how cities face their aging transportation systems

17 ○△×
• 2023년 9월 교육청(고1) 17번

언급된 도시가 아닌 것은? 정답률 94%

① Barcelona ② Amsterdam ③ London
④ Venice ⑤ Paris

Dictation

문제 풀이에 중요한 핵심 부분과 듣기에 자주 나오는 표현들에 빈칸 처리를 했습니다. 방송을 잘 듣고, 빈칸에 알맞은 말을 써 넣으세요.

Tip! 잘 들리지 않는 부분이 있을 때에는 정답을 확인 후, 똑같은 속도로 따라 읽기 연습을 해 보세요.

1

M: Good morning, students. This is your vice principal Richard Simpson. As you know, our school drone club __________ __________ __________ __________ at the Drone Show Contest. Actually, I asked the drone club to perform the show again for you. And they said, "Yes". So I would __________ __________ __________ __________ __________ at the school field tomorrow. Please come and see the club's drone performance, and __________ __________ __________. Thank you.

2

M: Clara, why the long face?

W: Aw, Dad, I bought this hair dryer, but the cool air mode doesn't work.

M: Where did you get it?

W: I bought it secondhand online.

M: Did you __________ __________ __________ before you ordered it?

W: I did, but I missed the seller's note that said the cool air mode doesn't work.

M: Oh dear. It's important to check all the details when you buy secondhand items.

W: You're right. I was just so excited because it was __________ __________ __________ __________ __________ __________.

M: Some secondhand items are almost like new, but others are not. So, you should __________ __________ __________ __________ __________ __________ __________.

W: Thanks, Dad. I'll keep that in mind.

3

W: Hello, listeners. This is Kelly Watson's *Love Yourself*. Have you ever thought about your social media use? Social media lets you stay connected with others easily. However, it can make you __________ __________ __________ __________, too. For example, a celebrity's post about going on a luxurious trip may make you jealous. Continuously making such comparisons stops you from looking at yourself the way you truly are. You might think, "Why can't I have a better life?" and __________ __________ __________ __________. As you can see, social media can __________ __________ __________ __________ __________ __________ __________. I'll be right back with some tips for healthy social media use.

4

M: Hi, Grace. What are you looking at on your phone?

W: Hi, James. It's a photo I took when I did some volunteer work. We painted pictures on a street wall.

M: Let me see. Wow, I like the __________ __________ __________ __________ __________.

W: I like it, too. How do you like the house under the whale?

M: It's beautiful. What are these two chairs for?

W: You can take a picture sitting there. The painting becomes the background.

M: Oh, I see. Look at this tree! It __________ __________ __________.

W: That's right. We named it the Love Tree.

M: The __________ __________ __________ __________ __________ is lovely, too.

W: I hope a lot of people enjoy the painting.

5

W: Dad, where are you going?

M: I'm going to the grocery store. We're having a surprise party this evening.

W: Really? Is it a special day today?

M: Yes. Mom __________ __________ __________ __________, so we're going to celebrate.

W: Oh, good for her. I'm sure she'll love the party.

M: I hope so. I'm thinking of making steak and seafood pasta for dinner.

W: Sounds perfect. Will there be any guests?

M: Yes. I invited a couple of our friends.

W: Good. I also want to help. Shall I __________ __________ __________ __________ for the dinner table?

M: No. I'll do that. Can you __________ __________ __________ __________ instead?

W: Sure. I'll make it neat and tidy before you come back.

M: Thanks. That's very kind of you.

6

W: Hello. How can I help you?

M: Hi. I want to buy some mini apple pies. How much are they?

W: They're four dollars each.

M: Good. I'll take three. And this bacon and egg sandwich looks delicious. How much is it?

W: It's five dollars. But this week if you buy two, __________ __________ __________ __________.

M: Well, that sounds like a good deal, but three sandwiches are too many. I'll just buy one. That's it.

W: Great. Do you have a store membership?

M: No, but __________ __________ __________ __________. Can I use it?

W: Sure. You'll __________ __________ __________ __________ of the total.

M: Good. Here's my credit card.

7

[Cell phone rings.]

M: Hey, Suji. Where are you?

W: I'm in the library checking out books. I'll be heading out to the science lab for our experiment in a couple of minutes.

M: I guess you haven't checked my message yet. We can't do the experiment today.

W: Really? __________ __________ __________ __________ today?

M: Yes, it is, but I canceled our reservation.

W: Why? Are you still __________ __________ __________ __________?

M: No, I'm fine now.

W: That's good. Then why aren't we doing the experiment today? We need to hand in the science report by next Monday.

M: Unfortunately, the __________ __________ __________ __________ __________ __________. It'll arrive tomorrow.

W: Oh, well. The experiment has to wait one more day, then.

8

W: Hey, Alex. Have you seen the announcement for the Victory Marathon?

M: Not yet, but I'm curious about it. When's the event?

W: It's __________ __________, __________ __________.

M: Nice. Where will the race start?

W: It will start at William Stadium.

M: Oh, great. How much __________ __________ __________ __________ __________?

W: It costs $30.

M: That's reasonable. How many participants are they expecting?

W: Last year, there were around 5,000. They say they __________ __________ __________ __________ this year.

M: I didn't know that many people love marathons. I'm in!

W: Great. I look forward to running with you.

9

W: Hello, students! This is your science teacher Jane Brown. I have some good news. This Saturday we're having Science Day at our school. In the morning, coding experts will teach you how to make a computer program. You can also ___________ ___________ ___________ ___________ ___________ in the school hall. In the afternoon, your science teachers will ___________ ___________ ___________ ___________ for you. It's a good chance to experiment with what you've learned from the textbooks. You can sign up for Science Day by scanning the QR codes on the school board. For the participants, ___________ ___________ ___________ ___________. Come and enjoy Science Day!

10

M: Jessica, what are you doing?

W: I'm trying to buy one of these five frying pans.

M: Let me see. This frying pan seems pretty expensive.

W: Yeah. I don't want to ___________ ___________ ___________ ___________.

M: Okay. And I think 9 to 12-inch frying pans will work for most of your cooking.

W: I think so, too. An 8-inch frying pan seems too small for me.

M: What about the material? Stainless steel pans are good for fast cooking.

W: I know, but they are heavier. I'll ___________ ___________ ___________ ___________.

M: Then you have two options left. Do you need a lid?

W: Of course. A lid ___________ ___________ ___________ ___________ ___________. I'll buy this one.

M: Good choice.

11

M: Have you finished your team's short-movie project?

W: Not yet. I'm still ___________ ___________ ___________ ___________.

M: Oh, you edit? ___________ ___________ ___________ ___________ to do that?

W: (I learned it by myself through books.)

12

W: I easily catch a cold these days.

M: That's too bad. It's a good idea to ___________ ___________ ___________ in your room.

W: Oh, how does that ___________ ___________ ___________ ___________?

M: (If it's too dry inside, you can easily get a cold.)

13

M: Hi, Cindy! What are you doing this weekend?

W: I'm going to play badminton with my friends.

M: You play badminton quite often.

W: It's my new hobby. It ___________ ___________ ___________ ___________.

M: How nice! I've been looking for something to reduce stress.

W: Well, you don't have to think too hard. Just think of something that makes you happy.

M: Hmm.... But nothing comes to mind right away.

W: Then, why don't you ___________ ___________ ___________ ___________ with me this Saturday? You'll like it, too, I think.

M: Really? Is it okay if I join you?

W: Of course, it is! We meet at the sports center every Saturday morning.

M: Thanks a lot! Do I ___________ ___________ ___________ ___________?

W: (Just bring your racket and some comfortable clothes.)

14

W: Hi, Andrew. I heard that your tennis club is competing in the City Tennis Tournament.
M: Yes. We've been practicing a lot these days.
W: I'm sure you'll do well.
M: Thanks. But our school tennis court is going to be under construction starting next week, so we ________ ________ ________ ________ ________ ________.
W: What about the community center? It has several tennis courts.
M: We already checked. But all the courts are fully booked.
W: That's too bad. Oh, wait! My sister told me her school tennis courts would be ________ ________ ________ ________ starting this Saturday.
M: Really? That's great news. Do I need a reservation?
W: Yes. I remember she said that ________ ________ ________ at 9 a.m. tomorrow.
M: (I hope I can reserve a court to continue practicing.)

15

W: Alex and Olivia have been close friends since they were children. They grew up in the same town, and they attend the same high school. One day, Alex tells Olivia that his father got a new job so his family has to move to another city. That's why he's going to ________ ________ ________ ________ ________ next week. Olivia feels sad because they have been friends for such a long time. Alex also hopes to ________ ________ ________ ________ ________. So, Alex wants to suggest that they ________ ________ ________ ________ even after he leaves the city. In this situation, what would Alex most likely say to Olivia?
Alex: (Let's keep in touch even after we part.)

16~17

M: Good afternoon, everyone. Last time, we learned that overtourism happens when there are too many visitors to a particular destination. Today, we'll learn how cities deal with the ________ ________ ________ ________. First, some cities limit the number of hotels so there are fewer places for visitors to stay. In Barcelona, building new hotels is not allowed in the city center. Second, other cities ________ ________ ________ ________ ________ ________. For instance, Amsterdam encourages tourists to visit less-crowded areas. Third, many cities have tried to limit access. For example, Venice has tried to reduce tourism overall by stopping large cruise ships from docking on the island. Similarly, Paris has ________ ________ ________ ________ to certain parts of the city by having car-restricted areas. Now, let's watch some video clips.

Dictation Answers

1. was awarded first prize / recommend you watch the performance / show your support
2. check the condition / much cheaper than other hair dryers / read every detail of the item carefully
3. compare yourself with others / feel small about yourself / have a negative effect on your self-esteem
4. whale with the flower pattern / has heart-shaped leaves / butterfly on the tree branch
5. was promoted at work / go buy some flowers / clean the living room
6. you get one free / I have this coupon / get 2 dollars off
7. Isn't the lab available / suffering from your cold / experiment kit hasn't been delivered yet
8. on Saturday, July 13th / does it cost to participate / expect about the same
9. operate some robots by yourself / run some experimental booths / lunch will be provided
10. spend more than $50 / buy an aluminum pan / keeps the oil from splashing
11. editing the video clip / How did you learn
12. keep some moisture / relate to a cold
13. helps me reduce stress / come and play badminton / need to prepare anything
14. won't have a place to practice / open to the public / reservations would start
15. transfer to a new school / keep his friendship with her / remain in close touch

16~17. problems caused by overtourism / promote areas away from popular sites / focused on reducing tourism

제2회 초급 모의고사

맞은 개수: 2점 문항 ___개, 3점 문항 ___개
알고 푼 문항은 ○, 찍어서 맞힌 문제는 △에 표시하고, △와 ×는 다시 복습하세요.

1번부터 17번까지는 듣고 답하는 문제입니다. 1번부터 15번까지는 한 번만 들려주고, 16번부터 17번까지는 두 번 들려줍니다. 방송을 잘 듣고 답을 하시기 바랍니다.

1 ○△× • 2022년 3월 교육청(고1) 1번

다음을 듣고, 남자가 하는 말의 목적으로 가장 적절한 것을 고르시오. 정답률 87%

① 농구 리그 참가 등록 방법의 변경을 알리려고
② 확정된 농구 리그 시합 일정을 발표하려고
③ 농구 리그의 심판을 추가 모집하려고
④ 농구 리그 경기 관람을 권장하려고
⑤ 농구 리그 우승 상품을 안내하려고

2 ○△× • 2018년 9월 교육청(고1) 4번

대화를 듣고, 여자의 의견으로 가장 적절한 것을 고르시오. 정답률 85%

① 공상 과학 소설을 읽으면 과학에 대한 흥미를 키울 수 있다.
② 다양한 주제의 책을 읽는 것이 창의력 향상에 도움이 된다.
③ 책을 읽을 때에는 배경지식을 활용하는 것이 중요하다.
④ 꾸준한 독서를 통해 작문 실력을 향상시킬 수 있다.
⑤ 책의 내용을 반복해서 읽어야 기억에 오래 남는다.

3 ○△× • 2025년 6월 교육청(고1) 3번

다음을 듣고, 남자가 하는 말의 요지로 가장 적절한 것을 고르시오. 정답률 94%

① 햇빛을 쬐는 것은 신체와 정신의 건강에 도움이 된다.
② 자외선 차단제를 바르는 것은 피부 노화를 예방한다.
③ 건강을 위해 다양한 영양소를 고루 섭취해야 한다.
④ 몸과 마음이 건강하면 삶의 만족도가 높아진다.
⑤ 야외 활동 시 안전 수칙을 준수해야 한다.

4 ○△× • 2023년 9월 교육청(고1) 4번

대화를 듣고, 그림에서 대화의 내용과 일치하지 않는 것을 고르시오. 정답률 86%

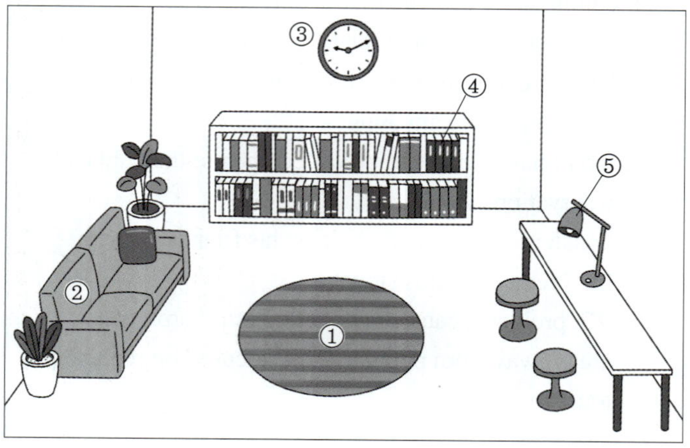

5 고득점 ○△× • 2017년 3월 교육청(고1) 7번

대화를 듣고, 남자가 여자를 위해 할 일로 가장 적절한 것을 고르시오. 정답률 63%

① 동아리 안내 책자 가져다주기
② 동아리 모임 장소 예약하기
③ 동아리 방에 함께 가기
④ 동아리 모임 일정 짜기
⑤ 동아리 가입 신청서 대신 제출하기

6 ○△× • 2020년 6월 교육청(고1) 9번

대화를 듣고, 여자가 지불할 금액을 고르시오. [3점] 정답률 86%

① $15 ② $23 ③ $27 ④ $30 ⑤ $33

7 ○△× • 2023년 9월 교육청(고1) 7번

대화를 듣고, 여자가 스키 여행을 갈 수 없는 이유를 고르시오. 정답률 94%

① 카페에서 일해야 해서
② 숙소를 예약하지 못해서
③ 역사 시험 공부를 해야 해서
④ 수술받은 고양이를 돌봐야 해서
⑤ 캐나다에 사는 친척을 방문해야 해서

8 ○△× • 2022년 3월 교육청(고1) 8번

대화를 듣고, Stanville Free-cycle에 관해 언급되지 않은 것을 고르시오. 정답률 90%

① 참가 대상 ② 행사 장소 ③ 주차 가능 여부
④ 행사 시작일 ⑤ 금지 품목

9 ○△× • 2024년 6월 교육청(고1) 9번

Violet Hill Mentorship에 관한 다음 내용을 듣고, 일치하지 않는 것을 고르시오. 정답률 95%

① 다음 주 금요일에 개최될 예정이다.
② 대학 생활에 관한 조언이 제공된다.
③ 신청 시 질문을 미리 제출해야 한다.
④ 신청 마감일은 다음 주 화요일이다.
⑤ 전공별 참가 가능한 인원은 20명이다.

10 ○△× · 2025년 3월 교육청(고1) 10번

다음 표를 보면서 대화를 듣고, 여자가 수강할 운동 수업을 고르시오. 정답률 78%

Exercise Classes

	Class	Fee	Time	Exercise Type	Level
①	A	$25	9:00 a.m.	Dancing	Beginner
②	B	$35	10:00 a.m.	Dancing	Advanced
③	C	$35	10:00 a.m.	Tennis	Beginner
④	D	$35	2:00 p.m.	Boxing	Beginner
⑤	E	$45	10:00 a.m.	Boxing	Advanced

11 ○△× · 2025년 3월 교육청(고1) 12번

대화를 듣고, 남자의 마지막 말에 대한 여자의 응답으로 가장 적절한 것을 고르시오. 정답률 74%

① Thanks. But I'm not hungry now.
② I agree. Printing it out is such a waste.
③ Of course not. I'll help you at any time.
④ Great idea! It'll catch the students' attention.
⑤ No worries. I like the menu of our school cafeteria.

12 고득점 ○△× · 2022년 9월 교육청(고1) 11번

대화를 듣고, 여자의 마지막 말에 대한 남자의 응답으로 가장 적절한 것을 고르시오. 정답률 69%

① You can join the tour, too.
② The bike wasn't that expensive.
③ I haven't decided the place, yet.
④ I'm going to rent a bike in the park.
⑤ Autumn is the best season for the tour.

13 ○△× · 2024년 6월 교육청(고1) 13번

대화를 듣고, 남자의 마지막 말에 대한 여자의 응답으로 가장 적절한 것을 고르시오. [3점] 정답률 85%

Woman: ______________________

① Yes. I can give you the phone number of the clinic I visited.
② I agree. Last evening's badminton match was awesome.
③ No problem. I'll teach you how to serve this time.
④ Too bad. I hope you recover from your knee injury soon.
⑤ You're right. Maybe I should start taking badminton lessons.

14 ○△× · 2019년 3월 교육청(고1) 13번

대화를 듣고, 여자의 마지막 말에 대한 남자의 응답으로 가장 적절한 것을 고르시오. [3점] 정답률 86%

Man: ______________________

① There's no room for a new member in our club.
② I'm sorry that you didn't pass the club interview.
③ That's true. We can't trust all the information there.
④ Thanks, but I don't want to take the drone class again.
⑤ Right. I'll post an ad for a drone club I'm going to make.

15 ○△× · 2024년 6월 교육청(고1) 15번

다음 상황 설명을 듣고, Laura가 Tony에게 할 말로 가장 적절한 것을 고르시오. 정답률 84%

Laura: ______________________

① I don't like visiting a hospital for medical checkups.
② I appreciate you taking me to the doctor today.
③ You'd better take a break for a few days.
④ You should finish your work before the deadline.
⑤ I'm afraid I can't reduce your workload right now.

[16~17] 다음을 듣고, 물음에 답하시오.

16 ○△× · 2021년 9월 교육청(고1) 16번

여자가 하는 말의 주제로 가장 적절한 것은? 정답률 96%

① different animals that are popular in different cultures
② unique sleeping habits that animals use for survival
③ wild animals that are becoming endangered species
④ how animals have changed their ways of eating
⑤ animals that bring people good luck

17 ○△× · 2021년 9월 교육청(고1) 17번

언급된 동물이 아닌 것은? 정답률 95%

① bats ② ducks ③ chimpanzees
④ giraffes ⑤ dolphins

초급 2회

Dictation

문제 풀이에 중요한 핵심 부분과 듣기에 자주 나오는 표현들에 빈칸 처리를 했습니다. 방송을 잘 듣고, 빈칸에 알맞은 말을 써 넣으세요.

Tip! 잘 들리지 않는 부분이 있을 때에는 정답을 확인 후, 똑같은 속도로 따라 읽기 연습을 해 보세요.

1

M: Good afternoon, everybody. This is Student President Sam Wilson. As you know, the lunch basketball league will begin soon. Many students are interested in __________ __________ __________ and waiting for the signup sheet to be handed out at the gym. For easier access, we've decided to __________ __________ __________ __________. Instead of going to the gym to register, simply log into the school website and __________ __________ __________ __________ __________ __________. Thank you for listening and let's have a good league.

2

W: Daniel, I see you're reading a book. What's it about?

M: Hello, Ms. Williams. It's about time travel. I'm a big fan of science fiction.

W: I know that. But why do you only read science fiction?

M: I feel like reading science fiction __________ __________ __________ __________.

W: I see. But if you really want to improve your creativity, you shouldn't just read science fiction. It would be better to read books on various topics.

M: What does that have to do with improving my creativity?

W: Reading many kinds of books will make you see things __________ __________ __________ __________.

M: That makes sense. With more perspectives, I can be more creative.

W: Exactly! Reading books on various topics will help you __________ __________ __________ __________.

M: Okay, I'll try it. Thank you for your advice.

3

M: Hello, listeners! This is Thomas White's *Living Well*. What do you do to stay healthy? Maybe you exercise regularly and eat healthy food. Those are both great habits. But I have one more simple tip for you. Go outside and __________ __________ __________! Sunlight is important for your body and mind. Getting sunlight can __________ __________ __________ __________ __________ and can reduce anxiety. It's an easy way to help you stay healthy __________ __________ __________ __________. I'll be right back with more after the break.

4

W: Come look at the new reading room in the library.

M: Wow! It's much better than I thought.

W: Same here. I like the rug in the center of the room.

M: The striped pattern of the rug makes the room feel warm.

W: I agree. I think __________ __________ __________ __________ __________ __________ was a good idea.

M: Right. We can sit there and read for hours.

W: There's a round clock on the wall.

M: I have the same clock at home. Oh, the bookshelf under the clock __________ __________ __________ __________.

W: We can read the books at the long table.

M: Yeah, it looks like a good place to read. The __________ __________ __________ __________ will make it easy to focus.

W: Good lighting is important for reading.

M: I can't wait to start using the reading room.

5

W: What are you doing, Sam?
M: I'm ___________ ___________ ___________ ___________ to join the school movie club.
W: Really? I'm also interested in that club.
M: Let's join together then.
W: I'd love to, but I already belong to the science club.
M: You can join both.
W: You're right. I'll have to check the movie club's meeting schedule first, though.
M: Then I'll ___________ ___________ ___________ ___________ ___________ ___________ for you from the club room later.
W: That'll be great. Thanks.
M: No problem. I'll have to go ___________ ___________ ___________ ___________ anyway.

6

[Telephone rings.]
M: Good evening, John's Food Delivery. How may I help you?
W: Hi. I'd like to order some dinners.
M: Okay. What would you like?
W: How much is a cheeseburger set?
M: ___________ ___________ ___________. How many would you like?
W: I need two sets. Is there anything else you can recommend?
M: Yes, our newest item, the avocado sandwich, is very delicious. It's seven dollars.
W: Good. ___________ ___________ ___________ ___________ to my order, please.
M: So two cheeseburger sets and two avocado sandwiches, right?
W: Yes. And I have a discount coupon for new customers.
M: Okay, then you'll ___________ ___________ ___________ ___________ ___________. Where would you like your food delivered?
W: 101 Fifth St., please.

7

M: You seem busy this morning, Olivia.
W: I am. I had to see Professor Martin about my history test.
M: Oh, I see. Do you remember that our club's ski trip is this weekend?
W: Yeah. I heard that a nice ski resort has been booked for the trip.
M: I didn't know that. I'm so excited to go skiing at a nice resort.
W: I bet it'll be great, but I don't think I can go this time.
M: Why? You ___________ ___________ ___________ ___________ ___________ on the weekends, do you?
W: No, I don't. But I need to take care of my cat. She's ___________ ___________ ___________.
M: Isn't there anyone else who can ___________ ___________ ___________ ___________?
W: No one but me. My parents are visiting relatives in Canada. They won't be back for two weeks.
M: I'm sorry that you can't join us.
W: Me, too. Have fun this weekend.

8

W: Honey, did you see the poster about the Stanville Free-cycle?
M: Free-cycle? What is that?
W: It's another way of recycling. You give away items you don't need and anybody can take them for free.
M: Oh, it's like one man's garbage is another man's treasure. Who can participate?
W: It's ___________ ___________ ___________ ___________ ___________ Stanville.
M: Great. Where is it taking place?
W: At Rose Park on Second Street.
M: When does the event start?
W: It ___________ ___________ ___________ ___________ and runs for a week.
M: Let's see what we can free-cycle, starting from the cupboard.
W: Okay. But breakable items like glass dishes or cups ___________ ___________ ___________.
M: I see. I'll keep that in mind.

초급 2회

9

M: Good morning, students of Violet Hill High School. This is your principal speaking. I'm delighted to announce that the annual Violet Hill Mentorship __________ __________ __________ __________ __________. Our school graduates who are now majoring in English literature, bioengineering, and theater and film will be __________ __________ __________ __________ __________ __________. To register for this event, visit our school website and submit two questions you would like to ask them in advance. The deadline for registration is next Tuesday, so don't wait too long. And remember, the maximum number of __________ __________ __________ __________ __________ __________ __________. For more information, visit our school website.

10

M: Sweetie, what are you doing?

W: I'm looking at the schedule for exercise classes. Would you like to help me choose?

M: Sure. What's your budget for it?

W: Well, I don't want to __________ __________ __________ __________ __________.

M: Okay. Then, forget about this one. What about class time?

W: As you know, I have things to do in the afternoon.

M: In that case, let's cross this one out. Now you have dancing and tennis left.

W: I heard the tennis class is held outside. I __________ __________ __________ __________.

M: Okay. Then, we have only two exercise classes left. Which level is good for you?

W: Since I've already taken the beginner's class, __________ __________ __________ __________ __________ this time.

11

M: Ashley, do you remember the digital poster we made to upload on social media?

W: Yes, of course. It __________ __________ __________ __________, right?

M: Exactly. Let's print it out and __________ __________ __________ __________ __________ in our school cafeteria.

W: (Great idea! It'll catch the students' attention.)

12

W: Kevin, is this bike yours?

M: Yes, I bought it __________ __________ __________ __________.

W: Really? __________ __________ __________ __________ __________ __________?

M: (I haven't decided the place, yet.)

13

M: Hey, Cindy. Have you been playing a lot of badminton these days?

W: No, I've been experiencing some pain in my knee since a badminton match last weekend.

M: I'm sorry to hear that. Did you go see a doctor?

W: Yes, I visited a local clinic yesterday.

M: I hope you feel better soon. By the way, have you ever __________ __________ __________ __________?

W: No, I haven't. Why are you asking?

M: In my experience, that kind of injury can come from bad posture. A lesson might __________ __________ __________ __________ __________ __________ __________.

W: Well, I thought I didn't need those lessons.

M: Cindy, if you want to keep playing badminton without any injuries, it's important to learn from an instructor to __________ __________ __________ __________.

W: (You're right. Maybe I should start taking badminton lessons.)

14

W: Hi, David. What are you looking at?
M: School club posters.
W: Is there any club you want to join?
M: I'm interested in drones, but there's no drone club.
W: That's too bad. Why don't you ___________ ___________ ___________ ___________ ___________?
M: Oh, I haven't thought about it. What do I have to do first?
W: You'll need at least five people to start a club.
M: Then I have to find people ___________ ___________ ___________ ___________ ___________.
W: How about ___________ ___________ ___________? It's an easy way to attract people.
M: (Right. I'll post an ad for a drone club I'm going to make.)

15

W: Laura and Tony are close coworkers. Laura notices that Tony has been ___________ ___________ ___________ ___________ ___________ ___________. One day, she asks Tony if he's not been feeling well lately, but Tony says he's just a bit tired from work. Laura knows that Tony sometimes works even on weekends ___________ ___________ ___________ ___________ or getting any rest. However, this time, she is really worried about him and wants him to take at least ___________ ___________ ___________ ___________ ___________. In this situation, what would Laura most likely say to Tony?
Laura: (You'd better take a break for a few days.)

16~17

W: Everyone loves a good night's sleep, but for wild animals, finding the right time and place can be difficult. Whether it's staying safe, keeping warm, or remembering to breathe, animals have a lot to consider before they go to bed. As a result, they've come up with some clever and interesting solutions. To start with, bats sleep in caves while hanging upside down. Doing that not only ___________ ___________ ___________ ___________ ___________ but also means they are in the perfect position to fly away if necessary. Meanwhile, ducks sleep side by side in rows. The ducks on the outside of the rows sleep with one eye open ___________ ___________ ___________ ___________, while the ducks on the inside sleep with both eyes closed. Giraffes require little rest, sleeping for only five minutes at a time or as little as 30 minutes a day. They ___________ ___________ ___________ ___________, sometimes sitting down or even standing up, so that they're ready to run. Finally, dolphins have to consciously think in order to breathe, even when they're sleeping. They only let part of their brain relax and keep one eye open as they sleep.

Dictation Answers

1. joining the league / change the registration method / fill out the registration form online
2. makes me more creative / from many different perspectives / think outside the box
3. get some sunlight / prevent you from getting sick / both physically and mentally
4. putting the sofa between two plants / is full of books / two lamps on the table
5. filling out an application / pick up the movie club's brochure / submit this application form
6. It's eight dollars / Add two avocado sandwiches / get 10% off the total
7. don't work at the cafe / recovering from surgery / look after your cat
8. open to everyone living in / starts on April 12 / won't be accepted
9. will be held next Friday / giving some tips on university life / participants for each major is 30 people
10. spend more than forty dollars / don't like outdoor sports / I'll take the other one
11. was about food waste / put it on the wall
12. for my bike tour / Where are you planning to go
13. taken a badminton lesson / reduce the risk of any further injury / develop the right posture
14. make a new club yourself / who are interested in drones / using social media
15. looking unusually tired and pale recently / without taking a break / a couple of days off

16~17. keeps them away from enemies / to watch for danger / sleep in short intervals

제3회 초급 모의고사

맞은 개수: 2점 문항 ___개, 3점 문항 ___개
알고 푼 문항은 ○, 찍어서 맞힌 문제는 △에 표시하고, △와 ×는 다시 복습하세요.

1번부터 17번까지는 듣고 답하는 문제입니다. 1번부터 15번까지는 한 번만 들려주고, 16번부터 17번까지는 두 번 들려줍니다. 방송을 잘 듣고 답을 하시기 바랍니다.

1 ○△× • 2023년 3월 교육청(고1) 1번

다음을 듣고, 남자가 하는 말의 목적으로 가장 적절한 것을 고르시오. 정답률 87%

① 아이스하키부의 우승을 알리려고
② 아이스하키부 훈련 일정을 공지하려고
③ 아이스하키부 신임 감독을 소개하려고
④ 아이스하키부 선수 모집을 안내하려고
⑤ 아이스하키부 경기의 관람을 독려하려고

2 ○△× • 2025년 3월 교육청(고1) 2번

대화를 듣고, 여자의 의견으로 가장 적절한 것을 고르시오. 정답률 82%

① 학급 뮤지컬은 다양한 음악을 활용해야 한다.
② 학급 뮤지컬은 학생이 공연하기 쉬워야 한다.
③ 학급 뮤지컬은 인기 있는 소재를 다루어야 한다.
④ 학급 뮤지컬은 의미 있는 교훈을 전달해야 한다.
⑤ 학급 뮤지컬은 학생 모두가 역할을 맡아야 한다.

3 ○△× • 2024년 3월 교육청(고1) 3번

다음을 듣고, 여자가 하는 말의 요지로 가장 적절한 것을 고르시오. 정답률 92%

① 학업 목표를 분명히 설정하는 것이 필요하다.
② 친구와의 협력은 학교생활의 중요한 덕목이다.
③ 과제 제출 마감 기한을 확인하고 준수해야 한다.
④ 적절한 휴식은 성공적인 과업 수행의 핵심 요소이다.
⑤ 할 일의 목록을 활용하는 것이 시간 관리에 유용하다.

4 ○△× • 2024년 9월 교육청(고1) 4번

대화를 듣고, 그림에서 대화의 내용과 일치하지 않는 것을 고르시오. 정답률 85%

5 ○△× • 2025년 3월 교육청(고1) 5번

대화를 듣고, 남자가 할 일로 가장 적절한 것을 고르시오. 정답률 83%

① 숲지도 다운로드 하기
② 산책 장소 찾아보기
③ 숲 입장권 구매하기
④ 식당 메뉴 찾아보기
⑤ 식당 예약하기

6 ○△× • 2017년 3월 교육청(고1) 9번

대화를 듣고, 남자가 지불할 금액을 고르시오. 정답률 88%

① $8 ② $10 ③ $12 ④ $14 ⑤ $16

7 ○△× • 2021년 9월 교육청(고1) 7번

대화를 듣고, 남자가 헬스장 회원권을 연장하지 않은 이유를 고르시오. 정답률 96%

① 어깨 부상이 회복되지 않아서
② 운동에 흥미를 잃어서
③ 샤워 시설이 낡고 좁아서
④ 가격이 인상되어서
⑤ 방과후 수업에 참여해야 해서

8 ○△× • 2025년 6월 교육청(고1) 8번

대화를 듣고, Fireworks Festival 자원봉사에 관해 언급되지 않은 것을 고르시오. 정답률 86%

① 기간
② 지원 가능 연령
③ 준비물
④ 활동 내용
⑤ 신청 기한

9 ○△× • 2024년 3월 교육청(고1) 9번

Triwood High School Volunteer Program에 관한 다음 내용을 듣고, 일치하지 않는 것을 고르시오. 정답률 94%

① 노인을 도와주는 봉사 활동이다.
② 봉사자는 대면으로 활동한다.
③ 스마트폰 사용 방법 교육을 한다.
④ 봉사자는 매주 토요일에 세 시간씩 참여한다.
⑤ 지원자는 이메일로 참가 신청서를 보내야 한다.

10 ○△× ········· 2019년 3월 교육청(고1) 12번

다음 표를 보면서 대화를 듣고, 남자가 구입할 운동 매트를 고르시오. 정답률 80%

Exercise Mats

	Model	Thickness	Price	Non-slip Surface
①	A	4mm	$24	×
②	B	6mm	$33	○
③	C	8mm	$38	×
④	D	8mm	$45	○
⑤	E	10mm	$55	○

11 고득점 ○△× ········· 2017년 9월 교육청(고1) 2번

대화를 듣고, 남자의 마지막 말에 대한 여자의 응답으로 가장 적절한 것을 고르시오. 정답률 56%

① The conductor was really impressive.
② There was heavy traffic, so I arrived late.
③ My dad gave me two tickets for the concert.
④ Classical music always makes me feel relaxed.
⑤ I kept coughing and didn't want to bother anyone.

12 ○△× ········· 2022년 3월 교육청(고1) 12번

대화를 듣고, 여자의 마지막 말에 대한 남자의 응답으로 가장 적절한 것을 고르시오. 정답률 80%

① That's not fair. I booked this seat first.
② Thank you. My friend will be glad to know it.
③ You're welcome. Feel free to ask me anything.
④ Not at all. I don't mind changing seats with you.
⑤ That's okay. I think the seat next to it is available.

13 고득점 ○△× ········· 2024년 9월 교육청(고1) 14번

대화를 듣고, 남자의 마지막 말에 대한 여자의 응답으로 가장 적절한 것을 고르시오. [3점] 정답률 65%

Woman: ____________________

① Trust me. When we eat makes a big difference.
② Okay. I'll check my meals to get in better shape.
③ Thank you for your tip. But I don't think I can do it.
④ Of course. I'll make sure to follow your workout routine.
⑤ Sure. That's why I didn't succeed at keeping a balanced diet.

14 ○△× ········· 2020년 3월 교육청(고1) 13번

대화를 듣고, 여자의 마지막 말에 대한 남자의 응답으로 가장 적절한 것을 고르시오. [3점] 정답률 88%

Man: ____________________

① I have, but he didn't take it seriously.
② Don't worry. I have no problem with him.
③ Well, he always keeps the bathroom clean.
④ Sorry. I delayed moving out of the apartment.
⑤ Of course. I'll help you move into a new apartment.

15 ○△× ········· 2023년 9월 교육청(고1) 15번

다음 상황 설명을 듣고, Brian이 Melissa에게 할 말로 가장 적절한 것을 고르시오. [3점] 정답률 89%

Brian: ____________________

① Let's clean the classroom after art class.
② Did you remove the stickers from the board?
③ Please turn off the heater when you leave the room.
④ When is the final date to sign up for the design class?
⑤ Will you design stickers that encourage energy saving?

[16~17] 다음을 듣고, 물음에 답하시오.

16 ○△× ········· 2018년 6월 교육청(고1) 16번

남자가 하는 말의 주제로 가장 적절한 것은? 정답률 79%

① ways to prevent food allergies
② common ingredients in cold medicines
③ how to make a tea for relieving cough
④ different types of tea and their origins
⑤ increasing popularity of homemade foods

17 ○△× ········· 2018년 6월 교육청(고1) 17번

언급된 재료가 아닌 것은? 정답률 82%

① ginger ② honey ③ lemon
④ peppermint ⑤ cinnamon

초급 3회

Dictation

문제 풀이에 중요한 핵심 부분과 듣기에 자주 나오는 표현들에 빈칸 처리를 했습니다. 방송을 잘 듣고, 빈칸에 알맞은 말을 써 넣으세요.

Tip! 잘 들리지 않는 부분이 있을 때에는 정답을 확인 후, 똑같은 속도로 따라 읽기 연습을 해 보세요.

1

M: Hello, Villeford High School students. This is principal Aaron Clark. __________ __________ __________ __________ __________ the Villeford ice hockey team, I'm very excited about the upcoming National High School Ice Hockey League. As you all know, the first game will be held in the Central Rink at 6 p.m. this Saturday. I want as many of you as possible to come and __________ __________ __________ __________ __________. I've seen them put in an incredible amount of effort __________ __________ __________ __________. It will help them play better just to see you there cheering for them. I really hope to see you at the rink. Thank you.

2

W: Ryan, did you enjoy the musical "Tigers" yesterday?

M: Yes, I loved it. I can't believe we got tickets for such a popular show.

W: Yes, we were lucky. By the way, it __________ __________ __________ __________ __________ __________ that we have to prepare for the next month's school festival.

M: You read my mind! I think we should look for a musical with __________ __________ __________ __________.

W: Well, there might be something even more important than that.

M: Should we give the audience a meaningful lesson?

W: Not necessarily. Do you remember what we did last year?

M: Yes. We focused on preparing a musical that was easy to perform.

W: Right. But not everyone participated. I think __________ __________ __________ __________ __________ for the class musical.

M: That's a good point.

3

W: Hello, this is your student counselor, Susan Smith. You might be worried about your new school life as a freshman. You have a lot of things to do in the beginning of the year. Today, I'm going to give you a tip about time management. __________ __________ __________ __________! Write down the tasks you have to do on a list and __________ __________ __________ __________ __________, one by one. By doing this, you won't miss the things you need to do. Using a to-do list will help you __________ __________ __________ __________. Good luck to you and don't forget to start today.

4

M: Hey, Amy. Here is the new recording studio for our band. How do you like it?

W: Wow, these two speakers are impressive!

M: Yes, they are. The sound quality is excellent.

W: Also, the __________ __________ __________ __________ __________ looks great.

M: Yeah. And on the desk, there is a microphone. We can use it to give recording directions.

W: Nice. Oh, this chair looks comfortable. It could be helpful for long recordings.

M: Agreed. And the rug under the chair __________ __________ __________ __________ __________ __________, doesn't it?

W: Yes, and I like the __________ __________ __________ __________ __________.

M: I like it, too. How about the poster on the wall?

W: It's cool. This studio feels like where music truly comes alive!

M: I'm glad you like this place.

W: Absolutely. I can't wait to start recording here.

5

W: Honey, the flowers are really beautiful these days. Why don't we take a walk this weekend?
M: Wow, that sounds great. Do you have any particular place in mind?
W: Yes, I'd like to visit the Grand Forest. I've already downloaded the map of the forest.
M: That's nice. Do we have to ________ ________ ________?
W: Yes. We can buy tickets online. I'll buy two tickets in the afternoon.
M: Great. Let's have a nice lunch there, too. There's a restaurant called Treehouse Pasta in the Grand Forest.
W: Nice. Do we have to make a reservation?
M: Yes. ________ ________ ________ ________ right away.
W: Then, I'll ________ ________ ________ ________ of the restaurant.
M: Thanks.

6

M: Good morning, Jennifer.
W: Good morning, Robin. How may I help you today?
M: This bagel sandwich looks so delicious. How much is it?
W: It was originally five dollars, but it's three dollars now. We're having a sale to ________ ________ ________ ________.
M: Great. I'll take two bagel sandwiches.
W: Okay. What about coffee?
M: ________ ________ ________ ________, too?
W: Sure. You can take ________ ________ ________ ________ ________ ________.
M: Wow! I'll order two cappuccinos.
W: Anything else?
M: That's all. Here's my credit card.

7

M: Mom, I'm home.
W: Hi. Did you go to the gym?
M: Yes. My membership ended today, but I didn't renew it.
W: Why? Does your shoulder still hurt?
M: No, ________ ________ ________ ________ ________.
W: So, what's the problem? I thought you were enjoying exercising.
M: I was. It's actually been fun.
W: Then why didn't you ________ ________ ________?
M: Well, the ________ ________ ________ ________ ________ are too old, and there's not enough space in the shower stalls.
W: I see. Why don't you check out the new health club nearby? It may be more expensive, but the facilities are probably a lot better.
M: Okay. Maybe I should visit there tomorrow on my way home after school.
W: That sounds like a good plan!

8

W: Jay, did you hear about the Fireworks Festival?
M: Yeah, I heard it's going to be amazing.
W: I'm thinking of volunteering there. Take a look at this poster about it.
M: The ________ ________ ________ ________ ________ ________, June 14th and 15th.
W: That's right. Would you like to join?
M: I'd love to. But can just anyone apply to be a volunteer?
W: ________ ________ ________ ________ can apply. So, we're both good.
M: I see. What exactly will we do during the festival?
W: It says we'll check tickets, run activity booths, or take photos for the festival website.
M: Sounds interesting. And look! We have to ________ ________ ________ ________ ________.
W: Really? We don't have much time. Let's do it right now.

9

W: Hello, students! Are you looking for a chance to help others? Then, I recommend you to join Triwood High School Volunteer Program to help senior citizens. You're supposed to __________ __________ __________ __________ __________. You teach them how to use their smartphones for things such as sending text messages or taking pictures. You will also teach seniors __________ __________ __________ __________ __________. The program will require volunteers to __________ __________ __________ __________ __________ __________. If you are interested in joining our program, please send us an application form through email.

10

W: Good morning. How may I help you?

M: I'm looking for an exercise mat for home training.

W: Okay. Here are our best-selling models.

M: They all look nice. Are thicker mats better?

W: Not really. But I think it should be at least __________ __________ __________ __________.

M: I see. Then I have to choose from these four.

W: How about this one? It's the most popular.

M: It's too expensive. I don't want to __________ __________ __________ __________.

W: Out of these two options left, I recommend this model with a non-slip surface. It __________ __________ __________ __________ __________.

M: Okay. Safety is important. I'll take it.

11

M: Did you go to the classical music concert yesterday?

W: Yes, I did. But I had to leave __________ __________ __________ __________ __________ __________.

M: Oh, really? __________ __________ __________ __________?

W: (I kept coughing and didn't want to bother anyone.)

12

W: Excuse me. __________ __________ __________ __________ __________ __________ here?

M: I'm sorry, but __________ __________ __________ __________. He'll be back in a minute.

W: Oh, I didn't know that. Sorry for bothering you.

M: (That's okay. I think the seat next to it is available.)

13

M: Hey, Emily! You're looking great these days.

W: Thanks, Isaac. I've been trying hard to get in better shape.

M: Good for you! __________ __________ __________ __________ __________, too. But it's tough.

W: Haven't you been working out a lot lately?

M: Yeah, but I __________ __________ __________ __________ __________. What's your secret?

W: Well, I started being careful about when I eat.

M: You mean like not eating right before bed?

W: Kind of. I noticed I was eating a lot at night. So now I don't eat after 7 p.m.

M: Hmm... __________ __________ __________ __________ __________ __________ to get me in better shape.

W: (Trust me. When we eat makes a big difference.)

14

W: Hey, Chris. What are you looking at on your cell phone?

M: I'm looking for an apartment to rent.

W: Aren't you sharing an apartment with William?

M: Yeah, but I'm __________ __________ __________ __________.

W: Why? I thought you two get along well with each other.

M: There have been a lot of problems between us. One thing __________ __________ __________.

W: Oh, what is it?

M: Actually, __________ __________ __________ __________. The kitchen and the bathroom are always messy.

W: That's awful. Have you talked about this issue with him?

M: (I have, but he didn't take it seriously.)

15

W: Brian is a class leader. He is __________ __________ __________ __________ and saving energy. Recently, he's noticed that his classmates don't turn the lights off when they leave the classroom. Brian thinks this is very careless. He wants to make stickers that __________ __________ __________ __________ __________ __________ by turning off the lights. He tells this idea to his classmate Melissa, and she agrees it's a good idea. Brian knows Melissa is a great artist, so he wants to __________ __________ __________ __________ __________ that encourage their classmates to save energy. In this situation, what would Brian most likely say to Melissa?

Brian: (Will you design stickers that encourage energy saving?)

16~17

M: Hello, listeners, and welcome to *Health Matters*. This is Dr. David Harvey. Coughing is one of __________ __________ __________ __________ of a cold. To relieve it, you might only think of going to a doctor or taking medicine. However, __________ __________ __________ can be an excellent way to warm you up and soothe your throat and cough. This kind of tea is __________ __________ __________ __________ __________ anybody can do it. First, get two inches of fresh ginger and slice it thinly. Next, boil the ginger slices in two cups of water for at least 10 minutes. Then, turn off the heat and add some honey. Squeeze a lemon and put the juice in the tea. You can add a bit of cinnamon at the end for flavor. I hope you'll enjoy your hot tea and stay healthy.

Dictation Answers

1. As a big fan of / cheer our team to victory / to win the league
2. reminded me of the class musical / a variety of music / everyone should have a role
3. Make a to-do list / check off what you finish / manage your time efficiently
4. long desk between the speakers / gives the room a cozy feeling / flower patterns on the rug
5. buy entrance tickets / I'll make the reservation / look up the menu
6. celebrate our 10th anniversary / Is it on sale / any coffee for just two dollars
7. my shoulder feels completely fine / renew your membership / shower facilities at the gym
8. volunteer period is for two days / Only people over 18 / sign up by this Friday
9. help the senior citizens face-to-face / how to use various apps / participate for two hours every Saturday
10. 5mm for home trainers / spend more than $40 / keeps you from sliding around
11. in the middle of the concert / Why did you leave
12. Would you mind if I sit / it's my friend's seat
13. I'm trying to get fit / don't see a big difference / I don't know if that's enough
14. thinking about moving out / especially bothers me / he never cleans up
15. passionate about environmental issues / remind his classmates to save energy / ask her to design stickers

16~17. the most common symptoms / drinking homemade tea / so easy to make that

제4회 초급 모의고사

맞은 개수: 2점 문항 ___개, 3점 문항 ___개
알고 푼 문항은 ○, 찍어서 맞힌 문제는 △에 표시하고, △와 ×는 다시 복습하세요.

1번부터 17번까지는 듣고 답하는 문제입니다. 1번부터 15번까지는 한 번만 들려주고, 16번부터 17번까지는 두 번 들려줍니다. 방송을 잘 듣고 답을 하시기 바랍니다.

1 ○△× · 2025년 9월 교육청(고1) 1번

다음을 듣고, 여자가 하는 말의 목적으로 가장 적절한 것을 고르시오. 정답률 87%

① 학부모 간담회 참석을 독려하려고
② 학부모 상담 기간 연기를 안내하려고
③ 교직원 회의 시간 변경에 대한 협조를 요청하려고
④ 학부모 간담회를 위한 교직원 주차 장소 변경을 알리려고
⑤ 지역 주민 행사를 위한 주말 교내 주차 허용을 공지하려고

2 ○△× · 2022년 3월 교육청(고1) 2번

대화를 듣고, 여자의 의견으로 가장 적절한 것을 고르시오. 정답률 96%

① 평소에 피부 상태를 잘 관찰할 필요가 있다.
② 여드름을 치료하려면 피부과 병원에 가야 한다.
③ 얼굴을 손으로 만지는 것은 얼굴 피부에 해롭다.
④ 지성 피부를 가진 사람은 자주 세수를 해야 한다.
⑤ 손을 자주 씻는 것은 감염병 예방에 도움이 된다.

3 ○△× · 2025년 3월 교육청(고1) 3번

다음을 듣고, 남자가 하는 말의 요지로 가장 적절한 것을 고르시오. 정답률 89%

① 건강을 지키기 위해서 규칙적인 운동이 필수적이다.
② 바쁜 일상에서 휴식을 취하는 것은 건강에 중요하다.
③ 집중력을 높이는 것은 업무 수행 능력을 향상시킨다.
④ 운동 부족을 보완하려면 적절한 식이 요법이 필요하다.
⑤ 다양한 인간관계가 스트레스를 줄이는 데 도움이 된다.

4 ○△× · 2021년 3월 교육청(고1) 4번

대화를 듣고, 그림에서 대화의 내용과 일치하지 않는 것을 고르시오. 정답률 83%

5 ○△× · 2024년 6월 교육청(고1) 5번

대화를 듣고, 남자가 할 일로 가장 적절한 것을 고르시오. 정답률 83%

① 과학 캠프 지원하기
② 참가 실험 결정하기
③ 체크리스트 작성하기
④ 실험 계획서 보여주기
⑤ 자기 소개 영상 촬영하기

6 ○△× · 2025년 6월 교육청(고1) 6번

대화를 듣고, 여자가 지불할 금액을 고르시오. [3점] 정답률 82%

① $80 ② $90 ③ $100 ④ $110 ⑤ $120

7 ○△× · 2017년 9월 교육청(고1) 8번

대화를 듣고, 여자가 building expo에 갈 수 없는 이유를 고르시오. 정답률 75%

① 오디션에 참가해야 해서
② 건축학 특강을 들어야 해서
③ 연극 관람을 하러 가야 해서
④ 다른 박람회에 갈 계획이어서
⑤ 집짓기 봉사 활동을 해야 해서

8 ○△× · 2021년 3월 교육청(고1) 8번

대화를 듣고, Spring Virtual Run에 관해 언급되지 않은 것을 고르시오. 정답률 91%

① 달리는 거리
② 참가 인원
③ 달리는 장소
④ 참가비
⑤ 기념품

9 ○△× · 2023년 3월 교육청(고1) 9번

2023 Career Week에 관한 다음 내용을 듣고, 일치하지 않는 것을 고르시오. 정답률 90%

① 5일 동안 열릴 것이다.
② 미래 직업 탐색을 돕는 프로그램이 있을 것이다.
③ 프로그램 참가 인원에 제한이 있다.
④ 특별 강연이 마지막 날에 있을 것이다.
⑤ 등록은 5월 10일에 시작된다.

10 ○△×

• 2025년 9월 교육청(고1) 10번

다음 표를 보면서 대화를 듣고, 남자가 주문할 스마트 배낭을 고르시오. 정답률 90%

Smart Backpacks

	Model	Price	Size	Safety Feature	Charging Port
①	A	$75	13 inches	×	Internal
②	B	$85	15 inches	○	External
③	C	$90	16 inches	○	Internal
④	D	$95	16 inches	×	External
⑤	E	$110	17 inches	○	External

11 ○△×

• 2024년 6월 교육청(고1) 11번

대화를 듣고, 남자의 마지막 말에 대한 여자의 응답으로 가장 적절한 것을 고르시오. 정답률 71%

① Fine. Let's talk about it over dinner.
② Okay. Be more responsible next time.
③ Great. I already ordered some pet food.
④ Too bad. I hope your cat gets well soon.
⑤ Sorry. I can't take care of your cat tonight.

12 고득점 ○△×

• 2022년 6월 교육청(고1) 11번

대화를 듣고, 여자의 마지막 말에 대한 남자의 응답으로 가장 적절한 것을 고르시오. 정답률 63%

① All children's books are 20% off.
② It takes time to write a good article.
③ I like to read action adventure books.
④ There are too many advertisements on TV.
⑤ The store has been closed since last month.

13 ○△×

• 2023년 9월 교육청(고1) 14번

대화를 듣고, 남자의 마지막 말에 대한 여자의 응답으로 가장 적절한 것을 고르시오. [3점] 정답률 80%

Woman: ______________________________

① No. It isn't difficult for me to learn Spanish.
② I'm glad you finally passed the vocabulary test.
③ Exactly. Learning a language starts with repetition.
④ It's very helpful to use a dictionary while writing.
⑤ You should turn in your homework by this afternoon.

14 ○△×

• 2023년 9월 교육청(고1) 13번

대화를 듣고, 여자의 마지막 말에 대한 남자의 응답으로 가장 적절한 것을 고르시오. 정답률 89%

Man: ______________________________

① You're right. I won't skip meals anymore.
② Thank you for the lunch you prepared for me.
③ You need to check when the cafeteria is open.
④ Trust me. I can teach you good table manners.
⑤ No problem. We'll finish the science project on time.

15 ○△×

• 2022년 3월 교육청(고1) 15번

다음 상황 설명을 듣고, Brian이 Sally에게 할 말로 가장 적절한 것을 고르시오. [3점] 정답률 90%

Brian: ______________________________

① You shouldn't touch a guide dog without permission.
② The dog would be happy if we give it some food.
③ I'm sure it's smart enough to be a guide dog.
④ I suggest that you walk your dog every day.
⑤ I'm afraid that dogs are not allowed in here.

[16~17] 다음을 듣고, 물음에 답하시오.

16 ○△×

• 2022년 3월 교육청(고1) 16번

여자가 하는 말의 주제로 가장 적절한 것은? 정답률 77%

① activities that help build muscles
② ways to control stress in daily life
③ types of joint problems in elderly people
④ low-impact exercises for people with bad joints
⑤ importance of daily exercise for controlling weight

17 ○△×

• 2022년 3월 교육청(고1) 17번

언급된 운동이 아닌 것은? 정답률 92%

① swimming
② cycling
③ horseback riding
④ bowling
⑤ walking

Dictation

문제 풀이에 중요한 핵심 부분과 듣기에 자주 나오는 표현들에 빈칸 처리를 했습니다. 방송을 잘 듣고, 빈칸에 알맞은 말을 써 넣으세요.

Tip! 잘 들리지 않는 부분이 있을 때에는 정답을 확인 후, 똑같은 속도로 따라 읽기 연습을 해 보세요.

1

W: Hello, this is Karen Smith, the principal of Sunnyfield High School. I would like to inform all staff about an important plan for next week's Parent-Teacher Meeting. Due to limited parking on campus, all teachers and staff should __________ __________ __________ __________ __________ __________ on Wednesday. It is only a five-minute walk from the school. This plan will ensure that parents attending the meeting __________ __________ __________ __________ __________. Your cooperation will greatly assist in making this event a __________ __________ __________ __________. Thank you in advance for your cooperation with the parking arrangements.

2

W: Daniel, what are you doing in front of the mirror?

M: I have skin problems these days. I'm trying to pop these pimples on my face.

W: Pimples are really annoying, but I wouldn't do that.

M: Why not?

W: When you pop them with your hands, you're touching your face.

M: Are you saying that I __________ __________ __________ __________?

W: Exactly. You know our hands are covered with bacteria, right?

M: So?

W: You'll be __________ __________ __________ __________ __________ __________ with your hands. It could worsen your skin problems.

M: Oh, I didn't know that.

W: Touching your face with your hands is __________ __________ __________ __________.

M: Okay, I got it.

3

M: Welcome to the *Healing Tip Podcast*. I'm Dr. Smith. In our busy lives, what do you think is just as important as exercising or eating well for your health? It's rest. __________ __________ __________ __________ __________ in maintaining your overall wellbeing. It allows your body to heal and recharge, while also helping your mind relax and improving focus. That's why I want to __________ __________ __________ __________ __________ for your health. Taking time to rest can prevent stress and __________ __________ __________ __________. So, don't skip those breaks!

4

W: Is that the photo of our school's new studio?

M: Yes. We can shoot online lectures here.

W: Can I have a look?

M: Sure. Do you see that __________ __________ __________ __________? It's the latest model.

W: I see. What is that ring on the stand next to the camera?

M: That's the lighting. It's to __________ __________ __________ __________.

W: Hmm.... The __________ __________ __________ __________ __________ looks simple and modern.

M: Teachers can check the time on the clock while shooting.

W: The microphone on the table looks very professional.

M: It really does. Also, I like the tree in the corner. It goes well with the studio.

5

M: Hey, Alice. I applied for the science camp next week. What about you?

W: Me, too. But I didn't know that there were so many things to do before the camp.

M: Right. Would you like to __________ __________ __________ __________ __________?

W: Hmm, let's see. Did you upload your introduction video to the website?

M: Yes, I tried to show my interest in science. Oh, hey, have you picked which experiment to work on?

W: Yes. I decided to participate in a biology experiment.

M: Me, too. Wasn't it difficult to __________ __________ __________ __________ __________ __________?

W: Actually, I haven't even started yet because I've never written a plan for a biology experiment before.

M: __________ __________ __________ __________ after class. Maybe you can get some ideas.

W: Really? That'd be great. See you soon.

6

M: Welcome to Lake Boat Tours. How can I help you?

W: Hello. I'd like to buy some tickets for today.

M: We have daytime tickets and sunset tickets. Which would you like?

W: We'd like sunset tickets, please. How much are they?

M: __________ __________ __________ __________ and $20 for children. How many tickets do you want?

W: Two adult tickets and one child ticket, please.

M: Okay. And, we __________ __________ __________ __________ __________ __________. Would you like them?

W: Yes. Snacks for all three of us, please.

M: Alright. Do you need anything else?

W: No, that's it.

M: So, that's two adults and __________ __________ __________ __________ __________ __________, all with snacks.

W: Perfect. Here's my credit card.

7

M: The Central Park Museum will __________ __________ __________ __________ soon.

W: What's it about?

M: It's a building expo titled "New Home Builders."

W: Sounds interesting. When does it open?

M: It will start tomorrow at nine a.m. I'm going to the exhibition in the afternoon. Do you want to go with me?

W: I'm sorry, but I can't.

M: Why not? You're interested in architecture, aren't you?

W: Yes, but I __________ __________ __________ __________ __________.

M: What's your plan?

W: Actually, I'm __________ __________ __________ __________ __________ tomorrow.

M: Oh, I see now. I hope you make it.

8

W: Hi, Asher. What are you doing on the computer?

M: I'm signing up for an event called the Spring Virtual Run.

W: The Spring Virtual... Run?

M: It's a race. Participants upload their record after running either a three-mile race or a ten-mile race.

W: Can you __________ __________ __________ __________?

M: Yes. I can choose any place in the city.

W: That sounds interesting. I want to participate, too.

M: Then you should sign up online and __________ __________ __________ __________. It's twenty dollars.

W: Twenty dollars? That's pretty expensive.

M: But __________ __________ __________ in the fee. All participants will get a T-shirt and a water bottle.

W: That's reasonable. I'll sign up.

초급 4회

9

W: Hello, Rosehill High School students! I'm your school counselor, Ms. Lee. I'm so happy to announce a special event, the 2023 Career Week. It'll be held from May 22nd for five days. There will be many programs to help you ___________ ___________ ___________ ___________. Please kindly note that the number of participants for each program ___________ ___________ ___________ ___________. A special lecture on future career choices will ___________ ___________ ___________ ___________ ___________ ___________. Registration begins on May 10th. For more information, please visit our school website. I hope you can come and enjoy the 2023 Career Week!

10

W: Hey, John. What are you looking at?

M: You know I'm planning to travel abroad, so I'm checking out smart backpacks. Want to help me pick one?

W: Sure, let me see. *[Pause]* The prices are different.

M: Yeah, but I don't want to spend more than 100 dollars.

W: Got it. Let's check the size.

M: I usually carry a laptop, so it should be ___________ ___________ ___________ ___________.

W: There's also an option with a safety feature. Do you need that?

M: Definitely. It will help ___________ ___________ ___________ ___________ while traveling. That narrows it down to just two models.

W: Now, how about a charging port? I think an ___________ ___________ ___________ ___________ ___________ ___________.

M: Sounds great. I'll pick the one with an external port. I'll order it right now.

11

M: Mom, I want to have a cat. Have you ever thought about ___________ ___________ ___________ ___________?

W: Sweetie, having a pet requires a lot of responsibility.

M: I'm totally ready for it. Mom, we could ___________ ___________ ___________ ___________.

W: (Fine. Let's talk about it over dinner.)

12

W: Justin, what are you reading?

M: An advertisement. ___________ ___________ ___________ ___________ at Will's Bookstore downtown.

W: ___________ ___________ ___________ ___________ ___________ ___________?

M: (All children's books are 20% off.)

13

M: Excuse me, Ms. Lopez. Can I ask you something?

W: Sure, Tony. What can I do for you?

M: I want to ___________ ___________ ___________ ___________, but I don't know how to improve.

W: You seem to do well during class. Do you study when you're at home?

M: I do all my homework and try to learn 20 new words every day.

W: That's a good start. Do you also practice ___________ ___________ ___________ ___________?

M: Do I need to do that? That sounds like it'll take a lot of time.

W: It does. But since you're still a beginner, you have to put in more effort to get used to new words.

M: I see. So are you suggesting that I ___________ ___________ ___________ ___________ ___________?

W: (Exactly. Learning a language starts with repetition.)

14

W: I haven't seen you in the cafeteria this week. Where have you been?
M: I've been in the library working on my science project.
W: Does that mean ___________ ___________ ___________ ___________?
M: Yeah. This project is really important for my grade.
W: You shouldn't do that. It's not good for your health.
M: Don't worry. I always have a big dinner when I get home.
W: That's the problem. Skipping meals ___________ ___________ ___________ ___________.
M: I hadn't thought of that. Then what should I do?
W: It's simple. You should ___________ ___________ ___________ ___________ ___________.
M: (You're right. I won't skip meals anymore.)

15

M: Brian and Sally are walking down the street together. A blind man and his guide dog are walking towards them. Sally likes dogs very much, so she ___________ ___________ ___________ ___________ ___________ ___________ ___________. Brian doesn't think that Sally should do that. The guide dog needs to concentrate on guiding the blind person. If someone touches the dog, the dog can ___________ ___________ ___________. So Brian wants to tell Sally not to touch the guide dog ___________ ___________ ___________ ___________ ___________ ___________ ___________. In this situation, what would Brian most likely say to Sally?
Brian: (You shouldn't touch a guide dog without permission.)

16~17

W: Hello, everybody. Welcome to the health workshop. I'm Alanna Reyes, the head trainer from Eastwood Fitness Center. As you know, joints are body parts that link bones together. And doing certain physical activities puts stress on the joints. But the good news is that people with bad joints can still do certain exercises. They have ___________ ___________ ___________ ___________ ___________ ___________. Here are some examples. The first is swimming. While swimming, the water supports your body weight. The second is cycling. You put almost ___________ ___________ ___________ ___________ ___________ ___________ when you pedal smoothly. Horseback riding is another exercise that puts very little stress on your knees. Lastly, walking is great because it's low-impact, unlike running. If you have bad joints, ___________ ___________ ___________ ___________. Instead, stay active and stay healthy!

Dictation Answers

1. park at the nearby community center / have easy access to parking / smooth and successful experience
2. shouldn't touch my face / spreading bacteria all over your face / bad for your skin
3. Rest plays a crucial role / emphasize how important rest is / boost your overall wellness
4. camera facing the chair / brighten the teacher's face / round clock on the wall
5. go over my checklist together / make a plan for your experiment / I'll show you mine
6. It's $30 for adults / offer snacks for $10 per person / one child for the sunset tour
7. have a special expo / have to do something else / auditioning for the school play
8. run at any location / pay the registration fee / souvenirs are included
9. explore various future jobs / is limited to 20 / be presented on the first day
10. at least 15 inches / keep my belongings safe / external port would be more convenient
11. us adopting a cat / at least consider it
12. There's a special event / What kind of event is it
13. do better in Spanish / saying those words repeatedly / practice them over and over
14. you've been skipping lunch / makes you overeat later / eat regularly to stay healthy
15. reaches out to touch the guide dog / lose its focus / without the permission of the dog owner

16~17. relatively low impact on the joints / no stress on the knee joints / don't give up exercising

제5회 초급 모의고사

맞은 개수: 2점 문항 ___개, 3점 문항 ___개
알고 푼 문항은 ○, 찍어서 맞힌 문제는 △에 표시하고,
△와 ×는 다시 복습하세요.

1번부터 17번까지는 듣고 답하는 문제입니다. 1번부터 15번까지는 한 번만 들려주고, 16번부터 17번까지는 두 번 들려줍니다. 방송을 잘 듣고 답을 하시기 바랍니다.

1 ○△× • 2025년 6월 교육청(고1) 1번

다음을 듣고, 여자가 하는 말의 목적으로 가장 적절한 것을 고르시오. 정답률 96%

① 학생회관 리모델링 일정을 공지하려고
② 새로운 학습 자료를 제공하려고
③ 학생용 프린터 설치를 알리려고
④ 학생회장 선출 방법을 안내하려고
⑤ 프린터 고장 시 해결 방법을 설명하려고

2 ○△× • 2021년 6월 교육청(고1) 2번

대화를 듣고, 여자의 의견으로 가장 적절한 것을 고르시오. 정답률 90%

① 독서 습관을 기르자.
② 지역 서점을 이용하자.
③ 지역 특산품을 애용하자.
④ 중고 서점을 활성화시키자.
⑤ 온라인을 통한 도서 구입을 늘리자.

3 ○△× • 2020년 3월 교육청(고1) 5번

대화를 듣고, 두 사람의 관계를 가장 잘 나타낸 것을 고르시오. 정답률 82%

① 정원사 — 집주인
② 출판사 직원 — 작가
③ 가구 판매원 — 손님
④ 관광 가이드 — 관광객
⑤ 인테리어 디자이너 — 잡지 기자

4 ○△× • 2022년 3월 교육청(고1) 4번

대화를 듣고, 그림에서 대화의 내용과 일치하지 않는 것을 고르시오. 정답률 76%

5 ○△× • 2018년 3월 교육청(고1) 7번

대화를 듣고, 남자가 할 일로 가장 적절한 것을 고르시오. 정답률 86%

① 동아리 가입 신청서 제출하기
② 학교 신문 기사 작성하기
③ 입학식 안내장 배부하기
④ 입학식 사진 보내 주기
⑤ 사진 편집 도와주기

6 ○△× • 2020년 3월 교육청(고1) 9번

대화를 듣고, 여자가 지불할 금액을 고르시오. [3점] 정답률 89%

① $140 ② $180 ③ $200 ④ $220 ⑤ $280

7 ○△× • 2019년 9월 교육청(고1) 8번

대화를 듣고, 여자가 El Bistro 레스토랑을 선택한 이유를 고르시오. 정답률 89%

① 호텔에서 가까워서
② 오랜 전통이 있어서
③ 프랑스 요리로 유명해서
④ TV 프로그램에 소개되어서
⑤ 지역 주민에게 인기가 많아서

8 ○△× • 2023년 3월 교육청(고1) 8번

대화를 듣고, Youth Choir Audition에 관해 언급되지 않은 것을 고르시오. 정답률 88%

① 지원 가능 연령
② 날짜
③ 심사 기준
④ 참가비
⑤ 지원 방법

9 고득점 ○△× • 2022년 9월 교육청(고1) 9번

Lakewoods Plogging에 관한 다음 내용을 듣고, 일치하지 않는 것을 고르시오. 정답률 66%

① 참가자는 운동복과 운동화를 착용해야 한다.
② 쓰레기를 담을 봉투가 배부된다.
③ 10월 1일 오전 7시부터 진행될 것이다.
④ 학교 웹사이트에서 신청할 수 있다.
⑤ 참가자 모두 스포츠 양말을 받을 것이다.

10 ○△×

• 2021년 3월 교육청(고1) 10번

다음 표를 보면서 대화를 듣고, 여자가 구매할 스마트 워치를 고르시오. 정답률 86%

Smart Watches

	Model	Waterproof	Warranty	Price
①	A	×	2 years	$90
②	B	○	3 years	$110
③	C	○	1 year	$115
④	D	×	2 years	$120
⑤	E	○	4 years	$125

11 ○△×

• 2023년 9월 교육청(고1) 12번

대화를 듣고, 남자의 마지막 말에 대한 여자의 응답으로 가장 적절한 것을 고르시오. 정답률 83%

① Let's take the leftovers home.
② I prefer fried chicken over pizza.
③ I don't want to go out for lunch today.
④ I'll call the restaurant and check our order.
⑤ The letter was delivered to the wrong address.

12 ○△×

• 2020년 6월 교육청(고1) 1번

대화를 듣고, 여자의 마지막 말에 대한 남자의 응답으로 가장 적절한 것을 고르시오. 정답률 87%

① I already did, but I couldn't find it.
② Okay, I'll wait in the living room.
③ You need to fix the cellphone.
④ I called the Lost and Found.
⑤ Wi-Fi is not available here.

13 ○△×

• 2025년 6월 교육청(고1) 14번

대화를 듣고, 남자의 마지막 말에 대한 여자의 응답으로 가장 적절한 것을 고르시오. [3점] 정답률 82%

Woman: ____________________

① You're right. That's how I found the book.
② Well, I think the food will be delivered soon.
③ Thanks. I guess I haven't lost my chef skills.
④ Really? I didn't know that you loved to cook.
⑤ I know. That's the reason I quit being a chef.

14 ○△×

• 2022년 6월 교육청(고1) 13번

대화를 듣고, 여자의 마지막 말에 대한 남자의 응답으로 가장 적절한 것을 고르시오. 정답률 88%

Man: ____________________

① I'm excited to buy a new guitar.
② Summer vacation starts on Friday.
③ You can find it on the school website.
④ Let's go to the school festival together.
⑤ You can get some rest during the vacation.

15 ○△×

• 2023년 3월 교육청(고1) 15번

다음 상황 설명을 듣고, John이 Ted에게 할 말로 가장 적절한 것을 고르시오. [3점] 정답률 82%

John: ____________________

① How can we find the best sunrise spot?
② Why do you go mountain climbing so often?
③ What time should we get up tomorrow morning?
④ When should we come down from the mountain top?
⑤ Where do we have to stay in the mountain at night?

[16~17] 다음을 듣고, 물음에 답하시오.

16 ○△×

• 2024년 6월 교육청(고1) 16번

남자가 하는 말의 주제로 가장 적절한 것은? 정답률 75%

① relationships between media and voters
② common ways of promoting school policy
③ guidelines for student election campaigns
④ requirements for becoming a candidate
⑤ useful tips for winning school debates

17 ○△×

• 2024년 6월 교육청(고1) 17번

언급된 매체가 아닌 것은? 정답률 96%

① social media ② poster
③ pamphlet ④ school newspaper
⑤ school website

Dictation

문제 풀이에 중요한 핵심 부분과 듣기에 자주 나오는 표현들에 빈칸 처리를 했습니다. 방송을 잘 듣고, 빈칸에 알맞은 말을 써넣으세요.

Tip! 잘 들리지 않는 부분이 있을 때에는 정답을 확인 후, 똑같은 속도로 따라 읽기 연습을 해 보세요.

1

W: Good morning, everyone. I'm your student council president, Kelly Green. Many ___________ ___________ ___________ that there are no printers available for them to use. To solve this problem, next week we will ___________ ___________ ___________ ___________ ___________ in the student council room. Students will be able to use the printers for homework, projects, or any other school tasks. We hope this will help you ___________ ___________ ___________ ___________ ___________ and make your school life easier. Thank you.

2

M: Irene, where are you heading?

W: Hello, Mason. I'm going to the bookstore to buy some books.

M: The bookstore? Isn't it more convenient to order books online?

W: Yes, but I like to ___________ ___________ ___________ ___________ at bookstores.

M: Yeah, but buying books online is cheaper.

W: Right. But we ___________ ___________ ___________ ___________ when we buy books from them.

M: I guess you're right. The bookstore near my house shut down last month.

W: It's a pity to see ___________ ___________ ___________ ___________ ___________ ___________ nowadays.

M: I agree. Next time I need a book, I'll try to go to a local bookstore.

3

M: Come on in, Ms. Miller. It's been a while since your last visit.

W: Good morning, Mr. Stevens. I've been in Europe for the last two months.

M: Wow. Are you preparing for your second book?

W: Yes, I'm working on it.

M: I'm looking forward to it. So, what brings you here today?

W: I'd like to ___________ ___________ ___________ ___________.

M: I see. Do you ___________ ___________ ___________ ___________ ___________ ___________?

W: Just a plain rectangular one would be great.

M: Okay. What color would you like?

W: I was thinking dark brown.

M: Great. We have a ___________ ___________ ___________ ___________ downstairs. Come this way.

W: All right.

4

W: Yesterday, I decorated my fish tank like a beach.

M: I'd like to see it. Do you have a picture?

W: Sure. Here. *[Pause]* Do you recognize the ___________ ___________ ___________ ___________ ___________ ___________?

M: Yes. It's the one I gave you, isn't it?

W: Right. It looks good in the fish tank, doesn't it?

M: It does. I love the ___________ ___________ ___________ ___________ ___________.

W: Yeah. I like it, too.

M: I see a starfish next to the chair.

W: Isn't it cute? And do you see ___________ ___________ ___________ ___________ on the right side of the picture?

M: Yeah. I like how you put both of them side by side.

W: I thought that'd look cool.

M: Your fish in the top left corner looks happy with its new home.

W: I hope so.

5

M: Hi, Theresa. What are you looking at on your smartphone?

W: These are the __________ __________ __________ at the entrance ceremony.

M: You took a lot of pictures. What are they for?

W: They're for the school newspaper. I'm __________ __________ __________ about the entrance ceremony.

M: I see.

W: But I don't think I can use any of these pictures. They don't look good.

M: Maybe I can help you. I also took some pictures at the ceremony.

W: Ah, you're in the school's Photo Club! Do you have them with you now?

M: No, they're on my computer. I'll __________ __________ __________ __________ by email.

W: That'd be great. Thank you.

6

M: Good afternoon. How can I help you?

W: I'd like to buy some wireless earphones for my children. How much is this pair?

M: It's __________ __________ __________ __________. It's a very popular model.

W: Great. I'll take two pairs.

M: I see. Is there anything else you need?

W: Oh, I also need a portable speaker.

M: These two are the latest models.

W: How much are they?

M: __________ __________ __________ __________ __________ and the pink one is $100.

W: I'll take the black one.

M: Okay. Is that all you need?

W: Yes. Oh, I have this discount coupon. Can I use it?

M: Sure. You can __________ __________ __________ __________ __________ __________ with this coupon.

W: Great. Here's the coupon and here's my credit card.

7

M: Agnes, what are you doing?

W: I'm surfing the Internet to find a nice restaurant for my trip this weekend.

M: All the places on the website look nice.

W: Yes, but I've finally decided where to go. It's this French restaurant called El Bistro.

M: Oh, I've watched a travel TV show about that restaurant.

W: Have you?

M: Yes. It said it's so popular among the local people that they have to __________ __________ __________ __________ __________ to get in.

W: I know. I don't like crowded places, but I think it'll be worth the wait because of __________ __________ __________. The family's been running it since 1890.

M: Wow, that long?

W: Yes. I like __________ __________ __________ __________ __________ __________. It's far from my hotel, but I'm willing to go anyway.

M: I'm sure you'll enjoy the meal there.

8

M: Lucy, look at this.

W: Wow. It's about the Youth Choir Audition.

M: Yes. It's open to __________ __________ __________ __________ __________.

W: I'm interested in joining the choir. When is it?

M: April 2nd, from 9 a.m. to 5 p.m.

W: The place for the audition is the Youth Training Center. It's really far from here.

M: I think you should leave early in the morning.

W: That's no problem. __________ __________ __________ __________ __________?

M: No, it's free.

W: Good. I'll apply for the audition.

M: Then you should __________ __________ __________ __________ __________ on this website.

W: All right. Thanks.

초급 5회

9

M: Hello, Lakewoods High School students! I'm Lawrence Cho, president of the student council. I'm happy to announce a special new event to reduce waste around our school: Lakewoods Plogging! Since plogging is the activity of picking up trash while running, all participants should __________ __________ __________ __________ __________. We provide eco-friendly bags for the trash, so you don't need to bring any. The event __________ __________ __________ __________ __________ __________ from 7 a.m. to 9 a.m. You can sign up for the event on the school website starting tomorrow. __________ __________ __________ __________ __________ __________ a pair of sports socks. For more information, please visit our school website. Don't miss this fun opportunity!

10

M: Hi, how can I help you today?

W: Hi, I'm looking for a smart watch.

M: Sure. We have these five models.

W: Hmm.... I want to wear it when I swim.

M: Then you're __________ __________ __________ __________ __________.

W: That's right. Do you think a one-year warranty is too short?

M: Yes. I recommend one that has a __________ __________ __________ __________ __________.

W: Okay. I'll take your advice.

M: That leaves you with these two options. I'd __________ __________ __________ __________ because it's as good as the other one.

W: I see. Then I'll go with the cheaper one.

M: Good choice.

11

M: Becky, did you order our food for dinner?

W: Yes. I ordered pizza __________ __________ __________ __________.

M: An hour ago? Delivery usually __________ __________ __________ __________ __________.

W: (I'll call the restaurant and check our order.)

12

W: Jimmy, what are you looking for?

M: My cellphone. I __________ __________ __________ __________ __________.

W: Why don't you __________ __________ __________ __________ __________ __________ first?

M: (I already did, but I couldn't find it.)

13

M: Grandma, look what I found in the garage. It's an old cookbook.

W: Oh, I haven't seen that for years.

M: It says here, "Recipes for Fine Dishes."

W: __________ __________ __________ __________ __________ when I was a chef before you were born.

M: Really? You were a professional chef?

W: Yeah, I used to work in a restaurant. Look! These were my special dishes.

M: Wow, they look fantastic! Did you __________ __________ __________ __________ in the book?

W: Yes. I really loved cooking and was good at it back then.

M: You're still good at cooking!

W: Do you really think so?

M: Of course! I've always thought __________ __________ __________ __________.

W: (Thanks. I guess I haven't lost my chef skills.)

14

M: Jenny, what class do you want to take this summer vacation?

W: Well, *[Pause]* I'm thinking of the guitar class.

M: Cool! I'm interested in __________ __________ __________, too.

W: Really? It would be exciting if we took the class together.

M: I know, but I am thinking of ___________ ___________ ___________ ___________ instead. I didn't do well on the final exam.

W: Oh, there is a math class? I didn't know that.

M: Yes. Mrs. Kim said she is offering a math class for first graders.

W: That might be a good chance to improve my skills, too. ___________ ___________ ___________ ___________ ___________ ___________ for the math class?

M: (You can find it on the school website.)

15

M: Ted and John are college freshmen. They are climbing Green Diamond Mountain together. Now they ___________ ___________ ___________ ___________ near the mountain top. After climbing the mountain all day, they have a relaxing time at the campsite. While drinking coffee, Ted suggests to John that they ___________ ___________ ___________ at the mountain top the next morning. John thinks it's a good idea. So, now John wants to ask Ted ___________ ___________ ___________ ___________ ___________ ___________ to see the sunrise. In this situation, what would John most likely say to Ted?

John: (What time should we get up tomorrow morning?)

16~17

M: Hello, Lincoln High School. This is David Newman, your current student representative, and I'm speaking to you today to let you know about the upcoming election for next year's student representative. Candidates can now begin their campaigns, ___________ ___________ ___________. First, they can share short promotional video clips on their social media, but the video clips must not be longer than 3 minutes. Second, ___________ ___________ ___________ ___________ only in allowed areas, and it's important to keep the size to A3 or smaller, as larger posters will be removed without warning. Third, the ___________ ___________ ___________ ___________ ___________, but they must only be distributed within the school campus. Lastly, ___________ ___________ ___________ ___________ ___________ ___________ ___________ on our school website among the candidates three days before the election. It's important to be respectful toward the other candidates during the debate. Let's make this election a success.

Dictation Answers

1. students have complained / set up several new printers / do your work more efficiently
2. flip through the pages / can help bookstore owners / local bookstores going out of business
3. buy a wooden desk / have a particular design in mind / perfect one for you
4. boat in the bottom left corner / beach chair in the center / these two surf boards
5. pictures I took / writing an article / send them to you
6. $60 for a pair / This black one is $80 / get 10% off the total price
7. wait in a long line / its long tradition / old places that maintain their tradition
8. anyone aged 13 to 18 / Is there an entry fee / fill out an application form
9. wear workout clothes and sneakers / will be held on October 1st / The first 30 participants will get
10. looking for one that's waterproof / warranty longer than one year / get the cheaper one
11. about an hour ago / takes less than 40 minutes
12. forgot where I left it / look for it in your room
13. That's the cookbook I wrote / create all the recipes / your food tastes amazing
14. playing the guitar / taking a math class / Where can I check the schedule
15. have reached the campsite / watch the sunrise / how early they should wake up

16~17. following these instructions / candidates can display posters / use of pamphlets is allowed / there will be an online debate broadcast

제6회 초급 모의고사

맞은 개수: 2점 문항 ___개, 3점 문항 ___개
알고 푼 문항은 ○, 찍어서 맞힌 문제는 △에 표시하고,
△와 ×는 다시 복습하세요.

1번부터 17번까지는 듣고 답하는 문제입니다. 1번부터 15번까지는 한 번만 들려주고, 16번부터 17번까지는 두 번 들려줍니다. 방송을 잘 듣고 답을 하시기 바랍니다.

1 ○△×
• 2021년 9월 교육청(고1) 1번

다음을 듣고, 남자가 하는 말의 목적으로 가장 적절한 것을 고르시오. 정답률 82%

① 시민 자율 방범 단원을 모집하려고
② 어린이 안전 교육 장소를 안내하려고
③ 초등학교 개교 기념행사를 홍보하려고
④ 학교 주변 제한 속도 준수를 독려하려고
⑤ 시청에서 열리는 공청회 일정을 공지하려고

2 ○△×
• 2019년 3월 교육청(고1) 4번

대화를 듣고, 여자의 의견으로 가장 적절한 것을 고르시오. 정답률 88%

① 무리한 여행 계획은 여행을 망칠 수 있다.
② 관광지에서 자연환경을 훼손하지 말아야 한다.
③ 여행할 지역의 문화를 미리 조사해 보는 것이 필요하다.
④ 남들이 추천하는 음식점에 꼭 가 볼 필요는 없다.
⑤ 여행을 가면 현지 음식을 먹어 보는 것이 좋다.

3 ○△×
• 2020년 6월 교육청(고1) 5번

대화를 듣고, 두 사람의 관계를 가장 잘 나타낸 것을 고르시오. 정답률 89%

① 구직자 — 채용 담당 직원 ② 소설가 — 영화감독
③ 배우 — 방송 작가 ④ 서점 직원 — 출판업자
⑤ 뮤지컬 배우 — 무대 감독

4 ○△×
• 2024년 6월 교육청(고1) 4번

대화를 듣고, 그림에서 대화의 내용과 일치하지 않는 것을 고르시오. 정답률 95%

5 ○△×
• 2022년 9월 교육청(고1) 5번

대화를 듣고, 여자가 할 일로 가장 적절한 것을 고르시오. 정답률 77%

① 식료품 주문하기 ② 자동차 수리 맡기기
③ 보고서 제출하기 ④ 고객 센터에 전화하기
⑤ 냉장고에 식료품 넣기

6 ○△×
• 2023년 9월 교육청(고1) 6번

대화를 듣고, 남자가 지불할 금액을 고르시오. [3점] 정답률 83%

① $37 ② $45 ③ $55 ④ $60 ⑤ $80

7 ○△×
• 2018년 6월 교육청(고1) 8번

대화를 듣고, 남자가 일본 여행을 가지 못한 이유를 고르시오. 정답률 83%

① 할머니 생신 파티에 가야 해서
② 가족 중 아픈 사람이 있어서
③ 날씨 때문에 비행 편이 취소되어서
④ 아들의 여권을 잃어버려서
⑤ 여행이 가을로 연기되어서

8 ○△×
• 2025년 9월 교육청(고1) 8번

대화를 듣고, Topas Beachcombing에 관해 언급되지 않은 것을 고르시오. 정답률 96%

① 날짜 ② 등록 방법 ③ 준비물
④ 참가 인원 ⑤ 참가비

9 ○△×
• 2023년 6월 교육청(고1) 9번

Eastville Dance Contest에 관한 다음 내용을 듣고, 일치하지 않는 것을 고르시오. 정답률 84%

① 처음으로 개최되는 경연이다.
② 모든 종류의 춤이 허용된다.
③ 춤 영상을 8월 15일까지 업로드해야 한다.
④ 학생들은 가장 좋아하는 영상에 투표할 수 있다.
⑤ 우승팀은 상으로 상품권을 받게 될 것이다.

10 ○△× • 2025년 6월 교육청(고1) 10번

다음 표를 보면서 대화를 듣고, 두 사람이 구매할 책가방을 고르시오. 정답률 93%

School Backpacks

	Model	Price	Shape	Color	Waterproof
①	A	$50	Round	Black	×
②	B	$55	Square	Black	×
③	C	$60	Square	White	○
④	D	$65	Square	Black	○
⑤	E	$75	Round	White	○

11 ○△× • 2024년 9월 교육청(고1) 12번

대화를 듣고, 남자의 마지막 말에 대한 여자의 응답으로 가장 적절한 것을 고르시오. 정답률 78%

① Awesome. The new bookshelf looks good in your room.
② Right. Then, shall we sell them at a used bookstore?
③ I see. Can you borrow them from the library?
④ Okay. I'll buy you books in a good condition.
⑤ I'm sorry. I haven't finished the book yet.

12 ○△× • 2023년 3월 교육청(고1) 12번

대화를 듣고, 여자의 마지막 말에 대한 남자의 응답으로 가장 적절한 것을 고르시오. 정답률 85%

① All right. I'll come pick you up now.
② I'm sorry. The library is closed today.
③ No problem. You can borrow my book.
④ Thank you so much. I'll drop you off now.
⑤ Right. I've changed the interior of my office.

13 ○△× • 2021년 6월 교육청(고1) 13번

대화를 듣고, 남자의 마지막 말에 대한 여자의 응답으로 가장 적절한 것을 고르시오. 정답률 84%

Woman: ______________________

① I'm in charge of giving the presentation.
② I think you're the right person for that role.
③ It's important to choose your team carefully.
④ The assignment is due the day after tomorrow.
⑤ I hope we don't stay up late to finish the project.

14 고득점 ○△× • 2024년 9월 교육청(고1) 13번

대화를 듣고, 여자의 마지막 말에 대한 남자의 응답으로 가장 적절한 것을 고르시오. [3점] 정답률 62%

Man: ______________________

① I'll clarify each group member's specific role.
② I'll collect more data for our group research.
③ I should challenge myself for the competition.
④ I need to change the topic of our group project.
⑤ I'll let you know how to analyze data effectively.

15 ○△× • 2022년 9월 교육청(고1) 15번

다음 상황 설명을 듣고, Ms. Olson이 Steven에게 할 말로 가장 적절한 것을 고르시오. [3점] 정답률 75%

Ms. Olson: ______________________

① You can come see me any time you want.
② I'm happy to hear that you've met the CEO.
③ Why do you want to run a gaming company?
④ How about going to your role model's book-signing?
⑤ You should buy more books written by your role model.

[16~17] 다음을 듣고, 물음에 답하시오.

16 ○△× • 2025년 6월 교육청(고1) 16번

남자가 하는 말의 주제로 가장 적절한 것은? 정답률 93%

① native plants of various countries
② wild plants and their medical uses
③ endangered flowers across the world
④ roles of flowers in national ceremonies
⑤ national flowers with symbolic meanings

17 ○△× • 2025년 6월 교육청(고1) 17번

언급된 국가가 아닌 것은? 정답률 94%

① Philippines ② Denmark ③ Germany
④ France ⑤ United States

Dictation

문제 풀이에 중요한 핵심 부분과 듣기에 자주 나오는 표현들에 빈칸 처리를 했습니다. 방송을 잘 듣고, 빈칸에 알맞은 말을 써 넣으세요.

Tip! 잘 들리지 않는 부분이 있을 때에는 정답을 확인 후, 똑같은 속도로 따라 읽기 연습을 해 보세요.

1

M: Hello, citizens of Portland. This is Jerry Wilson, your Mayor. As you know, Port Elementary School has opened, and it is so nice to hear the kids playing. __________ __________ __________ __________ of the students at the school, we've been communicating with the New Jersey State Police and requested that they enforce speed limits __________ __________ __________ __________ __________ __________. This is in response to the many complaints City Hall has received regarding excessive speeding, especially in front of the school. Please __________ __________ __________ for the safety of the kids and your fellow citizens. Thank you for your cooperation. Stay safe and healthy.

2

W: Hey, Daniel. How are you getting ready for your trip to Seoul?

M: Hi, Claire. Everything is going great, but I'm __________ __________ __________.

W: Why?

M: I heard that Korean food is very hot and spicy. I think I should bring some food with me.

W: Oh, aren't you going to try any Korean food?

M: Well, I __________ __________ __________ __________ __________. I feel comfortable with what I'm used to.

W: But __________ __________ __________ is the beauty of travel. It's the best way to get to the heart of the culture.

M: Maybe you're right. I'll give it a try during my travels.

W: Good thinking. You can find some good Korean restaurants on the web.

M: Okay. Thanks.

3

[Telephone rings.]

M: Hello, this is Daniel Johnson.

W: Hello, Mr. Johnson. It's Elena Roberts. Have you thought about my proposal?

M: Yes. You said you wanted to __________ __________ __________ __________ __________ __________, right?

W: That's right. I loved your novel, and it would make a great movie.

M: I'm glad to hear that. And if __________ __________ __________ __________, it would be a great honor for me.

W: Thank you for __________ __________ __________. I'd like us to speak about the details of the story in person.

M: Then, shall I go to your office?

W: That would be great. Can you come tomorrow?

M: Sure. I'll be there by 10 a.m.

4

W: Honey, I love this park!

M: Me, too. This park is so cool. But, oh, look! What's that in the tree?

W: It's just a __________ __________ __________ __________ __________ __________.

M: I guess some kids went home without their kite.

W: By the same tree, a woman is walking her dog. They look so lovely.

M: What about the little girl beside her?

W: You mean the girl __________ __________ __________ __________ __________?

M: Right. She's adorable. And look there! Did you __________ __________ __________ __________ __________ __________ on the picnic mat?

W: Yes, right. It adds a touch of romance to the scene.

M: I think so, too. Oh, there's a fountain. Next to it, a man is playing the violin.

W: The melody is beautiful. I'm glad we came here.

5

M: Honey, there's a box in the doorway. What is it?
W: I ordered some groceries online. Would you bring it in?
M: Sure. Is this for the housewarming party today?
W: Yeah. Since I had to __________ __________ __________ __________, I couldn't go shopping yesterday.
M: Sorry, I should've taken you to the market.
W: That's okay. You worked late to meet the deadline for your report. Would you open the box for me?
M: Sure. *[Pause]* Oh no, some eggs are broken! Have a look.
W: Ah... that's never happened before.
M: Why don't we __________ __________ __________ __________ about it?
W: Okay. I'll do it right now.
M: While you do that, I'll __________ __________ __________ __________ __________ __________ __________.
W: Thanks.

6

W: Welcome to Libby's Flowers. How can I help you?
M: I'd like to order a rose basket for my parents' wedding anniversary.
W: All right. Our rose baskets come in two sizes.
M: What are the options?
W: The regular size is 30 dollars, and the large size is 50 dollars.
M: Hmm.... I think __________ __________ __________ __________ __________.
W: Good choice. So, you'll get one rose basket in the large size. By the way, we're __________ __________ __________ __________ on all purchases this week.
M: Excellent! When will my order be ready?
W: It'll be ready around 11 a.m. If you can't pick it up, we offer a delivery service. It's 10 dollars.
M: Oh, great. __________ __________ __________ __________ __________ __________. Here's my credit card.

7

M: Emily, how was your weekend?
W: Good. I went to my grandmother's birthday party. How was yours? Did you __________ __________ __________ __________ to Japan?
M: Well, unfortunately things did not go as planned. We couldn't go to Japan.
W: Why not? Was someone in the family ill?
M: No, that was not the reason.
W: __________ __________ __________ __________ because of the weather?
M: Not that either. Just before getting on the plane, my wife and I found that we __________ __________ __________ __________ __________.
W: Oh, no! You must all have been very disappointed.
M: Yes, we were. So we're thinking about planning another family trip in the fall.

8

M: Hey, Emma, what are you reading?
W: Hi. I'm reading a post about the Topas Beachcombing activity.
M: What is that? I've never heard of it.
W: It's an activity where you go along the beach and collect garbage and make something useful or creative with it.
M: Great! When is it?
W: This Saturday, __________ __________ __________ __________, at 10 a.m. on Sunset Beach.
M: Oh, it's near my house. How can I join the activity?
W: You can __________ __________ __________ __________ __________.
M: Do I need to bring anything?
W: Yes, we'll __________ __________ __________ __________ __________ for the garbage.
M: No problem. Is there a participation fee?
W: No, it's free.
M: Perfect! It sounds meaningful and fun.

초급 6회

9

M: Hello, Eastville High School students. This is your P.E. teacher, Mr. Wilson. I'm pleased to let you know that we're hosting the first Eastville Dance Contest. Any Eastville students who love dancing can participate in the contest as a team. ___________ ___________ ___________ ___________ ___________ ___________. If you'd like to participate, please upload your team's dance video to our school website by August 15th. Students can ___________ ___________ ___________ ___________ ___________ from August 16th to 20th. The winning team will ___________ ___________ ___________ ___________ ___________ ___________. Don't miss this great opportunity to show off your talents!

10

W: Honey, we need to buy Robert a backpack for school.

M: Right, let's search for one online.

W: *[Clicking Sound]* Wow, there are so many options. What should we consider first?

M: Well, let's start with budget.

W: We already spent a lot on his other school supplies. I'd like to ___________ ___________ ___________ ___________.

M: All right. What shape should we get him, a square one?

W: Yeah, it's better for carrying school supplies. Then, what about the color?

M: White ones get dirty easily, so we should ___________ ___________ ___________ ___________ ___________.

W: Sounds good. And does it ___________ ___________ ___________ ___________?

M: Definitely. It'll be useful on rainy days.

W: Then, this is the one. Let's buy it.

11

M: Mom, the bookshelf in my room is full of books. There's ___________ ___________ ___________ ___________ ___________.

W: Well, how about throwing away the books you don't read anymore?

M: But some of them are in ___________ ___________ ___________ ___________ ___________ ___________.

W: (Right. Then, shall we sell them at a used bookstore?)

12

[Cell phone rings.]

W: Daddy, are you still working now?

M: No, Emma. ___________ ___________ ___________ ___________ ___________ my car and drive home.

W: Great. Can you ___________ ___________ ___________ ___________? I'm at the City Library near your office.

M: (All right. I'll come pick you up now.)

13

M: Why do you look so busy?

W: I'm ___________ ___________ ___________ ___________ ___________.

M: What's it about?

W: It's about 'Climate Change.'

M: Sounds interesting. Who's on your team?

W: You know Chris? He's the leader.

M: I know him very well. He's responsible and smart.

W: Jenny is ___________ ___________ ___________ and Alex is making the slides.

M: What a nice team! Then ___________ ___________ ___________?

W: (I'm in charge of giving the presentation.)

14

W: Hey, Peter. How's your group project going?

M: Hello, Ms. Adams. It's my first time as a leader, so it's quite challenging.

W: I thought your group was working well together.

M: Yes. We're all ___________ ___________ ___________ ___________, but progress is slow.

W: Well, what are you all working on at this moment?

M: Everyone is focusing on gathering data as much as possible.

W: Hmm, did you __________ __________ __________ __________ __________ __________?

M: Oh, we haven't discussed it yet. We're not exactly sure who does what.

W: That's crucial. Otherwise, it can lead to overlapping tasks in a group project.

M: That makes sense. That's why __________ __________ __________ __________ __________ __________.

W: Then, as the leader, what do you think you should do now?

M: (I'll clarify each group member's specific role.)

15

W: Steven is a high school student and Ms. Olson is a career counselor at his school. Steven has much interest in the video game industry. A few days ago, Ms. Olson recommended a book written by a CEO who runs a famous gaming company. After reading the book, Steven told her that the CEO is his role model. This morning, Ms. Olson hears the news that the CEO is going to __________ __________ __________ at a bookstore nearby. She thinks Steven would love to __________ __________ __________ __________ __________ __________. So, Ms. Olson wants to tell Steven that he __________ __________ __________ __________ __________ at the event. In this situation, what would Ms. Olson most likely say to Steven?

Ms. Olson: (How about going to your role model's book-signing?)

16~17

M: Hello, class! Last time, we learned about the national flags of various countries. Today, we'll talk about different countries' __________ __________ __________ __________ __________ __________. First, the Philippines' national flower is jasmine. Because it means good luck, people often give big necklaces made of this flower to welcome special guests. Next, Denmark's flower is the daisy and __________ __________ __________. Children express happiness by making daisy chains during their traditional games. In France, the national flower is the iris. Throughout history, French people have thought of this flower __________ __________ __________ __________ __________. Lastly, the United States uses the rose as its national flower. Americans consider it a symbol of love. So you can find many roses in American weddings. Now, let's watch a short video to look at these flowers up close.

Dictation Answers

1. To ensure the safety / in the area around the school / obey speed limits
2. worried about food / don't like trying new food / trying local food
3. turn my novel into a movie / you directed the movie / accepting my offer
4. kite stuck in the tree's branches / holding balloons in her hand / notice a basket full of flowers
5. have my car repaired / call the customer center / put the other food in the fridge
6. the bigger one is better / giving a 10-percent discount / I'd like it to be delivered
7. enjoy your family trip / Was your flight cancelled / had lost our son's passport
8. the 25th of September / sign up on their website / need gloves and a bag
9. All kinds of dance are allowed / vote for their favorite video / receive a trophy as a prize
10. keep it under $70 / go with a black one / need to be waterproof
11. no space for new ones / too good condition to throw away
12. I'm about to get in / give me a ride
13. working on a team project / doing the research / what's your role
14. motivated and working hard / assign individual tasks to each member / our progress is not that fast
15. have a book-signing / meet his role model in person / should go see the CEO

16~17. national flowers and what they symbolize / it represents happiness / as a symbol of perfection

제7회 초급 모의고사

맞은 개수: 2점 문항 ___개, 3점 문항 ___개
알고 푼 문항은 ○, 찍어서 맞힌 문제는 △에 표시하고,
△와 ×는 다시 복습하세요.

1번부터 17번까지는 듣고 답하는 문제입니다. 1번부터 15번까지는 한 번만 들려주고, 16번부터 17번까지는 두 번 들려줍니다. 방송을 잘 듣고 답을 하시기 바랍니다.

1 ○△× • 2020년 6월 교육청(고1) 3번

다음을 듣고, 여자가 하는 말의 목적으로 가장 적절한 것을 고르시오. 정답률 75%

① 축제 관련자 안전 교육 참석을 공지하려고
② 정해진 장소에서 활동할 것을 요청하려고
③ 다양한 공연을 준비할 것을 독려하려고
④ 동아리 담당 교사 변경을 안내하려고
⑤ 적극적인 동아리 활동을 부탁하려고

2 ○△× • 2020년 9월 교육청(고1) 4번

대화를 듣고, 두 사람이 하는 말의 주제로 가장 적절한 것을 고르시오. 정답률 86%

① 코딩 학습의 이점
② 코딩 시 주의할 점
③ 코딩 기술이 필요한 직업
④ 조기 코딩 교육의 문제점
⑤ 코딩 초보자를 위한 학습법

3 ○△× • 2019년 6월 교육청(고1) 5번

대화를 듣고, 두 사람의 관계를 가장 잘 나타낸 것을 고르시오. 정답률 92%

① 호텔 직원 — 투숙객
② 식당 지배인 — 요리사
③ 여행 가이드 — 여행객
④ 열쇠 수리공 — 집주인
⑤ 부동산 중개인 — 세입자

4 ○△× • 2024년 3월 교육청(고1) 4번

대화를 듣고, 그림에서 대화의 내용과 일치하지 않는 것을 고르시오. 정답률 92%

5 ○△× • 2020년 9월 교육청(고1) 7번

대화를 듣고, 여자가 할 일로 가장 적절한 것을 고르시오. 정답률 87%

① Tom에게 전화하기
② 화학 과제 제출하기
③ 인터뷰 사진 촬영하기
④ Cindy와 발표 준비하기
⑤ 인터뷰 질문지 작성하기

6 고득점 ○△× • 2018년 9월 교육청(고1) 9번

대화를 듣고, 여자가 지불할 금액을 고르시오. 정답률 53%

① $216 ② $225 ③ $240 ④ $250 ⑤ $270

7 ○△× • 2024년 3월 교육청(고1) 7번

대화를 듣고, 남자가 체육 대회 연습을 할 수 없는 이유를 고르시오. 정답률 95%

① 시험공부를 해야 해서
② 동아리 면접이 있어서
③ 축구화를 가져오지 않아서
④ 다리가 완전히 회복되지 않아서
⑤ 가족 식사 모임에 참석해야 해서

8 ○△× • 2023년 9월 교육청(고1) 8번

대화를 듣고, Street Photography Contest에 관해 언급되지 않은 것을 고르시오. 정답률 90%

① 참가 대상
② 주제
③ 심사 기준
④ 제출 마감일
⑤ 우승 상품

9 ○△× • 2017년 6월 교육청(고1) 11번

Book Review Contest에 관한 다음 내용을 듣고, 일치하지 않는 것을 고르시오. [3점] 정답률 82%

① 독서의 달을 기념하는 행사이다.
② 학생들은 누구나 참여할 수 있다.
③ 지정 도서에 대한 독후감을 작성해야 한다.
④ 독후감은 이달 말까지 제출해야 한다.
⑤ 우수작 세 편은 학교 잡지에 실릴 것이다.

10 ○△× • 2022년 3월 교육청(고1) 10번

다음 표를 보면서 대화를 듣고, 여자가 주문할 소형 진공청소기를 고르시오. 정답률 86%

Handheld Vacuum Cleaners

	Model	Price	Working Time	Weight	Washable Filter
①	A	$50	8 minutes	2.5 kg	×
②	B	$80	12 minutes	2.0 kg	○
③	C	$100	15 minutes	1.8 kg	○
④	D	$120	20 minutes	1.8 kg	×
⑤	E	$150	25 minutes	1.6 kg	○

11 ○△× • 2020년 3월 교육청(고1) 1번

대화를 듣고, 남자의 마지막 말에 대한 여자의 응답으로 가장 적절한 것을 고르시오. 정답률 89%

① No thanks. I'm already full.
② Sure. The onion soup is great here.
③ No idea. I've never been here before.
④ Yes. I recommend you be there on time.
⑤ I agree. Let's go to a Mexican restaurant.

12 ○△× • 2021년 6월 교육청(고1) 12번

대화를 듣고, 여자의 마지막 말에 대한 남자의 응답으로 가장 적절한 것을 고르시오. 정답률 73%

① No thank you. I've had enough.
② Great. I'll book for five people at six.
③ That's a good choice. The food is wonderful.
④ Okay. I'll set a place and time for the meeting.
⑤ Sorry to hear that. I'll cancel the reservation now.

13 ○△× • 2020년 9월 교육청 (고1) 14번

대화를 듣고, 남자의 마지막 말에 대한 여자의 응답으로 가장 적절한 것을 고르시오. [3점] 정답률 77%

Woman: ______________________________

① Sure. Write as many activities as possible.
② Of course. The more specific, the better.
③ Thanks. But I'll do it my way this time.
④ Great. You've finally made it to college.
⑤ That's right. First come, first served.

14 ○△× • 2025년 9월 교육청(고1) 14번

대화를 듣고, 여자의 마지막 말에 대한 남자의 응답으로 가장 적절한 것을 고르시오. [3점] 정답률 84%

Man: ______________________________

① Good decision. I'm sure you'll do a good job.
② Yes. Let's remove the kitchen table for more space.
③ I don't think so. I could never do something like that.
④ Exactly. You'd rather work harder to earn more money.
⑤ No way. You should stick to your usual spending habits.

15 ○△× • 2024년 9월 교육청(고1) 15번

다음 상황 설명을 듣고, Julia가 Sophie에게 할 말로 가장 적절한 것을 고르시오. 정답률 81%

Julia: ______________________________

① Could you help me assemble my desk?
② Can you share where you bought your desk?
③ How about choosing a new computer together?
④ Why don't you repair the furniture by yourself?
⑤ Do you have any ideas for decorating my room?

[16~17] 다음을 듣고, 물음에 답하시오.

16 ○△× • 2022년 9월 교육청(고1) 16번

남자가 하는 말의 주제로 가장 적절한 것은? 정답률 87%

① tips for caring for musical instruments
② ways to choose a good musical instrument
③ effects of the weather on musical instruments
④ benefits of learning musical instruments as a child
⑤ difficulties of making your own musical instruments

17 ○△× • 2022년 9월 교육청(고1) 17번

언급된 악기가 아닌 것은? 정답률 96%

① flutes ② trumpets ③ pianos
④ drums ⑤ guitars

초급 7회

Dictation

문제 풀이에 중요한 핵심 부분과 듣기에 자주 나오는 표현들에 빈칸 처리를 했습니다. 방송을 잘 듣고, 빈칸에 알맞은 말을 써 넣으세요.

Tip! 잘 들리지 않는 부분이 있을 때에는 정답을 확인 후, 똑같은 속도로 따라 읽기 연습을 해 보세요.

1

W: Hello, students. This is vice principal Susan Lee. I know all of you are busy preparing for the upcoming school festival. There are club activities going on in every part of our school building. You may __________ __________ __________ __________ __________ during activities. But I'd like to ask you to work in the place __________ __________ __________ __________ __________ __________. Your teachers want to make your safety the top priority. Once again, make sure to prepare for the festival __________ __________ __________ __________. Thank you for your cooperation.

2

M: Hey, Sarah. What are you going to choose for your afterschool activity?

W: I'm not sure, Dad.

M: What about taking a coding course?

W: A coding course? Why should I do that?

M: I think learning to code can __________ __________ __________ __________ for the future.

W: Oh, I remember my teacher saying that coding is a skill that can increase the chances of getting a job. But it sounds difficult.

M: It might be, but it can help you __________ __________ __________ __________ __________ __________ __________ __________.

W: Good to know. And I heard coding helps with math. Right?

M: Definitely. Plus, it __________ __________ __________ __________.

W: Cool! I think I'm going to take the course.

3

W: Good afternoon. How may I help you?

M: I made a reservation online. It's under the name of Stennis.

W: Could you spell it, sir?

M: Sure. S-T-E-N-N-I-S.

W: All right. You've __________ __________ __________ __________ with an ocean view for two nights. Is that correct?

M: Yes. And I want to stay on a higher floor if possible.

W: Let me check. *[Typing sound]* __________ __________ __________ __________ on the 15th and 19th floors. Which one would you prefer?

M: 19th is better.

W: Okay. You'll be staying in Room 1911. Here are your __________ __________ __________ __________.

M: Thanks. When does the morning buffet begin?

W: You can have breakfast from 7 to 9 a.m. at the restaurant on the first floor. Have a nice stay.

4

M: Hi, Amy. I heard that you've joined the English Newspaper Club.

W: Yes, Tom. I went to the club room yesterday and took a picture of it. Look.

M: Wow, the place looks nice. I like the lockers on the left.

W: Yes, they're good. We also have a __________ __________ __________ __________ __________.

M: It looks cool. What's that on the bookshelf?

W: Oh, that's the __________ __________ __________ __________ for 'Club of the Year'.

M: You must be very proud of it. There's also a computer __________ __________ __________ __________ __________ __________ __________.

W: Yeah, we use the computer when we need it.

M: Great. I can see a newspaper on the table.

W: Yes, it was published last December.

5

W: Chris, what are you doing?

M: I'm writing interview questions for the feature story of our next school magazine.

W: Who are you interviewing?

M: The new English teacher. I'm going to interview him tomorrow.

W: Do you need ________ ________ ________ ________ ________ ________?

M: No, I'm almost done. But I'm still ________ ________ ________ ________ ________ ________ during the interview.

W: Why don't you ask Cindy? She's good at taking photos.

M: I already asked her, but she said she has an important presentation tomorrow.

W: Well, how about Tom? He's a member of the photo club.

M: You mean the one in our chemistry class?

W: Yes. I think he's the right person. Do you want me to call him to ________ ________ ________ ________ tomorrow?

M: That would be great. Thanks.

6

M: Hello. How can I help you?

W: Hi, I'd like to ________ ________ ________ for a rafting trip this Sunday.

M: Lovely. We have two options. A full-day trip costs $100, and a half-day trip costs $40. Children under 10 are half price.

W: All right. Do the prices include lunch?

M: Only a full-day trip includes a riverside barbecue lunch.

W: Okay, then I'd like to book a full-day trip for two adults and one eight-year-old child.

M: Beautiful! A full-day trip for ________ ________ ________ ________ ________.

W: That's right. Can I use this coupon from your website?

M: Sure. With this coupon, ________ ________ ________ ________ ________ the total price.

W: Great! I'll pay in cash.

7

W: Hey, Jake! How was your math test yesterday?

M: ________ ________ ________ ________.

W: That's great. Let's go and practice for Sports Day.

M: I'm so sorry but I can't make it.

W: Come on, Jake! Sports Day is just around the corner.

M: I know. That's why I brought my soccer shoes.

W: Then, why can't you practice today? Do you ________ ________ ________ ________?

M: No, I already had the interview last week.

W: Then, does your leg still hurt?

M: Not really, it's okay, now. Actually, I have to ________ ________ ________ ________ ________ tonight for my mother's birthday.

W: Oh, that's important! Family always comes first. Are you available tomorrow, then?

M: Sure. Let's make up for the missed practice.

8

W: What are you doing, Tim?

M: I'm looking at the Street Photography Contest website.

W: I've heard about that. It's a contest for college students, right?

M: Actually, it's ________ ________ ________ ________ ________, too. Why don't you try it?

W: Really? Maybe I will. Does the contest have a theme?

M: Sure. This year's ________ ________ ________ ________.

W: That sounds interesting. When is the deadline?

M: You have to ________ ________ ________ by September 15.

W: That's sooner than I expected.

M: You should hurry and choose your photos. The winner will receive a laptop as a prize.

W: Okay! Wish me luck.

초급 7회

9

W: Good morning, Central High School. This is Kathy Miller, the school librarian. In order to celebrate this year's reading month, our school is going to hold a Book Review Contest. All students are invited to __________ __________ __________ __________. You can write a review __________ __________ __________ __________ __________, but the review must be your own original work. You can download a form from our school website. Reviews __________ __________ __________ __________ __________ by the end of this month. The best three works will be selected and published in our school magazine. For more details, please visit the school website. Thank you.

10

W: Ben, do you have a minute?

M: Sure. What is it?

W: I'm trying to buy a handheld vacuum cleaner among these five models. Could you help me choose one?

M: Okay. How much are you willing to spend?

W: __________ __________ __________ __________.

M: Then we can cross this one out. What about the working time?

W: I think it should be __________ __________ __________ __________.

M: Then that narrows it down to these three.

W: Should I go with one of the lighter ones?

M: Yes. __________ __________ __________ __________ __________ __________ while cleaning.

W: All right. What about the filter?

M: The one with a washable filter would be a better choice.

W: I got it. Then I'll order this one.

11

M: This restaurant looks great. Have you been here before?

W: Yeah, it's __________ __________ __________ __________ __________. Let's see the menu.

M: Everything looks so good. __________ __________ __________ __________?

W: (Sure. The onion soup is great here.)

12

W: Honey, we can't eat out tomorrow evening.

M: Why not? I've already __________ __________ __________ at the restaurant.

W: I'm sorry. I __________ __________ __________ __________ __________ at that time.

M: (Sorry to hear that. I'll cancel the reservation now.)

13

W: Hey, Minho. What are you doing?

M: Hi, Mrs. Sharon. I'm writing an application letter for college.

W: Can I take a look at it?

M: Of course. Please give me some advice after you're finished reading it.

W: Hmm.... You only listed the activities you've done __________ __________ __________.

M: Yeah. Isn't it good to include as many activities as possible?

W: No. If you do that, your application letter __________ __________ __________.

M: But I thought if I wrote down a lot of activities, I would stand out.

W: It's actually the opposite. You should focus on a few things and __________ __________ __________ __________ __________.

M: I never thought about that. Do you really think it'll work?

W: (Of course. The more specific, the better.)

14

W: Kevin, what are you writing about?

M: Hi, Eva. I'm writing about the money-saving challenge I completed.

W: The money-saving challenge? What's that?

M: It's a challenge where you __________ __________ __________ __________ __________ and do not buy unnecessary things for a set time. I did it for a month.

W: Really? Wasn't it so hard?

M: Not that much. I spent money on things I really needed.
W: Why did you decide to do that?
M: At first, it was just to save money. But it also made me realize that I have wasted money on too many extra things.
W: Oh, I see. So it's about ___________ ___________ ___________ ___________?
M: Exactly. And I found free ways to have fun. For example, cooking more at home, instead of eating out!
W: ___________ ___________ ___________ ___________ ___________. I'll do the same!
M: (Good decision. I'm sure you'll do a good job.)

15

M: Julia is a college student, living in the dormitory. Recently, she ordered a new computer desk. Upon receiving the desk, she realized that the desk was a DIY product. It means she needs to ___________ ___________ ___________ ___________ to build the desk. However, it was complicated to assemble it by herself. Julia knows that Sophie, her best friend, ___________ ___________ ___________ ___________ ___________ ___________ and enjoys it. So, Julia wants to ask Sophie to ___________ ___________ ___________ ___________ ___________. In this situation, what would Julia most likely say to Sophie?
Julia: (Could you help me assemble my desk?)

16~17

M: Hello, students. Last class, we took a brief look at how to tune your musical instruments. Today, we're going to talk a bit about how to ___________ ___________ ___________ ___________ ___________ ___________ ___________. First, let's take flutes. They may have moisture from the air blown through them, so you should clean and wipe the mouth piece before and after playing. Next are trumpets. They can be taken apart, so you should air dry the parts in a cool dry place, away from direct sunlight. And as for pianos, they don't need everyday care, but it's ___________ ___________ ___________ ___________ ___________ by covering them with a protective pad when not in use. The last ones are string instruments like guitars. Their strings need replacement. When you replace the strings, it's good to do it gradually, one at a time. ___________ ___________ ___________ ___________ ___________ ___________ of your musical instruments. I hope this lesson helps you to keep your musical instruments safe from damage.

Dictation Answers

1. want to move between places / where you are supposed to be / in your prearranged places
2. give you important skills / learn how to plan and organize your thoughts / improves your problem-solving skills
3. booked a double room / We have rooms available / key and breakfast coupons
4. star-shaped mirror on the wall / trophy my club won / on the right side of the room
5. any help with the interview questions / looking for someone to take photos / see if he's available
6. make a reservation / two adults and one child / you get 10 percent off
7. Better than I expected / have a club interview / attend a family dinner gathering
8. open to high school students / theme is Daily Life / submit your photographs
9. participate in the contest / on any type of book / should be submitted through e-mail
10. No more than $130 / longer than 10 minutes / Lighter ones are easier to handle
11. one of my favorite restaurants / Can you recommend anything
12. booked a table / have an important business meeting
13. without being specific / won't be memorable / write about them in detail
14. try to reduce your spending / cutting out unnecessary spending / That sounds difficult but rewarding
15. put the pieces together / is good at assembling DIY furniture / help her with the desk
16~17. take care of and maintain your instruments / essential to protect the keys / Proper care can lengthen the lifespan

제8회 초급 모의고사

맞은 개수: 2점 문항 ___개, 3점 문항 ___개
알고 푼 문항은 ○, 찍어서 맞힌 문제는 △에 표시하고, △와 ×는 다시 복습하세요.

1번부터 17번까지는 듣고 답하는 문제입니다. 1번부터 15번까지는 한 번만 들려주고, 16번부터 17번까지는 두 번 들려줍니다. 방송을 잘 듣고 답을 하시기 바랍니다.

1 ○△× • 2024년 9월 교육청(고1) 1번

다음을 듣고, 여자가 하는 말의 목적으로 가장 적절한 것을 고르시오. 정답률 90%

① 축제 기간 연장을 요청하려고
② 신설된 지하철 노선을 홍보하려고
③ 축제 당일의 지하철 연장 운행을 안내하려고
④ 축제 방문객에게 안전 수칙 준수를 당부하려고
⑤ 축제 기간 중 도심 교통 통제 구간을 공지하려고

2 ○△× • 2023년 3월 교육청(고1) 2번

대화를 듣고, 여자의 의견으로 가장 적절한 것을 고르시오. 정답률 91%

① 과다한 항생제 복용을 자제해야 한다.
② 오래된 약을 함부로 폐기해서는 안 된다.
③ 약을 복용할 때는 정해진 시간을 지켜야 한다.
④ 진료 전에 자신의 증상을 정확히 확인해야 한다.
⑤ 다른 사람에게 처방된 약을 복용해서는 안 된다.

3 ○△× • 2017년 6월 교육청(고1) 5번

대화를 듣고, 두 사람의 관계를 가장 잘 나타낸 것을 고르시오. 정답률 88%

① 교사 — 학부모
② 의사 — 환자
③ 간병인 — 보호자
④ 상담사 — 학생
⑤ 편집장 — 신문 기자

4 고득점 ○△× • 2021년 6월 교육청(고1) 4번

대화를 듣고, 그림에서 대화의 내용과 일치하지 않는 것을 고르시오. 정답률 69%

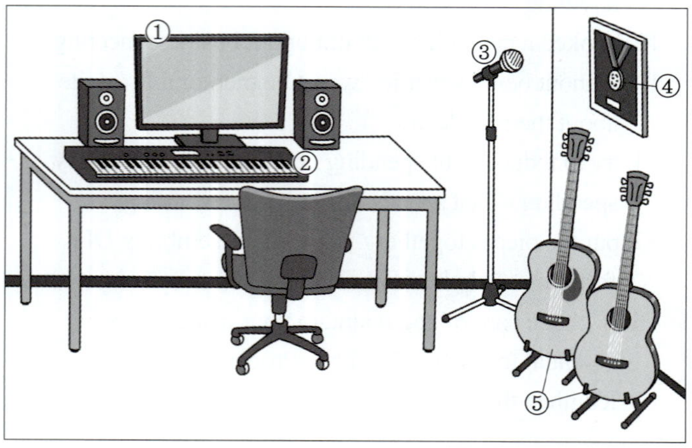

5 ○△× • 2025년 6월 교육청(고1) 5번

대화를 듣고, 남자가 할 일로 가장 적절한 것을 고르시오. 정답률 92%

① 시식용 사탕 고르기
② 가격표 붙이기
③ 홍보 포스터 게시하기
④ 스피커 점검하기
⑤ 음악 재생 목록 만들기

6 ○△× • 2023년 6월 교육청(고1) 6번

대화를 듣고, 여자가 지불할 금액을 고르시오. [3점] 정답률 84%

① $54 ② $60 ③ $72 ④ $76 ⑤ $80

7 ○△× • 2018년 9월 교육청(고1) 8번

대화를 듣고, 남자가 Jamie의 송별회에 갈 수 없는 이유를 고르시오. 정답률 82%

① 남동생을 돌봐야 해서
② 과학 숙제를 해야 해서
③ 할아버지 병문안을 가야 해서
④ 부모님을 병원에 모시고 가야 해서
⑤ 친구에게 줄 선물을 준비하기 위해서

8 ○△× • 2020년 9월 교육청(고1) 10번

대화를 듣고, Mind-Up Program에 관해 언급되지 않은 것을 고르시오. 정답률 87%

① 목적
② 특별 강연
③ 개최 장소
④ 시작 시간
⑤ 입장료

9 ○△× • 2022년 3월 교육청(고1) 9번

River Valley Music Camp에 관한 다음 내용을 듣고, 일치하지 않는 것을 고르시오. 정답률 91%

① 4월 11일부터 5일 동안 진행된다.
② 학교 오케스트라 단원이 아니어도 참가할 수 있다.
③ 자신의 악기를 가져오거나 학교에서 빌릴 수 있다.
④ 마지막 날에 공연을 촬영한다.
⑤ 참가 인원에는 제한이 없다.

10 ○△×

2019년 6월 교육청(고1) 12번

다음 표를 보면서 대화를 듣고, 여자가 구입할 전기면도기를 고르시오. 정답률 89%

Electric Shaver

	Model	Price	Battery Life	Waterproof	Color
①	A	$55	20 minutes	×	black
②	B	$70	40 minutes	×	white
③	C	$85	60 minutes	○	black
④	D	$90	70 minutes	○	white
⑤	E	$110	80 minutes	○	black

11 ○△×

2023년 6월 교육청(고1) 11번

대화를 듣고, 남자의 마지막 말에 대한 여자의 응답으로 가장 적절한 것을 고르시오. 정답률 77%

① Great. We don't have to wait in line.
② All right. We can come back later.
③ Good job. Let's buy the tickets.
④ No worries. I will stand in line.
⑤ Too bad. I can't buy that car.

12 ○△×

2025년 6월 교육청(고1) 12번

대화를 듣고, 여자의 마지막 말에 대한 남자의 응답으로 가장 적절한 것을 고르시오. 정답률 93%

① No. I made all these cakes by myself.
② Sure. I'm looking forward to my 30th birthday.
③ Actually, I don't mind if you eat my carrot cake.
④ Not really. It's hard to remember all the anniversaries.
⑤ Yes, I'd like a heart-shaped cake with a message on it.

13 ○△×

2025년 9월 교육청(고1) 13번

대화를 듣고, 남자의 마지막 말에 대한 여자의 응답으로 가장 적절한 것을 고르시오. [3점] 정답률 88%

Woman: ______________________________

① Sure. I'll recommend a list of courses you might like.
② Okay. Choose a course you think you'll score well in.
③ Cheer up! You'll make up with Henry soon.
④ Well, the time to choose courses is over.
⑤ No worries. I think you did your best!

14 ○△×

2020년 11월 교육청(고1) 14번

대화를 듣고, 여자의 마지막 말에 대한 남자의 응답으로 가장 적절한 것을 고르시오. [3점] 정답률 92%

Man: ______________________________

① Don't worry. I'll send you a notice by email.
② Great. Let me know how to use your services.
③ I don't agree. You can get a refund without a receipt.
④ Good. I'm looking forward to watching a movie tonight.
⑤ Okay. I'll call customer service to cancel the membership.

15 ○△×

2025년 9월 교육청(고1) 15번

다음 상황 설명을 듣고, Liam이 Sophia에게 할 말로 가장 적절한 것을 고르시오. 정답률 86%

Liam: ______________________________

① Can I borrow your mini oven to practice baking cookies?
② Are you using the recipe for cookies that I gave you?
③ Do you want to learn how to bake cookies together?
④ Where will you buy a mini oven to use at home?
⑤ How do you make your cookies taste so good?

[16~17] 다음을 듣고, 물음에 답하시오.

16 ○△×

2024년 9월 교육청(고1) 16번

여자가 하는 말의 주제로 가장 적절한 것은? 정답률 84%

① material trends in the fashion industry
② benefits of making clothes from nature
③ tips to purchase natural material clothes
④ development of clothes washing methods
⑤ proper ways to wash natural material clothes

17 ○△×

2024년 9월 교육청(고1) 17번

언급된 소재가 아닌 것은? 정답률 94%

① cotton ② silk ③ leather
④ linen ⑤ wool

Dictation

문제 풀이에 중요한 핵심 부분과 듣기에 자주 나오는 표현들에 빈칸 처리를 했습니다. 방송을 잘 듣고, 빈칸에 알맞은 말을 써 넣으세요.

Tip! 잘 들리지 않는 부분이 있을 때에는 정답을 확인 후, 똑같은 속도로 따라 읽기 연습을 해 보세요.

1

W: Hello! I'm Olivia Parker from Pineview City Subway. I have an announcement for this Saturday's fireworks festival. Many people are expected to visit and enjoy the festival late into the night. For smooth transportation and visitor safety, we're ___________ ___________ ___________ ___________ of the subway on the day of the festival. The subway will ___________ ___________ ___________ ___________ ___________ ___________ after the regular last train from the festival area stations. For a comfortable and safe journey from the event, we encourage you to ___________ ___________ ___________ ___________ ___________ ___________ ___________. We hope you enjoy this fantastic festival with convenience. Thank you!

2

W: Honey, are you okay?

M: I'm afraid I've caught a cold. I've got a sore throat.

W: Why don't you go see a doctor?

M: Well, I don't think it's necessary. I've found some medicine in the cabinet. I'll take it.

W: You ___________ ___________ ___________ ___________. That's what I got prescribed last week.

M: My symptoms are similar to yours.

W: Honey, you shouldn't take medicine ___________ ___________ ___________.

M: It's just a cold. I'll get better if I take your medicine.

W: It could be dangerous to ___________ ___________ ___________ ___________.

M: Okay. Then I'll go see a doctor this afternoon.

3

[Telephone Rings.]

W: Hello. This is Monica Jones.

M: Hello. This is John Lewis, Sally's father.

W: Hello, Mr. Lewis. Has Sally ___________ ___________ ___________?

M: Yes. She doesn't have a high fever anymore.

W: Glad to hear that.

M: But the doctor said that Sally needs to ___________ ___________ ___________ ___________.

W: I see. Do you think she'll ___________ ___________ ___________ ___________ ___________?

M: I think so. But, Sally's worried that she won't be able to submit her school newspaper article on time.

W: Oh, please tell her not to worry about it. The newspaper editor is also taking my class, so I'll talk to him.

M: Thank you so much.

4

M: Grace, let me show you my newly designed room.

W: Wow, Jake! It's so cool.

M: Look at the ___________ ___________ ___________ ___________. I changed my old monitor for this new one.

W: Looks nice. But isn't your desk too crowded to put your electric keyboard on it?

M: It's fine with me. I find it convenient there.

W: Is that a ___________ ___________ ___________ ___________? Do you sing?

M: Yes. Singing is my all-time favorite hobby.

W: What's that ___________ ___________ ___________ ___________ ___________? Where did you get it?

M: I won that medal at a guitar contest with my dad.

W: Incredible! Do you often practice the guitar with your dad?

M: Sure. That's why there're two guitars in the room.

5

W: Brian, I think we're almost ready for our candy shop's opening event.
M: That's right. What do we have left to do?
W: Well, let's see. Is the background music playlist ready?
M: Yes, I chose some cheerful songs and __________ __________ __________.
W: Great! What about the bluetooth speakers?
M: I tested them and __________ __________ __________. Did you choose the sample candies for customers to try?
W: Yeah. Look! I put them in these pretty little baskets.
M: Thanks! They look nice.
W: And all the other candies are nicely placed around the shop.
M: Wait, how about the price tags?
W: Oh, we almost forgot. Could you __________ __________ __________ __________ __________ __________?
M: Of course. I'll do it right away.

6

M: Good morning! How can I help you?
W: Hi. I'm looking for a blanket and some cushions for my sofa.
M: Okay. We've got some on sale. Would you like to have a look?
W: Yes. How much is this green blanket?
M: __________ __________.
W: Oh, I love the color green. Can you also show me some cushions that go well with this blanket?
M: Sure! How about these?
W: They look good. I need two of them. How much are they?
M: The __________ __________ __________ __________.
W: Okay. I'll take one green blanket and two cushions. Can I use this coupon?
M: Sure. It will __________ __________ __________ __________ __________ __________.
W: Thanks! Here's my credit card.

7

W: David, have you handed in the science assignment?
M: Yes, I'm happy that I finally finished it! By the way, are you going to Jamie's farewell party tonight?
W: Yes, I am. It's so __________ __________ __________ __________ __________ that far away. You're coming, too, right?
M: I really wish I could, but I need to go home early today.
W: Why do you need to go home early?
M: My grandfather is in the hospital, and my parents are going to visit him tonight.
W: I'm sorry to hear that. Do you have to go, too?
M: No, my little brother will be at home alone, so __________ __________ __________ __________ __________.
W: I see. You will take care of him.
M: Yes. Can you please give this present to Jamie and tell her that I'm sorry I __________ __________ __________ __________ __________?
W: No problem. I'm sure she'll understand your situation.

8

W: Hey, Sam. Have you heard about the Mind-Up Program?
M: No, I haven't. What is it?
W: It's a program for high school students. Its purpose is to encourage us to __________ __________ __________ __________. You should come.
M: It sounds interesting. Please tell me more about it.
W: There will be a lot of activities to help relieve stress. Also, we'll get to listen to __________ __________ __________ __________ __________ __________.
M: Awesome! I should sign up. When is it?
W: This Friday. It starts at 6 p.m.
M: Cool. How much is the admission fee?
W: __________ __________ __________ __________ __________. You can apply for the program on our school website.
M: Great. I'll do it now.

9

M: Hello, River Valley High School students. This is your music teacher, Mr. Stailor. __________ __________ __________ __________, we are going to have the River Valley Music Camp for five days. You don't need to be a member of the school orchestra to join the camp. You may bring your own instrument or you can borrow one from the school. On the last day of camp, we are going to __________ __________ __________ and play it on screen at the school summer festival. Please keep in mind the camp __________ __________ __________ __________ __________. Signups start this Friday, on a first-come-first-served basis. Come and make music together!

10

M: Katie, what are you doing with your smartphone?
W: I'm searching for an electric shaver for my dad's birthday. Will you help me find a good one?
M: Sure. Let me see... *[Pause]* How about this one?
W: Well, that's too expensive. I can't spend more than $100.
M: Okay. And I think a 20-minute battery life is __________ __________ __________ __________ __________.
W: I think so, too. It needs frequent charging.
M: You're right. Does it __________ __________ __________ __________?
W: Of course. He shaves in the shower every morning.
M: Then we have only two options left. Which color do you think is better?
W: Dad likes black, so I'll __________ __________ __________ __________.
M: I think it's a nice choice.

11

M: Let's get inside. I'm so excited to see this auto show.
W: Look over there. So many people are already __________ __________ __________ to buy tickets.
M: Fortunately, I __________ __________ __________ __________ __________.
W: (Great. We don't have to wait in line.)

12

W: Welcome to Emily's Cake Shop. How can I help you today?
M: I'd like to __________ __________ __________. It's to celebrate my first wedding anniversary.
W: Congratulations on your anniversary! Do you __________ __________ __________ __________ __________ __________?
M: (Yes, I'd like a heart-shaped cake with a message on it.)

13

M: Hello, Ms. Taylor.
W: Hi, Luke. What brings you in my office?
M: I'm not sure about __________ __________ __________ __________ for next year. I'm thinking of taking the same courses as my friend, Henry.
W: I understand why you feel that way. However, it's not a good idea to just __________ __________ __________ __________ __________ what's best for you.
M: But, I don't even know where to begin. Can you give me some guidance?
W: What do you enjoy doing?
M: Umm. I guess I like creating video clips.
W: That is the starting point. You can choose courses related to that.
M: Ah! I see. Could you help me __________ __________ __________ __________ __________?
W: (Sure. I'll recommend a list of courses you might like.)

14

W: Honey, look at this bill. Have you been using a movie streaming service?
M: No. But a few months ago, I __________ __________ __________ __________ __________.
W: Look. A $15 membership fee has been charged for three months.
M: Oh, no! There must be something wrong.
W: Did you get any notice about that?
M: Well, I did, but I didn't pay much attention to it when I signed up for it.

W: Let's check it now.
M: Wait. *[Clicking sound]* Hmm, it says the ___________ ___________ ___________ ___________ ___________ if I don't cancel it after the free trial.
W: Well, one of my friends was in the same situation and she tried to get a refund but she couldn't.
M: Then, what should I do?
W: Hmm, the only thing you can do is to ___________ ___________ ___________.
M: (Okay. I'll call customer service to cancel the membership.)

15

M: Liam and Sophia are college students and friends. Liam recently learned how to bake cookies in a cooking class and wants to ___________ ___________ ___________ ___________ ___________. However, he doesn't have a mini oven, and he cannot afford to buy one right now. He remembers that Sophia has a mini oven at home and often ___________ ___________ ___________ ___________ to class. So, he wants to ask her if she can ___________ ___________ ___________ ___________ ___________.
In this situation, what would Liam most likely say to Sophia?
Liam: (Can I borrow your mini oven to practice baking cookies?)

16~17

W: Hello, *Family-Life* subscribers! These days, many people are looking for clothes made from natural materials for their family. Today, I'd like to introduce some tips for how to ___________ ___________ ___________ ___________ ___________. First, for cotton, like 100% cotton t-shirts, you should hand-wash in cool water to avoid shrinking or wrinkling. Second, ___________ ___________ ___________ ___________ ___________ and quickly to keep its shape and color. Also, when you dry silk clothes such as blouses, avoid direct sunlight and dry them in the shade. Third, linen is a ___________ ___________ ___________ ___________. For example, to wash linen jackets, use vinegar instead of fabric softener. Lastly, for wool, the best way is to ___________ ___________ ___________ ___________ ___________.
If you have to wash wool sweaters, use special wool washing soap. Apply these tips so you can keep and enjoy natural clothes for a longer time!

Dictation Answers

1. extending the operational hours / run for an extra two hours / take advantage of our extended subway services
2. shouldn't take that medicine / prescribed for others / take someone else's prescription
3. gotten any better / stay home this week / come to school next Monday
4. monitor between the speakers / microphone in the corner / star-shaped medal on the wall
5. made a playlist / they're working fine / put them on the candy boxes
6. That's $40 / cushions are $20 each / give you 10% off the total
7. sad that she is moving / I have to babysit him / have to miss her party
8. build a positive mindset / special lectures from successful young CEOs / It's free for all students
9. Starting on April 11 / film our performance / is limited to 50 students
10. too short to use conveniently / need to be waterproof / buy the black one
11. standing in line / bought our tickets in advance
12. order a cake / have a specific design in mind
13. which courses to pick / follow your friend without considering / find courses that fit me
14. used a one-month free trial / membership fee will be charged / end the membership
15. practice the recipe at home / brings freshly baked cookies / lend him her mini oven

16~17. properly wash natural material clothes / silk should be washed separately / sensitive material to wash / wash as little as possible

제9회 초급 모의고사

맞은 개수: 2점 문항 ___개, 3점 문항 ___개
알고 푼 문항은 ○, 찍어서 맞힌 문제는 △에 표시하고, △와 ×는 다시 복습하세요.

1번부터 17번까지는 듣고 답하는 문제입니다. 1번부터 15번까지는 한 번만 들려주고, 16번부터 17번까지는 두 번 들려줍니다. 방송을 잘 듣고 답을 하시기 바랍니다.

1 ○△× • 2020년 3월 교육청(고1) 3번

다음을 듣고, 남자가 하는 말의 목적으로 가장 적절한 것을 고르시오. 정답률 94%

① 미세 먼지 수치가 높을 때 대처 요령을 안내하려고
② 교실 내 공기 정화기 설치 일정을 알리려고
③ 체육 실기 시험 준비 방법을 설명하려고
④ 미세 먼지 방지용 마스크 배부 행사를 홍보하려고
⑤ 미세 먼지 감축을 위해 대중교통 이용을 독려하려고

2 ○△× • 2024년 3월 교육청(고1) 2번

대화를 듣고, 여자의 의견으로 가장 적절한 것을 고르시오. 정답률 89%

① 전기 자전거 이용 전에 배터리 상태를 점검하여야 한다.
② 전기 자전거 운행에 관한 규정이 더 엄격해야 한다.
③ 전기 자전거의 속도 규정에 대한 논의가 필요하다.
④ 전기 자전거 구입 시 가격을 고려해야 한다.
⑤ 전기 자전거 이용 시 헬멧을 착용해야 한다.

3 ○△× • 2022년 3월 교육청(고1) 3번

대화를 듣고, 두 사람의 관계를 가장 잘 나타낸 것을 고르시오. 정답률 90%

① 방송 작가 — 연출자
② 만화가 — 환경 운동가
③ 촬영 감독 — 동화 작가
④ 토크쇼 진행자 — 기후학자
⑤ 제품 디자이너 — 영업 사원

4 ○△× • 2021년 9월 교육청(고1) 4번

대화를 듣고, 그림에서 대화의 내용과 일치하지 않는 것을 고르시오. 정답률 71%

5 ○△× • 2023년 3월 교육청(고1) 5번

대화를 듣고, 남자가 할 일로 가장 적절한 것을 고르시오. 정답률 91%

① 티켓 디자인하기
② 포스터 게시하기
③ 블로그 개설하기
④ 밴드부원 모집하기
⑤ 콘서트 장소 대여하기

6 고득점 ○△× • 2024년 6월 교육청(고1) 6번

대화를 듣고, 여자가 지불할 금액을 고르시오. [3점] 정답률 54%

① $50 ② $55 ③ $60 ④ $65 ⑤ $70

7 ○△× • 2025년 3월 교육청(고1) 7번

대화를 듣고, 남자가 휴대 전화를 수리받지 못한 이유를 고르시오. 정답률 88%

① 수리점의 위치를 찾지 못해서
② 예약 없이 수리점을 방문해서
③ 수학 시험을 준비하느라 바빠서
④ 수리점에서 오래 기다려야 해서
⑤ 버스에서 휴대 전화를 잃어버려서

8 ○△× • 2019년 3월 교육청(고1) 10번

대화를 듣고, Royal Botanic Garden에 관해 언급되지 않은 것을 고르시오. 정답률 88%

① 위치
② 크기
③ 프로그램
④ 입장료
⑤ 개관 시간

9 ○△× • 2021년 6월 교육청(고1) 9번

Sharing Friday Movement에 관한 다음 내용을 듣고, 일치하지 않는 것을 고르시오. [3점] 정답률 91%

① 매주 금요일에 2달러씩 기부하는 운동이다.
② 2001년 핀란드에서 시작되었다.
③ 기부금은 가난한 지역에 깨끗한 물을 공급하는 데 쓰인다.
④ 올해 20명의 학생에게 장학금을 지급했다.
⑤ 추가 정보는 홈페이지를 통해 얻을 수 있다.

10 ○△× 2022년 6월 교육청(고1) 10번

다음 표를 보면서 대화를 듣고, 여자가 구입할 운동화를 고르시오. 정답률 87%

Sneakers

	Model	Price	Style	Waterproof	Color
①	A	$50	casual	×	black
②	B	$60	active	×	white
③	C	$65	casual	○	black
④	D	$70	casual	○	white
⑤	E	$85	active	○	white

11 ○△× 2025년 6월 교육청(고1) 11번

대화를 듣고, 남자의 마지막 말에 대한 여자의 응답으로 가장 적절한 것을 고르시오. [3점] 정답률 77%

① I see. Then you should leave now to go see a doctor.
② Good idea. I can put you in another group next class.
③ Too bad. You should have taken some medicine first.
④ Never mind. I hope you do better on the final exam.
⑤ Thank you. I'll go to the nurse's office right now.

12 ○△× 2024년 3월 교육청(고1) 12번

대화를 듣고, 여자의 마지막 말에 대한 남자의 응답으로 가장 적절한 것을 고르시오. 정답률 79%

① Thank you. Everything looks delicious.
② Yes. I have an appointment this Saturday.
③ You're welcome. I made it with my dad's recipe.
④ Sounds good. What time did you make a reservation?
⑤ That's too bad. Why don't we try another restaurant?

13 고득점 ○△× 2019년 3월 교육청(고1) 14번

대화를 듣고, 남자의 마지막 말에 대한 여자의 응답으로 가장 적절한 것을 고르시오. 정답률 59%

Woman: ______________________________

① You're right. That's why I chose this book.
② That makes sense. I'll switch to an easier book.
③ Okay. I'll choose one from the bestseller list next time.
④ Don't worry. It's not too difficult for me to read.
⑤ Yeah. I'll join the book club to read more books.

14 ○△× 2025년 6월 교육청(고1) 13번

대화를 듣고, 여자의 마지막 말에 대한 남자의 응답으로 가장 적절한 것을 고르시오. 정답률 93%

Man: ______________________________

① I see. You've always preferred dogs over cats.
② Okay. I'll ask him if you can look after his cat.
③ Sorry. I don't have time to take care of your cat.
④ No problem. I'll take his pet to the animal hospital.
⑤ I agree. I know for sure he's a great pet caretaker.

15 ○△× 2023년 6월 교육청(고1) 15번

다음 상황 설명을 듣고, Violet이 Peter에게 할 말로 가장 적절한 것을 고르시오. 정답률 93%

Violet: ______________________________

① Will you join the science club together?
② Is it okay to use a card to pay for the drinks?
③ Why don't we donate our books to the library?
④ How about going to the cafeteria to have lunch?
⑤ Can you borrow the books for me with your card?

[16~17] 다음을 듣고, 물음에 답하시오.

16 ○△× 2020년 9월 교육청(고1) 16번

여자가 하는 말의 주제로 가장 적절한 것은? 정답률 83%

① benefits of using LEDs
② how the LED was invented
③ misunderstandings about LEDs
④ competition in the LED market
⑤ ways to advance LED technology

17 ○△× 2020년 9월 교육청(고1) 17번

언급된 물건이 아닌 것은? 정답률 91%

① lamps
② clocks
③ a television
④ traffic lights
⑤ a computer keyboard

Dictation

문제 풀이에 중요한 핵심 부분과 듣기에 자주 나오는 표현들에 빈칸 처리를 했습니다. 방송을 잘 듣고, 빈칸에 알맞은 말을 써 넣으세요.

Tip! 잘 들리지 않는 부분이 있을 때에는 정답을 확인 후, 똑같은 속도로 따라 읽기 연습을 해 보세요.

1

M: Hello, students. This is Mike Smith, your P.E. teacher. These days, the fine dust problem is getting serious. So, I'd like to explain what you should do when the ______ ______ ______ ______ ______. First, close all the classroom windows to keep out the dust. Second, ______ ______ ______ ______ ______ in the classroom. The air purifier will help keep the air clean. Third, drink water and wash your hands as often as possible. Last, ______ ______ ______ ______ ______ ______ when you're outside. Thank you for listening.

2

W: Brian, I heard that you are thinking of buying an electric bicycle.

M: Yes, that's right.

W: That's good. But be careful when you ride it.

M: Yeah, I know what you mean. On my way here I saw a man riding an electric bicycle without wearing a helmet.

W: Some riders ______ ______ ______ ______ ______ ______.

M: What do you mean by that?

W: These days many people ______ ______ ______ ______ ______.

M: Yes, it's so dangerous.

W: Right. ______ ______ ______ ______ ______ about riding electric bicycles.

M: I totally agree with you.

3

M: Excuse me. You're Chloe Jones, aren't you?

W: Yes, I am. Have we met before?

M: No, but I'm a big fan of yours. I've watched your speeches on climate change, and they're very inspiring.

W: Thank you. I'm so glad to hear that.

M: And, I also think your campaign about plastic pollution has been very successful.

W: ______ ______ ______ ______, that means a lot to me.

M: May I make a suggestion? I thought it'd be nice if ______ ______ ______ ______ ______ ______.

W: That's what I was thinking. Do you have any good ideas?

M: Actually, I'm a cartoonist. Perhaps I ______ ______ ______ ______ based on your work.

W: That is a wonderful idea. Can I contact you later to discuss it more?

M: Sure. By the way, my name is Jack Perse. Here's my business card.

4

W: Hi, Tim. How's everything going with the festival?

M: Hey, Julie! It's going great. This is a picture of what our booth will look like.

W: What will people do at your booth?

M: They'll be asked to answer questions and be given snacks if they answer correctly.

W: Okay, that sounds good. I like the banner that says 'Guessing Time' in the center.

M: Thanks. What do you think about the photos that are under the clock?

W: Great idea! What are you ______ ______ ______ ______ ______?

M: We're going to put the snacks on it.

W: That makes sense. Then, what about the ______ ______ ______ ______?

M: It's for choosing countries. We're going to ask people geography questions.

W: That should be interesting. What's ______ ______ ______ ______ ______ ______?

M: That's a photo zone for all participants.
W: Cool. I can't wait for this year's festival!

5

M: Hi, Stella. How are you doing these days?
W: Hi, Ryan. ________ ________ ________ ________ my granddad with his concert. He made a rock band with his friends.
M: There must be a lot of things to do.
W: Yeah. I ________ ________ ________ for the concert yesterday.
M: What about posters and tickets?
W: Well, I've just finished designing a poster.
M: Then I think I can help you.
W: Really? How?
M: Actually, I have a music blog. I think I can upload the poster there.
W: That's great!
M: Just send the poster to me, and ________ ________ ________ ________.
W: Thanks a lot.

6

W: Hi, I'm looking for a backpack for my niece. She's going on a camping trip this summer.
M: Great. We have this blue backpack that has multiple pockets.
W: It looks stylish and functional. How much is it?
M: It's $50, but we have a ________ ________ ________ ________ ________ today. Every backpack is 10% off.
W: That's a great deal! I'll take it.
M: I'm sure your niece will love it. Do you need anything else?
W: Yes. I like this camping hat. How much is it?
M: It's $10, ________ ________ ________, though.
W: That's okay. I'll take it as well.
M: Gift wrapping for them ________ ________ ________ ________ ________ ________. Would you like gift wrapping?
W: Yes, please. Here's my credit card.

7

W: Hi, Brian. Why didn't you answer my text message yesterday? I wanted to ask about the math exam.
M: Hi, Sarah. I'm really sorry. I broke my cell phone yesterday, so I couldn't read it.
W: Oh, no! What happened to it?
M: Well, I dropped it while getting off the bus. And now, it doesn't work at all.
W: Why didn't you ________ ________ ________?
M: I wanted to, but I couldn't.
W: Was it because you ________ ________ ________ ________ ________? There's one right by the bus stop near our school.
M: I went there to get it fixed, but I couldn't.
W: Oh, did you have to wait too long?
M: No, I didn't. Actually, I didn't know I had to ________ ________ ________ ________ ________. So I just went back home.
W: Ah! That's too bad!

8

W: Honey, it's spring. How about visiting the new botanic garden this weekend?
M: Do you mean the Royal Botanic Garden ________ ________ Redwood Valley?
W: Yes, it's not far from here. It's one of the biggest botanic gardens in the country.
M: That's right. I heard its size is about ________ ________ ________ ________ ________ ________ ________.
W: Yeah. You know, they offer interesting programs such as tree planting and guided tours.
M: Sounds great. Our kids will love planting trees.
W: Definitely. Let's go this Saturday. What time shall we leave?
M: How about 9 in the morning? The botanic garden is ________ ________ ________ ________ ________ ________ ________.
W: Okay. It'll be fun.

9

W: Good afternoon, listeners. Why don't you join the Sharing Friday Movement and __________ __________ __________ __________ __________ every Friday? This movement started in 2001 in Finland as an idea to __________ __________ __________ __________ __________. Since then, this idea has grown into a global movement. Most of the donations go to poor areas across the world and __________ __________ __________ __________ __________. This year, scholarships were given to 100 students in these areas to celebrate our 20th anniversary. Please join us, and help make a difference. If you want to get more information, visit our homepage.

10

W: Kyle, I'm looking for some sneakers. Can you help me find some good ones?

M: Of course. Let me see... *[Pause]* Look. These are the five bestselling ones.

W: Wow, they all look so cool. It's hard to choose among them.

M: Well, __________ __________ __________?

W: I don't want to spend more than 80 dollars.

M: All right. Which style do you want, active or casual?

W: I prefer casual ones. I think they match my clothes better.

M: Good. And I'd like to __________ __________ __________ for rainy days.

W: Okay, I will take your advice.

M: So you have two options left. Which color do you prefer?

W: Most of my shoes are black, so __________ __________ __________ __________ this time.

M: You made a good choice.

11

M: Ms. Adams, I'm not feeling well. __________ __________ __________ __________ __________.

W: Oh, sorry to hear that, Jack. Have you taken some medicine?

M: Yes, I took some an hour ago, but I don't think I __________ __________ __________ __________.

W: (I see. Then you should leave now to go see a doctor.)

12

W: Honey, what do you have in mind for lunch this Saturday?

M: I was thinking we should __________ __________ __________ __________ __________.

W: Hmm... I heard that __________ __________ __________ __________ __________ __________ there these days.

M: (That's too bad. Why don't we try another restaurant?)

13

M: What are you reading, Lily?

W: It's a book for my English class, Dad. We have to read a book and write a review.

M: Do you like the book?

W: Well, I'm not sure. Frankly it's __________ __________ __________ __________.

M: Why did you choose to read that book then?

W: It was __________ __________ __________ __________ and it looked interesting. It's very challenging, though.

M: Maybe you should try another book that __________ __________ __________.

W: I know what you mean, but wouldn't I learn more from reading a difficult book?

M: Well, what's the use of reading it if you can't understand it?

W: (That makes sense. I'll switch to an easier book.)

14

W: Dad, look at the cat over there!

M: Oh, it's so cute.

W: I've wanted a cat for a long time. Can we get one?

M: You know, __________ __________ __________ __________ __________, Rebecca.

W: I understand. But I promise I'd love it with all my heart.

M: It's not just about love. It's __________ __________ __________ __________.

W: Trust me, Dad. I know I can handle it.

M: Hmm... Then, how about practicing first? Uncle Tony is looking for someone to take care of his cat during his business trip.

W: That sounds great! If I do a good job with his cat, will you let me get my own cat?

M: I'll definitely think about it if you __________ __________ __________ __________ __________ __________.

W: Thanks, Dad. Please tell Uncle Tony that I want to do it.

M: (Okay. I'll ask him if you can look after his cat.)

15

W: Violet and Peter are classmates. They're doing their science group assignment together. On Saturday morning, they meet at the public library. They decide to find the books they need in different sections of the library. Violet __________ __________ __________ __________ and tries to check them out. Unfortunately, she suddenly realizes that she __________ __________ __________ __________ __________. At that moment, Peter walks up to Violet. So, Violet wants to ask Peter to __________ __________ __________ __________ __________ __________ because she knows he has his library card. In this situation, what would Violet most likely say to Peter?

Violet: (Can you borrow the books for me with your card?)

16~17

W: Hello, class! Last time we learned about LED technology. I hope all of you have a clear idea of what an LED is now. Today, I'll talk about __________ __________ __________ __________ __________ __________. First, one of the advantages of LEDs is the long lifespan. LED bulbs are used in lamps and last for over 17 years before you need to change them. Second, LEDs __________ __________ __________ __________ __________ __________. For example, a television using LEDs in its backlight saves a lot of energy. Next, LEDs are brighter than traditional bulbs. So, they __________ __________ __________ __________ __________ in foggy conditions. Finally, thanks to their small size, LEDs can be used in various small devices. Any light you see on a computer keyboard is an LED light. Now, let's think about other products that use LEDs.

Dictation Answers

1. fine dust level is high / turn on the air purifier / it's important to wear a mask
2. don't even follow basic traffic rules / ride electric bicycles on sidewalks / There should be stricter rules
3. As an environmental activist / more children could hear your ideas / can make comic books
4. using the round table for / globe on the floor / that crown on the left side
5. I've been busy helping / reserved a place / I'll post it online
6. special discount only on backpacks / not on sale / would be a total of $5
7. get it fixed / couldn't find a repair shop / make a reservation in advance
8. located in / four times larger than a soccer field / open from 10 a.m. to 6 p.m.
9. donate two dollars to our fund / encourage people to do good / help people get clean water
10. what's your budget / recommend waterproof shoes / I'll buy white ones
11. I have a bad headache / can stay in class
12. try the new Italian restaurant / it's hard to make a reservation
13. too difficult for me / on the bestseller list / suits your level
14. raising a cat isn't easy / about effort and responsibility / take good care of his cat
15. finds two useful books / didn't bring her library card / check out the books for her

16~17. how LEDs make our lives better / use very low amounts of power / make traffic lights more visible

다빈출 코드

영어 듣기

PART 2

중급 모의고사

X

1 ~ 9회

고2 교육청 학력평가
기출에서 선별한
우수 문항 모의고사

제1회 중급 모의고사

맞은 개수: 2점 문항 ___개, 3점 문항 ___개
알고 푼 문항은 ○, 찍어서 맞힌 문제는 △에 표시하고,
△와 ×는 다시 복습하세요.

1번부터 17번까지는 듣고 답하는 문제입니다. 1번부터 15번까지는 한 번만 들려주고, 16번부터 17번까지는 두 번 들려줍니다. 방송을 잘 듣고 답을 하시기 바랍니다.

1 ○△× 2022년 9월 교육청(고2) 1번

다음을 듣고, 여자가 하는 말의 목적으로 가장 적절한 것을 고르시오. 정답률 86%

① 설문조사 참여를 독려하려고
② 설문조사 결과를 공유하려고
③ 설문조사 기간 변경을 공지하려고
④ 학교 홈페이지 가입을 요청하려고
⑤ 학교 홈페이지 점검 시간을 안내하려고

2 ○△× 2024년 3월 교육청(고2) 2번

대화를 듣고, 여자의 의견으로 가장 적절한 것을 고르시오. 정답률 90%

① 플래시 카드를 퀴즈에 활용하면 단어를 즐겁게 익힐 수 있다.
② 퀴즈를 내는 활동을 통해 학습자의 약점을 파악할 수 있다.
③ 단어 학습에 가장 효과적인 방법은 개인마다 차이가 있다.
④ 그림과 글이 함께 포함된 플래시 카드는 학습에 효과적이다.
⑤ 플래시 카드를 활용한 단어 학습 프로그램 개발이 필요하다.

3 ○△× 2024년 3월 교육청(고2) 3번

다음을 듣고, 남자가 하는 말의 요지로 가장 적절한 것을 고르시오. 정답률 92%

① 깔끔한 방을 유지하기 위해 필요 없는 물건을 없애야 한다.
② 쓰레기를 버릴 때는 환경에 미칠 악영향을 고려해야 한다.
③ 공간의 기능과 종류에 따라 효과적인 정리 방법이 다르다.
④ 사용하지 않는 물건은 보관하기보다 기부하는 것이 낫다.
⑤ 상자를 이용하면 물건을 효과적으로 보관할 수 있다.

4 ○△× 2024년 3월 교육청(고2) 4번

대화를 듣고, 그림에서 대화의 내용과 일치하지 않는 것을 고르시오. 정답률 94%

5 ○△× 2023년 9월 교육청(고2) 5번

대화를 듣고, 남자가 할 일로 가장 적절한 것을 고르시오. 정답률 94%

① 상자 가져오기
② 거실 청소하기
③ 전구 구입하기
④ 세탁물 맡기기
⑤ 바이올린 레슨 신청하기

6 ○△× 2020년 9월 교육청(고2) 9번

대화를 듣고, 남자가 지불할 금액을 고르시오. [3점] 정답률 79%

① $41 ② $46 ③ $51 ④ $56 ⑤ $60

7 ○△× 2022년 6월 교육청(고2) 7번

대화를 듣고, 여자가 벼룩시장에 갈 수 없는 이유를 고르시오. 정답률 96%

① 결혼식에서 피아노를 연주해야 해서
② 빵집에서 아르바이트를 해야 해서
③ 티셔츠를 교환하러 가야 해서
④ 건강 검진을 받아야 해서
⑤ 과제를 제출해야 해서

8 ○△× 2025년 3월 교육청(고2) 8번

대화를 듣고, 2025 Aquathlon에 관해 언급되지 않은 것을 고르시오. 정답률 94%

① 경기 종목
② 경기 날짜
③ 등록 방법
④ 참가비
⑤ 경기 장소

9 ○△× 2023년 9월 교육청(고2) 9번

2023 Board Game Design Contest에 관한 다음 내용을 듣고, 일치하지 않는 것을 고르시오. 정답률 91%

① 참가 연령에 제한이 없다.
② 1라운드에서는 게임 소개 영상을 제출해야 한다.
③ 2라운드에서는 게임 디자이너의 도움을 받지 못한다.
④ 최종 우승자는 1,000달러를 받는다.
⑤ 9월 15일에 등록이 마감된다.

10 ○△×

• 2018년 9월 교육청(고2) 12번

다음 표를 보면서 대화를 듣고, 여자가 구입할 오븐을 고르시오. 정답률 75%

Ovens

	Model	Size	Timer (Minutes)	Customer Rating	Price
①	A	Small	75	5 stars	$55
②	B	Medium	60	4.5 stars	$79
③	C	Medium	75	3 stars	$85
④	D	Big	75	5 stars	$90
⑤	E	Big	90	4.5 stars	$105

11 ○△×

• 2022년 9월 교육청(고2) 12번

대화를 듣고, 여자의 마지막 말에 대한 남자의 응답으로 가장 적절한 것을 고르시오. 정답률 82%

① No way. We need the international program.
② Don't worry. I can exchange my book with yours.
③ Not bad. That's a good example of a topic sentence.
④ I understand. I was really nervous during the presentation.
⑤ Okay. Let's find one that is easy and interesting to talk about.

12 고득점 ○△×

• 2019년 6월 교육청(고2) 2번

대화를 듣고, 남자의 마지막 말에 대한 여자의 응답으로 가장 적절한 것을 고르시오. 정답률 64%

① Right, the whole room is too bright.
② Cleaning will be finished in a minute.
③ Okay, wash your hair in the bathroom.
④ The carpenter is expected to arrive here.
⑤ Then, I'll go and buy a new one right now.

13 ○△×

• 2023년 9월 교육청(고2) 14번

대화를 듣고, 여자의 마지막 말에 대한 남자의 응답으로 가장 적절한 것을 고르시오. [3점] 정답률 82%

Man: ______________________

① Thanks for letting me know. I should try using them.
② It tastes good. I'm curious about the recipe for this juice.
③ Don't worry. I don't care about the kinds of straws I use.
④ You're right. I'd better not use a silicone straw from now on.
⑤ I've tried all of them already, but I still prefer paper straws.

14 ○△×

• 2017년 3월 교육청(고2) 13번

대화를 듣고, 남자의 마지막 말에 대한 여자의 응답으로 가장 적절한 것을 고르시오. [3점] 정답률 77%

Woman: ______________________

① Yes, it was a wonderful essay.
② Well, let's ask the teacher about it.
③ No, I haven't decided on the topic yet.
④ No, I'm not interested in Indian culture.
⑤ Oh, your topic is far different from mine.

15 ○△×

• 2023년 6월 교육청(고2) 15번

다음 상황 설명을 듣고, Nick이 Annie에게 할 말로 가장 적절한 것을 고르시오. 정답률 75%

Nick: ______________________

① I'd like to replace my content with yours right away.
② We'd better ask our professor about which source to trust.
③ Your information is different from what's on the Internet.
④ You should have done more research for the presentation.
⑤ I believe that Van Gogh started painting in his early teens.

[16~17] 다음을 듣고, 물음에 답하시오.

16 고득점 ○△×

• 2021년 9월 교육청(고2) 16번

남자가 하는 말의 주제로 가장 적절한 것은? 정답률 71%

① animals' abilities to count
② reasons for animals' migrating
③ hunting habits of wild animals
④ necessity of protecting animal rights
⑤ ways to conserve endangered animals

17 ○△×

• 2021년 9월 교육청(고2) 17번

언급된 동물이 아닌 것은? 정답률 94%

① wolves ② frogs ③ chickens
④ snakes ⑤ desert ants

Dictation

문제 풀이에 중요한 핵심 부분과 듣기에 자주 나오는 표현들에 빈칸 처리를 했습니다. 방송을 잘 듣고, 빈칸에 알맞은 말을 써 넣으세요.

Tip! 잘 들리지 않는 부분이 있을 때에는 정답을 확인 후, 똑같은 속도로 따라 읽기 연습을 해 보세요.

1

W: Hello, Princeton High School students. As you know, our school's website is going to be redesigned. Our goals are to make our website more accessible to everyone and to strengthen online security. To better prepare our new website, __________ __________ __________ __________ to gather your opinions and suggestions. __________ __________ __________ __________ __________. The survey must be completed by this Thursday. For more information, please refer to our school bulletin board. Remember that __________ __________ __________ __________ to everyone in our school's community. Thank you!

2

W: Liam, what's that bunch of paper in your hand?

M: It's a deck of __________ __________ __________ __________ __________, but it doesn't work well for me.

W: Really? Why not? I think flashcards are helpful for learning vocabulary.

M: I thought so, too. But looking at the word on one side of the card and the meaning on the back is too boring.

W: Hmm, how about using them __________ __________ __________ __________ __________?

M: A more interesting way to use flashcards? What do you mean?

W: Ask a friend to read the meaning on the back, and you shout out the word as the answer.

M: Oh, you mean like asking and answering questions in a quiz?

W: That's right. __________ __________ __________ __________ __________, you can learn new words while having fun.

M: I like your idea a lot. I'll give it a try!

3

M: Hello, everyone. I'm Charlie Goodman, your speaker today. I'll be discussing the most effective way to __________ __________ __________ __________. Let's start by reflecting on the items in your room. Do you really use everything every day? Probably not. The most important thing to do to keep a clean room is to get rid of __________ __________ __________ __________ __________. Don't keep your room filled with items untouched for more than six months. If you haven't used an item in six months, it likely means you won't use it again! If you __________ __________ __________, you can keep your room nice and neat.

4

W: I've just finished setting up my booth to sell used items. How does it look?

M: Wow! Everything looks nice, especially the __________ __________ __________ __________ __________. People can see it well.

W: I think so, too. I also hope people like this striped dress in the corner.

M: I bet they will. What about the wooden box here? Is it a used one, too?

W: Yes. To make it look better, I put some flowers in it.

M: They really catch the eye. Also, the __________ __________ __________ __________ look almost new.

W: I haven't worn them much because they are a bit small for me. So I've decided to sell them. The __________ __________ __________ __________ is almost new, too.

M: Oh, I like it the most. I hope you can sell everything you prepared!

5

M: Mom, I'm home.

W: Hi, Brian. How was your violin lesson?

M: It was fun. I think my violin skills have improved a lot.

W: Good! By the way, did you see the __________ __________ __________ in the living room?

M: Yeah. I wore those clothes when I was a little kid. Are you going to throw them away?

W: No. I'm going to __________ __________ __________ __________ today.

M: Oh, so you want to donate the clothes?

W: Yes. They're all in good condition and they've been dry-cleaned.

M: That's great. Is there anything I can help you with?

W: Well, I __________ __________ __________ to put the clothes in.

M: No worries. I'll bring some from the garage.

W: Thanks, but be careful. The lights in the garage aren't working.

M: I got it, Mom. I'll be right back.

6

W: Good afternoon. How can I help you?

M: Hi. I'm looking for a gift for my newborn niece. What would you recommend?

W: These pajama sets and dresses are the best-selling clothes for babies.

M: They're so cute. How much are they?

W: This pajama set is 40 dollars, and __________ __________ __________ __________ __________.

M: Hmm.... I'd like to buy the dress you recommended.

W: Okay. Anything else?

M: Do you have any other items that would go well with the dress?

W: How about this hat? It's usually 10 dollars, but it's on sale. You can __________ __________ __________ __________ __________ __________.

M: That sounds great! I'll take it.

W: Wonderful. So, one dress and one hat, right?

M: Yes. I also have this 5 dollar discount coupon. Can I use it?

W: Let me see. *[Pause]* Unfortunately, no. This coupon only __________ __________ __________ __________ __________ __________.

M: All right. I'll pay with this credit card.

7

W: Hi, Jason. I like your T-shirt.

M: Thanks. I bought it for just $3 at the flea market.

W: What a bargain! I want to buy a T-shirt like yours, too.

M: Then, how about __________ __________ __________ __________ __________ together? It'll be held this Saturday.

W: This Saturday? I'd love to, but I can't.

M: Oh, I know you work at Tom's Bakery. Do you work on Saturdays?

W: No, I only work on weekdays.

M: I see. Then is it because of the medical check-up you reserved last week?

W: I did make an appointment, but I __________ __________ __________ to next Friday.

M: So, then what's your plan for Saturday?

W: Actually, it's my uncle's wedding day. I __________ __________ __________ __________ __________ for him at the ceremony.

M: Great! Maybe some other time, then.

8

M: Have you heard about the 2025 Aquathlon?

W: No, I haven't. What is it?

M: It's a competition that __________ __________ __________ __________. It's coming up soon.

W: That sounds great! I've competed in several swimming events, but never anything like this. Are you going to participate?

M: Absolutely. I've been training for both swimming and running.

W: When is the event?

M: It's on May 24th.

W: I'd like to join, too. Have you completed the registration process?

M: Not yet. I heard we need to __________ __________ __________ __________ __________ __________ __________. Let's sign up together.

W: Sounds good. How about training together before the event?

M: Great idea. The competition will be held at Blue River. Why don't we __________ __________ __________ __________ __________ __________?

W: I know the best place. Let's get started this weekend!

9

W: Hello, viewers. The 2023 Board Game Design Contest is an annual event for designing board games. It's open to board game fans __________ __________ __________ around the world. The contest is split into two rounds. In round one, contestants must submit a 2-minute video introducing their games. In round two, contestants must __________ __________ __________ __________ that explains how to play their game. During round two, contestants get the chance to work with experienced game designers who will help each contestant with establishing the rules for their game. The final winner of the contest receives $1,000, plus a chance to __________ __________ __________ __________ __________. Registration closes on Friday, September 15th. Show us your skills as a game designer!

10

M: Anna, what are you doing?

W: I'm searching the Internet to buy a new oven. Can you help me choose from this list?

M: What do you plan to make with it?

W: Well, I really enjoy baking, but I'd like to use it to make other things, too.

M: Then, I think you need a medium or big size oven.

W: All right. I'll cross out this item. Which timer do you think will be best?

M: If you're making many kinds of food, then I think the timer should __________ __________ __________ __________ __________.

W: Yeah. You have a good point. So, we have three options left.

M: Let's compare the customer ratings here.

W: Hmm. This one only got three stars. I want one with __________ __________ __________ __________.

M: Okay. Look! Between these two, this one is cheaper than that one.

W: Then, I'll __________ __________ __________ __________.

11

W: Our teacher said we __________ __________ __________ __________ __________ at the International Exchange Program next week.

M: Next week? We should hurry, then. What should we do first?

W: Let me see. First, I think __________ __________ __________ __________ __________ __________ for our presentation.

M: (Okay. Let's find one that is easy and interesting to talk about.)

12

M: Oh, Susan! The light in the bathroom went out.

W: I know, but don't worry. We only have to __________ __________ __________ __________. I'll buy one tomorrow.

M: But, it's __________ __________ __________ __________ __________.

W: (Then, I'll go and buy a new one right now.)

13

W: Fred, I got the blueberry juice we ordered.

M: Thanks, Kathy. Oh, it has a paper straw. Don't they have a plastic one?

W: What's wrong with a paper straw?

M: It can get soaked and fall apart while drinking. So I prefer a plastic straw.

W: But plastic straws can harm the environment.

M: Protecting the environment is all good, but my drink __________ __________ __________ __________ __________.

W: If so, there are other types of straws to enjoy your drink that __________ __________ __________ __________ __________ __________.

M: I didn't know there were other kinds. Can you name some of them?

W: Have you heard of a silicone straw?

M: No, I haven't. It sounds interesting.

W: There are also straws __________ __________ __________ __________ __________. They're reusable and don't affect the taste of your drink.

M: (Thanks for letting me know. I should try using them.)

14

W: How is it going with your essay on the cultures of other countries?

M: Not so well. How about you?

W: I've just started working on it.

M: For me, it was hard to __________ __________ __________ __________.

W: Same with me. Also, it's not easy __________ __________ __________ __________ __________ in the essay as the teacher required.

M: I know. He always regards our own opinions as the most important part.

W: So, what is your topic?

M: It's about India and its culture.

W: Oh, my! That's exactly __________ __________ __________ __________ __________ __________.

M: Really? I'm not sure if it's okay to have the same topic. Should one of us change it?

W: (Well, let's ask the teacher about it.)

15

M: Nick and Annie are partners for an art project. They are supposed to make a presentation on the life of Vincent van Gogh. However, while researching and working on their project, they realized that some of the content they found was conflicting. For example, __________ __________ __________ __________ about when exactly Van Gogh started painting. Nick gathered his information from the books in the library, while Annie collected hers from the Internet. Nick and Annie are not sure __________ __________ __________ __________. Nick wants their presentation to be as precise as possible, so he thinks that they should ask their professor for help with deciding __________ __________ __________ __________ __________. In this situation, what would Nick most likely say to Annie?

Nick: (We'd better ask our professor about which source to trust.)

16~17

M: Hello, everyone. I'm Dr. Martin Muller. Do you know that __________ __________ __________ __________ in the animal kingdom? Many biologists have suggested that counting is not unique to humans. For instance, wolves use strength in numbers while hunting. Wolves have optimal group sizes for hunting different prey. In addition, female frogs __________ __________ __________ __________ __________ in a male frog's cry. They can do this for phrases up to 10 notes long. Despite what you may have heard, chickens are quite smart. Research shows that newly hatched chicks and adult chickens can count and __________ __________ __________. Lastly, the real math wizards of the animal kingdom are desert ants. They are able to find their way back home after leaving their nests for food by counting steps. Now, we will watch a video about these animals.

Dictation Answers

1. we're conducting a survey / Your participation is strongly encouraged / your input is valuable
2. flashcards for memorizing new words / in a more interesting way / By using flashcards for quizzes
3. maintain an organized room / things you no longer need / remove unnecessary items
4. banner hanging under the roof / shoes on the table / guitar beside the table
5. pile of clothes / give them to charity / need some boxes
6. this dress is 50 dollars / get 40 percent off that price / applies to purchases over 100 dollars
7. going to the flea market / changed the date / promised to play the piano
8. combines swimming and running / register online by filling out a form / find a similar place to practice
9. of all ages / hand in a document / release his or her game
10. last at least 75 minutes / more than four stars / order the cheaper one
11. have to make a presentation / we'd better decide on the topic
12. replace the light bulb / uncomfortable to use the bathroom
13. tastes bad with paper straws / cause less harm to the environment / made of glass or metal
14. find an interesting topic / to put my personal opinions / what I'm going to write about
15. there was a disagreement / which one to trust / which source is more reliable

16~17. mathematical ability is widespread / count the number of pulses / do basic math

제2회 중급 모의고사

맞은 개수: 2점 문항 ___개, 3점 문항 ___개
알고 푼 문항은 ○, 찍어서 맞힌 문제는 △에 표시하고, △와 ×는 다시 복습하세요.

1번부터 17번까지는 듣고 답하는 문제입니다. 1번부터 15번까지는 한 번만 들려주고, 16번부터 17번까지는 두 번 들려줍니다. 방송을 잘 듣고 답을 하시기 바랍니다.

1 ○△× • 2021년 9월 교육청(고2) 1번

다음을 듣고, 남자가 하는 말의 목적으로 가장 적절한 것을 고르시오. 정답률 89%

① 학교 급식 일정 변경을 알리려고
② 학교 식당 이용 시 주의 사항을 안내하려고
③ 학교 급식 설문 조사 기간 연장을 공지하려고
④ 설문 조사로 선정된 학교 급식 메뉴를 소개하려고
⑤ 학교 급식 개선을 위한 토론회 참석을 요청하려고

2 ○△× • 2025년 6월 교육청(고2) 2번

대화를 듣고, 남자의 의견으로 가장 적절한 것을 고르시오. 정답률 92%

① 물건을 충동적으로 구매하지 않아야 한다.
② 지출을 기록하는 것은 금전 관리에 도움이 된다.
③ 부모로부터 경제적으로 독립하는 것이 필요하다.
④ 현명한 소비는 자기 만족감을 향상시킬 수 있다.
⑤ 기억력 향상을 위해 메모하는 습관을 길러야 한다.

3 ○△× • 2023년 9월 교육청(고2) 3번

대화를 듣고, 두 사람의 관계를 가장 잘 나타낸 것을 고르시오. 정답률 92%

① 방송 연출가 — 배우
② 영화 각본가 — 과학자
③ 신문 기자 — 환경 운동가
④ 영화감독 — 영화 비평가
⑤ 잡지 구독자 — 잡지 편집장

4 ○△× • 2023년 9월 교육청(고2) 4번

대화를 듣고, 그림에서 대화의 내용과 일치하지 않는 것을 고르시오. 정답률 92%

5 ○△× • 2024년 3월 교육청(고2) 5번

대화를 듣고, 여자가 남자에게 부탁한 일로 가장 적절한 것을 고르시오. 정답률 86%

① 설문 결과 정리하기
② 원인 조사하기
③ 그래프 제작하기
④ 사진 고르기
⑤ 데이터 전송하기

6 고득점 ○△× • 2024년 6월 교육청(고2) 6번

대화를 듣고, 여자가 지불할 금액을 고르시오. [3점] 정답률 72%

① $14 ② $19 ③ $24 ④ $28 ⑤ $33

7 ○△× • 2020년 9월 교육청(고2) 8번

대화를 듣고, 여자가 보드게임을 하러 갈 수 없는 이유를 고르시오. 정답률 91%

① 병문안을 가야 해서
② 시험공부를 해야 해서
③ 방과 후 수업이 있어서
④ 생일 파티에 참석해야 해서
⑤ 스키용품을 사러 가야 해서

8 ○△× • 2020년 3월 교육청(고2) 10번

대화를 듣고, Dream Bio Research Project에 관해 언급되지 않은 것을 고르시오. 정답률 84%

① 연구원 수
② 예산 규모
③ 연구 목적
④ 연구 장소
⑤ 연구 기간

9 ○△× • 2022년 6월 교육청(고2) 9번

Space Science Camp에 관한 다음 내용을 듣고, 일치하지 않는 것을 고르시오. 정답률 96%

① 8월 21일부터 8월 23일까지 진행된다.
② 우주 여행에 관한 특별 강연이 있다.
③ 참가자에게는 별을 관측할 기회가 있다.
④ 예약 페이지는 캠프 3주 전에 열린다.
⑤ 참가비는 1인당 50달러이다.

10 ○△× • 2024년 6월 교육청(고2) 10번

다음 표를 보면서 대화를 듣고, 두 사람이 구매할 반지를 고르시오. 정답률 82%

Gold Rings

	Model	Price	Color	Stone	Gift-Wrapping Service
①	A	$300	White	Ruby	×
②	B	$330	Yellow	Ruby	×
③	C	$350	White	Emerald	○
④	D	$380	Rose	Ruby	○
⑤	E	$430	Rose	Emerald	×

11 ○△× • 2022년 6월 교육청(고2) 12번

대화를 듣고, 여자의 마지막 말에 대한 남자의 응답으로 가장 적절한 것을 고르시오. 정답률 78%

① Sorry. I've already made a reservation at that restaurant.
② Oh, no. I must find another place as soon as possible.
③ Great. Let's have the phone fixed right now.
④ No way! It is too far away to go there.
⑤ Thanks. I'll definitely go to your party.

12 ○△× • 2025년 3월 교육청(고2) 11번

대화를 듣고, 남자의 마지막 말에 대한 여자의 응답으로 가장 적절한 것을 고르시오. 정답률 80%

① Thanks. I've always wanted to see their live performance.
② You're right. The concert is going to be canceled anyway.
③ Sorry. I can't make it to the live chat with the band.
④ Oh, no. You shouldn't have missed this special opportunity.
⑤ Wonderful! I look forward to seeing you play in the festival.

13 ○△× • 2024년 6월 교육청(고2) 14번

대화를 듣고, 여자의 마지막 말에 대한 남자의 응답으로 가장 적절한 것을 고르시오. 정답률 87%

Man: ______________________________

① Don't worry. He'll get his driver's license soon.
② Really? I didn't know you were interested in my car.
③ Oh, no. Then I should take my car to the repair shop.
④ No problem. We can schedule a time with my brother.
⑤ Never mind. I'm going to buy a different one tomorrow.

14 ○△× • 2019년 9월 교육청(고2) 14번

대화를 듣고, 남자의 마지막 말에 대한 여자의 응답으로 가장 적절한 것을 고르시오. [3점] 정답률 80%

Woman: ______________________________

① Don't worry. It'll only filter out the ads.
② Be careful. Don't trust online ads too much.
③ You're right. I'll consider using the program.
④ That can put your private information at risk.
⑤ Downloading the program will slow your computer.

15 ○△× • 2025년 3월 교육청(고2) 15번

다음 상황 설명을 듣고, Anthony가 Emma에게 할 말로 가장 적절한 것을 고르시오. [3점] 정답률 80%

Anthony: ______________________________

① I'm not sure. I won't be a responsible leader like you.
② I don't think I can help you. I've already joined another team.
③ I'm afraid I can't. But I'll recommend a close friend instead.
④ My pleasure! I'm honored to be able to join the team again.
⑤ That's right. I had to quit the badminton team due to injury.

[16~17] 다음을 듣고, 물음에 답하시오.

16 ○△× • 2022년 6월 교육청(고2) 16번

남자가 하는 말의 주제로 가장 적절한 것은? 정답률 84%

① misunderstandings about recycled products
② processes and outputs of recycling
③ issues caused by waste pollution
④ the history of recycling systems
⑤ tips for reducing trash

17 ○△× • 2022년 6월 교육청(고2) 17번

언급된 소재가 아닌 것은? 정답률 95%

① paper ② metals ③ fabrics
④ glass ⑤ plastics

Dictation

문제 풀이에 중요한 핵심 부분과 듣기에 자주 나오는 표현들에 빈칸 처리를 했습니다. 방송을 잘 듣고, 빈칸에 알맞은 말을 써 넣으세요.

Tip! 잘 들리지 않는 부분이 있을 때에는 정답을 확인 후, 똑같은 속도로 따라 읽기 연습을 해 보세요.

1

M: Hello, students. I'm the school nutritionist, Mr. Jackson. Over the past week, we have __________ __________ __________ on the school website about the meals you ate this semester. I want to thank those of you who have responded. Unfortunately, less than 50 percent of students answered the survey. We don't have enough data to make your school meals better. Therefore, we decided to __________ __________ __________ __________ by one week. The meal survey is now open until next Wednesday. We hope that giving you another week to __________ __________ __________ __________ will help improve the quality of your school meals. Thank you for listening.

2

M: Hey, sweetie. Why are you so quiet?

W: Dad, I feel bad today.

M: What's the matter?

W: I can't buy the running shoes I want.

M: How come? You just got paid from your part-time job!

W: Yeah, but I spent it all. I feel like I __________ __________ __________ __________.

M: Have you tried writing down __________ __________ __________ __________ __________?

W: No, I haven't. Do you think writing it down is helpful?

M: Totally. Once you see where your money goes, you'll be more careful with it.

W: Oh, that's a good point, Dad.

M: It's crucial to __________ __________ __________ __________ __________ __________. That'll help you manage your money wisely.

W: Okay, I'll remember that.

3

[Phone rings.]

W: Hello.

M: Hello. Can I speak to Ms. Norton?

W: This is she.

M: Hi, this is Mark Kelly from Polaris Studio. I heard you were a scientific advisor on the movie *Space Dynasty*.

W: Yes, I helped the writers with the script.

M: I thought the script was well written and had many entertaining scenes related to science.

W: Thank you. It was a lot of fun.

M: I'm actually __________ __________ __________ for a science fiction movie right now, and I was wondering if you could help me with your expertise.

W: Okay. What's the movie about?

M: It's about natural disasters caused by global warming. I __________ __________ __________ __________ __________ like you to make it more realistic.

W: I'd be interested. I've __________ __________ __________ __________ __________ __________ on global warming in my lab. My findings might be useful for you.

M: Fantastic! I'll send you my script. Thank you so much.

4

M: Hello, Ms. Clark. How's it going with __________ __________ __________?

W: Good morning, Mr. Cooper. It's almost done. Do you want to see a picture of what it looks like?

M: Sure. *[Pause]* Oh, I see a round clock on the wall. It looks nice.

W: Yes. I replaced the old clock with a new one.

M: I also like the bookcase under the window.

W: I put it there to make it easier for students to read books. How do you like the stripe-patterned rug?

M: I like it. It __________ __________ __________ __________ __________. By the way, what are the two boxes on the table for?

W: I'll put some classroom supplies in them. I also __________ __________ __________ __________ __________ __________ __________.

M: Great idea! I think your students will really like the new classroom.

W: Thank you.

5

W: We're almost done with our report on climate change. Why don't we check it together to see if everything is okay?

M: That's a good idea. Are you sure we included every graph we made?

W: Yes, they are all there in the report. They clearly __________ __________ __________ __________ __________ __________ that we've researched.

M: Good to hear that. How about the pictures? We've chosen the five best pictures.

W: They look very convincing. What do you think about the part discussing the students' awareness? Many of our friends __________ __________ __________ __________.

M: The survey results show that many students know how serious it is. How about the action plans?

W: We have two action plans here, but I think we need more. Could you __________ __________ __________ __________ from our research?

M: Sure. I'll send the data this afternoon.

6

M: Welcome to the World History Museum. How may I help you?

W: Hi, I'd like to purchase three admission tickets. What's the fee for an adult?

M: An adult ticket is $10.

W: What about for seniors?

M: If you look at the price board, people over 65 years of age __________ __________ __________.

W: Okay, then I'll buy one senior ticket, and two adult tickets.

M: May I see an identification card for the senior?

W: Yeah, just a moment. Here it is.

M: Thank you. And today is National Museum Day, so you can __________ __________ __________ __________ __________ __________.

W: Wow, that's amazing!

M: If you __________ __________ __________, they're $5 each.

W: No, thanks. Only the tickets, please. Here's my credit card.

7

W: I'm so happy our exams are over.

M: Me, too. They were really tough this time.

W: I know. Getting a cold made me even more stressed.

M: Are you still sick?

W: No, I feel all right now. What are you doing after school today?

M: Some of our classmates __________ __________ __________ __________ __________ __________ to celebrate the end of exams. Do you want to come?

W: I'd love to go, but I can't.

M: Why not?

W: Did I tell you my family is __________ __________ __________ __________ __________ this weekend?

M: No, you didn't. Why are you going skiing?

W: It's my dad's birthday, so we planned this trip for him.

M: That sounds like a perfect gift for your dad.

W: I hope so. I need to __________ __________ __________ __________ and a ski suit for myself today.

M: Oh, I see. Have a nice trip.

8

M: Hello, Dr. Peterson. How are you doing these days?

W: Hello, Dr. Collins. Good, I'm working on the Dream Bio Research Project.

M: You mean the medical research project sponsored by the government?

W: That's right. __________ __________ __________ __________ __________ __________ in the project and I'm the head researcher.

M: Wow, you're in charge of a really big job. How big is the budget for the project?

W: We're allowed to __________ __________ __________ __________ on the project.

M: That's a really huge amount. It's a project to __________ __________ __________ __________ for lung cancer, isn't it?

W: That's right.

M: How long will the research project last?

W: It's a 5-year project. I hope we can develop the drug within this period.

M: I wish you success, Dr. Peterson.

W: Thank you, Dr. Collins.

9

W: Good morning, everyone. I'm Olivia Benson, the president of Golden Star Observatory. We'll be hosting Space Science Camp for teenagers this summer vacation. It's a 3-day camp which goes from August 21st to August 23rd. Our programs will help you learn more about space. A former astronaut, Dr. Michael Russell, will __________ __________ __________ __________ about space travel. Participants will even have a chance to __________ __________ __________ __________ __________ __________. If you want to join this camp, you should sign up at our website. The reservation page will __________ __________ __________ __________ __________ __________. The participation fee is $50 per person. We hope to see you then. Thank you.

10

W: Hey Adam, Mom's birthday is coming up. Why don't we buy a gold ring for her present?

M: Good idea. I heard that jewelry online is cheaper than in stores. So let's buy one online.

W: Okay. Let me see... Rings are pretty expensive. What's our budget?

M: We spent a lot for Mother's Day last month, so I don't think we can __________ __________ __________ __________ on her present this time.

W: You're right. Let's decide on a color now. We have three options: white, yellow, and rose.

M: Mom already has several yellow gold rings. We __________ __________ __________.

W: Good point. Both the white and rose ones look better anyway.

M: That's true. What about a stone for the ring?

W: How about a ruby? It would __________ __________ __________ Mom's red earrings.

M: I agree. Oh, this one provides a gift-wrapping service.

W: We don't need that. I'd rather wrap it myself.

M: Okay, then let's order this one.

11

W: Richard, have you chosen a place for Mom's birthday party? It's already next week!

M: I've been trying to make a reservation at Palace Bistro, but the restaurant __________ __________ __________ __________.

W: Haven't you heard? It's __________ __________ __________ __________ __________ __________!

M: (Oh, no. I must find another place as soon as possible.)

12

M: Olivia, did you hear the news about the music festival this weekend?

W: No, I didn't. Is there __________ __________ __________ __________?

M: Actually, I heard your __________ __________ __________ __________ __________ __________ __________ at the festival on Sunday. I thought you might like it.

W: (Thanks. I've always wanted to see their live performance.)

13

M: Hi, Sandra. You look excited.

W: Yeah, I just got my driver's license.

M: Congratulations! Are you planning to buy a car?

W: Actually, I've been browsing cars online. But they're more expensive than I expected.

M: Then, what about a used car? My brother happens to __________ __________ __________ __________.

W: I was considering buying a used car, too. Can I see some pictures of his car?

M: Let me check... Here you go. He's had it for about three years.

W: Wow, it looks as shiny as new. Also, it's in my favorite color and design.

M: I'm glad you like it. You'll be even more satisfied when you __________ __________ __________ __________.

W: I hope so! Do you know how much he's selling it for?

M: He wants $10,000 for it.

W: That's within my budget. But I'd __________ __________ __________ __________ __________.

M: (No problem. We can schedule a time with my brother.)

14

W: Jay, why do you look so annoyed?

M: I've been surfing the Internet, but __________ __________ __________ __________ __________.

W: What kinds of ads?

M: Pop-up advertisements. Whenever I open a new website, ads pop up. It takes a lot of time for me to close all of them.
W: That used to happen to me, too. Maybe I can help you.
M: Is there a way to stop them?
W: I'm using a program that ________ ________ ________.
M: Is it difficult to use?
W: It's very simple and easy. Just install a pop-up blocker on your computer, and it'll prevent ads from popping up.
M: That sounds good. But what if I ________ ________ ________ ________ ________ that are not advertisements?
W: (Don't worry. It'll only filter out the ads.)

15

M: Emma is the captain of her school badminton team. Her team is planning to participate in the upcoming tournament, but one of the team members ________ ________ ________. Emma feels a strong responsibility to ________ ________ ________ as the team leader. Then she thinks of Anthony, who used to be a badminton team member. So she asks Anthony to ________ ________ ________ ________ ________. However, Anthony is very busy preparing for an important presentation next week. He thinks he cannot accept Emma's request and thinks of another way to help her. He ________ ________ ________ ________ of his close friends instead. His friend is not only good at badminton, but has always wanted to join the badminton team. In this situation, what would Anthony most likely say to Emma?
Anthony: (I'm afraid I can't. But I'll recommend a close friend instead.)

16~17

M: Hello, students. Last time, we talked about the problem of wasting materials. Today, we're going to discuss ________ ________ ________ ________ ________ and turned into new products. Used paper is usually cut down into small pieces and sent into a machine to remove any ink or glue on it. Then it can be used for making things such as toilet paper and paper bags. Metals like steel and iron are also valuable as recyclable materials. They are ________ ________ ________ ________ ________ into car parts, frames, foils, and other things. Glass is another special material that can be recycled endlessly. Like metals, glass is also melted down after being crushed, and then it is made into new bottles and jars. Plastics are complicated to recycle because there are so many types. After sorting and melting the plastics, they can be ________ ________ ________ ________ like bottles and toys through a special process. Now, let's take a look at some video clips and then we'll discuss them in detail.

Dictation Answers

1. conducted a survey / extend the survey period / participate in the survey
2. never have enough money / where you spend your money / keep a record of your spending
3. writing a script / need advice from science experts / done a lot of scientific research
4. rearranging your classroom / goes well with the classroom / put a flower pot in the corner
5. show the causes of climate change / participated in our survey / send me the data
6. are charged $8 / get 50% off the total price / need audio guides
7. are going to play board games / going on a ski trip / go shopping for goggles
8. More than 20 researchers are involved / spend one million dollars / develop a new drug
9. give a special lecture / look at stars through our telescopes / open two weeks before the camp
10. spend more than $400 / shouldn't choose yellow / go well with
11. never answers my calls / closed for repairs until next month
12. anything special about it / favorite band will be playing music live
13. be selling his car / see it in person / need to test-drive it first
14. there are so many ads / blocks pop-up advertisements / can't see important pop-up messages
15. recently got injured / find a replacement / join the team once again / decides to recommend one

16~17. how used materials are recycled / melted down and easily transformed / turned into new products

제3회 중급 모의고사

맞은 개수: 2점 문항 ___개, 3점 문항 ___개
알고 푼 문항은 ○, 찍어서 맞힌 문제는 △에 표시하고, △와 ×는 다시 복습하세요.

1번부터 17번까지는 듣고 답하는 문제입니다. 1번부터 15번까지는 한 번만 들려주고, 16번부터 17번까지는 두 번 들려줍니다. 방송을 잘 듣고 답을 하시기 바랍니다.

1 ○△×
2023년 9월 교육청(고2) 1번

다음을 듣고, 남자가 하는 말의 목적으로 가장 적절한 것을 고르시오. 정답률 93%

① 학생회 운영 방침을 설명하려고
② 학교 웹사이트 활용을 독려하려고
③ 진학 설명회 일정 변경을 공지하려고
④ 교내 봉사 활동 시 유의점을 안내하려고
⑤ 캠퍼스 투어 행사 자원봉사자를 모집하려고

2 ○△×
2017년 9월 교육청(고2) 4번

대화를 듣고, 남자의 의견으로 가장 적절한 것을 고르시오. 정답률 87%

① 달리는 것보다 빨리 걷는 것이 열량 소모가 더 크다.
② 저녁 시간에 하는 격렬한 운동은 수면에 좋지 않다.
③ 격렬한 운동 후에는 충분한 휴식이 필요하다.
④ 자신의 건강 상태에 맞는 운동을 선택해야 한다.
⑤ 운동의 강도를 서서히 높여야 부상을 예방할 수 있다.

3 ○△×
2024년 6월 교육청(고2) 3번

다음을 듣고, 여자가 하는 말의 요지로 가장 적절한 것을 고르시오. 정답률 95%

① 감정 일기 쓰기는 자신의 감정을 이해하는 데 도움이 된다.
② 자신의 감정을 절제하며 의견을 전달하는 것이 필요하다.
③ 타인과의 유대감은 감정 일기의 공유를 통해 증진된다.
④ 일기 쓰기는 규칙적인 생활 습관 형성에 효과적이다.
⑤ 가족과의 대화로 부정적인 감정을 해소할 수 있다.

4 ○△×
2016년 6월 교육청(고2) 6번

대화를 듣고, 그림에서 대화의 내용과 일치하지 않는 것을 고르시오. 정답률 78%

5 ○△×
2022년 6월 교육청(고2) 5번

대화를 듣고, 남자가 할 일로 가장 적절한 것을 고르시오. 정답률 93%

① 날씨 확인하기
② 렌트카 예약하기
③ 호텔 방 변경하기
④ 비행기표 예매하기
⑤ 할인 쿠폰 다운받기

6 고득점 ○△×
2023년 3월 교육청(고2) 6번

대화를 듣고, 여자가 지불할 금액을 고르시오. [3점] 정답률 70%

① $36 ② $39 ③ $47 ④ $52 ⑤ $55

7 ○△×
2019년 9월 교육청(고2) 8번

대화를 듣고, 여자가 개를 키울 수 없는 이유를 고르시오. 정답률 92%

① 낮에 개를 돌볼 사람이 없어서
② 부모님이 허락하지 않아서
③ 개를 키울 마당이 없어서
④ 동생이 개를 무서워해서
⑤ 개 알레르기가 있어서

8 ○△×
2021년 3월 교육청(고2) 8번

대화를 듣고, West Lake Fun Run에 관해 언급되지 않은 것을 고르시오. 정답률 91%

① 개최 날짜 ② 코스 길이 ③ 출발 시간
④ 참가비 ⑤ 모금액 용도

9 ○△×
2023년 3월 교육청(고2) 9번

Afterschool Math Festival에 관한 다음 내용을 듣고, 일치하지 않는 것을 고르시오. 정답률 90%

① 다음 주 월요일부터 3일간 진행된다.
② 9개의 활동 중 3개까지 참가할 수 있다.
③ 모든 활동의 예상 소요 시간은 같다.
④ 강연에 참석한 학생에게 강연자의 책이 무료로 제공된다.
⑤ 구내식당에서 특별한 간식과 음료가 제공된다.

10 ○△×
• 2022년 6월 교육청(고2) 10번

다음 표를 보면서 대화를 듣고, 두 사람이 구매할 식기세척기를 고르시오. 정답률 89%

Dishwashers

	Model	Price	Color	Type	Warranty Period
①	A	$650	black	portable	6 months
②	B	$680	black	built-in	6 months
③	C	$720	white	portable	1 year
④	D	$760	silver	built-in	1 year
⑤	E	$850	silver	built-in	2 years

11 ○△×
• 2020년 11월 교육청(고2) 12번

대화를 듣고, 여자의 마지막 말에 대한 남자의 응답으로 가장 적절한 것을 고르시오. 정답률 80%

① I see. I'll take another road then.
② Really? Go to the hospital right now.
③ That's too bad. You should've left earlier.
④ Sorry. I got a speeding ticket on the highway.
⑤ Okay. I'll make a reservation for the restaurant.

12 고득점 ○△×
• 2023년 3월 교육청(고2) 12번

대화를 듣고, 남자의 마지막 말에 대한 여자의 응답으로 가장 적절한 것을 고르시오. 정답률 70%

① I'm afraid I handed in my paper late.
② If so, applying hand cream might help.
③ Be careful when you use fabric scissors.
④ Well, the gloves are too big for my son.
⑤ Let's bring a paper grocery bag this time.

13 ○△×
• 2022년 3월 교육청(고2) 13번

대화를 듣고, 여자의 마지막 말에 대한 남자의 응답으로 가장 적절한 것을 고르시오. [3점] 정답률 82%

Man: ______________________________

① Okay, I'll visit the repair cafe you recommended before.
② Well, I saw a repair cafe next to the post office.
③ Sure, you can easily find a place to volunteer at.
④ Yes, the new bike shop offers good deals.
⑤ Sorry, but I'm too busy to fix your bike.

14 ○△×
• 2023년 9월 교육청(고2) 13번

대화를 듣고, 남자의 마지막 말에 대한 여자의 응답으로 가장 적절한 것을 고르시오. [3점] 정답률 85%

Woman: ______________________________

① Okay. I'll go there to check if I can find more caps.
② Wait. I forgot to separate the caps from the bottles.
③ Good. We can use bottle caps for our artwork.
④ No worries. I've already taken out the trash.
⑤ No, thanks. We have enough toothbrushes.

15 ○△×
• 2024년 6월 교육청(고2) 15번

다음 상황 설명을 듣고, Bill이 Susan에게 할 말로 가장 적절한 것을 고르시오. 정답률 87%

Bill: ______________________________

① I think you need to find the right time to relax.
② Getting good grades is not the most important thing.
③ There must be many benefits to studying at the library.
④ Why don't you make a study plan to prepare for exams?
⑤ How about changing where you study to regain your focus?

[16~17] 다음을 듣고, 물음에 답하시오.

16 ○△×
• 2020년 6월 교육청(고2) 16번

여자가 하는 말의 주제로 가장 적절한 것은? 정답률 85%

① lucky numbers in ancient times
② numbers that bring wealth to people
③ relationship between numbers and religion
④ symbolic meanings of numbers across cultures
⑤ danger of using favorite numbers in passwords

17 ○△×
• 2020년 6월 교육청(고2) 17번

언급된 숫자가 아닌 것은? 정답률 89%

① four ② seven ③ nine
④ ten ⑤ thirteen

중급 3회

Dictation

문제 풀이에 중요한 핵심 부분과 듣기에 자주 나오는 표현들에 빈칸 처리를 했습니다. 방송을 잘 듣고, 빈칸에 알맞은 말을 써 넣으세요.

Tip! 잘 들리지 않는 부분이 있을 때에는 정답을 확인 후, 똑같은 속도로 따라 읽기 연습을 해 보세요.

1

M: Good afternoon. I'm Tom Anderson, the student council president. I'm glad to announce that the student council is __________ __________ __________ __________ __________ __________ __________. Next Saturday, our school will be welcoming middle schoolers who are interested in attending our school. Student volunteers will show the middle schoolers around our campus, and __________ __________ __________ __________ __________ about our school's extracurricular activities and traditions. __________ __________ __________ __________ __________, please visit our school website. Your participation will be a great help to those who wish to attend our school.

2

M: Hi, Monica. I haven't seen you at the gym in a while.

W: Yes. I've been out of town on business.

M: Glad to see you again. I saw you running very quickly on the treadmill.

W: Right. These days I'm gaining weight. So, I decided to __________ __________ __________ __________.

M: Hmm.... That's not a good idea this late at night.

W: Well, I heard that running fast helps burn calories.

M: That's right. But intense evening exercise __________ __________ __________ __________ __________.

W: Oh, it's not? I thought exercising before bedtime could make me exhausted and help me sleep.

M: I'm afraid you're mistaken. Heavy exercise in the evening raises your heart rate and body temperature, so it prevents you from __________ __________ __________ __________ __________.

W: I see. Now I know why people say, "Evening walk, morning run."

3

W: Good afternoon, listeners! Do you have a hard time __________ __________ __________ __________? Have you suddenly gotten really angry but didn't know exactly what made you feel that way? If so, keeping an emotion diary can be a __________ __________ __________ __________ __________ __________. In an emotion diary, you write down in detail how you feel in each situation. This will give you an opportunity to understand why you're feeling a certain way. Writing an emotion diary won't be easy at first, but __________ __________ __________ __________ __________ __________. After the break, I'll tell you how to keep an emotion diary effectively. Stay tuned!

4

W: How was the magic show last night?

M: Fantastic! Let me show you a picture.

W: The man wearing the hat must be the magician.

M: Right. Look at the bird __________ __________ __________ __________. At the start of the show, the bird came out of the magician's hat.

W: Wonderful! And who is the lady with glasses on next to the magician?

M: She was a member of the audience.

W: What did she do?

M: She made sure that the box was empty and put it on the table.

W: __________ __________ __________ __________ __________?

M: Yes, unbelievably, the magician pulled flowers out of the box. That's why the __________ __________ __________ __________ __________.

W: Wow, it must have been awesome!

M: Absolutely! I couldn't take my eyes off of the stage.

5

W: Billy, I'm so excited about our first trip to Jeju Island next week.
M: Indeed, honey. We've been waiting so long for it.
W: Yeah. I __________ __________ __________ __________, and it says it will be nice.
M: Good. Is there anything we're forgetting to do before going?
W: Hmm... Oh! I forgot to make a reservation for a rental car.
M: Don't worry. I've already made one at a reasonable price.
W: What a relief! How about our plan to change our room from a city view to an ocean view?
M: I've already called the hotel and changed it to have an ocean view.
W: Great. I heard that the Jeju Tourism Organization is having a special event. They __________ __________ __________ __________ __________ __________.
M: Really? How can we get some?
W: We can __________ __________ __________ __________ __________.
M: Okay, I'll do that right away.

6

M: Honey, we need four extra cups for our housewarming party.
W: Okay. Let's buy them online. *[Typing Sound]* Look, I love this floral tea cup.
M: I like it too, and it only costs $8.
W: Hold on. The __________ __________ __________, "Buy one cup, get one cup free."
M: Fantastic! We only have to pay for two cups. Then, we can __________ __________ __________ __________ __________ __________ as well.
W: That's a good idea. Let's buy one that matches the tea cups.
M: I like the __________ __________ __________ __________ __________.
W: Okay. Let's pay for two tea cups and one teapot. Do we also have to pay for shipping?
M: Yes. The total shipping fee is $3. Do we need anything else?
W: Not really. Let me pay with my credit card.

7

W: What a cute dog! Is it yours?
M: Yes. I adopted him from an animal rescue center.
W: I've always wanted a dog. But I can't have one.
M: Why? Are you allergic to animal hair?
W: I'm __________ __________ __________ __________ __________. Dogs are totally fine.
M: What's the problem, then? Your house has a big backyard, so I think it's a __________ __________ __________ __________.
W: I think so, too. It's a really dog-friendly environment.
M: Do your parents not like dogs?
W: No, they love dogs. But I'm worried about a dog __________ __________ __________ __________ __________.
M: Is there nobody who can look after a dog?
W: There is no one at home during the day. My parents work, and my brother and I go to school.
M: Oh, I see. That's why you can't get a dog.

8

M: Amy, what are you reading?
W: Our school newsletter. It says our school is holding the West Lake Fun Run.
M: Sounds interesting. When is it?
W: It'll be __________ __________ __________ __________.
M: I see. How long is the course?
W: It's 5km long. Starting at the school, participants will run through Vincent Park and Central Stadium, and finish at West Lake.
M: Cool!
W: Why don't we sign up together?
M: Good idea. __________ __________ __________ __________ __________ __________?
W: It's $5 per person. The money raised will be __________ __________ __________ __________ __________ __________.
M: Great. It's so old. It'll be wonderful to have a new gym.
W: I agree.

중급 3회

9

M: Good morning, math lovers of Hamington High School. I'm your math teacher, Allen Steward. We have a special announcement for you. The Afterschool Math Festival will be held for three days starting next Monday. Nine activities are planned, and you may participate in ________ ________ ________ ________ ________. Keep in mind that activities such as the Math Escape Room and the Math Quiz Show will take longer than other activities. This year, we are also ________ ________ ________ ________. Our lecturer, Dr. Hilbert will tell us the stories behind famous mathematicians. Students who attend this special lecture will ________ ________ ________ of his book for free. Lastly, during the festival, special snacks and drinks will be served at the cafeteria. See you there.

10

W: Tom, we have so many dishes to wash after every meal.
M: You're right. Let's buy a dishwasher from this online mall.
W: Well, what's our budget for that?
M: We ________ ________ ________ ________ ________. We've already spent too much this month.
W: I agree. Well, dishwashers get dirty easily, so white is not a good choice for the color.
M: Right. Plus, silver or black would match our kitchen cabinets.
W: Okay. Which would you prefer, a portable or a built-in type?
M: ________ ________ ________ ________. We would have more space with a built-in.
W: Besides, it would look more stylish.
M: Good point. Then, there are two options left. Which one would be better?
W: Definitely this one. When it comes to warranty periods, ________ ________, ________ ________.
M: Perfect! Then let's order this one.

11

[Cell phone rings.]
W: Hi, David. I'm almost ________ ________ ________ ________. Where are you?
M: Hi, Amy. I just finished work and got in my car. I'll take the highway, so I'll arrive on time.
W: I heard on the radio that there has been a ________ ________ ________ ________ ________. So you're going to get stuck.
M: (I see. I'll take another road then.)

12

M: Ouch! I ________ ________ ________ ________.
W: Are you okay? I know how painful paper cuts are.
M: This is the third time this week. Maybe ________ ________ ________ ________ ________ that I get paper cuts too easily.
W: (If so, applying hand cream might help.)

13

M: Sandy, what are you doing with your bike?
W: Oh, hi, Jack. I'm checking it out. It makes strange sounds when I ride it.
M: Let me take a look. *[Pause]* Hmm.... I think the brakes are ________ ________ ________.
W: Oh, no. I should get them fixed at the bike shop. It'll cost too much.
M: Why don't you try a repair cafe? You can save money.
W: A repair cafe? What's that?
M: It's a place where you can fix your broken stuff on your own. The cafe provides tools and materials.
W: Well, I don't think I can ________ ________ ________ ________ ________.
M: Don't worry. Expert volunteers will be around to help you out there. There are many repair cafes around town.
W: That's great. I'll give it a try. Do you know ________ ________ ________ ________ ________?
M: (Well, I saw a repair cafe next to the post office.)

14

W: Dad, did you throw away all the empty plastic bottles?
M: Yes. Why?
W: I need plastic bottle caps for our school's zero waste challenge.
M: Interesting. So what are you doing with the caps?

W: We'll ___________ ___________ ___________ ___________ ___________ ___________, and they make products like chairs and hairpins from the caps.
M: That's cool.
W: Yeah, and the teacher said if we bring in ___________ ___________ ___________ ___________ ___________, she'll give us a bamboo toothbrush as a prize.
M: Great. How many bottle caps have you collected so far?
W: I've collected only eight bottle caps. I need some more.
M: Hmm, I threw the plastic bottles away just an hour ago, so they should be ___________ ___________ ___________ ___________.
W: (Okay. I'll go there to check if I can find more caps.)

15

W: Bill and Susan are second-grade high school students and friends. They are preparing for their final exams at the library after school. It used to be easy for Susan to focus on studying. However, these days she's noticing that she ___________ ___________ ___________ at the library and doesn't know why she cannot maintain her attention. So, she decides to get some advice from Bill, who gets high scores in school. When Bill hears her problem, he's suddenly reminded of ___________ ___________ ___________ ___________ ___________ ___________. He recalls that he changed his study location and that really helped him get back his concentration. Therefore, he wants to suggest that Susan try ___________ ___________ ___________ ___________ ___________ to find her focus again. In this situation, what would Bill most likely say to Susan?
Bill: (How about changing where you study to regain your focus?)

16~17

W: Welcome back, students. Last time we talked about your favorite numbers. They might come from your birth date or the date of a special occasion in your life. Interestingly, some beliefs about numbers seem to depend on one's culture. Today, we're talking about what ___________ ___________ ___________ ___________ ___________ of the world. In Asia, the number four is considered extremely unlucky, but Western people think it is promising. In Islam, the ___________ ___________ ___________ ___________. "Seven heavens" is one example of this number's importance. Ten is considered a good number in Japan because it is pronounced "joo", like the Japanese word for "enough." In the Western world, the number thirteen is believed ___________ ___________ ___________ ___________ by millions of people. So, to satisfy anxious customers, airlines and hotels often don't use the number thirteen. Numbers can be captivating and mystical. Numbers are also just fun to play around with. Let's enjoy learning more about numbers together.

Dictation Answers

1. recruiting volunteers for our campus tour event / provide them with useful information / To sign up to volunteer
2. work out more intensely / is not good for sleep / falling into a deep sleep
3. figuring out your emotions / powerful tool for understanding your feelings / you'll soon get used to it
4. sitting on the branch / That box on the table / flowers are on the floor
5. checked the weather forecast / provide discount coupons to fancy restaurants / download them from their website
6. store's promotion says / afford to buy a new teapot / white one that costs $20
7. only allergic to cat hair / perfect place for dogs / being alone during the day
8. held on April 17th / How much is the entry fee / used to renovate the school gym
9. up to three different activities / offering a guest lecture / get a copy
10. can't spend more than $800 / I'd prefer a built-in / the longer, the better
11. halfway to the restaurant / car accident on the highway
12. got a paper cut / my hands are so dry
13. not working properly / fix my bike by myself / where the nearest place is
14. send them to an upcycling company / more than 20 bottle caps / in the recycling area
15. gets distracted easily / his own experience of losing focus / studying in a different place

16~17. numbers symbolize in different parts / number seven is important / to be the unluckiest

제4회 중급 모의고사

맞은 개수: 2점 문항 ___개, 3점 문항 ___개
알고 푼 문항은 ○, 찍어서 맞힌 문제는 △에 표시하고, △와 ×는 다시 복습하세요.

1번부터 17번까지는 듣고 답하는 문제입니다. 1번부터 15번까지는 한 번만 들려주고, 16번부터 17번까지는 두 번 들려줍니다. 방송을 잘 듣고 답을 하시기 바랍니다.

1 ○△× • 2025년 3월 교육청(고2) 1번

다음을 듣고, 남자가 하는 말의 목적으로 가장 적절한 것을 고르시오. 정답률 91%

① 자판기 추가 설치가 완료되었음을 알리려고
② 자판기 설치 장소가 변경된 이유를 설명하려고
③ 자판기 설치에 관한 의견 수렴 결과를 공유하려고
④ 자판기 고장으로 인해 사용이 제한됨을 공지하려고
⑤ 자판기 판매 희망 품목에 관한 설문 참여를 요청하려고

2 ○△× • 2024년 6월 교육청(고2) 2번

대화를 듣고, 남자의 의견으로 가장 적절한 것을 고르시오. 정답률 94%

① 운동을 마친 후 스트레칭을 하는 것이 필요하다.
② 천천히 걷는 것은 근육통 완화에 도움이 된다.
③ 과도한 스트레칭은 부상을 유발할 수 있다.
④ 자신의 몸에 맞는 식단을 구성하는 것이 중요하다.
⑤ 몸과 마음의 건강을 위해 규칙적인 운동을 해야 한다.

3 ○△× • 2019년 6월 교육청(고2) 5번

대화를 듣고, 두 사람의 관계를 가장 잘 나타낸 것을 고르시오. 정답률 88%

① 도서관 사서 — 학생
② 작가 — 출판사 직원
③ 문학 평론가 — 기자
④ 영화 감독 — 신인 배우
⑤ 문학 교사 — 학부모

4 ○△× • 2024년 6월 교육청(고2) 4번

대화를 듣고, 그림에서 대화의 내용과 일치하지 않는 것을 고르시오. 정답률 88%

5 ○△× • 2018년 9월 교육청(고2) 7번

대화를 듣고, 여자가 할 일로 가장 적절한 것을 고르시오. 정답률 82%

① 연습 시간 확인하기
② 코치에게 전화 걸기
③ 담임 선생님과 상담하기
④ 학교에서 아들 데려오기
⑤ 축구 경기 좌석 예약하기

6 ○△× • 2025년 6월 교육청(고2) 6번

대화를 듣고, 여자가 지불할 금액을 고르시오. [3점] 정답률 86%

① $70 ② $72 ③ $90 ④ $94 ⑤ $100

7 ○△× • 2023년 9월 교육청(고2) 7번

대화를 듣고, 남자가 식당에서 식사를 하지 못한 이유를 고르시오. 정답률 83%

① 반려견을 데려가서
② 예약을 하지 않아서
③ 보수 공사 중이어서
④ 대기자가 너무 많아서
⑤ 음식 재료가 다 떨어져서

8 ○△× • 2021년 6월 교육청(고2) 8번

대화를 듣고, Friday Night Walk에 관해 언급되지 않은 것을 고르시오. 정답률 94%

① 행사 목적
② 코스 종류
③ 참가비
④ 기념품
⑤ 신청 방법

9 ○△× • 2024년 6월 교육청(고2) 9번

Library Plus에 관한 다음 내용을 듣고, 일치하지 않는 것을 고르시오. 정답률 83%

① 도서관 자원봉사자들이 책을 집으로 배송한다.
② 도서관 회원은 무료로 이용할 수 있다.
③ 한 번에 최대 5권의 책을 빌릴 수 있다.
④ 전화로 대출 기간을 연장할 수 있다.
⑤ 직접 도서관에 방문하여 책을 반납해야 한다.

10 ○△×

• 2017년 9월 교육청(고2) 12번

다음 표를 보면서 대화를 듣고, 여자가 구입할 소형 프로젝터를 고르시오. 정답률 80%

Best Mini Projectors of 2017

	Model	Battery Life	Wireless Support	Weight	Price
①	A	2 hours	○	500g	$580
②	B	1.5 hours	×	800g	$500
③	C	2.5 hours	○	500g	$620
④	D	2.5 hours	×	600g	$600
⑤	E	2 hours	○	700g	$550

11 ○△×

• 2020년 6월 교육청(고2) 2번

대화를 듣고, 여자의 마지막 말에 대한 남자의 응답으로 가장 적절한 것을 고르시오. 정답률 84%

① All right! It's perfect for walking outside.
② Wonderful! The movie is a must-see.
③ Thanks. I'll park the car by myself.
④ Sorry. I didn't check the weather.
⑤ Whew! I can't walk any longer.

12 ○△×

• 2025년 9월 교육청(고2) 12번

대화를 듣고, 남자의 마지막 말에 대한 여자의 응답으로 가장 적절한 것을 고르시오. 정답률 87%

① You're right. The construction is now complete.
② I see. I'll take the subway tomorrow instead.
③ No way. I've just missed the bus to school.
④ No problem. I can drive you to work.
⑤ Of course. I'll come home early.

13 ○△×

• 2018년 3월 교육청(고2) 13번

대화를 듣고, 여자의 마지막 말에 대한 남자의 응답으로 가장 적절한 것을 고르시오. [3점] 정답률 85%

Man: ______________________________

① No problem. You can teach me how to play the game.
② All right. I won't let him use my phone too long.
③ Okay. Let's take more photos with my phone.
④ Well, lack of sleep can cause poor eyesight.
⑤ Sure. I already had my eyes checked.

14 고득점 ○△×

• 2025년 3월 교육청(고2) 13번

대화를 듣고, 남자의 마지막 말에 대한 여자의 응답으로 가장 적절한 것을 고르시오. [3점] 정답률 73%

Woman: ______________________________

① Yes. I'll copy motivational quotes in my planner.
② Of course. Reminders have already been sent to me.
③ I guess so. Using apps can be distracting sometimes.
④ Exactly! You need to submit your report on your own.
⑤ Absolutely! This app will help you solve your problem.

15 ○△×

• 2025년 9월 교육청(고2) 15번

다음 상황 설명을 듣고, Jack이 Emma에게 할 말로 가장 적절한 것을 고르시오. 정답률 91%

Jack: ______________________________

① I wonder how I could decorate my booth.
② Please donate your items for the flea market.
③ You should always be kind to your customers.
④ Who will participate in the charity event with us?
⑤ Can you tell me what items sell well at flea markets?

[16~17] 다음을 듣고, 물음에 답하시오.

16 ○△×

• 2025년 6월 교육청(고2) 16번

여자가 하는 말의 주제로 가장 적절한 것은? 정답률 89%

① strategies animals use to protect themselves
② benefits of the unique appearances of animals
③ importance of saving endangered wild animals
④ difficulties that animals face when finding food
⑤ skills that animals develop to defend their young

17 ○△×

• 2025년 6월 교육청(고2) 17번

언급된 동물이 아닌 것은? 정답률 95%

① skunk ② chameleon ③ frog
④ lizard ⑤ zebra

Dictation

문제 풀이에 중요한 핵심 부분과 듣기에 자주 나오는 표현들에 빈칸 처리를 했습니다. 방송을 잘 듣고, 빈칸에 알맞은 말을 써 넣으세요.

Tip! 잘 들리지 않는 부분이 있을 때에는 정답을 확인 후, 똑같은 속도로 따라 읽기 연습을 해 보세요.

1

M: Good morning, students. This is the head of the student council and I have an important announcement today. Recently, our school has ________ ________ ________ ________ ________ ________. But many students have complained that the items in the vending machines do not ________ ________ ________ ________. To address this, we are conducting an online survey to ________ ________ ________ on what products you'd like to see in the vending machines. The survey link will be sent to you in a text message after this announcement. Please take a few minutes to ________ ________ ________ ________ ________ ________. Your opinion is important, and we're looking forward to receiving your ideas. Thank you!

2

M: Jane, are you feeling okay?

W: Well, I exercised at the gym and my muscles are hurting a bit now, Dad.

M: Did you stretch after exercising?

W: No. I only stretched before.

M: Oh. You should definitely ________ ________ ________ ________ ________.

W: Really? I thought stretching after working out would put more pressure on my muscles.

M: That's not true. Stretching afterward helps to ________ ________ ________ ________ and reduce injuries.

W: That makes sense. Are there any other benefits?

M: Absolutely. It allows both your body and mind to slow down and ________ ________ ________ ________.

W: All right. I'll give it a try. Thanks for your tip, Dad.

3

W: Hello, what can I do for you?

M: I went to the literature section, but I couldn't find *Romeo and Juliet* by Shakespeare.

W: Let me check.... *[Typing sound]* Oh, someone just borrowed it.

M: Oh, no. I really need it for my school assignment. When can I borrow the book, then?

W: I'm not sure, but it ________ ________ ________ ________ ________ in a week.

M: Then, are there any other books by Shakespeare? My teacher wants me to ________ ________ ________ ________ on a work by Shakespeare.

W: Okay. *[Typing sound]* We have several books by Shakespeare. How about *Hamlet*?

M: Oh, I've heard about that story. I'll read that book instead, then.

W: *Hamlet* is ________ ________ ________ ________. I can show you where it is if you want.

M: No, that's okay. I can go get it. Thank you so much.

W: You're welcome.

4

M: Hi, Julia. You were amazing in the play yesterday.

W: Thanks, Mason! Here's a picture from the dressing room after the play. Do you want to take a look?

M: Sure. *[Pause]* I see you're holding the flowers I gave you.

W: They're so beautiful. Thanks again.

M: My pleasure. What are those two boxes on the floor?

W: I ________ ________ ________ ________ ________ ________ in them. I needed many items because I played both a prisoner and the queen.

M: You wore that ________ ________ ________ ________ ________ as a prisoner, right?

W: Yes. Do you remember that crown on the table?

M: I remember! You wore that as the queen. Wasn't it difficult to change your costume during the play?

W: Not really. But it was hard to see my ________ ________ ________ ________ ________ ________ on the wall.

M: I understand. Anyway, you did a great job.

5

[Phone rings.]

W: Hey, honey. What's going on?

M: I got a call from Jeff's soccer coach. He said they ________ ________ ________ ________ to next Thursday.

W: Oh, Jeff must be disappointed.

M: Yeah. And since there's no game today, we need to pick Jeff up right after school.

W: His school ends at three, right? Can you go and ________ ________ ________ ________ ________ ________?

M: I'm afraid I can't. Work is really busy today.

W: I see. But, aren't you meeting with his homeroom teacher at 4:30?

M: That's why I called you. Can you pick Jeff up at 3:00 instead of me? Otherwise, he'll wait for over an hour and a half.

W: No worries. I'll leave work early and ________ ________ ________.

M: Thank you, honey.

6

M: Hello! Welcome to Tom's Party Supplies. How can I help you?

W: Hi. I want to get something for my grandma's birthday party.

M: You've ________ ________ ________ ________ ________. What do you have in mind?

W: I'm looking for some balloons and gift bags.

M: I see. This set of birthday balloons is very popular, and it's ________ ________ ________ ________.

W: Excellent. I'll take two sets. Can you show me some gift bags?

M: Certainly. These are our gift bags. We can also ________ ________ ________ ________ ________, if you'd like.

W: Awesome. Is it possible to put my grandma's picture on this bag?

M: Sure. That would be $2 for each bag with a picture.

W: Great. Then, I'll take 30.

M: So two sets of balloons and 30 special gift bags, right?

W: Yes. I have this discount coupon. Can I use it now?

M: Of course. That'll ________ ________ ________ ________ ________ ________.

W: Good. Here's my credit card.

7

W: Hey, Mike. How was dinner at the French restaurant downtown last weekend? I heard it was recently renovated.

M: Well, I went there, but I didn't get to eat anything.

W: Why? Were there too many people ________ ________ ________?

M: Not really. There were tables available.

W: Did you bring your dog and the restaurant said no?

M: No, I checked their website and it said I could ________ ________ ________ ________ at an outdoor table.

W: Okay, so then why couldn't you eat anything?

M: The restaurant said they ________ ________ ________ ________, so I left.

W: Oh, you must have been disappointed. How about we go there for lunch this Saturday?

M: Sounds great! They don't take reservations on weekends, so we should get there early.

W: Good idea. I look forward to it.

8

M: Honey, check out this poster. Friday Night Walk is going to be held this month.

W: Friday Night Walk? Is it walking through the city at night?

M: Well, yes. But its purpose is to ________ ________ ________ ________ ________.

W: That's meaningful. And we can ________ ________ ________ ________ ________ at night. Why don't we join it?

M: All right. Let's do it.

W: Great. Look. There are two walking courses we can choose from, a 5km course and a 10km one.

M: Hmm... How about the 10km one? It would be a lot more exercise.

W: Good idea. The ________ ________ ________ ________ for the 10km course.

M: I see. How can we sign up for the event?

W: It says we must register on their website.

M: Okay. Let's register right away.

9

M: Hello, I'm Tony Jones, a librarian at Greenfield Library. We're thrilled to tell you about a brand-new service called Library Plus. Our library volunteers will __________ __________ __________ __________ __________ __________. Our book delivery service is here to provide more people with the opportunity to read. All library members can use this service free of charge. In order to get started, use the library's mobile application on your phone. You can borrow a maximum of __________ __________ __________ __________ __________. Books may be borrowed for two weeks, but you can extend the borrowing period simply by giving us a call. You don't even need to come to the library to return your books. We'll __________ __________ __________ __________ __________ __________ __________. For more information, visit our website. Thank you.

10

M: Anna, what are you looking at?

W: It's a list of the five best mini projectors of 2017. I'm looking for one I could use for camping.

M: Do you have anything specific in mind?

W: I'd like one with a battery that __________ __________ __________ __________ __________ after it's charged.

M: Okay. Do you need wireless support for your projector?

W: Sure, I want to connect the projector to my smartphone __________ __________ __________ __________.

M: I see. What about the weight? If you're going to carry it around a lot, I guess __________ __________ __________ __________.

W: I agree. Then this leaves me with these two models.

M: How much are you willing to pay for your projector?

W: I don't want to spend more than 600 dollars.

M: Then you have only one choice.

W: Right, I'll buy that one.

11

W: Honey, what a beautiful Sunday! I don't want to stay home all day.

M: Neither do I. Why don't we __________ __________ __________ __________ __________ __________ or go to watch a movie?

W: We went to the movies last weekend. __________ __________ __________ __________ __________ this time!

M: (All right! It's perfect for walking outside.)

12

M: Cassie, I think you'll have to __________ __________ __________ to get to school tomorrow instead of taking the bus.

W: Why, Dad? The bus is the fastest way to school.

M: I know. But the road on your bus route __________ __________ __________ __________ tomorrow, so traffic will be heavy.

W: (I see. I'll take the subway tomorrow instead.)

13

W: Honey, would you stop letting Kevin use your smartphone?

M: Why? He's just playing a game. He looks so happy.

W: It's been an hour. That's too long for a 6-year-old boy.

M: It's natural for him to be __________ __________ __________ __________.

W: The problem is when he plays with your phone, he __________ __________ __________ __________ __________.

M: Well, could it be a problem?

W: Come on, honey! Kevin __________ __________ __________ __________ later on.

M: Hmm.... Now I see what you mean.

W: Honey, I can't fix this problem without your help.

M: (All right. I won't let him use my phone too long.)

14

M: Jenny, I'm __________ __________ __________ __________ __________ __________ __________ these days. How do you handle it?

W: For me, things have improved a lot since I started using a scheduling app.

M: Really? I'd love to hear more.

W: It's called "Study Detector," and it has several useful features that __________ __________ __________ __________ __________.

M: What features does it have?
W: First of all, it tracks how much time I study each day, week, and month, and then provides me with a report of my progress.
M: That's amazing!
W: It is! It also sends me reminders that help me __________ __________ __________ __________ __________.
M: That sounds great! Are there any other features?
W: Yes. It even sends me famous quotes that __________ __________ __________ __________.
M: Oh, I think I really need to try that app. Do you think it will help me too?
W: (Absolutely! This app will help you solve your problem.)

15

M: Jack and Emma are close friends. Emma invites Jack to join her at a local charity flea market this upcoming weekend. While Emma has participated in flea markets several times before, Jack is new to this kind of event. He's looking forward to it, and __________ __________ __________ __________ __________ __________. But he wonders what kinds of things __________ __________ __________ at flea markets. He thinks Emma can help him choose the right items to sell. So, Jack wants to ask Emma about __________ __________ __________ __________ __________ __________ __________ at flea markets. In this situation, what would Jack most likely say to Emma?
Jack: (Can you tell me what items sell well at flea markets?)

16~17

W: Hello, students! In our last lesson, we learned how animals use their senses to find food. Today, we'll talk about ways some animals __________ __________ __________ __________. First, one of the most well-known of these animals is the skunk. Skunks spray a bad-smelling liquid __________ __________ __________ __________. Skunk spray does not cause any lasting damage, though its smell is hard to remove. Second, chameleons change the color of their skin to match their surroundings, __________ __________ __________ __________ __________. That's one clever way to hide from their enemies! Next, we have frogs. By making themselves look bigger, they __________ __________ __________. Another animal that uses its body for survival is the lizard. Interestingly, lizards can cut off their own tails to escape. But don't worry — the tail eventually grows back! So far, we've looked at animals' defense strategies. In our next lesson, we'll cover plants that have similar ways to protect themselves.

Dictation Answers

1. installed vending machines in the dormitory / fully meet their tastes / gather your suggestions / answer the survey by this Friday
2. stretch after you finish exercising / loosen your tight muscles / helps you feel relaxed
3. is supposed to be returned / write a book review / in literature section H
4. stored some items for the play / striped T-shirt on the hanger / entire outfit in that star-shaped mirror
5. rescheduled their practice match / pick him up when he finishes / drive him home
6. come to the right place / only $20 per set / make special ones for you / give you 10% off the total
7. waiting in line / sit with my dog / ran out of ingredients
8. raise money for children's hospitals / enjoy the beautiful city views / participation fee is $20
9. deliver books straight to your home / five books at a time / pick up the books at your place
10. lasts at least two hours / without using a cord / the lighter the better
11. take a walk in a park / Let's enjoy the nice weather
12. find another way / will be under construction
13. interested in digital devices / rubs his eyes a lot / might have poor eyesight
14. having trouble sticking to my study plans / help me stay on track / stay focused on my schedule / motivate me to study
15. excitedly searches for items to sell / attract more customers / what kinds of items would be popular

16~17. defend themselves from enemies / to keep enemies away / making them hard to spot / appear more threatening

제5회 중급 모의고사

맞은 개수: 2점 문항 ___개, 3점 문항 ___개
알고 푼 문항은 ○, 찍어서 맞힌 문제는 △에 표시하고,
△와 ×는 다시 복습하세요.

1번부터 17번까지는 듣고 답하는 문제입니다. 1번부터 15번까지는 한 번만 들려주고, 16번부터 17번까지는 두 번 들려줍니다. 방송을 잘 듣고 답을 하시기 바랍니다.

1 ○△× • 2020년 3월 교육청(고2) 3번

다음을 듣고, 남자가 하는 말의 목적으로 가장 적절한 것을 고르시오. 정답률 78%

① 병실 사용 시 유의 사항을 설명하려고
② 병문안 시 면회 시간 준수를 당부하려고
③ 병원 내 새로운 편의 시설을 소개하려고
④ 병원 주변 도로 통제 구역을 공지하려고
⑤ 병원 일부 출입구의 사용 제한을 안내하려고

2 ○△× • 2022년 9월 교육청(고2) 2번

대화를 듣고, 남자의 의견으로 가장 적절한 것을 고르시오. 정답률 85%

① 논쟁은 더 나은 결정을 위한 기회가 된다.
② 의사 결정에 있어서 전원의 합의가 필수적이다.
③ 고민이 있을 때는 전문가에게 조언을 구해야 한다.
④ 리더로서 팀원들과 수평적 관계를 유지하는 것이 중요하다.
⑤ 팀 프로젝트의 성공을 위해서는 리더의 결단력이 필요하다.

3 ○△× • 2025년 3월 교육청(고2) 3번

다음을 듣고, 남자가 하는 말의 요지로 가장 적절한 것을 고르시오. 정답률 92%

① 노인에게 디지털 기술 활용 교육을 제공해야 한다.
② 노인을 위한 맞춤형 디지털 기기를 개발해야 한다.
③ 노인을 위한 대면 서비스를 계속 운영해야 한다.
④ 노인을 대상으로 하는 금융 범죄를 예방해야 한다.
⑤ 노인이 디지털 기술에 적응하지 못하는 이유를 이해해야 한다.

4 ○△× • 2022년 6월 교육청(고2) 4번

대화를 듣고, 그림에서 대화의 내용과 일치하지 않는 것을 고르시오. 정답률 93%

5 ○△× • 2017년 9월 교육청(고2) 7번

대화를 듣고, 남자가 여자를 위해 할 일로 가장 적절한 것을 고르시오. 정답률 86%

① 도서 구입하기
② 동영상 보내기
③ 병원 예약하기
④ 강좌 등록하기
⑤ 강사 추천하기

6 ○△× • 2024년 3월 교육청(고2) 6번

대화를 듣고, 남자가 지불할 금액을 고르시오. [3점] 정답률 77%

① $25 ② $29 ③ $31 ④ $34 ⑤ $36

7 ○△× • 2019년 6월 교육청(고2) 8번

대화를 듣고, 남자가 직장을 옮기려고 하는 이유를 고르시오. 정답률 84%

① 다른 지방으로 이사를 가게 되어서
② 여가 시간을 더 많이 가지고 싶어서
③ 다른 회사에서 일할 것을 제안 받아서
④ 일에 대한 더 많은 보수를 받기 위해서
⑤ 새롭게 도전하여 능력을 개발하고 싶어서

8 ○△× • 2023년 3월 교육청(고2) 8번

대화를 듣고, Nari Island 패키지 여행에 관해 언급되지 않은 것을 고르시오. 정답률 91%

① 여행 기간
② 방문 장소
③ 최소 출발 인원
④ 이동 수단
⑤ 가격

9 ○△× • 2024년 9월 교육청(고2) 9번

Short-form Video Course에 관한 다음 내용을 듣고, 일치하지 않는 것을 고르시오. 정답률 89%

① 무료 온라인 강좌이다.
② 세 단계로 이루어져 있다.
③ 웹사이트에서 등록할 수 있다.
④ 언제든지 반복해서 수강할 수 있다.
⑤ 모든 참가자의 작품에 대해 피드백을 제공한다.

10 ○△×

• 2023년 9월 교육청(고2) 10번

다음 표를 보면서 대화를 듣고, 두 사람이 주문할 제품을 고르시오. 정답률 81%

Electric Mug Warmer Sets

	Set	Price	Mug Material	Mug Capacity	LED Display
①	A	$26	Glass	250ml	×
②	B	$32	Ceramic	350ml	○
③	C	$37	Ceramic	450ml	×
④	D	$42	Stainless Steel	550ml	○
⑤	E	$55	Stainless Steel	590ml	×

11 ○△×

• 2024년 6월 교육청(고2) 11번

대화를 듣고, 남자의 마지막 말에 대한 여자의 응답으로 가장 적절한 것을 고르시오. [3점] 정답률 77%

① Sorry. We can't finish our art class project today.
② Oh, it's such a shame that you missed the chance.
③ I don't think so. The tickets are not that expensive.
④ Yeah, just let me make sure it's okay with my mom first.
⑤ Why not? My mom and I don't have any plans on Sunday.

12 ○△×

• 2023년 9월 교육청(고2) 12번

대화를 듣고, 여자의 마지막 말에 대한 남자의 응답으로 가장 적절한 것을 고르시오. 정답률 82%

① Then, I'll apply for the poetry club.
② Yeah, I can recommend a good club for you.
③ No way. We can't accept any new members.
④ Great! I'll see you at the history club after school.
⑤ Really? Thank you for allowing me to join this club.

13 고득점 ○△×

• 2018년 6월 교육청(고2) 13번

대화를 듣고, 남자의 마지막 말에 대한 여자의 응답으로 가장 적절한 것을 고르시오. 정답률 55%

Woman: ______________________________

① We got peace, but the cost was big.
② Improving confidence is the best education.
③ I thought you were supposed to join the army.
④ The museum was closed, which made us upset.
⑤ Soldiers insist that their pay should be increased.

14 ○△×

• 2025년 3월 교육청(고2) 14번

대화를 듣고, 여자의 마지막 말에 대한 남자의 응답으로 가장 적절한 것을 고르시오. [3점] 정답률 87%

Man: ______________________________

① Cheer up! You can win the competition next time.
② I agree. Focusing on contemporary art is important.
③ Not really. I've never found any helpful drawing classes.
④ Good for you! You might have a more meaningful experience.
⑤ Never mind. I can start fresh on a new social media platform.

15 ○△×

• 2023년 3월 교육청(고2) 15번

다음 상황 설명을 듣고, Jane이 David에게 할 말로 가장 적절한 것을 고르시오. 정답률 82%

Jane: ______________________________

① I'm sure you can play the solo part beautifully.
② It's all my fault. I should have been more careful.
③ How about giving your solo part to someone else?
④ Too bad. We should postpone our concert for a week.
⑤ I will do my best to participate in the Spring Concert.

[16~17] 다음을 듣고, 물음에 답하시오.

16 ○△×

• 2024년 6월 교육청(고2) 16번

남자가 하는 말의 주제로 가장 적절한 것은? 정답률 92%

① various drawing styles used by artists
② objects used as symbols in Western art
③ impact of religious objects on Western culture
④ changes in painting tools through history
⑤ how to paint objects in a realistic way

17 ○△×

• 2024년 6월 교육청(고2) 17번

언급된 사물이 아닌 것은? 정답률 95%

① mirrors ② candles ③ shells
④ books ⑤ flowers

중급 5회

Dictation

문제 풀이에 중요한 핵심 부분과 듣기에 자주 나오는 표현들에 빈칸 처리를 했습니다. 방송을 잘 듣고, 빈칸에 알맞은 말을 써 넣으세요.

Tip! 잘 들리지 않는 부분이 있을 때에는 정답을 확인 후, 똑같은 속도로 따라 읽기 연습을 해 보세요.

1

M: May I have your attention, please? This is from the management office of Vincent Hospital. The west entrance facing Main Street ___________ ___________ ___________, so it cannot be used. We'd like to remind you all to ___________ ___________ ___________ ___________ ___________. The east entrance is on Wilson Street, and it is open during regular visiting hours from 8 a.m. to 6 p.m. And during non-visiting hours, please use the north entrance facing Hyde Street. The west entrance will ___________ ___________ ___________ ___________ ___________. We're sorry for any inconvenience this might cause. Thank you for your cooperation.

2

M: Kate, you don't look good. Are you okay?
W: Yes, I'm fine. It's nothing.
M: Are you sure? You seem really stressed.
W: Well, I'm having a hard time being the leader of a team project.
M: What's the problem?
W: ___________ ___________ ___________ ___________ ___________ because my teammates get into arguments easily.
M: I understand, however, arguments can ___________ ___________ ___________ ___________ ___________ ___________.
W: Do you really think so?
M: Absolutely! Arguments happen all the time. ___________ ___________ ___________ ___________ ___________ as a way to reach a better decision.
W: That's good advice. I'll try to remember that.

3

M: Hello, everyone. Today, I am going to talk about how we can ___________ ___________ ___________ ___________ ___________ ___________ ___________. You may have heard that many seniors are struggling with digital technologies in their daily lives, such as ordering food at kiosks or using mobile banking apps. Because they are ___________ ___________ ___________ ___________ ___________ ___________, seniors may find it difficult to keep up with all the changes in today's world. That's why we need to ___________ ___________ ___________ ___________ ___________. By teaching seniors how to utilize digital skills, we can help them navigate modern life smoothly and they won't feel left behind.

4

M: Rebecca, look at this picture.
W: Sure. What is it?
M: This is the garage in my new house. I finally have one.
W: Great. It was your dream to have your own garage, right?
M: Right. Look at this ___________ ___________ ___________ ___________ ___________. It's very convenient for hanging tools.
W: Good. And you ___________ ___________ ___________ ___________ ___________ ___________.
M: Yes, I use it for repairing broken things. Can you see the skateboard in the box? I changed its wheels all by myself.
W: Awesome. But isn't it boring to work alone?
M: Yes, that's why I ___________ ___________ ___________ ___________ ___________ ___________ ___________ to listen to music.
W: Cool. Is that your new bicycle near the door?
M: Yes, now I can safely store it inside the garage.
W: That's good. You were always worried about your bicycle when it rained. Congratulations.

5

M: Reina, what are you reading?
W: Hi, Peter. This is a book that introduces simple yoga poses.
M: I didn't know you're interested in yoga.
W: I became interested in it recently since I heard yoga could help __________ __________ __________ __________ __________.
M: Well, why don't you go to see a doctor first?
W: Actually I did, and the doctor recommended yoga for me.
M: I see. Then how about taking a yoga class at the community center?
W: When I checked, the __________ __________ __________ __________ __________ __________. So, I'm looking for some simple yoga poses I can do every day from this book.
M: Then I'll __________ __________ __________ __________ __________ __________ through email. You can follow the poses while watching them.
W: Oh, that would be great. Thanks a lot.

6

W: Honey, how about getting a pizza from Toby's Place for dinner?
M: Sounds great! Let's try the new delivery app that I downloaded recently. *[Pause]* Hmm... How about a potato pizza?
W: I like that idea. How much is one large potato pizza?
M: It's $25. Oh, we have to order __________ __________ __________ __________ __________ __________.
W: Then we can add some drinks. How much is a cola?
M: One small can is $2, and a large one is $3.
W: Then let's order two large cans.
M: Great, one large potato pizza and two large cans of cola. Now we can __________ __________ __________.
W: Is there a delivery fee?
M: __________ __________ __________ __________ __________ __________, but it's free now because of the app promotion. So I'll pay using the app.
W: Thank you. I'm starving. I hope it gets here quickly.

7

W: Hey, Mark! You look serious. What's up?
M: I'm thinking of __________ __________ __________.
W: Why? Did you get a job offer from another company?
M: Not yet, but I've __________ __________ __________ __________ __________ __________.
W: I thought you were satisfied with your work and salary.
M: Well, the pay is good and I'm comfortable with this job.
W: Then, why do you want to leave?
M: If I don't look for a new challenge, I will get used to doing the same easy job and I won't develop.
W: You mean you want to __________ __________ __________ by challenging yourself with different work, don't you?
M: Exactly. I would be happier with a job that can help me improve my career.
W: I understand, but you'd better make the decision after considering the matter carefully.
M: Thank you for your advice.

8

M: Hi, Jessica. Are you ready for the trip to Nari Island?
W: Not yet. I've been too busy to __________ __________ __________ __________.
M: Then, how about booking a package tour? There should be some package tours on the island.
W: Really? Let me check online. *[Typing Sound]* This one runs for 5 days, from April 3 to April 7. It __________ __________ __________ __________.
M: It provides a guided tour to beautiful caves and cliffs.
W: I think I'd enjoy it. I like to explore geological sites.
M: And a minivan will __________ __________ __________ __________.
W: It sounds convenient. What do you think of the price?
M: I think $600 for each person is quite reasonable.
W: Perfect. I'll book it right away.

9

W: Hello, listeners. Have you ever thought about boosting your business with short-form videos? Then how about joining our Short-form Video Course? It's a free online course that is open to everyone interested in __________ __________ __________ __________ __________ __________. The course is made up of three stages that will teach you the art of __________, __________, __________ __________ __________ like a professional. Please visit our website at www.shortformclass.com to sign up. The best part of this course is that you can take it at any time, over and over again. And guess what? We'll __________ __________ __________ __________ __________ __________ and give feedback on their work. Don't miss this chance to level up your business!

10

W: Sean, look what I found for mom for her birthday.

M: Oh, an electric mug warmer set? What is it?

W: It's a set that includes a mug and a warmer, and the warmer keeps beverages warm.

M: Cool! How much can we spend on this?

W: Well, we didn't buy a cake yet, so __________ __________ __________ __________ more than $50.

M: I see. The mugs come in three different materials. Which one would she like?

W: She already has glass mugs, so let's __________ __________ __________ __________ __________.

M: Good idea. How about the capacity of the mug?

W: I think __________ __________ __________ __________ __________ __________.

M: Yeah, that makes sense. Do you think it's better to buy a set with the LED display?

W: Yes. I think it's better because it allows you to check the temperature.

M: I like it, too. Let's order this one.

11

M: Katie, we have to go to the Modern Art Center sometime this month for our art class project. How about this Sunday?

W: I have __________ __________ __________ __________ that day. Let's go another day.

M: But they have a special artist lecture only this Sunday. Would you __________ __________ __________ __________?

W: (Yeah, just let me make sure it's okay with my mom first.)

12

W: Harry, have you decided what school club you will join?

M: Not yet. I'm __________ __________ __________ either the poetry club or the history club.

W: I've heard the history club is already full, so they're not __________ __________ __________ __________ __________.

M: (Then, I'll apply for the poetry club.)

13

M: Daisy, how was your school trip to the War Memorial Museum?

W: The museum was __________ __________ __________ __________ __________ __________, Dad.

M: Great! Tell me about it.

W: It's huge! There were lots of __________ __________ __________ about the Korean War.

M: Then you saw many things about the war.

W: Absolutely. The museum gave me a feeling for what the Korean War was like.

M: Hmm, I've actually never thought about the war that seriously.

W: Me, either. But the countless names of dead people on a memorial stone there __________ __________ __________ __________ __________.

M: I didn't know the war was such a tragedy.

W: And, you know what? People from other countries were listed among the soldiers on the stone.

M: Right. So, I wonder what you learned from your visit.

W: (We got peace, but the cost was big.)

14

W: I've been feeling down lately about my art.

M: Really? What's wrong?

W: I keep posting my drawings online, but only a few people view my blog to look at them. It's so disappointing.
M: I understand how you feel, but isn't it great to __________ __________ __________ __________ __________?
W: Of course it is. But I'd like to share my art with other people and hear from them about my work.
M: Then how about finding another way to __________ __________ __________ __________ __________ __________ __________?
W: Another way? Like what?
M: You can join an art community or local art club and __________ __________ __________ __________ __________ at offline meetings.
W: That's a good idea. I've never thought about connecting with people in person. I think I'll look into it.
M: (Good for you! You might have a more meaningful experience.)

15

W: Jane and David are both violinists in the school orchestra. They have been practicing together for a month for the Spring Concert. Just three days before the concert, Jane __________ __________ __________ and her doctor recommends taking a rest for at least a week. Since Jane cannot play at the concert, David should __________ __________ __________ __________. They have been practicing together and David knows Jane's part. However, David says that he is too nervous to play the solo part. Jane knows that David is a skilled violinist. So, Jane wants to encourage David __________ __________ __________ __________. In this situation, what would Jane most likely say to David?
Jane: (I'm sure you can play the solo part beautifully.)

16~17

M: Good evening, viewers. Last time, I introduced some paintings by well-known Western artists. Today, I'd like to talk about __________ __________ __________ __________ __________ in Western art. Let's begin with mirrors. The reflection seen in mirrors can reveal a hidden truth or expose a lie. As you might imagine, a broken mirror generally represents bad luck. Second, candles. They can __________ __________ __________ __________ __________ or show a timeline. This is seen in how much of the candles have burned. Third, let's talk about books. Books often represent a higher educational status. They're also a symbol of learning or of giving knowledge. Lastly, flowers can be a symbol of life. Blooming flowers are used to __________ __________ __________ __________. In a moment, I'll present some paintings with these symbols.

Dictation Answers

1. is being repaired / use the east entrance today / be in use from tomorrow
2. It's hard handling different opinions / lead people to make better decisions / Try to think of arguments
3. support senior citizens in the digital age / not familiar with these digital services / provide them with digital education
4. tool board on the wall / put a table below the board / put a big speaker in the corner
5. to relieve my back pain / class hours didn't fit my schedule / send you some yoga video clips
6. a minimum of $30 for delivery / place the order / Normally we have to pay $5
7. leaving my job / submitted applications to some other companies / develop your abilities
8. make a detailed plan / matches my holiday schedule / be offered for transportation
9. using social media for their business / planning, shooting, and editing videos / randomly pick some of the participants
10. we'd better not spend / choose from the other materials / less than 500ml will be appropriate
11. plans with my mom / consider changing your plans
12. thinking of joining / accepting any more new members
13. much more impressive than I expected / collections and displays / made my heart feel heavy
14. create something meaningful for yourself / connect with people and share your work / discuss your work with others
15. sprains her wrist / take her solo part / to be more confident

16~17. objects that have symbolic meanings / symbolize the passing of time / show power and growth

제6회 중급 모의고사

맞은 개수: 2점 문항 ___개, 3점 문항 ___개
알고 푼 문항은 ○, 찍어서 맞힌 문제는 △에 표시하고, △와 ×는 다시 복습하세요.

1번부터 17번까지는 듣고 답하는 문제입니다. 1번부터 15번까지는 한 번만 들려주고, 16번부터 17번까지는 두 번 들려줍니다. 방송을 잘 듣고 답을 하시기 바랍니다.

1 ○△×
2025년 6월 교육청(고2) 1번

다음을 듣고, 여자가 하는 말의 목적으로 가장 적절한 것을 고르시오. 정답률 94%

① 보건실 이용에 대해 안내하려고
② 구급약 사용 방법을 설명하려고
③ 보건실 환경 개선을 건의하려고
④ 학생 식당 위치를 알려주려고
⑤ 학사 일정 변경을 공지하려고

2 ○△×
2025년 9월 교육청(고2) 2번

대화를 듣고, 남자의 의견으로 가장 적절한 것을 고르시오. 정답률 93%

① 냉장고 문을 자주 여닫으면 전기가 낭비된다.
② 과도한 육류 섭취는 영양 불균형의 원인이 된다.
③ 한 번 해동한 음식은 다시 냉동하지 않는 것이 좋다.
④ 음식을 밀폐해서 보관하면 세균 증식을 억제할 수 있다.
⑤ 오랫동안 냉동 보관한 음식을 먹는 것은 해로울 수 있다.

3 ○△×
2018년 6월 교육청(고2) 5번

대화를 듣고, 두 사람의 관계를 가장 잘 나타낸 것을 고르시오. 정답률 83%

① 아버지 — 딸
② 삽화가 — 동화 작가
③ 미술관 관장 — 기자
④ 서점 주인 — 출판사 직원
⑤ 미술 교사 — 학생

4 ○△×
2024년 9월 교육청(고2) 4번

대화를 듣고, 그림에서 대화의 내용과 일치하지 않는 것을 고르시오. 정답률 96%

5 ○△×
2021년 9월 교육청(고2) 5번

대화를 듣고, 여자가 남자에게 부탁한 일로 가장 적절한 것을 고르시오. 정답률 80%

① 에어컨 수리 요청하기
② 야구 경기 티켓 구매하기
③ 주문한 음식 찾아오기
④ 박물관 투어 취소하기
⑤ 식사 장소 예약하기

6 ○△×
2025년 3월 교육청(고2) 6번

대화를 듣고, 남자가 지불할 금액을 고르시오. 정답률 88%

① $18 ② $27 ③ $30 ④ $36 ⑤ $40

7 ○△×
2023년 3월 교육청(고2) 7번

대화를 듣고, 남자가 내일 봉사 활동에 같이 갈 수 없는 이유를 고르시오. 정답률 79%

① 봉사 활동 장소가 너무 멀어서
② 독감 예방 주사를 맞지 않아서
③ 가족과 저녁 식사를 해야 해서
④ 참여 가능한 나이가 되지 않아서
⑤ 스포츠 프로그램에 참여해야 해서

8 ○△×
2022년 3월 교육청(고2) 8번

대화를 듣고, Modern Architecture Expo에 관해 언급되지 않은 것을 고르시오. 정답률 79%

① 개최 장소
② 주최 기관
③ 개최 기간
④ 입장료
⑤ 강연자 수

9 ○△×
2023년 6월 교육청(고2) 9번

Ocean World에 관한 다음 내용을 듣고, 일치하지 않는 것을 고르시오. 정답률 90%

① 주제는 심해 탐험이다.
② 오전 10시부터 오후 6시까지 운영된다.
③ 중앙 홀에서 영상을 시청할 수 있다.
④ 물고기 모양의 쿠키를 만들 수 있다.
⑤ 사전 예약제로 운영된다.

10 ○△× • 2019년 9월 교육청(고2) 12번

다음 표를 보면서 대화를 듣고, 두 사람이 구매할 Air Fryer를 고르시오. 정답률 82%

Air Fryer

	Model	Price	Automatic Switch Off	Capacity (liters)	Warranty
①	A	$59	×	2	1 year
②	B	$68	○	2	1 year
③	C	$84	○	4	1 year
④	D	$95	○	4	2 year
⑤	E	$109	×	5	2 year

11 ○△× • 2024년 6월 교육청(고2) 12번

대화를 듣고, 여자의 마지막 말에 대한 남자의 응답으로 가장 적절한 것을 고르시오. 정답률 87%

① Good idea. You can cook instead of me.
② My fault! I should have paid for the dinner.
③ Unfortunately, the restaurant is closed tonight.
④ Okay, then I guess we should cancel our plans.
⑤ Right. I'll check if there's any public parking nearby.

12 ○△× • 2025년 6월 교육청(고2) 11번

대화를 듣고, 남자의 마지막 말에 대한 여자의 응답으로 가장 적절한 것을 고르시오. [3점] 정답률 86%

① Absolutely. You can donate them next time instead.
② Don't worry. I'm going to the supermarket right now.
③ Never mind. We've already got things we need to use.
④ Sure. Let's first pick out some items in good condition.
⑤ Sorry. I didn't have enough money to buy toys for kids.

13 고득점 ○△× • 2018년 6월 교육청(고2) 14번

대화를 듣고, 여자의 마지막 말에 대한 남자의 응답으로 가장 적절한 것을 고르시오. [3점] 정답률 72%

Man: ______________________________

① I'll use my tablet for my online lessons.
② I surely appreciate their help for fixing it.
③ I'll check the warranty period of this product.
④ I don't think I can live without my cell phone.
⑤ I think I'll buy a new one of a different brand.

14 ○△× • 2022년 6월 교육청(고2) 13번

대화를 듣고, 남자의 마지막 말에 대한 여자의 응답으로 가장 적절한 것을 고르시오. [3점] 정답률 86%

Woman: ______________________________

① Don't worry. I've already ordered it.
② You're right. I'll take care of it tomorrow.
③ My fault! I wrote the wrong address on it.
④ I'm sorry. I'll wake you up early next time.
⑤ Sure. You'd better return the borrowed item now.

15 ○△× • 2022년 3월 교육청(고2) 15번

다음 상황 설명을 듣고, Sandra가 Mr. Wilson에게 할 말로 가장 적절한 것을 고르시오. 정답률 79%

Sandra: ______________________________

① Will you tell me how to run the student council meetings?
② Can we hold a sports competition for student health?
③ Please provide new sports equipment to students.
④ Is it possible for you to join our regular meetings?
⑤ Let us enter the sports league on behalf of our school.

[16~17] 다음을 듣고, 물음에 답하시오.

16 ○△× • 2019년 9월 교육청(고2) 16번

여자가 하는 말의 주제로 가장 적절한 것은? 정답률 76%

① useful tips to finding parking spaces in cities quickly
② efforts in Europe to handle air pollution from traffic
③ impacts of greenhouse gases on the environment
④ causes of traffic jams in European capital cities
⑤ various renewable energy sources in Europe

17 ○△× • 2019년 9월 교육청(고2) 17번

언급된 나라가 아닌 것은? 정답률 87%

① Denmark ② France ③ Belgium
④ Switzerland ⑤ Germany

Dictation

문제 풀이에 중요한 핵심 부분과 듣기에 자주 나오는 표현들에 빈칸 처리를 했습니다. 방송을 잘 듣고, 빈칸에 알맞은 말을 써 넣으세요.

Tip! 잘 들리지 않는 부분이 있을 때에는 정답을 확인 후, 똑같은 속도로 따라 읽기 연습을 해 보세요.

1

W: Good morning, students! This is your school nurse, Emma Lee. What do you think of high school life so far? Since this is your first semester, I'm going to give you some guidelines for __________ __________ __________ __________. First, the clinic is located on the third floor next to the school cafeteria. And it's open Monday through Friday, from 9 a.m. to 4 p.m. I'll be there to help you with anything you need like __________ __________ __________ __________. Lastly, when you are in the clinic, please be careful not to __________ __________ __________ __________. I hope you have a safe and healthy school life. Thank you.

2

W: Honey, how about having beef for dinner tonight? We have some in the freezer.

M: Great idea, but that beef has been in the freezer for so long. __________ __________ __________ __________ __________.

W: Well, it's been frozen this whole time, so it should be fine.

M: Not really. Eating food that's been kept frozen for a long time can be harmful.

W: Really? I thought it would be alright.

M: Well, while freezing can slow bacteria growth in food, it cannot completely stop them from growing.

W: Hmm, that makes sense.

M: Besides, if we open the freezer often, the __________ __________ __________ __________ __________.

W: Oh. That might also encourage bacteria growth.

M: Correct! That's why it can be harmful to eat food that's __________ __________ __________ for a long time.

W: I see. Let's go grocery shopping for some beef then.

3

W: Hello, Mr. Smith.

M: Oh, Mrs. Roberts, I'm glad to work with you again.

W: Me, too. It was a pleasure to __________ __________ __________ __________ __________ __________.

M: Your pictures made my book more attractive to children. The little bear was especially cute.

W: Thank you. Is there anything you want to __________ __________ __________ __________ of your new book?

M: Yes. The story is about a father and his daughter. So, I want to show the father's love clearly.

W: Then, I'll draw the father putting his arms around his daughter.

M: That's great. How about drawing her with a big smiling face?

W: Then the daughter will look more cheerful.

M: That's exactly what I want.

W: Okay. After __________ __________ __________ __________ __________, I will e-mail my first draft to you.

M: Alright. I look forward to seeing your work soon.

4

M: Hello, Cindy. What are you looking at on your phone?

W: Hi, Tom. This is my own space in the metaverse.

M: Wow, it's amazing. Oh, there's a heart-shaped door in your house. That's unique.

W: Yes. I can __________ __________ __________ __________ __________ __________ like a real house.

M: Fantastic! Is it possible to ride the bicycle next to the tree?

W: Of course. We can do everything in virtual reality.

M: Awesome. I love the __________ __________ __________ __________ __________ __________.

W: Yeah, they make my place so lovely.

M: I agree. I also like that __________ __________ __________ __________ __________.

W: Thanks.

M: Oh, there's a girl sitting on the bench. She looks a lot like you.

W: Yes, she's my avatar in the metaverse.

M: That's so cool. I also want to design my own space like yours.

정답 및 해설 p.81

5

W: Henry, the weather's so nice today. We should do some of the outdoor activities Los Angeles has.

M: I agree. Because it's been so hot, we've been going to museums to enjoy the air conditioning.

W: I'm ready to enjoy the real Los Angeles. How should we spend the day?

M: We could go to the beach for lunch first, and I think there's a baseball game that we can go to in the evening.

W: That sounds great. I've always wanted to see the local team play.

M: Should we prepare a __________ __________ __________ __________ __________ __________? The restaurants there might be crowded.

W: I think it would be better to __________ __________ __________ __________ __________ on the way there.

M: Okay. What about tickets to the baseball game? They might sell out.

W: Oh, you're right. __________ __________ __________ __________ __________? I'll search for a place where we can pick up food for our lunch.

M: All right. I'll take care of that now.

6

W: Welcome to Gardener's! How can I help you?

M: Hi! I'd like to add some new flowers to my garden.

W: That's wonderful! __________ __________ __________ __________ __________ __________ __________?

M: I like lilies. How much are they?

W: They're $4 each.

M: I'll take five lilies. Can you recommend any other flowers? I was thinking of __________ __________ __________ __________ __________.

W: In that case, how about pairing them with some tulips?

M: Oh, that sounds great. How much are the tulips?

W: They're __________ __________ __________ __________ __________ — just $2 each.

M: Great. I'll take five tulips, then.

W: Five lilies and five tulips, right? When you buy 10 flowers or more, we offer a 10% discount.

M: Thank you. Here's my credit card.

7

W: Michael, what do you think about doing some volunteer work tomorrow?

M: Well, I thought we're going to join a sports program tomorrow.

W: You haven't heard? It's been cancelled.

M: Oh. Then, tell me more about the volunteer work.

W: We'll pick up meals at the community center and then __________ __________ __________ __________ __________ in the neighborhood.

M: Hmm.... When does it end? I'm having a family dinner.

W: Before noon. We'll be working for three hours in the morning.

M: Sounds good. Are there __________ __________ __________ __________?

W: Yes. You have to be 16 or older to participate.

M: Then, I'm qualified. I just turned 16 last February.

W: Oh, I almost forgot. You also __________ __________ __________ __________ __________ since you'll meet the elderly in person.

M: I haven't got a flu shot yet. I'm afraid I can't come.

W: Too bad. Maybe next time then.

8

M: Emily, come have a look at this leaflet. It's about the Modern Architecture Expo.

W: Oh, it looks interesting.

M: We both have an interest in architecture. Why don't we go there together?

W: Good idea. __________ __________ __________ __________ the Grand Convention Center. It's close to our school.

M: Great! When should we go?

W: It starts on April 1 and ends on April 15. Can you make it on Saturday, April 9?

M: Yes, I can. Look here. __________ __________ __________ __________ __________.

W: Oh, that's quite expensive.

M: I'm sure it'll be worth it. __________ __________ __________ __________ __________ __________ on their best architectural works. We can attend as many of them as we want.

W: Cool! It'll be great to see them in person.

9

W: Hello, I'm Grace, a manager of Dream Marine Museum. This year, our museum has a special program, called Ocean World. The topic of the program is deep-sea exploration. Through this program, children will __________ __________ __________ __________ __________ and fish living deep in the ocean. It runs from 10 a.m. to 6 p.m. this Saturday, October 28. This event will be held __________ __________ __________ __________. You can watch videos of deep-sea exploration on a huge screen in the central hall. There will be a photo booth where you can take selfies __________ __________ __________ __________ __________ __________. In addition, you can make fish-shaped cookies with a chef. Anyone can participate in Ocean World for free without having to make a reservation. I hope to see you all there.

10

M: Honey, what are you looking at?

W: A website that sells air fryers. I want one so we can cook more healthily.

M: Good idea. We can fry foods using less oil if we buy one. How much do you think we should spend?

W: Well, I don't want to spend more than 100 dollars.

M: Okay. Then how about these models?

W: Hmm... it's safer to buy one that will __________ __________ __________ __________ __________ __________ __________.

M: You're right. Let's choose one with the automatic switch off function.

W: What about capacity? My friend bought one that could only hold two liters. She regretted not buying a bigger one.

M: In that case, we should get one with a __________ __________ __________ __________ __________ __________. Now we have these two to choose from.

W: They both look good. But I think the one __________ __________ __________ __________ is better.

M: I agree. Let's order this one.

11

W: Jake, are we going to drive to the restaurant for the dinner meeting with our client?

M: Yes. It would be best to go by car. The problem is the place __________ __________ __________ __________ __________.

W: I'm sure we can __________ __________ __________ for the car around the restaurant.

M: (Right. I'll check if there's any public parking nearby.)

12

M: Mom, our school is having a flea market for charity this weekend. So I'm __________ __________ __________ __________ __________ __________.

W: Oh, that sounds like a great idea! It'll really help others.

M: Yes, but I'm not sure what to give. Could you help me with __________ __________ __________ __________ __________?

W: (Sure. Let's first pick out some items in good condition.)

13

W: Harry, you look angry. What's wrong?

M: My tablet PC is __________ __________ __________.

W: That's too bad. Have you been to customer service to repair it?

M: Yes, I have, but I was shocked at the cost.

W: How much would it cost to get your tablet fixed?

M: It's __________ __________ __________ __________ __________ of a new one!

W: You bought that one last year. Isn't it still under warranty?

M: I had a one-year warranty, and the tablet died when it was one year and one week old.

W: How about asking the staff to be __________ __________ __________ __________ __________? It was just one week!

M: Actually, I did, but the staff said the company is very strict regarding their warranty policies.

W: I'm sorry for that. So, what do you think you'll do?

M: (I think I'll buy a new one of a different brand.)

14

M: Sarah, where did you get those bananas?

W: I just took them out of the parcel box in front of the door.

M: What box? I haven't ordered anything recently.
W: Really? I thought you ordered them, so I ate some.
M: Let's check the address on the box.
W: Oh no! __________ __________ __________ __________. This is not our address.
M: Umm... The bananas were supposed to be delivered to our next-door neighbor, Mr. Jones.
W: What should I do?
M: I think it would be good to __________ __________ __________ __________ __________ __________ __________. And we should buy him some new bananas.
W: Okay. I'll tell him what happened right away.
M: Wait! It's too late. Mr. Jones usually __________ __________ __________ __________ __________, so I don't think it's a good idea to wake him up now.
W: (You're right. I'll take care of it tomorrow.)

15

M: Sandra is the president of the student council of her school. Today the student council is having their regular meeting. One of the issues at today's meeting is about how to __________ __________ __________ __________ __________ __________. These days, many students have health problems because they don't get much exercise. The student council agrees that it'd be good to __________ __________ __________ __________ to improve the students' health. After the meeting, Sandra goes to the principal's office and tells Mr. Wilson about what they discussed. Now she wants to __________ __________ __________ __________ to host the sports event for the sake of the students. In this situation, what would Sandra most likely say to Mr. Wilson?
Sandra: (Can we hold a sports competition for student health?)

16~17

W: Hello, students. As you all know, heavy traffic is a major source of air pollution. To tackle this problem, many European cities are taking various actions. For instance, in Copenhagen, the capital of Denmark, large parts of the city have been closed to vehicles for decades, and the city __________ __________ __________ __________ __________ by 2025. Also, Paris, in France, bans cars in many historic districts on weekends and encourages car and bikesharing programs. In Belgium, the city of Brussels operates "Mobility Week" to __________ __________ __________ __________ __________. And for one day every September, all cars are banned from the entire city center. Lastly, cities in Germany are establishing "green zones" in city centers. If vehicles don't have a sticker showing they __________ __________ __________ __________ __________, they can't enter those places. Now, I'll show you some pictures that illustrate this.

Dictation Answers

1. visiting our school clinic / medicine or some treatment / disturb the other students
2. We'd better not eat it / temperature inside doesn't stay constant / been stored frozen
3. draw pictures for your last book / emphasize on the cover / finishing the book cover design
4. enter my home through the door / two dogs looking at each other / striped-patterned mat on the ground
5. lunch to take to the beach / pick up something to eat / Will you buy the tickets
6. What flowers do you have in mind / mixing a few different types / half the price of lilies
7. deliver them to the elderly / any restrictions for applicants / need a flu vaccination record
8. It'll be held at / Admission is $20 for students / Ten great architects will be giving lectures
9. become interested in the plants / on the first floor / wearing various masks of ocean creatures
10. turn off if it gets too hot / capacity of at least four liters / with the longer warranty
11. doesn't have a parking lot / find a place
12. thinking of donating my old stuff / selecting the things for donation
13. out of order / as much as the cost / flexible about the warranty period
14. The package was misdelivered / explain to him why you took them / goes to bed really early
15. improve students' mental and physical health / hold a sports competition / ask him for permission
16~17. plans to become carbon neutral / encourage public over private transportation / have an acceptable emission level

제7회 중급 모의고사

맞은 개수: 2점 문항 ___개, 3점 문항 ___개
알고 푼 문항은 ○, 찍어서 맞힌 문제는 △에 표시하고, △와 ×는 다시 복습하세요.

1번부터 17번까지는 듣고 답하는 문제입니다. 1번부터 15번까지는 한 번만 들려주고, 16번부터 17번까지는 두 번 들려줍니다. 방송을 잘 듣고 답을 하시기 바랍니다.

1 ○△× • 2024년 3월 교육청(고2) 1번

다음을 듣고, 남자가 하는 말의 목적으로 가장 적절한 것을 고르시오. 정답률 91%

① 꽃 사진 촬영 동아리 회원을 모집하려고
② 꽃 사진 촬영 시 유의 사항을 당부하려고
③ 꽃 사진 촬영 행사가 취소됨을 공지하려고
④ 꽃 사진 촬영에 적합한 장비를 소개하려고
⑤ 꽃 사진을 촬영하기에 좋은 장소를 안내하려고

2 ○△× • 2021년 3월 교육청(고2) 2번

대화를 듣고, 남자의 의견으로 가장 적절한 것을 고르시오. 정답률 94%

① 오디오 북은 다른 활동을 하면서 듣기에 편리하다.
② 오디오 북은 책의 내용을 깊이 이해하는 데 도움이 된다.
③ 운동을 할 때는 오디오 북보다 음악을 듣는 것이 더 낫다.
④ 도서관은 다양한 장르의 오디오 북을 구비해야 한다.
⑤ 오디오 북은 조용한 장소에서 들을 필요가 있다.

3 ○△× • 2022년 9월 교육청(고2) 3번

대화를 듣고, 두 사람의 관계를 가장 잘 나타낸 것을 고르시오. 정답률 90%

① 학생 — 문화 인류학 교수
② 미술관 관장 — 건축가
③ 여행 작가 — 삽화가
④ 신문 기자 — 전시 기획자
⑤ 구호 활동가 — 후원자

4 ○△× • 2022년 3월 교육청(고2) 4번

대화를 듣고, 그림에서 대화의 내용과 일치하지 않는 것을 고르시오. 정답률 90%

5 ○△× • 2019년 6월 교육청(고2) 7번

대화를 듣고, 여자가 할 일로 가장 적절한 것을 고르시오. 정답률 86%

① 간식 구매하기
② 여벌 옷 챙기기
③ 등산화 빌리기
④ 여행 가방 챙기기
⑤ 친구 집 방문하기

6 ○△× • 2023년 6월 교육청(고2) 6번

대화를 듣고, 남자가 지불할 금액을 고르시오. [3점] 정답률 81%

① \$80 ② \$90 ③ \$100 ④ \$108 ⑤ \$120

7 ○△× • 2020년 6월 교육청(고2) 8번

대화를 듣고, 남자가 전시회에 갈 수 없는 이유를 고르시오. 정답률 89%

① 봉사활동을 해야 해서
② 축구 경기를 해야 해서
③ 과학 과제를 해야 해서
④ 아르바이트를 해야 해서
⑤ 기말고사 준비를 해야 해서

8 ○△× • 2021년 9월 교육청(고2) 8번

대화를 듣고, Electronics Fair에 관해 언급되지 않은 것을 고르시오. 정답률 93%

① 프로그램
② 장소
③ 종료일
④ 참가 업체
⑤ 티켓 가격

9 ○△× • 2022년 3월 교육청(고2) 9번

2022 Opera in School에 관한 다음 내용을 듣고, 일치하지 않는 것을 고르시오. 정답률 83%

① Romeo and Juliet을 공연할 것이다.
② 3월 25일 학교 강당에서 열릴 것이다.
③ 공연은 45분간 진행될 것이다.
④ 질의응답 시간 전에 가수들과 사진을 찍을 수 있다.
⑤ 참석하려면 사전에 등록해야 한다.

10 ○△× • 2024년 3월 교육청(고2) 10번

다음 표를 보면서 대화를 듣고, 두 사람이 구매할 사진첩을 고르시오. 정답률 93%

Photo Albums

	Model	Cover Material	Pages	Cover Color	Price
①	A	paper	20	white	$16
②	B	paper	30	blue	$19
③	C	fabric	30	white	$22
④	D	fabric	40	blue	$25
⑤	E	leather	40	brown	$30

11 ○△× • 2020년 11월 교육청(고2) 11번

대화를 듣고, 남자의 마지막 말에 대한 여자의 응답으로 가장 적절한 것을 고르시오. 정답률 88%

① No problem. Just let me know when you're ready.
② I'm afraid I can't. I lost my library card yesterday.
③ Sure. You can borrow my books anytime you want.
④ I'm sorry. The sunlight is too strong to go outside.
⑤ Of course. I'm going to walk to the library myself.

12 고득점 ○△× • 2018년 3월 교육청(고2) 1번

대화를 듣고, 여자의 마지막 말에 대한 남자의 응답으로 가장 적절한 것을 고르시오. 정답률 69%

① He's working on a new novel.
② There'll be a book signing in New York.
③ His new novel will be published in April.
④ It's in the new-release section over there.
⑤ You can find a bigger bookstore down the street.

13 ○△× • 2024년 3월 교육청(고2) 14번

대화를 듣고, 남자의 마지막 말에 대한 여자의 응답으로 가장 적절한 것을 고르시오. [3점] 정답률 78%

Woman: ______________________________

① Right. It's better to hide weaknesses whenever possible.
② Good luck. Show them who you are, and you'll make it.
③ Of course. You can handle your homework effectively.
④ I agree. You can make your schedule using a planner.
⑤ Be careful! A weakness keeps you from growing up.

14 고득점 ○△× • 2020년 11월 교육청(고2) 14번

대화를 듣고, 여자의 마지막 말에 대한 남자의 응답으로 가장 적절한 것을 고르시오. [3점] 정답률 72%

Man: ______________________________

① Don't worry. I know they'll definitely support your opinion.
② Of course not. We're not able to switch our club leaders now.
③ I understand. I'm going to look for another research topic then.
④ All right. That way we'll satisfy more members than last time.
⑤ Never mind. We can reschedule a time for our group discussion.

15 ○△× • 2025년 6월 교육청(고2) 15번

다음 상황 설명을 듣고, Ben이 Amy에게 할 말로 가장 적절한 것을 고르시오. 정답률 77%

Ben: ______________________________

① How about putting our ideas together for the project?
② Let me tell you how to reduce food waste at school.
③ Why don't we do a campaign about recycling?
④ You need to get the teacher's permission right away.
⑤ I think we should share his ideas with our classmates.

[16~17] 다음을 듣고, 물음에 답하시오.

16 ○△× • 2025년 9월 교육청(고2) 16번

여자가 하는 말의 주제로 가장 적절한 것은? 정답률 92%

① animals that can cause damage to buildings
② various functions of structures built by animals
③ construction skills that humans can learn from animals
④ effective ways for animals to escape from danger
⑤ creative hunting strategies of different animals

17 ○△× • 2025년 9월 교육청(고2) 17번

언급된 동물이 아닌 것은? 정답률 90%

① beavers ② ants ③ spiders
④ bees ⑤ birds

Dictation

문제 풀이에 중요한 핵심 부분과 듣기에 자주 나오는 표현들에 빈칸 처리를 했습니다. 방송을 잘 듣고, 빈칸에 알맞은 말을 써 넣으세요.

Tip! 잘 들리지 않는 부분이 있을 때에는 정답을 확인 후, 똑같은 속도로 따라 읽기 연습을 해 보세요.

1

M: Good morning, students. This is your vice principal, Mr. Gunning. I have an announcement regarding our 'Spring Flower Photo Day' event this afternoon. As you know, we __________ __________ __________ __________ of beautiful spring flowers as we walk around our neighborhood. I regret to inform you that the event __________ __________ __________ __________ __________ __________. I understand you've been looking forward to it, but unfortunately it appears we won't be able to get the best photos today. We __________ __________ __________ __________ for a sunny day in the near future. Please understand that this decision was made to ensure that the event will be a success.

2

W: Hi, Chris. Where are you going?

M: I'm going to the library to __________ __________ __________ __________. Do you want to come along?

W: Well, I don't often read books these days. I'm busy helping with housework, exercising, and so on.

M: Why don't you try audio books then? They're convenient to listen to while you're doing other things.

W: I've never tried it. Do you think it'll work for me?

M: Sure. It's an __________ __________ __________ __________ __________ even if you have a busy schedule. I always listen to a short story when I take a walk.

W: Cool! I guess I could try listening to audio books while I do chores.

M: I'm sure you'll enjoy listening to books __________ __________ __________ __________ __________.

W: Can you recommend some audio books to me?

M: I have a few in mind. I'll text you a list later.

3

W: Hello, Mr. Baker. Thank you for doing this interview.

M: My pleasure. I really like __________ __________ __________ __________ __________ __________ in your newspaper.

W: Thank you so much. I'm honored to __________ __________ __________ __________ who organized the Modern Asia exhibition at the National Art Museum.

M: Thank you. I'm very surprised it has gotten so much attention.

W: It certainly has. Our readers have expressed interest in it, too. What was the idea behind it?

M: The idea was to show contemporary Asia to the public.

W: I see. Are you planning to __________ __________ __________ __________?

M: Yes. I'm planning to do one about contemporary Africa. It will contain paintings featuring people, cities, and homes from around the continent.

W: That sounds great. I look forward to checking it out.

M: You won't be disappointed.

W: Thanks again for your time, Mr. Baker.

4

W: Hi, David. You look happy.

M: I won a prize at the science fair. Look at this photo from the fair.

W: Wow! Congratulations. Oh, the __________ __________ __________ __________ __________ __________ above the board. Cool!

M: Yeah, I'm so proud.

W: You set up your board on the round table. I see your topic was 'Lemon Battery.' What did you do?

M: I showed how to make a battery using lemons.

W: Interesting. So that's why there is a __________ __________ __________ __________ __________ __________ __________.

M: That's right.

W: Who is this woman wearing a flower-patterned dress?

M: That's my grandmother. She came to congratulate me.

W: How nice! Oh, you're holding __________ __________ __________ __________. They're so beautiful.

M: Thanks. It was a great day.

5

W: Tom, did you pack everything for tomorrow's backpacking trip?
M: I'm almost done, Mom. I just need a few more things.
W: Good! Don't forget to __________ __________ __________ __________!
M: Sure, I did. Just in case!
W: Well done! What about hiking boots? Didn't you say you were __________ __________ __________ Jake's?
M: Yes, he told me to pick them up in the afternoon.
W: That's so sweet of him. Anything else?
M: There is just one more important thing left. I have to go to the __________ __________ __________ __________ __________ __________!
W: Snacks are important. I'm going to the grocery store right now. I could buy them for you if you want.
M: Could you? That would be great!
W: Sure, sweetie. No problem.
M: Then all I have to do is get the boots from Jake!

6

W: Good afternoon, sir. May I help you?
M: Yes, please. I'm looking for swimming goggles for my kids.
W: We have several kinds. Take a look at this display.
M: All right, thank you. *[Pause]* Oh, how much are these? These would be perfect for my children.
W: They're 50 dollars each. They're anti-fog, which guarantees clear vision for fast swimming.
M: I see. They're a little bit expensive, though.
W: In that case, there are cheaper ones __________ __________ __________ __________ __________. How about these? They cost 40 dollars each.
M: Sounds better. I'll buy two pairs of these. I also need a swimming cap for myself.
W: I recommend this new cap. It __________ __________ __________ and costs only 20 dollars.
M: Okay. Then I'll buy two pairs of swimming goggles and one swimming cap.
W: We also have brand-new swimsuits in our store. Are you interested?
M: No, thanks. These are enough.
W: Sounds good. We __________ __________ __________ this week, so you can get a 10% discount on the total amount.
M: That's great. Here's my credit card.

7

W: Jake. There's going to be a Vincent van Gogh exhibition in the Art Center.
M: Really? He's my favorite artist.
W: Mine, too. How about going to the exhibition together this Sunday?
M: This Sunday? I'd really love to, but I'm afraid I can't go.
W: Come on. Do you __________ __________ __________ __________ __________ on that day?
M: No, I usually volunteer on Saturdays.
W: Oh, I remember. You said __________ __________ __________ __________ __________?
M: I did, but our game was delayed because of weather.
W: Then, do you have another appointment?
M: Actually, I have to __________ __________ __________ __________ __________. It's due next Monday.
W: You must be busy then.
M: Yeah. I hope you have a good time.

8

M: How was your visit to the Electronics Fair, Christine?
W: It was spectacular. You should check it out if you have time.
M: I might. What was there to do at the fair?
W: There were __________ __________ __________ __________ __________ of electronic devices and new technology.
M: Wow! You must have seen a lot of brand-new electronic devices! Did you participate in any hands-on activities there?
W: Of course I did. Various programs were available including 3-D printing, VR games, and __________ __________ __________.
M: I want to try talking with AI. Where is the fair held?
W: It takes place at Dream Expo Center.
M: That's near here! When does the fair end?
W: It __________ __________ __________ __________.
M: Can you tell me what the price of a ticket is?
W: It's 5 dollars. But if you purchase it online, you can buy it for 3 dollars.
M: Great! I'll order my ticket now.

9

W: Hello, students. This is Ms. Miller, your music teacher. Are you interested in operas? Then, we invite you to 2022 Opera in School. Five professional opera singers will come to our school and present *Romeo and Juliet* to you. They'll bring the classic story to life with opera costumes and sets. The show will __________ __________ __________ __________ __________ __________ on March 25, starting at 6 p.m. It'll __________ __________ __________ __________ and be followed by a question and answer session. You can take photos with the singers after the __________ __________ __________ __________ __________ __________. There's no admission fee, but to attend, you must register in advance. I hope to see you there.

10

W: Dad, I found a website that provides a service to make photo albums. How about creating one with the photos from our winter holiday?

M: Great! Let me see. *[Pause]* Oh, it says all we need to do is choose a few options and upload our photos.

W: Right. First, let's __________ __________ __________ __________.

M: Umm... Leather might be too heavy.

W: You're right. Let's choose __________ __________ __________ __________.

M: Okay. For the number of pages, is 40 too many?

W: Yes. Let's just go for 20 or 30 pages. What color would be good for the cover?

M: I want it to __________ __________ __________ __________. How about white?

W: Perfect. That leaves us with two options.

M: Then, let's choose the cheaper one.

W: Sounds great. I'll choose the best pictures and upload them.

11

M: Mom, I have to borrow some books from the library today. But it's raining outside.

W: Don't worry. I'll __________ __________ __________ __________. Do you want to leave now?

M: Yes. But I need to look for my library card first. Could you __________ __________ __________ __________?

W: (No, problem. Just let me know when you're ready.)

12

W: Excuse me. Do you have Gilbert Norton's new novel, *Space War*?

M: Yes, we do. __________ __________ __________ __________ yesterday.

W: Great. I've been waiting for it. __________ __________ __________ __________ __________?

M: (It's in the new-release section over there.)

13

M: Ms. Williams! Do you have a minute?

W: Sure. What is it?

M: I have to write an essay to get a scholarship, but I don't know what to write about.

W: Maybe you can start by __________ __________ __________ __________ __________ and school life.

M: I already wrote about that, but it doesn't seem good enough.

W: Umm... How about __________ __________ __________ __________ __________ __________?

M: Weakness? Wouldn't that be a bad idea for an essay?

W: Not necessarily. If you describe how you've been trying to deal with it, your story will show your potential.

M: Well, I used to __________ __________ __________ __________ until the last minute. But by using a planner, I make my schedule on an hourly basis. Now I no longer have any trouble finishing my work on time.

W: That's perfect! That will be a great story to include in your essay for the scholarship.

M: Thank you for your help! That actually makes me __________ __________ __________ __________ __________.

W: (Good luck. Show them who you are, and you'll make it.)

14

W: Hi, Steve. I have something to tell you.

M: Hi. What is it, Sophie?

W: We need to __________ __________ __________ __________ __________ for our science club.

M: Yeah. What topic do you have in mind?

W: I don't have any specific idea. Why don't we ask the other members for their opinions?

M: I'm not sure about that. I think it's our job to determine a research topic as club leaders.
W: But do you remember last semester? We chose the research topic ourselves, and some members didn't like it.
M: You're right. Then, how can we __________ __________ __________?
W: Well, we'll have time to discuss with all of our club members next week.
M: That sounds good. But what if they have too many different ideas?
W: Then we can __________ __________ __________ __________ __________ __________ __________ and choose what most members want for the topic.
M: (All right. That way we'll satisfy more members than last time.)

15

M: Ben and Amy are in the same environmental club in high school. They are doing an environmental campaign project and discussing ideas together. Ben sees that students sometimes throw away trash without recycling. So he wants to __________ __________ __________ __________ all the time. Meanwhile, Amy feels that __________ __________ __________ __________ __________ __________ is also a good idea because she notices a lot of leftovers in the school cafeteria. Ben thinks that both ideas will certainly help students to think more about the environment. So he wants to suggest that they __________ __________ __________ in their project. In this situation, what would Ben most likely say to Amy?
Ben: (How about putting our ideas together for the project?)

16~17

W: Hello, students. As you know, animals __________ __________ __________ __________ in the natural world. Today, we'll talk about the different functions that these structures have. First, an important function of animal-built structures is to __________ __________ __________ __________. For example, beavers build dams to create ponds where they can construct their homes. These structures provide a shelter from predators. Next, animal structures can also __________ __________ __________ __________ __________. Some species of ants use their own bodies to create bridges. These bridges provide a path over obstacles and allow them to search for food at an increased speed. In addition, animal structures can serve as traps. This can be observed in web-building spiders, who weave elaborate webs of sticky spider silk that capture prey. Finally, animal structures can serve __________ __________ __________ __________ __________ __________. During mating season, some species of birds collect small branches, leaves, and colorful objects to create structures that attract the attention of females. Now, let's watch a short video about these incredible animal structures.

Dictation Answers

1. planned to take pictures / is canceled due to heavy rain / will reschedule the event
2. check out some books / easy way to enjoy books / while dealing with other stuff
3. reading your articles on modern painting / be interviewing the person / do any other exhibitions
4. prize ribbon is on the wall / basket of lemons next to the battery / flowers in your hand
5. pack some extra clothes / going to borrow / grocery store to buy some snacks
6. with basically the same function / uses high-quality materials / have a promotion
7. have to do volunteer work / you're going to play soccer / work on a science assignment
8. displays for the latest models / chatting with AI / ends on November 30th
9. be held at the school auditorium / last for 45 minutes / question and answer session is finished
10. choose the cover material / either paper or fabric / reflect our winter holiday
11. give you a ride / wait for a second
12. It just came in / Where can I find it
13. expressing your passion for learning / mentioning a weakness you've worked on / put my work off / feel a lot more confident
14. decide on a research topic / hear everyone's opinion / put the research topic to the vote
15. encourage them to recycle / asking students to reduce food waste / include both ideas

16~17. build many different structures / provide protection from predators / play a role in transportation / as a means of attracting mates

제8회 중급 모의고사

맞은 개수: 2점 문항 ___개, 3점 문항 ___개
알고 푼 문항은 ○, 찍어서 맞힌 문제는 △에 표시하고, △와 ×는 다시 복습하세요.

1번부터 17번까지는 듣고 답하는 문제입니다. 1번부터 15번까지는 한 번만 들려주고, 16번부터 17번까지는 두 번 들려줍니다. 방송을 잘 듣고 답을 하시기 바랍니다.

1 ○△× · 2023년 3월 교육청(고2) 1번

다음을 듣고, 여자가 하는 말의 목적으로 가장 적절한 것을 고르시오. 정답률 86%

① 학교 실내 체육관의 임시 폐쇄를 안내하려고
② 학교 실내 체육관의 방과 후 이용을 권장하려고
③ 학교 실내 체육관 개관 10주년 기념식에 초대하려고
④ 학교 실내 체육관 시설 보수를 위한 의견을 모으려고
⑤ 학교 실내 체육관 이용 후 운동 기구 정리를 당부하려고

2 ○△× · 2021년 6월 교육청(고2) 2번

대화를 듣고, 남자의 의견으로 가장 적절한 것을 고르시오. 정답률 95%

① 올바른 역사관을 가지는 것이 중요하다.
② 암기력은 학습 효과를 높이는 데 중요한 요인이다.
③ 역사 만화책을 읽는 것이 역사 공부에 도움이 된다.
④ 다양한 주제의 독서를 통해 창의력을 키울 수 있다.
⑤ 만화 그리기는 아이들의 상상력을 풍부하게 해 준다.

3 ○△× · 2020년 9월 교육청(고2) 5번

대화를 듣고, 두 사람의 관계를 가장 잘 나타낸 것을 고르시오. 정답률 91%

① 디자이너 — 패션모델 ② 영화감독 — 영화배우
③ 출판사 직원 — 소설가 ④ 잡지사 기자 — 웹툰 작가
⑤ 미술관 큐레이터 — 화가

4 ○△× · 2022년 9월 교육청(고2) 4번

대화를 듣고, 그림에서 대화의 내용과 일치하지 않는 것을 고르시오. 정답률 85%

5 ○△× · 2024년 9월 교육청(고2) 5번

대화를 듣고, 여자가 할 일로 가장 적절한 것을 고르시오. 정답률 86%

① 운동 장비 대여하기 ② 축구공 개수 확인하기
③ 스포츠 클럽 방문하기 ④ 경기 규칙 유인물 만들기
⑤ 자원봉사자들에게 전화하기

6 고득점 ○△× · 2021년 3월 교육청(고2) 6번

대화를 듣고, 남자가 지불할 금액을 고르시오. [3점] 정답률 64%

① $60 ② $65 ③ $70 ④ $75 ⑤ $80

7 ○△× · 2018년 6월 교육청(고2) 8번

대화를 듣고, 여자가 친구의 병문안을 갈 수 없는 이유를 고르시오. 정답률 84%

① 어머니의 생신 파티에 가야 해서
② 스키 캠프에 참가해야 해서
③ 다리에 부상을 입어서
④ 가족 여행이 예정되어서
⑤ 태권도 수업을 들어야 해서

8 ○△× · 2019년 3월 교육청(고2) 10번

대화를 듣고, Romance City에 관해 언급되지 않은 것을 고르시오. 정답률 86%

① 첫 방영 날짜 ② 주연 배우 ③ 줄거리
④ 감독 ⑤ 원작 소설

9 ○△× · 2020년 6월 교육청(고2) 11번

Highland Movie Night에 관한 다음 내용을 듣고, 일치하지 않는 것을 고르시오. 정답률 84%

① 매월 개최하는 행사이다.
② Highland 주민에게는 무료이다.
③ Lincoln 도서관에서 열린다.
④ 사전에 등록해야 한다.
⑤ 음식물 반입이 허용된다.

10 ○△× 2023년 3월 교육청(고2) 10번

다음 표를 보면서 대화를 듣고, 두 사람이 구매할 자외선 칫솔 소독기를 고르시오. 정답률 93%

UV Toothbrush Sanitizers

	Model	Number of Slots	Built-in Battery	Drying Function	Price
①	A	3	×	×	$39
②	B	4	○	○	$48
③	C	4	×	×	$40
④	D	5	○	×	$50
⑤	E	6	○	○	$54

11 ○△× 2022년 6월 교육청(고2) 11번

대화를 듣고, 남자의 마지막 말에 대한 여자의 응답으로 가장 적절한 것을 고르시오. 정답률 84%

① It's important to grow a lot of plants for the Earth.
② You need to water them once every three days.
③ Too much sunlight can be bad for the plants.
④ I'd better save water for the environment.
⑤ We should drink one liter of water a day.

12 고득점 ○△× 2021년 3월 교육청(고2) 12번

대화를 듣고, 여자의 마지막 말에 대한 남자의 응답으로 가장 적절한 것을 고르시오. 정답률 60%

① Yes. I'll give you a call when I'm available.
② Well, you're not doing any project at the moment.
③ All right. We can talk now since the visitor just left.
④ Why not? You can join the project anytime.
⑤ Sure. I have 30 minutes for you now.

13 ○△× 2021년 3월 교육청(고2) 13번

대화를 듣고, 남자의 마지막 말에 대한 여자의 응답으로 가장 적절한 것을 고르시오. 정답률 92%

Woman: ______________________________

① You're right. He's been eating too much lately.
② That's not fair. I don't want to walk him all week.
③ Sorry. I don't have time to take him to the vet now.
④ Okay. I'll take him out for a walk on weekends then.
⑤ Not really. Too much exercise is not good for his health.

14 ○△× 2025년 9월 교육청(고2) 13번

대화를 듣고, 여자의 마지막 말에 대한 남자의 응답으로 가장 적절한 것을 고르시오. [3점] 정답률 90%

Man: ______________________________

① Okay. I'll let you know if I find any.
② Right. I have to finish my experiment.
③ No thanks. I already used some earlier.
④ Not really. I don't need any special effects.
⑤ Never mind. I'll take care of it after your show.

15 고득점 ○△× 2017년 3월 교육청(고2) 15번

다음 상황 설명을 듣고, Katie가 Jeff에게 할 말로 가장 적절한 것을 고르시오. [3점] 정답률 69%

Katie: ______________________________

① I hope you get better soon.
② I appreciate your kind offer.
③ I'll visit you tomorrow afternoon.
④ I'll do the presentation myself.
⑤ I finished my presentation with your help.

[16~17] 다음을 듣고, 물음에 답하시오.

16 ○△× 2025년 3월 교육청(고2) 16번

여자가 하는 말의 주제로 가장 적절한 것은? 정답률 85%

① etiquette for using digital devices in museums
② modern technologies transforming museum experiences
③ problems caused by rapid technological changes in museums
④ obstacles in integrating technologies in museum exhibitions
⑤ architectural technologies used in building museums

17 ○△× 2025년 3월 교육청(고2) 17번

언급된 기술이 아닌 것은? 정답률 93%

① virtual reality
② motion tracking
③ 3D animation
④ laser projection
⑤ 3D printing

Dictation

문제 풀이에 중요한 핵심 부분과 듣기에 자주 나오는 표현들에 빈칸 처리를 했습니다. 방송을 잘 듣고, 빈칸에 알맞은 말을 써 넣으세요.

Tip! 잘 들리지 않는 부분이 있을 때에는 정답을 확인 후, 똑같은 속도로 따라 읽기 연습을 해 보세요.

1

W: Good morning, students. This is your principal, Ms. Perez. I have an important announcement about our indoor gym. Since its opening, it has been a popular destination for students who'd like to stay fit. However, the gym has been in use for more than 10 years and most __________ __________ __________ __________ __________. So, our school has decided to __________ __________ __________. This means the gym will be __________ __________ __________ __________ __________. We apologize for any inconvenience this may cause. Please check our school website for updates on the reopening of the gym. Thank you for your understanding.

2

W: Dylan, what are you doing?

M: I'm learning about the history of Rome.

W: Hmm... But you are reading a comic book, aren't you?

M: Yes, it's a comic book about history. It's very helpful.

W: I think __________ __________ __________ __________ __________ would be more helpful.

M: Maybe. But __________ __________ __________ __________ __________ has many good points.

W: Why do you think so?

M: Comic books use pictures to convey information, so you can __________ __________ __________ __________ __________ and remember them for a long time.

W: That makes sense. Anything else?

M: Most importantly, comic books are interesting to read.

W: I see. Then I'll give it a try.

3

W: Hello, Mr. Stevenson. I'm Rachel Adams from *Entertainment Monthly*. Thank you for meeting with me today.

M: Hello, Ms. Adams. It's my pleasure.

W: Congratulations on gaining more than one million subscribers on your work, *The Invisible*. Why do you think __________ __________ __________ __________ __________ __________?

M: I think many people enjoy the comic because my style of drawing really makes the story come alive.

W: I agree. I especially love Jimmy, the character who wants to be a fashion model.

M: Yes, many of my subscribers like him.

W: I heard you'll finish it soon. The readers of our magazine have been asking if you have any plans to __________ __________ __________ __________ __________ __________ or make it into a movie.

M: If there's a chance, I'd love to.

W: You'll have to let our readers __________ __________ __________ __________ __________ if you do.

M: Of course! I hope I can bring you good news soon.

4

M: Look at this photo from our family camping trip last year.

W: I remember that trip. We parked our camping van between the two trees.

M: Right. You guys really loved the camping van.

W: Yes, we did. And you __________ __________ __________ __________ __________ for us.

M: That's right. You guys enjoyed playing board games on that table.

W: Yeah, that was so fun! And do you remember the __________ __________ __________ __________ __________?

M: Yes. I played the guitar and we sang songs together while we sat on the blanket.

W: That star-patterned blanket was our dogs' favorite.

M: __________ __________ __________ __________ __________, Rex and Rover. They look really happy in the picture.

W: Yeah. They started to run around and bark while we were singing. That was so funny.

M: Yeah, that was hilarious! We had such a good time.

5

M: Hey, Sarah, the school's sports day is just a week away. Let's go over our plan for the event.
W: Definitely, Alex. We're doing relays, a tug-of-war, and soccer, right?
M: Yes. I'll __________ __________ __________, including whistles and the ropes.
W: Thanks. Can you also check our stock for soccer balls?
M: Sure. I'll look into it. And, Sarah, I think we need some volunteers to __________ __________ __________ __________ as staff.
W: I already recruited some from the school's sports clubs.
M: Perfect. I think we should make sure they know the basic rules of the games.
W: I agree. Let's have a meeting with the volunteers tomorrow. I'll __________ __________ __________ __________ __________ about the meeting.
M: Good idea. Then, __________ __________ __________ __________ for the games' rules.
W: Deal. Let's make this sports day a success!

7

M: Hi, Emily. How was your family trip last weekend?
W: It was fantastic! Did you have a nice weekend, too?
M: It was fine, but Jenny __________ __________ __________ __________, so she is absent from school today.
W: Oh, what happened to her?
M: She broke her leg at a ski camp.
W: That's too bad. Is she in a hospital now?
M: Yeah, so tomorrow some of her friends and I will visit her after school. Can you join us?
W: I'm afraid I can't. __________ __________ __________ __________ for tomorrow.
M: Are you still learning Taekwondo every afternoon?
W: No, my lessons ended last week. We're having a __________ __________ __________ __________ __________.
M: Oh, I see. You can't miss that.
W: Thanks for understanding. Anyway, I'll give Jenny a call later.

6

W: Honey, we're running out of fine dust masks. Don't we need to order some more?
M: Oh, right. *[Typing sound]* Let's order them on this website. The masks are \$2 each and a pack of 10 masks is \$15.
W: Then it's cheaper to __________ __________ __________ __________. Let's get four packs.
M: Okay. We also need some hand wash, right?
W: Yes. Is there __________ __________ __________ __________ __________?
M: Let me see. *[Pause]* Oh, there is. We can buy three bottles of hand wash for \$10. It was originally \$5 per bottle.
W: That's a good deal. Let's buy three bottles then.
M: All right. Do we need anything else?
W: No, that's all. Oh, hang on. Look here. If we spend more than \$50, we can __________ __________ __________ __________.
M: Great. I'll place the order now with my credit card.

8

M: Maria, what are you watching?
W: I'm watching the __________ __________ __________ __________ __________ __________, *Romance City*.
M: *Romance City*? When does it start?
W: The first episode will be __________ __________ __________ __________.
M: Oh, it's this Saturday!
W: Yes, my favorite actor, Liam Collins, is the main character.
M: Oh, he is? I like him, too.
W: The director is Sam Adams. He also directed *Dreamcatcher*.
M: Really? I loved that drama.
W: You know what? *Romance City* __________ __________ __________ __________ __________ __________ of the same title.
M: Have you read the novel?
W: Of course. I enjoyed it very much.

9

W: Hello, Highland residents. I'm Jenny Walker, the community center manager. We host the Highland Movie Night every month. This event gives you a __________ __________ __________ __________ __________. It is free for all Highland residents. This month, we will show *The Amazing Wizard Harry*. The movie will start at seven p.m. this Saturday. As usual, it'll be held at the Lincoln Library. Due to the limited space, you __________ __________ __________ __________. You can reserve seats on our website until Friday. To keep the library clean, you __________ __________ __________ __________ __________ __________ __________. For more information, feel free to call us. Thank you.

10

M: Honey, why don't we buy a UV toothbrush sanitizer? This online store is __________ __________ __________ __________.

W: That's great. How about choosing one from these five models?

M: Fine. First, we need to __________ __________ __________ __________ __________.

W: For our family, we need four or more slots.

M: Right. Do you think we need one with a built-in battery?

W: Yes. It'd be easier to install.

M: Okay. And I think it's important to keep the brushes dry.

W: I agree. It prevents bacteria from growing on the brushes. We should definitely go with one that has a drying function.

M: That leaves us with these two models.

W: How about __________ __________ __________ __________?

M: Good. Let's order the cheaper one.

11

M: Emily, the __________ __________ __________ __________ __________ __________.

W: When taking care of plants, giving them enough sunlight and water is very important.

M: I think there's enough sunlight. But __________ __________ __________ __________ __________ the plants?

W: (You need to water them once every three days.)

12

W: Mr. Johnson, do you have a minute? I need your opinion on the project I'm doing.

M: I'd love to discuss that with you, but I'm __________ __________ __________ in 10 minutes. Is 10 minutes enough?

W: I'm afraid it'll take longer than that. Shall I __________ __________ __________?

M: (Yes. I'll give you a call when I'm available.)

13

W: Dad, I'm home. Where's Max?

M: He's sleeping in his house. I took him to the vet this morning. He hasn't been eating well lately.

W: What did the vet say?

M: She said there's nothing wrong with him. He just needs more exercise.

W: More exercise? We take him out for a walk regularly.

M: That's true, but we don't walk him every day. The vet said he needs at least an __________ __________ __________ __________ __________.

W: Oh, I didn't know that.

M: I think we should exercise him every day from now on.

W: I agree. What if we all __________ __________ __________ __________?

M: Good idea. Your mom and I will do it on weekdays. You're __________ __________ __________ __________ during the weekdays.

W: (Okay. I'll take him out for a walk on weekends then.)

14

W: Hi, Matt. Have you finished your science club experiment?

M: Yeah, I just __________ __________ __________. How's your magic club's show coming along?

W: It's going well. But I still have one thing left to do.

M: What do you have to do?

W: I need to set up the stage in the hall, but I've __________ __________ __________ __________.

M: What's wrong?

W: I need some dry ice for my performance, but I don't have any.
M: Why do you need dry ice?
W: I need it to create special effects. It's really important.
M: Actually, our science club used dry ice yesterday. There might be __________ __________ __________ __________ __________ __________.
W: Really? Could you go and check? It'd be great if I could use some.
M: (Okay. I'll let you know if I find any.)

15

W: Katie and Jeff have been working on an important presentation. They are __________ __________ __________ __________ __________ together tomorrow afternoon. Unfortunately, this morning, Katie fell down the stairs and broke her leg. She is in the hospital now and has to stay there for at least a week. Now she is very much worried about the presentation. Jeff hears the news and calls Katie to tell her he can __________ __________ __________ __________ about the presentation himself. Katie thinks that she has no other choice and __________ __________ __________ __________.
In this situation, what would Katie most likely say to Jeff?
Katie: (I appreciate your kind offer.)

16~17

W: Hello, students. Have any of you visited a museum recently? If so, you may have noticed some remarkable changes taking place. Today, I'd like to share some __________ __________ __________ __________ __________ __________ __________.
Now, traditional museums are being transformed by modern technologies. The first technology I want to introduce is virtual reality. Museums around the world are adopting virtual reality to change how __________ __________ __________ __________ __________.
For instance, visitors can now explore ancient buildings as if they were real. Another technology being used in museums is 3D animation. This brings historical scenes to life, showing how people lived in the past. Animated displays allow visitors to experience historical events in a more engaging way. Also, laser projection creates dynamic effects on gallery walls. Using this technology, museums can highlight specific artworks and __________ __________ __________ that enhance the viewing experience. Finally, 3D printing has opened up new possibilities for museums. This technology makes it possible to __________ __________ __________ of delicate or rare items that cannot be exposed to the public. These technological innovations are making museum collections more accessible, interactive, and engaging than ever before.

Dictation Answers

1. sports equipment is now outdated / renovate the gym / temporarily closed until further notice
2. reading a general history book / learning history through comic books / understand historical events more easily
3. so many people read your webcomic / publish your work as a book / be the first to know
4. set up that square table / guitar next to the table / Look at our two dogs
5. manage the equipment / assist with the event / give them a phone call / I'll make the handout
6. buy them in packs / any special promotion going on / get a 5-dollar discount
7. had an accident yesterday / I have other plans / birthday party for my mom
8. preview of the new TV drama / aired on March 9th / is based on the best-selling novel
9. chance to enjoy classic movies / should register in advance / are not allowed to bring any food
10. offering a good deal / consider the number of slots / staying under 50 dollars
11. plants you gave me are dying / how often should I water
12. expecting a visitor / come back later
13. hour of exercise every day / take turns doing it / busy with your schoolwork
14. wrapped it up / run into a problem / some left in the storage room
15. supposed to give the presentation / take care of everything / feels grateful toward him

16~17. insights about the changes happening in museums / visitors interact with historical objects / create fascinating environments / display accurate copies

제9회 중급 모의고사

맞은 개수: 2점 문항 ___개, 3점 문항 ___개
알고 푼 문항은 ○, 찍어서 맞힌 문제는 △에 표시하고, △와 ×는 다시 복습하세요.

1번부터 17번까지는 듣고 답하는 문제입니다. 1번부터 15번까지는 한 번만 들려주고, 16번부터 17번까지는 두 번 들려줍니다. 방송을 잘 듣고 답을 하시기 바랍니다.

1 ○△× • 2020년 6월 교육청(고2) 3번

다음을 듣고, 남자가 하는 말의 목적으로 가장 적절한 것을 고르시오. 정답률 91%

① 오디션 개최를 공지하려고
② 뮤지컬 공연을 홍보하려고
③ 과제 제출 방법을 설명하려고
④ 재능 기부 방법을 안내하려고
⑤ 연극 수업 참여를 독려하려고

2 ○△× • 2020년 9월 교육청(고2) 4번

대화를 듣고, 여자의 의견으로 가장 적절한 것을 고르시오. 정답률 90%

① 다양한 신체활동은 어린이의 창의력 신장에 필수적이다.
② 그림 그리기는 어린이의 집중력 향상에 도움이 된다.
③ 그림책을 읽어 주는 것은 자녀의 정서 안정에 좋다.
④ 부모와의 많은 대화는 자녀의 언어발달을 촉진한다.
⑤ 독서는 어린이의 상상력을 키우는 데 효과가 있다.

3 ○△× • 2019년 9월 교육청(고2) 5번

대화를 듣고, 두 사람의 관계를 가장 잘 나타낸 것을 고르시오. 정답률 86%

① 학생 — 사서교사
② 독자 — 소설가
③ 출판사 편집자 — 삽화가
④ 관객 — 무용가
⑤ 시나리오 작가 — 영화감독

4 고득점 ○△× • 2021년 9월 교육청(고2) 4번

대화를 듣고, 그림에서 대화의 내용과 일치하지 않는 것을 고르시오. 정답률 73%

5 ○△× • 2018년 3월 교육청(고2) 7번

대화를 듣고, 여자가 할 일로 가장 적절한 것을 고르시오. 정답률 90%

① 지하철 타기
② 음료 구매하기
③ 영화표 예매하기
④ 관람할 영화 고르기
⑤ 상영관 확인하기

6 ○△× • 2022년 6월 교육청(고2) 6번

대화를 듣고, 여자가 지불할 금액을 고르시오. [3점] 정답률 80%

① $30 ② $35 ③ $40 ④ $45 ⑤ $50

7 ○△× • 2025년 9월 교육청(고2) 7번

대화를 듣고, 여자가 특강에 참석할 수 없는 이유를 고르시오. 정답률 96%

① 발표 자료를 만들어야 해서
② 배구 경기에 참가해야 해서
③ 물리학 과제를 해야 해서
④ 아르바이트가 있어서
⑤ 무릎을 다쳐서

8 ○△× • 2024년 6월 교육청(고2) 8번

대화를 듣고, Noodle Cooking Contest에 관해 언급되지 않은 것을 고르시오. 정답률 76%

① 참가 대상
② 대회 날짜
③ 대회 장소
④ 우승 상금
⑤ 지원 방법

9 ○△× • 2017년 6월 교육청(고2) 11번

ABC Cable Network에 관한 다음 내용을 듣고, 일치하지 않는 것을 고르시오. [3점] 정답률 78%

① 150개 채널을 제공한다.
② 오락, 뉴스, 영화를 즐길 수 있다.
③ 올해 가장 많은 사람들이 시청한 케이블 방송사이다.
④ 신규 고객에게는 모든 채널이 무료이다.
⑤ 구체적인 정보는 웹 사이트에서 안내한다.

10 ○△×
2020년 9월 교육청(고2) 12번

다음 표를 보면서 대화를 듣고, 여자가 구입할 무선 이어폰을 고르시오. 정답률 89%

Wireless Earbuds

	Model	Price	Play Time (from a single charge)	Noise Canceling	Color
①	A	$135	5 hours	×	Silver
②	B	$145	8 hours	×	Silver
③	C	$160	8 hours	○	White
④	D	$180	10 hours	○	Black
⑤	E	$205	10 hours	○	Black

11 ○△×
2020년 3월 교육청(고2) 2번

대화를 듣고, 남자의 마지막 말에 대한 여자의 응답으로 가장 적절한 것을 고르시오. 정답률 79%

① I have no more clothes to donate.
② You can pick them up this afternoon.
③ Let me check if we can accept them.
④ I forgot to separate whites and colors.
⑤ Please bring the receipt to get a refund.

12 ○△×
2025년 3월 교육청(고2) 12번

대화를 듣고, 여자의 마지막 말에 대한 남자의 응답으로 가장 적절한 것을 고르시오. 정답률 80%

① You have to be careful not to lose your locker key.
② You can borrow an extra copy from our school library.
③ You shouldn't have sold your book to a second-hand bookstore.
④ You are allowed to take notes in your science textbook.
⑤ You could have chosen another topic for the project.

13 고득점 ○△×
2023년 6월 교육청(고2) 13번

대화를 듣고, 남자의 마지막 말에 대한 여자의 응답으로 가장 적절한 것을 고르시오. 정답률 73%

Woman: ______________________________

① How kind of her! I was worried that I wouldn't find it.
② Then, I'll tell her it was my fault, not yours.
③ Could you stop by again when it's raining?
④ Thanks for lending me your brand-new umbrella.
⑤ Why don't you ask her what she wants to do next time?

14 ○△×
2024년 3월 교육청(고2) 13번

대화를 듣고, 여자의 마지막 말에 대한 남자의 응답으로 가장 적절한 것을 고르시오. [3점] 정답률 92%

Man: ______________________________

① Don't worry. You can pay with a credit card.
② I see. Then this one is a perfect choice for him.
③ It'll be fine. Your husband can drop by and pick it up.
④ Really? You'd better apply sunscreen before going out.
⑤ Exactly. A product with strong sun protection is better.

15 ○△×
2020년 9월 교육청(고2) 15번

다음 상황 설명을 듣고, Brian이 Jennifer에게 할 말로 가장 적절한 것을 고르시오. 정답률 85%

Brian: ______________________________

① We should work out together more often.
② Don't waste money buying so many tumblers.
③ We'd better drink more water while we exercise.
④ When does the convenience store near the gym close?
⑤ Why don't you get a tumbler and bring it to the gym?

[16~17] 다음을 듣고, 물음에 답하시오.

16 ○△×
2023년 3월 교육청(고2) 16번

남자가 하는 말의 주제로 가장 적절한 것은? 정답률 89%

① reasons national flags have simple designs and colors
② geographical features affecting the national identity
③ common colors and their meanings in national flags
④ most frequently used symbols in national flags
⑤ differences in color preference across cultures

17 ○△×
2023년 3월 교육청(고2) 17번

언급된 색이 <u>아닌</u> 것은? 정답률 95%

① red ② blue ③ white
④ black ⑤ green

Dictation

문제 풀이에 중요한 핵심 부분과 듣기에 자주 나오는 표현들에 빈칸 처리를 했습니다. 방송을 잘 듣고, 빈칸에 알맞은 말을 써 넣으세요.

Tip! 잘 들리지 않는 부분이 있을 때에는 정답을 확인 후, 똑같은 속도로 따라 읽기 연습을 해 보세요.

1

M: Hello, everyone. This is Ted Williams, the drama teacher. As you know, there's a musical in the school festival every year. And the auditions for actors are going to be held soon. Even if you don't think you're talented, that's okay. Most importantly, I'm looking for students with passion. All interested students __________ __________ __________ __________ to me no later than June 23rd. The __________ __________ __________ __________ __________ __________ on June 24th from three to five p.m. in the school auditorium. If you need more information, please check the poster on the bulletin board. I'm looking forward to __________ __________ __________ __________ __________. Thank you.

2

W: Hi, Mike. You look distracted. Is something bothering you?

M: Well, my son's preschool teacher told me he's having trouble focusing while reading and during conversations. I don't know what I should do.

W: Oh, I see. *[Pause]* Maybe drawing classes could help.

M: How could they __________ __________ __________ __________?

W: Children develop their ability to focus as they __________ __________ __________ __________ __________ while drawing.

M: That's reasonable. Is that why your daughter takes drawing classes?

W: Exactly. When my daughter was 8 years old, she had a similar problem to your son.

M: Did you __________ __________ __________ __________ when she started drawing?

W: Sure. She concentrates better on reading and conversations now. It might help your son, too.

M: Okay, I'll look for a class right away.

3

M: Excuse me, are you Anna Zimmerman? I can't believe I'm seeing you here!

W: Oh, hello. Have we met before?

M: No, but I'm a big fan of yours.

W: Thank you. I love meeting my fans.

M: I just __________ __________ __________ __________, *The Beautiful Days*. I read the whole thing in a day.

W: I'm flattered. What did you like most?

M: I really liked the part where Emma and Jason first dance.

W: That's my favorite moment, too. It took me more than two weeks to __________ __________ __________.

M: Wow! It was worth it. It was so beautifully described. I hope this book will be made into a movie.

W: I'm so glad you like it that much.

M: I think you're one of the best novelists in the world. Can I __________ __________ __________, please?

W: Sure.

4

M: Honey, I've finished decorating the living room for Halloween. Can you come here and take a look?

W: Sure. *[Pause]* Is the carpet on the floor the one you ordered last week?

M: Yeah. I chose the round one because it looks cute. What do you think?

W: It looks really good there. I also love the __________ __________ __________ that you put on the wall above the piano.

M: Thanks. I thought it would help create the Halloween mood.

W: It definitely does. *[Pause]* Oh! The __________ __________ __________ __________ __________ __________ are so cool.

M: Totally. The faces we carved into the pumpkins look excellent.

W: Didn't you say you were planning to put flying ghost stickers under the window? Did you change your mind?

M: I did. I think the bat sticker looks better under the window.

W: Good choice. I prefer the bat, too. What's that

__________ __________ __________ __________
__________ for? Is it for trick-or-treating?

M: Right. We can use it when trick-or-treaters visit our house on Halloween.

W: That's a great plan. You did a terrific job decorating the room.

5

[Cell phone rings.]

W: Hello, Brian. Are you coming?

M: Yes, I'm on my way. Are you at the movie theater?

W: Yeah, I'm waiting for you. Where are you?

M: I've just arrived at Lincoln Square Station.

W: Don't rush. We still have 20 minutes before the movie starts.

M: Okay. I'll meet you in front of the box office.

W: __________ __________ __________ __________ __________ on the website, didn't you?

M: I did, but I have to get the tickets from the machine.

W: I see. You can use the one in the lobby.

M: Okay. I will. __________ __________ __________ __________ __________ __________?

W: Sure. __________ __________ __________ at the snack bar.

M: Thanks. I'm almost there.

6

M: Welcome to Sky Cable Car. How may I help you?

W: Hi. I want to buy tickets. I see two types of cable cars. What's the difference between the Regular and the Crystal Cable Car?

M: The Crystal Cable Car has a glass floor, so you can see below you.

W: That must be thrilling! How much is it for an adult?

M: An __________ __________ __________ __________.

W: Is that round-trip?

M: No, this is a one-way ticket. You need to __________ __________ __________ __________ __________ for round-trip tickets.

W: Then I'll buy round-trip tickets for two adults.

M: So round-trip Crystal Cable Car tickets for two adults, right?

W: Yes, and I have a discount coupon for local residents. Can I use it?

M: Let me take a look. *[Pause]* Yes. You can __________ __________ __________ __________ off the total.

W: Very good. Here's my credit card.

7

M: Sarah, have you heard about the special lecture at the community center this Saturday?

W: Yeah, Brian. It's a lecture on how to __________ __________ __________ __________, right?

M: Exactly! It'll help you create impressive presentations. Do you want to sign up for it with me?

W: I'd love to, but I can't attend.

M: Oh. Is it because you have a part-time job on weekends?

W: No. I don't work on weekends anymore.

M: Hmm. Then, do you have to __________ __________ __________ __________ __________?

W: I already finished it. Actually, I'm __________ __________ __________ __________ __________.

M: Really? You told me that you wouldn't play this time, didn't you?

W: __________ __________ __________ for Judy. She injured her knee last week.

M: I see. Good luck!

8

W: Honey, I picked up a flyer about the Noodle Cooking Contest.

M: What is it about?

W: It's a competition to cook the most creative dish using noodles.

M: Sounds interesting. Who can participate?

W: Any city resident can participate. Why don't you give it a try?

M: Let me take a look at the flyer. I should check the date first.

W: Here. It's __________ __________ __________ __________ __________. Are you free then?

M: Luckily, I don't have any plans that day. Maybe I can apply for the contest.

W: You should! The __________ __________ __________ __________.

M: Great! It says I have to __________ __________ __________ __________ __________ to apply for the contest. Any suggestions?

W: Well, do you remember the cold noodle salad you made for my birthday? It was so good. You should use that recipe.

M: That's a great idea. I'll do it.

9

M: Hello, listeners and viewers! Are you tired of only getting a few television channels? Then it's time to switch to ABC Cable Network. With 150 channels, ABC Network is one of the leading cable providers in the country. For a small monthly service fee, you can enjoy __________ __________ __________ __________ __________ __________, local and international news, and a good selection of movies. This year, we were recognized as __________ __________ __________ __________ __________. To celebrate this achievement, new customers can have a one-month free trial for our network channels, __________ __________ __________. If you want more specific information on our service plans, visit our website at www.ABCNet.co.ca.

10

M: Hey, Tiffany. What are you doing?

W: I'm thinking of buying some wireless earbuds. Do you want to help me choose from these five options?

M: Sure. How much can you spend?

W: I don't want to spend more than 200 dollars.

M: These models are __________ __________ __________.

W: What do you think would be a good play time from a single charge?

M: Hmm.... I think it __________ __________ __________ __________ __________ __________ so you don't have to charge them very often.

W: That's a good point. I'll cross out this one. What is noise canceling?

M: It reduces unwanted sound using active noise control.

W: Does that make a big difference?

M: It can really improve the sound quality of what you listen to.

W: I see. Then, I'll __________ __________ __________ __________ __________ __________.

M: Good choice. There are only two models left. Which color do you prefer?

W: I don't want white ones because they'll get dirty too easily. So, I'll buy this model.

11

M: Good afternoon. I'd like to __________ __________ __________ __________ to this charity.

W: Thank you. Are they all in good condition?

M: Yes, but the __________ __________ __________ __________ __________ __________ a bit.

W: (Let me check if we can accept them.)

12

W: I can't find my science textbook anywhere! I really need it now for my science project.

M: That sounds frustrating. Maybe you __________ __________ __________ __________ __________ __________ or in your school locker.

W: I __________ __________ __________ __________, but I couldn't find it. What should I do?

M: (You can borrow an extra copy from our school library.)

13

M: Hello, is there anything I can do for you?

W: My umbrella is missing. I thought I might have left it in the restroom, but when I checked, it wasn't there.

M: Which restroom did you use?

W: The one __________ __________ __________ __________.

M: What does your umbrella look like? Could you describe it?

W: It's yellow and it __________ __________ __________ __________. There's a big picture of a flower on it.

M: Okay, I'll check if it's in the Lost and Found box right now... *[Pause]* Oh! We have an umbrella that looks like yours. Is this it?

W: Wow, that's mine!

M: Wait. Here's a note that says a lady __________ __________ __________ __________ __________ to us.

W: (How kind of her! I was worried that I wouldn't find it.)

14

M: Hello, welcome to Glow Cosmetics Shop. How can I help you?

W: Hi, I'm looking for sunscreen.

M: Certainly. Is it for you, or someone else?

W: It's for my husband. He __________ __________ __________ __________ __________ for him.

M: Okay, does your husband spend much time outdoors, playing sports, or working outside?
W: No, not really. He works in an office and usually stays at home after work.
M: In that case, he might not need one with strong sun protection. A __________ __________ __________ __________ __________ for him.
W: Okay. I'll go with that.
M: We have two types of sunscreen, spray and cream type. Which one would he prefer?
W: I'm not sure but I guess he __________ __________ __________ __________ __________.
M: (I see. Then this one is a perfect choice for him.)

15

W: Brian and Jennifer are good friends who go to the gym together almost every day. When they're working out, they drink a lot of water. Brian always __________ __________ __________ __________ with him while Jennifer always buys a bottle of water at the convenience store before going to the gym. Brian thinks that buying a bottle of water every day is not only a waste of money but is also __________ __________ __________ __________. One day at the gym, Jennifer makes a comment about how much she likes Brian's tumbler. Brian thinks this is a good chance to suggest that she __________ __________ __________ __________ __________ to the gym. In this situation, what would Brian most likely say to Jennifer?
Brian: (Why don't you get a tumbler and bring it to the gym?)

16~17

M: Good afternoon, students. Today we are going to talk about different national flags. There are some __________ __________ __________ __________ __________. The most common color is red, which makes up about 30 percent of all colors used in national flags. Usually red means life, courage, and revolution. For example, the red stripes of the United State's national flag __________ __________ __________ __________ __________. The next is blue, with about a 20 percent share. The color often symbolizes the natural element of water or sky. For example, the blue in Greece's national flag means the seas surrounding the country. The next two most common colors are white and green. In some countries' flags, white means peace and honesty, such as in the United Kingdom's flag. Green is often __________ __________ __________, such as grasslands and forests. Can you guess what the green in Brazil's national flag means? Of course, it's the Amazon Rainforest. Now, let's look at the shapes of national flags.

Dictation Answers

1. should submit an application / auditions are going to be held / seeing you at the auditions
2. help with his concentration / pay attention to small details / notice a big change
3. finished your latest book / write that chapter / get your autograph
4. spider web decoration / two carved pumpkins on the bookshelf / empty basket on the table
5. You bought tickets in advance / Why don't we get some drinks / I'll buy some
6. adult ticket is $20 / pay an additional $5 each / get a $5 discount
7. design effective presentation materials / work on your physics assignment / participating in a volleyball match / I'm filling in
8. on the 20th of June / winner will receive $500 / send a recipe by email
9. a wide variety of entertainment programs / the most watched cable network / excluding movie channels
10. within your budget / should be longer than six hours / go with ones with noise canceling
11. donate these old clothes / colors of some shirts have changed
12. left it in your desk drawer / already checked both places
13. on the third floor / has a wooden handle / found it and brought it
14. asked me to buy one / mild one is probably best / is used to cream type
15. brings his own tumbler / harmful to the environment / bring her own reusable bottle

16~17. colors commonly used in national flags / symbolize the struggle for independence / related to nature

다빈출 코드

영어 듣기

PART 2

고 급
모의고사

X

1 ~ 6회

수능 기출에서 선별한
우수 문항 모의고사

제1회 고급 모의고사

맞은 개수: 2점 문항 ___개, 3점 문항 ___개
알고 푼 문항은 ○, 찍어서 맞힌 문제는 △에 표시하고, △와 ×는 다시 복습하세요.

1번부터 17번까지는 듣고 답하는 문제입니다. 1번부터 15번까지는 한 번만 들려주고, 16번부터 17번까지는 두 번 들려줍니다. 방송을 잘 듣고 답을 하시기 바랍니다.

1 ○△× 2019학년도 수능 3번

다음을 듣고, 남자가 하는 말의 목적으로 가장 적절한 것을 고르시오. 정답률 97%

① 경기 취소를 공지하려고 ② 팬클럽 가입을 권유하려고
③ 경기장 개장을 홍보하려고 ④ 웹 사이트 점검을 안내하려고
⑤ 시상식 일정 변경을 사과하려고

2 ○△× 2023학년도 수능 2번

대화를 듣고, 여자의 의견으로 가장 적절한 것을 고르시오. 정답률 99%

① 사과를 먹으면 장운동이 원활해진다.
② 사과 껍질은 피부 상태 개선에 도움이 된다.
③ 충분한 수면은 건강한 피부 유지에 필수적이다.
④ 사과를 먹기 전에 껍질을 깨끗이 씻어야 한다.
⑤ 주기적인 수분 섭취는 피부 노화를 늦춘다.

3 고득점 ○△× 2024학년도 수능 3번

다음을 듣고, 여자가 하는 말의 요지로 가장 적절한 것을 고르시오. 정답률 89%

① 일정한 실내 온도 유지는 건강에 중요한 역할을 한다.
② 충분한 햇빛 노출은 수면 호르몬 분비를 촉진한다.
③ 정서 안정을 위해서는 양질의 수면이 필요하다.
④ 수면 안대를 착용하면 잠드는 데 도움이 될 수 있다.
⑤ 적당한 밝기의 조명은 일의 능률을 향상시킬 수 있다.

4 ○△× 2022학년도 수능 4번

대화를 듣고, 그림에서 대화의 내용과 일치하지 않는 것을 고르시오. 정답률 98%

5 ○△× 2026학년도 수능 5번

대화를 듣고, 여자가 할 일로 가장 적절한 것을 고르시오. 정답률 87%

① 재료 배송 확인하기 ② 파이 사진 찍기
③ 포크와 접시 준비하기 ④ 제품 목록 완성하기
⑤ 소셜 미디어에 홍보하기

6 ○△× 2025학년도 수능 6번

대화를 듣고, 여자가 지불할 금액을 고르시오. 정답률 93%

① $100 ② $150 ③ $180 ④ $200 ⑤ $220

7 고득점 ○△× 2020학년도 수능 8번

대화를 듣고, 남자가 요리 대회 참가를 포기한 이유를 고르시오. 정답률 84%

① 다친 팔이 낫지 않아서
② 조리법을 완성하지 못해서
③ 다른 대회와 일정이 겹쳐서
④ 입학시험 공부를 해야 해서
⑤ 대회 전에 유학을 떠나야 해서

8 ○△× 2018학년도 수능 10번

대화를 듣고, Winter Discovery Camp에 관해 언급되지 않은 것을 고르시오. 정답률 97%

① 참가 대상 ② 활동 내용 ③ 기간
④ 기념품 ⑤ 참가비

9 ○△× 2021학년도 수능 9번

National Baking Competition에 관한 다음 내용을 듣고, 일치하지 않는 것을 고르시오. 정답률 97%

① 해마다 열리는 행사이다.
② 올해의 주제는 건강한 디저트이다.
③ 20명이 결선에 진출할 것이다.
④ 수상자들의 조리법이 잡지에 실릴 것이다.
⑤ 웹 사이트에서 생중계될 것이다.

10 ○△×
2021학년도 수능 10번

다음 표를 보면서 대화를 듣고, 여자가 주문할 재사용 빨대 세트를 고르시오. 정답률 96%

	Set	Material	Price	Length (inches)	Carrying Case
①	A	Bamboo	$5.99	7	×
②	B	Glass	$6.99	7	○
③	C	Glass	$7.99	8	×
④	D	Silicone	$8.99	8	○
⑤	E	Stainless Steel	$11.99	9	○

11 ○△×
2025학년도 수능 11번

대화를 듣고, 남자의 마지막 말에 대한 여자의 응답으로 가장 적절한 것을 고르시오. [3점] 정답률 93%

① Great idea! Let's ask him to come to the party.
② That's okay. I'll check if I can change the order.
③ I can't believe it! We finally won a tennis match.
④ No thanks. I don't really like cakes with nuts on them.
⑤ No problem. I won't eat foods that cause allergic reactions.

12 고득점 ○△×
2021학년도 수능 11번

대화를 듣고, 여자의 마지막 말에 대한 남자의 응답으로 가장 적절한 것을 고르시오. 정답률 89%

① I see. Then I'll park somewhere else.
② It's all right. I'll bring your car over here.
③ No thanks. I don't want my car to be painted.
④ Never mind. I'll pay the parking fee later.
⑤ Okay. I'll choose another car instead.

13 ○△×
2022학년도 수능 14번

대화를 듣고, 남자의 마지막 말에 대한 여자의 응답으로 가장 적절한 것을 고르시오. 정답률 94%

Woman: ______________________________

① Please check it again. The hotel can't be fully booked.
② Too bad. I should've checked out as early as possible.
③ Sure. I'm very satisfied with your cleaning service.
④ I'm sorry. You can't switch your room with mine.
⑤ Perfect. That's high enough to avoid the smell.

14 ○△×
2017학년도 수능 14번

대화를 듣고, 여자의 마지막 말에 대한 남자의 응답으로 가장 적절한 것을 고르시오. [3점] 정답률 92%

Man: ______________________________

① That's a good idea. I'll get rid of it right away.
② I think it's closed. Turn in the book tomorrow.
③ I hope you're right. I'll check with them.
④ It's too late. The tickets are all sold out.
⑤ Here's the wallet. Take it to the station.

15 고득점 ○△×
2022학년도 수능 15번

다음 상황 설명을 듣고, Jason이 Sarah에게 할 말로 가장 적절한 것을 고르시오. [3점] 정답률 77%

Jason: ______________________________

① Good luck. I hope you finish your work in time.
② Okay. Let's meet to discuss the changes to the sculpture.
③ That's terrible. I'm sorry that the reopening was postponed.
④ Hurry up. You have to send the final design immediately.
⑤ Don't worry. I can get the job done before the deadline.

[16~17] 다음을 듣고, 물음에 답하시오.

16 ○△×
2018학년도 수능 16번

남자가 하는 말의 주제로 가장 적절한 것은? 정답률 95%

① relationship between music and civilization
② materials used to make musical instruments
③ trends in modern art around the world
④ ways to preserve ancient instruments
⑤ use of music for rest and relaxation

17 ○△×
2018학년도 수능 17번

언급된 나라가 아닌 것은? 정답률 97%

① China ② Mongolia ③ Nigeria
④ Australia ⑤ Colombia

Dictation

문제 풀이에 중요한 핵심 부분과 듣기에 자주 나오는 표현들에 빈칸 처리를 했습니다. 방송을 잘 듣고, 빈칸에 알맞은 말을 써 넣으세요.

Tip! 잘 들리지 않는 부분이 있을 때에는 정답을 확인 후, 똑같은 속도로 따라 읽기 연습을 해 보세요.

1

M: Attention, Whittenberg Dragons and Westbrook Whales fans. This is an announcement about today's game at Estana Stadium. Today's baseball game __________ __________ __________ __________ __________ __________ __________. But it started raining one hour ago, and has not stopped. According to the forecast, the weather will only get worse. Because of this, we __________ __________ __________ __________ __________ __________. Tickets you purchased for today's event will be fully refunded. And information about the make-up game __________ __________ __________ __________ __________ __________ soon. Once again, today's game has been canceled due to heavy rain. Thank you for visiting our stadium, and we hope to see you again at our next game.

2

M: Honey, do you want some apples with breakfast?

W: Sounds great. Can you save the apple peels for me?

M: Why? What do you want them for?

W: I'm going to use them to make a face pack. Apple peels are __________ __________ __________ __________ __________.

M: Where did you hear about that?

W: I recently read an article about their __________ __________ __________ __________.

M: Interesting. What's in them?

W: It said apple peels are rich in vitamins and minerals, so they __________ __________ __________ __________ __________ __________ __________.

M: That's good to know.

W: Also, they remove oil from our skin and have a cooling effect.

M: Wow! Then I shouldn't throw them away.

W: Right. Apple peels can help improve our skin condition.

M: I see. I'll save them for you.

3

W: Hello, listeners. This is Dr. Graham's One-minute Health Tips. Getting a good night's sleep is __________ __________ __________ __________. But recently, more and more people are experiencing trouble falling asleep. If that's your case, wearing an eye mask for sleeping can __________ __________ __________ __________. If your room doesn't get dark enough, it'll be difficult to fall asleep. This is because light interferes with the release of the hormone that makes you sleepy. An eye mask __________ __________ __________ __________, which makes it easier for you to fall asleep. Why not try one tonight? I'll be back with more tips next time!

4

M: Wow, Ms. Peters! It looks like everything is ready for the exchange student welcoming ceremony.

W: Almost, Mr. Smith. What do you think?

M: It looks great. There's a basket beside the stairs. What is it for?

W: We're going to put flowers in it for the exchange students.

M: That'll be nice. I like the __________ __________ __________ __________ __________. It makes the table look fancy.

W: Yeah, I'm going to put water bottles there. What do you think about the balloons next to the welcome banner?

M: They really brighten up the stage. Oh, look at the __________ __________ __________ __________. It's cute.

W: Yes. It's the symbol of the exchange students' school.

M: I see. And you __________ __________ __________ __________.

W: It's because there'll be two MCs.

M: Good idea. Everything looks perfect.

5

M: Honey, I'm excited that we're opening our homemade-pie store tomorrow.

W: Me, too. Do you think everything's ready?

M: I do. But let's go over what we've done.

W: Good idea. I __________ __________ __________ __________ for sale. Did you take photos of the pies?

M: I took photos of the walnut, pumpkin, blueberry, and apple pies.

W: Perfect. What about __________ __________ __________ __________ __________?

M: Don't worry. I advertised our pies on social media.

W: I hope it brings in a lot of customers. I also prepared forks and plates for customers on our opening day.

M: One more thing, don't forget to __________ __________ __________ __________ __________ __________ for making more pies.

W: Right. I'll do that this afternoon.

M: Wonderful. See, we're ready for tomorrow.

6

M: Welcome to Camoo Traditional Village. How can I help you?

W: Hi. I'd like to buy admission tickets for my family. Is there a __________ __________ __________ __________?

M: Yes. Regular tickets are $30 each, and senior tickets are $20 each for people over 65 years old.

W: Good. My parents are in their 70s. So I'll take two regular tickets and two senior tickets.

M: Great. Would you also like lunch tickets? We serve traditional local food. __________ __________ __________ __________.

W: I'd love that. Is the lunch ticket cheaper for senior citizens?

M: No. I'm sorry. It's the same price.

W: Ah, okay. I'll __________ __________ __________ __________ __________ __________.

M: Alright. So you want two regular tickets and two senior tickets with four lunch tickets, right?

W: That's right. Here's my credit card.

7

W: Hi, Michael.

M: Hi, Sarah. Did you __________ __________ __________ __________ __________?

W: I did. I've already finished developing a recipe.

M: That's great. Actually, I gave up participating in it.

W: Why? Is your arm still hurt?

M: No, it's fully healed.

W: Is your recipe not ready yet?

M: I already created a unique recipe for the contest.

W: Then, what made you __________ __________ __________ __________?

M: You know I've planned to study abroad. The cooking school in Italy just informed me that I've been accepted. The problem is I have to __________ __________ __________ __________ __________.

W: I'm sorry you'll miss the contest. But it's good for you since you've always wanted to study in Italy.

M: I think so, too. I wish you luck in the contest.

W: Thanks. I'll do my best.

8

M: Honey, I'm looking at the Natural History Museum's website. The museum's going to hold the Winter Discovery Camp.

W: What's it about?

M: It says here that the theme is dinosaurs.

W: That sounds interesting. You know our son Peter loves dinosaurs.

M: He does. The camp is __________ __________ __________ __________, so it's perfect for him.

W: What activities will they do?

M: The camp offers fun, hands-on activities. For example, participants will __________ __________ __________ __________ __________ in sand and then put them together.

W: I'm sure Peter will love the camp. When is it?

M: It'll be __________ __________ __________ __________ __________ __________.

W: That's good. It won't overlap with our family trip. And how much does it cost?

M: The participation fee is $20.

W: That's not bad. I'll ask Peter if he wants to go.

M: Okay.

9

W: Hello, listeners. I'm Carla Jones from the National Baking Association. I'm glad to announce that we're hosting the National Baking Competition on December 20th. It's an annual event aimed to discover people with a __________ __________ __________ __________ __________. This year, the theme of the competition is "healthy desserts." We had the most applicants in the history of this competition, and only 10 participants will __________ __________ __________ __________ __________. The top three will win the grand prize of $10,000 each, and the recipes of the winners will __________ __________ __________ __________. You can enjoy watching the entire competition from home. It'll be __________ __________ __________ __________ __________ starting from 9 a.m. If you're a food lover, you won't want to miss watching this event.

10

M: Hi, Nicole. What are you doing?

W: Hi, Jack. I'm trying to buy a reusable straw set on the Internet. Do you want to see?

M: Sure. *[Pause]* These bamboo ones seem good. They're __________ __________ __________ __________.

W: That's true, but I'm worried they may not dry quickly.

M: Okay. Then let's look at straws made from other materials. How much are you willing to spend on a set of straws?

W: I don't want to spend more than $10.

M: __________ __________. How about length?

W: To use with my tumbler, eight or nine inches should be perfect.

M: Then you're down to these two. A carrying case would be very useful when going out.

W: Good point. I'll __________ __________ __________ and order this set now.

11

M: Jane, __________ __________ __________ __________ __________ for our tennis coach's farewell party next week?

W: Yes, I ordered a walnut cake with pistachio nuts on top. I'll pick it up next Wednesday afternoon from the bakery.

M: Oh, no. I should have told you that he's __________ __________ __________ __________ __________ __________.

W: (That's okay. I'll check if I can change the order.)

12

W: Excuse me, sir. I'm from the management office. You cannot park here because we're __________ __________ __________ __________ __________ __________ of the parking lot.

M: Why? What's going on here?

W: We're going to __________ __________ __________ __________ __________ __________. If there are cars parked here, we cannot start our work.

M: (I see. Then I'll park somewhere else.)

13

[Telephone rings.]

M: Front desk. How may I help you?

W: I'm in Room 201. I specifically booked a non-smoking room, but I __________ __________ __________ __________ __________ __________.

M: We're sorry about that. Let me check that for you. *[Typing sound]* You're Wendy Parker, right?

W: Yes, that's correct.

M: Hmm, the record says we assigned you a non-smoking room.

W: Then why do I smell cigarette smoke here?

M: Well, since your room is close to the ground level, cigarette smoke must have come in from outside. Sorry for the inconvenience. __________ __________ __________ __________ __________ __________?

W: Yes, please. The smell is really bothering me.

M: Let me first check if there are any rooms available.

W: If it's possible, I'd like to __________ __________ __________ __________ __________. Maybe higher than the 5th floor?

M: Okay. *[Typing sound]* Oh, we have one. Room 908 __________ __________ __________ __________ __________ __________.

W: (Perfect. That's high enough to avoid the smell.)

14

M: Alice, why didn't you come to the music festival yesterday?

W: I was busy doing my homework. I wish I could've gone. How was it?

M: It was great! My favorite band signed my ticket.

W: Wow! Can I see it?

M: Sure. It's in my wallet. *[Pause]* Wait! My wallet! __________ __________!

W: Really? Look in your coat pockets. Maybe it's there.

M: It's not here. Oh, no! What should I do?

W: When was the last time you saw your wallet?

M: Umm... I remember __________ __________ __________ __________ __________ __________. Did I leave it there?

W: You should __________ __________ __________ __________ __________ __________ right away.

M: But what if someone already took it?

W: Don't worry. Someone with a good heart might have __________ __________ __________.

M: (I hope you're right. I'll check with them.)

15

W: Jason is a sculptor and Sarah is the head of a local library. A few days ago, Sarah hired Jason to create a sculpture for the library's reopening by the end of next month. This morning, Sarah received the final design of the sculpture from Jason. She likes his design, but it looks quite complicated to her. She's worried __________ __________ __________ __________ __________ __________, so she calls him to express her concern. However, Jason thinks that he __________ __________ __________ __________ __________ __________ since he has worked on these types of sculptures before. So Jason wants to tell Sarah that he can finish it in time and that __________ __________ __________ __________ __________ __________. In this situation, what would Jason most likely say to Sarah?

Jason: (Don't worry. I can get the job done before the deadline.)

16~17

M: Good morning, everyone. Last class, we learned about different kinds of musical instruments around the world. Today, we'll talk about __________ __________ __________ __________ used to make them. One common source of materials is __________ __________ __________ __________. For example, in China, a wing bone from a large bird was made into a flute about 8,000 years ago. Another example of making musical instruments from animals comes from Mongolia. There, people made a stringed instrument __________ __________ __________ around a frame and horsehair for the strings. In another part of the world, people in Nigeria dig out clay from the ground to make a traditional drum. The entire process of __________ __________ __________ __________ takes around a month. Lastly, in Australia, the material of choice is hardwood from local trees. It's made into a type of wind instrument by the native people there. Now let's take a look at some photos, and then we'll discuss them in detail.

Dictation Answers

1. was supposed to begin in twenty minutes / have decided to cancel today's game / will be updated on our website
2. effective for improving skin condition / benefits for our skin / moisturize our skin and enhance skin glow
3. important for your health / help you fall asleep / can block the light
4. striped tablecloth on the table / bear on the flag / set up two microphones
5. completed the product list / uploading information onto social media / confirm the delivery of the ingredients
6. discount for senior citizens / It's $25 per person / buy four lunch tickets as well
7. apply for the cooking contest / give up the contest / leave before the contest begins
8. for elementary school students / look for dinosaur bones hidden / held from January 11 to 13
9. talent and passion for baking / advance to the final round / appear in our magazine / broadcast live on our website
10. made from natural materials / That's reasonable / take your recommendation
11. have you ordered a cake / allergic to all kinds of nuts
12. about to close off this section / paint the walls in this section
13. smell cigarette smoke in my room / Would you like to switch rooms / move to a higher floor / on the 9th floor is available
14. It's gone / having it at the subway station / contact the station's lost and found / turned it in
15. whether he can finish in time / has enough time to make it / she doesn't have to be concerned

16~17. a variety of materials / different parts of animals / using animal skin / making this musical instrument

제2회 고급 모의고사

맞은 개수: 2점 문항 ___개, 3점 문항 ___개
알고 푼 문항은 ○, 찍어서 맞힌 문제는 △에 표시하고,
△와 ×는 다시 복습하세요.

1번부터 17번까지는 듣고 답하는 문제입니다. 1번부터 15번까지는 한 번만 들려주고, 16번부터 17번까지는 두 번 들려줍니다. 방송을 잘 듣고 답을 하시기 바랍니다.

1 ○△× • 2025학년도 수능 1번

다음을 듣고, 여자가 하는 말의 목적으로 가장 적절한 것을 고르시오. 정답률 95%

① 학교 종소리 교체 계획을 알리려고
② 학교 수업 시간 단축을 공지하려고
③ 등교 시간 변경을 안내하려고
④ 학부모 상담 신청서 제출을 독려하려고
⑤ 학교 행사 후 교실 정리 정돈을 당부하려고

2 ○△× • 2017학년도 수능 4번

대화를 듣고, 남자의 의견으로 가장 적절한 것을 고르시오. 정답률 95%

① 효과적인 독서를 위해서 집중력을 길러야 한다.
② 학습자의 수준에 맞는 영어 도서를 선택해야 한다.
③ 도전 욕구를 불러일으키는 과제는 학습 동기를 높인다.
④ 학습자의 흥미를 고려한 영어 읽기 자료를 개발해야 한다.
⑤ 사전을 활용한 어휘 학습은 영어 읽기 능력 향상에 도움이 된다.

3 ○△× • 2018학년도 수능 5번

대화를 듣고, 두 사람의 관계를 가장 잘 나타낸 것을 고르시오. 정답률 97%

① 시민 — 경찰관
② 환자 — 간호사
③ 학생 — 소방관
④ 고객 — 차량 정비사
⑤ 학부모 — 영양사

4 ○△× • 2021학년도 수능 4번

대화를 듣고, 그림에서 대화의 내용과 일치하지 않는 것을 고르시오. 정답률 97%

5 ○△× • 2025학년도 수능 5번

대화를 듣고, 남자가 할 일로 가장 적절한 것을 고르시오. 정답률 92%

① 트로피 가져오기
② 사진 출력하기
③ 이메일 확인하기
④ 스티커 주문하기
⑤ 게시판 사용 허락받기

6 ○△× • 2024학년도 수능 6번

대화를 듣고, 남자가 지불할 금액을 고르시오. [3점] 정답률 96%

① $63 ② $70 ③ $72 ④ $78 ⑤ $80

7 ○△× • 2021학년도 수능 7번

대화를 듣고, 남자가 텐트를 반품하려는 이유를 고르시오. 정답률 98%

① 크기가 작아서
② 캠핑이 취소되어서
③ 운반하기 무거워서
④ 설치 방법이 어려워서
⑤ 더 저렴한 제품을 찾아서

8 ○△× • 2020학년도 수능 10번

대화를 듣고, Ten Year Class Reunion Party에 관해 언급되지 않은 것을 고르시오. 정답률 91%

① 장소 ② 날짜 ③ 회비
④ 음식 ⑤ 기념품

9 ○△× • 2019학년도 수능 11번

2018 Upcycling Workshop에 관한 다음 내용을 듣고, 일치하지 않는 것을 고르시오. 정답률 97%

① 3일간 진행될 것이다.
② 세미나실에서 열릴 것이다.
③ 패션 디자이너가 가르칠 것이다.
④ 모든 재료가 제공된다.
⑤ 참가 연령에 제한이 없다.

10 ○△× • 2018학년도 수능 12번

다음 표를 보면서 대화를 듣고, 여자가 구입할 재킷을 고르시오. 정답률 95%

Blackhills Hiking Jackets

	Model	Price	Pockets	Waterproof	Color
①	A	$40	3	×	brown
②	B	$55	4	○	blue
③	C	$65	5	○	yellow
④	D	$70	6	×	gray
⑤	E	$85	6	○	black

11 ○△× • 2024학년도 수능 12번

대화를 듣고, 남자의 마지막 말에 대한 여자의 응답으로 가장 적절한 것을 고르시오. 정답률 85%

① That's too bad. I was looking forward to seeing you there.
② Thank you. I'm so glad you could make it to the party.
③ That's okay. The birthday party has already finished.
④ Sure. I'll arrange the business trip for you and your team.
⑤ Don't worry. My boss will return from the trip this Monday.

12 고득점 ○△× • 2024학년도 수능 11번

대화를 듣고, 여자의 마지막 말에 대한 남자의 응답으로 가장 적절한 것을 고르시오. 정답률 69%

① Right. We should've watched them.
② Why not? Just put the mat on the shelf.
③ Great. We can store some snacks at home.
④ I'm sorry. I can't find the parking lot.
⑤ No problem. I'll take care of it.

13 ○△× • 2023학년도 수능 13번

대화를 듣고, 남자의 마지막 말에 대한 여자의 응답으로 가장 적절한 것을 고르시오. [3점] 정답률 80%

Woman: ________________________________

① Not really. It's better to speak in simple sentences.
② Yes. Try to memorize words by learning the root words.
③ That's right. I'm glad you've studied the proper examples.
④ Exactly. That way you can use the proper words in context.
⑤ I don't think so. Always use an Italian-to-Italian dictionary.

14 ○△× • 2020학년도 수능 13번

대화를 듣고, 여자의 마지막 말에 대한 남자의 응답으로 가장 적절한 것을 고르시오. 정답률 95%

Man: ________________________________

① It's worthwhile to spend money on my suit.
② It would be awesome to borrow your brother's.
③ Your brother will have a fun time at the festival.
④ I'm looking forward to seeing you in a new suit.
⑤ You're going to build a great reputation as an MC.

15 고득점 ○△× • 2025학년도 수능 15번

다음 상황 설명을 듣고, Sophia가 Jack에게 할 말로 가장 적절한 것을 고르시오. [3점] 정답률 52%

Sophia: ________________________________

① I think it'll be better to stick to your plan.
② Let's head out for the concert far in advance.
③ We can ask for a seat change so we can sit together.
④ Don't you think we need to rehearse one more time?
⑤ How about leaving the concert early to avoid traffic?

[16~17] 다음을 듣고, 물음에 답하시오.

16 ○△× • 2022학년도 수능 16번

남자가 하는 말의 주제로 가장 적절한 것은? 정답률 90%

① effects of incorporating painting into math education
② mathematical analysis of the art industry's growth
③ application of mathematics in different types of art
④ historical review of important concepts in the arts
⑤ challenges of harmonizing mathematics and art

17 ○△× • 2022학년도 수능 17번

언급된 예술 분야가 아닌 것은? 정답률 98%

① music ② painting ③ photography
④ dance ⑤ cinema

Dictation

문제 풀이에 중요한 핵심 부분과 듣기에 자주 나오는 표현들에 빈칸 처리를 했습니다. 방송을 잘 듣고, 빈칸에 알맞은 말을 써 넣으세요.

Tip! 잘 들리지 않는 부분이 있을 때에는 정답을 확인 후, 똑같은 속도로 따라 읽기 연습을 해 보세요.

1

W: Good morning, students. This is your vice principal, Ms. Morris. I want to inform you that __________ __________ __________ __________ __________ __________ from 50 minutes to 40 minutes next Tuesday. Due to the parent-teacher conferences that will be held on that day, school will end __________ __________ __________ __________ __________. You'll still take the same classes that you normally would on that day. The starting and ending bells will ring according to the reduced class time schedule. Once again, please keep in mind that next Tuesday's class periods __________ __________ __________ __________ __________ __________ each. Thank you.

2

M: Ji-na, what are you reading?

W: Hi, Mr. Brown. It's an English book titled *The Global Economy*.

M: That sounds difficult.

W: It is. I spend so much time __________ __________ __________ __________ in the dictionary.

M: Hmm. You should __________ __________ __________ __________ __________ __________. You'll be able to read faster without distractions.

W: That makes sense. But I thought I would learn English better if I read difficult things.

M: Well, when learners read English books that are too hard, they __________ __________ and give up their studies easily.

W: So, do you mean I need to read something that's not so hard?

M: Yes. Reading at an appropriate level is more enjoyable and __________ __________ __________ __________ __________.

W: I see what you mean.

M: Why don't you drop by the library and choose an English book that's appropriate for your level?

W: I think that's a good idea. Thank you, Mr. Brown.

3

W: Mr. Thomson. Thank you for your demonstration. I learned a lot today.

M: Glad to hear that. Everyone should know what to do in emergencies.

W: Right. Can I ask you some questions? I'm thinking of getting a job in your field after graduation.

M: Sure. Go ahead.

W: __________ __________ __________ __________ __________ __________. But what other things do you do?

M: One thing we do is search for and __________ __________ __________ __________ __________ like floods.

W: Wonderful. I'd love to learn more.

M: Well, we provide a __________ __________ __________ __________ __________ __________ on weekday afternoons at our fire station.

W: Really? I think I have time after school. What would I do there?

M: You'll practice how to use various equipment for extinguishing fires. You can also check out the fire trucks.

W: Sounds great. __________ __________ __________ __________ __________?

M: Your teacher has some pamphlets, so you can ask her.

4

W: Wow, Sam. You turned the student council room into a hot chocolate booth.

M: Yes, Ms. Thompson. We're ready to sell hot chocolate to raise money for children in need.

W: Excellent. What are you going to put on the __________ __________ __________ __________ __________?

M: I'll post information letting people know where the profits will go.

W: Good. I like the banner on the wall.

M: Thanks. I designed it myself.

W: Awesome. Oh, I'm glad you put my stripe-patterned tablecloth on the table.

M: Thanks for letting us use it. Did you notice the snowman drawing that's __________ __________ __________ __________?

W: Yeah. I remember it was drawn by the child you helped last year. By the way, there are __________ __________ __________ __________ __________. What are they for?

M: We're going to fill those up with donations of toys and books.

W: Sounds great. Good luck.

5

W: Hey, Brian. The Playful Cat Photo Contest is only two days away.

M: That's right, Lisa. Many students are excited about our club's contest.

W: Yeah. Let's check the preparations we've done so far.

M: Alright. I checked our email and confirmed that all the __________ __________ __________ __________ __________.

W: Great. I'll print them out tomorrow.

M: Okay. What about the bulletin board in the school lobby? We'll need it to post the photos on.

W: Don't worry. I already __________ __________ __________ __________ __________. Have you ordered stickers yet?

M: Yes, I ordered enough for everyone to use when voting for their favorite photos.

W: Good. What about the trophy for the winner?

M: It's at my house. __________ __________ __________ __________.

W: Thanks. I think we're all set.

6

W: Welcome to Jamie's Gift Shop! What can I do for you?

M: Hi. I need to get Christmas gifts for my friends. Is there anything you can recommend?

W: Sure. How about this photo tumbler? You can __________ __________ __________ of your friends into the tumbler to decorate it.

M: Ooh, my friends will love it. How much is it?

W: It's $30.

M: It __________ __________ __________ __________, but I like it. I'll take two of them.

W: Okay. Anything else?

M: These Christmas key chains look cute. Oh, they're $5 each.

W: Yes. __________ __________ __________ __________ __________.

M: Are they? I'll take four then. I think that's all.

W: So, that's two tumblers and four key chains.

M: That's right.

W: And you __________ __________ __________ __________ __________ __________ for our Christmas promotion.

M: Great. Here's my credit card.

7

W: Honey, I'm home.

M: How was your day?

W: Alright. Hey, did you order something? There's a large box outside the door.

M: It's the tent we bought online for our camping trip. I'm returning it.

W: Is it because of the size? I remember you said it might be a little small to fit all of us.

M: Actually, when I set up the tent, it seemed __________ __________ __________ __________ __________ __________.

W: Then, did you find a cheaper one on another website?

M: No, __________ __________ __________ __________ __________.

W: Then, why are you returning the tent?

M: It's __________ __________ __________ __________ __________. We usually have to walk a bit to get to the campsite.

W: I see. Is someone coming to pick up the box?

M: Yes. I already scheduled a pickup.

8

W: Hi, Ross. How's everything going for our Ten Year Class Reunion Party?

M: I think we're done, Jennifer.

W: Then let's go over what we've prepared.

M: I already booked the Silver Corral Restaurant for the party.

W: Good. It must have been very difficult to get a reservation because our party is __________ __________ __________.

M: Yeah, we were lucky.

W: __________ __________ __________ __________ __________?

M: Their steak, spaghetti, and pizza are famous, so that's what I ordered.

W: Sounds delicious. And the __________ __________ __________ __________ __________ __________, too.

M: You ordered mugs for souvenirs, right?

W: Yes, I did. I'll bring them that day.

M: Perfect. It's going to be a great party.

9

W: Attention, please. I'm Jenny Stone, the manager of the community center. I'm going to tell you about the 2018 Upcycling Workshop. Upcycling is creative reuse. It gives new life to old objects. The workshop __________ __________ __________ __________, from November 23rd to 25th. It'll run from 1 to 4 p.m. The workshop will be held in the seminar room. And we have a special treat this time. The famous fashion designer, Elizabeth Thompson, will teach you in the workshop. You'll __________ __________ __________ __________ from her. For example, you'll remake plastic bags into rugs and old shirts into hats. All materials are provided. And there's no participation fee. The workshop is __________ __________ __________ __________ __________ __________. We're looking forward to seeing you.

10

M: Alice, Blackhills Hiking Jackets is having a big sale this weekend.

W: Nice. I need a jacket for the hiking trip next week, Jason.

M: Here. Have a look at their online catalog.

W: Wow! They all look nice. But I __________ __________ __________ __________ __________ __________ __________.

M: Then you should choose from these four. How many pockets do you want?

W: The more the better. __________ __________ __________ __________ __________.

M: Does it need to be waterproof?

W: Of course. It's really important because it often rains in the mountains.

M: Then there're two options left.

W: I like this yellow one.

M: It looks nice, but __________ __________ __________ __________ __________.

W: That's true. Then I'll buy the other one.

M: I think that's a good choice.

11

M: Hey, Tina. I have something to tell you about your birthday party this Saturday.

W: Oh, Clark. You're coming, right? I'd really love it __________ __________ __________ __________. All our friends will be there.

M: I'm afraid __________ __________ __________ __________ this time. I have to go on a business trip with my boss this weekend.

W: (That's too bad. I was looking forward to seeing you there.)

12

W: Dad, we should leave soon to watch the fireworks in the park. Shall we bring something to eat?

M: Yeah, we might get hungry. Oh, we also need the picnic mat to sit on. I think I __________ __________ __________ __________ __________ __________ __________ in the storage room, but I'm not sure.

W: Then, could you __________ __________ __________ while I pack some snacks and soft drinks?

M: (No problem. I'll take care of it.)

13

M: Can I come in, Professor Rossini?

W: Of course. Come on in, Ben. What brings you here?

M: I __________ __________ __________ __________ __________ on studying Italian.

W: Is there anything specific you're having trouble with?

M: Yes. I'm __________ __________ __________ __________ __________. Could I get some tips?

W: Sure. First, let me ask how you use your dictionary.

M: Well, I use it to look up words that I don't know the meanings of.

W: Dictionaries provide example sentences for most words. Do you read them, too?

M: No, __________ __________ __________ __________ __________ the example sentences.

W: Knowing the meaning of words is important, but you should also understand the context in which the words are properly used.

M: I see. So you're suggesting that I __________ __________ __________ __________ __________ __________, right?

W: (Exactly. That way you can use the proper words in context.)

14

W: Hi, Justin. I heard you're going to be the MC at the school festival.

M: Yes, I am, Cindy.

W: Do you have everything ready?

M: Mostly. I __________ __________ __________ __________ __________ and I've practiced a lot.

W: I'm sure you'll do a great job.

M: I hope so, too. But there's one thing I'm worried about.

W: What is it?

M: I need a suit, so I'm thinking of buying one. But it's expensive, and I don't think I'll wear it after the festival.

W: Well, if you want, I can ask my older brother to __________ __________ __________ __________ __________ __________. He has a lot of them.

M: Could you please?

W: I'd be happy to.

M: Thanks. But will __________ __________ __________ __________ __________?

W: It will. You and my brother pretty much have the same build.

M: (It would be awesome to borrow your brother's.)

15

M: Sophia and Jack are sister and brother. They're going to their favorite singer's concert tonight. The concert starts at 7 p.m., and since it takes an hour to get to the concert, Jack __________ __________ __________ __________ __________ __________ at 6 p.m. While this is Jack's first time going to a concert, Sophia has been to several concerts. She knows that even after they arrive at the concert site, it takes a long time to __________ __________ __________ __________ __________ and get to their seats. Also, she wants to take pictures and __________ __________ __________ __________ __________ before the concert. So, Sophia wants to suggest to Jack that they should __________ __________ __________ __________ __________ __________ than he proposed. In this situation, what would Sophia most likely say to Jack?

Sophia: (Let's head out for the concert far in advance.)

16~17

M: Good morning, students. You might think that math is all about boring formulas, but actually it involves much more. Today, we'll learn __________ __________ __________ __________ __________ __________. First, let's take music. Early mathematicians found that dividing or multiplying sound frequencies created different musical notes. Many __________ __________ __________ __________ __________ __________ to make harmonized sounds. Second, painting frequently uses math concepts, particularly the "Golden Ratio." Using this, great painters created masterpieces that display accurate proportions. The *Mona Lisa* is __________ __________ __________ __________ __________. Photography is another example of using mathematical ideas. Photographers divide their frames into 3 by 3 sections and place their subjects along the lines. By doing so, the photo becomes balanced, thus more pleasing. Lastly, dance __________ __________ __________ __________ __________ on the stage. In ballet, dancers calculate distances between themselves and other dancers, and adjust to the size of the stage. This gives the impression of harmonious movement. I hope you've gained a new perspective on mathematics.

Dictation Answers

1. each class period will be reduced / one hour earlier than usual / will be shortened by 10 minutes
2. looking up new words / choose a more level-appropriate English book / get exhausted / motivates learners to keep going
3. Fighting fires is your main duty / rescue people during natural disasters / job experience program for high schoolers / How do I sign up
4. bulletin board under the clock / hanging on the tree / three boxes on the floor
5. participants had submitted their photos / got permission to use it / I'll bring it tomorrow
6. insert a picture / seems a bit pricey / They're only available this month / get 10% off the total cost
7. big enough to hold us all / price is not the issue / too heavy to carry around
8. on December 24th / What food will they serve / souvenirs for the party are ready
9. will last three days / learn many upcycling methods / open to people 18 and older
10. don't want to spend more than $80 / Three pockets are not enough / yellow can get dirty easily
11. if you could come / I can't make it
12. put it on one of the shelves / find the mat
13. came to ask for advice / experiencing difficulty using words properly / I don't pay attention to / study the example sentences as well
14. have all the introductions ready / lend you one of his suits / his suit be my size
15. proposes that they leave their house / go through the security line / stop by the gift shops / leave for the concert much earlier

16~17. how mathematics is used in the arts / musicians started applying this mathematical concept / well-known for its accurate proportionality / applies mathematics to position dancers

제3회 고급 모의고사

맞은 개수: 2점 문항 ___개, 3점 문항 ___개
알고 푼 문항은 ○, 찍어서 맞힌 문제는 △에 표시하고, △와 ×는 다시 복습하세요.

1번부터 17번까지는 듣고 답하는 문제입니다. 1번부터 15번까지는 한 번만 들려주고, 16번부터 17번까지는 두 번 들려줍니다. 방송을 잘 듣고 답을 하시기 바랍니다.

1 ○|△|× • 2024학년도 수능 1번

다음을 듣고, 여자가 하는 말의 목적으로 가장 적절한 것을 고르시오. 정답률 97%

① 축구 경기장 사용 수칙을 설명하려고
② 지역 아동 병원의 개원을 홍보하려고
③ 자선 축구 경기의 변경된 일정을 공지하려고
④ 축구 경기 티켓의 구매 사이트를 소개하려고
⑤ 자선 축구 경기 자원봉사자 모집을 안내하려고

2 ○|△|× • 2018학년도 수능 4번

대화를 듣고, 남자의 의견으로 가장 적절한 것을 고르시오. 정답률 95%

① 운동과 숙면은 밀접한 관계가 있다.
② 시골 생활은 건강한 삶에 도움이 된다.
③ 규칙적인 식습관은 장수의 필수 조건이다.
④ 야외 활동은 스트레스 해소에 효과적이다.
⑤ 가정의 화목은 가족 간의 대화에서 시작된다.

3 ○|△|× • 2022학년도 수능 3번

대화를 듣고, 두 사람의 관계를 가장 잘 나타낸 것을 고르시오. 정답률 97%

① 라디오 쇼 진행자 — 제빵사
② 리포터 — 과수원 주인
③ 광고주 — 요리사
④ 방송 작가 — 경제학자
⑤ 유통업자 — 농부

4 ○|△|× • 2017학년도 수능 6번

대화를 듣고, 그림에서 대화의 내용과 일치하지 않는 것을 고르시오. 정답률 97%

5 ○|△|× • 2022학년도 수능 5번

대화를 듣고, 남자가 할 일로 가장 적절한 것을 고르시오. 정답률 98%

① 리본 가져오기
② 선글라스 주문하기
③ 사진사 섭외하기
④ 설문 조사 실시하기
⑤ 졸업 연설문 작성하기

6 고득점 ○|△|× • 2020학년도 수능 9번

대화를 듣고, 여자가 지불할 금액을 고르시오. [3점] 정답률 85%

① $72 ② $74 ③ $76 ④ $78 ⑤ $80

7 ○|△|× • 2026학년도 수능 7번

대화를 듣고, 여자가 Morning Tea Club에 참석할 수 없는 이유를 고르시오. 정답률 98%

① 비즈니스 미팅이 있어서
② 아침 식사를 해야 해서
③ 차를 가져오지 않아서
④ 과도한 업무로 피곤해서
⑤ 의사가 차를 마시지 말라고 해서

8 ○|△|× • 2025학년도 수능 8번

대화를 듣고, Outstanding Octopuses 행사에 관해 언급되지 않은 것을 고르시오. 정답률 98%

① 목적
② 프로그램
③ 후원 기관
④ 입장료
⑤ 기간

9 ○|△|× • 2018학년도 수능 11번

Global Design Conference에 관한 다음 내용을 듣고, 일치하지 않는 것을 고르시오. 정답률 96%

① Chicago에서 매년 개최된다.
② 유명 디자이너들의 강연이 있을 것이다.
③ 100명의 디자이너가 제작한 작품들이 전시될 것이다.
④ 6월 20일에 시작한다.
⑤ 등록비는 환불이 가능하다.

10 ○△× • 2025학년도 수능 10번

다음 표를 보면서 대화를 듣고, 여자가 구입할 식물 씨앗 키트를 고르시오. 정답률 93%

Plant Seed Kits

	Kit	Price	Plant Varieties	Pot Material	Plant Growing Guide
①	A	$40	3	Plastic	×
②	B	$45	4	Wood	○
③	C	$45	5	Metal	×
④	D	$50	5	Ceramic	○
⑤	E	$60	6	Glass	○

11 ○△× • 2018학년도 수능 1번

대화를 듣고, 여자의 마지막 말에 대한 남자의 응답으로 가장 적절한 것을 고르시오. 정답률 97%

① Not yet. I forgot to send it.
② Of course. You can have it.
③ Sorry. We're sold out of pictures.
④ Right. You shouldn't buy a book.
⑤ No, thanks. I don't want an album.

12 ○△× • 2019학년도 수능 1번

대화를 듣고, 남자의 마지막 말에 대한 여자의 응답으로 가장 적절한 것을 고르시오. 정답률 93%

① No. You can't study with us.
② Okay. I'll do the report by myself.
③ Sure. I'll call you when I'm done.
④ Yes. I'm pleased to join your team.
⑤ Sorry. You have to finish by tomorrow.

13 고득점 ○△× • 2021학년도 수능 14번

대화를 듣고, 여자의 마지막 말에 대한 남자의 응답으로 가장 적절한 것을 고르시오. [3점] 정답률 79%

Man: ______________________________

① Don't worry. I already found his briefcase.
② Of course. You deserve to receive the award.
③ Don't mention it. I just did my duty as a citizen.
④ Definitely. I want to go to congratulate him myself.
⑤ Wonderful. It was the best ceremony I've ever been to.

14 ○△× • 2019학년도 수능 14번

대화를 듣고, 남자의 마지막 말에 대한 여자의 응답으로 가장 적절한 것을 고르시오. 정답률 94%

Woman: ______________________________

① I agree. The actors performed well in the musical.
② You're right. Let's wait for the reviews of the musical.
③ Good. Now, we should rewrite the script of the musical.
④ Great. I need a new musical instrument for our performance.
⑤ Thanks. Then, I'll read the novel before I watch the musical.

15 고득점 ○△× • 2024학년도 수능 15번

다음 상황 설명을 듣고, Jake가 Yuna에게 할 말로 가장 적절한 것을 고르시오. [3점] 정답률 87%

Jake: ______________________________

① Could you please take my picture again with the rock in it?
② I'd appreciate it if you could come to the mountain with me.
③ You shouldn't take any photos while climbing the rock.
④ I'm wondering if you can pose in front of the rock.
⑤ Why don't you take a selfie in the national park?

[16~17] 다음을 듣고, 물음에 답하시오.

16 ○△× • 2020학년도 수능 16번

남자가 하는 말의 주제로 가장 적절한 것은? 정답률 92%

① animals used in delivering mail in history
② difficulty of training animals from the wild
③ animals' adaptation to environmental changes
④ endangered animals in different countries
⑤ ways animals sent each other messages

17 ○△× • 2020학년도 수능 17번

언급된 동물이 아닌 것은? 정답률 94%

① horses ② pigeons ③ eagles
④ dogs ⑤ camels

고급 3회

Dictation

문제 풀이에 중요한 핵심 부분과 듣기에 자주 나오는 표현들에 빈칸 처리를 했습니다. 방송을 잘 듣고, 빈칸에 알맞은 말을 써 넣으세요.

Tip! 잘 들리지 않는 부분이 있을 때에는 정답을 확인 후, 똑같은 속도로 따라 읽기 연습을 해 보세요.

1

W: Hello, Timberglade High School students. This is your P.E. teacher, Ms. Larsen. I'd like to announce that we're looking for volunteers to __________ __________ __________ __________ __________ __________ next month. As you know, our best players will compete against our graduates at Ebanwood Stadium. Volunteers will __________ __________ __________ __________ __________ __________ and tidy up after the match. All the money from the ticket sales will get donated to the local children's hospital. This will be a great opportunity to __________ __________ __________ __________ __________. Please don't hesitate to apply for this volunteer work at our charity soccer match. For more information, you can check the school website. Thank you.

2

M: Honey, I heard the Smith family moved out to the countryside. I really envy them.

W: Really? Why is that?

M: I think we can __________ __________ __________ __________ __________ __________ __________ __________.

W: Hmm, can you be more specific?

M: Here in the city the air is polluted, but it's cleaner in the country.

W: That makes sense because there're fewer cars.

M: Right. And it's __________ __________ __________ __________ __________, too. We'll be less stressed.

W: I guess we could also sleep better since there isn't constant noise at night.

M: Plus, we can even __________ __________ __________ __________ __________ __________.

W: That'd be nice. We can have a healthier diet.

M: Definitely. I'm sure country living will help us enjoy a healthy life.

W: I agree.

3

W: Hello, Mr. Newton. Welcome to the *Delicacies Show*.

M: Thanks for inviting me.

W: I want to first start talking about your famous apple bread. Can you briefly introduce it __________ __________ __________ __________ __________?

M: Sure. Instead of sugar, I use home-made apple sauce when I bake bread.

W: That's interesting. What __________ __________ __________?

M: Well, one day, I saw a news report about local apple farmers. They were experiencing difficulty due to decreasing apple consumption.

W: So you created this new recipe to __________ __________ __________ __________.

M: Yes. I also thought that the apple's sweetness could add a special flavor.

W: Sounds delicious. I'll __________ __________ __________ __________ __________ and try some of your bread.

M: Actually, I brought some for you and your radio show staff.

W: Oh, thank you. We'll be back after a commercial break.

4

M: Hello, Ms. Miller. I'm Joshua's father.

W: Hi, Mr. Smith. Thanks for coming to our parent-teacher meeting.

M: It's nice to meet you. This room looks great. Wow! Look at the wall.

W: You know, Joshua loves the elephant between the lion and the panda.

M: Does he like the __________ __________ __________ __________ __________, too?

W: He does. The children made it together.

M: They did a wonderful job. That toy dinosaur next to the bookshelf looks good.

W: Oh, I put it there because the children have been learning about dinosaurs.

M: That sounds fun. There are __________ __________ __________ __________ __________ __________. What are they for?

W: They're presents for the class. We've got some candies for the kids.

M: Aha. The Christmas tree is decorated so nicely. The __________ __________ __________ __________ __________ __________ looks very pretty.

W: Thanks. The meeting will start soon. Let's go upstairs, Mr. Smith.

5

W: Brian. I'm so excited about our school club photo this Friday.

M: Me, too. The photo will be included in our graduation album. Let's check our preparations for it.

W: All right. I'm going to decorate our club's room with ribbons.

M: You said you'll bring some from home, right?

W: Yes. When is the photographer coming?

M: The photographer is coming after lunch.

W: Great. That gives us time to get ready. You know I surveyed our club members about what to wear for the photo.

M: Right. What were the results?

W: Most of our members __________ __________ __________ __________ __________. Now all that's left is to buy them for our members.

M: I know a good online store. __________ __________ __________ __________ __________.

W: Could you? That'll be great.

M: No problem. __________ __________ __________ __________ __________.

6

M: Welcome to the Science and Technology Museum. How can I help you?

W: Hi. I want to buy admission tickets.

M: Okay. They're __________ __________ __________ and __________ __________ __________.

W: Good. Two adult tickets and two child tickets, please. And I'm a member of the National Robot Club. Do I get a discount?

M: Yes. You get 10 percent off __________ __________ __________ __________ __________ with your membership.

W: Excellent.

M: We also have the AI Robot program. You can play games with the robots and take pictures with them.

W: That sounds interesting. How much is it?

M: It's just $5 per person. But the membership discount __________ __________ __________ __________ __________ __________.

W: Okay. I'll take four tickets.

M: So two adult and two child admission tickets, and four AI Robot program tickets, right?

W: Yes. Here are my credit card and membership card.

7

M: Good morning, Ms. Lee. Are you heading to Morning Tea Club?

W: Not today, Mr. Thomson. I can't attend it this time.

M: Really? But you enjoy starting the workday by drinking tea with co-workers. Did you __________ __________ __________ __________ __________?

W: No, I always keep it in my bag.

M: Are you just too tired this morning because you worked late last night?

W: Not at all. I feel fine, just like usual.

M: Then, has your doctor told you __________ __________ __________ __________ __________ __________?

W: No, my doctor actually encourages me to drink tea. He says it's good for my health.

M: Oh, I see. Something else must have come up then.

W: Yes. I have an early __________ __________ __________ __________ __________ __________ __________ __________.

M: That's too bad. I hope your meeting goes well.

8

M: Honey, did you hear that the local aquarium is holding an event called Outstanding Octopuses?

W: Outstanding Octopuses? What's it for?

M: The purpose of the event is to promote World Octopus Day.

W: Sounds interesting. What programs does the event have?

M: There are several programs. They __________ __________ __________ __________ from the Pacific Ocean and showing a documentary about how to protect them.

W: Really? Let me search for more information on my phone. *[Pause]* Oh, __________ __________ __________ the Aqua Life Council.

M: I'm glad that they're helping people realize how remarkable these creatures are.

W: I agree. The event started on October 4th and __________ __________ __________ __________ __________.

M: Good. We still have a lot of time to visit.

W: You're right. Let's make plans to go soon.

9

W: Welcome back to Design Talk. Today I have exciting news for you. One of the world's largest design conferences is coming soon. It's the Global Design Conference. The conference is held every year in Chicago. It aims to keep people informed about the current trends in design. This year __________ __________ __________ __________ __________ __________ and practical workshops. In addition, the works made by 100 designers will be displayed. These selected works will change the way you look at design. The conference __________ __________ __________ __________ and ends on the 22. Registration is only available on the conference website. The registration fee is $30, and __________ __________. If design is important to you, mark your calendar now!

10

W: Jason, what's that in your hand?

M: It's a flyer from the neighborhood flower shop, Mom.

W: Oh, they're selling plant seed kits! I want one. Can you help me choose?

M: Sure. I don't think you need the most expensive kit since it's your first try.

W: Right. But __________ __________ __________ __________. So, at least four kinds of plants would be nice.

M: Okay. What about the pots? They __________ __________ __________ __________.

W: I don't want the ceramic one. It'll be too heavy for me.

M: Good point. I think the one that __________ __________ __________ __________ __________ __________ would be helpful for you.

W: Yes, I can easily find out how to grow plants.

M: Then this seed kit is perfect for you.

W: Thanks for helping me. I'll buy that one.

11

W: Dad, I want to send this book to Grandma. __________ __________ __________ __________ __________?

M: Yeah. I've got this one to put photo albums in, but it's a bit small.

W: The box looks __________ __________ __________ __________ __________. Can I use it?

M: (Of course. You can have it.)

12

M: Amy, you said you're going to study at Donna's house tonight, right?

W: Yes, Dad. We have to __________ __________ __________ __________ __________ by midnight.

M: I think you'll be quite late. __________ __________ __________ __________ __________?

W: (Sure. I'll call you when I'm done.)

13

[Cell phone rings.]

M: Hello, Joe Burrow speaking.

W: Hello. This is Officer Blake from the Roselyn Police Station.

M: Oh, it's good to speak to you again.

W: Nice to speak to you, too. Do you remember the boy who found your briefcase and brought it here?

M: Sure. I wanted to __________ __________ __________ __________. But he wouldn't accept it.

W: I remember you saying that before.

M: Yeah. I'd still like to somehow __________ __________ __________ __________ __________.

W: Good. That's why I'm calling you. __________ __________ __________ next Friday at 10 a.m.?

M: Yes. I'm free at that time. Why?

W: The boy will receive the Junior Citizen Award for what he's done for you.

M: That's great news!

W: There'll be a ceremony for him at the police station, and he __________ __________ __________ __________ __________. I was wondering if you can make it.

M: (Definitely. I want to go to congratulate him myself.)

14

M: Hey, Jessica. You got here early.

W: You too, Mike. What are you reading?

M: __________ __________ __________ __________ __________ about the musical *Spring Empire*.

W: Oh, *Spring Empire*? I'm going to see it next week. What does the article say?

M: It mentions that the leading actors are geniuses and that the musical is going to be so popular.

W: Wow, I really can't wait to see it.

M: Actually, I've seen it already. Since you haven't watched the musical, __________ __________ __________ __________ __________ __________ __________ first.

W: Why do you say that?

M: The storyline is complicated. In my case, reading the novel first helped me fully understand and better enjoy the musical.

W: Then, I need to get a copy of the book.

M: I have one. __________ __________ __________ __________ __________ __________ if you want.

W: (Thanks. Then, I'll read the novel before I watch the musical.)

15

M: Jake and Yuna are members of a climbing club. Today, they're visiting a national park with other club members. At the top of the mountain, Jake sees a beautiful rock. He starts __________ __________ __________ __________. When Yuna sees Jake, she offers to take photos for him. Jake __________ __________ __________ __________ to take a photo with the rock and gives Yuna his smartphone. After Yuna takes some photos of him, Jake looks at the photos and notices that the rock is not in them. So Jake wants to ask Yuna to get another shot of him and __________ __________ __________ __________ __________. In this situation, what would Jake most likely say to Yuna?

Jake: (Could you please take my picture again with the rock in it?)

16~17

M: How did people send mail before they had access to cars and trains? There were simple options out there, like delivery by animal. Horses were frequently ___________ ___________ ___________ ___________ ___________ ___________ ___________. In the 19th century, a mail express system that used horses serviced a large area of the United States. Pigeons may be seen as a problem by many people today. However, in ancient Greece, they were used to mail people the results of the Olympics between cities. Alaska and Canada are known for their cold winters. In their early days, dogs were utilized to deliver mail because they've ___________ ___________ ___________ ___________ ice and snow. Maybe the most fascinating of all delivery animals is the camel. Australia imported camels from the Middle East and utilized them to transfer mail across vast deserts. They were ideally suited to this job because they can ___________ ___________ ___________ for quite a while. Fortunately, we've developed faster and more reliable delivery systems, but we should not ___________ ___________ ___________ ___________ these animals played in the past.

Dictation Answers

1. help with the charity soccer match / show the audience to their seats / get involved in helping children
2. stay healthy if we live in the country / less noisy in the country / grow our own fruits and vegetables
3. to our radio show listeners / inspired the recipe / help the local economy / definitely go to your bakery
4. mobile hanging from the ceiling / two boxes under the Christmas tree / star on top of the tree
5. wanted to wear heart-shaped sunglasses / I can order the sunglasses / I'll take care of that
6. \$20 for adults / \$10 for children / all of those admission tickets / does not apply to this program
7. forget to bring your tea / not to drink too much tea / business meeting that overlaps with the tea club
8. include exhibiting various octopuses / it's sponsored by / will end on December 8th
9. there'll be lectures by famous designers / begins on June 20 / it's non-refundable
10. I'd like some variety / come in different materials / comes with a plant growing guide
11. Do you have a box / big enough for the book
12. submit our team report online / Should I pick you up
13. give him a reward / express my thanks in person / Are you available / invited you as his guest
14. I'm reading a magazine article / I recommend you read the original novel / I can lend it to you
15. taking selfies with it / finds a great spot / this time include the rock

16~17. utilized in delivery of letters and messages / adapted to run over / go without water / ignore the important roles

제4회 고급 모의고사

맞은 개수: 2점 문항 ___개, 3점 문항 ___개
알고 푼 문항은 ○, 찍어서 맞힌 문제는 △에 표시하고, △와 ×는 다시 복습하세요.

1번부터 17번까지는 듣고 답하는 문제입니다. 1번부터 15번까지는 한 번만 들려주고, 16번부터 17번까지는 두 번 들려줍니다. 방송을 잘 듣고 답을 하시기 바랍니다.

1 ○△× ········ 2023학년도 수능 1번

다음을 듣고, 남자가 하는 말의 목적으로 가장 적절한 것을 고르시오. 정답률 97%

① 도서관의 변경된 운영 시간을 안내하려고
② 독후감 쓰기 대회의 일정을 공지하려고
③ 책갈피 디자인 대회 참가를 독려하려고
④ 기한 내 도서 반납을 촉구하려고
⑤ 전자책 이용 방법을 설명하려고

2 ○△× ········ 2019학년도 수능 4번

대화를 듣고, 여자의 의견으로 가장 적절한 것을 고르시오. 정답률 95%

① 실패한 실험을 분석하면 실험에 성공할 수 있다.
② 과학 수업에서는 이론과 실습이 병행되어야 한다.
③ 과학자가 되기 위해서는 인문학적 소양도 필요하다.
④ 실험 일지는 실험 보고서 작성에 도움이 된다.
⑤ 실험을 할 때마다 안전 교육을 해야 한다.

3 ○△× ········ 2020학년도 수능 5번

대화를 듣고, 두 사람의 관계를 가장 잘 나타낸 것을 고르시오. 정답률 95%

① 곤충학자 — 학생
② 동물 조련사 — 사진작가
③ 농부 — 잡지기자
④ 요리사 — 음식 평론가
⑤ 독자 — 소설가

4 ○△× ········ 2020학년도 수능 6번

대화를 듣고, 그림에서 대화의 내용과 일치하지 않는 것을 고르시오. 정답률 96%

5 ○△× ········ 2024학년도 수능 5번

대화를 듣고, 여자가 할 일로 가장 적절한 것을 고르시오. 정답률 95%

① 신입 회원 선물 준비하기
② 대회 일정 인쇄하기
③ 음악 재생 목록 만들기
④ 식당 예약하기
⑤ 문자 메시지 보내기

6 ○△× ········ 2021학년도 수능 6번

대화를 듣고, 여자가 지불할 금액을 고르시오. 정답률 95%

① \$180 ② \$190 ③ \$200 ④ \$210 ⑤ \$230

7 ○△× ········ 2025학년도 수능 7번

대화를 듣고, 남자가 Streamline Broadcasting Workshop에 갈 수 없는 이유를 고르시오. 정답률 98%

① 동아리 공연에 참여해야 해서
② 교내 방송 준비를 해야 해서
③ 야구 경기를 보러 가야 해서
④ 생일 파티에 참석해야 해서
⑤ 선물을 사러 가야 해서

8 ○△× ········ 2026학년도 수능 8번

대화를 듣고, Autumn Treasure Hunt 행사에 관해 언급되지 않은 것을 고르시오. 정답률 99%

① 장소
② 날짜
③ 상품
④ 신청 방법
⑤ 후원 기관

9 고득점 ○△× ········ 2023학년도 수능 9번

Greenville Houseplant Expo에 관한 다음 내용을 듣고, 일치하지 않는 것을 고르시오. 정답률 76%

① 3일 동안 진행될 것이다.
② 식물 관리 방법에 관한 강의가 매일 있을 것이다.
③ 희귀종을 포함한 다양한 식물을 구입할 수 있다.
④ 티켓 구입은 온라인으로만 가능하다.
⑤ 에메랄드 컨벤션 센터에서 열릴 것이다.

10 ○△× • 2017학년도 수능 12번

다음 표를 보면서 대화를 듣고, 여자가 구매할 램프를 고르시오. 정답률 96%

Floor Lamps for Sale

	Model	Height (cm)	LED Bulbs	Price ($)	Color
①	A	120	×	30	Black
②	B	140	○	40	Black
③	C	150	○	45	White
④	D	160	○	55	Black
⑤	E	170	×	55	White

11 ○△× • 2021학년도 수능 11번

대화를 듣고, 남자의 마지막 말에 대한 여자의 응답으로 가장 적절한 것을 고르시오. 정답률 93%

① I don't feel like going out today.
② You must get to the airport quickly.
③ How about going to the cafe over there?
④ I didn't know you wanted to go sightseeing.
⑤ Why didn't you wear more comfortable shoes?

12 고득점 ○△× • 2025학년도 수능 12번

대화를 듣고, 여자의 마지막 말에 대한 남자의 응답으로 가장 적절한 것을 고르시오. 정답률 80%

① In that case, let's give it a try.
② I don't know. It's a bit expensive.
③ That's the best class we've ever taken.
④ I'd be happy to teach yoga to beginners.
⑤ You're right. The hotel's view is amazing.

13 고득점 ○△× • 2021학년도 수능 13번

대화를 듣고, 남자의 마지막 말에 대한 여자의 응답으로 가장 적절한 것을 고르시오. [3점] 정답률 87%

Woman: ______________________________

① Sorry. I don't think I can wait until tomorrow for this one.
② I agree. The displayed one may be the best option for me.
③ Oh, no. It's too bad you don't sell the displayed model.
④ Good. Call me when my washing machine is repaired.
⑤ Exactly. I'm glad that you bought the displayed one.

14 ○△× • 2019학년도 수능 13번

대화를 듣고, 여자의 마지막 말에 대한 남자의 응답으로 가장 적절한 것을 고르시오. [3점] 정답률 94%

Man: ______________________________

① Absolutely! You should go and see a doctor.
② No problem. I'll visit you on my business trip.
③ Sure. You can check the directions before driving.
④ Okay. I'll ask my team so I can take the medicine.
⑤ Right. Taking a trip is a great way to relieve stress.

15 고득점 ○△× • 2018학년도 수능 15번

다음 상황 설명을 듣고, David가 Julia에게 할 말로 가장 적절한 것을 고르시오. [3점] 정답률 86%

David: ______________________________

① We need to check what we did last year.
② Why don't we cancel the program this year?
③ Let me assign this work to the other teachers.
④ How about joining the program after school?
⑤ Let's ask the students what they prefer to do.

[16~17] 다음을 듣고, 물음에 답하시오.

16 ○△× • 2026학년도 수능 16번

여자가 하는 말의 주제로 가장 적절한 것은? 정답률 94%

① fast growing plants used for science experiments
② how scientists preserve diverse species of plants
③ factors to consider when buying plants
④ what crucial conditions make plants grow fast
⑤ reasons why certain plants grow faster than others

17 ○△× • 2026학년도 수능 17번

언급된 식물이 아닌 것은? 정답률 98%

① bamboo ② lettuce ③ sunflowers
④ peas ⑤ corn

Dictation

문제 풀이에 중요한 핵심 부분과 듣기에 자주 나오는 표현들에 빈칸 처리를 했습니다. 방송을 잘 듣고, 빈칸에 알맞은 말을 써 넣으세요.

Tip! 잘 들리지 않는 부분이 있을 때에는 정답을 확인 후, 똑같은 속도로 따라 읽기 연습을 해 보세요.

1

M: Hello, Lockwood High School students. This is your school librarian, Mr. Wilkins. I'm sure you're aware that our school library __________ __________ __________ __________ __________ __________. I encourage students of all grades to participate in the competition. The winning designs will be made into bookmarks, which will be distributed to library visitors. We're also giving out a variety of other prizes. So __________ __________ __________ __________ __________ __________ __________. Since the registration period for the bookmark design competition ends this Friday, make sure you visit our school library __________ __________ __________ __________. Come and participate to display your creativity and talents.

2

W: Andrew, you look unhappy. What's wrong?

M: Hi, Ms. Benson. I've been trying this chemical reaction experiment again and again, but it's not working.

W: Why isn't it working?

M: I don't know. Maybe I don't have much talent for chemistry.

W: __________ __________ __________ __________ __________ __________.

M: So what should I do?

W: I believe that the path to success is through analyzing failure.

M: Analyzing failure? What do you mean?

W: __________ __________ __________ __________ __________ in your experiment, you can do it right.

M: Hmm. You mean that even though my experiment didn't work, I can learn something from failure?

W: Exactly. If you __________ __________ __________ __________ __________ it didn't work, you can succeed at your experiment.

M: Now I understand. I'll review my experiment. Thanks.

3

M: Hello, I'm Ted Benson. You must be Ms. Brown.

W: Hi, Mr. Benson. Thank you for __________ __________ __________ __________ __________. I've wanted to meet you since you won the "Best Rice Award."

M: I'm honored. I'm a __________ __________ __________ __________ __________. The articles are very informative.

W: Thank you. Can you tell me the secret to your success?

M: __________ __________ __________ without using any chemicals to kill harmful insects. It's organic.

W: How do you do that?

M: I put ducks into my fields, and they eat the insects.

W: So that's how you grew the best rice in the country. What a great idea!

M: Yeah, that's the know-how I've got from __________ __________ __________ __________ __________ __________.

W: Well, it's amazing. May I take a picture of you in front of your rice fields for my magazine article?

M: Go ahead.

4

W: What are you looking at, honey?

M: Aunt Mary sent me a picture. She's already set up a room for Peter.

W: Wow! She's excited for him to stay during the winter vacation, isn't she?

M: Yes, she is. I like the blanket with the ________ ________ ________ ________ ________.

W: I'm sure it must be very warm. Look at the ________ ________ ________ ________.

M: It looks comfortable. He could sit there and read.

W: Right. I guess that's why Aunt Mary put the bookcase next to it.

M: That makes sense. Oh, there's a ________ ________ ________ ________ ________.

W: It looks real. I think it's a gift for Peter.

M: Yeah, I remember she mentioned it. And do you see the ________ ________ ________ ________ ________?

W: It's nice. It looks like the one Peter has here at home.

M: It does. Let's show him this picture.

5

W: Oliver, I'm so excited about the party for the new members of our tennis club this Friday.

M: Me, too. Let's go through the to-do list. I want it to be perfect.

W: Agreed. Did you ________ ________ ________ ________ downtown for the party?

M: Yes, I did. The restaurant is spacious, so it's perfect for a party like ours.

W: Plus, the food there is terrific. And you prepared gifts for the new members, right?

M: Yeah, they're in my car. Did you remind the members about the party?

W: I've just ________ ________ ________ ________ to everyone.

M: Great. What about the tennis competition schedule? ________ ________ ________ ________ ________?

W: Oh, I almost forgot. I'll do it tonight. Um, is the music ready?

M: Uh-huh. I made a playlist last night.

W: That's great. I think we're good to go!

6

M: Welcome to the Chestfield Hotel. How may I help you?

W: Hi, I'm Alice Milford. I made a reservation for me and my husband.

M: *[Typing sound]* Here it is. You reserved one room for one night ________ ________ ________ ________ ________ ________.

W: Can I use this 10% discount coupon?

M: Sure, you can.

W: Fantastic. And is it possible to ________ ________ ________ ________?

M: Let me check. *[Mouse clicking sound]* Yes, the same room is available for tomorrow.

W: Good. Do I get a discount for the second night, too?

M: Sorry. The coupon doesn't ________ ________ ________ ________ ________. It'll be $100. Do you still want to stay an extra night?

W: Yes, I do.

M: Great. Will you and your husband have breakfast? It's ________ ________ ________ for each day.

W: No thanks. We'll be going out early to go shopping. Here's my credit card.

고급 4회

7

W: Hey, John. Come and look at this poster.

M: Hi, Sharon. The Streamline Broadcasting Workshop? What's that?

W: It's a student workshop that offers an opportunity __________ __________ __________ __________ __________ __________. How about going together?

M: Oh, it's on Friday. I wish I could, but I can't.

W: Why not? Is your dance club's performance on that day?

M: No, the __________ __________ __________ __________.

W: Then, is your little brother's birthday party on Friday?

M: No, it was last week. I got him a hat as a present.

W: So why can't you go to the workshop?

M: Actually, I'm going to see a baseball game on that day. I __________ __________ __________ __________ __________.

W: Oh, I see. I hope your team wins.

8

W: Hey, Nathan. Have you heard of the Autumn Treasure Hunt event that is coming soon?

M: Autumn Treasure Hunt? That's interesting. Where will it take place?

W: __________ __________ __________ __________ Pinenut Park. Participants can search for hidden treasure there.

M: Sounds fun. You know I'm a great treasure hunter. When is it?

W: It's this Saturday, __________ __________.

M: Perfect. I'm free that day. There must be a big prize for the winner. Do you know what it is?

W: Yeah. If you collect the most treasure, you'll get a __________ __________ __________ __________ __________ __________ __________.

M: Wow, that's a big prize. How can I sign up for the Autumn Treasure Hunt event?

W: You can __________ __________ __________ __________ __________ __________.

M: Awesome! Let's go there together.

W: That'd be great.

9

W: Hello, listeners. I'm Melinda Jones from the organizing committee of the Greenville Houseplant Expo. I'm here to announce that the expo will __________ __________ __________ __________ starting on March 17th, 2023. Just on the opening day, there'll be a lecture on plant care methods. This lecture will be given by Dr. Evans, host of the TV show *Plants Love You*. Most importantly, you can __________ __________ __________ __________ __________, including rare species, exhibited in the expo. Due to its popularity, you'd better get your tickets early. Tickets are __________ __________ __________ __________ __________. If you're a plant lover, come to the expo, which will take place at the Emerald Convention Center, and refresh your houseplant collection.

10

M: Welcome to Jay's Lighting Store. How may I help you?
W: I'm here to look for a floor lamp for my living room.
M: Here, take a look at this catalog. We have five models you can choose from. Are you looking for anything specific?
W: Yes. It shouldn't be too short. I'd like to get one that's __________ __________ __________ __________ __________ __________ __________.
M: Then how about these four models? Would you like LED bulbs?
W: Yes, I would. They last longer than standard bulbs.
M: And they save energy. I definitely recommend LEDs. What's your price range?
W: Well, I don't want to __________ __________ __________ __________ __________.
M: Then you have two options left. Which color do you like better?
W: Hmm..., __________ __________ __________ __________ __________ __________.
M: Good choice. Would you like to pay in cash or by credit card?
W: I'll pay in cash.

11

M: Lisa, are you okay from all the walking we did today?
W: Actually, Dad, my feet are __________ __________ __________ __________ __________. Also, I'm thirsty because the weather is so hot out here.
M: Oh, then let's go somewhere inside and __________ __________ __________ __________. Where should we go?
W: (How about going to the cafe over there?)

12

W: Honey, the hotel __________ __________ __________ __________ __________ on the beach to the guests. Do you want to go with me tomorrow morning?
M: Oh, really? I definitely want to try yoga, but I'm afraid we __________ __________ __________ __________ __________.
W: Don't worry. This class is for true beginners who have never done yoga before. So why don't we take it?
M: (In that case, let's give it a try.)

고급 4회

13

W: Hi. Can I get some help over here?
M: Sure. What can I help you with?
W: I'm thinking of buying this washing machine.
M: Good choice. It's our best-selling model.
W: I really like its design and it ________ ________ ________ ________ ________ ________. I'll take it.
M: Great. However, you'll have to wait for two weeks. We're ________ ________ ________ ________ right now.
W: Oh, no. I need it today. My washing machine broke down yesterday.
M: Then how about ________ ________ ________ ________ ________?
W: Oh, I didn't know I could buy the displayed one.
M: Sure, you can. We can deliver and install it today.
W: That's just what I need, but it's not a new one.
M: Not to worry. It's never been used. Also, like with the new ones, you can ________ ________ ________ ________ ________ for up to three years.
W: That's good.
M: We can also give you a 20% discount on it. It's a pretty good deal.
W: (I agree. The displayed one may be the best option for me.)

14

W: Honey, what did the doctor say about your neck?
M: She said that it's not too bad. I just need to take these pills and get enough rest.
W: I'm relieved that it's not so serious.
M: But there's a problem. The doctor said I ________ ________ ________ ________ ________ ________. It can make me very sleepy.
W: Oh, no. What about your business trip on Monday?
M: Exactly. ________ ________ ________ ________ ________ ________ ________ since I know the area.
W: You cannot drive. It would be very dangerous.
M: Maybe I'll skip the medicine before I drive.
W: Wouldn't it delay your recovery and even make your neck pain worse?
M: Yeah. I do need to take the medicine regularly.
W: Then one solution would be to see if ________ ________ ________ ________ ________ ________ ________ instead of you.
M: (Okay. I'll ask my team so I can take the medicine.)

15

W: David and Julia are teachers working at the same high school. This year, they have to ________ ________ ________ ________ for first-year students. Before they get to work, they look at the last year's program, which was very successful. Julia thinks the program looks quite good and wants to do it again. However, David is unsure. He thinks that the students may ________ ________ ________ ________ ________ from what last year's students did. And he wants to first find out what this year's students would like to do. Therefore, he wants to suggest to Julia that they should ________ ________ ________ ________ ________ ________ ________. In this situation, what would David most likely say to Julia?
David: (Let's ask the students what they prefer to do.)

16~17

M: Hello, students. Do you know that plants often help scientists understand the wonders of nature? Let's look at some __________ __________ __________ __________ __________ __________ __________ because they grow quickly. First, bamboo is known for quick growth, with some varieties growing inches per day. Therefore, it absorbs a large amount of CO_2, so it's often used in studies about __________ __________ __________ __________ __________. Second, lettuce grows quickly and is sensitive to environmental conditions. So, scientists grow it to see the effects of various chemicals on plant growth. Third, sunflowers are __________ __________ __________ __________ __________ __________, sometimes reaching several feet in just a few months. That's why scientists use them to learn about the effects of soils on plant height. Finally, peas are classic plants for experiments about genetics __________ __________ __________ __________ and have easily observable characteristics like seed color and shape. For these reasons, the famous scientist, Mendel, studied them. After a short break, we'll look at other plants that are good for science experiments.

Dictation Answers

1. is hosting a bookmark design competition / don't let this great opportunity slip away / to submit your application
2. Don't be so hard on yourself / By examining what went wrong / figure out how and why
3. sparing time for this interview / regular reader of your magazine / I grow rice / my 30 years of farming life
4. checkered pattern on the bed / chair below the window / toy horse in the corner / round mirror on the wall
5. reserve the Mexican restaurant / sent a text message / Have you printed it out
6. at the regular rate of $100 / stay one more night / apply to the second night / $10 per person
7. to connect with experts in broadcasting / performance is next month / have tickets for that game
8. It'll be held in / November 22nd / gift card worth $100 as a reward / visit its website and register online
9. run for three days / buy a variety of plants / available through online purchase only
10. taller than one hundred and thirty centimeters / spend more than fifty dollars / I'll go with the white one
11. tired from all the sightseeing / get something to drink
12. offers a free yoga class / might be the only beginners
13. has a lot of useful features / out of this model / buying the one on display / get it repaired for free
14. shouldn't drive after taking the medicine / I'm supposed to drive my team members / somebody else in your team can drive
15. develop an after-school program / want to do different things / hear from the students about their preferences

16~17. plants that are perfect for science experiments / how to reduce climate change / known for their remarkable growth rate / as they grow quickly

제5회 고급 모의고사

맞은 개수: 2점 문항 ___개, 3점 문항 ___개
알고 푼 문항은 ○, 찍어서 맞힌 문제는 △에 표시하고, △와 ×는 다시 복습하세요.

1번부터 17번까지는 듣고 답하는 문제입니다. 1번부터 15번까지는 한 번만 들려주고, 16번부터 17번까지는 두 번 들려줍니다. 방송을 잘 듣고 답을 하시기 바랍니다.

1 ○△× • 2020학년도 수능 3번

다음을 듣고, 남자가 하는 말의 목적으로 가장 적절한 것을 고르시오. 정답률 97%

① 백화점 주말 특별 행사를 안내하려고
② 백화점 층별 신규 매장을 소개하려고
③ 주차장 이용 요금 변경을 공지하려고
④ 고객 만족도 조사 참여를 요청하려고
⑤ 백화점 회원 가입 방법을 설명하려고

2 ○△× • 2020학년도 수능 4번

대화를 듣고, 여자의 의견으로 가장 적절한 것을 고르시오. 정답률 97%

① 왼쪽 신체의 잦은 사용은 두뇌 활동을 촉진한다.
② 수면 시간과 심장 기능은 밀접한 관련이 있다.
③ 왼쪽으로 누워 자는 것은 건강에 도움이 된다.
④ 규칙적인 운동은 소화 불량 개선에 필수적이다.
⑤ 숙면은 정신 건강을 유지하는 데 중요한 요인이다.

3 ○△× • 2019학년도 수능 5번

대화를 듣고, 두 사람의 관계를 가장 잘 나타낸 것을 고르시오. 정답률 97%

① 모델 — 사진작가
② 기증자 — 박물관 직원
③ 영화 관람객 — 티켓 판매원
④ 인테리어 디자이너 — 건축가
⑤ 고객 — 가구점 직원

4 ○△× • 2019학년도 수능 6번

대화를 듣고, 그림에서 대화의 내용과 일치하지 않는 것을 고르시오. 정답률 96%

5 고득점 ○△× • 2023학년도 수능 5번

대화를 듣고, 남자가 할 일로 가장 적절한 것을 고르시오. 정답률 89%

① 음식 재료 주문하기
② 와인 잔 포장하기
③ 추가 메뉴 선정하기
④ 초대 문자 메시지 보내기
⑤ 노래 목록 확인하기

6 ○△× • 2022학년도 수능 6번

대화를 듣고, 여자가 지불할 금액을 고르시오. [3점] 정답률 95%

① $36 ② $45 ③ $50 ④ $54 ⑤ $60

7 ○△× • 2018학년도 수능 8번

대화를 듣고, 여자가 영화를 보고 있는 이유를 고르시오. 정답률 97%

① 맡은 배역을 더 잘 이해하고 싶어서
② 훌륭한 영화감독이 되고 싶어서
③ 좋아하는 장르의 작품이어서
④ 주연 배우들을 좋아해서
⑤ 작문 숙제를 해야 해서

8 ○△× • 2023학년도 수능 8번

대화를 듣고, 졸업 사진 촬영에 관해 언급되지 않은 것을 고르시오. 정답률 97%

① 날짜
② 장소
③ 복장
④ 참여 학생 수
⑤ 소요 시간

9 ○△× • 2020학년도 수능 11번

Green Ocean 영화 시사회에 관한 다음 내용을 듣고, 일치하지 않는 것을 고르시오. 정답률 96%

① 100명을 초대할 예정이다.
② 다음 주 토요일 오후 4시에 시작할 것이다.
③ 영화 출연 배우와 사진을 찍을 수 있다.
④ 입장권을 우편으로 보낼 예정이다.
⑤ 초대받은 사람은 극장에서 포스터를 받을 것이다.

10 ○△× • 2020학년도 수능 12번

다음 표를 보면서 대화를 듣고, 두 사람이 예약할 항공편을 고르시오. 정답률 95%

Flight Schedule to New York City Area

	Flight	Ticket Price	Departure Time	Arrival Airport	Stops
①	A	$600	6:00 a.m.	JFK	1 stop
②	B	$625	10:00 a.m.	Newark	Nonstop
③	C	$700	11:30 a.m.	JFK	1 stop
④	D	$785	2:30 p.m.	JFK	Nonstop
⑤	E	$810	6:30 p.m.	Newark	1 stop

11 ○△× • 2020학년도 수능 1번

대화를 듣고, 남자의 마지막 말에 대한 여자의 응답으로 가장 적절한 것을 고르시오. 정답률 96%

① Okay. I'll send the address to your phone.
② Yes. I'll have your dress cleaned by noon.
③ Of course. I'll open the shop tomorrow.
④ No. I'm not moving to a new place.
⑤ Too late. I'm already back at home.

12 고득점 ○△× • 2020학년도 수능 2번

대화를 듣고, 여자의 마지막 말에 대한 남자의 응답으로 가장 적절한 것을 고르시오. 정답률 85%

① Unbelievable. I'm really going to be on stage today.
② Absolutely. I'm so eager to see him sing in person.
③ Not really. He wasn't as amazing as I expected.
④ Sure. I'll find someone else to perform instead.
⑤ Oh, no. You shouldn't have missed his performance.

13 ○△× • 2024학년도 수능 14번

대화를 듣고, 남자의 마지막 말에 대한 여자의 응답으로 가장 적절한 것을 고르시오. 정답률 86%

Woman: ______________________________

① No worries. I can go pick it up now.
② All right. Just be sure to return it tomorrow.
③ That's okay. We can fix the system next week.
④ Sorry to hear that. You can buy it next time.
⑤ Never mind. I'll bring a new copy for you.

14 ○△× • 2023학년도 수능 14번

대화를 듣고, 여자의 마지막 말에 대한 남자의 응답으로 가장 적절한 것을 고르시오. [3점] 정답률 93%

Man: ______________________________

① I had the photos from our trip printed out yesterday.
② The problem is that I already put out the campfire.
③ I gladly accept his invitation to the fishing camp.
④ Then I'll ask him to come with me on this trip.
⑤ Remember not to set up your tent near a river.

15 고득점 ○△× • 2021학년도 수능 15번

다음 상황 설명을 듣고, Ben이 Stacy에게 할 말로 가장 적절한 것을 고르시오. [3점] 정답률 79%

Ben: ______________________________

① Feel free to take the tomatoes from my backyard.
② Tell me if you need help when planting tomatoes.
③ Do you want the ripe tomatoes I picked yesterday?
④ Why don't we grow tomatoes in some other places?
⑤ Let me take care of your tomatoes while you're away.

[16~17] 다음을 듣고, 물음에 답하시오.

16 ○△× • 2021학년도 수능 16번

남자가 하는 말의 주제로 가장 적절한 것은? 정답률 91%

① color change in nature throughout seasons
② various colors used in traditional English customs
③ differences in color perceptions according to culture
④ why expressions related to colors are common in English
⑤ how color-related English expressions gained their meanings

17 ○△× • 2021학년도 수능 17번

언급된 색깔이 아닌 것은? 정답률 98%

① blue ② white ③ green
④ red ⑤ yellow

Dictation

문제 풀이에 중요한 핵심 부분과 듣기에 자주 나오는 표현들에 빈칸 처리를 했습니다. 방송을 잘 듣고, 빈칸에 알맞은 말을 써 넣으세요.

Tip! 잘 들리지 않는 부분이 있을 때에는 정답을 확인 후, 똑같은 속도로 따라 읽기 연습을 해 보세요.

1

M: Shoppers, may I have your attention please? Thank you for visiting Miracle Department Store. We'd like to __________ __________ __________ __________ __________ __________ going on through this weekend. First, we're offering a 50 percent discount on certain electronics and sporting goods on the seventh floor. Second, we're __________ __________ __________ __________ at our coffee shop on the first floor to shoppers who spend over $50. Third, we're also __________ __________ __________ __________ __________ to all shoppers who spend over $100. Last but not least, you don't have to worry about parking fees this weekend. __________ __________ __________. We hope you enjoy this weekend's special events at our department store.

2

W: Hi, Sam. How are you?

M: Fine. How about you, Christine?

W: I feel really good.

M: Wow! What happened to you? You usually say you're tired.

W: Well, I changed how I sleep. I __________ __________ __________ __________ __________ __________, and it has improved my health.

M: Really?

W: Yeah. I've done it for a week, and __________ __________ __________ __________ __________.

M: I didn't know how we sleep has something to do with digestion.

W: It does. Sleeping on your left side __________ __________ __________ __________ because your stomach is on the left.

M: I can see that. But does improving digestion make you that much healthier?

W: Sleeping on the left side does more than that. I think it's good for health because it also __________ __________ __________ __________ __________ __________.

M: That makes sense. I guess I should try it.

3

[Cell phone rings.]

W: Hello.

M: Hello, Ms. Monroe. This is John Brown. I'm calling to invite you to a special event.

W: Oh, thank you for calling. What's the event?

M: Our museum will __________ __________ __________ __________ __________ __________, including the old pictures and tools you donated, under the theme *Life in the 1800s*.

W: That's wonderful. When is it?

M: It'll be from December 3rd to 7th. And it's all thanks to generous people like you.

W: It's my pleasure. I __________ __________ __________ __________ __________ __________ learn about the past.

M: Thank you. The antique items you donated have really improved our collection.
W: I'm glad to hear that. I'm looking forward to visiting the exhibition.
M: I'll send you the invitation letter soon.
W: Great. I'll be waiting for it.
M: Again, on behalf of our museum, __________ __________ __________ __________.

4

M: Mom, I think the backyard is ready for Dad's birthday party.
W: Really? Let's see.
M: *[Pause]* I __________ __________ __________ __________ __________ __________.
W: That's nice.
M: I think he'll enjoy watching our old family videos there.
W: I'm sure he will. Oh, did you buy the __________ __________ __________ __________ __________?
M: Yes. I got it from Dad's favorite bakery.
W: He'll love it. What are the two boxes under the chair?
M: They're gifts from Grandma and Grandpa.
W: How nice of them. Hmm. I think the __________ __________ __________ __________ __________ is too small. We cannot all sit there.
M: You're right. I'll bring more chairs.
W: Good idea. And you put the grill next to the garden lamp.
M: Yeah. As you know, Dad loves barbecue.
W: Right. We're almost ready for the party.

5

W: Honey, I'm so excited for our restaurant's reopening event tomorrow.
M: So am I. Let's see. We've ordered enough ingredients, right?
W: I think so. We need to remind our loyal customers of the event.
M: I __________ __________ __________ __________.
W: Good. I hope people like the new menu items that we added.
M: Don't worry. We have a great chef. So I'm sure the new dishes will be a hit.
W: What about the live music? Did you __________ __________ __________ __________ with the band?
M: Not yet. And we also __________ __________ __________ __________ __________ to give as gifts for the customers.
W: Okay. Could you wrap them?
M: Sure. I'll do it now.
W: Great! Then I'll contact the band.

6

M: Welcome to Daisy Valley Restaurant.
W: Hi. I'd like to __________ __________ __________ __________ __________. How much is the shrimp pasta and the chicken salad?
M: The shrimp pasta is $20, and the chicken salad is $10.
W: I'll take two shrimp pastas and one chicken salad, please.
M: Sure. Would you like some dessert, too?
W: Yes. What do you recommend?
M: The mini cheese cake is one of the best sellers in our restaurant. __________ __________ __________.
W: Great! I'll order two of them.
M: Okay. __________ __________ __________ __________ __________. Two shrimp pastas, one chicken salad, and two mini cheese cakes. Is that correct?
W: Yes. And I have a birthday coupon here. Can I use it?
M: Let me see. *[Pause]* Yes. You can get a __________ __________ __________ __________ __________.
W: Terrific. I'll use this coupon. Here's my credit card.

고급 5회

7

M: Ellen, what are you looking at on your smart phone?
W: Hey, John. I'm watching the movie *Romeo and Juliet*.
M: I didn't know you're interested in romantic movies.
W: To be honest, I like action movies.
M: Then, is it __________ __________ __________ __________? You said you needed to write a paper on Shakespeare.
W: No, I've already finished it.
M: Well, do you __________ __________ __________ __________ __________ __________?
W: Not really. Actually, I'm going to play Juliet in the school play. And I'm watching this because I want to __________ __________ __________ __________.
M: Oh, that's a good idea. I'm sure it'll help you.
W: I hope so. I really want to do well.
M: Don't worry. You'll do great.
W: Thanks. You should come and watch the play.

8

[Telephone rings.]
W: Hello, Jennifer Porter speaking.
M: Hi, Ms. Porter. This is Steve Jackson from Lifetime Photo Studio.
W: Oh, how are you?
M: Good. I'm scheduled to shoot your school's graduation photos __________ __________, __________ __________. So, I'm calling to confirm the details.
W: Sure. As we previously discussed, the place will be Lily Pond Park.
M: Okay. Could you tell me the exact number of students taking part in the photo session?
W: Let me check. *[Pause]* Well, __________ __________ __________ __________.
M: I see. The same as you said before.
W: That's right. How long will it take to shoot the photos?
M: __________ __________ __________ __________ __________. We should finish by noon.
W: Great. Is there any other information you need?
M: No, I'm all set. Bye.

9

W: Hello, listeners. Welcome to *Good Day Movie*. We'd like to let you know about a great chance to __________ __________ __________ of the movie *Green Ocean* by Feather Pictures. One hundred people will be invited to the event. It'll begin at the Glory Theater at 4 p.m. next Saturday. After watching the movie, you can __________ __________ __________ __________ __________ __________ __________ of the movie. If you're interested, apply for admission tickets on the *Green Ocean* homepage, and the tickets will be __________ __________ __________ __________ to the first 100 people who apply. Those who are invited will be __________ __________ __________ __________ __________ __________. Hurry up and don't miss this chance to watch *Green Ocean* in advance. Now we'll be back after the commercial break. So stay tuned.

10

M: Ms. Roberts, we're going on a business trip to New York City next week. Why don't we __________ __________ __________ on this website?
W: Okay, Mr. White. Let's take a look at the flight schedule.
M: Sure. How much can we spend on the flight?
W: Our company policy doesn't allow us to spend __________ __________ __________ __________ __________.
M: I see. And what about the departure time? I have to take my daughter to daycare early in the morning that day.
W: Then how about choosing __________ __________ __________ __________ __________?
M: That'll be great. Which airport should we arrive at?
W: JFK is closer to the company we're visiting.
M: Oh, you're right. Let's go there.
W: Then we have two options left, nonstop or one stop.
M: I don't want to spend hours waiting for a connecting flight.
W: Me, neither. We should __________ __________ __________ __________.
M: Okay. Let's book the flight now.

11

[Cell phone rings.]

M: Honey, I've just left work. I'll be home in half an hour.

W: Good. Is it possible for you to __________ __________ __________ __________ __________ __________ and pick up my dress?

M: Sure. Can you tell me __________ __________ __________ __________ __________?

W: (Okay. I'll send the address to your phone.)

12

W: David, look at this advertisement! Jason Stevens is going to sing at the opening of City Concert Hall next Saturday.

M: Wow! You know I'm a big fan of him, Mom. Luckily, I __________ __________ __________ __________ that day.

W: Great. __________ __________ __________ __________ __________ __________, so you don't miss his performance.

M: (Absolutely. I'm so eager to see him sing in person.)

13

W: Excuse me. Can you tell me where the non-fiction books are?

M: Sure. They're right over here. Are you looking for anything in particular?

W: I __________ __________ __________ __________ __________ __________ by Harriot Braun.

M: You mean *Follow Your Own Trail*?

W: Yes, that's the book.

M: Sorry. We __________ __________ __________ __________ __________ at the moment.

W: I can't believe it. It just came out three weeks ago.

M: The book is so popular that it sold out very quickly. Do you want me to find out if any of our other stores has a copy?

W: Yes, please. I really need to buy one for my book club meeting tomorrow. Could you __________ __________ __________ __________? It's on my way home.

M: Certainly. Let me look it up in our system. *[Typing sound]* Oh, there's one copy left there, but unfortunately we __________ __________ __________ __________ __________.

W: (No worries. I can go pick it up now.)

14

W: Dad, I found these old photos of our camping trip from 25 years ago.

M: Oh, I remember this trip. You were about the same age as your son, Peter.

W: Right. It was a really fun trip.

M: Yeah. I still go camping often, but that's __________ __________ __________ __________.

W: I agree. I want Peter to have that experience, too. But he always refuses to go.

M: Why doesn't he want to go camping?

W: He just wants to stay home and spend all his time on his smartphone.

M: Don't worry. I'm sure Peter will like camping __________ __________ __________ __________ __________ __________ __________.

W: You're probably right. Dad, when is the next time you're going camping?

M: This weekend. We should all go together.

W: That'd be great. Peter __________ __________ __________ __________ if his favorite grandpa invites him.

M: (Then I'll ask him to come with me on this trip.)

15

W: Ben and Stacy are neighbors. Ben has been growing tomatoes in his backyard for several years. Ben shares his tomatoes with Stacy every year because she loves his fresh tomatoes. Today, Ben notices that his tomatoes will __________ __________ __________ __________ __________ in about a week. However, he __________ __________ __________ __________ __________ __________ tomorrow. He's worried that there'll be no fresh tomatoes left in his backyard by the time he comes back. He'd like Stacy to have them while __________ __________ __________ __________ __________. So, Ben wants to tell Stacy that she can come and get the tomatoes from his backyard whenever she wants. In this situation, what would Ben most likely say to Stacy?

Ben: (Feel free to take the tomatoes from my backyard.)

16~17

M: Hello, students. Last time, I gave you a list of __________ __________ __________ __________ __________. Today, we'll learn how these expressions got their meanings. The first expression is "out of the blue," meaning something happens unexpectedly. It came from the phrase "a lightning bolt out of the blue," which expresses the idea that it's unlikely to see lightning when there's a clear blue sky. The next expression, "white lie," means a harmless lie to __________ __________ __________ __________ __________ __________. This is because the color white traditionally symbolizes innocence. Another expression, "green thumb," refers to a __________ __________ __________ __________ __________. Planting pots were often covered with tiny green plants, so those who worked in gardens had green-stained hands. The last expression, "to see red," means to suddenly get very angry. Its origin possibly comes from the belief that bulls __________ __________ __________ __________ when a bullfighter waves a red cape. I hope this lesson helps you remember these phrases better.

Dictation Answers

1. inform you of the special events / providing a free beverage / giving away $10 gift certificates / Parking is free
2. started sleeping on my left side / my digestion has got better / helps the digestive process / helps blood circulation to the heart
3. hold an exhibition of antique items / want my donation to help people / we appreciate your donation
4. hung a screen between the trees / heart-shaped cake on the table / striped mat on the grass
5. already sent text messages / confirm the song list / need to wrap wine glasses
6. order some food to go / It's $5 each / Let me confirm your order / 10% discount off the total
7. for your writing assignment / like the actors in the movie / better understand my role
8. on Wednesday / November 23rd / it'll be 180 students / It'll take almost three hours
9. see the preview / meet and take pictures with the actors / sent by text message / given a poster at the theater
10. book the flight / more than $800 per ticket / a flight after 9 a.m. / choose the nonstop flight
11. stop by the dry cleaner's shop / where the shop is located
12. don't have anything scheduled / Mark the date on your calendar
13. want to buy the latest book / don't have any copies left / check the store downtown / can't hold it for you
14. the most memorable one / once he experiences how fun it is / might come as well
15. be ready to be picked / leaves for a month-long business trip / they are fresh and ripe

16~17. English expressions containing color terms / protect someone from a harsh truth / great ability to cultivate plants / get angry and attack

제6회 고급 모의고사

맞은 개수: 2점 문항 ___개, 3점 문항 ___개
알고 푼 문항은 ○, 찍어서 맞힌 문제는 △에 표시하고, △와 ×는 다시 복습하세요.

1번부터 17번까지는 듣고 답하는 문제입니다. 1번부터 15번까지는 한 번만 들려주고, 16번부터 17번까지는 두 번 들려줍니다. 방송을 잘 듣고 답을 하시기 바랍니다.

1 ○△× • 2021학년도 수능 1번

다음을 듣고, 남자가 하는 말의 목적으로 가장 적절한 것을 고르시오. 정답률 98%

① 헬스클럽 할인 행사를 안내하려고
② 동영상 업로드 방법을 설명하려고
③ 스포츠 중계방송 중단을 예고하려고
④ 체육관 보수 공사 일정 변경을 공지하려고
⑤ 운동 방법에 관한 동영상 채널을 홍보하려고

2 ○△× • 2021학년도 수능 2번

대화를 듣고, 여자의 의견으로 가장 적절한 것을 고르시오. 정답률 96%

① 별 관찰은 아이들이 수학 개념에 친숙해지도록 도와준다.
② 아이들은 별 관찰을 통해 예술적 영감을 얻는다.
③ 야외 활동이 아이들의 신체 발달에 필수적이다.
④ 아이들은 자연을 경험함으로써 인격적으로 성장한다.
⑤ 수학 문제 풀이는 아이들의 논리적 사고력을 증진시킨다.

3 ○△× • 2023학년도 수능 3번

대화를 듣고, 두 사람의 관계를 가장 잘 나타낸 것을 고르시오. 정답률 97%

① 평론가 — 영화감독
② 심판 — 수영 선수
③ 작가 — 수영 코치
④ 서점 주인 — 유치원 교사
⑤ 잡지사 편집장 — 광고주

4 ○△× • 2018학년도 수능 6번

대화를 듣고, 그림에서 대화의 내용과 일치하지 않는 것을 고르시오. 정답률 95%

5 ○△× • 2021학년도 수능 5번

대화를 듣고, 남자가 여자를 위해 할 일로 가장 적절한 것을 고르시오. 정답률 98%

① 사진 전송하기
② 그림 그리기
③ 휴대 전화 찾기
④ 생물 보고서 제출하기
⑤ 야생화 개화 시기 검색하기

6 ○△× • 2026학년도 수능 6번

대화를 듣고, 남자가 지불할 금액을 고르시오. 정답률 96%

① $63 ② $70 ③ $81 ④ $90 ⑤ $108

7 ○△× • 2022학년도 수능 7번

대화를 듣고, 남자가 탁구 연습을 할 수 없는 이유를 고르시오. 정답률 99%

① 학교 도서관에 자원봉사를 하러 가야 해서
② 과학 퀴즈를 위한 공부를 해야 해서
③ 연극부 모임에 참가해야 해서
④ 역사 숙제를 제출해야 해서
⑤ 어깨에 통증이 있어서

8 ○△× • 2021학년도 수능 8번

대화를 듣고, Bradford Museum of Failure에 관해 언급되지 않은 것을 고르시오. 정답률 96%

① 전시품
② 설립 목적
③ 개관 연도
④ 입장료
⑤ 위치

9 ○△× • 2026학년도 수능 9번

2025 Court Visit Program에 관한 다음 내용을 듣고, 일치하지 않는 것을 고르시오. 정답률 98%

① 11월 19일에 개최된다.
② 판사와 변호사를 만날 기회를 제공한다.
③ 참가자에게 수료증을 준다.
④ 개인별로 신청해야 한다.
⑤ 무료 점심 식사를 포함한다.

10 ○△× • 2019학년도 수능 12번

다음 표를 보면서 대화를 듣고, 여자가 구매할 도마를 고르시오.
정답률 94%

Cutting Boards at Camilo's Kitchen

	Model	Material	Price	Handle	Size
①	A	plastic	$ 25	×	medium
②	B	maple	$ 35	○	small
③	C	maple	$ 40	×	large
④	D	walnut	$ 45	○	medium
⑤	E	walnut	$ 55	○	large

11 ○△× • 2022학년도 수능 11번

대화를 듣고, 여자의 마지막 말에 대한 남자의 응답으로 가장 적절한 것을 고르시오. 정답률 95%

① Just give me about ten minutes.
② It took an hour for us to get back home.
③ I think you need to focus on your work.
④ It was nice of you to invite my co-workers.
⑤ Call me when you finish sending the email.

12 고득점 ○△× • 2022학년도 수능 12번

대화를 듣고, 남자의 마지막 말에 대한 여자의 응답으로 가장 적절한 것을 고르시오. 정답률 88%

① Excellent. I like the camera you bought for me.
② Good. I'll stop by and get it on my way home.
③ Never mind. I'll drop off the camera tomorrow.
④ I see. Thanks for taking those pictures of me.
⑤ No way. That's too expensive for the repair.

13 고득점 ○△× • 2024학년도 수능 13번

대화를 듣고, 여자의 마지막 말에 대한 남자의 응답으로 가장 적절한 것을 고르시오. [3점] 정답률 89%

Man: ______________________________

① Don't give up! You've inspired me to be a painter.
② Cheer up! The fashion market is open to everybody.
③ You have a point. I don't have any fashion sense at all.
④ I agree. You should make a balance between work and life.
⑤ Be positive. You can start pursuing your dream at any time.

14 ○△× • 2017학년도 수능 13번

대화를 듣고, 남자의 마지막 말에 대한 여자의 응답으로 가장 적절한 것을 고르시오. [3점] 정답률 92%

Woman: ______________________________

① Probably not. You'd better see a doctor.
② It's my fault. I should've told you earlier.
③ That's too bad. We waited for you today.
④ No problem. I can explain how to get there.
⑤ That's right. We met in the library yesterday.

15 고득점 ○△× • 2020학년도 수능 15번

다음 상황 설명을 듣고, Brian의 어머니가 Brian에게 할 말로 가장 적절한 것을 고르시오. [3점] 정답률 80%

Brian's mother: ______________________________

① Make sure to call me whenever you go somewhere new.
② School trips are good opportunities to make friends.
③ I believe traveling broadens your perspective.
④ How about carrying the luggage on your own?
⑤ Why don't you pack your bag by yourself for the trip?

[16~17] 다음을 듣고, 물음에 답하시오.

16 ○△× • 2017학년도 수능 16번

남자가 하는 말의 주제로 가장 적절한 것은? 정답률 95%

① several ways flowers attract animals
② popular professions related to animals
③ various animals that feed from flowers
④ major factors that pose a threat to animals
⑤ endangered animals living on tropical islands

17 ○△× • 2017학년도 수능 17번

언급된 동물이 아닌 것은? 정답률 95%

① hummingbirds ② bats ③ lizards
④ parrots ⑤ squirrels

Dictation

문제 풀이에 중요한 핵심 부분과 듣기에 자주 나오는 표현들에 빈칸 처리를 했습니다. 방송을 잘 듣고, 빈칸에 알맞은 말을 써 넣으세요.

Tip! 잘 들리지 않는 부분이 있을 때에는 정답을 확인 후, 똑같은 속도로 따라 읽기 연습을 해 보세요.

1

M: Hello, viewers. Thank you for clicking on this video. I'm Ronnie Drain, and I've been a personal fitness trainer for over 15 years. Today, I'd like to tell you about my channel, *Build Your Body*. On my channel, you can watch videos showing you __________ __________ __________ __________ __________ __________ __________ that you can do at home or at your office. If you've experienced difficulty exercising regularly, my videos can provide __________ __________ __________ __________ __________ on exercise routines. New videos will be uploaded every Friday. __________ __________ __________ and build a stronger, healthier body.

2

W: Good morning, Chris.

M: Good morning, Julie. How was your weekend?

W: It was wonderful. I went to an event called Stargazing Night with my 7-year-old son.

M: Oh, so you went outdoors to look up at stars. Your son must have had a great time.

W: Yes. And I think it helped my son __________ __________ __________ __________ __________.

M: Interesting! How does it do that?

W: By counting the stars together, my son had a chance to __________ __________ __________ __________ __________.

M: Ah, that makes sense.

W: Also, he enjoyed __________ __________ __________ __________ __________ that stars form together.

M: Sounds like you had a magical and mathematical night!

W: Absolutely. I think looking at stars is a good way for kids to get used to mathematical concepts.

M: Maybe I should take my daughter to the event next time.

3

W: Hello, Mr. Roberts. I appreciate you taking the time to share your experience and knowledge.

M: My pleasure, Ms. Lee. __________ __________ __________ __________ __________ __________. So, I'm excited to help you.

W: Thanks. Since I'm writing about world-class athletes, I wanted to hear __________ __________ __________ __________ who became Olympic swimming champions.

M: Then we should start with what I observe on the first day of my swimming classes.

W: Do some children stand out right away?

M: Yes. Some kids are able to pick up my instructions quickly and easily.

W: I see. So did many of those kids go on to become Olympic champions?

M: Well, __________ __________ __________ __________ __________. Those who consistently practiced made great improvements and ultimately became champions.

W: This is good insight I can use in my book.

M: I hope it helps.

4

M: Honey, Aunt Sophie just called me and said we can stay at her house next weekend.

W: Wonderful. I really like the family room there.

M: She said she rearranged it and emailed me a photo. *[Clicking sound]* Here. Look.

W: Wow, the curtains on the window are pretty. I like their star pattern.

M: That's her favorite style.

W: Do you see the chair next to the sofa? It looks comfortable.

M: Maybe we should get one like that.

W: Good idea.

M: What do you think of the __________ __________ __________ __________ __________ __________ __________?

W: Oh, it's lovely. I also like the flowers in the vase.

M: Wait. I know those __________ __________ __________ __________ __________. They were our gift for her birthday.

W: That's right. Hey, look at the __________ __________ __________ __________ __________.

M: It looks cute. I can't wait to see it all in person.

5

M: Hi, Mary. You look worried. What's the matter?

W: Hi, Steve. Remember the report about wildflowers I've been working on?

M: Of course. That's for your biology class, right?

W: Yeah. I was able to get pictures of all the wildflowers in my report except for daisies.

M: I see. Can't you submit your report without pictures of daisies?

W: No. I really need them. I even tried to take pictures of daisies myself, but I found out that they usually __________ __________ __________ __________ __________.

M: You know what? This spring, I went hiking with my dad and __________ __________ __________ __________ __________.

W: Do you have them on your phone? Can I see them?

M: Sure. Have a look.

W: Oh, the flowers in the pictures are daisies! These will be great for my report.

M: Really? Then I'll __________ __________ __________ __________.

W: Thanks. That would be very helpful.

6

M: Welcome to Winter Land Mart. How may I help you?
M: Hi. I'm shopping for an electric heater.
W: How about this type? It's very popular.
M: Let me see. Oh, I like it.
W: Well, we have it in three sizes. The small one is $50, __________ __________ __________ __________, and the large is $100.
M: I'll take one medium-sized heater. Do you also have slippers?
W: Yes. We have wool and leather ones. A pair of wool slippers is $5, and a pair of leather ones is $10.
M: Hmm, I'll __________ __________ __________ __________ __________ __________.
W: Great. So, one medium-sized electric heater and two pairs of leather slippers. Is that correct?
M: Yes, that's right. Can I use this 10% off coupon?
W: I'll check. *[Pause]* Oh, I'm sorry. You cannot use this coupon because __________ __________ __________ __________.
M: That's okay. Here's my credit card.

7

W: Hey, Mike. How's your shoulder? Are you still in pain?
M: No, I feel totally fine, Emily. I should be ready for the table tennis tournament.
W: That's good to hear. Then do you want to practice with me now?
M: I'm sorry but I can't right now.
W: Why not? Do you have to __________ __________ __________ __________ __________?
M: No, I already submitted it to Mr. Jackson.
W: Oh, then I guess you have to __________ __________ __________ __________ __________, right?
M: I think I'm ready for it. Actually, I'm on my way to __________ __________ __________ __________ __________.
W: I see. Then, don't forget about our drama club meeting tomorrow.
M: Of course not. See you there.

8

M: Hey, Kelly. Have you been to the Bradford Museum of Failure?
W: I've never even heard of it.
M: Well, I went there yesterday and it was amazing.
W: What does the museum exhibit?
M: It __________ __________ __________ __________ from the world's best-known companies.
W: Interesting. That makes me curious about the purpose of founding the museum.
M: It was __________ __________ __________ __________ __________ that we need to admit our failures to truly succeed.
W: That's quite a message, and it makes a lot of sense. Did it just open?
M: No, it __________ __________ __________.
W: How come I've never heard of it?
M: I guess many people don't know about it. But visiting the museum was an eye-opening experience.
W: Where is it?
M: __________ __________ __________ Greenfalls, Hillside.
W: That's not too far from here. I'll be sure to visit it.

9

W: Hello, listeners. This is Lisa Cooperson from Leverin Radio Station. Are you considering a career related to law? The 2025 Court Visit Program will be held on November 19th at Woodfield County Courthouse. It allows high school students to experience working in law. This program offers an __________ __________ __________ __________ __________ __________ __________ and learn what happens in court. Its activities include a trial role-play. Also, the program __________ __________ __________ __________ that shows completion of the program. To join, you must apply as a team, __________ __________ __________ __________. Applications should be submitted to the courthouse by the end of this week. Lastly, the program __________ __________ __________ __________, so you won't need to bring your own. Don't miss this wonderful opportunity!

10

M: Welcome to Camilo's Kitchen.

W: Hello. I'm looking for a cutting board.

M: Let me show you our five top-selling models, all at affordable prices. Do you have a preference for any material? We have plastic, maple, and walnut cutting boards.

W: __________ __________ __________ __________ __________ __________ because I think plastic isn't environmentally friendly.

M: I see. What's your budget range?

W: __________ __________ __________ __________.

M: Okay. Do you prefer one with or without a handle?

W: I think a cutting board with a handle is easier to use. So __________ __________ __________ __________ __________ __________.

M: Then, which size do you want? You have two models left.

W: Hmm. A small-sized cutting board isn't convenient when I cut vegetables. I'll buy the other model.

M: Great. Then this is the cutting board for you.

11

W: Honey, I'm going out for a walk. Do you want to join me?

M: Sure. But can you wait for a moment? I __________ __________ __________ __________ __________ to one of my co-workers right now.

W: No problem. __________ __________ __________ __________ __________ __________ __________?

M: (Just give me about ten minutes.)

12

[Telephone rings.]

M: Hello, this is Bob's Camera Shop.

W: Hi, this is Clara Patterson. I'm calling to see __________ __________ __________ __________ __________ __________ __________ today.

M: Let me check. *[Clicking sound]* Yes. __________ __________ __________ your camera. It's ready to go.

W: (Good. I'll stop by and get it on my way home.)

13

W: Shaun, you really rocked the runway as a senior fashion model yesterday!

M: Thanks for coming to my first show, Grace.

W: My pleasure. You'll be an __________ __________ __________ __________ our age.

M: I'm so flattered.

W: It's amazing that you successfully switched careers.

M: Thank you. My dream has finally come true.

W: It couldn't have been easy to __________ __________ __________ in your 60s.

M: It wasn't. But I've always believed in myself, and age was never an issue for me.

W: You make me think of my old passion to be a painter, but I __________ __________ __________ __________ __________ __________.

M: Now is the time __________ __________ __________ __________ __________.

W: I think it's too late for that.

M: (Be positive. You can start pursuing your dream at any time.)

14

[Cell phone rings.]

W: Hello.

M: Hi, Cindy. It's Danny.

W: Hey, Danny. How are you?

M: I'm fine, but a little confused. I'm in the library, but none of our group members are here.

W: What? You're at the library now? We're not meeting until Thursday.

M: Really? I think there was __________ __________ __________ __________. I thought we were supposed to meet here at 12:30 this afternoon.

W: We were going to, but we __________ __________ __________ because we needed more time for individual work.

M: Huh? No one told me about it.

W: Don't you remember? We __________ __________ __________ __________ last Friday.

M: I wasn't there, Cindy. I stayed home sick.

W: Oh, no! That's right. You were absent last Friday when we changed the date! I was going to call you after school, but I forgot.

M: Oh, that explains it. Well, it's not a big deal.

W: (It's my fault. I should've told you earlier.)

15

W: Brian is a high school student. He has only traveled with his family before. Until now his mother has always __________ __________ __________ __________ __________ __________, so he doesn't have any experience preparing it himself. This weekend, Brian is supposed to go on a school trip with his friends. He asks his mother to get his stuff ready for his trip this time, too. However, she believes Brian is __________ __________ __________ __________ what he needs, and she thinks this time is a great opportunity for him to __________ __________ __________ __________ __________. So, she wants to tell Brian that he should get his things ready and put them in his bag without her help. In this situation, what would Brian's mother most likely say to Brian?

Brian's mother: (Why don't you pack your bag by yourself for the trip?)

16~17

M: Hello, class. Last time we learned about insects, their life cycles and what they eat. As you know, many insects get food from flowers, but they aren't the only creatures that do. Today, we'll learn about a variety of animals that __________ __________ __________ __________ __________ __________. First are hummingbirds. These birds use their long narrow beaks to __________ __________ __________ __________ __________ called nectar. Mysteriously, they only feed from upside down flowers. We still don't know why. Next are bats. Although most bats eat insects, some get their food from flowers. These bats have a strong sense of smell and sight compared to insect-eating bats. There are also lizards that drink nectar. These lizards are found on tropical islands that have few natural enemies. Finally, there is a type of squirrel that __________ __________ __________. Most nectar-drinking animals help flowers grow in numbers, but these squirrels often harm the plant. When drinking nectar, they __________ __________ __________ __________, which causes damage. Interesting, huh? What other animals use flowers in their diet? Take a minute to think, and then we'll talk about it.

Dictation Answers

1. how to do a variety of exercises / easy guidelines and useful resources / Visit my channel
2. become familiar with mathematical concepts / practice counting to high numbers / identifying shapes and tracing patterns
3. I've enjoyed all your bestselling books / how you've trained children / practicing is much more important
4. vase between the lamp and the book / two candles on the fireplace / round mirror on the wall
5. bloom from spring to fall / took some pictures of wildflowers / send them to you
6. the medium is $70 / take two pairs of leather ones / it isn't valid anymore
7. work on your history homework / study for the science quiz / volunteer at the school library
8. exhibits numerous failed products / founded to deliver the message / opened in 2001 / It's located in
9. opportunity to meet with judges and lawyers / gives participants a certificate / not as an individual / includes a free lunch
10. I don't want the plastic one / No more than $50 / I'll take one with a handle
11. have to send an email / How long do you think it'll take
12. if I can pick up my camera / I've finished repairing
13. inspiration to many people / realize your dream / put it off for too long / to give it a try
14. some kind of misunderstanding / changed the date / decided that in class
15. taken care of his travel bag / old enough to prepare / learn to be more independent

16~17. use flowers as a food source / get the flower's sweet liquid / feeds from flowers / bite through the flower

다빈출 코드

영어 듣기

PART 3

PATTERN PRACTICE

X

3 STEPS

STEP 1

문장을
3번씩 듣고
따라 읽는다.

▶

STEP 2

문장을
3번씩 듣고
받아 적는다.

▶

STEP 3

문장을 1번씩
듣고 의미를
파악한다.

多빈출 Pattern Practice 1

Pattern 01-10

STEP 1 다음 표현들을 3번씩 듣고 따라 읽으시오.

01. What do you think of ~? ~에 대해 어떻게 생각해?

1 2 3

What do you think of the vase between the lamp and the book? 전등과 책 사이에 있는 화병은 어떻게 생각해요? 2018학년도 수능
What do you think of the price? 가격에 대해 어떻게 생각해? 2023년 3월 고2

02. Why don't you[we] ~? ~하는 게 어때?

1 2 3

Why don't you give her something she likes when she sleeps?
그 애가 잘 때 그 애가 좋아하는 뭔가를 주는 게 어때요? 2023년 6월 고2

Honey, why don't we buy a UV toothbrush sanitizer? 여보, 우리 UV 칫솔 살균기를 사는 게 어때요? 2023년 3월 고2

03. I'd like to-v ~하고 싶다

1 2 3

I'd like to place an order. 주문하고 싶어요. 2015년 9월 고1
I'd like to make a reservation for March 21st. 3월 21일로 예약하고 싶습니다. 2015년 3월 고1

04. look forward to ~를 고대하다

1 2 3

We all have been looking forward to seeing you. 우리 모두 너를 보기를 고대하고 있었어. 2018년 3월 고2
I'm looking forward to it. 나는 그걸 고대하고 있어. 2023년 6월 고1

05. be going to-v ~할 것이다

1 2 3

More than 200 companies are going to participate. 200개가 넘는 회사가 참가할 예정이야. 2016년 3월 고1
We're going to ask people geography questions. 우리는 사람들에게 지리학 질문을 할 거야. 2021년 9월 고1

06. I'm thinking of v-ing 나는 ~할까 생각 중이다

1 2 3

I need a suit, so I'm thinking of buying one. 나는 정장이 필요해서, 한 벌 살까 생각 중이야. 2020학년도 수능
I'm thinking of buying a new one. 나는 새것을 살까 생각 중이야. 2017년 6월 고1

07. feel like ~하는 기분이다 / ~하고 싶다

1 2 3

I feel like I'm walking on air. 나는 공중을 걷는 기분이야. 2015년 6월 고1
I feel like taking art lessons, too. 나도 미술 수업을 듣고 싶어. 2015년 9월 고1

08. be supposed to-v ~하기로 되어 있다

1 2 3

This weekend, Brian is supposed to go on a school trip with his friends.
이번 주말에 Brian은 친구들과 함께 견학을 가기로 되어 있다. 2020학년도 수능

I thought we were supposed to meet here at 12:30 this afternoon.
난 우리가 오늘 오후 12시 30분에 여기서 만나기로 했다고 생각했어. 2017학년도 수능

09. it looks like ~ ~인 것처럼 보인다 / ~인 것 같다

1 2 3

It looks like he's blaming himself. 그는 자책하고 있는 것처럼 보인다. 2015년 3월 고1
It looks like your son is very happy on the swing. 아드님이 그네에서 아주 행복한 것처럼 보여요. 2015년 3월 고1

10. be planning to-v ~할 계획이다

1 2 3

I'm planning to watch that with my friend tonight. 오늘 밤 친구와 함께 그걸 볼 계획이야. 2019년 9월 고2
I'm planning to go camping with my family. 나는 가족과 함께 캠핑을 갈 계획이야. 2023년 6월 고1

Pattern 01-10

STEP 2 다음 문장을 3번씩 듣고, 각 문장의 빈칸을 채우시오.

1. ________ ________ ________ ________ ________ the price?

2. ________ ________ ________ watch that with my friend tonight.

3. I need a suit, so ________ ________ ________ ________ one.

4. I thought we ________ ________ ________ ________ here at 12:30 this afternoon.

5. ________ ________ ________ place an order.

6. ________ ________ ________ he's blaming himself.

7. We all have been ________ ________ ________ ________ you.

8. ________ ________ ________ ________ ________ ________ for March 21st.

9. This weekend, Brian ________ ________ ________ ________ on a school trip with his friends.

10. More than 200 companies ________ ________ ________ ________.

STEP 3 다음 문장을 1번씩 듣고, 해석과 같으면 ○, 다르면 ×표 하시오.

1 전등과 책 사이에 있는 화병은 어떻게 생각해요? (   )

2 왜 그녀가 잘 때 그녀가 좋아하는 것을 주니? (   )

3 우리는 사람들에게 지리학 질문을 하고 있어. (   )

4 나는 가족과 함께 캠핑을 갈 계획이야. (   )

5 나는 새것을 살까 생각 중이야. (   )

6 나는 공중을 걷는 기분이야. (   )

7 우리 UV 칫솔 살균기를 사는 게 어때요? (   )

8 아드님이 그네에서 아주 행복한 것처럼 보여요. (   )

9 나는 그걸 보고 있어. (   )

10 나도 미술 수업을 듣고 싶어. (   )

多빈출 Pattern Practice 2

Pattern 11-20

STEP 1 다음 표현들을 3번씩 듣고 따라 읽으시오.

11. What[How] about ~? ~는 어때?

1 ✓ 2 3

How about going shopping this Saturday? 이번 주 토요일에 쇼핑하러 가는 건 어때? 2022년 3월 고2
What about starting a school campaign to collect blankets and towels for the animals?
동물들을 위한 담요와 수건을 모으기 위해 학교 캠페인을 시작하는 게 어때? 2023년 3월 고2

12. Would you like to-v ~? ~하시겠습니까?

1 2 3

Would you like to switch rooms? 방을 바꾸시겠습니까? 2022학년도 수능
Would you like to have a look? 한 번 보시겠습니까? 2023년 6월 고1

13. Make sure ~ 반드시 ~해라, ~하는 것을 잊지 마라

1 2 3

Make sure to visit the observation deck on the 32nd floor. 반드시 32층에 있는 전망대를 가 보세요. 2021학년도 수능
Make sure you bring your own water. 반드시 각자의 물을 가져오세요. 2022년 3월 고2

14. be wondering if ~ ~인지 궁금하다

1 2 3

I was wondering if you can make it. 시간이 되시는지 궁금합니다. 2021학년도 수능
I was wondering if you had found any good locations yet. 네가 이미 좋은 장소를 찾았는지 궁금해하고 있었어. 2015학년도 수능

15. finish v-ing ~하는 것을 끝내다

1 2 3

Did you finish preparing for your hiking trip tomorrow? 내일 하이킹 여행 준비 끝냈니? 2023년 3월 고2
I finished designing the poster for our school's musical auditions.
나는 우리 학교 뮤지컬 오디션 포스터 디자인을 끝냈어. 2023년 9월 고2

16. Let me ~ 내가 ~할게

1 2 3

Let me take a look. 내가 한 번 볼게. 2017년 6월 고2
Alright, let me confirm your order. 알겠습니다, 주문을 확인하겠습니다. 2022년 9월 고2

17. it's time to-v ~할 시간이다

1 2 3

Now, it's time to let the other students know about the party. 이제 다른 학생들에게 파티에 대해 알릴 시간이야. 2020년 6월 고2
Honey, I think it's time to replace the kids' beds. 여보, 아이들 침대를 교체해야 할 때인 것 같아요. 2017학년도 수능

18. I'm afraid ~ ~할까 걱정이다, (유감이지만) ~할 것 같다

1 2 3

I think I can, but I'm afraid it'll be a problem for our friends.
그럴 수 있을 것 같은데 그게 우리 친구들에게 문제가 될까 걱정이야. 2018년 3월 고2
I'm afraid I can't make the reservation, then. 그러면 저는 예약을 할 수 없을 것 같아요. 2015년 3월 고1

19. Have you v-ed ~? ~해본 적이 있니?

1 2 3

Have you ever wondered what happens in the forest after dark?
어두워진 후에 숲속에서 무슨 일이 일어나는지 궁금해해본 적이 있나요? 2016년 3월 고2
Have you heard of a silicone straw? 실리콘 빨대를 들어봤니? 2023년 6월 고2

20. have ~ in mind ~을 염두에 두다

1 2 3

I have a model in mind. 염두에 두고 있는 모델이 있어요. 2016년 3월 고1
Do you have any special program in mind? 특별한 프로그램을 염두에 두고 있니? 2016년 9월 고2

Pattern 11-20

STEP 2 다음 문장을 3번씩 듣고, 각 문장의 빈칸을 채우시오.

1. ________ ________ ________ a school campaign to collect blankets and towels for the animals?

2. I ________ ________ ________ ________ ________.

3. ________ ________ ________ ________ what happens in the forest after dark?

4. I think I can, but ________ ________ it'll be a problem for our friends.

5. ________ ________ ________ ________ your own water.

6. ________ ________ ________ ________ you had found any good locations yet.

7. ________ ________ ________ ________ have a look?

8. Alright, ________ ________ ________ your order.

9. ________ ________ ________ ________ for your hiking trip tomorrow?

10. Honey, I think ________ ________ ________ ________ the kids' beds.

STEP 3 다음 문장을 1번씩 듣고, 해석과 같으면 ○, 다르면 ×표 하시오.

1 어떤 특별 프로그램이 있나요? (　　)

2 실리콘 빨대 있나요? (　　)

3 그러면 저는 예약을 할 수 없을 것 같아요. (　　)

4 이제 다른 학생들에게 파티에 대해 알릴 시간이야. (　　)

5 나는 우리 학교 뮤지컬 오디션 포스터 디자인을 끝냈어. (　　)

6 시간이 되시는지 궁금합니다. (　　)

7 내가 한 번 보여 줄게. (　　)

8 32층에 전망대가 있는지 가서 확인해 보세요. (　　)

9 방을 바꾸는 것을 좋아하십니까? (　　)

10 이번 주 토요일에 쇼핑하러 가는 건 어때? (　　)

多빈출 Pattern Practice 3

Pattern 21-30

STEP 1 다음 표현들을 3번씩 듣고 따라 읽으시오.

21. Could[Would] you ~? ~해 주시겠어요?

1 ✓ 2 3

Could you give me a discount? 할인해 주시겠어요? 2015년 3월 고1
Would you come take a look at this plant? 오셔서 이 식물을 한 번 봐주시겠어요? 2023년 3월 고2

22. 'd[had] better ~하는 것이 좋겠다

1 2 3

First, I think we'd better decide on the topic for our presentation. 우선, 우리의 발표 주제를 정하는 게 좋겠어. 2022년 9월 고2
You'd better use public transportation today. 오늘은 대중교통을 이용하는 게 좋겠어. 2019년 6월 고1

23. be interested in ~에 관심이 있다

1 2 3

I didn't know they were interested in my proposal. 그들이 제 제안에 관심이 있는지 몰랐어요. 2016학년도 수능
I'm interested in drones, but there's no drone club. 나는 드론에 관심이 있는데, 드론 동아리는 없어. 2019년 3월 고1

24. feel free to-v 마음껏 ~해라

1 2 3

For more information, feel free to call us. 더 많은 정보는, 편히 전화주세요. 2020년 6월 고2
As always, if you have any questions, please feel free to ask.
언제나처럼, 궁금한 점이 있으시면, 마음껏 질문하시길 바랍니다. 2019년 9월 고2

25. What if ~? ~라면 어쩌지?

1 2 3

What if I can't see important pop-up messages that are not advertisements?
광고가 아닌 중요한 팝업 메시지를 보지 못하면 어쩌지? 2019년 9월 고2
What if they don't know the answers? 그들이 답을 모르면 어쩌지? 2022년 9월 고1

26. be good at ~에 능숙하다

1 2 3

I'm good at washing dishes. 나는 설거지를 잘해. 2020학년도 수능
You know I'm good at finding information online. 너도 알겠지만 내가 온라인에서 정보 찾는 데 능숙하잖아. 2016학년도 수능

27. How ~ be going? 어떻게 되어 가나요?

1 2 3

How's it going with rearranging your classroom? 교실 재배치는 어떻게 되어 가나요? 2023년 9월 고2
How are your preparations going? 준비는 어떻게 되어 가니? 2022년 3월 고1

28. be busy v-ing[with] ~하느라[로] 바쁘다

1 2 3

I've been busy helping my granddad with his concert. 나는 할아버지의 연주회를 돕느라 바빴어. 2023년 3월 고1
I've been really busy with my science assignment. 나는 과학 과제로 정말 바빴어. 2016학년도 수능

29. on one's way to ~로 가는 도중[길]에

1 2 3

I'm on my way to volunteer at the school library. 학교 도서관에 자원봉사하러 가는 길이야. 2022학년도 수능
I'm meeting some friends on my way home. 나는 집에 가는 길에 친구 몇 명을 만날 거야. 2016년 6월 고2

30. be able to-v ~할 수 있다

1 2 3

I was able to fix your issue. 당신의 문제를 해결할 수 있었어요. 2023년 3월 고2
Luckily, I was able to fix it by myself. 다행히, 나는 나 혼자 그것을 고칠 수 있었어. 2022년 6월 고1

Pattern 21-30

STEP 2 다음 문장을 3번씩 듣고, 각 문장의 빈칸을 채우시오.

1. ___________ ___________ use public transportation today.

2. ___________ ___________ ___________ ___________ my granddad with his concert.

3. ___________ ___________ I can't see important pop-up messages that are not advertisements?

4. As always, if you have any questions, please ___________ ___________ ___________ ___________.

5. I'm meeting some friends ___________ ___________ ___________ ___________.

6. ___________ ___________ ___________ ___________ a discount?

7. ___________ ___________ ___________ with rearranging your classroom?

8. I didn't know ___________ ___________ ___________ ___________ my proposal.

9. I ___________ ___________ ___________ ___________ your issue.

10. You know ___________ ___________ ___________ finding information online.

STEP 3 다음 문장을 1번씩 듣고, 해석과 같으면 ○, 다르면 ×표 하시오.

1 오셔서 이 식물을 한 번 봐주시겠어요? (　　)

2 우리는 더 좋은 발표 주제를 정했어. (　　)

3 그들이 답을 모르면 어쩌지? (　　)

4 나는 설거지를 잘해. (　　)

5 정말 바빠서 과학 과제를 못 했어. (　　)

6 나는 드론에 관심이 있는데, 드론 동아리는 없어. (　　)

7 어떻게 갈 준비를 했니? (　　)

8 학교 도서관에 자원봉사하러 가는 길이야. (　　)

9 다행히, 나는 나 혼자 그것을 고칠 수 있었어. (　　)

10 더 많은 정보는, 편히 전화주세요. (　　)

多빈출 Pattern Practice 4

Pattern 31-40

STEP 1 다음 표현들을 3번씩 듣고 따라 읽으시오.

31. must have v-ed ~했음에 틀림없다

1 2 3

It must have been awesome! 그것은 틀림없이 멋졌겠구나! 2016년 6월 고2

You must have been busy. 너 틀림없이 바빴겠구나. 2019학년도 3월 고1

32. used to-v ~하곤 했다, ~했었다

1 2 3

You used to sit on the floor and watch me while I cleaned.
내가 청소하는 동안 너는 바닥에 앉아서 날 지켜보곤 했단다. 2018년 9월 고2

I used to have the same problem just like you. 나도 너처럼 똑같은 문제가 있었어. 2015년 11월 고2

33. that sounds ~하게 들리다, ~인 것 같다

1 2 3

That sounds like a lot of work. 일이 많은 것 같아. 2023년 9월 고1

That sounds quite demanding. 꽤 어렵게 들려. 2022학년도 수능

34. 'd[would] rather (차라리) ~하는 게 낫다

1 2 3

I'd rather have more space to store my keyboard. 나는 차라리 키보드를 보관할 공간을 더 두겠어. 2021년 9월 고2

I'd rather take a lesson in the morning. 나는 오전에 수업을 듣는 게 낫겠어. 2020년 11월 고1

35. I'm calling ~ 때문에[하려고] 전화드립니다

1 2 3

I'm calling to see if I can pick up my camera today. 오늘 제 카메라를 찾을 수 있는지 확인하려고 전화드려요. 2022학년도 수능

I'm calling about renting an apartment in Westford Village.
Westford Village에 있는 아파트를 임대하는 것에 대해 알아보려고 전화했어요. 2016학년도 수능

36. how to-v ~하는 방법

1 2 3

I don't know how to make QR codes. 나는 QR코드 만드는 방법을 몰라. 2023년 9월 고2

Now let's talk about how to use them in design for your brand.
이제 여러분의 브랜드 디자인에 그것들을 이용하는 방법에 대해 이야기해봅시다. 2023년 6월 고2

37. May I ~? ~해도 될까요?

1 2 3

May I ask your price range? 생각하시는 가격 범위를 여쭤봐도 될까요? 2017년 3월 고1

May I take a picture of you in front of your rice fields for my magazine article?
저희 잡지 기사에 쓰도록 논 앞에서 선생님 사진을 찍어도 될까요? 2020학년도 수능

38. seem like / seem to-v ~인 것 같다

1 2 3

It seems like they're looking for something. 그들은 뭔가를 찾고 있는 것 같아. 2021년 9월 고1

He seems to be in a serious condition. 그는 심각한 상태인 것 같아. 2015년 3월 고2

39. ask A to-v A에게 ~해 달라고 요청하다

1 2 3

I couldn't buy the wallet you asked me to buy. 네가 나에게 사달라고 요청한 지갑을 사지 못했어. 2023년 3월 고1

He wants to ask her to help him draw posters. 그는 그녀에게 그가 포스터 그리는 것을 도와달라고 요청하기를 원한다. 2022년 6월 고1

40. How long ~? 얼마나 ~하나요?

1 2 3

How long do you think it'll take? 얼마나 걸릴 거라고 생각하세요? 2022학년도 수능

How long will the research project last? 연구 프로젝트는 얼마나 지속될까요? 2020년 3월 고2

Pattern 31-40

STEP 2 다음 문장을 3번씩 듣고, 각 문장의 빈칸을 채우시오.

1. You ___________ ___________ ___________ on the floor and watch me while I cleaned.

2. ___________ ___________ ___________ a lesson in the morning.

3. Now let's talk about ___________ ___________ ___________ them in design for your brand.

4. You ___________ ___________ ___________ busy.

5. I couldn't buy the wallet you ___________ ___________ ___________ ___________.

6. ___________ ___________ will the research project last?

7. He ___________ ___________ ___________ in a serious condition.

8. ___________ ___________ ___________ ___________ if I can pick up my camera today.

9. ___________ ___________ ___________ a lot of work.

10. ___________ ___________ ___________ ___________ ___________ of you in front of your rice fields for my magazine article?

STEP 3 다음 문장을 1번씩 듣고, 해석과 같으면 ○, 다르면 ×표 하시오.

1 그것은 틀림없이 멋져야만 해! ( )

2 나는 너와 똑같은 문제를 사용했어. ( )

3 나는 차라리 키보드를 보관할 공간을 더 두겠어. ( )

4 그들은 무언가를 찾고 싶어 해. ( )

5 그는 그녀에게 그가 포스터 그리는 것을 도와달라고 요청하기를 원한다. ( )

6 나는 QR코드를 얼마나 만들어야 할지 모르겠어. ( )

7 얼마나 멀다고 생각하세요? ( )

8 생각하시는 가격 범위를 여쭤봐도 될까요? ( )

9 그걸 듣기는 꽤 어려워. ( )

10 Westford Village에 있는 아파트를 임대하는 것에 대해 알아보려고 전화했어요. ( )

多빈출 Pattern Practice 5

Pattern 41-50

STEP 1 다음 표현들을 3번씩 듣고 따라 읽으시오.

41. I prefer ~ ~을 선호한다

I prefer wearing hiking shoes that aren't too tight. 나는 너무 꽉 끼지 않는 등산화를 신는 것을 선호해. 2023년 9월 고2

I prefer wireless so that we can install it anywhere we want.
저는 우리가 원하는 어느 곳에든 설치할 수 있도록 무선을 선호해요. 2023년 6월 고2

42. should have v-ed ~했어야 했다

I should've told you earlier. 내가 네게 더 일찍 말했어야 했어. 2017학년도 수능

I think he should have been more careful. 나는 그가 더 신중했어야 한다고 생각해. 2016년 3월 고1

43. try to-v ~하려고 노력하다

I'll try to keep that in mind. 그것을 명심하도록 노력할게. 2018년 6월 고1

I'm trying to buy a trash can for my kitchen. 나는 내 주방에 놓을 쓰레기통을 사려고 하고 있어. 2018년 3월 고2

44. be about to-v 막 ~하려고 하다

She is about to call the card company to report the card missing.
그녀는 분실한 카드를 신고하기 위해 카드 회사에 막 전화하려 한다. 2018년 9월 고1

When Amy is about to leave work, she's given some tasks. Amy가 막 퇴근하려고 할 때, 그녀는 일을 받는다. 2022년 6월 고2

45. Don't forget ~을 잊지 마라

Don't forget to take pictures when they come in. 그들이 들어올 때 사진 찍는 거 잊지 마. 2016년 6월 고1

Don't forget that your small actions can make a big difference.
여러분의 작은 행동이 큰 변화를 가져올 수 있다는 것을 잊지 마십시오. 2015학년도 수능

46. be here to-v ~하러 여기에 왔다

I'm here to purchase city tour package tickets for today. 오늘 시티 투어 패키지 표를 구입하러 왔어요. 2016년 6월 고2

I'm here to announce that the expo will run for three days starting on March 17th, 2023.
2023년 3월 17일부터 3일간 엑스포가 진행될 것임을 알려드리기 위해 이 자리에 섰습니다. 2023학년도 수능

47. have an option/there's an option 선택(권)이 있다

We have just two options left. 우린 딱 두 가지 선택이 남아 있어. 2023년 9월 고1

There are two options left. 두 가지 선택권이 있어. 2022학년도 수능

48. That's why ~ 그게 ~한 이유이다 / **This is because ~** 이것은 ~ 때문이다

That's why there're two guitars in the room. 그래서 방에 기타가 두 개 있는 거야. 2021년 6월 고1

This is because the color white traditionally symbolizes innocence. 이는 흰색이 전통적으로 결백을 상징하기 때문이다. 2021학년도 수능

49. Do you have to+동사원형? 너는 ~해야 하니?

Do you have to prepare your presentation for biology class? 너는 생물학 수업을 위한 발표를 준비해야 하니? 2021년 6월 고2

Do you have to study for your economics exam? 경제학 시험 공부를 해야 하니? 2023학년도 수능

50. be looking for ~을 찾고 있다

I'm looking for swimming goggles for my kids. 우리 아이들을 위한 수경을 찾고 있어요. 2023년 6월 고1

I'm looking for some sneakers. 나는 운동화를 좀 찾고 있어. 2022년 6월 고1

Pattern 41-50

STEP 2 다음 문장을 3번씩 듣고, 각 문장의 빈칸을 채우시오.

1. ________ ________ ________ some sneakers.

2. ________ ________ ________ your small actions can make a big difference.

3. There are ________ ________ ________.

4. ________ ________ ________ ________ prepare your presentation for biology class?

5. She ________ ________ ________ ________ the card company to report the card missing.

6. ________ ________ ________ so that we can install it anywhere we want.

7. ________ ________ ________ swimming goggles for my kids.

8. ________ ________ ________ ________ ________ for your economics exam?

9. ________ ________ ________ ________ city tour package tickets for today.

10. I'm ________ ________ ________ a trash can for my kitchen.

STEP 3 다음 문장을 1번씩 듣고, 해석과 같으면 ○, 다르면 ×표 하시오.

1 우린 딱 두 가지 선택이 남아 있어. (　　)

2 그건 방에 기타가 두 개 있기 때문이야. (　　)

3 그것을 명심하도록 노력할게. (　　)

4 나는 분명 네게 더 일찍 말했어. (　　)

5 3일간 엑스포가 진행될 것임을 알려드리기 위해 이 자리에 섰습니다. (　　)

6 나는 너무 꽉 끼지 않는 등산화를 신는 것을 선호해. (　　)

7 Amy가 막 퇴근하려고 할 때, 그녀는 일을 받는다. (　　)

8 그래서 흰색이 전통적으로 결백을 상징한다. (　　)

9 그들이 들어올 때 사진 찍었던 거 잊지 마. (　　)

10 나는 그가 더 신중했어야 한다고 생각해. (　　)

MEMO

MEMO

MEMO

다빈출코드

빠른 정답 찾기

영어영역 **듣기**

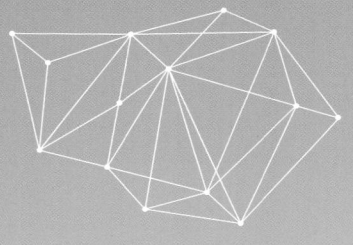

2027 수능대비 다빈출코드 빠른 정답 찾기

초급 모의고사(1~9회)

제1회	제2회	제3회	제4회	제5회	제6회	제7회	제8회	제9회
1④	1①	1⑤	1④	1③	1④	1②	1③	1①
2⑤	2②	2⑤	2③	2②	2⑤	2①	2⑤	2②
3③	3①	3⑤	3②	3③	3②	3①	3①	3②
4⑤	4⑤	4④	4③	4④	4⑤	4⑤	4④	4③
5④	5①	5⑤	5④	5④	5④	5①	5②	5②
6②	6③	6②	6④	6②	6③	6②	6③	6③
7①	7④	7③	7①	7②	7④	7⑤	7①	7②
8②	8③	8③	8②	8③	8④	8③	8③	8④
9③	9⑤	9④	9④	9⑤	9⑤	9③	9⑤	9④
10②	10②	10②	10②	10②	10④	10③	10③	10④
11②	11④	11⑤	11①	11④	11②	11②	11①	11①
12①	12③	12⑤	12①	12①	12①	12⑤	12⑤	12⑤
13④	13⑤	13①	13③	13③	13①	13②	13①	13②
14④	14⑤	14①	14①	14③	14①	14①	14⑤	14②
15③	15③	15⑤	15①	15③	15④	15①	15①	15⑤
16③	16②	16③	16④	16③	16⑤	16①	16⑤	16①
17③	17③	17④	17④	17④	17③	17④	17③	17②

중급 모의고사(1~9회)

제1회	제2회	제3회	제4회	제5회	제6회	제7회	제8회	제9회
1①	1③	1⑤	1⑤	1⑤	1①	1③	1①	1①
2①	2②	2②	2①	2①	2⑤	2①	2③	2②
3①	3②	3①	3①	3①	3②	3④	3④	3②
4④	4④	4⑤	4⑤	4④	4④	4⑤	4⑤	4⑤
5①	5⑤	5⑤	5④	5②	5②	5①	5⑤	5②
6④	6①	6②	6③	6③	6②	6②	6②	6④
7①	7⑤	7①	7⑤	7⑤	7②	7③	7①	7②
8④	8④	8③	8④	8③	8②	8④	8③	8③
9③	9④	9③	9⑤	9⑤	9⑤	9④	9⑤	9④
10④	10①	10④	10①	10②	10④	10①	10②	10④
11⑤	11②	11①	11①	11④	11⑤	11①	11②	11③
12⑤	12①	12②	12②	12①	12④	12④	12①	12②
13①	13④	13②	13②	13①	13⑤	13②	13④	13①
14②	14①	14①	14⑤	14④	14②	14④	14①	14②
15②	15③	15⑤	15⑤	15①	15②	15①	15②	15⑤
16①	16②	16④	16①	16②	16②	16②	16②	16③
17④	17③	17③	17⑤	17③	17④	17④	17②	17④

고급 모의고사(1~6회)

제1회	제2회	제3회	제4회	제5회	제6회
1①	1②	1⑤	1③	1①	1⑤
2②	2②	2②	2①	2③	2①
3④	3③	3①	3③	3②	3③
4④	4⑤	4④	4④	4④	4⑤
5①	5①	5②	5②	5②	5①
6④	6③	6②	6②	6④	6④
7⑤	7③	7①	7③	7①	7①
8④	8③	8④	8⑤	8③	8④
9③	9⑤	9⑤	9②	9④	9④
10④	10②	10②	10③	10④	10④
11②	11①	11②	11③	11①	11①
12①	12⑤	12③	12①	12②	12②
13⑤	13④	13④	13②	13①	13⑤
14③	14②	14⑤	14④	14④	14②
15⑤	15②	15①	15⑤	15①	15⑤
16②	16③	16①	16①	16⑤	16③
17⑤	17⑤	17③	17⑤	17⑤	17④

다빈출 코드

듣기

영어영역 고1 독해 / 고2 독해 / 듣기 / 어법·어휘

1. 최근 수능/학평 출제경향을 가장 잘 보여주는 기출 우수문항 선별 수록
2. 모든 지문에 대한 직독직해, 끊어 읽기, 구문해설, 오답풀이 제공

www.nebooks.co.kr ▼

NE 능률

빠른 독해를 위한 바른 선택

교재구성 미리 보기

시리즈 구성

- 기초세우기
- 구문독해
- 유형독해
- 수능실전

1 최신 수능 경향 반영

최신 수능 경향에 맞춘 독해 지문 교체와
수능 기출 문장 중심으로 구성 된 구문 훈련

2 실전 대비 기능 강화

실제 사용에 기반한 사례별 구문 학습과 최신 수능 경향을 반영한
수능 독해 Mini Test로 수능 유형 훈련

3 서술형 주관식 문제

내신 및 수능 출제 경향에 맞춘 서술형 및 주관식 문제 재정비

고등

BOOK LIST

도/서/목/록

어휘 · 문법 · 구문

능률 VOCA

대한민국 어휘서의 표준

초등 기본 | 초등 필수

중등 기본 | 중등 필수 | 중등 고난도 | 중등 숙어

고등 기본 | 수능 필수 | 수능 고난도

어원편 중등 | 어원편 고등

GRAMMAR ZONE

대한민국 영문법 교재의 표준

중등 기본 | 중등 필수 |

고등 기본 | 고등 필수 | Complete

필히 통하는 시리즈

시험에 필히 통하는 고등 영문법과 서술형

필히 통하는 고등 영문법 기본편 | 실력편

필히 통하는 고등 서술형 기본편 | 실전편

문마고

문제로 마스터하는 고등 영문법

천문장

구문이 독해로 연결되는 해석 공식

입문 | 기본 | 완성

다빈출 코드

2027 수능대비

수능기출문제집

영어영역

듣기

해설편

NE 능률

다빈출 코드

2027 수능대비

수능기출문제집

영어영역

듣기

해설편

01 목적

p.10

[코드 접속하기]

정답 I ③

선택지 선택비율	① 1%	② 0%	③ 98%	④ 0%	④ 1%

해석

남: 안녕하세요, 시청자 여러분. Ryan입니다. Only4Health 채널에 다시 오신 걸 환영합니다. ⓐ잠을 잘 자고 싶으신가요? 그렇다면 Nightly Journey 앱이 여러분께 딱 맞습니다. 이 앱은 차분한 소리, 평화롭고 조용한 음악, 그리고 잠자리 동화처럼 여러분이 숙면을 취하도록 도와주는 다양한 도움을 제공합니다. 또한 더 잘 자기 위해 호흡하는 방법을 가르쳐주는 오디오 연습도 제공합니다. 다음에 잠자리에 들 때, Nightly Journey를 고려해 보세요. 그러면 다음 날 아침에 상쾌한 기분으로 일어날 겁니다. ⓑ오늘 밤 이 앱을 사용해서 숙면을 취하는 건 어떨까요? 시청해 주셔서 감사합니다.

문제 풀이

ⓐⓑ숙면을 돕는 Nightly Journey 앱을 소개하며 사용을 권하고 있다.

오답 풀이

	선택지	오답 유도 방식
①	명상에 도움이 되는 호흡 방법을 설명하려고	더 잘 자기 위한 호흡 방법은 언급되었으나, 명상에 도움이 되는 호흡 방법에 관한 내용은 언급되지 않았다.
②	숙면을 위한 균형 잡힌 식단을 권장하려고	균형 잡힌 식단에 관한 언급은 없다.
③	아침에 듣기 좋은 음악 채널을 홍보하려고	도입부에 'Channel'이 나오지만, 음악 채널에 관한 언급은 없다.
④	수면 시간을 측정하는 앱 설치 방법을 안내하려고	수면 시간 측정에 대한 언급은 없다.

02 요지 · 의견 · 주장 · 주제

p.11

[코드 접속하기]

정답 I ②

선택지 선택비율	① 1%	② 98%	③ 0%	④ 0%	⑤ 0%

해석

남: Monica, 부산 여행 계획 짰니?
여: 네, 아빠. 오전에 해변에 가고 수족관에 갈 거예요. 그런 다음 수산시장에서 점심을 먹고 하이킹하러 갈 거예요.
남: 잠깐! ⓐ꽤 힘들겠구나.
여: 아시다시피, 대학 생활 시작하고 첫 여행이잖아요.
남: 알지, 하지만 ⓑ여행에 너무 많은 것을 계획하면 안 될 것 같구나.
여: 음, 하루밖에 없어서, 가능하면 많이 경험하고 싶어요.
남: ⓒ계획을 고수하려면 몹시 지칠 거야. 그리고 각 장소로 이동하는 데 걸리는 시간도 고려하렴.
여: 아빠 말씀이 맞는 것 같아요. 그리고 어떤 곳에서는 대기가 길 수도 있고요.
남: 맞아. 그게 바로 ⓓ여행 계획을 너무 많은 걸로 채우면 안 되는 이유야.
여: 알겠어요. 계획을 변경할게요.

문제 풀이

남자는 여자의 여행 계획을 듣고, ⓐ힘들겠다며 ⓑⓒⓓ여행에 너무 많은 것을 계획하고 지키려면 지치기 때문에 너무 많이 계획하면 안 된다고 말하고 있다.

오답 풀이

	선택지	오답 유도 방식
①	여행 전에 합리적으로 예산을 계획해야 한다.	여행 예산에 관한 언급은 없었다.
③	인생에서 자신의 원칙을 고수하는 것이 중요하다.	'You'll be worn out if you stick to your plan.'의 'stick to'를 활용한 오답이다.
④	여행은 사고의 폭을 확장시켜 사람을 성장하게 한다.	여행이 사람을 성장하게 한다는 내용은 언급되지 않았다.
⑤	보호자 없이 학생끼리 여행하는 것은 안전하지 않다.	'starting college'에서 여자가 대학생임을 유추할 수 있으나, 학생끼리 하는 여행의 안전성에 대한 내용은 아니다.

03 관계

p.12

[코드 접속하기]

정답 I ①

선택지 선택비율	① 96%	② 1%	③ 0%	④ 1%	⑤ 0%

해석

남: 안녕하세요, Watson 선생님. 제 인터뷰 요청을 수락해주셔서 감사합니다.
여: 별말씀을요. ⓐWindmore 고등학교의 Michael이시죠.
남: 네. ⓑ제가 다니고 있는 학교를 설계한 분을 인터뷰하게 되어 영광이에요.
여: 고맙습니다. 저는 그 설계에 자부심을 느껴요.
남: 디자인 컨셉이 뭐였나요?
여: 학교 건물 설계를 계획할 때, 거기에 자연의 요소를 포함하고 싶었어요.
남: 그렇군요. 이 컨셉을 다른 건물 설계에 적용하셨나요?
여: 네. Skyforest Tower요. 제 설계에는 층마다 있는 작은 정원과 옥상 정원을 포함하고 있어서, 건물을 솟아오른 숲처럼 보이게 했죠.
남: 인상적이네요. 실은 다음 주에 저희 미술 선생님께서 현장학습으로 저희를 그곳에 데려가실 거예요.
여: 정말요? 32층에 있는 전망대에 꼭 가 보세요. 전망이 장관을 이룬답니다.
남: 고맙습니다. ⓒ반 친구들과 볼게요.

문제 풀이

남자는 ⓐⓑWindmore 고등학교에 다니고 있다고 했고 ⓒ반 친구들을 언급한 것으로 보아 학생임을 알 수 있다. 여자는 ⓑ남자가 다니고 있는 학교를 설계했다고 했으므로 건축가임을 알 수 있다.

오답 풀이

	선택지	오답 유도 방식
②	신문 기자 – 화가	'design'이 언급된 것을 이용한 오답 선택지이다.
③	탐험가 – 환경 운동가	탐험에 대한 언급은 없다. 'nature'가 언급된 것을 환경 운동가의 단서로 생각하면 안 된다.
④	건물 관리인 – 정원사	'building'과 'mini gardens'가 언급된 것을 이용한 오답 선택지이다.

⑤	교사 – 여행사 직원	'my art teacher'와 'trip'이 언급된 것을 이용한 오답 선택지이다.

04 그림 일치 p.13

[코드 접속하기]

정답 | ④

선택지 선택비율	① 3%	② 1%	③ 2%	④ 90%	⑤ 4%

해석

남: Kayla, 네가 지난 주말에 거리에서 버스킹하러 갔다고 들었어.
여: 정말 놀라웠어! 여기 사진이 있어. 봐!
남: 아, ⓐ내가 준 모자를 쓰고 있네.
여: 응, 정말 마음에 들거든.
남: 좋아 보여. ⓑ네 옆에서 기타를 연주하는 이 남자아이는 네 남동생인 Kevin이겠구나.
여: 맞아. 내가 노래하는 동안 그 애가 연주했어.
남: 멋지다. 왜 ⓒ기타 케이스를 열어두었어?
여: 그건 관객을 위한 거야. 관객이 우리 공연이 마음에 들면, 우리에게 돈을 좀 주거든.
남: 아, 그리고 ⓓ스피커 두 대를 설치했구나!
여: 응. 최근에 샀어.
남: 그렇구나. 그리고 ⓔ벽에 있는 저 포스터는 네가 디자인했니?
여: 응. 내 동생과 내가 함께 작업했어.
남: 정말 즐거웠겠구나!

문제 풀이

ⓓ스피커 두 대를 설치했다고 했으므로, 그림 ④는 대화 내용과 일치하지 않는다.

오답 풀이

	선택지	오답 유도 방식
①		모자를 쓴 여자가 있다.
②		여자 옆에 기타를 연주하는 소년이 있다.
③		열어 둔 기타 케이스가 있다.
⑤		벽에 포스터가 있다.

05 할 일 · 부탁한 일 p.14

[코드 접속하기]

정답 | ②

선택지 선택비율	① 4%	② 82%	③ 7%	④ 6%	⑤ 1%

해석

여: Tony, ⓐ난 우리의 Go-Green 행사가 정말 기대돼!
남: 나도 그래. 행사가 거의 다가왔어. ⓑ준비 사항을 같이 점검하는 게 어때?
여: 좋아. 난 전시 부스가 우리 행사에 매우 중요하다고 생각해. 어떻게 돼 가고 있어?
남: 거의 준비됐어. 내가 오늘 오후에 부스 설치를 할 거야. 환영 선물은?
여: 내가 이미 친환경 가방을 준비했어.
남: 완벽해! 그다음은 뭐야?
여: 우리 행사 손님 명단을 확인해야 해.
남: 내가 명단은 두 번 확인했어. 하지만 ⓒ아직 온라인 초대장은 보내지 않았어.
여: 문제없어. ⓓ그건 내가 바로 처리할게. 음식과 음료는?
남: 내가 음식과 음료 서비스는 일정을 잡았고, 손님들에게 재사용 가능한 접시로 제공할 거야.
여: 좋다! 우리 행사가 큰 성공을 거둘 거라고 확신해.

문제 풀이

ⓐⓑGo-Green 행사 준비 사항을 점검하는 상황인데, 남자가 ⓒ아직 온라인 초대장을 보내지 않았다고 말하자 여자가 ⓓ자신이 바로 처리하겠다고 했다.

오답 풀이

	선택지	오답 유도 방식
①	선물 준비하기	여자가 이미 친환경 가방을 준비했다고 했다.
③	음식 주문하기	남자가 음식과 음료 서비스 일정을 잡았다고 했다.
④	초대 손님 명단 확인하기	남자가 손님 명단을 두 번 확인했다고 했다.
⑤	전시 부스 설치하기	남자가 오늘 오후에 부스를 설치할 것이라고 했다.

06 숫자 정보 p.15

[코드 접속하기]

정답 | ③

선택지 선택비율	① 1%	② 1%	③ 93%	④ 0%	⑤ 3%

해석

남: 안녕하세요, 이곳 Magic Unicorn 어린이 농장에서의 시간을 즐기고 계신가요?
여: 네, 고맙습니다. 동물들에게 먹이로 줄 간식을 좀 사고 싶어요.
남: 네. 동물들을 위한 두 가지 종류의 음식을 팔고 있어요. 채소 스틱과 썰은 과일이에요.
여: 얼마인가요?
남: ⓐ채소 스틱 한 봉지는 5달러이고 썰은 과일 한 봉지는 10달러예요.
여: ⓑ채소 스틱 열 봉지 할게요. 다른 활동이 있나요?
남: 승마를 제공하고 있어요. ⓒ농장 주위를 타는 티켓은 25달러예요.
여: 아, 제 아들과 딸이 좋아하겠어요. ⓓ티켓 두 장 주세요.
남: 그럼, ⓔ채소 스틱 네 봉지와 승마 티켓 두 장, 맞지요?
여: 네. 그리고 가을 판촉 행사로 10% 할인을 제공한다고 들었어요.
남: 죄송합니다. 그 행사는 지난주에 끝났어요.
여: 알겠습니다. 여기 제 신용카드요.

문제 풀이

여자는 ⓐⓑⓔ한 봉지에 5달러인 채소 스틱 네 봉지(5x4)와 ⓒⓓⓔ한 장에 25달러인 승마 티켓 두 장(25x2)을 구입하므로, 총 70달러를 지불할 것이다. 판촉 행사는 종료되어 10% 할인은 받지 못한다.

오답 풀이

	선택지	오답 유도 방식
①	$55	채소 스틱 네 봉지, 썰은 과일 한 봉지, 승마 티켓 한 장 값을 더한 금액이다.
②	$63	10% 할인받을 때의 금액으로 착각하면 안 된다.
④	$81	채소 스틱 네 봉지, 썰은 과일 두 봉지, 승마 티켓 두 장 값을 더한 금액에서 10% 할인받은 금액이다.
⑤	$90	채소 스틱 네 봉지, 썰은 과일 두 봉지, 승마 티켓 두 장 값을 더한 금액이다.

07 이유

p.16

[코드 접속하기]

정답 | ①

선택지 선택비율	① 85%	② 3%	③ 3%	④ 4%	⑤ 2%

해석

남: 안녕, Claire. 네 화학 발표는 어땠니?
여: 예상했던 것보다 더 잘 했어.
남: 잘됐네. 하지만 너 좀 피곤해 보여.
여: 어젯밤에 잠을 충분히 못 잤는데, 지금은 괜찮아. 우리 오늘 배드민턴 레슨 있는 거 알지, 그렇지?
남: 응, 하지만 난 못 갈 것 같아.
여: 아, 왼쪽 발목이 아직도 아프니?
남: 아니, 완전히 회복됐어.
여: 그럼, 왜?
남: 사실, ⓐ오늘 아침에 독감 예방 주사를 맞았거든.
여: 그렇구나. ⓑ나도 전에 독감 예방 주사를 맞고 나서 근육통이 심했어.
남: 음, 어쨌든, 오늘은 레슨을 빠지고 좀 쉬어야겠어.
여: 그래, 몸 잘 챙겨.

문제 풀이

남자가 ⓐ아침에 독감 예방 주사를 맞아서 오늘 배드민턴 레슨에 빠지겠다고 하자, 여자도 ⓑ전에 독감 예방 주사를 맞은 후 심한 근육통을 겪었다며 남자의 상황에 공감하고 있다.

오답 풀이

	선택지	오답 유도 방식
②	발표 준비를 해야 해서	남자가 언급한 'your chemistry presentation'을 단서로 생각하면 안 된다.
③	수면 시간이 부족해서	여자가 말한 'I didn't get enough sleep last night'을 이유로 혼동하면 안 된다.
④	왼쪽 발목을 다쳐서	'does your left ankle still hurt?'라는 여자의 물음에 남자는 완전히 회복했다고 답했다.
⑤	진료 예약이 있어서	여자가 남자에게 'does your left ankle still hurt?'라고 한 질문 때문에 남자가 진료가 있을 것이라 추측해서는 안 된다.

08 언급

p.17

[코드 접속하기]

정답 | ④

선택지 선택비율	① 0%	② 0%	③ 0%	④ 97%	⑤ 1%

해석

남: Christine, 당신 딸 Jennifer가 책 읽는 걸 아주 좋아한다고 들었어요. 안타깝게도, 우리 딸은 안 그래요.
여: 실은, Little Readers' Class를 수강하기 전까지는 Jennifer도 책 읽는 걸 즐기지 않았어요. 그 수업은 다양한 재미있는 읽기 활동을 제공해요.
남: 정말요? 우리 딸에게도 좋겠어요. 수업은 어디에서 하나요?
여: ⓐStonefield 도서관에서요. 내 전화기 어딘가에 전단 사진이 있어요. [잠시 후] 여깄네요.
남: 아. ⓑ수업이 매주 월요일 오후 4시부터 5시네요.
여: 딸에게 그 시간이 괜찮아요?
남: 네, 월요일 오후에는 한가해요.
여: 잘됐네요. ⓒ그 수업은 일곱 살에서 아홉 살까지 아이들을 위한 거예요. 당신 딸이 여덟 살이죠, 맞나요?
남: 네, 수업을 들을 수 있네요. 그럼, ⓓ등록하려면, 전단에 있는 주소로 이메일을 보내야겠네요.
여: 맞아요. 그 수업이 당신 딸을 읽기에 동참하게 하면 좋겠어요.

문제 풀이

ⓐ장소는 Stonefield 도서관, ⓑ시간은 매주 월요일 오후 4시부터 5시, ⓒ대상 연령은 일곱 살에서 아홉 살, ⓓ등록 방법은 전단에 있는 주소로 이메일 보내기라고 언급되었지만, 모집 인원은 언급되지 않았다.

오답 풀이

	선택지	오답 유도 방식
①	장소	'Where's it held?'은 수업이 어디서 하는지 묻는 질문이다.
②	시간	두 사람은 전단에서 수업 시간을 확인하고 있다.
③	대상 연령	'The class is for children ages'는 대상 연령을 언급하는 부분이다.
⑤	등록 방법	남자의 말 'to register, I should send an email to the address on the flyer'에서 언급되었다.

09 내용 일치

p.18

[코드 접속하기]

정답 | ③

선택지 선택비율	① 1%	② 0%	③ 92%	④ 2%	⑤ 3%

해석

남: 안녕하십니까, WBPR 청취자 여러분. 양질의 가족 시간을 즐길 기회를 찾고 계시나요? 그렇다면, 2021 Family Science Festival로 여러분을 초대합니다. ⓐ12월 7일에 시작하여 일주일간 시청 근처에 위치한 Bermont 과학 박물관에서 진행됩니다. 로봇 만들기와 VR 모의실험을 포함하여, 부모와 아이가 함께 즐길 수 있는 ⓑ8개의 프로그램이 제공될 것입니다. ⓒ어린이 과학 잡지도 무료로 나눠드릴 것입니다. 이 행사는 누구에게나 열려 있지만, ⓓ11세 미만 어린이들은 성인을 동반해야 한다는 걸 기억해 주세요. 등록비는 없지만, ⓔ참가하시려면 사전에 등록하셔야 합니다. 가족과 함께 오셔서 흥미로운 과학의 세계에 대해 배워보세요. 보다 많은 정보는 저희 웹사이트 www.wbpr.com을 방문해 주세요.

문제 풀이

ⓒ어린이 과학 잡지를 무료로 나눠줄 것이라고 했으므로, ③은 내용과 일치하지 않는다.

오답 풀이

	선택지	오답 유도 방식
①	12월 7일부터 일주일 동안 진행된다.	'It starts on December 7th and runs for one week'라고 직접적으로 언급되었다.
②	8개의 프로그램이 제공될 것이다.	'Eight programs will be offered'라고 언급되었다.
④	11세 미만의 어린이들은 성인을 동반해야 한다.	'all children under age 11 must be accompanied by an adult'라고 했다.
⑤	참가를 위해 미리 등록해야 한다.	'to participate, you must register in advance'라고 언급했다.

10 도표

p.19

[코드 접속하기]

정답 | ③

선택지 선택비율	① 5%	② 3%	③ 84%	④ 7%	⑤ 1%

해석

남: 여보, 인터넷에서 미니 오븐을 사려고 해요?
여: 네, 쿠키나 비스킷을 구우려면 그게 필요해요. 이 다섯 모델에 대해 어떻게 생각해요?
남: 어디 좀 볼게요. [잠시 후] 모두 좋아 보이지만, ⓐ미니 오븐에 100달러 넘게 쓰는 것은 너무 과한 것 같아요.
여: 동의해요. 그럼 이걸 없애야겠네요. 난 ⓑ용량이 적어도 10리터는 되어야 한다고 생각해요.
남: 그럼 이 셋 중에 하나를 선택합시다. 무게는요?
여: 가벼울수록 더 좋은 것 같아요. ⓒ6kg가 넘지 않으면 좋겠어요.
남: 좋아요. 이제 이 두 모델만 남았네요. ⓓ베이킹 팬이 있는 걸 선택해야 할까요?
여: ⓔ아니요. 우리가 이미 가지고 있는 팬을 사용하면 돼요.
남: 그렇군요. 그럼 나머지 다른 걸로 사죠.
여: 좋아요.

문제 풀이

두 사람은 ⓐ100달러가 넘지 않으며 ⓑ용량이 최소 10리터인 ⓒ6kg가 넘지 않는 무게의 ⓓⓔ베이킹 팬이 없는 미니 오븐을 구입하기로 했다.

오답 풀이

	선택지	오답 유도 방식
①	Model A	여자가 'I think the capacity should be at least 10 liters.'라고 했으므로 용량은 10리터 이상이 되어야 한다.
②	Model B	여자가 'I don't want it to be more than 6 kg.'라고 했으므로 무게가 6kg가 넘어서는 안 된다.
④	Model D	베이킹 팬은 집에 있는 것을 사용하면 되어서 베이킹 팬이 없는 것으로 구매하기로 했다.
⑤	Model E	남자가 'it seems too much to spend more than $100 for a mini oven'이라고 했으므로 가격이 100달러를 넘지 않아야 한다.

11 짧은 대화 응답

p.20

[코드 접속하기]

정답 | ①

선택지 선택비율	① 71%	② 19%	③ 2%	④ 4%	⑤ 3%

해석

남: Jane, ⓐ드론 설정 거의 다 했니?
여: 아직 못 했어. ⓑ사용 설명서를 이해하는 데 어려움을 겪고 있어.
남: ⓒ영상을 좀 보는 게 도움이 될 수도 있어. 분명 그걸 하는 방법을 보여 주는 걸 찾을 거야.
여: 좋은 생각이야! 온라인으로 영상을 좀 찾아볼게.

문제 풀이

남자가 여자에게 ⓐ드론 설정을 다 했는지 물었는데 여자는 ⓑ사용 설명서를 이해하기 어려워서 아직 못했다고 대답했다. 그러자 남자가 ⓒ영상을 보는 게 도움이 될 것이라고 조언했으므로, 온라인으로 영상을 찾아보겠다는 내용의 ①이 응답으로 가장 적절하다.
② 좋아! 내게 영상 만드는 법을 가르쳐 줘.
③ 우와! 너 드론 조종 잘 하는구나.
④ 알겠어. 같이 새 드론을 사러 가자.
⑤ 맞아. 나는 사용 설명서를 읽어야 해.

오답 풀이

	선택지	오답 유도 방식
②	Great! Teach me how to make a video clip.	남자는 드론 설정 방법을 보여 주는 영상을 찾아보라고 한 것이다. 'video clip'이라는 말 때문에 혼동하면 안 된다.
③	Wow! You're good at controlling the drone.	남자가 드론 조종을 잘 하는지 여부는 알 수 없다.
④	Okay. Let's go buy a new drone together.	여자는 드론 설정 방법을 잘 모르는 것이므로, 새 드론을 사러 가자는 말은 흐름상 적절하지 않다.
⑤	Right. I should read the instructions.	여자는 사용 설명서를 이미 읽어보았으나 이해하기 힘들다고 말했다.

12 긴 대화 응답

p.21

[코드 접속하기]

정답 | ⑤

선택지 선택비율	① 2%	② 15%	③ 4%	④ 1%	⑤ 78%

해석

[휴대전화가 울린다.]
남: 안녕, Rachel. 무슨 일이야?
여: 안녕, Kevin. 다음 주말에 계획 있어?
남: 아니, 나 시간 있어. 왜 물어봐?
여: 시 교통국이 주차장에서 자전거 경매를 개최한대. 같이 가볼래?
남: 재미있겠다. 새 자전거를 파는 거야?
여: 아니, 중고 자전거를 팔 거야. 사람들이 좋은 목적을 위해 그것들을 기부한 거야.
남: 목적이 뭔데?
여: 모금하는 모든 돈이 청소년 스포츠 클럽을 후원하는 데 쓰일 거라고 들었어.
남: 아, 그래? 그렇다면 ⓐ나도 경매에 기여하고 싶어. 사실 내가 더 이상 타지 않는 자전거가 하나 있어.
여: 잘됐다. ⓑ판매할 수 있을 만큼 상태가 괜찮은지만 확인하도록 해.
남: ⓒ걱정할 필요 없어. 두세 번밖에 사용하지 않았거든.
여: 훌륭해! 네 기부품은 분명 감사히 받아들여질 거야.

문제 풀이

ⓐ타지 않는 자전거가 있어 경매에 기여하고 싶다는 남자의 말에 여자는 ⓑ상태를 확인하라고 했고, 남자는 ⓒ두세 번밖에 사용하지 않아 걱정 없다고 했다. 따라서 남자의 기부품(자전거)이 가치가 있을 것이라는 긍정적인 칭찬과 격려의 말인 ⑤가 응답으로 가장 적절하다.
① 안됐다. 네가 잃어버린 자전거를 찾을 수 있길 바랄게.
② 잘했어. 곧 자전거 타는 데 익숙해질 거야.
③ 정말 좋아! 네 새 자전거를 내게 빌려줘서 고마워.
④ 죄송합니다. 저희 경매는 이미 끝났습니다.

오답 풀이

	선택지	오답 유도 방식
①	Too bad. I hope you can find your lost bike.	대화 속 'bike'를 활용한 오답이다. 자전거 분실이나, 자전거 타기, 자전거 빌리기는 대화 내용과 무관하다.
②	Good job. You'll get used to riding a bike soon.	
③	Awesome! Thank you for lending me your new bike.	

④	I'm sorry. I'm afraid our auction has already finished.	대화 속 'auction'을 활용한 오답으로, 여자는 경매의 주최측이 아니므로 'our auction'이라는 표현은 여자가 할 말로 적절하지 않다.

13 상황에 적절한 말

p.22

[코드 접속하기]

정답 | ②

선택지 선택비율	① 7%	② 76%	③ 5%	④ 5%	⑤ 4%

해석

남: Eve는 역사학을 전공하고 있는 대학생이다. 그녀는 졸업 후에 무엇을 해야 할지에 대해 불확실하기 때문에 진로에 대해 걱정해 왔다. 그래서, 직업 선택에 대해 더 알기 위해 대학에 있는 직업 상담가를 정기적으로 만난다. 그녀는 이것이 자신에게 많은 도움이 되었다고 느낀다. 어느 날, Eve는 반 친구 ⓐTom도 졸업 후에 무엇을 해야 할지에 대해 걱정하고 있다는 것을 알게 된다. ⓑEve는 Tom에게 직업 상담가를 만나러 가서 조언을 얻을 것을 제안하고 싶다. 이 상황에서, Eve는 Tom에게 뭐라고 말하겠는가?

Eve: 직업 상담가에게서 도움을 얻는 게 어때?

문제 풀이

ⓐ졸업 후 진로에 대해 걱정하는 Tom에게 Eve는 ⓑ직업 상담가의 도움을 받으라고 제안하고 싶다고 했다.

| 오답 풀이 |

	선택지	오답 유도 방식
①	You should find a job related to your field of study.	대화의 중요한 부분인 'career(직업)'와 비슷한 의미를 가진 job을 이용한 오답이다.
③	Do some research before choosing your major.	대화에서 'major(전공)'가 언급되었으나, 전공 선택이 아닌 졸업 후 진로가 핵심이다.
④	If I were you, I'd focus on studying history.	Eve가 역사학을 전공하고 있다는 내용을 이용한 오답이다.
⑤	Why don't you apply for an internship?	인턴십에 관한 언급은 전혀 없다.

14 세트 문항

p.23

[코드 접속하기]

정답 | 1. ⑤ 2. ④

선택지 선택비율					
1	① 5%	② 2%	③ 2%	④ 2%	⑤ 87%
2	① 4%	② 1%	③ 2%	④ 88%	⑤ 2%

해석

여: 안녕하세요, 여러분. 여러분은 아침으로 무엇을 먹었나요? 여러분 중 몇몇은 여러분이 가장 좋아하는 시리얼을 우유와 함께 먹었을 것으로 짐작되는데요. ⓐ여러분은 우유가 어디서 나오는지 궁금해해 본 적이 있나요? 대부분의 사람들은 그것이 젖소에서 나온다고 말할 것이고, 맞습니다. ⓑ캐나다와 미국의 우유의 약 90퍼센트는 젖소에서 나옵니다. 하지만 젖소가 유일한 우유 공급원은 아닙니다. ⓒ전 세계 사람들은 각기 다른 동물들로부터 우유를 얻습니다. 물소는 ⓓ인도에서 우유의 주요 공급원입니다. 그것들은 그 나라에서 소비되는 우유의 절반을 생산합니다. 순록이 그토록 추운 환경에서 살아남을 수 있는 유일한 착유 동물이기 때문에 ⓔ핀란드의 북쪽 지방에 있는 일부 사람들은 순록의 우유를 마십니다. ⓕ루마니아 사람들은 양에서 우유를 얻어 그것을 치즈를 만드는 데 사용합니다. 그것은 지방 함량이 소젖의 두 배입니다. 이제 이 동물들에 대한 영상을 보도록 하겠습니다.

문제 풀이

1. ⓐ우유가 어디에서 나오는지 궁금해해 본 적이 있냐는 질문을 던지며, ⓒ전 세계 사람들이 각기 다른 동물들로부터 우유를 얻는다고 말하고, 이어 각기 다른 나라들의 예를 들고 있다. 따라서 주제로는 ⑤ '각기 다른 나라의 다양한 우유 공급원'이 가장 적절하다.
① 유제품의 주요 수출 국가
② 규칙적으로 우유를 마시는 것의 건강상 이점
③ 세계의 독특한 음식 문화
④ 착유 동물에 적합한 환경
2. ⓑ캐나다, ⓓ인도, ⓔ핀란드, ⓕ루마니아는 언급했으나, 노르웨이(Norway)는 언급하지 않았다.

| 오답 풀이 |

1.

	선택지	오답 유도 방식
①	major exporting countries of dairy products	'dairy products'를 단서로 생각해서는 안 된다. 유제품 수출에 관한 언급은 전혀 없었다.
②	health benefits of drinking milk regularly	우유의 공급원에 대한 내용이지, 우유를 마시는 것의 이점에 관한 언급은 하지 않았다.
③	unique food cultures around the world	'around the world'를 단서로 생각해서는 안 된다. 전 세계의 다양한 우유 공급원에 관한 내용이지, 음식 문화에 관한 언급은 없었다.
④	suitable environments for dairy animals	'dairy animals'를 단서로 생각해서는 안 된다. 핀란드의 유일한 착유 동물이 순록이라는 언급은 있었으나, 착유 동물 전반에 있어 적합한 환경에 관한 내용은 아니다.

2.

	선택지	오답 유도 방식
①	Canada	캐나다와 미국의 우유의 약 90퍼센트는 젖소에서 나온다고 했다.
②	India	인도에서 물소는 우유의 주요 공급원이라고 언급되었다.
③	Finland	핀란드의 북쪽 지방 일부 사람들은 순록의 우유를 마신다고 언급되었다.
⑤	Romania	루마니아 사람들은 양으로부터 우유를 얻어 치즈를 만든다고 했다.

[코드 공략하기]

제1회 초급 모의고사

1	④	2	⑤	3	③	4	⑤	5	④	6	②
7	①	8	②	9	③	10	②	11	②	12	①
13	④	14	④	15	③	16	③	17	③		

1. ④ | 목적

선택지 선택비율	① 1%	② 7%	③ 1%	④ 88%	⑤ 3%

M: Good morning, students. This is your vice principal (교감) Richard Simpson. As you know, our school drone (드론, 무인 항공기) club was awarded (수여하다) first prize at the Drone Show Contest. Actually, I asked the drone club to perform the show again for you. And they said, "Yes". So ⓐI would recommend (권하다) you watch the performance at the school field tomorrow. ⓑPlease come and see the club's drone performance, and show your support (지지, 응원). Thank you.

해석

남: 안녕하세요, 학생 여러분. 저는 여러분의 교감 선생님인 Richard Simpson입니다. 여러분도 알다시피, 우리 학교 드론 동아리가 드론 쇼 대회에서 1등을 수상했습니다. 사실, 제가 여러분을 위해 다시 공연을 해 달라고 드론 동아리에 부탁했습니다. 그리고 그들이 "네."라고 했고요. 그래서 ⓐ저는 여러분이 내일 학교 운동장에서 그 공연을 보기를 권하고 싶습니다. ⓑ와서 동아리의 드론 공연을 관람하고 응원해 주기 바랍니다. 감사합니다.

문제 풀이

남자는 ⓐⓑ내일 학교 운동장에서 있을 드론 동아리의 공연을 관람하고 응원해 줄 것을 권하고 있다.

2. ⑤ | 의견

선택지 선택비율	① 1%	② 2%	③ 1%	④ 2%	⑤ 94%

M: Clara, why the long face?
W: Aw, Dad, I bought this hair dryer, but the cool air mode doesn't work.
M: Where did you get it?
W: I bought it secondhand (중고의) online.
M: Did you check the condition (상태) before you ordered it?
W: I did, but I missed the seller's note that said the cool air mode doesn't work.
M: Oh dear. ⓐIt's important to check all the details (세부 사항) when you buy secondhand items.
W: You're right. I was just so excited because it was much cheaper than other hair dryers.
M: Some secondhand items are almost like new, but others are not. So, ⓑyou should read every detail of the item carefully (주의 깊게, 면밀하게).
W: Thanks, Dad. I'll keep that in mind (~을 명심하다).

해석

남: Clara, 왜 우울한 얼굴이니?
여: 아, 아빠, 제가 이 헤어드라이어를 샀는데, 냉풍 모드가 작동하지 않아요.
남: 그걸 어디서 샀니?
여: 인터넷에서 중고로 샀어요.
남: 그걸 주문하기 전에 상태를 확인했니?
여: 했는데, 냉풍 모드가 작동하지 않는다는 판매자의 메모를 놓쳤어요.
남: 이런. ⓐ중고품을 살 때는 모든 세부 사항을 확인하는 것이 중요하단다.
여: 아빠 말씀이 맞아요. 이게 다른 헤어드라이어들보다 훨씬 더 저렴해서 그저 너무 신났었어요.
남: 어떤 중고품들은 거의 새것 같지만, 또 다른 것들은 그렇지 않단다. 그래서 ⓑ그 물건의 모든 세부 사항을 면밀하게 읽어야 해.
여: 고마워요, 아빠. 명심할게요.

문제 풀이

남자는 ⓐⓑ중고품을 살 때 모든 세부 사항을 면밀하게 확인해야 한다고 말하고 있다.

3. ③ | 요지

선택지 선택비율	① 4%	② 2%	③ 92%	④ 1%	⑤ 1%

W: Hello, listeners. This is Kelly Watson's *Love Yourself*. Have you ever thought about your social media use? Social media lets you stay connected (연결된) with others easily. However, it can make you compare (비교하다) yourself with others, too. For example, a celebrity (유명인)'s post (게시물) about going on a luxurious (호화로운) trip may make you jealous. Continuously (계속해서) making such comparisons stops you from looking at (stop A from v-ing: A가 ~하는 것을 막다) yourself the way you truly are. You might think, "Why can't I have a better life?" and feel small about yourself. As you can see, social media can have a negative (부정적인) effect on your self-esteem (자존감). I'll be right back with some tips for healthy social media use.

해석

여: 안녕하세요, 청취자 여러분. Kelly Watson의 'Love Yourself'입니다. 여러분은 소셜 미디어 이용에 대해 생각해 본 적 있나요? 소셜 미디어는 다른 사람들과 쉽게 연결을 유지하게 합니다. 하지만 자신을 다른 사람들과 비교하게 만들 수도 있습니다. 예를 들어, 호화로운 여행을 떠나는 것에 대한 한 유명인의 게시물은 여러분으로 하여금 질투심을 느끼게 만들 수 있습니다. 계속해서 이런 비교를 하는 것은 여러분이 자신의 진정한 모습을 바라보는 걸 막습니다. 여러분은 어쩌면 "왜 나는 더 나은 삶을 살지 못할까?"라고 생각하며 자신에 대해 초라하게 느낄지도 모릅니다. 보다시피, 소셜 미디어는 여러분의 자존감에 부정적인 영향을 미칠 수 있습니다. 건강한 소셜 미디어 이용을 위한 몇 가지 팁과 함께 곧 돌아오겠습니다.

문제 풀이

소셜 미디어 이용이 자신을 다른 사람과 계속해서 비교하게 하여 자존감에 부정적인 영향을 미칠 수 있다고 말하고 있다.

4. ⑤ | 그림 일치

선택지 선택비율	① 2%	② 4%	③ 4%	④ 1%	⑤ 89%

M: Hi, Grace. What are you looking at on your phone?
W: Hi, James. It's a photo I took when I did some volunteer work(자원봉사). We painted pictures on a street wall.
M: Let me see. Wow, I like ⓐthe whale(고래) with the flower pattern.
W: I like it, too. How do you like ⓑthe house under the whale?
M: It's beautiful. What are these ⓒtwo chairs for?
W: You can take a picture sitting there. The painting becomes the background(배경).
M: Oh, I see. Look at this tree! It has ⓓheart-shaped leaves.
W: That's right. We named it the Love Tree.
M: ⓔThe butterfly on the tree branch(나뭇가지) is lovely, too.
W: I hope a lot of people enjoy the painting.

해석

남: 안녕, Grace. 네 전화기로 무엇을 보고 있니?
여: 안녕, James. 내가 자원봉사를 할 때 찍은 사진이야. 우리는 거리 벽에 그림을 그렸어.
남: 어디 보자. 와, ⓐ꽃무늬가 있는 고래가 마음에 들어.
여: 나도 마음에 들어. ⓑ고래 아래에 있는 집은 어때?
남: 아름다워. 이 ⓒ의자 두 개는 뭘 위한 거야?
여: 거기 앉아서 사진을 찍을 수 있어. 그림이 배경이 되는 거지.
남: 아, 그렇구나. 이 나무를 봐! ⓓ하트 모양의 잎을 가지고 있네.
여: 맞아. 우리는 그걸 '사랑 나무'라고 이름 지었어.
남: ⓔ나뭇가지 위에 있는 나비도 사랑스럽다.
여: 많은 사람들이 이 그림을 즐기면 좋겠어.

문제 풀이

ⓔ나뭇가지 위에 나비가 있다고 했으므로, 그림 ⑤의 새는 대화 내용과 일치하지 않는다.

5. ④ | 부탁한 일

선택지 선택비율	① 3%	② 3%	③ 2%	④ 89%	⑤ 2%

W: Dad, where are you going?
M: I'm going to the grocery store(식품점, 슈퍼마켓). We're having a surprise party this evening.
W: Really? Is it a special day today?
M: Yes. Mom was promoted(승진시키다) at work, so we're going to celebrate(축하하다).
W: Oh, good for her. I'm sure she'll love the party.
M: I hope so. I'm thinking of making steak and seafood pasta for dinner.
W: Sounds perfect. Will there be any guests?
M: Yes. I invited a couple of(둘의) our friends.
W: Good. I also want to help. ⓐShall I go buy some flowers for the dinner table?
M: No. I'll do that. ⓑCan you clean the living room instead?
W: Sure. I'll make it neat and tidy(정돈된, 깔끔한 잘 정돈된) before you come back.
M: Thanks. That's very kind of you.

해석

여: 아빠, 어디 가세요?
남: 슈퍼마켓에 가는 중이야. 우린 오늘 저녁에 깜짝 파티를 할 거란다.
여: 정말이요? 오늘이 특별한 날인가요?
남: 응. 엄마가 직장에서 승진해서, 우리가 축하해 드릴 거란다.
여: 와, 잘됐네요. 엄마께서 분명 파티를 좋아하실 거예요.
남: 그러면 좋겠구나. 저녁으로 스테이크와 해산물 파스타를 만들까 생각 중이야.
여: 좋아요. 손님들도 오실 건가요?
남: 응. 친구 두 사람을 초대했단다.
여: 좋아요. 저도 돕고 싶어요. ⓐ제가 저녁 식탁에 놓을 꽃을 좀 사러 갈까요?
남: 아니. 그건 내가 할게. ⓑ대신에 거실을 청소해 줄 수 있니?
여: 물론이죠. 제가 아빠 돌아오시기 전까지 깔끔하게 잘 정돈해 놓을게요.
남: 고맙다. 정말 착하구나.

문제 풀이

남자는 여자에게 ⓑ거실 청소를 부탁하고 있다. ⓐ저녁 식탁에 놓을 꽃을 사러 가겠다는 여자의 제안과 혼동해서는 안 된다.

6. ② | 금액

선택지 선택비율	① 6%	② 71%	③ 7%	④ 10%	⑤ 3%

W: Hello. How can I help you?
M: Hi. I want to buy some mini apple pies. How much are they?
W: ⓐThey're four dollars each.
M: Good. ⓑI'll take three. And this bacon and egg sandwich looks delicious. How much is it?
W: ⓒIt's five dollars. But this week if you buy two, you get one free.
M: Well, that sounds like a good deal(거래), but three sandwiches are too many. ⓓI'll just buy one. That's it.
W: Great. Do you have a store membership(회원권)?
M: No, but ⓔI have this coupon. Can I use it?
W: Sure. ⓕYou'll get 2 dollars off of the total(총액).
M: Good. Here's my credit card.

해석

여: 안녕하세요. 무엇을 도와드릴까요?
남: 안녕하세요. 저는 미니 애플파이를 조금 사고 싶어요. 얼마인가요?
여: ⓐ각각 4달러예요.
남: 좋아요. ⓑ세 개를 살게요. 그리고 이 베이컨 계란 샌드위치가 맛있어 보이네요. 얼마인가요?
여: ⓒ5달러예요. 하지만 이번 주에는 두 개를 사시면 하나를 무료로 받으실 수 있어요.
남: 음, 좋은 거래인 것 같지만 샌드위치 세 개는 너무 많아요. ⓓ하나만 살게요. 그게 다예요.
여: 좋아요. 매장 회원권이 있으신가요?
남: 아니요, 하지만 ⓔ이 쿠폰이 있어요. 사용할 수 있나요?
여: 물론이죠. ⓕ총액에서 2달러를 할인받으실 거예요.
남: 좋아요. 여기 제 신용 카드입니다.

문제 풀이

남자는 ⓐⓑ4달러짜리 미니 애플파이 세 개, ⓒⓓ5달러짜리 베이컨 계란 샌드위치 한 개를 사며 ⓔⓕ쿠폰으로 2달러 할인을 받으므로, 남자가 지불할 금액은 15달러((4x3)+5−2=15)이다.

7. ① | 이유

선택지 선택비율	① 94%	② 1%	③ 3%	④ 1%	⑤ 1%

[Cell phone rings.]
M: Hey, Suji. Where are you?
W: I'm in the library checking out((책을) 대출하다) books. I'll be heading out to(~로 (향해) 가다) the science lab(실험실) for our experiment(실험) in a couple of minutes.
M: I guess you haven't checked my message yet. We can't do the experiment today.
W: Really? Isn't the lab available(이용 가능한) today?

M: Yes, it is, but I canceled our reservation.
예약

W: Why? Are you still suffering from your cold?
~로 고생하다

M: No, I'm fine now.

W: That's good. Then ⓐwhy aren't we doing the experiment today? We need to hand in the science report by next Monday.
~을 제출하다

M: Unfortunately, ⓑthe experiment kit hasn't been delivered yet. It'll arrive tomorrow.
배달하다

W: Oh, well. The experiment has to wait one more day, then.

해석

[휴대전화가 울린다.]
남: 얘, 수지야. 너 어디 있니?
여: 도서관에서 책을 대출하고 있어. 몇 분 후에 우리 실험을 위해 과학 실험실로 갈 거야.
남: 너 아직 내 메시지를 확인하지 않았나 보구나. 우리는 오늘 실험을 할 수 없어.
여: 정말? 오늘 실험실을 이용할 수 없니?
남: 아니, 이용할 수 있는데, 내가 예약을 취소했어.
여: 왜? 너 아직도 감기로 고생 중이니?
남: 아니, 지금은 괜찮아.
여: 다행이다. 그럼 ⓐ왜 오늘 실험을 하지 않는 거야? 우리 다음 주 월요일까지 과학 보고서를 제출해야 하잖아.
남: 안타깝게도 ⓑ실험용 키트가 아직 배달되지 않았어. 내일 도착할 거야.
여: 아, 음. 그렇다면 실험은 하루 더 기다려야겠네.

문제 풀이

ⓐ왜 오늘 실험을 하지 않냐는 여자의 질문에 남자는 ⓑ실험용 키트가 아직 배달되지 않았다고 했다.

8. ② | 언급

선택지 선택비율	① 1%	② 92%	③ 4%	④ 1%	⑤ 2%

W: Hey, Alex. Have you seen the announcement for the Victory Marathon?
소식, 공지

M: Not yet, but I'm curious about it. When's the event?
궁금한

W: It's on Saturday, ⓐJuly 13th.

M: Nice. Where will the race start?

W: It will ⓑstart at William Stadium.

M: Oh, great. How much does it cost to participate?
참가하다

W: ⓒIt costs $30.

M: That's reasonable. How many participants are they expecting?
(가격이) 적당한 / 참가자 / 예상하다

W: ⓓLast year, there were around 5,000. They say they expect about the same this year.

M: I didn't know that many people love marathons. I'm in!

W: Great. I look forward to running with you.

해석

여: 얘, Alex, 너 Victory Marathon 공지 봤어?
남: 아직 못 봤는데, 궁금하네. 행사가 언제야?
여: ⓐ7월 13일 토요일이야.
남: 좋네. 경주는 어디서 출발해?
여: ⓑWilliam Stadium에서 출발할 거야.
남: 아, 잘됐다. 참가하는 데 비용은 얼마야?
여: ⓒ30달러야.
남: 적당하네. 그들은 참가자를 몇 명으로 예상해?
여: ⓓ작년에는 5,000명 정도였어. 올해도 거의 같게 예상한다고 해.
남: 그렇게 많은 사람들이 마라톤을 좋아하는지 몰랐어. 나도 참여할래!
여: 좋아. 너와 같이 뛰는 거 기대할게.

문제 풀이

ⓐ행사 날짜, ⓑ출발 지점, ⓒ참가비, ⓓ예상 참가 인원은 언급되었지만, 신청 방법은 언급되지 않았다.

9. ③ | 내용 일치

선택지 선택비율	① 6%	② 3%	③ 84%	④ 2%	⑤ 5%

W: Hello, students! This is your science teacher Jane Brown. I have some good news. ⓐThis Saturday we're having Science Day at our school. In the morning, coding experts will teach you how to make a computer program. ⓑYou can also operate some robots by yourself in the school hall. ⓒIn the afternoon, your science teachers will run some experimental booths for you. It's a good chance to experiment with what you've learned from the textbooks. ⓓYou can sign up for Science Day by scanning the QR codes on the school board. ⓔFor the participants, lunch will be provided. Come and enjoy Science Day!
코딩, 프로그램 작성 / 전문가 / 작동하다 / 홀, 강당 / 운영하다 / 실험의 / 교과서 / ~을 신청하다 / 제공하다

해석

여: 안녕하세요, 학생 여러분! 저는 여러분의 과학 선생님인 Jane Brown입니다. 좋은 소식이 있습니다. ⓐ이번 주 토요일에 우리 학교에서 '과학의 날'이 열립니다. 오전에는 코딩 전문가들이 여러분에게 컴퓨터 프로그램 만드는 방법을 가르쳐 줄 것입니다. ⓑ여러분은 또한 학교 강당에서 직접 로봇을 작동해 볼 수도 있습니다. ⓒ오후에는 과학 선생님들이 여러분을 위해 실험 부스를 운영할 것입니다. 여러분이 교과서에서 배운 것을 실험해 볼 수 있는 좋은 기회입니다. 학교 게시판에 있는 ⓓQR 코드를 스캔하여 '과학의 날'에 신청할 수 있습니다. ⓔ참가자들에게는 점심이 제공될 것입니다. 와서 '과학의 날'을 즐기세요!

문제 풀이

ⓒ과학 선생님들이 오후에 실험 부스를 운영할 것이라고 했다.

10. ② | 도표

선택지 선택비율	① 5%	② 91%	③ 1%	④ 1%	⑤ 1%

M: Jessica, what are you doing?

W: I'm trying to buy one of these five frying pans.

M: Let me see. This frying pan seems pretty expensive.

W: Yeah. ⓐI don't want to spend more than $50.

M: Okay. And ⓑI think 9 to 12-inch frying pans will work for most of your cooking.

W: I think so, too. An 8-inch frying pan seems too small for me.

M: What about the material? Stainless steel pans are good for fast cooking.
재료, 소재

W: I know, but they are heavier. ⓒI'll buy an aluminum pan.

M: Then you have two options left. Do you need a lid?
뚜껑

W: Of course. ⓓA lid keeps the oil from splashing. I'll buy this one.
(물 등이) 튀다

M: Good choice.

해석

남: Jessica, 뭐 하고 있어요?
여: 이 다섯 개 프라이팬 중에 하나를 사려는 중이에요.
남: 어디 봐요. 이 프라이팬은 꽤 비싼 것 같네요.
여: 그러게요. ⓐ50달러 이상은 쓰고 싶지 않아요.

남: 좋아요. 그리고 ⓑ대부분의 요리에 9인치에서 12인치 프라이팬이 적당할 것 같아요.
여: 나도 그렇게 생각해요. 8인치 프라이팬은 내게 너무 작은 것 같아요.
남: 소재는요? 스테인리스 팬이 빠른 조리에 좋죠.
여: 알아요, 근데 더 무겁네요. ⓒ알루미늄 팬을 사야겠어요.
남: 그럼 두 가지 선택지가 남아있네요. 뚜껑이 필요해요?
여: 그럼요. ⓓ뚜껑이 기름 튀는 걸 막거든요. 이걸로 사야겠어요.
남: 좋은 선택이에요.

문제 풀이

여자는 ⓐ50달러 이하이면서 ⓑ9인치에서 12인치 사이 크기인 ⓒ알루미늄 소재의 ⓓ뚜껑이 있는 프라이팬을 구입하기로 했다.

11. ② | 짧은 대화 응답

선택지 선택비율	① 5%	② 88%	③ 2%	④ 3%	⑤ 2%

M: Have you finished your team's short-movie project?
W: Not yet. ⓐI'm still editing the video clip.
편집하다
M: Oh, you edit? ⓑHow did you learn to do that?
W: I learned it by myself through books.

해석

남: 너희 팀의 단편 영화 프로젝트는 다 끝냈니?
여: 아니. ⓐ내가 아직 영상 편집 중이야.
남: 아, 네가 편집하는 거야? ⓑ영상 편집하는 걸 어떻게 배웠어?
여: 책을 통해서 스스로 익혔어.

문제 풀이

여자가 ⓐ영상을 편집 중이라고 하자 남자가 ⓑ영상 편집하는 것을 어떻게 배웠냐고 물었으므로, 영상 편집을 배운 방법을 말하는 ②가 응답으로 가장 적절하다.
① 그때까지 편집을 끝내지 못할 것 같아.
③ 이 짧은 영화는 무척 재미있어.
④ 너는 또다른 영상을 만들어야 해.
⑤ 나는 팀 프로젝트에서 A+를 받았어.

12. ① | 짧은 대화 응답

선택지 선택비율	① 63%	② 7%	③ 10%	④ 15%	⑤ 5%

W: ⓐI easily catch a cold these days.
감기에 걸리다
M: That's too bad. ⓑIt's a good idea to keep some moisture in your room.
수분, 습기
W: Oh, ⓒhow does that relate to a cold?
~와 관련되다
M: If it's too dry inside, you can easily get a cold.

해석

여: 난 요즘 ⓐ쉽게 감기에 걸려.
남: 안됐다. ⓑ방에 약간의 습기를 유지하는 게 좋아.
여: 아, ⓒ그게 감기와 어떻게 관련이 있어?
남: 실내가 너무 건조하면, 쉽게 감기에 걸릴 수 있거든.

문제 풀이

ⓐ쉽게 감기에 걸린다는 여자에게 남자가 ⓑ방에 습기를 유지하는 것이 좋다고 말하자 ⓒ감기와 습기가 어떻게 관련이 있는지 묻고 있으므로, 감기와 습기의 상관관계를 알려주는 ①이 남자의 응답으로 가장 적절하다.
② 기침을 할 때는, 입을 가려야 해.
③ 감기에 걸리지 않으려면 손을 씻어야 해.
④ 몸을 따뜻하게 유지하는 것이 정말 중요해.
⑤ 물을 마시면 피부를 부드럽게 할 수 있어.

13. ④ | 긴 대화 응답

선택지 선택비율	① 2%	② 2%	③ 2%	④ 93%	⑤ 1%

M: Hi, Cindy! What are you doing this weekend?
W: I'm going to play badminton with my friends.
M: You play badminton quite often.
W: It's my new hobby. It helps me reduce stress.
줄이다
M: How nice! I've been looking for something to reduce stress.
W: Well, you don't have to think too hard. Just think of something that makes you happy.
M: Hmm.... But nothing comes to mind right away.
W: Then, ⓐwhy don't you come and play badminton with me this Saturday? You'll like it, too, I think.
M: Really? Is it okay if I join you?
W: Of course, it is! We meet at the sports center every Saturday morning.
M: Thanks a lot! ⓑDo I need to prepare anything?
준비하다
W: Just bring your racket and some comfortable clothes.
편한

해석

남: 안녕, Cindy! 이번 주말에 뭐 해?
여: 나는 친구들이랑 배드민턴 칠 거야.
남: 너 배드민턴 꽤 자주 치는구나.
여: 그게 내 새로운 취미야. 스트레스를 줄이는 데 도움이 되거든.
남: 정말 좋다! 나도 스트레스를 줄일 무언가를 찾고 있었거든.
여: 음, 너무 어렵게 생각할 필요 없어. 그냥 너를 즐겁게 만드는 걸 생각해 봐.
남: 음…. 근데 당장은 떠오르는 게 없네.
여: 그럼, ⓐ이번 토요일에 와서 나랑 같이 배드민턴 치는 게 어때? 내 생각에는, 너도 좋아할 거야.
남: 정말? 내가 같이 해도 괜찮아?
여: 물론 괜찮지! 우린 매주 토요일 아침에 스포츠 센터에서 만나.
남: 정말 고마워! ⓑ내가 뭔가 준비해야 해?
여: 그냥 네 라켓하고 편한 옷만 좀 가져오면 돼.

문제 풀이

여자가 ⓐ토요일에 함께 배드민턴 칠 것을 권하자 남자는 ⓑ무엇을 준비하면 될지 물었으므로, 여자의 응답으로는 준비물을 말하는 ④가 가장 적절하다.
① 독서도 좋은 취미가 될 수 있어.
② 너는 그 경기를 이기기 위해 연습을 많이 해야 했어.
③ 이번 토요일에 나랑 나가는 게 어때?
⑤ 만약 취미가 없다면, 스트레스를 더 받을 수 있어.

14. ④ | 긴 대화 응답

선택지 선택비율	① 3%	② 5%	③ 5%	④ 83%	⑤ 1%

W: Hi, Andrew. I heard that your tennis club is competing in the City Tennis Tournament.
compete: 경쟁하다, 참가하다
M: Yes. We've been practicing a lot these days.
W: I'm sure you'll do well.
M: Thanks. But ⓐour school tennis court is going to be under construction starting next week, so we won't have a place to practice.
공사 중인
W: What about the community center? It has several tennis courts.
M: We already checked. But all the courts are fully booked.
W: That's too bad. Oh, wait! ⓑMy sister told me her school tennis courts would be open to the public starting this Saturday.
대중
M: Really? That's great news. Do I need a reservation?
W: Yes. I remember she said that ⓒreservations would start at 9 a.m. tomorrow.

M: I hope I can reserve (예약하다) a court to continue practicing.

해석

여: 안녕, Andrew. 나는 너희 테니스 클럽이 시 테니스 토너먼트에 참가한다고 들었어.
남: 응. 우리는 요즘 연습을 많이 하고 있어.
여: 너는 분명 잘 할 거야.
남: 고마워. 하지만 ⓐ우리 학교 테니스장이 다음 주부터 공사 중일 예정이어서, 우리는 연습할 곳이 없을 거야.
여: 주민 센터는 어때? 그곳에는 테니스 코트가 여러 개 있어.
남: 이미 확인했어. 하지만 모든 코트가 모두 예약되었어.
여: 정말 유감이야. 아, 잠깐! ⓑ내 여동생이 그 애의 학교 테니스 코트가 이번 주 토요일부터 대중에게 개방될 거라고 나에게 말해 줬어.
남: 정말? 그거 좋은 소식이다. 예약이 필요하니?
여: 응. 그녀가 ⓒ내일 오전 9시에 예약이 시작될 것이라고 말한 게 기억나.
남: 계속 연습할 코트를 예약할 수 있으면 좋겠어.

문제 풀이

테니스 대회를 앞두고 있는 남자가 ⓐ자신의 학교 테니스장이 다음 주부터 공사 예정이어서 연습할 곳이 없다고 하자, 여자가 ⓑ자신의 여동생 학교 테니스 코트가 이번 주 토요일에 대중에게 개방될 것이라며 ⓒ내일 예약이 시작된다고 말했으므로, 남자의 응답으로는 ④가 가장 적절하다.
① 네 여동생이 그곳들을 예약하는 데 어려움을 겪었구나.
② 공사가 곧 끝날 것이라 확신해.
③ 주민 센터는 내일 이용 가능할 거야.
⑤ 그들이 우리가 체육관에서 연습하는 걸 허락할 것 같지 않아.

15. ③ | 상황에 적절한 말

선택지 선택비율	① 3%	② 7%	③ 66%	④ 7%	⑤ 15%

W: Alex and Olivia have been close friends since they were children. They grew up in the same town, and they attend (다니다) the same high school. One day, Alex tells Olivia that his father got a new job so his family has to move to another city. That's why ⓐhe's going to transfer to (전학 가다) a new school next week. Olivia feels sad because they have been friends for such a long time. Alex also hopes to keep his friendship with her. So, ⓑAlex wants to suggest (제안하다) that they remain (여전히 ~이다) in close touch (친밀한 관계) even after he leaves the city. In this situation, what would Alex most likely say to Olivia?
Alex: Let's keep in touch (연락하고 지내다) even after we part (헤어지다).

해석

여: Alex와 Olivia는 어렸을 때부터 가까운 친구였다. 그들은 같은 도시에서 자랐고 같은 고등학교를 다닌다. 어느 날, Alex는 Olivia에게 아버지가 새 일자리를 구해서서 식구가 다른 도시로 이사를 가야 한다고 말한다. 이가 바로 ⓐ그가 다음 주에 새로운 학교로 전학을 갈 예정인 이유이다. Olivia는 그들이 아주 오랫동안 친구였기 때문에 슬퍼한다. Alex도 그녀와의 우정을 지키길 희망한다. 그래서 ⓑAlex는 자신이 그 도시를 떠난 후에도 그들이 여전히 친밀한 관계이길 제안하고 싶다. 이 상황에서, Alex는 Olivia에게 뭐라고 말하겠는가?
Alex: 헤어진 후에도 연락하고 지내자.

문제 풀이

ⓐ다른 학교로 전학을 가게 된 Alex가 ⓑ친밀한 관계를 계속 유지하자고 Olivia에게 말하려고 하는 상황이므로, 헤어진 후에도 연락하고 지내자는 내용인 ③이 가장 적절하다.
① 네가 일자리를 구하다니 정말 다행이다.
② 네가 어디로 전학을 가야 하는지 네게 말해 줄게.
④ 난 너의 친절한 말에 깊이 감동받았어.
⑤ 네가 새로운 학교에 익숙해지길 바라.

16~17. | 세트 문항

16. ③ 17. ③

선택지 선택비율	① 2%	② 6%	③ 84%	④ 5%	⑤ 3%
	① 1%	② 2%	③ 94%	④ 3%	⑤ 1%

M: Good afternoon, everyone. Last time, we learned that overtourism happens (발생하다, 일어나다) when there are too many visitors to a particular (특정한) destination (목적지). Today, ⓐwe'll learn how cities deal with (~을 다루다) the problems caused by overtourism. First, some cities limit (제한하다) the number of hotels so there are fewer places for visitors to stay. In ⓑBarcelona, building new hotels is not allowed in the city center. Second, other cities promote (홍보하다) areas away from popular sites (장소). For instance, ⓒAmsterdam encourages (장려하다) tourists to visit less-crowded areas. Third, many cities have tried to limit access (접근). For example, ⓓVenice has tried to reduce tourism overall (종합[전반]적으로) by stopping large cruise ships from docking ((배를) 부두에 대다) on the island. Similarly, ⓔParis has focused on (~에 집중[주력]하다) reducing tourism (관광) to certain (특정한) parts of the city by having car-restricted (제한된) areas. Now, let's watch some video clips.

해석

남: 안녕하세요, 여러분. 지난 시간에, 우리는 특정 목적지에 방문하는 사람들이 너무 많을 때 과잉 관광이 일어난다는 것을 배웠습니다. 오늘은 ⓐ도시들이 과잉 관광으로 인해 야기된 문제들을 어떻게 다루는지 배울 것입니다. 첫째로, 일부 도시들은 호텔의 수를 제한해서 방문객들이 머무를 수 있는 장소가 더 적어지게끔 합니다. ⓑ바르셀로나에서는 도심에 새로운 호텔을 짓는 것이 허용되지 않습니다. 둘째로, 다른 도시들은 인기 있는 장소들로부터 떨어져 있는 지역을 홍보합니다. 예를 들어, ⓒ암스테르담은 관광객들로 하여금 덜 붐비는 지역을 방문하도록 장려합니다. 셋째로, 많은 도시들은 접근을 제한하려고 노력합니다. 예를 들어, ⓓ베니스는 대형 크루즈선들이 섬의 부두에 배를 대는 것을 막음으로써 전반적으로 관광을 줄이려고 노력합니다. 비슷하게, ⓔ파리는 자동차 제한 구역을 둠으로써 도시의 특정 지역으로의 관광을 줄이는 데 주력해왔습니다. 이제, 몇 개의 영상들을 봅시다.

문제 풀이

16. ⓐ도시들이 과잉 관광으로 인해 야기된 문제들을 어떻게 다루는지 배울 것이라고 했으므로, 주제로는 ③ '도시들이 과잉 관광 문제를 다루는 방법'이 가장 적절하다.
① 도시에서 주택을 임대하는 것의 장점
② 관광객들이 오래된 도시를 방문하는 것을 선호하는 이유
④ 도시 규모와 오버투어리즘 사이의 상관 관계
⑤ 도시들이 노후화된 교통 시스템에 어떻게 직면하는가

17. ⓑ바르셀로나, ⓒ암스테르담, ⓓ베니스, ⓔ파리는 언급되었으나, 런던(London)은 언급되지 않았다.

근드 +α 과잉 관광(overtourism)

overtourism은 지나치게 많다는 뜻의 'over'와 관광을 뜻하는 'tourism'이 결합된 말이다. 수용 가능한 적정 수준을 넘어서는 많은 관광객이 모여들어 이들이 지역을 점령하여 현지 주민들의 삶을 침범하게 되는 현상을 일컫는다. 교통난, 소음공해 등 인간의 삶뿐만 아니라 생태계를 파괴하는 등 환경에도 영향을 미친다.

[코드 공략하기]

제2회 초급 모의고사

1	①	2	②	3	①	4	⑤	5	①	6	③
7	④	8	③	9	⑤	10	②	11	④	12	③
13	⑤	14	⑤	15	③	16	②	17	③		

1. ① | 목적

선택지 선택비율	① 87%	② 5%	③ 2%	④ 5%	⑤ 1%

M: Good afternoon, everybody. This is Student President Sam Wilson. As you know, the lunch basketball league will begin soon. Many students are interested in joining the league and waiting for the signup sheet to be handed out at the gym. For easier access,
가입 ~을 나눠주다[배포하다] 체육관 접근
ⓐwe've decided to change the registration method. Instead of
등록 방법
going to the gym to register, ⓑsimply log into the school website
등록하다
and fill out the registration form online. Thank you for listening and
~을 작성하다[기입하다]
let's have a good league.

해석

남: 안녕하세요, 여러분. 학생회장 Sam Wilson입니다. 여러분도 알다시피, 점심시간 농구 리그가 곧 시작될 것입니다. 많은 학생들이 리그 참여에 관심을 가지고 체육관에서 가입 신청서가 배포되기를 기다리고 있습니다. 더 쉽게 접근할 수 있도록, ⓐ저희는 등록 방법을 변경하기로 결정했습니다. 등록하러 체육관에 가는 대신, ⓑ그저 학교 웹사이트에 로그인해서 온라인으로 등록 양식을 작성하십시오. 들어주셔서 감사하고 좋은 리그를 펼쳐 봅시다.

문제 풀이

ⓐ농구 리그 등록 방법의 변경을 알리며 ⓑ학교 웹사이트에 로그인해서 온라인으로 등록 양식을 작성하라고 말하고 있다.

2. ② | 의견

선택지 선택비율	① 3%	② 85%	③ 3%	④ 4%	⑤ 3%

W: Daniel, I see you're reading a book. What's it about?
M: Hello, Ms. Williams. It's about time travel. I'm a big fan of science
열혈 팬 공상 과학 소설
fiction.
W: I know that. But why do you only read science fiction?
M: I feel like reading science fiction makes me more creative.
창의적인
W: I see. ⓐBut if you really want to improve your creativity, you shouldn't
향상시키다 창의력
just read science fiction. It would be better to read books on various
다양한
topics.
M: What does that have to do with improving my creativity?
~와 관계가 있다
W: ⓑReading many kinds of books will make you see things from many different perspectives.
관점
M: That makes sense. With more perspectives, I can be more creative.
W: Exactly! ⓒReading books on various topics will help you think outside the box.
새로운 사고를 하다
M: Okay, I'll try it. Thank you for your advice.

해석

여: Daniel, 책을 읽고 있구나. 무엇에 관한 거니?
남: 안녕하세요, Williams 선생님. 시간 여행에 관한 거예요. 제가 공상 과학 소설을 정말 좋아하거든요.
여: 알지. 그런데 너는 왜 공상 과학 소설만 읽니?
남: 공상 과학 소설을 읽으면 제 창의력이 더 좋아지는 것 같아서요.
여: 그렇구나. ⓐ하지만 네가 정말 창의력을 높이고 싶다면 공상 과학 소설만 읽어서는 안 돼. 다양한 주제의 책을 읽는 것이 더 좋을 거야.
남: 그게 제 창의력을 높이는 것과 무슨 관계가 있죠?
여: ⓑ많은 종류의 책을 읽는 것이 네가 다양한 관점에서 사물을 보게 해 줄 거야.
남: 일리가 있네요. 더 많은 관점을 갖게 되면 창의력이 더 좋아질 수 있겠어요.
여: 그렇지! ⓒ다양한 주제의 책을 읽는 것은 네가 새로운 사고를 하는 데 도움이 될 거야.
남: 알겠어요, 그렇게 해 볼게요. 조언 감사합니다.

문제 풀이

여자는 ⓐ창의력을 높이고 싶으면 공상 과학 소설만 읽는 것보다는 다양한 주제의 책을 읽는 것이 더 좋으며, ⓑ많은 종류의 책을 읽으면 다양한 관점에서 사물을 보게 될 것이고, ⓒ새로운 사고를 하는 데 도움이 될 것이라고 말하고 있다.

3. ① | 요지

선택지 선택비율	① 94%	② 2%	③ 1%	④ 2%	⑤ 1%

M: Hello, listeners! This is Thomas White's *Living Well*. What do you do to stay healthy? Maybe you exercise regularly and eat healthy food.
규칙적으로
Those are both great habits. But I have one more simple tip for you.
습관
Go outside and get some sunlight! ⓐSunlight is important for your
햇빛
body and mind. Getting sunlight can prevent you from getting sick
막다, 예방하다
and can reduce anxiety. It's an easy way to ⓑhelp you stay healthy
줄이다 불안
both physically and mentally. I'll be right back with more after the
신체적으로 정신적으로
break.

해석

남: 안녕하세요, 청취자 여러분! Thomas White의 '건강하게 살기'입니다. 여러분은 건강을 지키기 위해 무엇을 하시나요? 아마 규칙적으로 운동을 하고 건강한 음식을 드실지도 모릅니다. 그 두 가지 모두 훌륭한 습관입니다. 하지만 제가 여러분에게 드릴 간단한 제안이 하나 더 있습니다. 밖에 나가서 햇빛을 좀 쬐세요! ⓐ햇빛은 여러분의 신체와 정신에 중요합니다. 햇빛을 쬐면 병에 걸리는 것을 막을 수 있고 불안을 줄일 수도 있습니다. ⓑ그것은 신체적, 정신적으로 모두 당신이 건강을 유지하는 데 도움이 되는 쉬운 방법입니다. 잠시 후에 더 많은 내용으로 돌아오겠습니다.

문제 풀이

ⓐ햇빛을 쬐면 병을 예방하고 불안을 줄일 수 있기 때문에 ⓑ신체와 정신 건강에 도움이 된다고 말하고 있다.

4. ⑤ | 그림 일치

선택지 선택비율	① 6%	② 2%	③ 2%	④ 4%	⑤ 86%

W: Come look at the new reading room in the library.
M: Wow! It's much better than I thought.
W: Same here. I like ⓐthe rug in the center of the room.
M: ⓑThe striped pattern of the rug makes the room feel warm.
줄무늬가 있는
W: I agree. I think ⓒputting the sofa between two plants was a good idea.
M: Right. We can sit there and read for hours.

W: There's ⓓa round clock on the wall.
M: I have the same clock at home. Oh, ⓔthe bookshelf under the clock is full of books.
책꽂이
be full of: ~로 가득 찬
W: We can read the books at the long table.
M: Yeah, it looks like a good place to read. ⓕThe two lamps on the table will make it easy to focus.
전등, 스탠드 / 집중하다
W: Good lighting is important for reading.
조명
M: I can't wait to start using the reading room.

해석

여: 와서 도서관의 새 열람실을 봐.
남: 와! 내가 생각한 것보다 훨씬 더 좋네.
여: 내 생각도 그래. 나는 ⓐ방 중앙에 있는 깔개가 마음에 들어.
남: ⓑ깔개의 줄무늬 패턴이 방을 따뜻하게 느껴지게 하네.
여: 맞아. ⓒ소파를 두 식물 사이에 둔 건 좋은 생각이었던 것 같아.
남: 그렇지. 우린 거기 앉아서 몇 시간이고 책을 읽을 수 있어.
여: ⓓ벽에 둥근 시계가 있네.
남: 나도 집에 똑같은 시계가 있어. 오, ⓔ시계 아래에 있는 책장은 책들로 가득 차 있네.
여: 우린 긴 책상에서 책을 읽을 수 있겠어.
남: 응, 책 읽기에 좋은 장소인 것 같아. ⓕ책상 위에 있는 스탠드 두 개가 집중하기 쉽게 하겠어.
여: 좋은 조명은 독서하는 데 중요하지.
남: 빨리 이 열람실을 이용하고 싶어.

문제 풀이

ⓕ책상 위에 스탠드 두 개가 있다고 했으므로, 그림 ⑤는 대화 내용과 일치하지 않는다.

5. ① | 할 일

선택지 선택비율	① 63%	② 5%	③ 15%	④ 6%	⑤ 10%

W: What are you doing, Sam?
M: I'm filling out an application to join the school movie club.
지원서, 신청서
W: Really? I'm also interested in that club.
M: Let's join together then.
W: I'd love to, but I already belong to the science club.
~에 속하다
M: You can join both.
W: You're right. I'll have to check the movie club's meeting schedule first, though.
일정, 시간표
M: Then I'll pick up the movie club's brochure for you from the club room later.
안내 책자
W: That'll be great. Thanks.
M: No problem. I'll have to go submit this application form anyway.
제출하다 / 신청서

해석

여: 너 뭐 하고 있니, Sam?
남: 학교 영화 동아리에 가입하려고 신청서를 작성하는 중이야.
여: 정말? 나도 그 동아리에 관심이 있어.
남: 그러면 같이 가입하자.
여: 나도 그러고 싶지만, 난 이미 과학 동아리에 속해 있어.
남: 둘 다 가입해도 돼.
여: 맞아. 하지만 난 먼저 영화 동아리의 회의 일정을 확인해야 할 거야.
남: 그러면 내가 나중에 동아리 방에서 영화 동아리 안내 책자를 네게 가져다줄게.
여: 그러면 좋겠네. 고마워.
남: 천만에. 난 어쨌든 이 신청서를 제출하러 가야겠어.

문제 풀이

남자는 여자에게 영화 동아리 안내 책자를 가져다주겠다고 했다.

6. ③ | 금액

선택지 선택비율	① 3%	② 3%	③ 86%	④ 4%	⑤ 1%

[Telephone rings.]
M: Good evening, John's Food Delivery. How may I help you?
배달
W: Hi. I'd like to order some dinners.
M: Okay. What would you like?
W: How much is a cheeseburger set?
M: ⓐIt's eight dollars. How many would you like?
W: ⓑI need two sets. Is there anything else you can recommend?
추천하다
M: Yes, our newest item, the avocado sandwich, is very delicious. ⓒIt's seven dollars.
최신의
W: Good. ⓓAdd two avocado sandwiches to my order, please.
M: So two cheeseburger sets and two avocado sandwiches, right?
W: Yes. And I have a discount coupon for new customers.
할인
M: Okay, then ⓔyou'll get 10% off the total. Where would you like your food delivered?
W: 101 Fifth St., please.

해석

[전화벨이 울린다.]
남: 안녕하세요. John의 음식 배달입니다. 무엇을 도와드릴까요?
여: 안녕하세요. 저녁식사를 좀 주문하고 싶습니다.
남: 네. 무엇을 드시겠어요?
여: 치즈버거 세트는 얼마인가요?
남: ⓐ8달러입니다. 몇 개 원하세요?
여: ⓑ두 세트 필요해요. 추천해 주실 수 있는 다른 게 있나요?
남: 네, 저희 최신 품목인 아보카도 샌드위치가 정말 맛있습니다. ⓒ그건 7달러입니다.
여: 좋아요. ⓓ제 주문에 아보카도 샌드위치 두 개를 추가해 주세요.
남: 그럼 치즈버거 세트 두 개와 아보카도 샌드위치 두 개네요, 맞죠?
여: 네. 그리고 신규 고객을 위한 할인 쿠폰이 있어요.
남: 네, 그러면 ⓔ총 금액에서 10% 할인받으실 겁니다. 어디로 음식을 배달받으시겠습니까?
여: 5번가 101로 부탁드립니다.

문제 풀이

여자는 ⓐ8달러인 ⓑ치즈버거 세트 두 개와 ⓒ7달러인 ⓓ아보카도 샌드위치 두 개를 주문했는데 ⓔ총 금액에서 10% 할인을 받으므로, 27달러를 지불하면 된다.

7. ④ | 이유

선택지 선택비율	① 1%	② 1%	③ 2%	④ 94%	⑤ 2%

M: You seem busy this morning, Olivia.
W: I am. I had to see Professor Martin about my history test.
M: Oh, I see. Do you remember that our club's ski trip is this weekend?
W: Yeah. I heard that a nice ski resort has been booked for the trip.
예약하다
M: I didn't know that. I'm so excited to go skiing at a nice resort.
W: I bet it'll be great, but I don't think I can go this time.
M: Why? You don't work at the cafe on the weekends, do you?
W: No, I don't. But I need to take care of my cat. She's recovering from surgery.
~을 돌보다 / 회복되다 / 수술

M: Isn't there anyone else who can look after your cat?
~을 돌보다
W: No one but me. My parents are visiting relatives in Canada. They
친척
won't be back for two weeks.
M: I'm sorry that you can't join us.
W: Me, too. Have fun this weekend.

해석

남: 오늘 아침 바빠 보여, Olivia.
여: 응. 역사 시험 때문에 Martin 교수님을 뵈어야 했어.
남: 아, 그렇구나. 우리 동아리 스키 여행이 이번 주말인 거 기억하지?
여: 응. 이번 여행에 좋은 스키장이 예약되어 있다고 들었어.
남: 그건 몰랐네. 좋은 리조트에 스키 타러 간다니 정말 기대돼.
여: 분명 좋을 것 같은데, 나는 이번에는 못 갈 것 같아.
남: 왜? 너 주말에는 카페에서 일하지 않잖아, 그렇지?
여: 응, 안 해. 하지만 내 고양이를 돌봐야 하거든. 고양이가 수술을 받고 회복 중이야.
남: 네 고양이를 돌봐줄 다른 누군가는 없니?
여: 나 외에는 아무도 없어. 부모님께서는 캐나다에 계신 친척들을 방문하실 예정이야. 2주 간 돌아오시지 않을 거야.
남: 네가 우리와 함께 할 수 없다니 아쉬워.
여: 나도 그래. 이번 주말 재미있게 보내.

문제 풀이

여자는 수술을 받고 회복 중인 자신의 고양이를 돌봐야 해서 스키 여행에 갈 수 없다고 했다.

코드 +α 확신을 나타내는 표현

I bet our team will win the game. (분명 우리 팀이 이길 거야.)
I'm sure that you can make it. (분명 너는 해낼 수 있어.)
There is no doubt that we don't have much time. (분명한 건 우리가 시간이 많지 않다는 거야.)

8. ③ | 언급

선택지 선택비율	① 3%	② 2%	③ 90%	④ 1%	⑤ 3%

W: Honey, did you see the poster about the Stanville Free-cycle?
M: Free-cycle? What is that?
W: It's another way of recycling. You give away items you don't need
거저 주다, 나눠 주다
and anybody can take them for free.
M: Oh, it's like one man's garbage is another man's treasure. Who can
쓰레기 보물
participate?
W: ⓐIt's open to everyone living in Stanville.
M: Great. Where is it taking place?
take place: 개최되다
W: ⓑAt Rose Park on Second Street.
M: When does the event start?
W: ⓒIt starts on April 12 and runs for a week.
계속되다
M: Let's see what we can free-cycle, starting from the cupboard.
찬장
W: Okay. But ⓓbreakable items like glass dishes or cups won't be
깨지기 쉬운
accepted.
M: I see. I'll keep that in mind.
~을 명심하다

해석

여: 여보, Stanville 프리사이클에 관한 포스터 봤어요?
남: 프리사이클이요? 그게 뭔데요?
여: 재활용의 또 다른 방법이에요. 당신이 필요 없는 물건을 나눠 주면 누구나 그걸 무료로 가져갈 수 있어요.
남: 아, 어떤 사람의 쓰레기가 다른 사람의 보물인 셈이네요. 누가 참가할 수 있나요?
여: ⓐStanville에 사는 모든 사람들에게 열려 있어요.
남: 좋아요. 어디서 개최되나요?
여: ⓑ2번가에 있는 Rose 공원에서요.
남: 그 행사는 언제 시작해요?
여: ⓒ4월 12일에 시작해서 일주일 동안 계속돼요.
남: 찬장부터 시작해서, 우리가 무엇을 프리사이클할 수 있을지 봅시다.
여: 좋아요. 하지만 ⓓ유리 접시나 컵처럼 깨지기 쉬운 물품은 받지 않아요.
남: 알겠어요. 명심할게요.

문제 풀이

ⓐ참가 대상, ⓑ행사 장소, ⓒ행사 시작일, ⓓ금지 품목은 언급되었지만, 주차 가능 여부는 언급되지 않았다.

9. ⑤ | 내용 일치

선택지 선택비율	① 1%	② 1%	③ 1%	④ 2%	⑤ 95%

M: Good morning, students of Violet Hill High School. This is your principal speaking. I'm delighted to announce that the annual Violet
교장 매우 기뻐하는 발표하다, 알리다 연례의
Hill Mentorship ⓐwill be held next Friday. Our school graduates
졸업생
who are now majoring in English literature, bioengineering, and
~을 전공하다 문학 생명 공학
theater and film will be ⓑgiving some tips on university life. To register for this event, visit our school website and ⓒsubmit two questions you would like to ask them in advance. ⓓThe deadline for
미리
registration is next Tuesday, so don't wait too long. And remember, ⓔthe maximum number of participants for each major is 30 people.
최대의 전공
For more information, visit our school website.

해석

남: 안녕하세요, Violet Hill 고등학교 학생 여러분. 교장입니다. 연례 Violet Hill 멘토십이 ⓐ다음 주 금요일에 개최될 것임을 알리게 되어 매우 기쁩니다. 현재 영문학, 생명공학, 연극 및 영화를 전공하고 있는 우리 학교 졸업생들이 ⓑ대학 생활에 관한 조언을 해줄 예정입니다. 이 행사에 등록하려면, 우리 학교 웹사이트를 방문하여 ⓒ그들에게 물어보고 싶은 질문 두 가지를 미리 제출하세요. ⓓ신청 마감일은 다음 주 화요일이니, 너무 시간을 끌지 마세요. 그리고 기억하세요, ⓔ각 전공의 최대 참가 인원은 30명입니다. 더 자세한 정보를 위해서는, 우리 학교 웹사이트를 방문하세요.

문제 풀이

ⓔ각 전공의 최대 참가 인원은 30명이라고 했다.

10. ② | 도표

선택지 선택비율	① 12%	② 78%	③ 5%	④ 4%	⑤ 1%

M: Sweetie, what are you doing?
W: I'm looking at the schedule for exercise classes. Would you like to
시간표
help me choose?
M: Sure. What's your budget for it?
예산
W: Well, I don't want to spend more than forty dollars.
M: Okay. Then, forget about this one. What about class time?
W: As you know, I have things to do in the afternoon.
M: In that case, let's cross this one out. ⓐNow you have dancing and
~을 지우다, ~을 삭제하다
tennis left.

W: I heard the tennis class is held outside. ⓑI don't like outdoor sports.
야외의

M: Okay. Then, we have only two exercise classes left. Which level is good for you?

W: ⓒSince I've already taken the beginner's class, I'll take the other one this time.
초보자, 초급 단계

해석

남: 여보, 뭐 하고 있어요?
여: 운동 수업 시간표를 보고 있어요. 내가 고르는 거 도와 줄래요?
남: 물론이죠. 예산은 얼마예요?
여: 음, 40달러 넘게는 쓰고 싶지 않아요.
남: 알겠어요. 그러면 이건 무시해요. 수업 시간은요?
여: 당신도 알다시피, 난 오후에는 할 일이 있어요.
남: 그렇다면 이것도 지워요. ⓐ이제 춤하고 테니스만 남았네요.
여: 테니스 수업은 야외에서 한다고 들었어요. ⓑ나는 야외 스포츠는 좋아하지 않아요.
남: 좋아요. 그러면 두 개의 운동 수업만 남았네요. 어떤 수준이 당신한테 좋을까요?
여: ⓒ내가 초급 수업은 이미 들었으니, 이번에는 다른 수업을 수강할래요.

문제 풀이

여자는 ⓐ테니스와 춤 수업 중에서 ⓑ테니스는 야외 스포츠를 좋아하지 않아 제외하고, ⓒ춤 수업 중에서 초급 수업이 아닌 다른 것을 수강하겠다고 했다.

11. ④ | 짧은 대화 응답

선택지 선택비율	① 5%	② 7%	③ 5%	④ 74%	⑤ 9%

M: Ashley, do you remember the digital poster we made to upload on social media?
올리다
소셜 미디어, 사회 관계망 서비스

W: Yes, of course. ⓐIt was about food waste, right?
쓰레기

M: Exactly. ⓑLet's print it out and put it on the wall in our school cafeteria.
~을 출력하다
구내식당

W: Great idea! It'll catch the students' attention.
주의, 관심

해석

남: Ashley, 우리가 소셜 미디어에 올리려고 만든 디지털 포스터 기억나?
여: 응, 물론이지. ⓐ그거 음식물 쓰레기에 관한 거였잖아, 그렇지?
남: 맞아. ⓑ그걸 출력해서 우리 학교 식당 벽에 붙이자.
여: 좋은 생각이야! 그게 학생들의 관심을 끌 거야.

문제 풀이

남자가 ⓐ음식물 쓰레기에 관한 포스터를 ⓑ출력해서 학교 식당 벽에 붙이자고 제안했으므로, 여자의 응답으로는 그것이 학생들의 관심을 끌 것이라며 호응하는 ④가 가장 적절하다.
① 고마워. 하지만 지금은 배가 고프지 않아.
② 동의해. 그걸 출력하는 건 정말 낭비야.
③ 물론 아니지. 내가 언제든 너를 도와줄게.
⑤ 걱정 마. 난 우리 학교 식당 메뉴가 마음에 들어.

12. ③ | 짧은 대화 응답

선택지 선택비율	① 3%	② 1%	③ 69%	④ 26%	⑤ 2%

W: Kevin, is this bike yours?
M: Yes, ⓐI bought it for my bike tour.
여행
W: Really? ⓑWhere are you planning to go?
M: I haven't decided the place, yet.

해석

여: Kevin, 이 자전거 네 거니?
남: 응, ⓐ자전거 여행을 위해 그걸 샀어.
여: 정말? ⓑ어디로 갈 계획이니?
남: 아직 장소는 정하지 않았어.

문제 풀이

ⓐ자전거 여행을 위해 자전거를 산 남자에게 여자가 ⓑ어디로 갈 계획인지 물었으므로, 구체적인 장소를 대답하거나 아직 장소를 정하지 않았다고 하는 ③이 응답으로 가장 적절하다.
① 너도 여행에 함께 할 수 있어.
② 그 자전거는 그렇게 비싸지 않았어.
④ 공원에서 자전거를 빌릴 거야.
⑤ 가을은 여행에 가장 좋은 계절이야.

13. ⑤ | 긴 대화 응답

선택지 선택비율	① 4%	② 4%	③ 5%	④ 2%	⑤ 85%

M: Hey, Cindy. Have you been playing a lot of badminton these days?
W: No, ⓐI've been experiencing some pain in my knee since a badminton match last weekend.
experience: 느끼다 통증
M: I'm sorry to hear that. Did you go see a doctor?
W: Yes, I visited a local clinic yesterday.
지역의 병원
M: I hope you feel better soon. By the way, have you ever taken a badminton lesson?
W: No, I haven't. Why are you asking?
M: In my experience, that kind of injury can come from bad posture. ⓑA lesson might reduce the risk of any further injury.
경험 부상 자세
줄이다 위험 더 이상의
W: Well, I thought I didn't need those lessons.
M: Cindy, ⓒif you want to keep playing badminton without any injuries, it's important to learn from an instructor to develop the right posture.
강사 발전시키다, 익히다
W: You're right. Maybe I should start taking badminton lessons.

해석

남: 안녕, Cindy. 요즘 배드민턴 많이 치고 있니?
여: 아니, ⓐ지난 주말 배드민턴 경기 이후로 무릎에 통증을 느끼고 있어.
남: 안됐다. 병원에 갔었니?
여: 응, 어제 동네 병원에 다녀왔어.
남: 빨리 나으면 좋겠다. 그런데, 너 배드민턴 레슨을 받아본 적 있어?
여: 아니, 없어. 왜 묻니?
남: 내 경험으로는, 그런 종류의 부상은 안 좋은 자세에서 올 수 있거든. ⓑ레슨을 받으면 더 이상의 부상 위험을 줄일지도 몰라.
여: 음, 나는 그런 레슨이 필요 없다고 생각했어.
남: Cindy, ⓒ부상 없이 계속 배드민턴을 치고 싶다면, 제대로 된 자세를 익히기 위해 강사에게 배우는 게 중요해.
여: 네 말이 맞아. 아마 배드민턴 레슨을 받기 시작해야겠네.

문제 풀이

ⓐ배드민턴 경기 후 무릎에 통증을 느끼고 있는 여자에게 남자가 ⓑⓒ부상 위험을 줄이기 위해 레슨을 받도록 재차 권하고 있으므로, 남자의 충고를 받아들여 배드민턴 레슨을 받기 시작해야겠다고 말하는 ⑤가 여자의 응답으로 가장 적절하다.
① 응. 내가 방문한 병원의 전화번호를 네게 알려줄 수 있어.
② 동의해. 어제 저녁의 배드민턴 경기는 굉장했어.
③ 문제없어. 이번에는 내가 서브 넣는 방법을 가르쳐 줄게.
④ 안됐다. 무릎 부상이 빨리 회복되길 바랄게.

14. ⑤ | 긴 대화 응답

선택지 선택비율	① 2%	② 3%	③ 3%	④ 4%	⑤ 86%

W: Hi, David. What are you looking at?
M: School club posters.
W: Is there any club you want to join?
가입하다
M: I'm interested in drones, but there's no drone club.
W: That's too bad. ⓐWhy don't you make a new club yourself?
M: Oh, I haven't thought about it. What do I have to do first?
W: You'll need at least five people to start a club.
적어도
M: ⓑThen I have to find people who are interested in drones.
W: ⓒHow about using social media? It's an easy way to attract people.
(사람을) 끌어모으다
M: Right. I'll post an ad for a drone club I'm going to make.
게시하다 광고 (= advertisement)

해석

여: 안녕, David. 뭘 보고 있니?
남: 학교 동아리 포스터.
여: 가입하고 싶은 동아리가 있니?
남: 난 드론에 관심이 있는데, 드론 동아리는 없어.
여: 안됐구나. ⓐ네가 직접 새 동아리를 만들지 그래?
남: 아, 그 생각은 안 해 봤어. 내가 가장 먼저 뭘 해야 하지?
여: 동아리를 개설하려면 적어도 다섯 명이 필요할 거야.
남: ⓑ그러면 드론에 관심 있는 사람들을 찾아야겠군.
여: ⓒ소셜 미디어를 이용하는 건 어때? 그게 사람들을 끌어모으는 쉬운 방법이잖아.
남: 맞아. 나는 내가 만들 드론 동아리 광고를 게시하겠어.

문제 풀이

ⓐ여자의 제안에 따라 드론 동아리를 만들기 위해 남자는 ⓑ드론에 관심 있는 사람들을 찾아야 하고 ⓒ그 방법으로 소셜 미디어를 이용할 것을 여자가 제안하고 있으므로, 소셜 미디어에 드론 동아리 광고를 게시하겠다는 내용의 ⑤가 응답으로 가장 적절하다.
① 우리 동아리에는 신입 회원이 들어올 자리가 없어.
② 네가 동아리 면접을 통과하지 못했다니 유감이야.
③ 맞아. 우리는 거기에 있는 모든 정보를 믿으면 안 돼.
④ 고맙지만, 나는 다시 드론 수업을 받고 싶지는 않아.

15. ③ | 상황에 적절한 말

선택지 선택비율	① 3%	② 5%	③ 84%	④ 5%	⑤ 3%

W: Laura and Tony are close coworkers. ⓐLaura notices that Tony has been looking unusually tired and pale recently. One day, she asks Tony if he's not been feeling well lately, but Tony says he's just a bit tired from work. Laura knows that Tony sometimes works even on weekends without taking a break or getting any rest. However, this time, ⓑshe is really worried about him and wants him to take at least a couple of days off. In this situation, what would Laura most likely say to Tony?
(직장 동료 / 알아차리다 / look pale: 안색이 나쁘다 / 평소와 달리, 유난히 / 최근에 / 요즘 / 조금, 약간 / take a break: 휴식을 취하다 / (근무·일을) 쉬는)
Laura: You'd better take a break for a few days.

해석

여: Laura와 Tony는 친한 직장 동료이다. ⓐLaura는 최근에 Tony가 유난히 피곤해 보이고 안색이 나쁘다는 것을 알아차린다. 어느 날, 그녀는 Tony에게 요즘 몸이 안 좋은지 물어보지만, Tony는 일 때문에 조금 피곤할 뿐이라고 말한다. Laura는 Tony가 가끔 주말에도 쉬지 않고 일한다는 것을 알고 있다. 하지만 이번에는 ⓑ그녀는 정말로 그가 걱정이 되어 그가 최소 며칠이라도 쉬길 바라고 있다. 이 상황에서, Laura는 Tony에게 뭐라고 말하겠는가?
Laura: 며칠 동안 휴식을 취하는 게 좋겠어요.

문제 풀이

ⓐLaura는 Tony가 최근에 유난히 피곤해 보이고 안색이 나쁜 것을 보고, ⓑ그가 걱정되는 마음에 최소 며칠이라도 쉬길 바라고 있으므로, ③이 가장 적절하다.
① 저는 건강 검진을 받으러 병원에 가는 걸 좋아하지 않아요.
② 오늘 저를 병원에 데려다줘서 고마워요.
④ 당신은 마감일 전에 일을 끝내야 해요.
⑤ 유감이지만 지금은 당신의 업무량을 줄여 줄 수 없어요.

16~17. | 세트 문항

16. ② 17. ③

선택지 선택비율					
16	① 1%	② 96%	③ 2%	④ 1%	⑤ 0%
17	① 1%	② 1%	③ 95%	④ 1%	⑤ 1%

W: Everyone loves a good night's sleep, but ⓐfor wild animals, finding the right time and place can be difficult. Whether it's staying safe, keeping warm, or remembering to breathe, animals have a lot to consider before they go to bed. As a result, ⓑthey've come up with some clever and interesting solutions. To start with, ⓒbats sleep in caves while hanging upside down. Doing that not only keeps them away from enemies but also means they are in the perfect position to fly away if necessary. Meanwhile, ⓓducks sleep side by side in rows. The ducks on the outside of the rows sleep with one eye open to watch for danger, while the ducks on the inside sleep with both eyes closed. ⓔGiraffes require little rest, sleeping for only five minutes at a time or as little as 30 minutes a day. They sleep in short intervals, sometimes sitting down or even standing up, so that they're ready to run. Finally, ⓕdolphins have to consciously think in order to breathe, even when they're sleeping. They only let part of their brain relax and keep one eye open as they sleep.
(숨을 쉬다 / 고려하다 / ~을 생각해 내다 / 우선 / enemy: 적 / 위치, 자리 / 한편 / 나란히 / 줄지어 / ~을 살피다 / 간격 / 의식적으로)

해석

여: 누구나 밤에 푹 자는 것을 좋아하지만, ⓐ야생동물들에게 있어, (잠자기) 적당한 시간과 장소를 찾는 것은 어려울 수 있습니다. 안전하게 머무는지, 따뜻함을 유지하는지, 또는 잊지 않고 숨을 쉬는지, 동물들은 잠자리에 들기 전에 고려할 것이 많습니다. 결과적으로, ⓑ그들은 몇 가지 영리하고 흥미로운 해결책을 생각해 냈습니다. 우선, ⓒ박쥐는 동굴 안에서 거꾸로 매달려 잡니다. 그렇게 하면 그들을 적으로부터 지켜줄 뿐만 아니라, 필요한 경우에 그들이 날아갈 수 있는 완벽한 위치에 있다는 것을 의미합니다. 한편, ⓓ오리는 나란히 줄지어 잡니다. 줄 바깥쪽에 있는 오리는 위험을 살피기 위해 한쪽 눈을 뜨고 자는 반면, 안쪽에 있는 오리는 두 눈을 감고 잡니다. ⓔ기린은 거의 쉼이 없는데요, 한 번에 겨우 5분, 또는 하루에 가급적 30분 잡니다. 그들은 짧은 간격으로 자면서, 때로는 앉아 있거나 심지어 서 있기도 하는데요, 그렇게 해서 그들은 달아날 준비를 하는 겁니다. 마지막으로, ⓕ돌고래는 숨을 쉬기 위해 의식적으로 생각을 해야 하는데요, 심지어 자고 있을 때조차도요. 그들은 잘 때 뇌 일부만 쉬게 하고 한쪽 눈은 뜨고 있답니다.

문제 풀이

16. ⓐⓑ잠자기 적당한 시간과 장소를 찾기 위한 야생동물의 해결책에 관해 말하고 있으므로, 주제는 ② '생존을 위해 동물들이 이용하는 독특한 수면 습관'이 가장 적절하다.
① 각 문화에서 인기 있는 각기 다른 동물
③ 멸종 위기에 처한 종이 되고 있는 야생동물

④ 동물이 식이 방법을 바꾼 방법
⑤ 사람들에게 행운을 가져다주는 동물

17. ⓒ박쥐, ⓓ오리, ⓔ기린, ⓕ돌고래는 언급되었으나, 침팬지(chimpanzees)는 언급되지 않았다.

[코드 공략하기]

제3회 초급 모의고사

1	⑤	2	⑤	3	⑤	4	④	5	⑤	6	②
7	③	8	③	9	④	10	②	11	⑤	12	⑤
13	①	14	①	15	⑤	16	③	17	④		

1. ⑤ | 목적

선택지 선택비율	① 3%	② 5%	③ 1%	④ 3%	⑤ 87%

M: Hello, Villeford High School students. This is principal(교장) Aaron Clark. As a big fan of the Villeford ice hockey team, I'm very excited about the upcoming(다가오는) National High School Ice Hockey League. As you all know, ⓐthe first game will be held in the Central Rink at 6 p.m. this Saturday. ⓑI want as many of you as possible to come and cheer(응원하다) our team to victory(승리). I've seen them put in(put effort: 노력을 쏟다) an incredible(믿을 수 없는) amount of effort to win the league. It will help them play better just to see you there cheering for them. I really hope to see you at the rink. Thank you.

해석

남: 안녕하세요, Villeford 고등학교 학생 여러분. 저는 교장 Aaron Clark입니다. Villeford 아이스하키팀의 열렬한 팬으로서, 다가오는 전국 고등학교 아이스하키 리그에 매우 흥분됩니다. 여러분 모두가 알다시피, ⓐ첫 경기는 이번 주 토요일 오후 6시에 Central 링크에서 열릴 예정입니다. ⓑ저는 여러분들이 가능한 한 많이 와서 우리 팀이 승리할 수 있도록 응원해주길 바랍니다. 저는 그들이 리그에서 승리하기 위해 엄청난 노력을 하는 것을 보았습니다. 여러분이 그곳에서 그들을 응원하는 것을 보는 것만으로도 그들이 경기를 더 잘할 수 있도록 도와줄 것입니다. 링크에서 여러분을 볼 수 있기를 간절히 바랍니다. 감사합니다.

문제 풀이

남자는 ⓐ이번 주 토요일 오후 6시에 아이스하키 첫 경기가 있음을 상기시키며 ⓑ아이스하키부 경기의 관람을 독려하고 있다.

2. ⑤ | 의견

선택지 선택비율	① 4%	② 9%	③ 2%	④ 2%	⑤ 82%

W: Ryan, did you enjoy the musical(뮤지컬) "Tigers" yesterday?
M: Yes, I loved it. I can't believe we got tickets for such a popular show.
W: Yes, we were lucky. By the way, it reminded(상기시키다, 떠올리게 하다) me of the class musical that we have to prepare for the next month's school festival.
M: You read my mind! I think we should look for a musical with a variety of(다양한) music.
W: Well, there might be something even more important than that.
M: Should we give the audience(관객, 청중) a meaningful(의미 있는) lesson?
W: Not necessarily. Do you remember what we did last year?
M: Yes. We focused on(~에 집중하다) preparing a musical that was easy to perform(공연하다).
W: Right. But not everyone participated(참여하다, 참가하다). I think everyone should have a role(역할) for the class musical.
M: That's a good point.

해석

여: Ryan, 어제 뮤지컬 〈Tigers〉 재미있었어?
남: 응, 정말 좋았어. 우리가 그렇게 인기 있는 공연 표를 구했다니 믿기지 않아.
여: 맞아, 우리가 운이 좋았지. 그런데 그게 다음 달 학교 축제를 위해 우리가 준비해야 할 학급 뮤지컬을 떠올리게 했어.
남: 내 마음을 읽었네! 나는 우리가 다양한 음악이 있는 뮤지컬을 찾아봐야 한다고 생각해.
여: 음, 어쩌면 그보다 훨씬 더 중요한 게 있을지도 몰라.
남: 관객에게 의미 있는 교훈을 줘야 할까?
여: 꼭 그런 건 아니야. 작년에 우리가 했던 거 기억나?
남: 응. 우리는 공연하기 쉬운 뮤지컬을 준비하는 데 집중했었지.
여: 맞아. 그런데 모두가 참여하지는 않았어. 나는 모두가 학급 뮤지컬에서 역할을 맡아야 한다고 생각해.
남: 좋은 지적이야.

문제 풀이

여자는 학급 뮤지컬에 모두가 참여해 역할을 맡아야 한다고 말하고 있다.

3. ⑤ | 요지

선택지 선택비율	① 3%	② 1%	③ 3%	④ 1%	⑤ 92%

W: Hello, this is your student counselor(상담사), Susan Smith. You might be worried about your new school life as a freshman(신입생). You have a lot of things to do in the beginning of the year. Today, I'm going to give you a tip about time management(시간 관리). Make a to-do list! Write down the tasks(일) you have to do on a list and check off what you finish, one by one. By doing this, you won't miss the things you need to do. Using a to-do list will help you manage(관리하다) your time efficiently(효율적으로). Good luck to you and don't forget to start today.

해석

여: 안녕하세요, 저는 여러분의 학생 상담사 Susan Smith입니다. 여러분은 신입생으로서 새로운 학교생활에 대해 걱정할 수도 있습니다. 연초에는 해야 할 일이 많죠. 오늘은 여러분에게 시간 관리에 대한 팁을 하나 드리겠습니다. 할 일의 목록을 만드세요! 해야 할 일을 목록에 적고, 끝내는 것을 하나씩 체크하세요. 이렇게 하면, 해야 할 일을 놓치지 않을 거예요. 할 일의 목록을 활용하면 여러분이 시간을 효율적으로 관리하는 데 도움이 될 겁니다. 행운을 빌어요, 그리고 잊지 말고 오늘 시작하세요.

문제 풀이

할 일의 목록을 활용하면 시간을 효율적으로 관리할 수 있다고 말하고 있다.

4. ④ | 그림 일치

선택지 선택비율	① 2%	② 3%	③ 3%	④ 85%	⑤ 8%

M: Hey, Amy. Here is the new recording(녹음) studio for our band. How do you like it?
W: Wow, ⓐthese two speakers are impressive(인상적인)!
M: Yes, they are. The sound quality(음질) is excellent.
W: Also, ⓑthe long desk between the speakers looks great.
M: Yeah. And ⓒon the desk, there is a microphone(마이크). We can use it to give recording directions(지시).
W: Nice. Oh, this chair looks comfortable(편안한). It could be helpful for long recordings.
M: Agreed. And the rug under the chair gives the room a cozy(아늑한) feeling, doesn't it?
W: Yes, and I like ⓓthe flower patterns on the rug.
M: I like it, too. How about ⓔthe poster on the wall?
W: It's cool. This studio feels like where music truly comes alive(come alive: 활기를 띠다)!
M: I'm glad you like this place.
W: Absolutely. I can't wait to start recording here.

해석

남: 안녕, Amy. 여기가 우리 밴드를 위한 새로운 녹음 스튜디오야. 어때?
여: 와, ⓐ이 스피커 두 대가 정말 인상적이네!
남: 응, 그렇지. 음질이 훌륭해.
여: 그리고 ⓑ스피커 사이에 있는 긴 책상도 멋져 보여.
남: 맞아. 그리고 ⓒ책상 위에는 마이크가 있어. 우린 녹음 지시를 하기 위해 그걸 사용할 수 있지.
여: 좋다. 오, 이 의자 편안해 보이네. 긴 녹음에 도움이 될 것 같아.
남: 동의해. 그리고 의자 밑에 있는 깔개가 방에 아늑한 느낌을 주네, 그렇지 않니?
여: 응, 그리고 난 ⓓ깔개의 꽃무늬가 마음에 들어.
남: 나도 마음에 들어. ⓔ벽에 있는 포스터는 어때?
여: 멋져. 이 스튜디오는 음악이 진짜 활기를 띠는 곳 같아!
남: 네가 이곳이 마음에 든다니 기뻐.
여: 물론이지. 빨리 여기서 녹음을 시작하고 싶어.

문제 풀이

ⓓ깔개에 꽃무늬가 있다고 했으므로, 그림 ④의 격자무늬 깔개는 대화 내용과 일치하지 않는다.

5. ⑤ | 부탁한 일

선택지 선택비율	① 1%	② 4%	③ 4%	④ 8%	⑤ 83%

W: Honey, the flowers are really beautiful these days. Why don't we take a walk(산책하다) this weekend?
M: Wow, that sounds great. Do you have any particular(특정한) place in mind?
W: Yes, I'd like to visit the Grand Forest. I've already downloaded the map of the forest(숲).
M: That's nice. Do we have to buy entrance tickets(입장권)?
W: Yes. We can buy tickets online. I'll buy two tickets in the afternoon.
M: Great. Let's have a nice lunch there, too. There's a restaurant called Treehouse Pasta in the Grand Forest.
W: Nice. Do we have to make a reservation(예약하다)?
M: Yes. I'll make the reservation right away.
W: Then, I'll look up(~을 찾아보다) the menu of the restaurant.
M: Thanks.

해석

여: 여보, 요즘 꽃이 정말 예쁘네요. 이번 주말에 산책하는 거 어때요?
남: 와, 좋은 생각이에요. 생각하는 특정 장소가 있어요?
여: 네, Grand Forest에 가고 싶어요. 숲지도도 벌써 다운로드해 놨어요.
남: 좋아요. 입장권을 사야 하나요?
여: 네. 온라인으로 표를 살 수 있어요. 오후에 내가 두 장 살게요.
남: 알았어요. 우리 거기서 맛있는 점심도 먹어요. Grand Forest 안에 Treehouse Pasta라는 식당이 있어요.
여: 좋아요. 예약해야 하나요?
남: 네. 내가 지금 바로 예약할게요.
여: 그럼 나는 식당 메뉴를 찾아볼게요.
남: 고마워요.

문제 풀이

남자가 지금 바로 식당 예약을 하겠다고 했다.

6. ② | 금액

선택지 선택비율	① 4%	② 88%	③ 2%	④ 3%	⑤ 1%

M: Good morning, Jennifer.
W: Good morning, Robin. How may I help you today?
M: This bagel sandwich looks so delicious. How much is it?
W: It was originally five dollars, but ⓐit's three dollars now. We're
원래
having a sale to celebrate our 10th anniversary.
경축하다, 기리다 기념일
M: Great. ⓑI'll take two bagel sandwiches.
W: Okay. What about coffee?
M: Is it on sale, too?
할인 중인
W: Sure. ⓒYou can take any coffee for just two dollars.
M: Wow! ⓓI'll order two cappuccinos.
W: Anything else?
M: That's all. Here's my credit card.
신용카드

해석

남: 안녕하세요, Jennifer.
여: 안녕하세요, Robin. 오늘은 어떻게 도와 드릴까요?
남: 이 베이글 샌드위치가 매우 맛있어 보이네요. 얼마인가요?
여: 그것은 원래 5달러였지만, ⓐ지금은 3달러에요. 10주년을 기념하기 위해 할인을 하고 있어요.
남: 좋아요. ⓑ베이글 샌드위치 두 개를 살게요.
여: 네. 커피는요?
남: 그것도 할인 중인가요?
여: 그럼요. ⓒ어떤 커피든 겨우 2달러에 드실 수 있으세요.
남: 와! ⓓ카푸치노 두 잔 주문할게요.
여: 또 다른 것은요?
남: 그게 다예요. 여기 제 신용카드입니다.

문제 풀이

ⓐ3달러인 ⓑ베이글 샌드위치 두 개와 ⓒ2달러인 ⓓ커피(카푸치노) 두 잔을 주문했으므로, 남자가 지불할 금액은 10달러이다.

7. ③ | 이유

선택지 선택비율	① 1%	② 1%	③ 96%	④ 1%	⑤ 1%

M: Mom, I'm home.
W: Hi. Did you go to the gym?
M: Yes. My membership ended today, but I didn't renew it.
갱신하다, 연장하다
W: Why? Does your shoulder still hurt?
M: No, my shoulder feels completely fine.
W: So, what's the problem? I thought you were enjoying exercising.
M: I was. It's actually been fun.
W: Then ⓐwhy didn't you renew your membership?
M: Well, ⓑthe shower facilities at the gym are too old, and there's not
facility: 시설
enough space in the shower stalls.
공간 샤워칸
W: I see. Why don't you check out the new health club nearby? It may be more expensive, but the facilities are probably a lot better.
M: Okay. Maybe I should visit there tomorrow on my way home after school.
W: That sounds like a good plan!

해석

남: 엄마, 저 왔어요.
여: 그래. 헬스장에 갔었니?
남: 네. 회원권이 오늘 끝났는데, 연장하지 않았어요.
여: 왜? 어깨가 아직도 아프니?
남: 아니요, 어깨는 완전히 좋아요.
여: 그러면 뭐가 문제니? 네가 운동을 즐기고 있다고 생각했는데.
남: 그랬어요. 사실 재미있었어요.
여: 그러면 ⓐ왜 회원권을 연장하지 않았니?
남: 음, ⓑ헬스장 샤워 시설이 너무 낡았고, 샤워칸 공간이 충분하지 않아요.
여: 그렇구나. 근처에 새 헬스장을 살펴보지 그러니? 더 비쌀지는 모르지만, 시설은 아마 훨씬 더 나을 거야.
남: 네. 아마도 내일 방과후에 집에 오는 길에 거기 들러봐야겠어요.
여: 좋은 계획 같구나!

문제 풀이

ⓐ왜 회원권을 연장하지 않았는지 묻는 여자의 말에, 남자는 ⓑ샤워 시설이 낡고 샤워칸 공간이 충분하지 않아서라고 답했다.

8. ③ | 언급

선택지 선택비율	① 1%	② 2%	③ 86%	④ 10%	⑤ 1%

W: Jay, did you hear about the Fireworks Festival?
불꽃놀이
M: Yeah, I heard it's going to be amazing.
W: I'm thinking of volunteering there. Take a look at this poster
자원봉사하다
about it.
M: The volunteer period is ⓐfor two days, June 14th and 15th.
기간
W: That's right. Would you like to join?
M: I'd love to. But can just anyone apply to be a volunteer?
신청하다, 지원하다 자원봉사자
W: ⓑOnly people over 18 can apply. So, we're both good.
M: I see. What exactly will we do during the festival?
정확히
W: It says ⓒwe'll check tickets, run activity booths, or take photos for the festival website.
M: Sounds interesting. And look! ⓓWe have to sign up by this Friday.
W: Really? We don't have much time. Let's do it right now.

해석

여: Jay, 불꽃놀이 축제 소식 들었어?
남: 응, 굉장할 거라고 들었어.
여: 나 거기서 자원봉사하려고 생각 중이야. 그것에 대한 이 포스터 좀 봐.
남: 자원봉사 기간은 ⓐ6월 14일과 15일 이틀 동안이네.
여: 맞아. 너도 같이 할래?
남: 하고 싶어. 그런데 아무나 자원봉사자에 지원할 수 있어?
여: ⓑ18세 이상만 지원할 수 있어. 그러니까 우리 둘 다 괜찮아.
남: 그렇구나. 축제 기간에 우리는 정확히 뭘 하는 거야?
여: ⓒ표 확인, 체험 부스 운영, 또는 축제 웹사이트용 사진 촬영을 할 거라고 하네.
남: 재미있겠다. 그런데 봐! ⓓ이번 주 금요일까지 신청해야 해.
여: 정말? 시간이 얼마 없네. 지금 바로 하자.

문제 풀이

ⓐ기간, ⓑ지원 가능 연령, ⓒ활동 내용, ⓓ신청 기한은 언급되었으나, 준비물은 언급되지 않았다.

9. ④ | 내용 일치

선택지 선택비율	① 3%	② 1%	③ 2%	④ 94%	⑤ 1%

W: Hello, students! Are you looking for (look for: ~을 찾다) a chance to help others? Then, I recommend (추천하다) you to join Triwood High School Volunteer Program ⓐto help senior (노인의) citizens (시민). You're supposed to ⓑhelp the senior citizens face-to-face (대면(으로)). You ⓒteach them how to use their smartphones for things such as sending text messages or taking pictures. You will also teach seniors how to use various (다양한) apps. The program will require (요구하다) volunteers to ⓓparticipate (참여하다) for two hours every Saturday. If you are interested in joining our program, please ⓔsend us an application form (신청서) through email.

해석

여: 안녕하세요, 학생 여러분! 다른 사람을 도울 기회를 찾고 있나요? 그렇다면 ⓐ노인을 돕는 Triwood 고등학교 봉사 프로그램에 참여할 것을 추천합니다. 여러분은 ⓑ노인을 대면해서 돕게 될 것입니다. 여러분은 그분들께 문자 메시지 보내기나 사진 찍기 같은 일에 ⓒ스마트폰을 어떻게 사용하는지 가르쳐 드립니다. 노인분들께 다양한 앱 사용법도 가르쳐 드릴 것입니다. 이 프로그램은 봉사자가 ⓓ매주 토요일에 두 시간씩 참여하는 것을 요합니다. 저희 프로그램에 참여하는 데 관심이 있다면, ⓔ저희에게 이메일로 신청서를 보내 주세요.

문제 풀이

ⓓ봉사자는 매주 토요일에 두 시간씩 참여해야 한다고 했다.

10. ② | 도표

선택지 선택비율	① 4%	② 80%	③ 6%	④ 6%	⑤ 2%

W: Good morning. How may I help you?
M: I'm looking for an exercise mat for home training.
W: Okay. Here are our best-selling (가장 잘 팔리는) models.
M: They all look nice. Are thicker (두꺼운) mats better?
W: Not really. But I think ⓐit should be at least (최소한) 5mm for home trainers.
M: I see. Then I have to choose from these four.
W: How about this one? It's the most popular (인기 있는).
M: It's too expensive. ⓑI don't want to spend more than $40.
W: Out of these two options (선택 사항) left, I recommend ⓒthis model with a non-slip (미끄럽지 않은) surface (표면). It keeps you from sliding around. (keep ~ from v-ing: ~가 …하는 것을 방지하다)
M: Okay. Safety (안전) is important. I'll take it.

해석

여: 안녕하세요. 어떻게 도와드릴까요?
남: 홈 트레이닝용 운동 매트를 찾고 있어요.
여: 그러시군요. 여기 있는 게 가장 잘 팔리는 모델들입니다.
남: 다 좋아 보이네요. 더 두꺼운 매트가 더 좋나요?
여: 꼭 그렇지는 않습니다. 하지만 제가 생각하기에 ⓐ홈 트레이닝을 하시는 분들께는 최소한 5mm는 되어야 합니다.
남: 알겠습니다. 그러면 이 네 가지 중에 골라야겠네요.
여: 이건 어떠세요? 가장 인기 있답니다.
남: 너무 비싸네요. ⓑ40달러 이상을 쓰고 싶진 않아요.
여: 남은 이 두 가지 선택권 중에, 저는 ⓒ표면이 미끄럽지 않은 이 모델을 추천드립니다. 미끄러지지 않게 해 주거든요.
남: 그래요. 안전이 중요하죠. 그걸로 할게요.

문제 풀이

남자는 ⓐ두께는 최소 5mm이고, ⓑ가격이 40달러가 넘지 않고, ⓒ표면이 미끄럽지 않은 모델을 구입하기로 했다.

11. ⑤ | 짧은 대화 응답

선택지 선택비율	① 4%	② 24%	③ 7%	④ 6%	⑤ 56%

M: Did you go to the classical music concert yesterday?
W: Yes, I did. But ⓐI had to leave in the middle of (~의 도중에) the concert.
M: Oh, really? ⓑWhy did you leave?
W: I kept coughing and didn't want to bother (신경 쓰이게 하다, 괴롭히다) anyone.

해석

남: 너 어제 클래식 음악 공연에 갔니?
여: 응, 갔어. 하지만 ⓐ공연 도중에 나와야 했어.
남: 아, 정말? ⓑ왜 나왔니?
여: 계속 기침을 해서 다른 사람들을 신경 쓰이게 하고 싶지 않았거든.

문제 풀이

ⓐ여자가 공연 도중에 나와야 했던 이유를 ⓑ남자가 묻고 있으므로 공연장을 떠난 이유를 말하는 내용의 ⑤가 가장 적절하다.
① 그 지휘자는 정말 인상적이었어.
② 교통 체증이 너무 심해서, 난 늦게 도착했어.
③ 우리 아빠가 내게 공연 티켓을 두 장 주셨어.
④ 클래식 음악은 항상 내 기분을 편안하게 만들어 줘.

12. ⑤ | 짧은 대화 응답

선택지 선택비율	① 3%	② 7%	③ 6%	④ 5%	⑤ 80%

W: Excuse me. ⓐWould you mind if I sit here?
M: I'm sorry, but ⓑit's my friend's seat. He'll be back in a minute (곧).
W: Oh, I didn't know that. ⓒSorry for bothering you.
M: That's okay. I think the seat next to it is available.

해석

여: 실례합니다. ⓐ여기 앉아도 될까요?
남: 죄송하지만, ⓑ제 친구 자리예요. 곧 돌아올 거예요.
여: 아, 몰랐어요. ⓒ귀찮게 해서 죄송합니다.
남: 괜찮아요. 그 옆자리는 이용 가능한 것 같아요.

문제 풀이

ⓐ자리에 앉아도 될지 묻는 여자에게 ⓑ친구의 자리라고 대답하자 여자가 ⓒ귀찮게 해서 미안하다고 사과했으므로, 괜찮다고 말하며 그 옆자리는 이용 가능한 것 같다고 말하는 ⑤가 남자의 응답으로 가장 적절하다.
① 그건 불공평해요. 제가 먼저 이 자리를 예약했어요.
② 고맙습니다. 제 친구가 그걸 알면 기쁠 거예요.
③ 천만에요. 뭐든 제게 편히 요청하세요.
④ 전혀요. 기꺼이 자리를 바꿔드리죠.

13. ① | 긴 대화 응답

선택지 선택비율	① 65%	② 24%	③ 3%	④ 3%	⑤ 5%

M: Hey, Emily! You're looking great these days.
W: Thanks, Isaac. I've been trying hard to get in better shape.
좋은 몸 상태(몸매)를 만들다
M: Good for you! I'm trying to get fit, too. But it's tough.
건강한 / 힘든
W: Haven't you been working out a lot lately?
운동하다
M: Yeah, but I don't see a big difference. ⓐWhat's your secret?
W: Well, I started being careful about when I eat.
신경을 쓰는
M: You mean like not eating right before bed?
W: Kind of. I noticed I was eating a lot at night. So now ⓑI don't eat after 7 p.m.
알아차리다
M: Hmm... ⓒI don't know if that's enough to get me in better shape.
W: Trust me. When we eat makes a big difference.
큰 차이를 만들다

해석

남: 안녕, Emily! 너 요즘 정말 좋아 보여.
여: 고마워, Isaac. 더 좋은 몸매를 만들려고 열심히 노력 중이야.
남: 잘하고 있네! 나도 건강해지려고 노력 중이야. 그런데 힘들어.
여: 너 요즘 운동 많이 하고 있지 않아?
남: 응, 하지만 큰 변화는 못 느끼겠어. ⓐ네 비결은 뭐야?
여: 음, 나는 언제 먹는지에 신경을 쓰기 시작했어.
남: 잠자기 직전에 먹지 않기 같은 것 말이지?
여: 그런 셈이지. 내가 밤에 많이 먹고 있다는 걸 알았거든. 그래서 이제 ⓑ저녁 7시 이후에는 먹지 않아.
남: 음… ⓒ그게 내가 더 좋은 몸매를 만드는 데 충분할지 모르겠네.
여: 내 말 믿어. 우리가 언제 먹는지는 큰 차이를 만들어.

문제 풀이

남자가 여자에게 ⓐ좋은 몸매를 만든 비결을 묻자 ⓑ저녁 7시 이후에는 먹지 않는다고 답했고, 이에 남자가 ⓒ그게 좋은 몸매를 만드는 데 충분할지 모르겠다고 했으므로, 자신의 말에 확신을 더하며 언제 먹는지가 큰 차이를 만든다는 ①이 여자의 응답으로 가장 적절하다.
② 알겠어. 더 좋은 몸매를 만들기 위해 내 식사를 점검할게.
③ 조언 고마워. 하지만 내가 그걸 할 수 있을 것 같진 않아.
④ 물론이지. 네 운동 루틴을 반드시 따를게.
⑤ 응. 그래서 내가 균형 잡힌 식단을 유지하는 데 성공하지 못한 거야.

14. ① | 긴 대화 응답

선택지 선택비율	① 88%	② 2%	③ 4%	④ 1%	⑤ 2%

W: Hey, Chris. What are you looking at on your cell phone?
M: I'm looking for an apartment to rent.
임차하다, 빌리다
W: Aren't you sharing an apartment with William?
share: 함께 쓰다
M: Yeah, but ⓐI'm thinking about moving out.
W: Why? I thought you two get along well with each other.
~와 잘 지내다
M: There have been a lot of problems between us. One thing especially bothers me.
W: Oh, what is it?
M: Actually, ⓑhe never cleans up. The kitchen and the bathroom are always messy.
지저분한
W: That's awful. ⓒHave you talked about this issue with him?
끔찍한 / 사안, 문제
M: I have, but he didn't take it seriously.

해석

여: 얘, Chris. 너 휴대전화로 뭘 보고 있니?
남: 임대할 아파트를 찾고 있어.
여: 너 William과 아파트를 함께 쓰고 있지 않니?
남: 맞아, 하지만 ⓐ난 이사 갈까 생각 중이야.
여: 왜? 난 너희 둘이 서로 잘 지내는 줄 알았는데.
남: 우리 사이에 많은 문제가 있었어. 한 가지가 특히 나를 신경 쓰이게 해.
여: 아, 그게 뭔데?
남: 사실, ⓑ그는 절대 청소를 안 해. 부엌과 화장실이 항상 지저분해.
여: 끔찍하네. ⓒ이 문제에 대해 그와 이야기해 본 적이 있니?
남: 해 봤는데, 그는 그것을 심각하게 받아들이지 않았어.

문제 풀이

남자는 아파트를 함께 쓰고 있는 William이 ⓑ청소를 하지 않아 부엌과 화장실이 항상 지저분해서 ⓐ이사할 집을 찾고 있는데, 여자가 ⓒ이 문제에 대해 이야기해 봤는지 물었으므로 이에 대한 응답으로는, 이야기했지만 소용이 없었다는 내용의 ①이 가장 적절하다.
② 걱정 마. 나는 그와 아무 문제가 없어.
③ 음, 그는 항상 화장실을 깨끗하게 유지해.
④ 미안해. 나는 아파트에서 이사 나가는 것을 연기했어.
⑤ 물론이지. 네가 새 아파트로 이사하는 것을 도와줄게.

15. ⑤ | 상황에 적절한 말

선택지 선택비율	① 2%	② 3%	③ 4%	④ 2%	⑤ 89%

W: Brian is a class leader. He is passionate about environmental issues and saving energy. Recently, he's noticed that his classmates don't turn the lights off when they leave the classroom. Brian thinks this is very careless. He wants to make stickers that remind his classmates to save energy by turning off the lights. He tells this idea to his classmate Melissa, and she agrees it's a good idea. Brian knows Melissa is a great artist, so he wants to ask her to design stickers that encourage their classmates to save energy. In this situation, what would Brian most likely say to Melissa?
열정적인 / 환경의 / save: 절약하다 / 부주의한 / 상기시키다 / 격려하다, 장려하다
Brian: Will you design stickers that encourage energy saving?

해석

여: Brian은 반장이다. 그는 환경 문제와 에너지 절약에 대해 열정적이다. 최근에, 그는 반 친구들이 교실을 떠날 때 불을 끄지 않는 것을 알게 되었다. Brian은 이것이 매우 부주의하다고 생각한다. 그는 반 친구들에게 불을 꺼서 에너지를 절약하도록 상기시키는 스티커를 만들고 싶다. 그는 이 생각을 반 친구인 Melissa에게 말하고, 그녀는 그것이 좋은 생각이라는 것에 동의한다. Brian은 Melissa가 미술을 아주 잘한다는 것을 알기에, 반 친구들로 하여금 에너지를 절약하도록 장려하는 스티커를 디자인해달라고 그녀에게 부탁하고 싶다. 이 상황에서, Brian은 Melissa에게 뭐라고 말하겠는가?
Brian: 네가 에너지 절약을 장려하는 스티커를 디자인해 줄래?

문제 풀이

남자는 여자에게 반 친구들로 하여금 에너지를 절약하도록 장려하는 스티커를 디자인해달라고 부탁하고 싶어 하므로, 이 상황에서 가장 적절한 말은 ⑤이다.
① 미술 수업 끝나고 교실 청소하자.
② 네가 게시판의 스티커를 제거했니?
③ 방에서 나갈 때 히터를 꺼줘.
④ 디자인 수업을 신청할 수 있는 마감일이 언제니?

16~17. | 세트 문항

16. ③ **17.** ④

선택지 선택비율	① 5%	② 7%	③ 79%	④ 4%	⑤ 2%
	① 5%	② 3%	③ 4%	④ 82%	⑤ 3%

M: Hello, listeners, and welcome to *Health Matters*. This is Dr. David Harvey. Coughing(기침) is one of the most common symptoms(증상) of a cold. To relieve(완화하다) it, you might only think of going to a doctor or taking medicine(약). ⓐHowever, drinking homemade(집에서 만든) tea can be an excellent way to warm you up and soothe(가라앉히다) your throat and cough. This kind of tea is so easy to make that anybody can do it. First, get two inches of fresh ⓑginger(생강) and slice(썰다) it thinly(얇게). Next, boil the ginger slices((얇게 썬) 조각) in two cups of water for at least 10 minutes. Then, turn off the heat and add some ⓒhoney. Squeeze(짜다, 짜내다) ⓓa lemon and put the juice((과일 · 채소의) 즙) in the tea. You can add a bit of ⓔcinnamon(계피) at the end for flavor(맛, 풍미). I hope you'll enjoy your hot tea and stay healthy.

해석

남: 안녕하세요, 청취자 여러분, 〈Health Matters〉에 오신 것을 환영합니다. 저는 David Harvey 박사입니다. 기침은 감기의 가장 흔한 증상 중 하나죠. 기침을 완화하기 위해서, 여러분은 병원에 가거나 약을 먹는 것만 생각하실지도 모릅니다. ⓐ하지만, 집에서 만든 차를 마시는 것은 몸을 따뜻하게 하고 목과 기침을 가라앉히는 훌륭한 방법이 될 수 있습니다. 이런 종류의 차는 만들기가 매우 쉬워서 누구나 할 수 있습니다. 첫 번째로, 신선한 ⓑ생강 2인치를 구해서 얇게 써세요. 다음으로, 두 잔 분량의 물에 생강 조각을 넣고 최소 10분 동안 끓이세요. 그런 다음, 불을 끄고 약간의 ⓒ꿀을 넣으세요. ⓓ레몬을 짜서 차에 그 즙을 넣으세요. 풍미를 위해서 마지막에 ⓔ계피를 약간 넣으셔도 됩니다. 여러분이 뜨거운 차를 즐기고 건강하시길 바랍니다.

문제 풀이

16. 남자는 ⓐ집에서 만든 차를 마시는 것은 기침을 가라앉히는 좋은 방법이라고 말하며 차를 만드는 과정을 설명하고 있으므로, 남자가 하는 말의 주제로 가장 적절한 것은 ③ '기침을 완화하기 위한 차를 만드는 방법'이다.
① 음식 알레르기 예방법
② 감기약의 흔한 재료
④ 차의 다양한 종류와 유래
⑤ 집에서 만든 음식의 인기 상승

17. ⓑ생강, ⓒ꿀, ⓓ레몬, ⓔ계피는 언급되었으나, 페퍼민트(peppermint)는 언급되지 않았다.

[코드 공략하기]

제4회 초급 모의고사

1	④	2	③	3	②	4	③	5	④	6	④
7	①	8	②	9	④	10	②	11	①	12	①
13	③	14	①	15	①	16	④	17	④		

1. ④ | 목적

선택지 선택비율	① 6%	② 1%	③ 2%	④ 87%	⑤ 4%

W: Hello, this is Karen Smith, the principal of Sunnyfield High School. I would like to inform(알리다) all staff about an important plan ⓐfor next week's Parent-Teacher Meeting. ⓑDue to(~ 때문에) limited(제한된) parking on campus, all teachers and staff should park at the nearby community center on Wednesday. It is only a five-minute walk from the school. This plan will ensure(반드시 ~하게 하다, 보장하다) that parents attending(참석하다) the meeting have easy access to(~을 이용하다) parking. Your cooperation(협조) will greatly assist(돕다) in making this event a smooth((일의 진행이) 순조로운) and successful experience. Thank you in advance(미리) for your cooperation with the parking arrangements(준비, 마련).

해석

여: 안녕하세요, 저는 Sunnyfield 고등학교 교장 Karen Smith입니다. 저는 모든 직원 여러분께 ⓐ다음 주 학부모 - 교사 간담회와 관련된 중요한 계획에 대해 알리고자 합니다. ⓑ교내 제한된 주차 공간으로 인해, 모든 교사와 직원분들은 수요일에 인근 주민센터에 주차해야 합니다. 그곳은 학교에서 불과 도보 5분 거리입니다. 이 계획은 간담회에 참석하는 학부모들이 편리하게 주차할 수 있도록 보장할 것입니다. 여러분의 협조는 이번 행사를 순조롭고 성공적인 일로 만드는 데 큰 도움이 될 것입니다. 주차 준비에 협조해 주시는 것에 대해 미리 감사합니다.

문제 풀이

여자는 ⓐ다음 주 학부모 간담회가 있는 ⓑ수요일에 교직원들로 하여금 인근 주민센터에 주차할 것을 당부하고 있다.

2. ③ | 의견

선택지 선택비율	① 2%	② 1%	③ 96%	④ 1%	⑤ 1%

W: Daniel, what are you doing in front of the mirror?
M: I have skin problems these days. I'm trying to pop(터뜨리다) these pimples(여드름) on my face.
W: Pimples are really annoying(신경에 거슬리는), but I wouldn't do that.
M: Why not?
W: When you pop them with your hands, you're touching your face.
M: Are you saying that I shouldn't touch my face?
W: Exactly. You know ⓐour hands are covered with bacteria(박테리아), right?
M: So?
W: ⓑYou'll be spreading(퍼뜨리다) bacteria all over your face with your hands. It could worsen(악화시키다) your skin problems.
M: Oh, I didn't know that.
W: ⓒTouching your face with your hands is bad for your skin.
M: Okay, I got it.

해석

여: Daniel, 거울 앞에서 뭐 하고 있어?
남: 요즘 내가 피부 문제가 있거든. 얼굴에 있는 이 여드름을 터뜨리려고 하고 있어.
여: 여드름은 정말 신경에 거슬리지만, 난 그렇게 하지 않을 거야.
남: 왜?
여: 네가 손으로 그걸 터뜨릴 때, 얼굴을 만지는 거잖아.
남: 얼굴을 만지면 안 된다는 말을 하는거니?
여: 맞아. 너 ⓐ우리 손이 박테리아로 덮여 있다는 거 알고 있지, 그렇지?
남: 그래서?
여: ⓑ네가 손으로 박테리아를 네 얼굴 전체에 퍼뜨릴 거야. 그건 네 피부 문제를 악화시킬 수 있어.
남: 아, 몰랐어.
여: ⓒ손으로 얼굴을 만지는 것은 피부에 해로워.
남: 응, 알겠어.

문제 풀이

여자는 ⓐ손이 박테리아로 덮여 있는데 ⓑ손으로 얼굴을 만지면 얼굴 전체에 박테리아를 퍼뜨리게 되므로 ⓒ손으로 얼굴을 만지는 것이 피부에 해롭다고 말하고 있다.

3. ② | 요지

선택지 선택비율	① 6%	② 89%	③ 2%	④ 1%	⑤ 2%

M: Welcome to the *Healing Tip Podcast*. I'm Dr. Smith. In our busy lives, what do you think is just as important as exercising or eating well for your health? It's rest. ⓐRest plays a crucial role in maintaining your overall well-being. It allows your body to heal and recharge, while also helping your mind relax and improving focus. That's why I want to emphasize how important rest is for your health. ⓑTaking time to rest can prevent stress and boost your overall wellness. So, don't skip those breaks!

팟캐스트, 인터넷 방송 / 휴식 / 중요한, 결정적인 / 유지하다, 지속하다 / 전반적인 / 치유되다 / 재충전하다 / 진정하다 / improve: 향상시키다 / 집중(력) / 강조하다 / 방지하다 / 신장시키다 / 건강 / 건너뛰다 / 휴식, 쉬는 시간

해석

남: 'Healing Tip Podcast'에 오신 것을 환영합니다. 저는 Smith 박사입니다. 우리의 바쁜 생활 속에서, 여러분은 건강을 위해 운동이나 잘 먹는 것만큼이나 중요한 것이 무엇이라고 생각하시나요? 바로 휴식입니다. ⓐ휴식은 여러분의 전반적인 건강을 유지하는 데 중요한 역할을 합니다. 그것은 여러분의 몸이 회복하고 재충전할 수 있게 해 주는 동시에, 또한 마음이 진정하는 것을 돕고 집중력을 향상시킵니다. 이것이 제가 여러분의 건강에 있어 휴식이 얼마나 중요한지를 강조하고 싶은 이유입니다. ⓑ시간을 내서 휴식을 취하는 것은 스트레스를 방지하고 여러분의 전반적인 건강을 신장시킬 수 있습니다. 그러니 그런 쉬는 시간을 건너뛰지 마세요!

문제 풀이

남자는 ⓐⓑ휴식을 취하는 것이 건강에 중요하다고 말하고 있다.

4. ③ | 그림 일치

선택지 선택비율	① 4%	② 2%	③ 83%	④ 6%	⑤ 3%

W: Is that the photo of our school's new studio?
M: Yes. We can shoot online lectures here.
촬영하다
W: Can I have a look?
M: Sure. Do you see ⓐthat camera facing the chair? It's the latest model.
face: 향하다, 마주보다 / 최신의
W: I see. What is ⓑthat ring on the stand next to the camera?
M: That's the lighting. It's to brighten the teacher's face.
조명 / 밝히다
W: Hmm.... ⓒThe round clock on the wall looks simple and modern.
현대적인
M: Teachers can check the time on the clock while shooting.
W: ⓓThe microphone on the table looks very professional.
마이크 / 전문적인
M: It really does. Also, I like ⓔthe tree in the corner. It goes well with the studio.
~와 잘 어울리다

해석

여: 저게 우리 학교 새 스튜디오 사진이니?
남: 응. 여기서 온라인 강의를 촬영할 수 있어.
여: 한 번 봐도 될까?
남: 그럼. ⓐ의자를 향해 있는 저 카메라 보이니? 최신 모델이야.
여: 그렇구나. ⓑ카메라 옆 세움대 위에 있는 저 고리는 뭐니?
남: 저건 조명이야. 교사 얼굴을 밝히기 위한 거지.
여: 음…. ⓒ벽에 있는 둥근 시계가 단순하고 현대적으로 보여.
남: 그 시계로 촬영 중에 교사가 시간을 확인할 수 있지.
여: ⓓ탁자 위에 있는 마이크가 무척 전문적으로 보여.
남: 실제로 그래. 그리고 나는 ⓔ모퉁이에 있는 나무가 마음에 들어. 스튜디오와 잘 어울려.

문제 풀이

여자는 ⓒ벽에 있는 둥근 시계라고 말했다.

5. ④ | 할 일

선택지 선택비율	① 3%	② 9%	③ 3%	④ 83%	⑤ 2%

M: Hey, Alice. I applied for the science camp next week. What about you?
apply for: ~에 지원하다
W: Me, too. But I didn't know that there were so many things to do before the camp.
M: Right. Would you like to go over my checklist together?
~을 점검[검토]하다
W: Hmm, let's see. Did you upload your introduction video to the website?
소개
M: Yes, I tried to show my interest in science. Oh, hey, have you picked which experiment to work on?
관심 / 고르다 / 실험
W: Yes. I decided to participate in a biology experiment.
생물학
M: Me, too. ⓐWasn't it difficult to make a plan for your experiment?
W: Actually, I haven't even started yet because I've never written a plan for a biology experiment before.
M: ⓑI'll show you mine after class. Maybe you can get some ideas.
W: Really? ⓒThat'd be great. See you soon.

해석

남: 안녕, Alice. 나 다음 주 과학 캠프에 지원했어. 너는?
여: 나도 했어. 근데 캠프 전에 할 일이 그렇게 많은지 몰랐어.
남: 맞아. 같이 내 체크리스트 점검할래?
여: 음, 어디 보자. 너 자기 소개 영상 웹사이트에 올렸니?
남: 응, 과학에 대한 나의 관심을 보여주려고 했어. 아, 너 어떤 실험을 할지 골랐어?
여: 응. 나는 생물학 실험에 참가하기로 했어.
남: 나도. ⓐ네 실험을 위한 계획 세우는 거 어렵지 않았어?
여: 사실, 전에 생물학 실험 계획서를 써 본 적이 한 번도 없어서, 아직 시작하지도 못했어.
남: ⓑ수업 끝나고 내 걸 보여줄게. 아이디어를 좀 얻을 수 있을지도 몰라.
여: 정말? ⓒ그러면 진짜 좋겠다. 곧 보자.

문제 풀이

남자가 여자에게 ⓐⓑ실험 계획 세우기 어렵지 않았냐며 자신의 실험 계획서를 보여주겠다고 하자 여자가 ⓒ좋다고 했다.

6. ④ | 금액

선택지 선택비율	① 4%	② 9%	③ 4%	④ 82%	⑤ 1%

M: Welcome to Lake Boat Tours. How can I help you?
W: Hello. I'd like to buy some tickets for today.
M: We have daytime(낮, 주간) tickets and sunset(일몰) tickets. Which would you like?
W: We'd like sunset tickets, please. How much are they?
M: It's ⓐ$30 for adults and ⓑ$20 for children. How many tickets do you want?
W: ⓒTwo adult tickets and ⓓone child ticket, please.
M: Okay. And, we offer(제공하다) ⓔsnacks for $10 per person. Would you like them?
W: Yes. ⓕSnacks for all three of us, please.
M: Alright. Do you need anything else?
W: No, that's it.
M: So, that's two adults and one child for the sunset tour, all with snacks.
W: Perfect. Here's my credit card.

해석

남: Lake Boat Tours에 오신 것을 환영합니다. 무엇을 도와드릴까요?
여: 안녕하세요. 오늘 표를 좀 사고 싶어요.
남: 저희는 주간 표와 야간 표가 있습니다. 어느 것을 원하시나요?
여: 야간 표로 부탁드립니다. 가격이 얼마인가요?
남: ⓐ성인은 30달러이고, ⓑ어린이는 20달러입니다. 표가 몇 장 필요하신가요?
여: ⓒ성인 표 두 장과 ⓓ어린이 표 한 장 주세요.
남: 알겠습니다. 그리고 저희가 ⓔ1인당 10달러에 간식을 제공하는데요. 원하시나요?
여: 네. ⓕ저희 세 명 모두 간식 부탁드려요.
남: 좋습니다. 다른 건 필요 없으신가요?
여: 아니요, 그게 다예요.
남: 그러면 성인 두 명과 어린이 한 명 야간 투어, 모두 간식 포함이네요.
여: 맞습니다. 여기 제 신용카드예요.

문제 풀이

ⓐ30달러인 성인 표 ⓒ두 장과 ⓑ20달러인 어린이 표 ⓓ한 장을 구매하며 ⓔ1인당 10달러인 간식을 ⓕ세 사람 모두 추가했으므로, 여자가 지불할 금액은 110달러이다.

7. ① | 이유

선택지 선택비율	① 75%	② 8%	③ 10%	④ 3%	⑤ 2%

M: The Central Park Museum will have a special expo(전람회, 박람회) soon.
W: What's it about?
M: It's a building expo titled "New Home Builders."
W: Sounds interesting. When does it open?
M: It will start tomorrow at nine a.m. I'm going to the exhibition in the afternoon. Do you want to go with me?
W: I'm sorry, but I can't.
M: Why not? You're interested in architecture(건축학, 건축), aren't you?
W: Yes, but I have to do something else.
M: What's your plan?
W: Actually, I'm auditioning(오디션을 보다) for the school play tomorrow.
M: Oh, I see now. I hope you make it.

해석

남: Central Park 박물관에서 곧 특별한 박람회가 있을 예정이야.
여: 무엇에 관한 건데?
남: '새로운 집을 짓는 사람들'이라는 제목의 건축 박람회야.
여: 재미있을 것 같아. 언제 열리니?
남: 내일 오전 9시에 시작할 거야. 난 오후에 전시회에 가려고 해. 나와 함께 가고 싶니?
여: 미안하지만, 난 못 가.
남: 왜 안 돼? 너 건축에 관심 있잖아, 그렇지 않니?
여: 맞아, 하지만 다른 걸 해야 해.
남: 네 계획은 뭔데?
여: 사실, 난 내일 학교 연극 오디션에 참가해.
남: 아, 그렇구나. 네가 잘 해내길 바랄게.

문제 풀이

여자는 내일 학교 연극 오디션에 참가해야 해서 남자와 함께 건축 박람회에 갈 수 없다고 했다.

8. ② | 언급

선택지 선택비율	① 1%	② 91%	③ 3%	④ 0%	⑤ 2%

W: Hi, Asher. What are you doing on the computer?
M: I'm signing up(등록하다) for an event called the Spring Virtual Run.
W: The Spring Virtual... Run?
M: It's a race. Participants(참가자) upload(올리다) their record after running ⓐeither a three-mile race or a ten-mile race.
W: ⓑCan you run at any location(장소)?
M: Yes. ⓒI can choose any place in the city.
W: That sounds interesting. I want to participate, too.
M: Then you should sign up online and ⓓpay the registration fee(등록비). ⓔIt's twenty dollars.
W: Twenty dollars? That's pretty expensive.
M: But souvenirs(기념품) are included(포함하다) in the fee(요금). ⓕAll participants will get a T-shirt and a water bottle.
W: That's reasonable(적당한). I'll sign up.

해석

여: Aher, 안녕하세요. 컴퓨터로 뭐 하고 있나요?
남: Spring Virtual Run이라고 하는 행사에 등록 중이에요.
여: Spring Virtual··· Run이요?
남: 경주예요. 참가자들이 ⓐ3마일 경주나 10마일 경주를 달린 후에 자신의 기록을 올리죠.
여: ⓑ아무 장소에서나 달릴 수 있나요?
남: 네. ⓒ도시 안 어느 곳이든 선택할 수 있어요.
여: 그거 재미있겠네요. 나도 참가하고 싶어요.
남: 그러면 온라인으로 등록하고 ⓓ등록비를 내야 해요. ⓔ20달러예요.
여: 20달러요? 꽤 비싸네요.
남: 하지만 요금에 기념품이 포함되어 있어요. ⓕ모든 참가자는 티셔츠와 물병을 받게 돼요.
여: 적당하네요. 등록할래요.

문제 풀이

ⓐ달리는 거리, ⓑⓒ달리는 장소, ⓓⓔ참가비, ⓕ기념품은 언급되었으나, 참가 인원은 언급되지 않았다.

9. ④ | 내용 일치

선택지 선택비율	① 2%	② 3%	③ 3%	④ 90%	⑤ 2%

W: Hello, Rosehill High School students! I'm your school counselor(상담사), Ms. Lee. I'm so happy to announce(발표하다) a special event, the 2023 Career Week. ⓐIt'll be held from May 22nd for five days. ⓑThere will be many programs to help you explore(탐구하다, 조사하다) various future jobs. Please kindly note(~에 주목[주의]하다) that ⓒthe number of participants for each program is

limited to 20. ⓓA special lecture on future career choices will be
제한하다
presented on the first day. ⓔRegistration begins on May 10th. For
진행하다 등록
more information, please visit our school website. I hope you can come and enjoy the 2023 Career Week!

해석

여: 안녕하세요, Rosehill 고등학교 학생 여러분! 저는 여러분의 학교 상담사 이 선생님입니다. 2023 Career Week라는 특별한 행사를 발표하게 되어 매우 기쁩니다. ⓐ행사는 5월 22일부터 5일간 개최될 예정입니다. ⓑ여러분이 다양한 미래 직업을 탐색할 수 있도록 돕는 많은 프로그램들이 있을 것입니다. ⓒ각 프로그램의 참가자 수는 20명으로 제한되어 있으니 주의하기 바랍니다. ⓓ첫째 날에 미래 직업 선택에 관한 특별 강연이 진행될 예정입니다. ⓔ등록은 5월 10일에 시작합니다. 더 많은 정보를 원하면, 저희 학교 웹사이트를 방문해 보세요. 여러분이 와서 2023 커리어 주간을 즐기길 바랍니다!

문제 풀이

ⓓ특별 강연은 첫째 날에 있을 예정이라고 했다.

10. ② | 도표

선택지 선택비율	① 2%	② 90%	③ 3%	④ 4%	⑤ 1%

W: Hey, John. What are you looking at?
M: You know I'm planning to travel abroad, so I'm checking out smart
해외로
backpacks. Want to help me pick one?
W: Sure, let me see. *[Pause]* The prices are different.
M: Yeah, but ⓐI don't want to spend more than 100 dollars.
W: Got it. Let's check the size.
M: I usually carry a laptop, so ⓑit should be at least 15 inches.
가지고 다니다 휴대용[노트북] 컴퓨터 최소한
W: ⓒThere's also an option with a safety feature. Do you need that?
안전 장치
M: ⓓDefinitely. It will help keep my belongings safe while traveling.
소지품
That narrows it down to just two models.
좁히다, 줄이다
W: Now, how about a charging port? I think an external port would be
충전 포트 외부의
more convenient.
편리한
M: Sounds great. ⓔI'll pick the one with an external port. I'll order it right now.

해석

여: 안녕, John. 뭐 보고 있어?
남: 알다시피 내가 해외여행을 갈 계획이잖아, 그래서 스마트 배낭을 알아보고 있어. 하나 고르는 거 도와줄래?
여: 물론이지, 어디 보자. [잠시 후] 가격들이 다르네.
남: 응, 하지만 ⓐ난 100달러 이상은 쓰고 싶지 않아.
여: 알겠어. 크기를 확인해 보자.
남: 나는 보통 노트북 컴퓨터를 들고 다녀서, ⓑ최소 15인치는 되어야 해.
여: ⓒ안전 장치가 있는 옵션도 있어. 그거 필요해?
남: ⓓ당연하지. 그게 여행 중에 내 소지품들을 안전하게 지키는 데 도움이 될 거야. 이제 딱 두 가지 모델로 좁혀지네.
여: 그럼, 충전 포트는 어때? 외부 포트가 더 편리할 것 같은데.
남: 좋은 생각이야. ⓔ외부 포트가 있는 걸로 고를게. 지금 바로 주문해야겠다.

문제 풀이

남자는 ⓐ100달러가 넘지 않는 ⓑ15인치 이상 사이즈의 ⓒⓓ안전 장치가 있고 ⓔ충전 포트가 외부에 있는 스마트 배낭을 주문하기로 했다.

11. ① | 짧은 대화 응답

선택지 선택비율	① 71%	② 15%	③ 3%	④ 3%	⑤ 8%

M: Mom, ⓐI want to have a cat. Have you ever thought about us adopting a cat?
입양하다
W: Sweetie, having a pet requires a lot of responsibility.
필요로 하다 책임(감)
M: I'm totally ready for it. Mom, ⓑwe could at least consider it.
완전히 고려하다
W: Fine. Let's talk about it over dinner.

해석

남: 엄마, ⓐ저 고양이 키우고 싶어요. 우리가 고양이를 입양하는 것에 대해 생각해 보신 적 있어요?
여: 얘야, 반려동물을 키우는 건 많은 책임을 필요로 한단다.
남: 저 그럴 준비가 완전히 됐어요. 엄마, ⓑ우리 최소한 고려라도 할 수 있잖아요.
여: 좋아. 저녁 먹으면서 얘기해보자.

문제 풀이

ⓐ고양이를 키우고 싶은 남자가 여자에게 ⓑ고려해보자고 했으므로, 저녁 먹으면서 함께 얘기해보자는 ①이 여자의 응답으로 가장 적절하다.
② 알겠어. 다음에는 더 책임감을 가지렴.
③ 좋아. 내가 이미 반려동물 먹이를 주문했단다.
④ 안됐구나. 네 고양이가 빨리 낫길 바랄게.
⑤ 미안해. 오늘 밤에는 네 고양이를 돌봐줄 수 없어.

12. ① | 짧은 대화 응답

선택지 선택비율	① 63%	② 8%	③ 21%	④ 6%	⑤ 2%

W: Justin, what are you reading?
M: An advertisement. ⓐThere's a special event at Will's Bookstore
광고
downtown.
시내에
W: ⓑWhat kind of event is it?
M: All children's books are 20% off.

해석

W: Justin, 뭘 읽고 있어?
M: 광고. ⓐ시내에 있는 Will's 서점에서 특별 행사가 있어.
W: ⓑ어떤 행사인데?
M: 모든 아동 도서가 20% 할인돼.

문제 풀이

남자가 ⓐ시내에 있는 Will's 서점에 특별 행사가 있다고 하자 여자가 ⓑ어떤 행사인지 물었으므로, 행사 내용에 대해 말하는 ①이 응답으로 가장 적절하다.
② 좋은 기사를 쓰려면 시간이 걸려.
③ 난 액션 모험 책을 읽는 것을 좋아해.
④ TV에 광고가 너무 많아.
⑤ 그 가게는 지난달 이후로 문을 닫았어.

13. ③ | 긴 대화 응답

선택지 선택비율	① 3%	② 2%	③ 80%	④ 10%	⑤ 5%

M: Excuse me, Ms. Lopez. Can I ask you something?
W: Sure, Tony. What can I do for you?
M: I want to do better in Spanish, but I don't know how to improve.
향상시키다
W: You seem to do well during class. Do you study when you're at home?

M: I do all my homework and ⓐtry to learn 20 new words every day.
W: That's a good start. ⓑDo you also practice saying those words repeatedly?
반복해서
M: Do I need to do that? That sounds like it'll take a lot of time.
W: It does. But since you're still a beginner, ⓒyou have to put in more
초보자
effort to get used to new words.
~에 익숙해지다
M: I see. ⓓSo are you suggesting that I practice them over and over?
제안하다, 추천하다 / 반복해서
W: Exactly. Learning a language starts with repetition.
반복

해석

남: 실례합니다, Lopez 선생님. 뭐 좀 여쭤봐도 될까요?
여: 물론이지, Tony. 뭘 도와줄까?
남: 저는 스페인어를 더 잘하고 싶은데, 어떻게 향상시켜야 할지 모르겠어요.
여: 수업 시간에 잘하는 것 같던데. 집에 있을 때 공부를 하니?
남: 저는 숙제를 다 하고 ⓐ매일 20개의 새로운 단어를 익히려고 노력해요.
여: 시작이 좋구나. ⓑ그 단어들을 반복해서 말하는 연습도 하니?
남: 그렇게 해야 하나요? 시간이 많이 걸릴 것 같아요.
여: 그렇지. 하지만 아직 초보자이기 때문에, ⓒ새로운 단어에 익숙해지기 위해서는 더 많은 노력을 해야 한단다.
남: 알겠습니다. ⓓ그럼 제가 그것들을 반복해서 연습해야 한다는 말씀이시죠?
여: 바로 그거야. 언어를 배우는 것은 반복에서부터 시작하니까.

문제 풀이

남자가 ⓐ스페인어 새로운 단어를 매일 20개씩 학습하고 있다고 하자, 여자는 ⓑ그 단어를 반복해서 말하기를 연습하냐고 물어보며 ⓒ새로운 단어에 익숙해지려면 더 많은 노력을 해야 한다고 말하고 있다. 남자가 마지막에 ⓓ그 단어들을 반복해서 연습해야 한다는 말이냐며 재차 확인하고 있으므로, 남자의 말에 동의하며 언어 학습은 반복에서부터 시작된다고 말하는 ③이 응답으로 가장 적절하다.
① 아니. 나는 스페인어를 배우는 것이 어렵지 않아.
② 네가 드디어 어휘 시험에 합격해서 기쁘구나.
④ 글을 쓸 때는 사전을 사용하는 것이 큰 도움이 돼.
⑤ 너는 오늘 오후까지 숙제를 제출해야 해.

14. ① | 긴 대화 응답

선택지 선택비율	① 89%	② 5%	③ 2%	④ 2%	⑤ 3%

W: I haven't seen you in the cafeteria this week. Where have you been?
M: I've been in the library working on my science project.
W: Does that mean ⓐyou've been skipping lunch?
(일을) 거르다[빼먹다]
M: Yeah. This project is really important for my grade.
성적
W: You shouldn't do that. It's not good for your health.
M: Don't worry. I always have a big dinner when I get home.
W: That's the problem. ⓑSkipping meals makes you overeat later.
과식하다
M: I hadn't thought of that. Then what should I do?
W: It's simple. ⓒYou should eat regularly to stay healthy.
규칙적으로
M: You're right. I won't skip meals anymore.

해석

여: 이번 주에는 널 구내식당에서 본적이 없네. 어디 있었어?
남: 도서관에서 과학 프로젝트를 하고 있었어.
여: 그럼 ⓐ점심을 안 먹었다는 거야?
남: 응. 이번 프로젝트는 내 성적에 정말 중요하거든.
여: 그러면 안 돼. 건강에 안 좋아.
남: 걱정하지 마. 집에 가면 항상 저녁을 푸짐하게 먹어.
여: 그게 문제야. ⓑ끼니를 거르면 나중에 과식하게 돼.
남: 그건 생각을 못 했네. 그럼 어떻게 해야 해?
여: 간단해. ⓒ건강하려면 규칙적으로 먹어야 해.
남: 네 말이 맞아. 더 이상 끼니를 거르지 않아야겠어.

문제 풀이

여자는 ⓐ남자가 최근 점심을 거르고 있다는 것을 알게 되자, ⓑ끼니를 거르면 나중에 과식하게 되므로 ⓒ건강하려면 규칙적으로 식사해야 한다고 조언하고 있다. 따라서 여자의 조언을 받아들이는 ①이 응답으로 가장 적절하다.
② 나를 위해 준비해 준 점심 잘 먹었어.
③ 구내식당이 언제 문을 여는지 확인해야 해.
④ 날 믿어. 너에게 좋은 식사 예절을 가르쳐 줄 수 있어.
⑤ 아니야. 과학 프로젝트는 제시간에 끝낼 거야.

코드+α 이해를 확인하는 표현

- **Do you mean to say** I'm lying? (내가 거짓말을 하고 있다는 말이야?)
- **You mean** there's an extra cost? (추가 비용이 있다는 말인가요?)
- **Does that mean** steaming is healthier than frying? (찌는 게 튀기는 것보다 더 건강하다는 말이야?)

15. ① | 상황에 적절한 말

선택지 선택비율	① 90%	② 1%	③ 2%	④ 3%	⑤ 2%

M: Brian and Sally are walking down the street together. A blind man and his guide dog are walking towards them. Sally likes dogs very
안내견 / ~을 향해서
much, so she reaches out to touch the guide dog. Brian doesn't
(손을) 뻗다
think that Sally should do that. The guide dog needs to concentrate
~에 집중하다
on guiding the blind person. If someone touches the dog, the dog can lose its focus. So Brian wants to tell Sally not to touch the guide
집중
dog without the permission of the dog owner. In this situation, what
허락
would Brian most likely say to Sally?
Brian: You shouldn't touch a guide dog without permission.

해석

남: Brian과 Sally가 함께 길을 걷고 있다. 한 시각 장애인과 안내견이 그들을 향해 걸어오고 있다. Sally는 개를 아주 많이 좋아해서, 그 안내견을 만지려고 손을 뻗는다. Brian은 Sally가 그렇게 하면 안 된다고 생각한다. 안내견은 시각 장애인을 안내하는 데 집중해야 한다. 누군가가 그 개를 만지면, 개는 집중을 잃을 수 있다. 그래서 Brian은 Sally에게 주인의 허락 없이 안내견을 만지지 말라고 말하고 싶다. 이 상황에서, Brian은 Sally에게 뭐라고 말하겠는가?
Brian: 허락 없이 안내견을 만지면 안 돼.

문제 풀이

Brian은 Sally에게 주인의 허락 없이 안내견을 만지지 말라고 말하고 싶어 하므로, ①이 가장 적절하다.
② 우리가 음식을 좀 준다면 그 개는 기쁠 거야.
③ 분명 그 개는 안내견을 할 만큼 충분히 똑똑해.
④ 나는 네가 네 개를 매일 산책시키는 걸 제안해.
⑤ 유감이지만 여기는 개가 허용되지 않아.

16~17. | 세트 문항

16. ④ 17. ④

선택지 선택비율	① 5%	② 11%	③ 2%	④ 77%	⑤ 6%
	① 2%	② 2%	③ 4%	④ 92%	⑤ 1%

W: Hello, everybody. Welcome to the health workshop. I'm Alanna Reyes, the head trainer from Eastwood Fitness Center. As you
수석
know, joints are body parts that link bones together. And doing
관절 연결하다
certain physical activities puts stress on the joints. But the good
육체[신체]의
news is that ⓐpeople with bad joints can still do certain exercises. They have relatively low impact on the joints. Here are some
비교적 충격, 영향
examples. The first is ⓑswimming. While swimming, the water supports your body weight. The second is ⓒcycling. You put almost
떠받치다, 지탱하다 체중
no stress on the knee joints when you pedal smoothly. ⓓHorseback
압박 페달을 밟다 부드럽게 승마
riding is another exercise that puts very little stress on your knees. Lastly, ⓔwalking is great because it's low-impact, unlike running. If you have bad joints, don't give up exercising. Instead, stay active
~을 포기하다
and stay healthy!

해석

여: 안녕하세요, 여러분. 건강 워크숍에 오신 것을 환영합니다. 저는 Eastwood 피트니스 센터의 수석 트레이너 Alanna Reyes입니다. 아시다시피, 관절은 뼈를 서로 연결하는 신체 부위입니다. 그리고 특정 신체 활동을 하는 것이 관절에 스트레스를 줍니다. 하지만 좋은 소식은 ⓐ관절이 좋지 않은 사람들도 특정 운동들을 할 수 있다는 것입니다. 그것들은 관절에 비교적 적은 영향을 미칩니다. 여기 몇 가지 예가 있습니다. 첫 번째는 ⓑ수영입니다. 수영하는 동안, 물은 여러분의 체중을 지탱합니다. 두 번째는 ⓒ자전거 타기입니다. 페달을 부드럽게 밟을 때, 무릎 관절에 거의 압박을 주지 않습니다. ⓓ승마는 무릎에 압박을 거의 주지 않는 또 다른 운동입니다. 마지막으로, ⓔ걷기는 달리기와 달리 충격이 적어서 아주 좋습니다. 관절이 안 좋더라도, 운동을 포기하지 마세요. 대신, 활동적이고 건강하게 지내세요!

문제 풀이

16. ⓐ관절이 좋지 않은 사람들도 상대적으로 관절에 미치는 영향이 적은 특정 운동들을 할 수 있다며 그러한 운동들의 예를 말하고 있으므로, 주제로는 ④ '관절이 나쁜 사람들을 위한 충격이 적은 운동들'이 가장 적절하다.
① 근육을 키우는 데 도움을 주는 활동들
② 일상 생활에서 스트레스를 조절하는 방법들
③ 노인들의 관절 문제 유형들
⑤ 체중 조절을 위해 매일 하는 운동의 중요성
17. ⓑ수영, ⓒ자전거 타기, ⓓ승마, ⓔ걷기는 언급되었으나, 볼링(bowling)은 언급되지 않았다.

[코드 공략하기]

제5회 초급 모의고사

1	③	2	②	3	③	4	④	5	④	6	②
7	②	8	③	9	⑤	10	②	11	④	12	①
13	③	14	③	15	③	16	③	17	④		

1. ③ | 목적

선택지 선택비율	① 1%	② 1%	③ 96%	④ 1%	⑤ 1%

W: Good morning, everyone. I'm your student council president, Kelly
학생회장
Green. Many students have complained that there are no printers
불평하다
available for them to use. To solve this problem, next week we will set up several new printers in the student council room. Students
~을 설치하다 몇몇의
will be able to use the printers for homework, projects, or any other school tasks. We hope this will help you do your work more
과업, 과제
efficiently and make your school life easier. Thank you.
효율적으로

해석

여: 안녕하세요, 여러분. 저는 여러분의 학생회장인 Kelly Green입니다. 많은 학생들이 사용할 수 있는 프린터가 없다고 불평해 왔습니다. 이 문제를 해결하기 위해, 다음 주에 학생회실에 새 프린터 몇 대를 설치할 예정입니다. 학생들은 숙제, 프로젝트, 또는 다른 학교 과제를 위해 이 프린터를 사용할 수 있을 것입니다. 이 조치가 여러분이 과제를 더 효율적으로 하는 데 도움이 되고 학교생활을 더 편하게 만들기 바랍니다. 감사합니다.

문제 풀이

여자는 다음 주에 학생회실에 새 프린터를 설치할 것임을 알리고 있다.

2. ② | 의견

선택지 선택비율	① 1%	② 90%	③ 1%	④ 6%	⑤ 1%

M: Irene, where are you heading?
가다, 향하다
W: Hello, Mason. I'm going to the bookstore to buy some books.
M: The bookstore? Isn't it more convenient to order books online?
편리한
W: Yes, but ⓐI like to flip through the pages at bookstores.
(책장을) 휙휙 넘기다
M: Yeah, but buying books online is cheaper.
W: Right. But ⓑwe can help bookstore owners when we buy books from them.
M: I guess you're right. The bookstore near my house shut down last
문을 닫다
month.
W: It's a pity to see local bookstores going out of business nowadays.
유감이다 지역의 폐업하다
M: I agree. Next time I need a book, I'll try to go to a local bookstore.

해석

남: Irene, 어디 가는 길이니?
여: Mason, 안녕. 책을 좀 사려고 서점에 가고 있어.
남: 서점? 온라인으로 책을 주문하는 게 더 편리하지 않니?
여: 응, 하지만 ⓐ난 서점에서 책장 넘겨보는 걸 좋아해.
남: 그래, 하지만 온라인에서 책을 사는 게 더 저렴해.
여: 맞아. 하지만 ⓑ서점에서 책을 사면 서점 주인에게 도움이 될 수 있어.

남: 네 말이 맞는 것 같아. 우리 집 근처에 있는 서점은 지난 달에 문을 닫았어.
여: 요즘 지역 서점들이 폐업하는 걸 보니 유감이야.
남: 동의해. 다음에 책이 필요할 때, 지역 서점에 가볼래.

문제 풀이

여자는 ⓐ서점에서 책장 넘겨보는 걸 좋아한다고 말하며, ⓑ지역 서점에서 책을 사면 서점 주인에게 도움이 될 수 있다는 지역 서점을 이용의 장점을 말하고 있다.

3. ③ | 관계

선택지 선택비율	① 4%	② 4%	③ 82%	④ 1%	⑤ 7%

M: Come on in, Ms. Miller. It's been a while since your last visit.
W: Good morning, Mr. Stevens. I've been in Europe for the last two months.
M: Wow. Are you preparing for your second book?
W: Yes, I'm working on it.
M: I'm looking forward to it. So, what brings you here today?
W: ⓐI'd like to buy a wooden desk.
나무로 된
M: I see. ⓑDo you have a particular design in mind?
특정한, 특별한
W: Just a plain rectangular one would be great.
평범한, 단순한 직사각형의
M: Okay. What color would you like?
W: I was thinking dark brown.
M: Great. ⓒWe have a perfect one for you downstairs. Come this way.
아래층에
W: All right.

해석

남: 들어오세요, Miller 씨. 마지막으로 방문하신 지 꽤 됐어요.
여: 안녕하세요, Stevens 씨. 지난 두 달 동안 유럽에 있었어요.
남: 와. 두 번째 책을 준비하고 계신가요?
여: 네, 지금 하고 있는 중이에요.
남: 기대하고 있어요. 그래서 오늘은 무슨 일로 오셨나요?
여: ⓐ나무 책상을 하나 사고 싶어요.
남: 그러시군요. ⓑ특정 디자인을 염두에 두고 있으신가요?
여: 그냥 평범한 직사각형 책상이 좋을 것 같아요.
남: 알겠습니다. 무슨 색을 원하세요?
여: 저는 짙은 갈색을 생각하고 있었어요.
남: 좋습니다. ⓒ아래층에 딱 맞는 것이 있어요. 이쪽으로 오세요.
여: 네.

문제 풀이

ⓐ나무 책상을 사고 싶다는 여자에게, 남자가 ⓑ어떤 디자인을 원하는지 묻고 ⓒ딱 맞는 것이 있다며 안내하는 것으로 보아, 가구 판매원과 손님의 대화임을 알 수 있다.

4. ④ | 그림 일치

선택지 선택비율	① 7%	② 1%	③ 4%	④ 76%	⑤ 11%

W: Yesterday, I decorated my fish tank like a beach.
장식하다 어항
M: I'd like to see it. Do you have a picture?
W: Sure. Here. *[Pause]* Do you recognize ⓐthe boat in the bottom left corner?
알아차리다 맨 아래 (부분)
M: Yes. It's the one I gave you, isn't it?
W: Right. It looks good in the fish tank, doesn't it?
M: It does. I love ⓑthe beach chair in the center.
W: Yeah. I like it, too.
M: I see ⓒa starfish next to the chair.
불가사리
W: Isn't it cute? And do you see ⓓthese two surf boards on the right side of the picture?
M: Yeah. I like how you put both of them side by side.
나란히
W: I thought that'd look cool.
M: ⓔYour fish in the top left corner looks happy with its new home.
W: I hope so.

해석

여: 어제, 난 내 어항을 해변처럼 장식했어.
남: 그걸 보고 싶어. 사진 있니?
여: 물론이지. 여기. [잠시 후] ⓐ왼쪽 맨 아래 모퉁이에 있는 배를 알아보겠니?
남: 응. 그거 내가 너한테 준 거지, 그렇지 않니?
여: 맞아. 어항 안에 잘 어울려, 그렇지 않니?
남: 그래. 난 ⓑ가운데 있는 해변의자가 정말 마음에 들어.
여: 응. 나도 그거 마음에 들어.
남: ⓒ의자 옆에 불가사리가 보이네.
여: 그거 귀엽지 않니? 그리고 ⓓ사진 오른쪽에 이 서핑 보드 두 개 보이니?
남: 응. 네가 그 둘 다를 나란히 놓은 방식이 마음에 들어.
여: 멋져 보일 것 같았지.
남: ⓔ왼쪽 맨 위 모퉁이에 있는 네 물고기가 새로운 집에 만족하는 것처럼 보여.
여: 그러면 좋겠어.

문제 풀이

ⓓ사진 오른쪽에 서핑 보드 두 개라고 했으므로, 서핑 보드 한 개가 있는 그림의 ④는 대화 내용과 일치하지 않는다.

5. ④ | 할 일

선택지 선택비율	① 3%	② 1%	③ 1%	④ 86%	⑤ 7%

M: Hi, Theresa. What are you looking at on your smartphone?
W: These are the pictures I took at the entrance ceremony.
입학식
M: You took a lot of pictures. What are they for?
W: They're for the school newspaper. I'm writing an article about the entrance ceremony.
기사
M: I see.
W: But I don't think I can use any of these pictures. They don't look good.
M: Maybe I can help you. ⓐI also took some pictures at the ceremony.
W: Ah, you're in the school's Photo Club! ⓑDo you have them with you now?
M: ⓒNo, they're on my computer. I'll send them to you by email.
W: That'd be great. Thank you.

해석

남: 안녕, Theresa. 스마트폰으로 무엇을 보고 있니?
여: 이건 내가 입학식에서 찍은 사진들이야.
남: 사진을 많이 찍었구나. 뭘 위한 거야?
여: 학교 신문을 위한 거야. 나는 입학식에 관한 기사를 쓰고 있어.
남: 그렇구나.
여: 하지만 나는 이 사진들을 하나도 쓸 수 없을 것 같아. 좋아 보이지 않아.
남: 아마 내가 도울 수 있을 것 같아. ⓐ나도 입학식에서 사진을 좀 찍었어.
여: 아, 너는 학교 사진 동아리에 있지! ⓑ지금 갖고 있니?
남: ⓒ아니, 내 컴퓨터에 있어. 네게 이메일로 보내 줄게.
여: 그게 좋겠다. 고마워.

문제 풀이

남자가 ⓐ입학식에서 사진을 찍었다고 하자 여자는 ⓑ그 사진을 지금 갖고 있는지 물었고 남자는 ⓒ컴퓨터에 있어서 이메일로 보내 주겠다고 했다.

6. ② | 금액

선택지 선택비율	① 4%	② 89%	③ 2%	④ 1%	⑤ 1%

M: Good afternoon. How can I help you?
W: I'd like to buy some wireless earphones for my children. How much is this pair?
(wireless: 무선의)
M: ⓐIt's $60 for a pair. It's a very popular model.
W: Great. ⓑI'll take two pairs.
M: I see. Is there anything else you need?
W: Oh, I also need a portable speaker.
(portable: 휴대용의)
M: These two are the latest models.
(latest: 최신의)
W: How much are they?
M: ⓒThis black one is $80 and the pink one is $100.
W: ⓓI'll take the black one.
M: Okay. Is that all you need?
W: Yes. Oh, I have this discount coupon. Can I use it?
(discount: 할인)
M: Sure. ⓔYou can get 10% off the total price with this coupon.
W: Great. Here's the coupon and here's my credit card.

해석

남: 안녕하세요. 무엇을 도와드릴까요?
여: 저희 아이들을 위해 무선 이어폰을 사고 싶어요. 이 쌍은 얼마에요?
남: ⓐ한 쌍에 60달러입니다. 그건 매우 인기 있는 모델이에요.
여: 좋아요. ⓑ두 쌍 살게요.
남: 알겠습니다. 그 밖에 더 필요한 건 없으신가요?
여: 아, 휴대용 스피커도 필요해요.
남: 이 두 가지가 최신 모델입니다.
여: 그것들은 얼마죠?
남: ⓒ이 검은색은 80달러이고 분홍색은 100달러입니다.
여: ⓓ검은색으로 할게요.
남: 알겠습니다. 그게 필요하신 전부인가요?
여: 네. 아, 이 할인 쿠폰이 있어요. 그걸 사용해도 되나요?
남: 물론이죠. 이 쿠폰으로 ⓔ총 금액에서 10%를 할인받으실 수 있습니다.
여: 좋아요. 여기 쿠폰이고 여기 신용카드요.

문제 풀이

여자는 ⓐ한 쌍에 60달러인 ⓑ이어폰 두 쌍과 ⓒ80달러인 ⓓ검은색 휴대용 스피커를 사려고 하는데, 쿠폰으로 ⓔ총 금액에서 10%를 할인받을 수 있다고 했으므로, 180달러를 지불하면 된다.

7. ② | 이유

선택지 선택비율	① 5%	② 89%	③ 2%	④ 2%	⑤ 1%

M: Agnes, what are you doing?
W: I'm surfing the Internet to find a nice restaurant for my trip this weekend.
(surf the Internet: 인터넷 서핑을 하다)
M: All the places on the website look nice.
W: Yes, but I've finally decided where to go. It's this French restaurant called El Bistro.
(decide: 결정하다)
M: Oh, I've watched a travel TV show about that restaurant.
W: Have you?
M: Yes. It said it's so popular among the local people that they have to wait in a long line to get in.
W: I know. I don't like crowded places, but I think ⓐit'll be worth the wait because of its long tradition. ⓑThe family's been running it since 1890.
(crowded: 붐비는, 복잡한 / tradition: 전통 / run: 운영하다)
M: Wow, that long?
W: Yes. ⓒI like old places that maintain their tradition. It's far from my hotel, but I'm willing to go anyway.
(maintain: 유지하다, 지키다 / far from: ~에서 멀리 / be willing to-v: 기꺼이 ~하다)
M: I'm sure you'll enjoy the meal there.
(meal: 식사)

해석

남: Agnes, 뭐 하고 있니?
여: 이번 주말 여행 때 갈 좋은 레스토랑을 찾으려고 인터넷 서핑을 하고 있어.
남: 웹사이트에 있는 곳들 모두 좋아 보이네.
여: 응, 하지만 마침내 어디 갈지 정했어. El Bistro라는 이 프랑스 요리 레스토랑이야.
남: 아, 그 레스토랑에 관한 여행 TV 프로그램 본 적 있어.
여: 그래?
남: 응. 지역 사람들에게 무척 인기 있어서 들어가려면 긴 줄을 서서 기다려야 한다더라.
여: 알고 있어. 붐비는 곳을 싫어하지만, ⓐ그 레스토랑의 오랜 전통 때문에 기다릴 가치가 있을 것이라고 생각해. ⓑ그 가문이 1890년부터 레스토랑을 운영해 오고 있거든.
남: 우와, 그렇게 오래?
여: 응. ⓒ난 전통을 지키는 오래된 곳이 좋아. 내가 머물 호텔에서는 멀지만, 어쨌든 기꺼이 갈 거야.
남: 분명 거기서 즐거운 식사를 하겠구나.

문제 풀이

ⓐⓑⓒ오랜 전통을 지키는 레스토랑이기 때문에 좋다고 했다.

8. ③ | 언급

선택지 선택비율	① 2%	② 1%	③ 88%	④ 6%	⑤ 2%

M: Lucy, look at this.
W: Wow. It's about the Youth Choir Audition.
(Choir: 합창단)
M: Yes. ⓐIt's open to anyone aged 13 to 18.
W: I'm interested in joining the choir. When is it?
M: ⓑApril 2nd, from 9 a.m. to 5 p.m.
W: The place for the audition is the Youth Training Center. It's really far from here.
M: I think you should leave early in the morning.
W: That's no problem. Is there an entry fee?
(entry fee: 참가비)
M: No, ⓒit's free.
W: Good. I'll apply for the audition.
(apply for: ~에 지원하다)
M: Then ⓓyou should fill out an application form on this website.
(fill out: ~을 작성하다 / application form: 지원서, 신청서)
W: All right. Thanks.

해석

남: Lucy, 이것 좀 봐.
여: 와. 청소년 합창단 오디션에 관한 거네.
남: 응. ⓐ13세부터 18세까지인 누구나 가능해.
여: 나 합창단 가입에 관심 있어. 언제니?
남: ⓑ4월 2일 오전 9시부터 오후 5시까지야.
여: 오디션 장소는 청소년 수련관이네. 여기서 정말 멀어.
남: 아침 일찍 출발하는 게 좋겠어.
여: 그건 문제없지. 참가비가 있니?
남: 아니, ⓒ무료야.
여: 좋아. 오디션에 지원해야겠다.
남: 그럼 ⓓ이 웹사이트에서 지원서를 작성해야 해.
여: 알았어. 고마워.

문제 풀이

ⓐ지원 가능 연령, ⓑ날짜, ⓒ참가비, ⓓ지원 방법은 언급되었지만, 심사 기준은 언급되지 않았다.

코드 +α 관심 표현하기

I'm interested in joining this club. (이 모임에 가입하는 데 관심이 있어요.)
Could you tell me more in detail? (상세히 더 말씀해주실래요?)
I'm really into K-pop these days. (요즘 나는 케이팝에 푹 빠졌어.)
The title of this movie **grabbed my interest**. (이 영화 제목이 내 관심을 끌었어.)

9. ⑤ | 내용 일치

선택지 선택비율	① 10%	② 12%	③ 9%	④ 3%	⑤ 66%

M: Hello, Lakewoods High School students! I'm Lawrence Cho, president of the student council(학생회). I'm happy to announce(발표하다) a special new event to reduce(줄이다) waste around our school: Lakewoods Plogging! Since plogging is the activity(활동) of picking up trash(쓰레기를 줍다) while running, ⓐall participants(참가자) should wear workout(운동) clothes and sneakers. ⓑWe provide eco-friendly(친환경적인) bags for the trash, so you don't need to bring any. ⓒThe event will be held on October 1st from 7 a.m. to 9 a.m. You ⓓcan sign up for(~을 신청하다) the event on the school website starting tomorrow. ⓔThe first 30 participants will get a pair of sports socks. For more information, please visit our school website. Don't miss this fun opportunity(기회)!

해석

남: 안녕하세요, Lakewoods 고등학교 학생들! 저는 학생회 회장 Lawrence Cho입니다. 저는 우리 학교 주변의 쓰레기를 줄이기 위한 새로운 특별 행사인 'Lakewoods 플로깅'을 발표하게 되어 기쁩니다! 플로깅은 달리면서 쓰레기를 줍는 활동이기 때문에, ⓐ모든 참가자들은 운동복과 운동화를 착용해야 합니다. ⓑ저희가 쓰레기를 담을 친환경 봉투를 제공하니, 아무것도 가져오지 않아도 됩니다. ⓒ행사는 10월 1일 오전 7시부터 9시까지 개최될 것입니다. 여러분은 내일부터 ⓓ학교 웹사이트에서 행사에 신청할 수 있습니다. ⓔ처음 30명의 참가자들은 스포츠 양말 한 켤레를 받을 것입니다. 더 많은 정보를 원하면, 우리 학교 웹사이트를 방문해 주세요. 이 즐거운 기회를 놓치지 마세요!

문제 풀이

ⓔ처음 30명의 참가자들은 스포츠 양말 한 켤레를 받을 것이라고 했다.

10. ② | 도표

선택지 선택비율	① 3%	② 86%	③ 8%	④ 0%	⑤ 1%

M: Hi, how can I help you today?
W: Hi, I'm looking for a smart watch.
M: Sure. We have these five models.
W: Hmm.... I want to wear it when I swim.
M: Then ⓐyou're looking for one that's waterproof(방수의).
W: That's right. Do you think a one-year warranty(보증 기간) is too short?
M: Yes. I recommend ⓑone that has a warranty longer than one year.
W: Okay. I'll take your advice.
M: That leaves you with these two options. I'd get the cheaper one because it's as good as the other one.
W: I see. Then ⓒI'll go with the cheaper one.
M: Good choice.

해석

남: 안녕하세요, 오늘은 뭘 도와드릴까요?
여: 안녕하세요, 스마트 워치를 찾고 있어요.
남: 네. 이 다섯 가지 모델이 있어요.
여: 음…. 수영할 때 차고 싶어요.
남: 그러면 ⓐ방수 모델을 찾으시겠네요.
여: 맞아요. 1년 보증 기간은 너무 짧을까요?
남: 네. ⓑ보증 기간이 1년 이상인 것을 추천드립니다.
여: 네. 조언을 따를게요.
남: 그러면 이 두 가지 선택이 남네요. 저라면 다른 것만큼 좋기 때문에 더 저렴한 것을 사겠어요.
여: 알겠습니다. 그러면 ⓒ더 저렴한 것으로 할게요.
남: 좋은 선택이에요.

문제 풀이

여자는 ⓐ방수가 되고, ⓑ보증 기간이 1년 이상인 두 가지 중에 ⓒ더 저렴한 모델을 사기로 했다.

11. ④ | 짧은 대화 응답

선택지 선택비율	① 5%	② 3%	③ 3%	④ 83%	⑤ 6%

M: Becky, did you order(주문하다) our food for dinner?
W: Yes. ⓐI ordered pizza about an hour ago.
M: An hour ago? ⓑDelivery(배달) usually takes less than 40 minutes.
W: I'll call the restaurant and check our order.

해석

남: Becky, 우리 저녁 식사 주문했어?
여: 응. ⓐ한 시간 전쯤에 피자를 주문했어.
남: 한 시간 전? ⓑ보통 배달은 40분이 안 걸리는데.
여: 내가 식당에 전화해서 주문을 확인해 볼게.

문제 풀이

여자가 ⓐ한 시간 전쯤에 피자를 주문했는데 남자가 ⓑ보통 배달은 40분 내로 된다고 말하고 있으므로, 다시 식당에 전화해서 주문을 확인해 보겠다는 ④가 응답으로 가장 적절하다.
① 남은 음식은 집으로 가져가자.
② 나는 피자보다 프라이드치킨을 더 좋아해.
③ 오늘은 점심 먹으러 나가고 싶지 않아.
⑤ 편지가 잘못된 주소로 배달되었어.

12. ① | 짧은 대화 응답

선택지 선택비율	① 87%	② 4%	③ 2%	④ 3%	⑤ 2%

W: Jimmy, what are you looking for(~을 찾다)?
M: My cellphone. I forgot where I left it.
W: Why don't you look for it in your room first?
M: I already did, but I couldn't find it.

해석

여: Jimmy, 너 뭘 찾고 있니?
남: 내 휴대전화. 그것을 어디에 두었는지 잊어버렸어.
여: 네 방 안에서 먼저 찾아보는 게 어때?
남: 벌써 찾아봤는데, 못 찾았어.

문제 풀이

남자의 방 안에서 휴대전화를 찾아보는 것이 어떻겠냐고 여자가 말했으므로, 이미 찾아봤지만 못 찾았다는 ①이 남자의 응답으로 가장 적절하다.

② 알겠어, 거실에서 기다릴게.
③ 너는 휴대전화를 고쳐야 해.
④ 난 분실물 보관소에 전화했어.
⑤ 이곳에서는 와이파이를 이용할 수 없어.

13. ③ | 긴 대화 응답

선택지 선택비율	① 2%	② 2%	③ 82%	④ 12%	⑤ 1%

M: Grandma, look what I found in the garage. It's an old cookbook.
차고 요리책
W: Oh, I haven't seen that for years.
M: It says here, "Recipes for Fine Dishes."
W: That's the cookbook I wrote when I was a chef before you were born.
요리사
M: Really? ⓐYou were a professional chef?
직업의, 전문적인
W: ⓑYeah, I used to work in a restaurant. Look! These were my special dishes.
used to-v: ~하곤 했다
M: Wow, they look fantastic! Did you create all the recipes in the book?
창조하다
W: Yes. ⓒI really loved cooking and was good at it back then.
M: You're still good at cooking!
W: Do you really think so?
M: Of course! ⓓI've always thought your food tastes amazing.
W: Thanks. I guess I haven't lost my chef skills.
기량, 솜씨

해석

남: 할머니, 제가 차고에서 뭘 찾았는지 보세요. 오래된 요리책이에요.
여: 아, 그거 몇 년 동안 못 봤던 거네.
남: 여기 "멋진 요리를 위한 레시피"라고 쓰여 있어요.
여: 그건 네가 태어나기 전에 내가 요리사였을 때 쓴 요리책이란다.
남: 정말요? ⓐ할머니가 전문 요리사였어요?
여: ⓑ그래, 예전에 식당에서 일했단다. 봐! 이게 내 특별 요리들이었어.
남: 와, 정말 멋져 보여요! 책에 있는 레시피들 전부 할머니가 만드신 거예요?
여: 그렇지. ⓒ그때는 요리를 정말 좋아하고 잘했단다.
남: 지금도 요리 잘하시잖아요!
여: 정말 그렇게 생각하니?
남: 물론이죠! ⓓ전 늘 할머니 음식이 정말 맛있다고 생각했어요.
여: 고맙구나. 아직 요리사 솜씨를 잃진 않은 것 같네.

문제 풀이

ⓑ과거에 식당에서 일하는 ⓐ전문 요리사로서 ⓒ요리를 정말 좋아하고 잘했다고 말하는 여자에게 남자가 ⓓ평소 음식 맛을 칭찬하고 있으므로, 고마움을 표하며 아직 솜씨를 잃지 않은 것 같다고 말하는 ③이 응답으로 가장 적절하다.
① 네 말이 맞아. 그렇게 해서 내가 그 책을 찾은 거야.
② 음, 곧 음식이 배달될 것 같아.
④ 정말? 네가 요리를 좋아하는 줄 몰랐어.
⑤ 알아. 그래서 내가 요리사를 그만둔 거야.

14. ③ | 긴 대화 응답

선택지 선택비율	① 1%	② 8%	③ 88%	④ 2%	⑤ 2%

M: Jenny, what class do you want to take this summer vacation?
W: Well, *[Pause]* I'm thinking of the guitar class.
M: Cool! I'm interested in playing the guitar, too.
W: Really? It would be exciting if we took the class together.
M: I know, but ⓐI am thinking of taking a math class instead. I didn't do well on the final exam.
W: Oh, there is a math class? I didn't know that.
M: Yes. Mrs. Kim said she is offering a math class for first graders.
(이용할 수 있도록) 내놓다[제공하다]
W: That might be a good chance to improve my skills, too. ⓑWhere can I check the schedule for the math class?
향상시키다
M: You can find it on the school website.

해석

남: Jenny, 이번 여름 방학에 무슨 수업을 듣고 싶니?
여: 음, [잠시 후] 난 기타 수업을 생각하고 있어.
남: 멋지다! 나도 기타 치는 것에 관심이 있어.
여: 정말? 우리가 함께 수업을 듣는다면 재미있을 거야.
남: 알아, 하지만 ⓐ난 대신 수학 수업을 들을 생각이야. 기말고사를 잘 못 봤거든.
여: 아, 수학 수업이 있어? 난 몰랐어.
남: 응. 김 선생님께서 1학년들을 위한 수학 수업을 해 주신다고 말씀하셨어.
여: 내 실력을 향상시킬 수 있는 좋은 기회가 될 수 있을지도 모르겠어. ⓑ수학 수업 시간표를 어디서 확인할 수 있어?
남: 학교 웹사이트에서 찾을 수 있어.

문제 풀이

남자가 ⓐ여름 방학에 수학 수업을 들을 생각이라고 하자 여자가 관심을 보이며 ⓑ수학 수업 시간표를 어디서 확인할 수 있는지 물었으므로, 시간표를 찾을 수 있는 곳을 말하는 ③이 남자의 응답으로 가장 적절하다.
① 새 기타를 사게 되어 신이 나.
② 여름 방학은 금요일에 시작해.
④ 우리 학교 축제에 함께 가자.
⑤ 넌 방학 동안 좀 쉴 수 있어.

15. ③ | 상황에 적절한 말

선택지 선택비율	① 7%	② 3%	③ 82%	④ 5%	⑤ 3%

M: Ted and John are college freshmen. They are climbing Green Diamond Mountain together. Now they have reached the campsite near the mountain top. After climbing the mountain all day, they have a relaxing time at the campsite. While drinking coffee, ⓐTed suggests to John that they watch the sunrise at the mountain top the next morning. John thinks it's a good idea. So, now ⓑJohn wants to ask Ted how early they should wake up to see the sunrise. In this situation, what would John most likely say to Ted?
대학교 freshman: 신입생 오르다
~에 도착하다
편안한
일출
John: What time should we get up tomorrow morning?

해석

남: Ted와 John은 대학교 신입생이다. 그들은 함께 Green Diamond 산을 오르고 있다. 이제 그들은 산 정상 근처의 캠프장에 도착했다. 하루 종일 산을 오른 후, 그들은 캠프장에서 편안한 시간을 보낸다. 커피를 마시면서, ⓐTed는 John에게 다음날 아침에 산 정상에서 일출을 보자고 제안한다. John은 이것이 좋은 생각이라고 생각한다. 그래서 이제 ⓑJohn은 Ted에게 일출을 보기 위해 얼마나 일찍 일어나야 하는지 묻고 싶다. 이 상황에서, John은 Ted에게 뭐라고 말하겠는가?
John: 내일 아침 몇 시에 일어나야 할까?

문제 풀이

ⓐTed가 John에게 다음날 아침 산 정상에서 일출을 보자고 제안했고, ⓑJohn은 Ted에게 그러려면 얼마나 일찍 일어나야 하는지 묻고 싶어 하므로, 상황에 가장 적절한 말은 ③이다.
① 어떻게 가장 좋은 일출 장소를 찾을 수 있을까?
② 왜 등산을 그렇게 자주 가니?
④ 산 정상에서 언제 내려가면 될까?
⑤ 우리가 밤에 산에서 지내야 하는 곳이 어디야?

16~17. | 세트 문항

16. ③ 17. ④

선택지 선택비율	① 2%	② 5%	③ 75%	④ 15%	⑤ 3%
	① 1%	② 1%	③ 1%	④ 96%	⑤ 1%

M: Hello, Lincoln High School. This is David Newman, your current
현재의
student representative, and I'm speaking to you today ⓐto let
대표
you know about the upcoming election for next year's student
다가오는 선거
representative. ⓑCandidates can now begin their campaigns,
후보자 선거 운동
following these instructions. First, they can share short promotional
지시, 지침 홍보의
video clips on their ⓒsocial media, but the video clips must not be longer than 3 minutes. Second, candidates can display ⓓposters
전시하다
only in allowed areas, and it's important to keep the size to A3 or
허가받은, 허용된
smaller, as larger posters will be removed without warning. Third,
제거하다 경고
the use of ⓔpamphlets is allowed, but they must only be distributed
나누어 주다
within the school campus. Lastly, there will be an online debate
토론
broadcast on our ⓕschool website among the candidates three
방송
days before the election. It's important to be respectful toward
존중하는
the other candidates during the debate. Let's make this election a success.
성공

해석

남: 안녕하세요, Lincoln 고등학교 학생 여러분. 저는 현재 학생 대표인 David Newman이고, 오늘은 여러분에게 ⓐ다가오는 내년 학생 대표 선거에 대해 알려드리고자 말씀드립니다. ⓑ후보자들은 이제 다음 지침에 따라 선거 운동을 시작할 수 있습니다. 첫째, 후보자들은 자신의 ⓒ소셜 미디어에 짧은 홍보 영상을 공유할 수 있지만, 영상은 3분보다 더 길지 않아야 합니다. 둘째, 후보자들은 허용된 구역에만 ⓓ포스터를 전시할 수 있으며, 더 큰 포스터는 경고 없이 제거될 예정이니, 포스터 크기를 A3나 그보다 더 작게 만드는 것이 중요합니다. 셋째, ⓔ전단지 사용은 허용되지만, 그것들은 학교 교정 내에서만 나눠주어야 합니다. 마지막으로, 선거 3일 전에 후보자들 간의 온라인 토론 방송이 ⓕ학교 웹사이트에서 있을 예정입니다. 토론 중에는 다른 후보자들에 대한 존중이 중요합니다. 이번 선거를 성공적으로 치러봅시다.

문제 풀이

16. ⓐⓑ내년 학생 대표 선거 운동의 지침에 대해 이야기하고 있으므로, 주제로는 ③ '학생 선거 운동 지침'이 가장 적절하다.
① 미디어와 유권자 간의 관계
② 학교 정책을 홍보하는 일반적인 방법
④ 후보자가 되기 위한 요건
⑤ 학교 토론에서 이기기 위한 유익한 조언

17. ⓒ소셜 미디어, ⓓ포스터, ⓔ전단지, ⓕ학교 웹사이트는 언급되었으나, 학교 신문(school newspaper)은 언급되지 않았다.

[코드 공략하기]

제6회 초급 모의고사

1	④	2	⑤	3	②	4	⑤	5	④	6	③
7	④	8	④	9	⑤	10	④	11	②	12	①
13	①	14	①	15	④	16	⑤	17	③		

1. ④ | 목적

선택지 선택비율	① 5%	② 5%	③ 5%	④ 82%	⑤ 2%

M: Hello, citizens of Portland. This is Jerry Wilson, your Mayor. As you know, Port Elementary School has opened, and it is so nice to hear the kids playing. To ensure the safety of the students at the school,
보장하다, 확보하다
we've been communicating with the New Jersey State Police and requested that ⓐthey enforce speed limits in the area around the
요청하다 강화하다 속도 제한
school. This is in response to the many complaints City Hall has
~에 대응하여 불평, 항의
received regarding excessive speeding, especially in front of the
~와 관련하여 과도한 속도위반
school. ⓑPlease obey speed limits for the safety of the kids and
따르다, 지키다
your fellow citizens. Thank you for your cooperation. Stay safe and
협조
healthy.

해석

남: 안녕하세요, Portland 시민 여러분. Jerry Wilson 시장입니다. 아시다시피, Port 초등학교가 개교하면서, 아이들이 노는 소리를 듣는 게 참 좋습니다. 학교에서의 학생들의 안전을 확보하기 위해서, New Jersey 주립 경찰과 이야기한 끝에 ⓐ학교 주변 지역에서 속도 제한을 강화할 것을 요청했습니다. 이는 특히 학교 앞에서의 과도한 속도위반과 관련하여 받았던 많은 시청 민원에 대한 대응입니다. ⓑ어린이, 그리고 시민의 안전을 위해 속도 제한을 따라 주시길 바랍니다. 협조 감사합니다. 평안하십시오.

문제 풀이

남자는 ⓐ학교 주변 지역에서 속도 제한을 강화할 것이므로, ⓑ이를 준수해 줄 것을 당부하고 있다.

2. ⑤ | 의견

선택지 선택비율	① 1%	② 1%	③ 5%	④ 3%	⑤ 88%

W: Hey, Daniel. How are you getting ready for your trip to Seoul?
M: Hi, Claire. Everything is going great, but I'm worried about food.
W: Why?
M: I heard that Korean food is very hot and spicy. I think I should bring
양념 맛이 강한
some food with me.
W: Oh, aren't you going to try any Korean food?
써 보거나 해 보다
M: Well, I don't like trying new food. I feel comfortable with what I'm
편한
used to.
be used to v-ing/명사: ~에 익숙하다
W: But trying local food is the beauty of travel. It's the best way to get
현지의 좋은 점
to the heart of the culture.
M: Maybe you're right. I'll give it a try during my travels.
시도해 보다
W: Good thinking. You can find some good Korean restaurants on the web.
M: Okay. Thanks.

해석

여: 얘, Daniel. 서울 여행 준비는 어떻게 돼 가니?
남: 안녕, Claire. 모든 게 잘 되고 있는데, 음식이 걱정이야.
여: 왜?
남: 한국 음식이 맵고 양념 맛이 강하다고 들었거든. 내 생각에 내가 음식을 좀 가져가야겠어.
여: 아, 한국 음식은 안 먹어 볼 거니?
남: 음, 난 새로운 음식 먹어 보는 걸 좋아하지 않아. 난 익숙한 게 편해.
여: 하지만 현지 음식을 먹어 보는 게 여행의 좋은 점인 걸. 그게 문화의 핵심을 찌르는 가장 좋은 방법이야.
남: 어쩌면 네 말이 맞을지도 몰라. 여행 동안 시도해 볼게.
여: 잘 생각했어. 웹에서 좋은 한식당을 찾을 수 있어.
남: 그래. 고마워.

문제 풀이

여자는 현지 음식을 먹어 보는 게 여행의 좋은 점으로, 문화의 핵심을 찌르는 방법이라고 말하고 있다.

3. ② | 관계

선택지 선택비율	① 2%	② 89%	③ 4%	④ 1%	⑤ 2%

[Telephone rings.]
M: Hello, this is Daniel Johnson.
W: Hello, Mr. Johnson. It's Elena Roberts. Have you thought about my proposal?
제안, 제의
M: Yes. ⓐYou said you wanted to turn my novel into a movie, right?
~을 …로 바꾸다
W: That's right. I loved your novel, and it would make a great movie.
M: I'm glad to hear that. And ⓑif you directed the movie, it would be a great honor for me.
(영화를) 감독하다 / 영광
W: Thank you for accepting my offer. I'd like us to speak about the details of the story in person.
받아들이다, 수락하다 / 제안 / 직접
M: Then, shall I go to your office?
W: That would be great. Can you come tomorrow?
M: Sure. I'll be there by 10 a.m.

해석

[전화벨이 울린다.]
남: 여보세요, Daniel Johnson입니다.
여: 안녕하세요, Johnson 씨. Elena Roberts입니다. 제 제안에 대해 생각해 보셨어요?
남: 네. ⓐ제 소설을 영화로 만들고 싶다고 하셨죠, 그렇죠?
여: 맞습니다. 저는 당신의 소설이 너무 좋았고, 그것은 훌륭한 영화가 될 거예요.
남: 그 말을 들으니 기쁘네요. 그리고 ⓑ만약 당신이 그 영화를 감독한다면, 그것은 제게 큰 영광이 될 겁니다.
여: 제 제안을 수락해 주셔서 감사합니다. 저희가 내용의 세부 사항에 대해서는 직접 이야기했으면 합니다.
남: 그러면 제가 사무실로 갈까요?
여: 그게 좋겠네요. 내일 오실 수 있나요?
남: 물론이죠. 오전 10시까지 그곳에 가도록 하겠습니다.

문제 풀이

ⓐ여자가 남자의 소설을 영화로 만들고 싶다고 제안했다고 했고, 남자는 ⓑ여자가 그 영화를 감독해 준다면 영광이라고 말한 것으로 보아, 남자는 소설가이고 여자는 영화감독임을 알 수 있다.

코드 +α 제안에 대한 응답

It would be a great honor for me. (그렇다면 영광입니다.)
Thank you for offering me this opportunity.
(저에게 이 기회를 주셔서 감사합니다.)
Unfortunately, I won't be able to accept your proposal.
(유감스럽게도 제안을 받아들일 수 없습니다.)

4. ⑤ | 그림

선택지 선택비율	① 1%	② 0%	③ 1%	④ 3%	⑤ 95%

W: Honey, I love this park!
M: Me, too. This park is so cool. But, oh, look! What's that in the tree?
W: It's just ⓐa kite stuck in the tree's branches.
연 / 갇힌, 빠져나갈 수 없는
M: I guess some kids went home without their kite.
W: By the same tree, ⓑa woman is walking her dog. They look so lovely.
M: What about the little girl beside her?
~ 옆에
W: You mean ⓒthe girl holding balloons in her hand?
M: Right. She's adorable. And look there! Did you notice ⓓa basket full of flowers on the picnic mat?
사랑스러운, 귀여운
W: Yes, right. It adds a touch of romance to the scene.
더하다 / 촉감, 기운 / 사랑, 설렘 / 장면, 상황, 광경
M: I think so, too. Oh, there's a fountain. Next to it, ⓔa man is playing the violin.
분수
W: The melody is beautiful. I'm glad we came here.

해석

여: 여보, 이 공원 정말 마음에 들어요!
남: 나도 그래요. 이 공원 정말 멋지네요. 그런데, 어, 봐요! 나무에 저게 뭐예요?
여: 그냥 ⓐ나뭇가지에 연이 걸린 것뿐이에요.
남: 아마 어떤 아이들이 연을 두고 집에 갔나 봐요.
여: 같은 나무 옆에, ⓑ한 여자가 개를 산책시키고 있어요. 정말 사랑스러워 보이네요.
남: 그 여자 옆에 있는 어린 여자아이는요?
여: ⓒ손에 풍선을 들고 있는 여자아이 말하는 거예요?
남: 그래요. 정말 귀여워요. 그리고 저기 봐요! ⓓ피크닉 매트 위에 꽃으로 가득 찬 바구니 봤어요?
여: 네, 봤어요. 그게 이 광경에 설렘의 기운을 더하네요.
남: 나도 그렇게 생각해요. 오, 분수가 있어요. 그 옆에서 ⓔ한 남자가 바이올린을 켜고 있네요.
여: 멜로디가 아름다워요. 여길 오길 잘했어요.

문제 풀이

ⓔ분수 옆에서 남자가 바이올린을 켜고 있다고 했으므로, 그림 ⑤의 사진을 찍고 있는 남자는 대화 내용과 일치하지 않는다.

5. ④ | 할 일

선택지 선택비율	① 7%	② 5%	③ 3%	④ 77%	⑤ 7%

M: Honey, there's a box in the doorway. What is it?
출입구
W: I ordered some groceries online. Would you bring it in?
grocery: 식료품
M: Sure. Is this for the housewarming party today?
집들이
W: Yeah. Since I had to have my car repaired, I couldn't go shopping
수리하다

yesterday.
M: Sorry, I should've taken you to the market.
W: That's okay. You worked late to meet the deadline for your report.
(기한 등을) 지키다 기한, 마감 시간
Would you open the box for me?
M: Sure. *[Pause]* Oh no, some eggs are broken! Have a look.
W: Ah... that's never happened before.
M: ⓐWhy don't we call the customer center about it?
W: Okay. ⓑI'll do it right now.
M: While you do that, I'll put the other food in the fridge.
냉장고
W: Thanks.

해석

남: 여보, 입구에 상자가 하나 있어요. 그거 뭐예요?
여: 온라인으로 식료품을 좀 주문했어요. 그것을 가지고 들어와 줄래요?
남: 물론이죠. 이게 오늘 집들이를 위한 건가요?
여: 네. 차를 수리해야 해서, 어제 쇼핑하러 못 갔거든요.
남: 미안해요, 내가 당신을 시장에 데려다줬어야 했는데요.
여: 괜찮아요. 당신은 보고서 마감일을 맞추려고 늦게까지 일했잖아요. 나 대신 상자를 열어 줄래요?
남: 알겠어요. [잠시 후] 오 이런, 계란 몇 개가 깨졌어요! 봐요.
여: 아… 전에는 그런 일이 한 번도 없었어요.
남: ⓐ이 일에 대해 고객 센터에 전화하는 게 어때요?
여: 네. ⓑ지금 바로 할게요.
남: 그러는 동안, 내가 다른 음식을 냉장고에 넣을게요.
여: 고마워요.

문제 풀이

ⓐ고객 센터에 전화해 보는 것이 어떻겠냐는 남자의 말에 여자가 ⓑ지금 바로 하겠다고 했다.

6. ③ | 금액

선택지 선택비율	① 2%	② 7%	③ 83%	④ 7%	⑤ 1%

W: Welcome to Libby's Flowers. How can I help you?
M: I'd like to order a rose basket for my parents' wedding anniversary.
결혼기념일
W: All right. Our rose baskets come in two sizes.
M: What are the options?
W: The regular size is 30 dollars, and ⓐthe large size is 50 dollars.
M: Hmm.... ⓑI think the bigger one is better.
W: Good choice. So, you'll get one rose basket in the large size. By the way, ⓒwe're giving a 10-percent discount on all purchases this
할인 구입, 구입한 것
week.
M: Excellent! When will my order be ready?
W: It'll be ready around 11 a.m. If you can't pick it up, we offer a delivery service. ⓓIt's 10 dollars.
M: Oh, great. ⓔI'd like it to be delivered. Here's my credit card.

해석

여: Libby의 꽃가게에 오신 걸 환영합니다. 무엇을 도와드릴까요?
남: 저희 부모님 결혼기념일을 위한 장미 바구니를 주문하고 싶은데요.
여: 알겠습니다. 저희 장미 바구니는 두 가지 사이즈가 있습니다.
남: 어떤 옵션이 있나요?
여: 보통 사이즈는 30달러이고, ⓐ큰 사이즈는 50달러입니다.
남: 음…. ⓑ더 큰 게 더 나을 것 같네요.
여: 좋은 선택이에요. 그럼 큰 사이즈 장미 바구니를 하나 하셨습니다. 그런데 ⓒ저희가 이번 주는 구매하시는 모든 것에 대해 10% 할인해 드리고 있어요.
남: 아주 좋네요! 주문한 게 언제쯤 준비될까요?
여: 오전 11시쯤에 준비될 예정입니다. 가지러 오실 수 없으면, 배달 서비스를 제공해 드려요. ⓓ10달러입니다.
남: 아, 잘됐네요. ⓔ배달해주시면 좋겠어요. 여기 제 신용카드입니다.

문제 풀이

ⓐⓑ50달러짜리 큰 사이즈의 장미 바구니를 구매했는데 ⓒ10% 할인을 받았고, ⓓⓔ배달비가 10달러이므로, 남자가 지불할 금액은 55달러이다.

코드+α 요청하는 표현

I'd like to order some room service. (룸서비스를 주문하고 싶어요.)
I'd like you to fill out this form. (이 양식을 작성해 주셨으면 합니다.)
Would you mind explaining that again? (그걸 다시 설명해 주시겠습니까?)

7. ④ | 이유

선택지 선택비율	① 4%	② 3%	③ 4%	④ 83%	⑤ 3%

M: Emily, how was your weekend?
W: Good. I went to my grandmother's birthday party. How was yours? Did you enjoy your family trip to Japan?
M: Well, unfortunately things did not go as planned. We couldn't go to
불행하게도 계획대로 진행되다
Japan.
W: Why not? Was someone in the family ill?
M: No, that was not the reason.
W: Was your flight cancelled because of the weather?
M: Not that either. Just before getting on the plane, my wife and I found that we had lost our son's passport.
W: Oh, no! You must all have been very disappointed.
must have p.p.: ~했음이 틀림없다
M: Yes, we were. So we're thinking about planning another family trip in the fall.

해석

남: Emily, 주말 어떻게 보냈니?
여: 좋았어. 나는 할머니 생신 잔치에 갔었어. 너는 어땠니? 일본 가족 여행은 즐거웠니?
남: 음, 불행히도 일이 계획대로 되지 않았어. 우리는 일본에 가지 못했어.
여: 왜? 가족 중에 누군가 아팠니?
남: 아니, 그런 이유가 아니었어.
여: 날씨 때문에 항공편이 취소되었니?
남: 그것도 아니야. 비행기에 타기 직전에 아내와 나는 우리 아들의 여권을 잃어버린 것을 알았어.
여: 안돼! 너희 모두 틀림없이 실망했겠구나.
남: 맞아. 그래서 우리는 가을에 또 다른 가족 여행 계획을 생각 중이야.

문제 풀이

남자는 아들의 여권을 잃어버려서 여행을 가지 못했다고 했다.

8. ④ | 언급

선택지 선택비율	① 1%	② 0%	③ 1%	④ 96%	⑤ 1%

M: Hey, Emma, what are you reading?
W: Hi. I'm reading a post about the Topas Beachcombing activity.
게시글 활동
M: What is that? I've never heard of it.
W: It's an activity where you go along the beach and collect garbage
~을 따라 가다 쓰레기
and make something useful or creative with it.
유용한 창의적인
M: Great! When is it?
W: This Saturday, ⓐthe 25th of September, at 10 a.m. on Sunset Beach.
M: Oh, it's near my house. How can I join the activity?
W: ⓑYou can sign up on their website.

M: Do I need to bring anything?
W: Yes, ⓒwe'll need gloves and a bag for the garbage.
M: No problem. Is there a participation fee?
참가비
W: No, ⓓit's free.
M: Perfect! It sounds meaningful and fun.
의미 있는

해석

남: 안녕, Emma. 뭐 읽고 있어?
여: 안녕. Topas Beachcombing 활동에 대한 게시글을 읽고 있어.
남: 그게 뭐야? 난 한 번도 들어본 적 없어.
여: 해변을 따라 가면서 쓰레기를 줍고, 그걸로 유용하거나 창의적인 걸 만드는 활동이야.
남: 멋지다! 언제 하는데?
여: 이번 토요일, ⓐ9월 25일 오전 10시에 Sunset 해변에서 해.
남: 오, 우리집 근처네. 어떻게 그 활동에 참가할 수 있어?
여: ⓑ웹사이트에서 등록할 수 있어.
남: 뭔가 가져가야 해?
여: 응, ⓒ장갑이랑 쓰레기 담을 봉투가 필요할 거야.
남: 문제없어. 참가비가 있어?
여: 아니, ⓓ무료야.
남: 좋아! 의미 있고 재미있을 것 같아.

문제 풀이

ⓐ날짜, ⓑ등록 방법, ⓒ준비물, ⓓ참가비는 언급되었으나, 참가 인원은 언급되지 않았다.

9. ⑤ | 내용 일치

선택지 선택비율	① 4%	② 3%	③ 3%	④ 6%	⑤ 84%

M: Hello, Eastville High School students. This is your P.E. teacher, Mr. Wilson. I'm pleased to let you know that ⓐwe're hosting the first Eastville Dance Contest. Any Eastville students who love dancing can participate in the contest as a team. ⓑAll kinds of dance are allowed. If you'd like to participate, please ⓒupload your team's dance video to our school website by August 15th. ⓓStudents can vote for their favorite video from August 16th to 20th. ⓔThe winning team will receive a trophy as a prize. Don't miss this great opportunity to show off your talents!
체육 / 기쁜 / 주최하다 / 참가하다 / ~에 투표하다 / 받다 / 트로피 / 기회 / ~을 자랑하다 / 재능

해석

남: 안녕하세요, Eastville 고등학교 학생 여러분. 여러분의 체육 교사인 Wilson입니다. ⓐ우리가 처음으로 Eastville 춤 경연을 주최하게 되었다는 것을 알리게 되어 기쁩니다. 춤을 사랑하는 Eastville 학생들은 누구나 팀을 이루어 경연에 참가할 수 있습니다. ⓑ모든 종류의 춤이 허용됩니다. 참가를 원하면, ⓒ8월 15일까지 우리 학교 웹사이트에 여러분 팀의 춤 영상을 업로드해 주세요. 학생들은 8월 16일부터 20일까지 ⓓ자신이 가장 좋아하는 영상에 투표할 수 있습니다. ⓔ우승팀은 상으로 트로피를 받을 것입니다. 여러분의 재능을 뽐낼 수 있는 이 좋은 기회를 놓치지 마세요!

문제 풀이

ⓔ우승팀은 상으로 상품권이 아닌 트로피를 받을 것이라고 했다.

10. ④ | 도표

선택지 선택비율	① 1%	② 3%	③ 2%	④ 93%	⑤ 0%

W: Honey, we need to buy Robert a backpack for school.
M: Right, let's search for one online.
~을 찾다
W: *[Clicking Sound]* Wow, there are so many options. What should we consider first?
고려하다
M: Well, let's start with budget.
예산
W: We already spent a lot on his other school supplies. ⓐI'd like to keep it under $70.
학용품
M: All right. What shape should we get him, ⓑa square one?
정사각형의, 네모난
W: ⓒYeah, it's better for carrying school supplies. Then, what about the color?
M: White ones get dirty easily, so ⓓwe should go with a black one.
W: Sounds good. And ⓔdoes it need to be waterproof?
방수의
M: ⓕDefinitely. It'll be useful on rainy days.
W: Then, this is the one. Let's buy it.

해석

여: 여보, Robert에게 학교에 가지고 다닐 책가방을 사 줘야 해요.
남: 맞아요, 온라인으로 하나 찾아봅시다.
여: [클릭하는 소리] 와, 선택지가 정말 많네요. 뭘 먼저 고려해야 할까요?
남: 음, 예산부터 시작하죠.
여: 우린 이미 그 애의 다른 학용품에 돈을 많이 썼어요. ⓐ70달러 미만으로 하고 싶어요.
남: 좋아요. 어떤 모양으로 사 줘야 할까요, ⓑ네모난 걸로요?
여: ⓒ네, 학용품을 가지고 다니기에는 그게 더 좋아요. 그럼 색깔은요?
남: 흰색은 쉽게 더러워지니까 ⓓ검은색으로 해야 해요.
여: 좋아요. 그리고 ⓔ방수 기능도 필요할까요?
남: ⓕ그럼요. 비 오는 날에 유용할 거예요.
여: 그렇다면 이게 딱이네요. 이걸로 사요.

문제 풀이

두 사람은 ⓐ70달러 미만의 ⓑⓒ네모난 모양이고 ⓓ검은색이며 ⓔⓕ방수 기능이 있는 책가방을 구매하기로 했다.

11. ② | 짧은 대화 응답

선택지 선택비율	① 4%	② 78%	③ 5%	④ 12%	⑤ 1%

M: Mom, the bookshelf in my room is full of books. There's no space for new ones.
책장 / 공간
W: Well, ⓐhow about throwing away the books you don't read anymore?
버리다
M: But ⓑsome of them are in too good condition to throw away.
상태
W: Right. Then, shall we sell them at a used bookstore?

해석

남: 엄마, 제 방에 있는 책장이 책으로 가득 찼어요. 새것을 놓을 공간이 없어요.
여: 음, ⓐ더 이상 읽지 않는 책들을 버리는 게 어떠니?
남: 하지만 ⓑ그 중 몇 권은 버리기에는 상태가 너무 좋아요.
여: 그렇구나. 그럼, 우리 그것들을 중고서점에 팔까?

문제 풀이

ⓐ더 이상 읽지 않는 책들을 버리는 것이 어떻겠냐는 여자의 말에 남자가 ⓑ버리기에는 상태가 너무 좋은 책들이 있다고 했으므로, 그 책들을 중고서점에 팔자고 제안하는 ②가 여자의 응답으로 가장 적절하다.
① 멋지다. 새 책장이 네 방에 잘 어울려.
③ 알겠어. 네가 도서관에서 그것들을 빌릴 수 있니?
④ 좋아. 상태가 좋은 책을 사줄게.
⑤ 미안해. 아직 그 책을 다 읽지 못했어.

12. ① | 짧은 대화 응답

선택지 선택비율	① 85%	② 6%	③ 5%	④ 2%	⑤ 2%

[Cell phone rings.]
W: Daddy, are you still working now?
M: No, Emma. ⓐI'm about to get in my car and drive home.
be about to-v: 막 ~하려는 참이다
W: Great. ⓑCan you give me a ride? I'm at the City Library near your office.
~을 태워주다
M: All right. I'll come pick you up now.

해석

[휴대전화가 울린다.]
여: 아빠, 지금도 일하고 계세요?
남: 아니, Emma. ⓐ이제 막 차를 타고 집에 가려던 중이란다.
여: 잘됐네요. ⓑ저 좀 태워주실 수 있으세요? 저 지금 아빠 사무실 근처에 있는 시립 도서관에 있거든요.
남: 좋아. 지금 데리러 갈게.

문제 풀이

ⓐ이제 막 퇴근하여 집에 가려던 남자에게 여자가 ⓑ사무실 근처 도서관에 있는 자신을 태워줄 수 있는지 묻고 있으므로, 이에 대한 응답으로 가장 적절한 것은 ①이다.
② 죄송합니다. 도서관은 오늘 휴관입니다.
③ 괜찮아. 내 책을 빌려도 돼.
④ 정말 고마워. 지금 내려줄게.
⑤ 맞아. 내가 사무실 인테리어를 바꿨어.

13. ① | 긴 대화 응답

선택지 선택비율	① 84%	② 6%	③ 2%	④ 2%	⑤ 3%

M: Why do you look so busy?
W: ⓐI'm working on a team project.
M: What's it about?
W: It's about 'Climate Change.'
M: Sounds interesting. Who's on your team?
W: You know Chris? ⓑHe's the leader.
M: I know him very well. He's responsible and smart.
책임감 있는
W: ⓒJenny is doing the research and Alex is making the slides.
조사하다
M: What a nice team! Then ⓓwhat's your role?
역할
W: I'm in charge of giving the presentation.
~을 맡아서[담당해서]

해석

남: 왜 이렇게 바빠 보이니?
여: ⓐ조별 과제를 하고 있어.
남: 뭐에 관한 건데?
여: '기후 변화'에 관한 거야.
남: 재미있겠다. 네 조에 누가 있니?
여: Chris 알지? ⓑ그 애가 조장이야.
남: 그 애 아주 잘 알지. 책임감 있고 똑똑하지.
여: ⓒJenny가 조사를 하고 있고 Alex가 슬라이드를 만들고 있어.
남: 좋은 조네! 그러면 ⓓ네 역할은 뭐니?
여: 나는 발표를 맡았어.

문제 풀이

여자는 ⓐ자신이 하고 있는 조별 과제에서 ⓑⓒ각 조원의 역할을 말하고 있고, 마지막에 남자가 ⓓ여자의 역할을 물었으므로, 맡은 역할을 말하는 ①이 응답으로 가장 적절하다.
② 네가 그 역할에 제격인 사람 같아.
③ 조를 신중하게 선택하는 게 중요해.
④ 과제는 내일모레까지야.
⑤ 나는 우리가 과제를 끝내려고 늦게까지 깨어 있지 않으면 좋겠어.

14. ① | 긴 대화 응답

선택지 선택비율	① 62%	② 14%	③ 11%	④ 9%	⑤ 4%

W: Hey, Peter. How's your group project going?
M: Hello, Ms. Adams. It's my first time as a leader, so it's quite challenging.
도전적인, 힘든
W: I thought your group was working well together.
M: Yes. We're all motivated and working hard, but progress is slow.
동기를 부여하다 / 진척, 진행
W: Well, what are you all working on at this moment?
M: Everyone is focusing on gathering data as much as possible.
~에 집중하다 / 모으다
W: Hmm, ⓐdid you assign individual tasks to each member?
(일·책임 등을) 맡기다[부과하다] / 각각의 / 일, 업무
M: Oh, we haven't discussed it yet. We're not exactly sure who does what.
논의하다
W: ⓑThat's crucial. Otherwise, it can lead to overlapping tasks in a group project.
중대한 / 그렇지 않으면 / ~을 이끌다[초래하다] / 중복된
M: That makes sense. That's why our progress is not that fast.
W: Then, ⓒas the leader, what do you think you should do now?
M: I'll clarify each group member's specific role.
명확하게 하다 / 구체적인

해석

여: 안녕, Peter. 너희 조별 과제는 어떻게 돼 가고 있니?
남: 안녕하세요, Adams 선생님. 제가 리더로는 처음이라, 꽤 힘들어요.
여: 너희 조는 함께 잘하고 있다고 생각했는데.
남: 네. 저희 모두 동기부여가 되어 있고 열심히 하고 있지만, 진행이 느려요.
여: 음, 지금 너희 모두 무엇을 하고 있니?
남: 모두가 가능한 한 많은 자료를 모으는 데 집중하고 있어요.
여: 흠, ⓐ각 조원에게 각각의 일을 맡겼니?
남: 아, 저희는 아직 그건 논의하지 않았어요. 누가 뭘 하는지 그다지 확실하지 않아요.
여: ⓑ그게 중대하단다. 그렇지 않으면 조별 과제에서 중복 작업이 생길 수 있어.
남: 그렇군요. 그래서 저희 진행이 그리 빠르지 않은 거네요.
여: 그러면, ⓒ리더로서 지금 너는 무엇을 해야 한다고 생각하니?
남: 각 조원들의 구체적인 역할을 명확하게 할게요.

문제 풀이

여자는 남자에게 ⓑ조별 과제에서는 작업이 중복될 수 있기 때문에 ⓐ각 조원들에게 각각의 일을 맡기는 것이 중요하며 ⓒ리더로서 무엇을 해야 할지 묻고 있으므로, 각 조원들의 구체적인 역할을 명확히 하겠다는 ①이 남자의 응답으로 가장 적절하다.
② 저희 조별 연구를 위해 더 많은 자료를 모을게요.
③ 그 대회를 위해 스스로 도전해야겠어요.
④ 저희 조별 과제의 주제를 바꿔야겠어요.
⑤ 자료를 효과적으로 분석하는 방법을 알려 드릴게요.

15. ④ | 상황에 적절한 말

선택지 선택비율	① 4%	② 11%	③ 4%	④ 75%	⑤ 5%

W: Steven is a high school student and Ms. Olson is a career counselor at his school. Steven has much interest in the video game industry. A few days ago, Ms. Olson recommended a book written by a CEO who runs a famous gaming company. After reading the book, ⓐSteven told her that the CEO is his role model. This morning,
상담사 / 산업 / 운영하다 / 역할 모델

ⓑMs. Olson hears the news that the CEO is going to have a book-signing at a bookstore nearby. She thinks Steven would love to meet his role model in person(직접). So, ⓒMs. Olson wants to tell Steven that he should go see the CEO at the event. In this situation, what would Ms. Olson most likely say to Steven?

Ms. Olson: How about going to your role model's book-signing?

해석

여: Steven은 고등학생이고 Olson 씨는 그의 학교의 진로 상담사이다. Steven은 비디오 게임 산업에 많은 관심을 가지고 있다. 며칠 전, Olson 씨는 유명한 게임 회사를 운영하는 CEO가 쓴 책을 추천했다. 책을 읽은 후, ⓐSteven은 그녀에게 그 CEO가 자신의 역할 모델이라고 말했다. 오늘 아침, ⓑOlson 씨는 그 CEO가 근처 서점에서 책 사인회를 할 것이라는 소식을 듣는다. 그녀는 Steven이 그의 역할 모델을 직접 만나고 싶어 할 것이라고 생각한다. 그래서 ⓒOlson 씨는 Steven에게 CEO를 보러 행사에 가야 한다고 말하고 싶어 한다. 이 상황에서, Olson 씨는 Steven에게 뭐라고 말하겠는가?

Ms. Olson: 네 역할 모델의 책 사인회에 가보는 게 어떠니?

문제 풀이

Orson 씨는 ⓐSteven의 역할 모델인 CEO가 ⓑ근처 서점에서 책 사인회를 할 것이라는 소식을 듣고 ⓒSteven에게 가야 한다고 말하고 싶어 하므로, 역할 모델의 사인회에 가보라고 권유하는 ④가 가장 적절하다.

① 네가 원할 때 언제든지 나를 보러 와도 돼.
② 네가 그 CEO를 만났다니 기쁘구나.
③ 왜 게임 회사를 운영하고 싶니?
⑤ 너는 네 역할 모델이 쓴 책을 더 많이 사야 해.

16~17. | 세트 문항

16. ⑤ 17. ③

선택지 선택비율					
	① 3%	② 1%	③ 1%	④ 1%	⑤ 93%
	① 2%	② 0%	③ 94%	④ 2%	⑤ 1%

M: Hello, class! Last time, we learned about the national flags(국기) of various(여러 가지의) countries. Today, we'll talk about ⓐdifferent countries' national flowers(국화) and what they symbolize(상징하다). First, ⓑthe Philippines' national flower is jasmine. Because it means good luck, people often give big necklaces made of this flower to welcome special guests(손님). Next, ⓒDenmark's flower is the daisy and it represents(나타내다, 상징하다) happiness. Children express(표현하다) happiness by making daisy chains(사슬, 목걸이) during their traditional(전통의) games. In ⓓFrance, the national flower is the iris. Throughout(~ 동안 쭉) history, French people have thought of this flower as a symbol(상징) of perfection(완벽). Lastly, ⓔthe United States uses the rose as its national flower. Americans consider(여기다) it a symbol of love. So you can find many roses in American weddings. Now, let's watch a short video to look at these flowers up close.

해석

남: 안녕하세요, 학생 여러분! 지난 시간에 우리는 여러 나라들의 국기에 대해 배웠습니다. 오늘은 ⓐ여러 나라의 국화와 그것이 상징하는 것에 대해 이야기해 보겠습니다. 첫째로, ⓑ필리핀의 국화는 재스민입니다. 그것은 행운을 뜻하기 때문에, 종종 사람들은 특별한 손님을 환영할 때 이 꽃으로 만든 큰 목걸이를 선물합니다. 다음으로, ⓒ덴마크의 국화는 데이지이고 이는 행복을 상징합니다. 아이들은 전통 놀이를 하면서 데이지 목걸이를 만들어 행복을 표현합니다. ⓓ프랑스에서 국화는 아이리스입니다. 유사 이래, 프랑스 사람들은 이 꽃을 완벽의 상징으로 여겨 왔습니다. 마지막으로, ⓔ미국은 국화로 장미를 사용합니다. 미국인들은 그것을 사랑의 상징으로 여깁니다. 그래서 미국의 결혼식에서 장미를 많이 볼 수 있습니다. 자, 이제 이 꽃들을 가까이서 살펴보기 위해 짧은 영상을 시청하겠습니다.

문제 풀이

16. ⓐ여러 나라의 국화와 그것이 상징하는 것에 대해 이야기하고 있으므로, 주제로는 ⑤ '상징적 의미를 지닌 국화'가 가장 적절하다.
① 여러 나라의 야생 식물
② 야생 식물과 그것들의 의학적 활용
③ 전 세계의 멸종 위기 꽃들
④ 국가 의식에서의 꽃의 역할

17. ⓑ필리핀, ⓒ덴마크, ⓓ프랑스, ⓔ미국은 언급되었으나, 독일(Germany)은 언급되지 않았다.

[코드 공략하기]

제7회 초급 모의고사

1	②	2	①	3	①	4	⑤	5	①	6	②
7	⑤	8	③	9	③	10	③	11	②	12	⑤
13	②	14	①	15	①	16	①	17	④		

1. ② | 목적

선택지 선택비율	① 12%	② 75%	③ 6%	④ 2%	⑤ 4%

W: Hello, students. This is vice principal Susan Lee. I know all of you are busy preparing for the upcoming school festival. There are club activities going on in every part of our school building. You may want to move between places during activities. But ⓐI'd like to ask you to work in the place where you are supposed to be. Your teachers want to make your safety the top priority. Once again, ⓑmake sure to prepare for the festival in your prearranged places. Thank you for your cooperation.

vice principal: 교감 / be busy v-ing: ~하느라 바쁘다 / upcoming: 다가오는 / be supposed to-v: ~하기로 되어 있다, ~해야 한다 / priority: 최우선 / make sure to-v: 반드시 ~하다 / prearranged: 미리 계획[준비]된 / cooperation: 협력, 협조

해석

여: 안녕하세요, 학생 여러분. 저는 Susan Lee 교감입니다. 여러분 모두가 다가오는 학교 축제를 준비하느라 바쁘다는 것을 알고 있습니다. 우리 학교 건물 곳곳에서는 동아리 활동들이 진행되고 있습니다. 여러분은 활동 중에 장소 간 이동을 원할 수 있습니다. 하지만 ⓐ여러분이 있어야 할 곳에서 활동해 달라고 부탁하고 싶습니다. 여러분의 선생님들은 여러분의 안전을 최우선으로 삼길 원합니다. 다시 한 번, ⓑ반드시 미리 계획된 장소에서 축제를 준비하도록 하세요. 협조 감사합니다.

문제 풀이

학교 축제 준비 시 안전을 위해 ⓐⓑ미리 정해진 장소에서만 활동해 달라고 요청하고 있다.

2. ① | 주제

선택지 선택비율	① 86%	② 2%	③ 2%	④ 1%	⑤ 6%

M: Hey, Sarah. What are you going to choose for your afterschool activity?
W: I'm not sure, Dad.
M: What about taking a coding course?
W: A coding course? Why should I do that?
M: I think ⓐlearning to code can give you important skills for the future.
W: Oh, I remember my teacher saying that ⓑcoding is a skill that can increase the chances of getting a job. But it sounds difficult.
M: It might be, but ⓒit can help you learn how to plan and organize your thoughts.
W: Good to know. And I heard ⓓcoding helps with math. Right?
M: Definitely. Plus, ⓔit improves your problem-solving skills.
W: Cool! I think I'm going to take the course.

increase: 증가시키다 / organize: 정리하다, 체계화[구조화]하다 / improve: 개선되다, 향상시키다 / problem-solving skill: 문제 해결 능력

해석

남: 얘, Sarah. 방과 후 활동으로 무엇을 선택할 거니?
여: 잘 모르겠어요, 아빠.
남: 코딩 강좌를 듣는 건 어때?
여: 코딩 강좌요? 제가 왜 그걸 들어야 하죠?
남: ⓐ코드 학습이 미래를 위한 중요한 기술을 줄 수 있다고 생각해.
여: 아, ⓑ코딩이 취업 기회를 증가시킬 수 있는 기술이라고 저희 선생님께서 말씀하셨던 것이 기억나요. 하지만 어렵게 들리네요.
남: 그럴 수도 있지만, ⓒ너의 생각을 계획하고 체계화하는 방법을 배우는 데 도움이 될 수 있어.
여: 알고 보니 좋네요. 그리고 ⓓ코딩이 수학에 도움이 된다고 들었어요. 맞죠?
남: 물론이지. 게다가, ⓔ너의 문제 해결 능력을 향상시킨단다.
여: 멋져요! 그 강좌를 들을 것 같아요.

문제 풀이

ⓐ미래를 위한 중요한 기술을 습득하고, ⓑ취업 기회를 높이며, ⓒ생각을 계획하고 체계화하는 방법을 배우고, ⓓ수학에 도움이 될 뿐 아니라, ⓔ문제 해결 능력을 향상시키는 등 코딩 학습의 이점에 대해 말하고 있다.

3. ① | 관계

선택지 선택비율	① 92%	② 1%	③ 2%	④ 1%	⑤ 1%

W: Good afternoon. How may I help you?
M: I made a reservation online. It's under the name of Stennis.
W: Could you spell it, sir?
M: Sure. S-T-E-N-N-I-S.
W: All right. ⓐYou've booked a double room with an ocean view for two nights. Is that correct?
M: Yes. And I want to stay on a higher floor if possible.
W: Let me check. *[Typing sound]* ⓑWe have rooms available on the 15th and 19th floors. Which one would you prefer?
M: 19th is better.
W: Okay. ⓒYou'll be staying in Room 1911. Here are your key and breakfast coupons.
M: Thanks. ⓓWhen does the morning buffet begin?
W: ⓔYou can have breakfast from 7 to 9 a.m. at the restaurant on the first floor. Have a nice stay.

make a reservation: 예약하다 / book: 예약하다 / view: 전망 / prefer: 선호하다 / stay: 묵다

해석

여: 안녕하세요. 어떻게 도와드릴까요?
남: 온라인에서 예약했는데요. Stennis 이름으로요.
여: 철자를 말씀해 주실 수 있을까요, 고객님?
남: 네. S-T-E-N-N-I-S예요.
여: 예. ⓐ바다 전망 더블룸 2박 예약하셨네요. 맞습니까?
남: 네. 그리고 가능하면 높은 층에 묵고 싶어요.
여: 확인해 보겠습니다. [타이핑하는 소리] ⓑ15층과 19층에 이용 가능한 방이 있네요. 어느 것을 선호하십니까?
남: 19층이 더 좋겠어요.
여: 알겠습니다. ⓒ1911호에 묵으실 거예요. 여기 열쇠와 아침 식사 쿠폰입니다.
남: 고맙습니다. ⓓ아침 뷔페가 언제 시작하나요?
여: ⓔ1층에 있는 레스토랑에서 오전 7시부터 9시까지 아침 식사를 하실 수 있습니다. 편히 머무십시오.

문제 풀이

여자는 ⓐⓑⓒⓔ호텔 예약과 이용 관련해서 설명하고 남자는 ⓓ아침 뷔페 시간에 대해 묻는 것으로 보아, 두 사람의 관계가 호텔 직원과 투숙객임을 알 수 있다.

4. ⑤ | 그림 일치

선택지 선택비율	① 1%	② 4%	③ 1%	④ 2%	⑤ 92%

M: Hi, Amy. I heard that you've joined the English Newspaper Club.
W: Yes, Tom. I went to the club room yesterday and took a picture of it. Look.

M: Wow, the place looks nice. I like ⓐthe lockers on the left.
사물함
W: Yes, they're good. We also have ⓑa star-shaped mirror on the wall.
거울 벽
M: It looks cool. What's that on the bookshelf?
W: Oh, that's ⓒthe trophy my club won for 'Club of the Year'.
트로피
M: You must be very proud of it. There's also ⓓa computer on the right side of the room.
W: Yeah, we use the computer when we need it.
M: Great. I can see ⓔa newspaper on the table.
W: Yes, it was published last December.
발행하다

해석

남: 안녕, Amy. 네가 영어 신문 동아리에 가입했다고 들었어.
여: 맞아, Tom. 어제 동아리 방에 가서 사진을 찍었어. 봐.
남: 와, 공간이 좋아 보인다. 나는 ⓐ왼쪽에 있는 사물함이 마음에 들어.
여: 응, 좋아. 우리는 ⓑ벽에 별 모양의 거울도 있어.
남: 멋져 보여. 책장 위에 저건 뭐야?
여: 아, 저건 ⓒ우리 동아리가 '올해의 동아리' 상으로 받은 트로피야.
남: 정말 자랑스럽겠다. ⓓ방 오른쪽에 컴퓨터도 있네.
여: 응, 우린 필요할 때 컴퓨터를 사용해.
남: 멋지다. ⓔ테이블 위에 신문이 보이네.
여: 응, 그건 지난 12월에 발행되었어.

문제 풀이

ⓔ테이블 위에 신문이 보인다고 했으므로, 그림 ⑤의 달력은 대화 내용과 일치하지 않는다.

5. ① | 할 일

선택지 선택비율	① 87%	② 3%	③ 3%	④ 2%	⑤ 2%

W: Chris, what are you doing?
M: I'm writing interview questions for the feature story of our next school magazine.
특집 기사
W: Who are you interviewing?
M: The new English teacher. I'm going to interview him tomorrow.
W: Do you need any help with the interview questions?
M: No, I'm almost done. But I'm still looking for someone to take photos during the interview.
W: Why don't you ask Cindy? She's good at taking photos.
M: I already asked her, but she said she has an important presentation tomorrow.
발표[설명]
W: Well, how about Tom? He's a member of the photo club.
M: You mean the one in our chemistry class?
화학
W: Yes. I think he's the right person. ⓐDo you want me to call him to see if he's available tomorrow?
시간[여유]이 있는
M: ⓑThat would be great. Thanks.

해석

여: Chris, 너 뭐 하고 있니?
남: 다음 번 학교 잡지의 특집 기사를 위해 인터뷰 질문을 작성하고 있어.
여: 누구를 인터뷰하는데?
남: 새로 오신 영어 선생님. 내일 그 선생님을 인터뷰할 거야.
여: 인터뷰 질문 작성에 도움이 필요하니?
남: 아니, 거의 다 했어. 하지만 인터뷰 동안 사진 찍어줄 사람을 여전히 찾고 있는 중이야.
여: Cindy에게 물어보는 게 어때? 사진을 잘 찍잖아.
남: 이미 물어봤는데, 내일 중요한 발표가 있대.
여: 음, Tom은 어때? 그 애는 사진 동아리 회원이야.
남: 우리 화학 수업의 그 아이 말이야?
여: 응. 난 그 애가 적임자라고 생각해. ⓐ내가 그 애한테 전화해서 내일 시간이 있는지 확인해 볼까?
남: ⓑ그거 좋겠다. 고마워.

문제 풀이

ⓐTom에게 전화해서 내일 시간이 있는지 확인해 주길 원하는지 묻는 여자의 질문에 남자가 ⓑ그렇게 해 주면 좋겠다고 했으므로, 여자의 할 일로 ①이 가장 적절하다.

6. ② | 금액

선택지 선택비율	① 18%	② 53%	③ 9%	④ 6%	⑤ 12%

M: Hello. How can I help you?
W: Hi, I'd like to make a reservation for a rafting trip this Sunday.
M: Lovely. We have two options. ⓐA full-day trip costs $100, and a half-day trip costs $40. ⓑChildren under 10 are half price.
반값
W: All right. Do the prices include lunch?
포함하다
M: Only a full-day trip includes a riverside barbecue lunch.
강가의
W: Okay, then ⓒI'd like to book a full-day trip for two adults and one eight-year-old child.
M: Beautiful! A full-day trip for two adults and one child.
W: That's right. Can I use this coupon from your website?
M: Sure. ⓓWith this coupon, you get 10 percent off the total price.
W: Great! I'll pay in cash.
현금으로

해석

남: 안녕하세요. 무엇을 도와드릴까요?
여: 안녕하세요, 저는 이번 주 일요일에 래프팅 여행을 예약하고 싶어요.
남: 좋아요. 두 가지 선택 사항이 있습니다. ⓐ전일 여행 비용은 100달러이고 반일 여행 비용은 40달러입니다. ⓑ10세 미만의 어린이는 반값입니다.
여: 좋아요. 가격에 점심도 포함되어 있나요?
남: 전일 여행에만 강가의 바비큐 점심이 포함되어 있습니다.
여: 알겠어요, 그러면 ⓒ어른 두 명과 8세 어린이 한 명의 전일 여행을 예약하고 싶습니다.
남: 좋아요! 어른 두 명과 아이 한 명의 전일 여행이요.
여: 맞아요. 웹사이트에서 받은 이 쿠폰을 사용할 수 있나요?
남: 물론이죠. ⓓ이 쿠폰으로 전체 가격에서 10퍼센트 할인을 받으세요.
여: 좋아요! 현금으로 계산할게요.

문제 풀이

ⓐ전일 여행 비용은 100달러이며 ⓑ10세 미만의 어린이는 반값($50)인데, 여자는 ⓒ어른 두 명과 8세 어린이 한 명의 전일 여행을 예약하겠다고 했으며 ⓓ쿠폰으로 전체 금액의 10퍼센트 할인을 받을 수 있으므로, 여자가 지불할 금액은 {(100x2)+50}x0.9=225달러이다.

7. ⑤ | 이유

선택지 선택비율	① 2%	② 1%	③ 1%	④ 1%	⑤ 95%

W: Hey, Jake! How was your math test yesterday?
M: Better than I expected.
예상하다
W: That's great. Let's go and practice for Sports Day.
연습
M: I'm so sorry but I can't make it.
W: Come on, Jake! Sports Day is just around the corner.
임박하여
M: I know. That's why I brought my soccer shoes.
W: Then, why can't you practice today? Do you have a club interview?
M: No, I already had the interview last week.
W: Then, does your leg still hurt?
아프다

M: Not really, it's okay, now. Actually, I have to attend a family dinner
참석하다
gathering tonight for my mother's birthday.
W: Oh, that's important! Family always comes first. Are you available tomorrow, then?
M: Sure. Let's make up for the missed practice.
보충하다

해석

여: 안녕, Jake! 어제 수학 시험 어땠어?
남: 예상한 것보다 더 잘 봤어.
여: 잘됐네. 우리 가서 체육 대회 연습하자.
남: 정말 미안하지만 나는 못 가.
여: Jake, 왜 그래! 체육 대회가 코앞이잖아.
남: 알아. 그래서 축구화도 챙겨왔어.
여: 그럼, 왜 오늘 연습 못 해? 동아리 면접 있어?
남: 아니, 면접은 지난주에 이미 봤어.
여: 그럼, 다리가 아직 아프니?
남: 아니, 이제 괜찮아. 사실 어머니 생신 때문에 오늘 저녁에 가족 저녁 식사 모임에 참석해야 해.
여: 아, 그거 중요하지! 가족이 항상 가장 먼저니까. 그럼 내일은 시간 되니?
남: 물론이지. 놓친 연습을 보충하자.

문제 풀이

남자는 오늘 어머니 생신을 맞아 가족 저녁 식사 모임에 참석해야 해서 체육 대회 연습을 할 수 없다고 했다.

8. ③ | 언급

선택지 선택비율	① 2%	② 3%	③ 90%	④ 3%	⑤ 3%

W: What are you doing, Tim?
M: I'm looking at the Street Photography Contest website.
사진술
W: I've heard about that. It's a contest for college students, right?
대학(교)
M: Actually, ⓐit's open to high school students, too. Why don't you try it?
W: Really? Maybe I will. Does the contest have a theme?
주제
M: Sure. ⓑThis year's theme is Daily Life.
일상생활
W: That sounds interesting. When is the deadline?
기한, 마감 시간[일자]
M: ⓒYou have to submit your photographs by September 15.
제출하다
W: That's sooner than I expected.
M: You should hurry and choose your photos. ⓓThe winner will receive
받다
a laptop as a prize.
노트북 컴퓨터 상, 상품
W: Okay! Wish me luck.

해석

여: 뭐 하는 중이야, Tim?
남: 길거리 사진 대회 웹사이트를 보고 있는 중이야.
여: 그것에 대해 들어봤어. 대학생들을 위한 대회잖아, 맞지?
남: 사실 ⓐ고등학생들도 참여 가능해. 너 한번 해보는 게 어때?
여: 정말? 한번 해볼까 싶네. 대회에 주제가 있니?
남: 응. ⓑ올해의 주제는 '일상생활'이야.
여: 재미있을 것 같아. 마감일이 언제니?
남: ⓒ9월 15일까지 사진을 제출해야 해.
여: 예상보다 이르네.
남: 서둘러서 사진을 골라야 해. ⓓ우승자는 노트북 컴퓨터를 상품으로 받을 거야.
여: 좋아! 행운을 빌어줘.

문제 풀이

ⓐ참가 대상, ⓑ주제, ⓒ제출 마감일, ⓓ우승 상품은 언급되었지만, 심사 기준은 언급되지 않았다.

코드+α 기원을 나타내는 표현

Best wish for a successful new year. (성공적인 새해를 기원합니다.)
I wish you all the best. (모두 잘 되길 바랍니다.)
Wish me luck. (내게 행운을 빌어줘.)
I'll cross my fingers for you. (행운을 빌게.)

9. ③ | 내용 일치

선택지 선택비율	① 6%	② 2%	③ 82%	④ 6%	⑤ 1%

W: Good morning, Central High School. This is Kathy Miller, the school librarian. ⓐIn order to celebrate this year's reading month, our
사서 기념하다
school is going to hold a Book Review Contest. ⓑAll students are invited to participate in the contest. ⓒYou can write a review on any
~에 참여하다 논평, 독후감
type of book, but the review must be your own original work. You
고유의, 독창적인
can download a form from our school website. ⓓReviews should be submitted through e-mail by the end of this month. ⓔThe best three works will be selected and published in our school magazine.
선정하다 게재하다
For more details, please visit the school website. Thank you.
세부 사항

해석

여: 안녕하세요, Central 고등학교 학생 여러분. 저는 학교 사서인 Kathy Miller입니다. ⓐ올해 독서의 달을 기념하기 위해, 우리 학교는 독후감 대회를 개최할 예정입니다. ⓑ모든 학생 여러분은 대회에 참여하도록 초대됩니다. ⓒ여러분은 어떤 종류의 책에 대해서든 독후감을 써도 되지만, 그 독후감은 반드시 여러분 본인의 독창적인 글이어야 합니다. 여러분은 학교 웹사이트에서 양식을 다운로드할 수 있습니다. ⓓ독후감은 이달 말까지 이메일로 제출되어야 합니다. ⓔ우수작 세 편이 선정되어 우리 학교 잡지에 게재될 것입니다. 더 많은 세부 사항을 위해서는, 학교 웹사이트를 방문해 주세요. 감사합니다.

문제 풀이

ⓒ어떤 종류의 책에 대해서든 독후감을 써도 된다고 했다.

10. ③ | 도표

선택지 선택비율	① 3%	② 6%	③ 86%	④ 2%	⑤ 3%

W: Ben, do you have a minute?
M: Sure. What is it?
W: I'm trying to buy a handheld vacuum cleaner among these five
소형 진공청소기
models. Could you help me choose one?
M: Okay. How much are you willing to spend?
be willing to-v: 흔쾌히 ~하다
W: ⓐNo more than $130.
M: Then we can cross this one out. What about the working time?
줄을 그어 ~을 지우다
W: ⓑI think it should be longer than 10 minutes.
M: Then that narrows it down to these three.
~을 좁히다
W: Should I go with one of the lighter ones?
~을 선택하다

M: Yes. ⓒLighter ones are easier to handle while cleaning.
다루다

W: All right. What about the filter?
M: ⓓThe one with a washable filter would be a better choice.
씻을 수 있는

W: I got it. Then I'll order this one.
주문하다

해석

여: Ben, 너 시간 좀 있니?
남: 응. 그게 뭐야?
여: 이 다섯 가지 모델 중에서 소형 진공청소기를 사려고 해. 하나 고르는 것 좀 도와줄래?
남: 좋아. 얼마를 쓸 의향이 있니?
여: ⓐ130달러 넘게는 아니야.
남: 그럼 이걸 지울 수 있겠다. 작동 시간은?
여: ⓑ10분 보다는 더 길어야 할 것 같아.
남: 그러면 이 세 가지로 좁혀지네.
여: 가벼운 것들 중 하나를 선택해야 할까?
남: 응. ⓒ가벼운 것이 청소할 때 다루기 더 쉬워.
여: 알겠어. 필터는?
남: ⓓ씻을 수 있는 필터가 있는 게 더 좋은 선택일 거야.
여: 알겠어. 그럼 이걸로 주문할게.

문제 풀이

여자는 ⓐ130달러가 넘지 않고 ⓑ10분 넘게 작동되는 ⓒ가볍고 ⓓ필터를 씻을 수 있는 소형 진공청소기를 주문하기로 했다.

11. ② | 짧은 대화 응답

선택지 선택비율	① 5%	② 89%	③ 1%	④ 2%	⑤ 1%

M: This restaurant looks great. Have you been here before?
W: Yeah, it's one of my favorite restaurants. Let's see the menu.
M: Everything looks so good. Can you recommend anything?
권하다, 추천하다

W: Sure. The onion soup is great here.

해석

남: 이 식당 좋아 보인다. 너 전에 여기 와본 적 있니?
여: 응, 내가 가장 좋아하는 식당들 중 한 곳이야. 메뉴를 봐 보자.
남: 다 정말 좋아 보여. 뭐 좀 추천해 줄래?
여: 물론이지. 여기는 양파 수프가 훌륭해.

문제 풀이

여자가 좋아하는 식당에서 남자가 여자에게 메뉴를 추천해 달라고 했으므로, 메뉴를 추천해 주는 ②가 응답으로 가장 적절하다.
① 괜찮아. 나는 이미 배불러.
③ 모르겠어. 나는 전에 여기에 와본 적이 없어.
④ 응. 나는 네가 그곳에 제시간에 가기를 권해.
⑤ 좋아. 멕시코 식당으로 가자.

12. ⑤ | 짧은 대화 응답

선택지 선택비율	① 1%	② 1%	③ 1%	④ 21%	⑤ 73%

W: Honey, ⓐwe can't eat out tomorrow evening.
외식하다

M: Why not? ⓑI've already booked a table at the restaurant.
W: I'm sorry. ⓒI have an important business meeting at that time.
M: Sorry to hear that. I'll cancel the reservation now.
취소하다 예약

해석

여: 여보, ⓐ우리 내일 저녁에 외식 못하겠어요.
남: 왜요? ⓑ이미 식당에 테이블을 예약했는데요.
여: 미안해요. ⓒ그때 중요한 업무 회의가 있어요.
남: 유감이네요. 지금 예약을 취소할게요.

문제 풀이

남자가 ⓑ이미 식당 예약을 했으나 여자는 ⓐⓒ중요한 업무 회의가 있어 외식을 하지 못한다고 했으므로, 유감이지만 예약을 취소하겠다는 ⑤가 응답으로 가장 적절하다.
① 괜찮아요. 충분히 먹었어요.
② 좋아요. 여섯 시에 다섯 명으로 예약할게요.
③ 좋은 선택이에요. 그 음식은 훌륭해요.
④ 알겠어요. 회의 장소와 시간을 정할게요.

13. ② | 긴 대화 응답

선택지 선택비율	① 14%	② 77%	③ 1%	④ 2%	⑤ 2%

W: Hey, Minho. What are you doing?
M: Hi, Mrs. Sharon. I'm writing an application letter for college.
지원서

W: Can I take a look at it?
M: Of course. Please give me some advice after you're finished reading it.
W: Hmm.... ⓐYou only listed the activities you've done without being specific.
열거하다 구체적인

M: Yeah. Isn't it good to include as many activities as possible?
W: No. If you do that, your application letter won't be memorable.
기억할 만한, 인상적인

M: But I thought if I wrote down a lot of activities, I would stand out.
눈에 띄다

W: It's actually the opposite. ⓑYou should focus on a few things and write about them in detail.
반대의 ~에 집중하다 상세하게

M: I never thought about that. Do you really think it'll work?
W: Of course. The more specific, the better.

해석

여: 얘, 민호야. 너 뭐 하고 있니?
남: 안녕하세요, Sharon 선생님. 대학 입학 지원서를 쓰고 있어요.
여: 내가 좀 봐도 될까?
남: 물론이죠. 다 읽으시면 제게 조언을 좀 주세요.
여: 음…. ⓐ너는 네가 한 활동들에 대해 구체적이지 않게 열거만 했구나.
남: 네. 가능한 한 많은 활동들을 포함시키는 게 좋지 않나요?
여: 아니야. 그렇게 하면, 네 지원서는 인상적이지 않을 거야.
남: 하지만 저는 많은 활동들을 적으면, 제가 눈에 띌 것이라고 생각했어요.
여: 사실은 반대란다. ⓑ몇몇 활동들에 집중해서 그것들에 대해 상세하게 적어야 해.
남: 그건 전혀 생각하지 못했어요. 정말 그것이 효과가 있을 거라고 생각하세요?
여: 물론이지. 더 구체적일수록, 더 좋단다.

문제 풀이

여자는 남자에게 대학 입학 지원서를 쓸 때, ⓐ자신이 한 활동에 대해 열거만 하는 게 아니라 ⓑ그것들에 대해 상세하게 적어야 한다고 조언하고 있으므로, 더 구체적일수록 더 좋다는 ②가 응답으로 가장 적절하다.
① 물론이지. 가능한 한 많은 활동들을 적으렴.
③ 고마워. 하지만 이번에는 내 방식대로 할게.
④ 훌륭해. 네가 마침내 대학에 합격했구나.
⑤ 맞아. 선착순이란다.

14. ① | 긴 대화 응답

선택지 선택비율	① 84%	② 3%	③ 3%	④ 7%	⑤ 4%

W: Kevin, what are you writing about?
M: Hi, Eva. I'm writing about the money-saving challenge I completed.
완료하다, 끝마치다
W: The money-saving challenge? What's that?
M: ⓐIt's a challenge where you try to reduce your spending and do not
줄이다
buy unnecessary things for a set time. I did it for a month.
불필요한
W: Really? Wasn't it so hard?
M: Not that much. I spent money on things I really needed.
W: Why did you decide to do that?
M: At first, it was just to save money. But ⓑit also made me realize that
깨닫다
I have wasted money on too many extra things.
필요 이상의
W: Oh, I see. So it's about cutting out unnecessary spending?
~을 그만두다
M: Exactly. And I found free ways to have fun. For example, cooking more at home, instead of eating out!
외식하다
W: That sounds difficult but rewarding. ⓒI'll do the same!
보람 있는
M: Good decision. I'm sure you'll do a good job.

해석

여: Kevin, 너 뭐에 대해 쓰고 있어?
남: 안녕, Eva. 내가 끝마친 돈 절약 챌린지에 대해 쓰고 있는 중이야.
여: 돈 절약 챌린지? 그게 뭐야?
남: ⓐ일정 기간 동안 지출을 줄이고 불필요한 것들을 사지 않도록 노력하는 챌린지야. 나는 한 달 동안 했어.
여: 정말? 엄청 힘들지 않았어?
남: 그렇게 힘들진 않았어. 내가 정말 필요한 것들에 돈을 썼거든.
여: 왜 그걸 하기로 한 거야?
남: 처음에는 그저 돈을 아끼기 위해서였어. 그런데 ⓑ그 덕분에 내가 너무 많은 필요 이상의 것들에 돈을 낭비해 왔다는 것도 깨닫게 되었지.
여: 아, 그렇구나. 그러니까 불필요한 지출을 그만두는 거네?
남: 맞아. 그리고 돈 안 들이고 즐길 방법들을 찾았어. 예를 들어, 외식 대신 집에서 요리를 더 많이 하는 거지!
여: 어렵지만 보람 있겠다. ⓒ나도 그렇게 해봐야겠다!
남: 좋은 결심이야. 너는 분명 잘할 수 있을 거야.

문제 풀이

남자가 ⓐ한 달 동안 지출을 줄이고 불필요한 것들을 사지 않는 돈 절약 챌린지를 함으로써 ⓑ자신이 필요 이상의 것들에 돈을 낭비했음을 깨닫게 되었다고 하자 여자도 ⓒ그렇게 해봐야겠다고 했으므로, 이 결심을 지지하며 격려하는 ①이 응답으로 가장 적절하다.
② 그래. 공간을 더 만들기 위해 주방 식탁을 치우자.
③ 나는 그렇게 생각하지 않아. 나는 그런 일을 절대 할 수 없어.
④ 맞아. 너는 차라리 돈을 더 벌기 위해 더 열심히 일하는 게 나아.
⑤ 절대 안 돼. 네 평소 소비 습관을 고수해야 해.

15. ① | 상황에 적절한 말

선택지 선택비율	① 81%	② 9%	③ 3%	④ 3%	⑤ 3%

M: Julia is a college student, living in the dormitory. Recently, she
기숙사
ordered a new computer desk. Upon receiving the desk, she
주문하다 / upon v-ing: ~하자마자 곧
realized that the desk was a DIY product. It means she needs to put
제품 / put ~ together: ~을 조립하다
the pieces together to build the desk. However, it was complicated
조각, 부품 / 복잡한
to assemble it by herself. Julia knows that Sophie, her best friend,
조립하다
is good at assembling DIY furniture and enjoys it. So, Julia wants to
가구
ask Sophie to help her with the desk. In this situation, what would Julia most likely say to Sophie?
Julia: Could you help me assemble my desk?

해석

남: Julia는 기숙사에 사는 대학생이다. 최근에 그녀는 새로운 컴퓨터 책상을 주문했다. 책상을 받자마자 곧, 그녀는 그 책상이 DIY 제품이라는 것을 깨달았다. 이는 그녀가 부품을 조립해서 책상을 만들어야 한다는 뜻이다. 하지만 그녀 혼자 그것을 조립하기에는 복잡했다. Julia는 자신의 가장 친한 친구인 Sophie가 DIY 가구 조립을 잘하고 그걸 즐긴다는 것을 알고 있다. 그래서 Julia는 Sophie에게 책상 조립을 도와달라고 부탁하고 싶어 한다. 이 상황에서, Julia는 Sophie에게 뭐라고 말하겠는가?
Julia: 내가 책상 조립하는 걸 도와줄 수 있니?

문제 풀이

Julia는 Sophie에게 책상 조립하는 것을 도와달라고 부탁하고 싶어 하므로, Julia가 Sophie에게 할 말로 ①이 가장 적절하다.
② 네 책상을 어디서 샀는지 공유해줄 수 있니?
③ 함께 새 컴퓨터를 고르는 게 어때?
④ 가구를 네가 직접 수리하는 게 어때?
⑤ 내 방을 꾸밀 아이디어가 있니?

16~17. | 세트 문항

16. ① 17. ④

선택지 선택비율	① 87%	② 5%	③ 3%	④ 3%	⑤ 2%
	① 1%	② 1%	③ 1%	④ 96%	⑤ 1%

M: Hello, students. Last class, we took a brief look at how to tune your
조율하다
musical instruments. Today, ⓐwe're going to talk a bit about how to
악기
take care of and maintain your instruments. First, let's take ⓑflutes.
유지하다 / 악기
They may have moisture from the air blown through them, so you
습기
should clean and wipe the mouth piece before and after playing.
닦다
Next are ⓒtrumpets. They can be taken apart, so you should air dry
take apart: ~을 분해하다 / 공기[자연] 건조하다
the parts in a cool dry place, away from direct sunlight. And as for
직사광선
ⓓpianos, they don't need everyday care, but it's essential to protect
필수적인
the keys by covering them with a protective pad when not in use.
건반
The last ones are string instruments like ⓔguitars. Their strings
현악기 / 현
need replacement. When you replace the strings, it's good to do it
교체 / 교체하다
gradually, one at a time. Proper care can lengthen the lifespan of
점차적으로 / 길게 하다, 늘이다 / 수명
your musical instruments. I hope this lesson helps you to keep your musical instruments safe from damage.
손상

해석

남: 안녕하세요, 학생 여러분. 지난 시간에는 악기를 조율하는 방법에 대해 간략하게 살펴보았습니다. 오늘은 ⓐ악기 관리와 유지 방법에 대해 이야기를 조금 나누어 보겠습니다. 먼저, ⓑ플루트를 예로 들어 봅시다. 그것을 통과하여 부는 공기로 인한 습기가 있을 수 있기 때문에, 연주 전후에 마우스피스를 청소하고 닦아야 합니다. 다음은 ⓒ트럼펫입니다. 그것은 분해될 수 있으니, 직사광선을 피해 시원하고 건조한 장소에서 부품들을 자연 건조해야 합니다. 그리고 ⓓ피아노에 관해 말하자면, 매일 관리할 필요는 없지만, 사용하지 않을 때는 보호 패드로 덮어 건반을 보호하는 것이 필수적입니다. 마지막은 ⓔ기타와 같은 현악기입니다. 그것들의 현은 교체가 필요합니다. 현을 교체할 때

는, 한 번에 하나씩 점차적으로 하는 것이 좋습니다. 적절한 관리는 악기의 수명을 늘릴 수 있습니다. 이 수업이 여러분이 악기를 손상으로부터 안전하게 지키는 데 도움이 되기를 바랍니다.

문제 풀이

16. ⓐ악기 관리와 유지 방법에 대해 이야기를 나누어 보겠다고 했으므로, 주제는 ① '악기 관리를 위한 조언'이 가장 적절하다.
② 좋은 악기를 고르는 방법
③ 악기에 미치는 날씨의 영향
④ 어렸을 때 악기를 배우는 것의 이점
⑤ 자신만의 악기를 만드는 것의 어려움

17. ⓑ플루트, ⓒ트럼펫, ⓓ피아노, ⓔ기타는 언급되었으나, 드럼(drums)은 언급되지 않았다.

[코드 공략하기]

제8회 초급 모의고사

1	③	2	⑤	3	①	4	④	5	②	6	③
7	①	8	③	9	⑤	10	③	11	①	12	⑤
13	①	14	⑤	15	①	16	⑤	17	③		

1. ③ ㅣ 목적

선택지 선택비율	① 2%	② 1%	③ 90%	④ 6%	⑤ 2%

W: Hello! I'm Olivia Parker from Pineview City Subway. I have an announcement(발표, 안내) for this Saturday's fireworks(불꽃놀이) festival. Many people are expected to visit and enjoy the festival late into the night. For smooth(원활한) transportation(교통) and visitor safety(안전), we're extending(연장하다) the operational(가동[운영]상의) hours of the subway on the day of the festival. The subway will run for an extra(추가의) two hours after the regular(평상시의) last train from the festival area stations(역). For a comfortable(편안한) and safe journey from the event, we encourage(권장하다, 장려하다) you to take advantage of(이용하다) our extended subway services. We hope you enjoy this fantastic festival with convenience(편리). Thank you!

해석

여: 안녕하세요! 저는 Pineview 도시 지하철의 Olivia Parker입니다. 이번 주 토요일 불꽃놀이 축제에 관한 안내가 있습니다. 많은 사람들이 방문해 밤늦게까지 축제를 즐길 것으로 예상됩니다. 원활한 교통과 방문객 안전을 위해, 축제 당일에 지하철 운행 시간을 연장할 예정입니다. 축제 지역 역에서는 평소 마지막 열차 이후 추가 2시간 동안 지하철이 운행할 예정입니다. 행사 후 편안하고 안전한 귀가를 위해, 연장된 지하철 서비스를 이용하시길 권장합니다. 이 멋진 축제를 편리하게 즐기시기 바랍니다. 감사합니다!

문제 풀이

불꽃놀이 축제 당일의 지하철 운행 시간 연장에 관해 안내하고 있다.

2. ⑤ ㅣ 의견

선택지 선택비율	① 2%	② 2%	③ 3%	④ 3%	⑤ 91%

W: Honey, are you okay?
M: I'm afraid I've caught a cold. I've got a sore throat.
W: Why don't you go see a doctor?
M: Well, I don't think it's necessary(필요한). I've found some medicine in the cabinet(보관장). I'll take it.
W: You shouldn't take that medicine. That's what I got prescribed(처방을 내리다) last week.
M: My symptoms(증상) are similar(비슷한) to yours.
W: Honey, ⓐyou shouldn't take medicine prescribed for others.
M: It's just a cold. I'll get better if I take your medicine.
W: ⓑIt could be dangerous(위험한) to take someone else's prescription(처방전, 처방된 약).
M: Okay. Then I'll go see a doctor this afternoon.

해석

여: 여보, 괜찮아요?
남: 감기에 걸린 것 같아요. 목이 아프네요.
여: 병원에 가보는 게 어때요?
남: 음, 그럴 필요는 없을 것 같아요. 보관장에서 약을 발견했어요. 그걸 먹어야겠어요.
여: 그 약은 먹으면 안 돼요. 그건 지난주에 내가 처방받은 거예요.
남: 내 증상이 당신의 증상과 비슷해요
여: 여보, ⓐ다른 사람에게 처방된 약을 복용하면 안 돼요.
남: 그냥 감기일 뿐인걸요. 당신의 약을 먹으면 나아질 거예요.
여: ⓑ다른 사람의 처방약을 먹으면 위험할 수 있어요.
남: 알았어요. 그럼 오늘 오후에 병원에 가보도록 할게요.

문제 풀이

여자는 ⓑ다른 사람에게 처방된 약을 먹으면 위험할 수 있기에 ⓐ복용하면 안 된다고 말하고 있다.

코드+α 제안·권유 표현

I think you should go see a doctor. (너 병원에 가봐야 할 것 같아.)
How about getting some rest? (좀 쉬는 게 어때?)
Why don't you join the volunteer club? (자원봉사 동아리에 가입하는 게 어때?)

3. ① | 관계

선택지 선택비율	① 88%	② 2%	③ 3%	④ 2%	⑤ 2%

[Telephone rings.]
W: Hello. This is Monica Jones.
M: Hello. ⓐThis is John Lewis, Sally's father.
W: Hello, Mr. Lewis. Has Sally gotten any better?
M: Yes. She doesn't have a high fever anymore. (fever: 열)
W: Glad to hear that.
M: But the doctor said that Sally needs to stay home this week.
W: I see. ⓑDo you think she'll come to school next Monday?
M: I think so. But, Sally's worried that she won't be able to submit her school newspaper article on time. (submit: 제출하다)
W: Oh, ⓒplease tell her not to worry about it. The newspaper editor is also taking my class, so I'll talk to him. (editor: 편집장, 편집자)
M: Thank you so much.

해석

[전화벨이 울린다.]
여: 여보세요. Monica Jones입니다.
남: 안녕하세요. ⓐSally의 아버지인 John Lewis입니다.
여: 안녕하세요, Lewis 씨. Sally는 좀 나아졌나요?
남: 네. 더 이상 고열은 나지 않습니다.
여: 그 말을 들으니 기쁘네요.
남: 하지만 의사 선생님께서 Sally가 이번 주는 집에 있어야 한다고 말씀하셨어요.
여: 알겠습니다. ⓑ그녀가 다음 주 월요일에는 등교할 것 같으세요?
남: 그럴 것 같아요. 그런데 Sally가 제 시간에 학교 신문 기사를 제출할 수 없을 것 같아 걱정하고 있습니다.
여: 아, ⓒ그것에 대해서는 걱정하지 말라고 말해 주세요. 신문 편집장도 제 수업을 듣고 있으니, 제가 그 애에게 말할게요.
남: 정말 감사합니다.

문제 풀이

남자가 여자에게 전화를 걸어 ⓐSally의 아버지라고 말하고, 여자는 ⓑSally가 언제 등교할지와 ⓒ학교 신문 기사 제출 문제에 대해 이야기하는 것으로 보아 두 사람의 관계가 교사와 학부모임을 알 수 있다.

4. ④ | 그림 일치

선택지 선택비율	① 9%	② 13%	③ 3%	④ 69%	⑤ 4%

M: Grace, let me show you my newly designed room.
W: Wow, Jake! It's so cool.
M: Look at ⓐthe monitor between the speakers. I changed my old monitor for this new one.
W: Looks nice. But ⓑisn't your desk too crowded to put your electric keyboard on it? (crowded: 복잡한)
M: It's fine with me. I find it convenient there. (convenient: 편리한)
W: ⓒIs that a microphone in the corner? Do you sing?
M: Yes. Singing is my all-time favorite hobby. (all-time: 불변의)
W: What's ⓓthat star-shaped medal on the wall? Where did you get it?
M: I won that medal at a guitar contest with my dad.
W: Incredible! Do you often practice the guitar with your dad? (Incredible: 믿기 힘든)
M: Sure. That's why ⓔthere're two guitars in the room.

해석

남: Grace, 새롭게 디자인한 내 방 보여줄게.
여: 우와, Jake! 정말 멋지다.
남: ⓐ스피커 사이에 있는 모니터를 봐. 오래된 모니터를 이 새것으로 바꿨어.
여: 좋아 보여. 하지만 ⓑ위에 전자 건반을 놓기에는 책상이 너무 복잡하지 않니?
남: 나는 괜찮아. 거기가 편리해.
여: ⓒ모퉁이에 저건 마이크니? 너 노래해?
남: 응. 노래 부르는 건 내 변하지 않는 가장 좋아하는 취미야.
여: ⓓ벽에 저 별 모양 메달은 뭐니? 어디서 땄니?
남: 아빠와 함께 기타 경연대회에서 저 메달을 땄어.
여: 믿어지지 않아! 아빠와 기타 연습을 자주 하니?
남: 그럼. 그래서 ⓔ방에 기타가 두 개 있잖아.

문제 풀이

ⓓ벽에 메달은 별 모양이라고 했다.

5. ② | 할 일

선택지 선택비율	① 4%	② 92%	③ 1%	④ 2%	⑤ 1%

W: Brian, I think we're almost ready for our candy shop's opening event.
M: That's right. What do we have left to do?
W: Well, let's see. Is the background music playlist ready? (background: 배경)
M: Yes, I chose some cheerful songs and made a playlist. (cheerful: 즐거운, 밝은)
W: Great! What about the bluetooth speakers?
M: I tested them and they're working fine. Did you choose the sample candies for customers to try? (customers: 손님)
W: Yeah. Look! I put them in these pretty little baskets.
M: Thanks! They look nice.
W: And all the other candies are nicely placed around the shop. (placed: 놓다, 배열하다)
M: Wait, ⓐhow about the price tags? (price tags: 가격표)
W: Oh, we almost forgot. ⓑCould you put them on the candy boxes?
M: Of course. ⓒI'll do it right away.

해석

여: Brian, 우리 사탕 가게 개점 행사 준비가 거의 다 된 것 같아요.
남: 그래요. 이제 할 게 뭐가 남았죠?
여: 음, 볼게요. 배경 음악 재생 목록은 준비됐어요?
남: 네, 밝은 노래들을 몇 곡 골라서 재생 목록을 만들었어요.

여: 좋아요! 그럼 블루투스 스피커는요?
남: 그것들을 점검해봤는데 잘 작동해요. 손님들이 맛볼 수 있는 시식용 사탕은 골랐어요?
여: 네. 봐요! 이 예쁜 작은 바구니들에 넣어두었어요.
남: 고마워요! 좋아 보이네요.
여: 그리고 다른 사탕들은 전부 가게 곳곳에 잘 놓여 있어요.
남: 잠시만요, ⓐ가격표는요?
여: 아, 잊을 뻔했네요. ⓑ그것들을 사탕 상자 위에 붙여줄래요?
남: 물론이죠. ⓒ제가 지금 바로 할게요.

문제 풀이

사탕 가게 개점 행사 준비 상황을 점검하던 중 남자가 ⓐ가격표에 대해 묻자, 여자가 잊을 뻔했다며 ⓑ가격표를 사탕 상자 위에 붙여 달라고 부탁했고, 남자가 ⓒ지금 바로 하겠다고 답했다.

6. ③ | 금액

선택지 선택비율	① 6%	② 3%	③ 84%	④ 4%	⑤ 3%

M: Good morning! How can I help you?
W: Hi. I'm looking for a blanket(담요) and some cushions for my sofa.
M: Okay. We've got some on sale. Would you like to have a look?
W: Yes. How much is this green blanket?
M: ⓐThat's $40.
W: Oh, I love the color green. Can you also show me some cushions that go well with(~와 잘 어울리다) this blanket?
M: Sure! How about these?
W: They look good. I need two of them. How much are they?
M: ⓑThe cushions are $20 each.
W: Okay. ⓒI'll take one green blanket and two cushions. Can I use this coupon?
M: Sure. ⓓIt will give you 10% off the total.
W: Thanks! Here's my credit card.

해석

남: 좋은 아침입니다! 무엇을 도와드릴까요?
여: 안녕하세요. 담요와 소파 쿠션을 좀 찾고 있는데요.
남: 네. 일부는 지금 할인 중이에요. 한번 보시겠어요?
여: 네. 이 초록색 담요는 얼마인가요?
남: ⓐ40달러입니다.
여: 아, 저는 초록색이 정말 좋아요. 이 담요와 잘 어울리는 쿠션도 좀 보여주시겠어요?
남: 네! 이것들은 어떠세요?
여: 좋아 보이네요. 두 개가 필요해요. 얼마인가요?
남: ⓑ쿠션은 한 개에 20달러입니다.
여: 알겠습니다. ⓒ초록색 담요 하나랑 쿠션 두 개 살게요. 이 쿠폰 사용 가능한가요?
남: 네. ⓓ총액에서 10% 할인해 드립니다.
여: 감사합니다! 여기 제 신용카드요.

문제 풀이

여자는 ⓐⓒ40달러짜리 담요 하나와 ⓑⓒ20달러짜리 쿠션 두 개를 구매하기로 했는데, ⓓ총액에서 10% 할인을 받았으므로 72달러를 지불하면 된다.

7. ① | 이유

선택지 선택비율	① 82%	② 2%	③ 9%	④ 3%	⑤ 1%

W: David, have you handed in(~을 제출하다) the science assignment(과제)?
M: Yes, I'm happy that I finally finished it! By the way, are you going to Jamie's farewell party(송별회) tonight?
W: Yes, I am. It's so sad that she is moving that far away. You're coming, too, right?
M: I really wish I could, but I need to go home early today.
W: Why do you need to go home early?
M: My grandfather is in the hospital, and my parents are going to visit him tonight.
W: I'm sorry to hear that. Do you have to go, too?
M: No, ⓐmy little brother will be at home alone, so I have to babysit(아이를 봐주다) him.
W: I see. You will take care of him.
M: Yes. ⓑCan you please give this present to Jamie and tell her that I'm sorry I have to miss her party?
W: No problem. I'm sure she'll understand your situation.

해석

여: David, 과학 과제를 제출했니?
남: 응, 마침내 끝내서 행복해! 그나저나 너는 오늘 밤에 Jamie의 송별회에 가니?
여: 응. 그녀가 그렇게 멀리 이사해서 슬퍼. 너도 오는 거지?
남: 정말 가고 싶지만 오늘 집에 일찍 가야 해.
여: 왜 집에 일찍 가야 하니?
남: 우리 할아버지가 병원에 있으셔서 부모님이 오늘 밤에 그에게 병문안을 가실 거야.
여: 그렇다니 안됐구나. 너도 가야 하는 거야?
남: 아니, ⓐ남동생이 집에 혼자 있을 거라서 내가 그 애를 봐야 해.
여: 그렇구나. 네가 그를 돌보겠구나.
남: 응. ⓑJamie에게 이 선물을 주면서 그녀의 송별회에 빠져야 해서 미안하다고 전해줄 수 있니?
여: 문제없어. 그녀는 분명히 네 상황을 이해할 거야.

문제 풀이

남자는 ⓐ집에 혼자 있을 남동생을 돌봐야 해서 여자에게 ⓑ송별회에 빠져서 미안하다는 말을 선물과 함께 Jamie에게 전해달라고 했다.

8. ③ | 언급

선택지 선택비율	① 4%	② 3%	③ 87%	④ 2%	⑤ 2%

W: Hey, Sam. Have you heard about the Mind-Up Program?
M: No, I haven't. What is it?
W: It's a program for high school students. ⓐIts purpose(목적) is to encourage us to build a positive mindset(사고방식, 태도). You should come.
M: It sounds interesting. Please tell me more about it.
W: There will be a lot of activities to help relieve((불쾌감·고통 등을) 없애[덜어] 주다) stress. Also, we'll get to listen to ⓑspecial lectures from successful young CEOs.
M: Awesome! I should sign up(참가하다, ~에 등록하다). When is it?
W: This Friday. ⓒIt starts at 6 p.m.
M: Cool. ⓓHow much is the admission fee(입장료)?
W: ⓔIt's free for all students. You can apply for(~에 지원하다) the program on our school website.
M: Great. I'll do it now.

해석

여: 얘, Sam. 마인드업 프로그램에 대해 들어본 적 있니?
남: 아니, 없어. 그게 뭔데?
여: 그것은 고등학생들을 위한 프로그램이야. ⓐ그것의 목적은 우리가 긍정적인 사고방식을 키울 수 있도록 장려하는 거야. 네가 와야 해.
남: 재미있겠다. 그것에 대해 내게 더 말해 줘.
여: 스트레스를 없애는 데 도움이 되는 많은 활동들이 있을 거야. 또, 우리는 ⓑ성공한 젊은 CEO들의 특강을 듣게 될 거야.
남: 굉장한데! 나 참가해야겠어. 언제야?
여: 이번 주 금요일. ⓒ오후 6시에 시작해.

남: 좋아. ⓓ입장료는 얼마니?
여: ⓔ모든 학생들에게 무료야. 우리 학교 웹사이트에서 그 프로그램에 지원할 수 있어.
남: 좋아. 나 지금 할래.

문제 풀이

마인드업 프로그램의 ⓐ목적, ⓑ특별 강연, ⓒ시작 시간, ⓓⓔ입장료는 언급되었으나, 개최 장소에 대한 언급은 없다.

9. ⑤ | 내용 일치

선택지 선택비율	① 2%	② 2%	③ 3%	④ 3%	⑤ 91%

M: Hello, River Valley High School students. This is your music teacher, Mr. Stailor. ⓐStarting on April 11, we are going to have the River Valley Music Camp for five days. ⓑYou don't need to be a member of the school orchestra(오케스트라) to join the camp. ⓒYou may bring your own instrument or you can borrow one from the school. ⓓOn the last day of camp, we are going to film(촬영하다) our performance(공연) and play it on screen at the school summer festival. Please keep in mind ⓔthe camp is limited(제한하다) to 50 students. Signups(등록, 가입) start this Friday, on a first-come-first-served basis(선착순). Come and make music together!

해석

남: 안녕하세요, River Valley 고등학교 학생 여러분. 여러분의 음악 선생님인 Stailor입니다. ⓐ4월 11일부터 5일간 River Valley 음악 캠프가 열릴 예정입니다. ⓑ캠프에 참가하기 위해 학교 오케스트라 단원일 필요는 없습니다. ⓒ자신의 악기를 가져와도 되고 학교에서 빌려도 됩니다. ⓓ캠프 마지막 날에는, 우리 공연을 촬영하여 학교 여름 축제에서 스크린으로 상영할 것입니다. ⓔ이 캠프는 50명의 학생으로 제한된다는 것을 명심해 주세요. 등록은 이번 주 금요일에 선착순으로 시작됩니다. 와서 함께 음악을 만드세요!

문제 풀이

ⓔ캠프는 50명의 학생으로 제한된다고 했다.

10. ③ | 도표

선택지 선택비율	① 2%	② 2%	③ 89%	④ 2%	⑤ 2%

M: Katie, what are you doing with your smartphone?
W: I'm searching for(~을 찾다) an electric shaver(전기면도기) for my dad's birthday. Will you help me find a good one?
M: Sure. Let me see... *[Pause]* How about this one?
W: Well, that's too expensive. ⓐI can't spend more than $100.
M: Okay. And I think ⓑa 20-minute battery life(배터리 수명) is too short to use conveniently(편리하게).
W: I think so, too. It needs frequent(잦은) charging(charge: 충전하다).
M: You're right. ⓒDoes it need to be waterproof(방수의)?
W: ⓓOf course. He shaves(면도하다) in the shower every morning.
M: Then we have only two options left. Which color do you think is better?
W: ⓔDad likes black, so I'll buy the black one.
M: I think it's a nice choice.

해석

남: Katie, 스마트폰으로 뭐 하고 있니?
여: 아빠 생신 선물로 전기면도기를 찾고 있어. 좋은 거 찾는 거 도와줄래?
남: 그래. 어디 보자… [잠시 후] 이건 어때?
여: 음, 그건 너무 비싸. ⓐ100달러 이상을 쓸 수는 없어.
남: 알겠어. 그리고 내 생각에 ⓑ편리하게 사용하기에 배터리 수명 20분은 너무 짧아.
여: 내 생각도 그래. 잦은 충전이 필요하지.
남: 맞아. ⓒ방수일 필요가 있니?
여: ⓓ물론이지. 매일 아침 샤워하면서 면도하시거든.
남: 그럼 두 가지 선택권만 남네. 어느 색이 나은 것 같아?
여: ⓔ아빠는 검은색을 좋아하시니까, 검은색으로 살래.
남: 잘 고른 것 같아.

문제 풀이

여자는 ⓐ100달러가 넘지 않고 ⓑ배터리 수명이 20분이 넘고 ⓒⓓ방수가 되는 ⓔ검은색 전기면도기를 구입할 것이다.

11. ① | 짧은 대화 응답

선택지 선택비율	① 77%	② 3%	③ 11%	④ 8%	⑤ 1%

M: Let's get inside. I'm so excited to see this auto(자동차) show.
W: Look over there. ⓐSo many people are already standing in line to buy tickets.
M: Fortunately(다행히, 운 좋게), ⓑI bought our tickets in advance(미리).
W: Great. We don't have to wait in line.

해석

남: 안으로 들어가자. 이 자동차 전시회를 보게 돼서 너무 신이 나.
여: 저기 봐. ⓐ벌써 표를 사려고 줄을 서 있는 사람들이 너무 많아.
남: 다행히 ⓑ내가 미리 표를 구매했지.
여: 잘됐다. 우린 줄 서서 기다릴 필요가 없겠네.

문제 풀이

ⓐ표를 사려고 줄을 서 있는 사람들이 많다는 여자의 말에 남자가 ⓑ자신이 표를 미리 구매해 두었다고 말하고 있으므로, 줄 서서 기다릴 필요가 없어서 좋다고 말하는 ①이 이에 대한 여자의 응답으로 가장 적절하다.
② 좋아. 우린 나중에 다시 오면 돼.
③ 잘했어. 표를 사자.
④ 걱정하지 마. 내가 줄을 설게.
⑤ 정말 안타까워. 저 차는 못 사겠네.

12. ⑤ | 짧은 대화 응답

선택지 선택비율	① 1%	② 2%	③ 2%	④ 2%	⑤ 93%

W: Welcome to Emily's Cake Shop. How can I help you today?
M: ⓐI'd like to order a cake. It's to celebrate my first wedding anniversary(결혼기념일).
W: Congratulations on your anniversary! ⓑDo you have a specific(특정한, 구체적인) design in mind?
M: Yes, I'd like a heart-shaped cake with a message on it.

해석

여: 'Emily의 케이크 가게'에 오신 걸 환영합니다. 오늘은 어떻게 도와드릴까요?
남: ⓐ케이크를 주문하고 싶습니다. 제 첫 번째 결혼기념일을 축하하려고요.
여: 결혼기념일 축하드립니다! ⓑ특별히 생각하고 계신 디자인이 있나요?
남: 네, 위에 메시지가 있는 하트 모양 케이크로 하고 싶습니다.

문제 풀이

ⓐ첫 번째 결혼기념일을 축하하기 위해 케이크를 주문하려는 남자에게 여자가 ⓑ특별히 생각하고 있는 디자인이 있는지 물었으므로, 원하는 디자인을 말하는 ⑤가 응답으로 가장 적절하다.

① 아니요. 이 케이크들은 전부 제가 직접 만들었어요.
② 물론이에요. 제 30번째 생일을 기대하고 있어요.
③ 사실, 당신이 제 당근 케이크를 먹어도 괜찮아요.
④ 꼭 그렇진 않아요. 모든 기념일을 기억하는 건 힘들어요.

13. ① | 긴 대화 응답

선택지 선택비율	① 88%	② 8%	③ 1%	④ 2%	⑤ 2%

M: Hello, Ms. Taylor.
W: Hi, Luke. What brings you in my office?
M: I'm not sure about which courses to pick for next year. I'm thinking
과정, (학)과목 고르다
of taking the same courses as my friend, Henry.
W: I understand why you feel that way. However, it's not a good idea to just follow your friend without considering what's best for you.
따르다 고려하다
M: But, I don't even know where to begin. Can you give me some guidance?
안내, 조언
W: What do you enjoy doing?
M: Umm. ⓐI guess I like creating video clips.
W: That is the starting point. ⓑYou can choose courses related to that.
~와 관련 있는
M: Ah! I see. ⓒCould you help me find courses that fit me?
맞다
W: Sure. I'll recommend a list of courses you might like.
추천하다

해석

남: 안녕하세요, Taylor 선생님.
여: 안녕, Luke. 무슨 일로 내 교무실에 왔니?
남: 내년에 어떤 과목들을 골라야 할지 잘 모르겠어요. 제 친구 Henry와 같은 과목들을 들을까 생각 중이에요.
여: 네가 왜 그렇게 생각하는지 이해해. 하지만 너에게 가장 좋은 게 뭔지 고려하지 않고 단순히 친구를 따르는 건 좋은 생각이 아니야.
남: 하지만 어디서부터 시작해야 할지조차 모르겠어요. 제게 조언을 좀 해 주실 수 있나요?
여: 네가 즐겨 하는 게 뭐니?
남: 음. ⓐ저는 동영상 만드는 걸 좋아하는 것 같아요.
여: 그게 출발점이야. ⓑ그와 관련된 과목들을 선택할 수 있지.
남: 아! 그렇군요. ⓒ제게 맞는 과목들을 찾는 걸 도와주실 수 있나요?
여: 물론이지. 네가 좋아할 만한 과목 목록을 추천해 줄게.

문제 풀이

남자가 ⓐ동영상 만드는 것을 좋아한다고 하자 여자는 ⓑ그것과 관련된 과목들을 선택하면 된다고 조언한다. 그러자 남자가 ⓒ자신에게 맞는 과목들 찾는 것을 도와줄 수 있는지 묻고 있으므로, 좋아할 만한 과목 목록을 추천해 주겠다는 ①이 응답으로 가장 적절하다.

② 알았어. 네가 점수를 잘 받을 거라고 생각하는 과목을 골라.
③ 힘내! 곧 Henry와 화해하게 될 거야.
④ 음, 과목 선택 기간은 끝났어.
⑤ 걱정 마. 난 네가 최선을 다했다고 생각해!

14. ⑤ | 긴 대화 응답

선택지 선택비율	① 2%	② 2%	③ 1%	④ 1%	⑤ 92%

W: Honey, look at this bill. Have you been using a movie streaming
영수증
service?
M: No. But a few months ago, ⓐI used a one-month free trial.
W: Look. ⓑA $15 membership fee has been charged for three months.
요금 요금을 청구하다
M: Oh, no! There must be something wrong.
W: Did you get any notice about that?
공지, 안내
M: Well, I did, but I didn't pay much attention to it when I signed up for
~에 주의를 기울이다
it.
W: Let's check it now.
M: Wait. *[Clicking sound]* Hmm, it says ⓒthe membership fee will be charged if I don't cancel it after the free trial.
취소하다
W: Well, one of my friends was in the same situation and she tried to get a refund but she couldn't.
환불받다
M: Then, what should I do?
W: Hmm, ⓓthe only thing you can do is to end the membership.
M: Okay. I'll call customer service to cancel the membership.

해석

여: 여보, 이 영수증 좀 봐요. 당신이 영화 스트리밍 서비스를 이용하고 있나요?
남: 아니요. 하지만 몇 달 전에, ⓐ1개월 무료 체험을 했어요.
여: 봐요. ⓑ3개월 동안 15달러 회원 요금이 청구되었어요.
남: 이런! 뭔가 잘못된 게 분명해요.
여: 그것에 관한 어떤 안내를 받았나요?
남: 음, 그러긴 했는데, 신청할 때 거기에 신경을 많이 안 썼어요.
여: 지금 확인해 보자고요.
남: 기다려 봐요. [클릭하는 소리] 음, ⓒ무료 체험 후에 취소하지 않으면 회원 요금이 청구될 것이라고 되어 있네요.
여: 음, 내 친구 한 명도 같은 상황에 처해서 환불받으려고 했지만 그러지 못했어요.
남: 그러면, 어떻게 해야 할까요?
여: 음, ⓓ당신이 할 수 있는 건 회원권을 종료하는 것뿐이에요.
남: 알겠어요. 고객 서비스 센터에 전화해서 회원권을 취소할게요.

문제 풀이

두 사람은 ⓐⓑⓒ1개월 무료 체험을 취소하지 않아 요금이 청구된 상황인데, 여자는 남자에게 ⓓ남자가 할 수 있는 일은 회원권을 종료하는 것뿐이라고 했으므로, 남자의 응답으로 가장 적절한 것은 회원권을 취소하겠다는 내용의 ⑤이다.

① 걱정하지 마요. 내가 당신에게 이메일로 안내문을 보내 줄게요.
② 잘됐네요. 서비스 이용 방법을 알려줘요.
③ 내 생각은 달라요. 영수증이 없어도 환불받을 수 있어요.
④ 좋아요. 오늘밤 영화 보는 걸 고대하고 있어요.

15. ① | 상황에 적절한 말

선택지 선택비율	① 86%	② 3%	③ 4%	④ 4%	⑤ 3%

M: Liam and Sophia are college students and friends. Liam recently
대학교 최근에
learned how to bake cookies in a cooking class and wants to practice the recipe at home. However, he doesn't have a mini oven,
연습하다 요리법, 레시피
and he cannot afford to buy one right now. He remembers that
cannot afford to-v: ~할 여유가 없다
Sophia has a mini oven at home and often brings freshly baked
갓 ~한
cookies to class. So, he wants to ask her if she can lend him her mini oven. In this situation, what would Liam most likely say to Sophia?
Liam: Can I borrow your mini oven to practice baking cookies?

해석

남: Liam과 Sophia는 대학생이자 친구이다. Liam은 최근 요리 수업에서 쿠키 굽는 법을 배웠고 집에서 그 레시피를 연습하고 싶어 한다. 하지만 그는 소형 오븐이 없고, 지금 당장 그것을 살 여유가 없다. 그는 Sophia가 집에 소형 오븐을 가지고 있고 종종 갓 구운 쿠키를 수업에 가져오는 것이 기억난다. 그래서 그는 그녀가 그에게 소형 오븐

을 빌려줄 수 있는지 물어보고 싶어 한다. 이 상황에서, Liam은 Sophia에게 뭐라고 말하겠는가?

Liam: 쿠키 굽는 것을 연습하기 위해 네 소형 오븐을 빌릴 수 있을까?

문제 풀이

Liam이 Sophia에게 소형 오븐을 빌려줄 수 있는지 물어보고 싶어 한다고 했으므로, Liam이 Sophia에게 할 말로는 ①이 가장 적절하다.

② 내가 너에게 준 쿠키 레시피를 활용하고 있니?
③ 같이 쿠키 굽는 법을 배우고 싶니?
④ 집에서 사용할 소형 오븐을 어디서 살 거니?
⑤ 어떻게 쿠키를 그렇게 맛있게 만드는 거니?

16~17. ǀ 세트 문항

16. ⑤ 17. ③

선택지 선택비율					
16	① 2%	② 1%	③ 10%	④ 3%	⑤ 84%
17	① 1%	② 1%	③ 94%	④ 3%	⑤ 1%

W: Hello, *Family-Life* subscribers! These days, many people are
구독자
looking for clothes made from natural materials for their family.
천연 소재
Today, ⓐI'd like to introduce some tips for how to properly wash
올바로
natural material clothes. First, for ⓑcotton, like 100% cotton
면
t-shirts, you should hand-wash in cool water to avoid shrinking or
피하다, 방지하다 줄어들다
wrinkling. Second, ⓒsilk should be washed separately and quickly
wrinkle: 주름이 생기다 별도로
to keep its shape and color. Also, when you dry silk clothes such as blouses, avoid direct sunlight and dry them in the shade. Third,
직접적인 그늘
ⓓlinen is a sensitive material to wash. For example, to wash linen
리넨 민감한
jackets, use vinegar instead of fabric softener. Lastly, for ⓔwool, the
식초 섬유 유연제 울
best way is to wash as little as possible. If you have to wash wool sweaters, use special wool washing soap. Apply these tips so you
적용하다
can keep and enjoy natural clothes for a longer time!

해석

여: 안녕하세요, 〈패밀리 라이프〉 구독자 여러분! 요즘 많은 사람들이 가족을 위해 천연 소재로 만들어진 옷을 찾고 있습니다. 오늘은 ⓐ천연 소재 옷을 올바로 세탁하는 방법에 관한 몇 가지 팁을 소개하고자 합니다. 먼저, 100% 면 티셔츠 같은 ⓑ면은 줄어들거나 주름이 생기는 것을 방지하기 위해 찬물에 손세탁을 해야 합니다. 두 번째로, ⓒ실크는 모양과 색을 유지하기 위해 별도로 빠르게 세탁해야 합니다. 또한, 블라우스 같은 실크 옷을 건조할 때는 직사광선을 피하고 그늘에서 건조해야 합니다. 세 번째로, ⓓ리넨은 세탁하기 민감한 소재입니다. 예를 들어, 리넨 재킷을 세탁하려면, 섬유 유연제 대신 식초를 사용하세요. 마지막으로, ⓔ울은 가능한 한 적게 세탁하는 것이 가장 좋은 방법입니다. 울 스웨터를 세탁해야 한다면, 특별한 세탁 비누를 사용하세요. 이 팁들을 적용해서 천연 소재 옷을 더 오래 유지하고 즐기세요!

문제 풀이

16. ⓐ천연 소재 옷을 올바로 세탁하는 방법에 관한 몇 가지 팁을 소개하겠다고 했으므로, 주제로는 ⑤ '천연 소재 옷을 세탁하는 올바른 방법'이 가장 적절하다.
① 패션 산업에서의 소재 동향
② 천연 소재로 옷을 만드는 이점
③ 천연 소재 옷을 구매하는 팁
④ 의류 세탁 방법의 발전

17. ⓑ면, ⓒ실크, ⓓ리넨, ⓔ울은 언급되었으나, 가죽(leather)은 언급되지 않았다.

[코드 공략하기]

제9회 초급 모의고사

1	①	2	②	3	②	4	③	5	②	6	③
7	②	8	④	9	④	10	④	11	①	12	⑤
13	②	14	②	15	⑤	16	①	17	②		

1. ① ǀ 목적

선택지 선택비율	① 94%	② 1%	③ 2%	④ 1%	⑤ 0%

M: Hello, students. This is Mike Smith, your P.E. teacher. These days,
체육(=physical education)
the fine dust problem is getting serious. So, I'd like to explain what
미세 먼지
you should do when the fine dust level is high. First, close all the classroom windows to keep out the dust. Second, turn on the air
~이 들어가지 않게 하다 공기청정기
purifier in the classroom. The air purifier will help keep the air clean. Third, drink water and wash your hands as often as possible. Last, it's important to wear a mask when you're outside. Thank you for listening.

해석

남: 안녕하세요, 학생 여러분. 저는 여러분의 체육 교사 Mike Smith입니다. 요즘 미세 먼지 문제가 심각해지고 있습니다. 그래서 미세 먼지 수치가 높을 때 어떻게 해야 할지 설명을 드리고 싶습니다. 첫째, 먼지가 들어가지 않게 하기 위해 모든 교실 창문들을 닫으세요. 둘째, 교실 안의 공기청정기를 켜세요. 공기청정기는 공기를 깨끗하게 유지하는 데 도움이 될 것입니다. 셋째, 가능한 한 자주 물을 마시고 손을 씻으세요. 마지막으로, 실외에 있을 때는 마스크를 착용하는 것이 중요합니다. 들어주셔서 고맙습니다.

문제 풀이

남자는 담화 초반부에 미세 먼지 수치가 높을 때 어떻게 해야 할지 설명하겠다고 밝히고 있다.

2. ② ǀ 의견

선택지 선택비율	① 2%	② 89%	③ 5%	④ 0%	⑤ 4%

W: Brian, I heard that you are thinking of buying an electric bicycle.
전기 자전거
M: Yes, that's right.
W: That's good. But be careful when you ride it.
M: Yeah, I know what you mean. On my way here I saw a man riding an electric bicycle without wearing a helmet.
W: Some riders don't even follow basic traffic rules.
기본적인 교통 법규
M: What do you mean by that?
W: These days many people ride electric bicycles on sidewalks.
보행로, 인도
M: Yes, it's so dangerous.
위험한
W: Right. There should be stricter rules about riding electric bicycles.
엄격한
M: I totally agree with you.

해석

여: Brian, 네가 전기 자전거를 사려고 생각 중이라고 들었어.
남: 응, 맞아.
여: 그거 좋다. 하지만 탈 때 조심해.
남: 응, 무슨 말인지 알아. 여기 오는 길에 헬멧을 착용하지 않고 전기 자전거를 타는 사람을 봤어.
여: 몇몇 자전거 타는 사람들은 기본적인 교통 법규조차 지키지 않아.

남: 그게 무슨 뜻이야?
여: 요즘 많은 사람들이 전기 자전거를 인도에서 타고 다녀.
남: 맞아, 정말 위험해.
여: 그래. 전기 자전거 운행에 관한 더 엄격한 규정이 있어야 해.
남: 완전 동의해.

문제 풀이

여자는 전기 자전거 운행에 관한 더 엄격한 규정이 있어야 한다고 말하고 있다.

3. ② | 관계

선택지 선택비율	① 2%	② 90%	③ 4%	④ 2%	⑤ 1%

M: Excuse me. You're Chloe Jones, aren't you?
W: Yes, I am. Have we met before?
M: No, but I'm a big fan of yours. I've watched your speeches on climate change(기후 변화), and they're very inspiring(고무적인).
W: Thank you. I'm so glad to hear that.
M: And, I also think ⓐyour campaign(캠페인) about plastic pollution has been very successful.
W: ⓑAs an environmental activist(환경 운동가), that means a lot to me.
M: May I make a suggestion(제안하다)? I thought it'd be nice if more children could hear your ideas.
W: That's what I was thinking. Do you have any good ideas?
M: Actually, ⓒI'm a cartoonist(만화가). Perhaps I can make comic books(만화책) based on your work.
W: That is a wonderful idea. Can I contact(연락하다) you later to discuss(상의하다, 논의하다) it more?
M: Sure. By the way, my name is Jack Perse. Here's my business card(명함).

해석

남: 실례합니다. Chloe Jones 씨죠, 그렇죠?
여: 네, 그렇습니다. 저희가 전에 만난 적이 있나요?
남: 아니요, 하지만 저는 당신의 열렬한 팬이에요. 기후 변화에 관한 연설을 봤는데요, 정말 고무적입니다.
여: 감사합니다. 그 말씀을 들으니 정말 기쁘네요.
남: 그리고 또 ⓐ플라스틱 오염에 관한 당신의 캠페인이 매우 성공적이었다고 생각합니다.
여: ⓑ환경 운동가로서, 그건 저에게 큰 의미가 있어요.
남: 제가 제안을 하나 해도 될까요? 더 많은 아이들이 당신의 생각을 들을 수 있으면 좋겠다고 생각했어요.
여: 저도 그렇게 생각하고 있었어요. 좋은 생각이 있으신가요?
남: 사실, ⓒ저는 만화가예요. 아마도 당신의 일을 바탕으로 만화책을 만들 수 있을 것 같아요.
여: 정말 좋은 생각이에요. 좀 더 상의하기 위해 나중에 연락 드려도 될까요?
남: 물론이죠. 그나저나, 제 이름은 Jack Perse입니다. 여기 제 명함입니다.

문제 풀이

남자가 ⓐ여자의 플라스틱 오염에 관한 캠페인이 성공적이었다고 말하자 여자는 ⓑ환경 운동가로서 그것이 자신에게 큰 의미가 있다고 했고, 남자가 ⓒ자신이 만화가임을 밝히며 여자의 일을 바탕으로 만화책을 만들고 싶다고 했으므로, 만화가와 환경 운동가의 대화임을 알 수 있다.

4. ③ | 그림 일치

선택지 선택비율	① 2%	② 3%	③ 71%	④ 15%	⑤ 9%

W: Hi, Tim. How's everything going with the festival?
M: Hey, Julie! It's going great. This is a picture of what our booth will look like.
W: What will people do at your booth?
M: They'll be asked to answer questions and be given snacks if they answer correctly.
W: Okay, that sounds good. I like ⓐthe banner that says 'Guessing Time' in the center.
M: Thanks. What do you think about ⓑthe photos that are under the clock?
W: Great idea! What are you using ⓒthe round table for?
M: We're going to put the snacks on it.
W: That makes sense. Then, what about ⓓthe globe(지구본) on the floor?
M: It's for choosing countries. We're going to ask people geography(지리학) questions.
W: That should be interesting. What's ⓔthat crown on the left side?
M: That's a photo zone for all participants.
W: Cool. I can't wait for this year's festival!

해석

여: 안녕, Tim. 축제는 모두 어떻게 되고 있니?
남: 안녕, Julie! 잘 되어 가고 있어. 우리 부스가 어떤 모습일지 이게 사진이야.
여: 너희 부스에서 사람들이 뭘 하게 되니?
남: 질문에 답하라는 요청을 받고 맞게 대답하면 간식을 받게 될 거야.
여: 그래, 좋아 보인다. ⓐ중심에 'Guessing Time'이라고 써 있는 현수막이 마음에 들어.
남: 고마워. ⓑ시계 아래에 있는 사진은 어떻게 생각해?
여: 좋은 아이디어야! ⓒ둥근 탁자는 뭐에 사용할 거니?
남: 그 위에 간식을 놓을 거야.
여: 타당하네. 그러면 ⓓ바닥에 있는 지구본은?
남: 국가를 선택하기 위한 거야. 사람들에게 지리학 질문을 할 거거든.
여: 재미있겠다. ⓔ왼편에 있는 저 왕관은 뭐니?
남: 모든 참가자들을 위한 포토존이야.
여: 멋지다. 올해 축제가 너무 기다려져!

문제 풀이

여자가 ⓒ둥근 탁자를 무엇에 사용할지 물었으므로, 그림의 네모난 탁자는 대화 내용과 일치하지 않는다.

5. ② | 할 일

선택지 선택비율	① 2%	② 91%	③ 5%	④ 1%	⑤ 1%

M: Hi, Stella. How are you doing these days?
W: Hi, Ryan. I've been busy helping my granddad with his concert. He made a rock band with his friends.
M: There must be a lot of things to do.
W: Yeah. I reserved(예약하다) a place for the concert yesterday.
M: What about posters and tickets?
W: Well, I've just finished designing a poster.
M: Then I think I can help you.
W: Really? How?
M: Actually, I have a music blog. I think I can upload the poster there.
W: That's great!
M: Just send the poster to me, and I'll post(게시하다) it online.
W: Thanks a lot.

해석

남: 안녕, Stella. 요즘 어떻게 지내니?
여: 안녕, Ryan. 나는 할아버지의 콘서트를 돕느라 바빴어. 할아버지께서 친구분들과 록 밴드를 만드셨거든.
남: 할 일이 많겠네.
여: 응. 어제는 콘서트 장소를 예약했어.
남: 포스터랑 티켓은?
여: 음, 이제 막 포스터 디자인을 마쳤어.

남: 그럼 내가 도와줄 수 있을 것 같아.
여: 정말? 어떻게?
남: 사실, 나에게 음악 블로그가 있거든. 거기에 포스터를 올리면 될 것 같아.
여: 잘됐다!
남: 나한테 포스터를 보내주기만 하면, 내가 인터넷에 게시할게.
여: 정말 고마워.

문제 풀이

여자가 포스터를 보내주면 남자가 포스터를 인터넷에 게시할 것이라고 했다.

6. ③ | 목적

선택지 선택비율	① 13%	② 28%	③ 54%	④ 4%	⑤ 2%

W: Hi, I'm looking for a backpack for my niece. She's going on a camping trip this summer.
M: Great. We have this blue backpack that has multiple pockets.
많은
W: It looks stylish and functional. How much is it?
기능성의
M: ⓐIt's $50, but we have a special discount only on backpacks today. ⓑEvery backpack is 10% off.
W: That's a great deal! I'll take it.
M: I'm sure your niece will love it. Do you need anything else?
W: Yes. I like this camping hat. How much is it?
M: ⓒIt's $10, not on sale, though.
W: That's okay. I'll take it as well.
역시, 또한
M: ⓓGift wrapping for them would be a total of $5. Would you like gift
포장
wrapping?
W: Yes, please. Here's my credit card.

해석

여: 안녕하세요, 제 조카에게 줄 배낭을 찾고 있어요. 그 애가 이번 여름에 캠핑을 가거든요.
남: 좋습니다. 주머니가 많은 이 파란 배낭이 있습니다.
여: 맵시 있고 기능성 있어 보이네요. 이건 얼마죠?
남: ⓐ50달러인데, 오늘 배낭만 특별 할인이 있어요. ⓑ모든 배낭이 10% 할인됩니다.
여: 정말 괜찮은 가격이네요! 그걸 살게요.
남: 분명 조카분이 그걸 좋아할 거예요. 다른 것도 필요하세요?
여: 네. 이 캠핑 모자가 마음에 드네요. 얼마죠?
남: ⓒ10달러인데, 할인은 안 됩니다.
여: 괜찮아요. 이것도 살게요.
남: ⓓ선물 포장을 하면 총 5달러입니다. 선물 포장을 원하시나요?
여: 네, 부탁드려요. 여기 제 신용카드요.

문제 풀이

여자는 ⓑ10% 할인 중인 ⓐ50달러짜리 배낭(45달러)과 ⓒ10달러인 캠핑 모자를 구매하며 ⓓ5달러 비용이 드는 선물 포장을 이용하므로, 총 60달러를 지불해야 한다.

7. ② | 이유

선택지 선택비율	① 2%	② 88%	③ 5%	④ 2%	⑤ 2%

W: Hi, Brian. Why didn't you answer my text message yesterday? I wanted to ask about the math exam.
M: Hi, Sarah. I'm really sorry. I broke my cell phone yesterday, so
break: 고장 내다
I couldn't read it.
W: Oh, no! What happened to it?
M: Well, I dropped it while getting off the bus. And now, it doesn't work
떨어뜨리다 ~에서 내리다
at all.
W: Why didn't you get it fixed?
M: I wanted to, but I couldn't.
W: Was it because you couldn't find a repair shop? There's one right by
수리점
the bus stop near our school.
M: I went there to get it fixed, but I couldn't.
W: Oh, did you have to wait too long?
M: No, I didn't. Actually, I didn't know I had to make a reservation in advance. So I just went back home.
미리, 사전에
W: Ah! That's too bad!

해석

여: 안녕, Brian. 왜 어제 내 문자 메시지에 답하지 않았어? 수학 시험에 대해서 물어보고 싶었거든.
남: 안녕, Sarah. 정말 미안해. 어제 내 휴대 전화를 고장 내서 문자 메시지를 읽을 수가 없었어.
여: 아, 이런! 무슨 일이 있었던 거야?
남: 그게, 내가 버스에서 내리다가 그걸 떨어뜨렸어. 그래서 지금 전혀 작동하지 않아.
여: 왜 수리를 안 받았어?
남: 그러고 싶었는데, 못했어.
여: 수리점을 못 찾아서야? 우리 학교 근처 버스 정류장 바로 옆에 하나 있잖아.
남: 거기 가서 고치려고 했는데, 못했어.
여: 아, 너무 오래 기다려야 했어?
남: 아니, 그렇진 않아. 사실은 미리 예약을 해야 한다는 걸 몰랐어. 그래서 그냥 집으로 돌아왔어.
여: 아! 그거 안됐다!

문제 풀이

남자는 예약을 하지 않고 수리점을 방문해서 휴대 전화를 수리받지 못한 채 그냥 집으로 돌아왔다고 했다.

8. ④ | 언급

선택지 선택비율	① 2%	② 3%	③ 3%	④ 88%	⑤ 1%

W: Honey, it's spring. How about visiting the new botanic garden this
식물원
weekend?
M: Do you mean ⓐthe Royal Botanic Garden located in Redwood
~에 위치한
Valley?
W: Yes, it's not far from here. It's one of the biggest botanic gardens in the country.
M: That's right. I heard ⓑits size is about four times larger than a soccer field.
W: Yeah. You know, ⓒthey offer interesting programs such as tree
제공하다 나무 심기
planting and guided tours.
M: Sounds great. Our kids will love planting trees.
W: Definitely. Let's go this Saturday. What time shall we leave?
그렇고말고
M: How about 9 in the morning? ⓓThe botanic garden is open from 10 a.m. to 6 p.m.
W: Okay. It'll be fun.

해석

여: 여보, 봄이잖아요. 이번 주말에 새로 생긴 식물원에 가는 게 어때요?
남: ⓐRedwood 계곡에 위치한 Royal 식물원 말하는 거예요?
여: 네, 여기서 안 멀어요. 국내 최대 식물원 중 하나죠.
남: 맞아요. ⓑ크기가 축구 경기장보다 약 네 배 더 크다고 들었어요.
여: 네. 알다시피, ⓒ나무 심기와 가이드 투어 같은 흥미로운 프로그램을 제공해요.
남: 그거 참 좋겠네요. 아이들이 나무 심기를 아주 좋아할 거예요.
여: 그렇고말고요. 이번 주 토요일에 가요. 몇 시에 출발할까요?
남: 아침 9시 어때요? ⓓ식물원이 오전 10시부터 오후 6시까지 개관하잖아요.
여: 좋아요. 재미있겠네요.

문제 풀이

ⓐ위치, ⓑ크기, ⓒ프로그램, ⓓ개관 시간은 언급되었으나, 입장료는 언급되지 않았다.

9. ④ | 내용 일치

선택지 선택비율	① 2%	② 2%	③ 2%	④ 91%	⑤ 0%

W: Good afternoon, listeners. Why don't you join the Sharing Friday Movement and ⓐdonate(기부하다) two dollars to our fund(기금) every Friday? This movement(운동) ⓑstarted in 2001 in Finland as an idea to encourage(장려하다) people to do good(착한 일을 하다). Since then, this idea has grown into a global(세계적인) movement. ⓒMost of the donations(기부(금)) go to poor areas across the world and help people get clean water. ⓓThis year, scholarships(장학금) were given to 100 students in these areas to celebrate our 20th anniversary(기념일). Please join us, and help make a difference. ⓔIf you want to get more information, visit our homepage.

해석

여: 안녕하세요, 청취자 여러분. Sharing Friday Movement에 동참하셔서 ⓐ매주 금요일에 저희 기금에 2달러를 기부하시면 어떨까요? 이 운동은 사람들에게 선행을 하도록 장려하고자 하는 아이디어의 일환으로 ⓑ2001년 핀란드에서 시작되었습니다. 그 이후로, 이 아이디어는 세계적인 운동으로 성장하였습니다. ⓒ기부금의 대부분은 전 세계의 가난한 지역으로 가서 사람들이 깨끗한 물을 얻도록 돕습니다. ⓓ올해에는 20번째 기념일을 축하하기 위하여 이 지역 학생 100명에게 장학금이 주어졌습니다. 저희와 함께 하시어, 변화를 만드는 데 도움을 주세요. ⓔ더 많은 정보를 원하시면, 저희 홈페이지를 방문해 주십시오.

문제 풀이

ⓓ올해 20명이 아니라 100명의 학생에게 장학금이 주어졌다고 했다.

10. ④ | 도표

선택지 선택비율	① 2%	② 1%	③ 10%	④ 87%	⑤ 1%

W: Kyle, I'm looking for some sneakers(운동화). Can you help me find some good ones?
M: Of course. Let me see... *[Pause]* Look. These are the five bestselling ones.
W: Wow, they all look so cool. It's hard to choose among them.
M: Well, what's your budget(예산)?
W: ⓐI don't want to spend more than 80 dollars.
M: All right. Which style do you want, active or casual?
W: ⓑI prefer casual ones. I think they match(어울리다) my clothes better.
M: Good. And ⓒI'd like to recommend waterproof(방수의) shoes for rainy days.
W: Okay, I will take your advice(조언, 충고).
M: So you have two options left. Which color do you prefer?
W: Most of my shoes are black, so ⓓI'll buy white ones this time.
M: You made a good choice.

해석

여: Kyle, 나 운동화를 좀 찾고 있어. 좋은 것 좀 찾게 도와줄 수 있니?
남: 물론이지. 어디 보자… [잠시 후] 봐. 이게 가장 잘 팔리는 다섯 가지야.
여: 와, 모두 정말 멋져 보인다. 그것들 중에서 고르기가 어려워.
남: 음, 예산은 얼마인데?
여: ⓐ80달러 넘게는 쓰고 싶지 않아.
남: 알겠어. 활동적인 스타일과 캐주얼한 스타일 중 어떤 스타일을 원하니?
여: ⓑ난 캐주얼한 것이 더 좋아. 내 옷과 더 잘 어울리는 것 같아.
남: 좋아. 그리고 비 오는 날을 대비해 ⓒ방수 신발을 추천하고 싶어.
여: 응, 네 조언을 받아들일게.
남: 그럼 두 가지 선택사항이 남았네. 어떤 색을 더 좋아하니?
여: 내 신발은 대부분 검은색이어서, ⓓ이번에는 흰색으로 살래.
남: 잘 선택했어.

문제 풀이

여자는 ⓐ80달러가 넘지 않고 ⓑ캐주얼한 스타일의 ⓒ방수가 되는 ⓓ흰색 운동화를 구입하기로 했다.

11. ① | 짧은 대화 응답

선택지 선택비율	① 77%	② 7%	③ 10%	④ 4%	⑤ 2%

M: Ms. Adams, I'm not feeling well(건강 상태가 좋다). ⓐI have a bad headache(두통).
W: Oh, sorry to hear that, Jack. Have you taken some medicine(약)?
M: Yes, ⓑI took some an hour ago, but I don't think I can stay in class.
W: I see. Then you should leave now to go see a doctor.

해석

남: Adams 선생님, 저 몸이 안 좋아요. ⓐ두통이 심해요.
여: 오, 안됐구나, Jack. 약은 좀 먹었니?
남: 네, ⓑ한 시간 전에 먹었는데, 수업에 계속 있을 수는 없을 것 같아요.
여: 그래. 그러면 지금 나가서 병원에 가봐야겠다.

문제 풀이

남자가 ⓐ심한 두통을 호소하며 ⓑ약을 먹었음에도 불구하고 수업에 더 이상 있을 수 없을 것 같다고 말하고 있으므로, 어서 병원에 가보라고 말하는 ①이 응답으로 가장 적절하다.
② 좋은 생각이야. 다음 수업에는 너를 다른 조에 넣어줄 수 있어.
③ 정말 안됐구나. 너는 먼저 약을 좀 먹었어야 했어.
④ 괜찮아. 기말시험에서는 더 잘하기를 바랄게.
⑤ 고맙습니다. 지금 바로 보건실에 갈게요.

12. ⑤ | 짧은 대화 응답

선택지 선택비율	① 2%	② 6%	③ 1%	④ 11%	⑤ 79%

W: Honey, what do you have in mind(~을 염두에 두다) for lunch this Saturday?
M: I was thinking ⓐwe should try the new Italian restaurant.
W: Hmm... I heard that ⓑit's hard to make a reservation(예약하다) there these days.
M: That's too bad. Why don't we try another restaurant?

해석

여: 여보, 이번 토요일 점심으로 염두에 둔 게 있나요?
남: ⓐ새로 생긴 이탈리아 음식점을 가볼까 생각 중이었어요.
여: 음… ⓑ요즘 그곳은 예약하기 어렵다고 들었어요.
남: 안타깝네요. 다른 식당을 가보는 게 어떨까요?

문제 풀이

ⓐ새로 생긴 이탈리아 음식점을 가보고 싶어 하는 남자에게 여자가 ⓑ요즘 그곳은 예약하기 어렵다고 했으므로, 아쉬움을 표하며 다른 곳을 가보자고 말하는 ⑤가 남자의 응답으로 가장 적절하다.
① 고마워요. 모든 게 맛있어 보여요.
② 네. 난 이번 토요일에 약속이 있어요.
③ 천만에요. 아빠의 요리법으로 만들었어요.
④ 좋아요. 몇 시로 예약했어요?

13. ② | 긴 대화 응답

선택지 선택비율	① 9%	② 59%	③ 12%	④ 13%	⑤ 4%

M: What are you reading, Lily?
W: It's a book for my English class, Dad. We have to read a book and write a review.
비평
M: Do you like the book?
W: Well, I'm not sure. Frankly ⓐit's too difficult for me.
솔직하게
M: Why did you choose to read that book then?
W: It was on the bestseller list and it looked interesting. ⓑIt's very challenging, though.
어려운 그러나
M: Maybe ⓒyou should try another book that suits your level.
W: I know what you mean, but wouldn't I learn more from reading a difficult book?
M: Well, ⓓwhat's the use of reading it if you can't understand it?
W: That makes sense. I'll switch to an easier book.
타당하다, 말이 되다 바꾸다

해석

남: Lily, 뭘 읽고 있니?
여: 영어 수업에 필요한 책을 읽고 있어요, 아빠. 책 한 권을 읽고 비평을 써야 해요.
남: 책은 마음에 드니?
여: 음, 잘 모르겠어요. 솔직히 ⓐ제게 너무 어려워요.
남: 그럼 왜 그 책을 읽기로 결정했니?
여: 베스트셀러 목록에 있고 재미있어 보였어요. 하지만 ⓑ무척 어려워요.
남: 아마 ⓒ네 수준에 맞는 다른 책을 시도해야겠구나.
여: 무슨 말씀인지 알겠지만, 어려운 책을 읽으면 더 많이 배우지 않을까요?
남: 음, ⓓ네가 그걸 이해하지 못한다면 읽는 게 무슨 소용이니?
여: 맞는 말씀이에요. 더 쉬운 책으로 바꿀게요.

문제 풀이

ⓐⓑ어려운 책을 읽고 있는 여자에게 남자는 ⓓ이해가 안 되는 책을 읽는 것은 소용이 없으니 ⓒ수준에 맞는 책을 읽을 것을 권하고 있다. 따라서 남자의 조언에 따라 더 쉬운 책을 읽겠다는 ②가 응답으로 가장 적절하다.
① 맞는 말씀이에요. 그래서 제가 이 책을 골랐어요.
③ 알겠어요. 다음에는 베스트셀러 목록에서 고를게요.
④ 걱정하지 마세요. 제가 읽기에 그리 어렵지 않아요.
⑤ 네. 독서 동아리에 가입해서 책을 더 많이 읽을게요.

14. ② | 긴 대화 응답

선택지 선택비율	① 1%	② 93%	③ 2%	④ 1%	⑤ 3%

W: Dad, look at the cat over there!
M: Oh, it's so cute.
W: I've wanted a cat for a long time. Can we get one?
M: You know, raising a cat isn't easy, Rebecca.
raise: 키우다, 기르다
W: I understand. But I promise I'd love it with all my heart.
약속하다
M: It's not just about love. It's about effort and responsibility.
노력 책임
W: Trust me, Dad. I know I can handle it.
믿다 다루다
M: Hmm... Then, how about practicing first? Uncle Tony is looking for someone to take care of his cat during his business trip.
~을 돌보다 출장
W: That sounds great! If I do a good job with his cat, will you let me get my own cat?
M: ⓐI'll definitely think about it if you take good care of his cat.
분명히, 틀림없이
W: Thanks, Dad. ⓑPlease tell Uncle Tony that I want to do it.
M: Okay. I'll ask him if you can look after his cat.
~을 돌보다

해석

여: 아빠, 저기 고양이 좀 보세요!
남: 오, 정말 귀엽구나.
여: 저 오랫동안 고양이를 키우고 싶었어요. 우리 한 마리 키워도 될까요?
남: 너도 알다시피, 고양이를 키우는 건 쉽지 않단다, Rebecca.
여: 알아요. 하지만 온 마음을 다해 사랑할 거라고 약속할게요.
남: 그저 사랑만으로 되는 게 아니란다. 노력과 책임이 필요해.
여: 저를 믿어 주세요, 아빠. 저 할 수 있어요.
남: 음… 그러면 먼저 연습을 해 보는 게 어떠니? Tony 삼촌이 출장 동안 그의 고양이를 돌봐줄 사람을 찾고 있어.
여: 정말 좋은 생각이에요! 제가 그 고양이를 잘 돌보면, 제 고양이를 키우게 해 주실 거예요?
남: ⓐ네가 그의 고양이를 잘 돌본다면, 틀림없이 생각해 보마.
여: 고마워요, 아빠. ⓑTony 삼촌께 제가 하고 싶다고 꼭 말씀드려 주세요.
남: 알겠어. 네가 고양이를 돌봐도 되는지 삼촌에게 물어볼게.

문제 풀이

남자가 ⓐ삼촌의 고양이를 잘 돌보면 고양이 키우는 것을 고려하겠다고 하자, 여자는 ⓑ자신이 그 고양이를 돌보고 싶다고 말한다. 따라서 삼촌에게 물어보겠다고 하는 ②가 응답으로 가장 적절하다.
① 그렇구나. 너는 항상 고양이보다 개를 더 좋아했지.
③ 미안해. 나는 네 고양이를 돌볼 시간이 없어.
④ 문제없어. 내가 그의 반려동물을 동물병원에 데려갈게.
⑤ 동의해. 그가 반려동물을 아주 잘 돌보는 사람이란 걸 확실히 알아.

15. ⑤ | 상황에 적절한 말

선택지 선택비율	① 1%	② 1%	③ 3%	④ 2%	⑤ 93%

W: Violet and Peter are classmates. They're doing their science group assignment together. On Saturday morning, they meet at the public library. They decide to find the books they need in different sections of the library. Violet finds two useful books and tries to check them out. Unfortunately, ⓐshe suddenly realizes that she didn't bring her library card. At that moment, Peter walks up to Violet. So, ⓑViolet wants to ask Peter to check out the books for her because she knows he has his library card. In this situation, what would Violet most likely say to Peter?
과제 공공의 구역 유용한 (도서관 등에서) 대출받다 유감스럽게도 갑자기 깨닫다 ~에 걸어서 다가가다
Violet: Can you borrow the books for me with your card?

해석

여: Violet과 Peter는 같은 반 친구이다. 그들은 과학 그룹 과제를 함께 하고 있다. 토요일 아침에, 그들은 공공 도서관에서 만난다. 그들은 도서관의 각기 다른 구역에서 그들이 필요한 책들을 찾기로 결정한다. Violet은 두 권의 유용한 책을 찾아서 그것들을 빌리려고 한다. 안타깝게도, ⓐ그녀는 갑자기 자신이 도서관 카드를 가져오지 않았다는 것을 깨닫는다. 그 순간, Peter가 Violet에게 걸어서 다가간다. 그래서, ⓑViolet은 Peter가 도서관 카드를 가지고 있다는 것을 알기 때문에 그 책들을 빌려달라고 그에게 부탁하고 싶다. 이 상황에서, Violet은 Peter에게 뭐라고 말하겠는가?
Violet: 네 카드로 내 대신 책들을 좀 빌려줄래?

문제 풀이

Violet이 ⓐ자신의 도서관 카드를 가져오지 않았다는 사실을 깨닫고, ⓑ도서관 카드가 있는 Peter에게 책을 대신 빌려달라고 부탁하고 싶어 하므로, 이 상황에 가장 적절한 말은 ⑤이다.
① 과학 동아리에 같이 가입할래?
② 음료를 카드로 계산해도 되나요?
③ 우리 도서관에 책을 기증하는 게 어때?

④ 점심 먹으러 구내식당에 가는 건 어때?

16~17. ㅣ 세트 문항

16. ① 17. ②

선택지 선택비율	① 83%	② 2%	③ 1%	④ 1%	⑤ 10%
	① 3%	② 91%	③ 1%	④ 1%	⑤ 1%

W: Hello, class! Last time we learned about LED technology(기술). I hope all of you have a clear idea of what an LED is now. Today, ⓐI'll talk about how LEDs make our lives better. First, one of the advantages(이점, 장점) of LEDs is the long lifespan(수명). LED bulbs(전구) are used in ⓑlamps and last(지속되다) for over 17 years before you need to change them. Second, LEDs use very low amounts of power. For example, ⓒa television using LEDs in its backlight(배면광) saves a lot of energy. Next, LEDs are brighter than traditional bulbs. So, they make ⓓtraffic lights more visible(보이는) in foggy(안개가 낀) conditions(날씨). Finally, thanks to their small size, LEDs can be used in various small devices(장치, 기구). Any light you see on ⓔa computer keyboard is an LED light. Now, let's think about other products(상품, 제품) that use LEDs.

해석

여: 안녕하세요, 학생 여러분! 우리는 지난 시간에 LED 기술에 대해 배웠습니다. 이제 여러분 모두가 LED가 무엇인지 확실히 알고 있기를 바랍니다. 오늘은 ⓐLED가 어떻게 우리의 삶을 더 좋게 만드는지에 대해 말하려고 합니다. 첫째, LED의 장점들 중 하나는 긴 수명입니다. LED 전구는 ⓑ전등에 사용되며 교체해야 하기까지 17년 이상 갑니다. 둘째, LED는 매우 적은 양의 전력을 사용합니다. 예를 들어, 배면광에 LED를 사용하는 ⓒ텔레비전은 많은 에너지를 절약합니다. 다음으로, LED는 전통적인 전구보다 더 밝습니다. 그래서 안개 낀 날씨에서 ⓓ교통 신호등을 더 잘 보이게 합니다. 마지막으로, 작은 크기 덕분에 LED는 다양한 작은 장치들에 사용될 수 있습니다. ⓔ컴퓨터 키보드에 보이는 모든 빛은 LED 조명입니다. 이제 LED를 사용하는 다른 제품에 대해 생각해 봅시다.

문제 풀이

16. ⓐLED가 어떻게 우리의 삶을 더 좋게 만드는지에 대해 말할 것이라고 했으므로, 여자가 하는 말의 주제로는 ① 'LED 사용의 장점들'이 가장 적절하다.
② 어떻게 LED가 발명되었는가
③ LED에 대한 오해들
④ LED 시장의 경쟁
⑤ LED 기술을 발전시키는 방법
17. ⓑ전등, ⓒ텔레비전, ⓓ교통 신호등, ⓔ컴퓨터 키보드는 언급되었으나, 시계(clocks)는 언급되지 않았다.

[코드 공략하기]

제1회 중급 모의고사

1	①	2	①	3	①	4	④	5	①	6	④
7	①	8	④	9	③	10	④	11	⑤	12	⑤
13	①	14	②	15	②	16	①	17	④		

1. ① | 목적

선택지 선택비율	① 86%	② 1%	③ 3%	④ 5%	⑤ 4%

W: Hello, Princeton High School students. As you know, our school's website is going to be redesigned. Our goals are to make our website more accessible(이용할 수 있는, 이해하기 쉬운) to everyone and to strengthen(강화하다) online security(보안). To better prepare our new website, we're conducting a((특정한 활동을) 하다) survey to gather(모으다) your opinions and suggestions. Your participation(참여) is strongly encouraged. The survey must be completed by this Thursday. For more information, please refer to((정보를 알아내기 위해) ~을 보다) our school bulletin board(게시판). Remember that your input((정보·의견의) 제공[투입]) is valuable(소중한) to everyone in our school's community. Thank you!

해석

여: 안녕하세요, Princeton 고등학교 학생 여러분. 여러분도 알다시피, 우리 학교 웹사이트가 새롭게 디자인될 예정입니다. 우리의 목표는 우리 웹사이트를 모든 사람들이 더 이해하기 쉽게 하고 온라인 보안을 강화하는 것입니다. 우리의 새 웹사이트를 더 잘 준비하고자, 여러분의 의견과 제안을 모으기 위해 설문조사를 하고 있습니다. 여러분의 참여를 적극 권장합니다. 설문조사는 이번 주 목요일까지 완료되어야 합니다. 더 많은 정보는 학교 게시판을 봐 주세요. 여러분의 의견 제공은 우리 학교 공동체의 모든 사람들에게 소중하다는 것을 기억하세요. 감사합니다!

문제 풀이

웹사이트 디자인을 위해 학생들의 의견과 제안을 받는 설문조사를 하고 있음을 알리며, 학생들의 참여를 적극적으로 권장하고 있다.

2. ① | 의견

선택지 선택비율	① 90%	② 7%	③ 1%	④ 1%	⑤ 1%

W: Liam, what's that bunch(묶음) of paper in your hand?

M: It's a deck((카드) 한 벌) of flashcards for memorizing(memorize: 외우다) new words, but it doesn't work well for me.

W: Really? Why not? I think flashcards are helpful for learning vocabulary(어휘).

M: I thought so, too. But looking at the word on one side of the card and the meaning on the back is too boring.

W: Hmm, how about using them in a more interesting way?

M: A more interesting way to use flashcards? What do you mean?

W: Ask a friend to read the meaning on the back, and you shout out the word as the answer.

M: Oh, you mean like asking and answering questions in a quiz?

W: That's right. By using flashcards for quizzes, you can learn new words while having fun.

M: I like your idea a lot. I'll give it a try(한번 해보다)!

해석

여: Liam, 네 손에 있는 저 종이 묶음은 뭐야?
남: 새로운 단어를 외우기 위한 플래시 카드 한 벌인데, 나한테는 별로 효과가 없네.
여: 정말? 왜 없어? 나는 플래시 카드가 어휘 학습에 도움이 된다고 생각해.
남: 나도 그렇게 생각했어. 그런데 카드 한 면의 단어와 뒷면의 뜻을 보는 게 너무 지루해.
여: 음, 그것들을 더 재미있는 방법으로 사용하는 게 어때?
남: 플래시 카드를 사용하는 더 재미있는 방법? 그게 무슨 말이야?
여: 친구에게 뒷면에 있는 뜻을 읽어달라고 하고, 너는 답으로 단어를 큰 소리로 말하는 거야.
남: 아, 퀴즈에서 문제를 내고 답하는 것처럼 말이지?
여: 맞아. 플래시 카드를 퀴즈에 활용하면, 즐기면서 새로운 단어를 배울 수 있어.
남: 네 아이디어가 아주 마음에 들어. 한번 해봐야겠다!

문제 풀이

플래시 카드를 퀴즈에 활용하면 즐기면서 새로운 단어를 배울 수 있다고 말하고 있다.

3. ① | 요지

선택지 선택비율	① 92%	② 1%	③ 2%	④ 4%	⑤ 2%

M: Hello, everyone. I'm Charlie Goodman, your speaker today. I'll be discussing the most effective(효과적인) way to maintain(유지하다) an organized(정돈된) room. Let's start by reflecting on(reflect on: ~에 대해 곰곰이 생각해 보다) the items in your room. Do you really use everything every day? Probably not. The most important thing to do to keep a clean room is to get rid of(~을 없애다[제거하다]) things you no longer need. Don't keep your room filled with items untouched(손대지 않은) for more than six months. If you haven't used an item in six months, it likely means you won't use it again! If you remove(없애다, 제거하다) unnecessary(불필요한) items, you can keep your room nice and neat.

해석

남: 안녕하세요, 여러분. 오늘 여러분의 강연자인 Charlie Goodman입니다. 저는 정돈된 방을 유지하는 가장 효과적인 방법에 대해 의견을 나눌 예정입니다. 여러분의 방에 있는 물건들에 대해 곰곰이 생각해 보는 것으로 시작해 봅시다. 매일 모든 물건을 정말 사용하고 있나요? 아마 그렇지 않을 겁니다. 깨끗한 방을 유지하기 위해 가장 중요한 할 일은 더 이상 필요하지 않은 물건을 없애는 겁니다. 6개월 넘게 손대지 않은 물건들로 방을 가득 차 있게 하지 마세요. 어떤 물건을 6개월 동안 사용하지 않았다면, 다시는 그것을 사용하지 않을 거라는 의미일 가능성이 큽니다! 불필요한 물건을 없애면, 방을 깔끔하고 정돈된 상태로 유지할 수 있습니다.

문제 풀이

불필요한 물건을 없애면 방을 깔끔하고 정돈된 상태로 유지할 수 있다고 말하고 있다.

4. ④ | 그림 일치

선택지 선택비율	① 1%	② 1%	③ 1%	④ 94%	⑤ 3%

W: I've just finished setting up(set up: ~을 설치하다) my booth to sell used items. How does it look?

M: Wow! Everything looks nice, especially ⓐthe banner(현수막) hanging under(걸려 있다) the roof(지붕). People can see it well.

W: I think so, too. I also hope people like ⓑthis striped(줄무늬의) dress in the corner.

M: I bet they will. What about ⓒthe wooden(나무로 된) box here? Is it a used one, too?

W: Yes. To make it look better, ⓓI put some flowers in it.
M: They really catch the eye. Also, ⓔthe shoes on the table look almost new.
W: I haven't worn them much because they are a bit small for me. So I've decided to sell them. ⓕThe guitar beside the table is almost new, too.
M: Oh, I like it the most. I hope you can sell everything you prepared!

해석

여: 내 중고품 판매 부스 설치를 막 마쳤어. 어때 보여?
남: 와! 모든 게 좋아 보여, 특히 ⓐ지붕 아래 걸려 있는 현수막 말이야. 사람들이 그걸 잘 볼 수 있겠어.
여: 내 생각도 그래. 그리고 사람들이 ⓑ모퉁이에 있는 이 줄무늬 드레스를 마음에 들어하면 좋겠어.
남: 분명 그럴 거야. 여기에 있는 ⓒ나무 상자는? 이것도 중고품이야?
여: 응. 더 좋아 보이게 하려고 ⓓ그 안에 꽃을 좀 놓았어.
남: 그게 정말 시선을 사로잡아. 그리고 ⓔ탁자 위에 있는 신발은 거의 새것처럼 보여.
여: 나에게는 약간 작아서 많이 안 신었어. 그래서 팔기로 결심했지. ⓕ탁자 옆에 있는 기타도 거의 새거야.
남: 아, 난 그게 제일 마음에 들어. 네가 준비한 것 모두 팔 수 있으면 좋겠다!

문제 풀이

ⓔ탁자 위에 있는 신발이 거의 새것처럼 보인다고 했으므로, 그림 ④의 곰인형은 대화 내용과 일치하지 않는다.

5. ① | 할 일

선택지 선택비율	① 94%	② 1%	③ 1%	④ 3%	⑤ 0%

M: Mom, I'm home.
W: Hi, Brian. How was your violin lesson?
M: It was fun. I think my violin skills have improved(향상되다) a lot.
W: Good! By the way, did you see the pile(더미) of clothes in the living room?
M: Yeah. I wore those clothes when I was a little kid. Are you going to throw them away?
W: No. I'm going to give them to charity(자선 단체) today.
M: Oh, so you want to donate(기부하다) the clothes?
W: Yes. They're all in good condition(상태) and they've been dry-cleaned(드라이클리닝하다).
M: That's great. ⓐIs there anything I can help you with?
W: Well, ⓑI need some boxes to put the clothes in.
M: No worries. ⓒI'll bring some from the garage(차고).
W: Thanks, but be careful. The lights in the garage aren't working.
M: I got it, Mom. I'll be right back.

해석

남: 엄마, 저 왔어요.
여: 그래, Brian. 바이올린 수업은 어땠니?
남: 재미있었어요. 제 바이올린 실력이 많이 향상된 것 같아요.
여: 잘됐구나! 그런데 거실에 있는 옷 더미 봤니?
남: 네. 제가 어린아이였을 때 입었던 옷이잖아요. 그거 버리실 거예요?
여: 아니. 오늘 자선단체에 줄 거야.
남: 아, 옷을 기부하시려는 거예요?
여: 응. 모두 상태가 좋고 드라이클리닝을 한 거란다.
남: 좋네요. ⓐ제가 도와드릴 수 있는 게 있나요?
여: 음, ⓑ옷을 넣을 상자가 좀 필요해.
남: 걱정 마세요. ⓒ차고에서 좀 가져올게요.
여: 고맙구나, 하지만 조심하렴. 차고 등이 작동하지 않거든.
남: 알겠어요, 엄마. 바로 돌아올게요.

문제 풀이

ⓐ도와줄 게 있냐는 남자의 말에 여자는 ⓑ옷을 넣을 상자가 필요하다고 했고, 이에 남자는 ⓒ상자를 가져오겠다고 했다.

6. ④ | 금액

선택지 선택비율	① 2%	② 10%	③ 4%	④ 79%	⑤ 2%

W: Good afternoon. How can I help you?
M: Hi. I'm looking for a gift for my newborn(갓 난) niece(조카딸). What would you recommend?
W: These pajama sets and dresses are the best-selling clothes for babies.
M: They're so cute. How much are they?
W: This pajama set is 40 dollars, and ⓐthis dress is 50 dollars.
M: Hmm.... I'd like to buy the dress you recommended.
W: Okay. Anything else?
M: Do you have any other items that would go well(잘 어울리다) with the dress?
W: How about this hat? ⓑIt's usually 10 dollars, but it's on sale. You can get 40 percent off that price.
M: That sounds great! I'll take it.
W: Wonderful. So, one dress and one hat, right?
M: Yes. I also have this 5 dollar discount coupon. Can I use it?
W: Let me see. *[Pause]* Unfortunately, no. This coupon only applies to(apply to: ~에 적용되다) purchases(구입, 구매) over 100 dollars.
M: All right. I'll pay with this credit card.

해석

여: 안녕하세요. 무엇을 도와드릴까요?
남: 안녕하세요. 저는 갓 태어난 조카딸에게 줄 선물을 찾고 있는데요. 어떤 것을 추천해 주시겠어요?
여: 이 잠옷 세트와 원피스가 가장 잘 팔리는 아기 옷이에요.
남: 정말 귀엽네요. 그것들은 얼마인가요?
여: 이 잠옷 세트는 40달러이고, ⓐ이 원피스는 50달러입니다.
남: 음…. 추천해 주신 원피스를 사고 싶어요.
여: 알겠습니다. 다른 건요?
남: 원피스에 잘 어울릴 만한 다른 상품은 없나요?
여: 이 모자는 어떠세요? ⓑ원래 10달러인데, 세일 중이에요. 그 가격에서 40퍼센트 할인받으실 수 있어요.
남: 좋아요! 그걸 사도록 할게요.
여: 멋지네요. 그럼, 원피스 하나와 모자 하나 맞으시죠?
남: 네. 그리고 이 5달러 할인 쿠폰도 있어요. 그걸 사용해도 될까요?
여: 확인해 볼게요. [잠시 후] 안타깝지만 사용하실 수 없네요. 이 쿠폰은 100달러 이상 구매 시에만 적용됩니다.
남: 알겠습니다. 이 신용카드로 결제할게요.

문제 풀이

남자는 ⓐ50달러인 원피스 하나와 ⓑ10달러에서 40퍼센트 할인 중인 모자를 하나 사기로 했으므로, 56달러를 지불하면 된다. 5달러 할인 쿠폰은 사용하지 못했다.

7. ① | 이유

선택지 선택비율	① 96%	② 1%	③ 2%	④ 1%	⑤ 1%

W: Hi, Jason. I like your T-shirt.
M: Thanks. I bought it for just $3 at the flea market(벼룩시장).
W: What a bargain(싸게 사는 물건)! I want to buy a T-shirt like yours, too.
M: Then, how about going to the flea market together? It'll be held this Saturday.

W: This Saturday? I'd love to, but I can't.
M: Oh, I know you work at Tom's Bakery. Do you work on Saturdays?
W: No, I only work on weekdays.
M: I see. Then is it because of the medical check-up you reserved last
건강 검진 예약하다
week?
W: I did make an appointment, but I changed the date to next Friday.
예약하다
M: So, then what's your plan for Saturday?
W: Actually, it's my uncle's wedding that day. I promised to play the piano for him at the ceremony.
M: Great! Maybe some other time, then.

해석

여: 안녕, Jason. 네 티셔츠가 마음에 들어.
남: 고마워. 벼룩시장에서 단돈 3달러에 샀어.
여: 정말 싸게 샀네! 나도 네 것 같은 티셔츠를 사고 싶어.
남: 그럼 같이 벼룩시장에 가는 게 어때? 이번 주 토요일에 열릴 거야.
여: 이번 주 토요일? 그러고 싶지만, 갈 수가 없어.
남: 아, 네가 Tom's 제과점에서 일하는 거 알아. 토요일에도 일하니?
여: 아니, 평일에만 일해.
남: 그렇구나. 그럼 지난주에 예약한 건강 검진 때문이니?
여: 예약을 하긴 했는데, 다음 주 금요일로 날짜를 바꿨어.
남: 그럼, 토요일 계획이 뭐니?
여: 사실, 그날이 우리 삼촌의 결혼식이야. 내가 결혼식에서 삼촌을 위해 피아노를 연주하기로 약속했거든.
남: 멋지다! 그럼 다른 날에 가자.

문제 풀이

여자는 토요일에 삼촌 결혼식에서 피아노를 연주해야 하기 때문에 벼룩시장에 갈 수 없다고 했다.

8. ④ | 언급

선택지 선택비율	① 1%	② 2%	③ 1%	④ 94%	⑤ 2%

M: Have you heard about the 2025 Aquathlon?
W: No, I haven't. What is it?
M: ⓐIt's a competition that combines swimming and running. It's
대회, 경기 결합시키다, 합치다
coming up soon.
W: That sounds great! I've competed in several swimming events, but
(시합 등에) 참가하다
never anything like this. Are you going to participate?
M: Absolutely. I've been training for both swimming and running.
W: When is the event?
M: ⓑIt's on May 24th.
W: I'd like to join, too. Have you completed the registration process?
완료하다, 끝마치다 등록
M: Not yet. I heard ⓒwe need to register online by filling out a form.
등록하다 서식을 작성하다
Let's sign up together.
신청하다
W: Sounds good. How about training together before the event?
M: Great idea. ⓓThe competition will be held at Blue River. Why don't we find a similar place to practice?
W: I know the best place. Let's get started this weekend!

해석

남: 2025 Aquathlon에 대해 들어봤어?
여: 아니, 못 들어봤어. 그게 뭐야?
남: ⓐ수영과 달리기를 결합한 경기야. 곧 열릴 거야.
여: 멋지다! 나는 여러 수영 경기에 참가한 적이 있지만, 이런 건 없었어. 너는 참가할 거야?
남: 물론이지. 수영이랑 달리기 둘 다 훈련해 오고 있는 중이야.
여: 경기가 언제야?
남: ⓑ5월 24일이야.
여: 나도 참가하고 싶어. 너는 등록 절차를 마쳤어?
남: 아니, 아직. ⓒ온라인으로 서식을 작성해서 등록해야 한다고 들었어. 같이 신청하자.
여: 좋아. 경기 전에 같이 훈련하는 건 어때?
남: 좋은 생각이야. ⓓ경기가 Blue River에서 열릴 예정이거든. 연습할 비슷한 장소를 찾는 게 어때?
여: 내가 딱 좋은 장소를 알아. 이번 주말에 시작하자!

문제 풀이

ⓐ경기 종목, ⓑ경기 날짜, ⓒ등록 방법, ⓓ경기 장소는 언급되었지만, 참가비는 언급되지 않았다.

9. ③ | 내용 일치

선택지 선택비율	① 4%	② 2%	③ 91%	④ 1%	⑤ 2%

W: Hello, viewers. The 2023 Board Game Design Contest is an annual event for designing board games. It's open to board game
연례의
fans ⓐof all ages around the world. The contest is split into two
나누다
rounds. ⓑIn round one, contestants must submit a 2-minute video
참가자 제출하다
introducing their games. In round two, contestants must hand in
introduce: 소개하다 ~을 제출하다
a document that explains how to play their game. ⓒDuring round
문서
two, contestants get the chance to work with experienced game
경험이 풍부한
designers who will help each contestant with establishing the rules
수립하다
for their game. ⓓThe final winner of the contest receives $1,000, plus a chance to release his or her game. ⓔRegistration closes on
출시하다
Friday, September 15th. Show us your skills as a game designer!

해석

여: 안녕하세요, 시청자 여러분. 2023 보드게임 디자인 경연대회는 보드게임 디자인을 위한 연례 행사입니다. 이 경연대회는 세계의 ⓐ모든 연령의 보드게임 팬들에게 열려 있습니다. 경연대회는 2라운드로 나뉩니다. ⓑ1라운드에서 참가자들은 자신의 게임을 소개하는 2분짜리 영상을 제출해야 합니다. 2라운드에서 참가자들은 게임을 하는 방법을 설명하는 문서를 제출해야 합니다. ⓒ2라운드에서 참가자들은 각 참가자들이 게임 규칙을 수립하는 데 도움을 줄 경험이 풍부한 게임 디자이너와 함께 일할 기회를 갖게 됩니다. 경연대회의 ⓓ최종 우승자는 1,000달러를 받고, 이에 더하여 자신의 게임을 출시할 기회를 얻습니다. ⓔ등록은 9월 15일 금요일에 마감됩니다. 게임 디자이너로서의 여러분의 기술을 보여주세요!

문제 풀이

ⓒ2라운드에서 게임 규칙 수립에 도움을 줄 경험이 풍부한 게임 디자이너과 협업한다고 했다.

10. ④ | 도표

선택지 선택비율	① 4%	② 10%	③ 7%	④ 75%	⑤ 1%

M: Anna, what are you doing?
W: I'm searching the Internet to buy a new oven. Can you help me choose from this list?
M: What do you plan to make with it?
W: Well, I really enjoy baking, but I'd like to use it to make other things, too.
M: Then, I think ⓐyou need a medium or big size oven.
W: All right. I'll cross out this item. Which timer do you think will be
선을 그어 지우다
best?

M: If you're making many kinds of food, then I think ⓑthe timer should last at least 75 minutes.
지속되다
W: Yeah. You have a good point. So, we have three options left.
M: Let's compare the customer ratings here.
비교하다 평가
W: Hmm. This one only got three stars. ⓒI want one with more than four stars.
M: Okay. Look! Between these two, this one is cheaper than that one.
W: Then, ⓓI'll order the cheaper one.

해석

남: Anna, 너 뭐하고 있니?
여: 새 오븐을 사기 위해 인터넷을 검색하고 있어. 내가 이 목록에서 고르는 것을 도와줄 수 있니?
남: 그것으로 무엇을 만들 계획이니?
여: 음, 나는 빵 굽는 것을 정말로 좋아하지만, 다른 것들을 만들기 위해서도 그것을 사용하고 싶어.
남: 그렇다면, 내 생각에 ⓐ너는 중간이나 큰 크기의 오븐이 필요하겠어.
여: 좋아. 이 품목은 지울게. 너는 어느 타이머가 가장 좋을 것 같니?
남: 네가 많은 종류의 음식을 만들 거라면, 내 생각에 ⓑ타이머가 최소한 75분 동안 지속되어야 할 것 같아.
여: 맞아. 좋은 지적이야. 그러면, 우리는 세 가지 선택 사항이 남네.
남: 여기 고객 평가를 비교해 보자.
여: 음. 이것은 겨우 별 세 개를 받았네. ⓒ나는 별 네 개 이상 받은 것을 원해.
남: 좋아. 봐! 이 두 개 중에, 이게 저것보다 가격이 더 싸.
여: 그렇다면, ⓓ가격이 더 싼 것으로 주문할게.

문제 풀이

여자는 ⓐ중간이거나 큰 크기에, ⓑ타이머가 최소 75분 동안 지속되며, ⓒ별 네 개 이상의 고객 평가를 받은 오븐 중 ⓓ가격이 더 싼 것을 구입할 것이다.

11. ⑤ | 짧은 대화 응답

선택지 선택비율	① 1%	② 2%	③ 6%	④ 9%	⑤ 82%

W: Our teacher said ⓐwe have to make a presentation at the International Exchange Program next week.
발표하다
M: Next week? We should hurry, then. What should we do first?
W: Let me see. ⓑFirst, I think we'd better decide on the topic for our presentation.
~을 (결)정하다 주제
M: Okay. Let's find one that is easy and interesting to talk about.

해석

여: ⓐ우리가 다음 주에 국제 교류 프로그램에서 발표를 해야 한다고 선생님께서 말씀하셨어.
남: 다음 주에? 그럼 서둘러야겠네. 먼저 뭘 해야 할까?
여: 어디 보자. ⓑ우선 발표 주제를 정하는 게 좋을 것 같아.
남: 좋아. 이야기하기 쉽고 재미있는 것을 찾아보자.

문제 풀이

ⓐ여자가 다음 주 국제 교류 프로그램에서 발표를 해야 하는데 ⓑ우선 발표 주제를 정하는 것이 좋을 것 같다고 했으므로, 발표 주제를 제안하는 ⑤가 응답으로 가장 적절하다.
① 말도 안 돼. 우리는 국제적인 프로그램이 필요해.
② 걱정하지 마. 내 책을 네 것과 맞바꿀 수 있어.
③ 나쁘지 않아. 그건 주제문의 좋은 본보기야.
④ 이해해. 난 발표 동안 정말 긴장됐어.

12. ⑤ | 짧은 대화 응답

선택지 선택비율	① 7%	② 13%	③ 10%	④ 3%	⑤ 64%

M: Oh, Susan! ⓐThe light in the bathroom went out.
go out: (불·전깃불이) 꺼지다[나가다]
W: I know, but don't worry. We only have to replace the light bulb. ⓑI'll buy one tomorrow.
바꾸다, 교체하다 전구
M: But, ⓒit's uncomfortable to use the bathroom.
불편한
W: Then, I'll go and buy a new one right now.

해석

남: 오, Susan! ⓐ욕실 등이 나갔네요.
여: 알고 있는데, 걱정하지 마요. 전구만 교체하면 돼요. ⓑ내가 내일 살게요.
남: 하지만 ⓒ욕실을 사용하기 불편하잖아요.
여: 그럼 지금 가서 새것을 살게요.

문제 풀이

ⓐ욕실 등이 나갔다는 남자의 말에 여자가 ⓑ내일 전구를 사겠다고 하자, 남자는 ⓒ욕실 사용이 불편하다고 했다. 이에 가장 적절한 응답은 ⑤이다.
① 그래요, 방 전체가 너무 밝아요.
② 청소는 곧 끝날 거예요.
③ 좋아요, 욕실에서 머리를 감도록 해요.
④ 목수가 여기로 올 예정이에요.

13. ① | 긴 대화 응답

선택지 선택비율	① 82%	② 3%	③ 2%	④ 10%	⑤ 2%

W: Fred, I got the blueberry juice we ordered.
M: Thanks, Kathy. Oh, it has a paper straw. Don't they have a plastic one?
빨대
W: What's wrong with a paper straw?
M: It can get soaked and fall apart while drinking. So I prefer a plastic straw.
흠뻑 젖시다 다 허물어질 정도이다
W: But plastic straws can harm the environment.
해를 끼치다 환경
M: Protecting the environment is all good, but my drink tastes bad with paper straws.
보호하다
W: If so, ⓐthere are other types of straws to enjoy your drink that cause less harm to the environment.
유발하다 해
M: I didn't know there were other kinds. ⓑCan you name some of them?
이름을 대다
W: ⓒHave you heard of a silicone straw?
M: No, I haven't. It sounds interesting.
W: ⓓThere are also straws made of glass or metal. They're reusable and don't affect the taste of your drink.
재사용할 수 있는 영향을 미치다
M: Thanks for letting me know. I should try using them.

해석

여: Fred, 우리가 주문한 블루베리 주스를 받았어요.
남: 고마워요, Kathy. 아, 종이 빨대네요. 플라스틱 빨대는 없나요?
여: 종이 빨대에 문제가 있나요?
남: 마실 때 젖어서 다 허물어질 수 있어서요. 그래서 플라스틱 빨대가 더 좋아요.
여: 하지만 플라스틱 빨대는 환경에 해를 끼칠 수 있어요.
남: 환경을 보호하는 건 좋지만, 종이 빨대로 먹는 음료는 맛이 없어요.
여: 그렇다면, ⓐ음료를 즐기는 데 환경에 해를 덜 유발하는 다른 형태의 빨대들이 있어요.

남: 다른 종류가 있는지 몰랐어요. ⓑ이름을 말해볼래요?
여: ⓒ실리콘 빨대 들어봤나요?
남: 아니요. 흥미롭네요.
여: ⓓ유리나 금속으로 만들어진 빨대도 있어요. 그것들은 재사용할 수 있고 음료 맛에 영향을 미치지 않아요.
남: 알려줘서 고마워요. 그걸 사용해봐야겠네요.

문제 풀이

ⓐ환경에 해를 덜 끼치는 빨대가 있다는 여자의 말에 남자는 ⓑ이름을 알려달라고 했고, 여자는 ⓒ실리콘 빨대와 ⓓ유리나 금속으로 만든 빨대를 말해주었다. 따라서 그 빨대를 사용해보겠다는 내용의 ①이 응답으로 가장 적절하다.
② 맛이 좋네요. 이 주스의 레시피가 궁금해요.
③ 걱정하지 마요. 난 내가 사용하는 빨대 종류에 관심 없어요.
④ 당신 말이 맞아요. 앞으로는 실리콘 빨대를 사용하지 않는 게 낫겠어요.
⑤ 난 이미 그것들을 모두 사용해봤지만, 여전히 종이 빨대가 더 좋아요.

14. ② | 긴 대화 응답

선택지 선택비율	① 6%	② 77%	③ 6%	④ 6%	⑤ 2%

W: How is it going with your essay on the cultures of other countries?
M: Not so well. How about you?
W: I've just started working on it.
M: For me, it was hard to find an interesting topic.
W: Same with me. Also, it's not easy to put my personal opinions in the essay as the teacher required(요구하다).
M: I know. He always regards(생각하다, 여기다) our own opinions as the most important part.
W: So, what is your topic?
M: It's about India and its culture.
W: Oh, my! ⓐThat's exactly what I'm going to write about.
M: Really? ⓑI'm not sure if it's okay to have the same topic. Should one of us change it?
W: Well, let's ask the teacher about it.

해석

여: 다른 나라의 문화에 대한 에세이 잘 쓰고 있니?
남: 그리 잘 안 되고 있어. 넌 어때?
여: 난 이제 막 쓰기 시작했어.
남: 나에게 있어선, 재미있는 주제를 찾는 것이 어려웠어.
여: 나도 그래. 그리고 선생님께서 요구하신 대로 내 개인적인 의견을 에세이에 쓰는 것이 쉽지 않아.
남: 알아. 선생님께서는 항상 우리 자신의 의견을 가장 중요한 부분으로 여기시잖아.
여: 그래서, 네 주제는 뭐니?
남: 인도와 인도 문화에 대한 거야.
여: 아, 이런! ⓐ그게 바로 내가 쓰려는 건데.
남: 정말? ⓑ같은 주제로 써도 괜찮을지 모르겠네. 우리 중 한 명이 주제를 바꿔야 할까?
여: 음, 그것에 대해서 선생님께 여쭤보자.

문제 풀이

ⓐ여자가 쓰려 하는 에세이의 주제가 남자의 것과 똑같다고 하자, ⓑ남자가 둘 중 한 명이 주제를 바꿔야 하는지 궁금해하고 있으므로, 그것에 대해 선생님께 여쭤보자는 내용의 ②가 응답으로 가장 적절하다.
① 그래, 그것은 멋진 에세이였어.
③ 아니, 아직 주제를 결정하지 않았어.
④ 아니, 나는 인도 문화에 관심이 없어.
⑤ 오, 네 주제는 내 것과 크게 달라.

15. ② | 상황에 적절한 말

선택지 선택비율	① 3%	② 75%	③ 9%	④ 10%	⑤ 3%

M: Nick and Annie are partners for an art project. They are supposed to make a presentation on the life of Vincent van Gogh. However, while researching(연구[조사]하다) and working on their project, ⓐthey realized that some of the content(내용) they found was conflicting(모순되는, 상충되는). For example, there was a disagreement(의견 충돌, 불일치) about when exactly Van Gogh started painting. Nick gathered(모으다) his information from the books in the library, while Annie collected(모으다) hers from the Internet. Nick and Annie are not sure which one to trust(신뢰하다). Nick wants their presentation to be as precise(정확한) as possible, so ⓑhe thinks that they should ask their professor(교수) for help with deciding which source((자료의) 출처) is more reliable(믿을 만한). In this situation, what would Nick most likely say to Annie?
Nick: We'd better ask our professor about which source to trust.

해석

남: Nick과 Annie는 미술 프로젝트의 파트너이다. 그들은 빈센트 반 고흐의 삶에 대한 발표를 하기로 되어 있다. 하지만 그들의 프로젝트에 대해 조사하고 작업하는 동안, ⓐ그들이 찾은 내용 중 일부가 상충된다는 것을 깨달았다. 예를 들어, 정확히 언제 반 고흐가 그림을 그리기 시작했는지에 대한 의견 차이가 있었다. Nick은 도서관에 있는 책들로부터 그의 정보를 모은 반면, Annie는 인터넷으로부터 그녀의 정보를 모았다. Nick과 Annie는 어느 것을 믿어야 할지 확신하지 못한다. Nick은 그들의 발표가 가능한 한 정확하기를 원하기에, ⓑ어떤 출처가 더 신뢰할 만한지 결정하는 데 있어서 그들의 교수님께 도움을 요청해야 한다고 생각한다. 이 상황에서, Nick은 Annie에게 뭐라고 말하겠는가?
Nick: 어떤 출처를 신뢰해야 할지 교수님께 여쭤보는 게 좋을 것 같아.

문제 풀이

남자는 빈센트 반 고흐에 대해 조사하는 과정에서, ⓐ그들이 찾은 내용 중 일부가 상충된다는 것을 깨닫고, ⓑ어떤 자료의 출처가 더 신뢰할 만한지 결정하는 데 있어서 교수님께 도움을 요청해야 한다고 생각하고 있으므로, 교수님께 어떤 출처를 신뢰해야 할지 물어보자는 ②가 가장 적절하다.
① 내 내용을 지금 당장 네 것으로 교체하고 싶어.
③ 네 정보는 인터넷에 있는 정보와 달라.
④ 넌 발표를 위해 더 많은 조사를 했어야 했어.
⑤ 나는 반 고흐가 10대 초반에 그림을 그리기 시작했다고 생각해.

16~17. | 세트 문항

16. ① 17. ④

선택지 선택비율	①	②	③	④	⑤
16	① 71%	② 2%	③ 22%	④ 2%	⑤ 2%
17	① 3%	② 1%	③ 1%	④ 94%	⑤ 1%

M: Hello, everyone. I'm Dr. Martin Muller. ⓐDo you know that mathematical(수학의) ability is widespread(널리 퍼진) in the animal kingdom? Many biologists(생물학자) have suggested that counting is not unique to humans. For instance, ⓑwolves use strength in numbers while hunting. Wolves have optimal(최적의, 최상의) group sizes for hunting different prey. In addition, female ⓒfrogs count the number of pulses(리듬) in a male frog's cry. They can do this for phrases(악구) up to 10 notes(음) long. Despite what you may have heard, ⓓchickens are quite smart. Research shows

that newly hatched chicks and adult chickens can count and do
부화하다
basic math. Lastly, the real math wizards of the animal kingdom are ⓔdesert ants. They are able to find their way back home after leaving their nests for food by counting steps. Now, we will watch
둥지, 집
a video about these animals.

해석

남: 안녕하세요, 여러분. Martin Muller 박사입니다. ⓐ동물 왕국에 수학 능력이 널리 퍼져 있다는 것을 알고 있나요? 많은 생물학자들은 수를 세는 것이 인간에게만 고유한 것이 아님을 시사해 왔습니다. 예를 들어, ⓑ늑대는 사냥을 할 때 수에 있어서의 강점을 이용합니다. 늑대는 각기 다른 먹이 사냥을 위해 최적의 그룹 크기를 이룹니다. 게다가, 암컷 ⓒ개구리는 수컷 개구리의 울음소리의 리듬 수를 셉니다. 10개 음 길이 악구까지 셀 수 있죠. 들어본 적이 있을지는 모르지만, ⓓ닭은 꽤 영리합니다. 갓 부화한 병아리와 다 자란 닭은 수를 세고 기본적인 수학을 할 수 있다는 것을 연구가 보여줍니다. 마지막으로, 동물 왕국의 진정한 수학의 귀재는 ⓔ사막 개미인데요. 걸음 수를 셈으로써 먹이를 찾아 집을 떠났다가 돌아오는 길을 찾을 수 있습니다. 이제, 이런 동물들에 관한 영상을 보겠습니다.

문제 풀이

16. 남자는 ⓐ동물들에게 수학 능력이 있어 수를 세는 것이 인간에게만 있는 고유한 능력이 아니라는 것을 말하고 있으므로, ① '동물의 수 세기 능력'이 남자가 하는 말의 주제로 가장 적절하다.
② 동물들이 이주하는 이유
③ 야생동물의 사냥 습관
④ 동물권 보호의 필요성
⑤ 멸종 위기에 처한 동물들을 보호하는 방법
17. ⓑ늑대, ⓒ개구리, ⓓ닭, ⓔ사막 개미는 언급되었으나, 뱀(snakes)은 언급되지 않았다.

[코드 공략하기]

제2회 중급 모의고사

1	③	2	②	3	②	4	④	5	⑤	6	①
7	⑤	8	④	9	④	10	①	11	②	12	①
13	④	14	①	15	③	16	②	17	③		

1. ③ | 목적

선택지 선택비율	① 3%	② 1%	③ 89%	④ 4%	⑤ 3%

M: Hello, students. I'm the school nutritionist, Mr. Jackson. Over the
영양사
past week, we have conducted a survey on the school website
설문 조사를 실시하다
about the meals you ate this semester. I want to thank those of
학기
you who have responded. Unfortunately, less than 50 percent of
응하다, 응답하다
students answered the survey. We don't have enough data to make your school meals better. Therefore, we decided to extend the
연장하다
survey period by one week. The meal survey is now open until next
기간
Wednesday. We hope that giving you another week to participate
~에 참여하다
in the survey will help improve the quality of your school meals.
향상시키다
Thank you for listening.

해석

남: 안녕하세요, 학생 여러분. 학교 영양사 Jackson입니다. 지난 주 동안, 이번 학기에 여러분이 먹은 식사에 관해 학교 웹사이트에서 설문 조사를 실시했는데요. 응해 주신 분들께 감사하고 싶습니다. 안타깝게도, 50퍼센트 미만의 학생들이 설문 조사에 답해 주셨습니다. 저희는 여러분의 학교 급식을 더 좋게 하기에 충분한 자료를 얻지 못했습니다. 따라서 설문 조사 기간을 일주일 연장하기로 결정했습니다. 급식 설문 조사는 현재 다음 주 수요일까지 열려 있습니다. 여러분께 설문 조사에 참여할 한 주를 더 드리는 것이 학교 급식의 질을 향상시키는 데 도움이 되길 바랍니다. 들어 주셔서 감사합니다.

문제 풀이

남자는 학교 급식 설문 조사가 일주일 연장되었음을 말하고 있다.

2. ② | 의견

선택지 선택비율	① 3%	② 92%	③ 1%	④ 2%	⑤ 2%

M: Hey, sweetie. Why are you so quiet?
W: Dad, I feel bad today.
M: What's the matter?
W: I can't buy the running shoes I want.
M: How come? You just got paid from your part-time job!
W: Yeah, but I spent it all. I feel like I never have enough money.
M: ⓐHave you tried writing down where you spend your money?
W: No, I haven't. Do you think writing it down is helpful?
M: Totally. ⓑOnce you see where your money goes, you'll be more careful with it.
W: Oh, that's a good point, Dad.
M: ⓒIt's crucial to keep a record of your spending. That'll help you
매우 중요한 기록하다
manage your money wisely.
관리하다 현명하게
W: Okay, I'll remember that.

해석

남: 얘야, 왜 이렇게 조용하니?
여: 아빠, 오늘 기분이 안 좋아요.
남: 무슨 일이야?
여: 제가 원하는 운동화를 살 수가 없어요.
남: 왜? 너 얼마전에 아르바이트비 받았잖아!
여: 맞아요, 하지만 그걸 다 썼어요. 늘 돈이 충분하지 않은 느낌이에요.
남: ⓐ네가 돈을 쓰는 곳을 적어보려고 한 적 있니?
여: 아니요, 그런 적 없어요. 그걸 적는 게 도움이 된다고 생각하세요?
남: 물론이지. ⓑ네 돈이 쓰이는 곳을 알면, 더 신중해질 거야.
여: 아, 좋은 말씀이에요, 아빠.
남: ⓒ지출을 기록하는 건 매우 중요하단다. 그게 돈을 현명하게 관리하도록 도울 거야.
여: 네, 기억할게요.

문제 풀이

남자는 ⓐⓑⓒ돈을 어디에 쓰는지 지출을 기록하면 더 신중해져 돈을 현명하게 관리할 수 있다고 말하고 있다.

3. ② | 관계

선택지 선택비율	① 3%	② 92%	③ 1%	④ 4%	⑤ 0%

[Phone rings.]
W: Hello.
M: Hello. Can I speak to Ms. Norton?
W: This is she.
M: Hi, this is Mark Kelly from Polaris Studio. I heard you were a scientific advisor on the movie *Space Dynasty*.
고문, 조언자
W: Yes, I helped the writers with the script.
대본
M: I thought the script was well written and had many entertaining scenes related to science.
재미있는 / 장면 / ~와 관련 있는
W: Thank you. It was a lot of fun.
M: ⓐI'm actually writing a script for a science fiction movie right now, and I was wondering if you could help me with your expertise.
공상과학영화 / 전문 지식
W: Okay. What's the movie about?
M: It's about natural disasters caused by global warming. ⓑI need advice from science experts like you to make it more realistic.
자연재해 / 지구 온난화 / 조언 / 전문가 / 현실적인
W: I'd be interested. I've done a lot of scientific research on global warming in my lab. My findings might be useful for you.
조사, 연구 / 실험실 / 연구 결과
M: Fantastic! I'll send you my script. Thank you so much.

해석

[전화벨이 울린다.]
여: 여보세요.
남: 여보세요. Norton 씨 계신가요?
여: 전데요.
남: 안녕하세요, 저는 Polaris 스튜디오의 Mark Kelly입니다. 영화 Space Dynasty의 과학 고문이셨다고 들었습니다.
여: 네, 작가님의 대본에 도움을 드렸죠.
남: 대본이 잘 쓰여졌고 과학과 관련 있는 재미있는 장면이 많았던 것 같아요.
여: 고맙습니다. 굉장히 재미있었어요.
남: ⓐ실은 제가 지금 공상과학영화 대본을 쓰고 있는데요, 선생님의 전문 지식으로 저를 도와주실 수 있는지 궁금합니다.
여: 좋아요. 무엇에 관한 영화인가요?
남: 지구 온난화로 야기된 자연재해에 관한 거예요. 영화를 더 현실적으로 만들기 위해서 ⓑ선생님 같은 과학 전문가의 조언이 필요합니다.
여: 관심이 생기네요. 제 실험실에서 지구 온난화에 관한 과학 연구를 많이 했거든요. 제 연구 결과가 유용할지도 모르겠어요.
남: 정말 좋네요! 제 대본을 보내드리겠습니다. 정말 고맙습니다.

문제 풀이

남자는 ⓐ공상과학영화 대본을 쓰고 있다고 했고, 여자에게 ⓑ과학 전문가의 조언이 필요하다고 했으므로, 두 사람의 관계가 영화 각본가와 과학자임을 알 수 있다.

4. ④ | 그림 일치

선택지 선택비율	① 2%	② 0%	③ 2%	④ 92%	⑤ 1%

M: Hello, Ms. Clark. How's it going with rearranging your classroom?
rearrange: 재배치하다
W: Good morning, Mr. Cooper. It's almost done. Do you want to see a picture of what it looks like?
M: Sure. *[Pause]* Oh, I see ⓐa round clock on the wall. It looks nice.
W: Yes. I replaced the old clock with a new one.
교체하다
M: I also like ⓑthe bookcase under the window.
책장
W: I put it there to make it easier for students to read books. How do you like ⓒthe stripe-patterned rug?
M: I like it. It goes well with the classroom. By the way, what are ⓓthe two boxes on the table for?
W: I'll put some classroom supplies in them. I also put ⓔa flower pot in the corner.
물품 / 화분
M: Great idea! I think your students will really like the new classroom.
W: Thank you.

해석

남: 안녕하세요, Clark 선생님. 교실 재배치는 어떻게 돼 가나요?
여: 좋은 아침이에요, Cooper 선생님. 거의 다 됐어요. 어떻게 생겼는지 사진 보시겠어요?
남: 좋아요. [잠시 후] 아, ⓐ벽에 둥근 시계가 보이네요. 좋아 보여요.
여: 네. 오래된 시계를 새것으로 교체했어요.
남: ⓑ창문 아래 책장도 마음에 들어요.
여: 학생들이 책 읽기 더 쉽게 하려고 거기에 그걸 뒀어요. ⓒ줄무늬 깔개는 어때요?
남: 마음에 들어요. 교실과 잘 어울려요. 그런데 ⓓ탁자 위에 있는 상자 두 개는 뭘 위한 거예요?
여: 학급 물품을 그 안에 둘 거예요. ⓔ모퉁이에 화분도 두었어요.
남: 좋은 생각이네요! 학생들이 새 교실을 정말 좋아할 것 같아요.
여: 고마워요.

문제 풀이

ⓓ탁자 위에 상자 두 개가 있다고 했으므로, 그림 ④의 탁자 위 상자 한 개는 대화 내용과 일치하지 않는다.

5. ⑤ | 부탁한 일

선택지 선택비율	① 4%	② 8%	③ 1%	④ 1%	⑤ 86%

W: We're almost done with our report on climate change. Why don't we check it together to see if everything is okay?
기후 변화
M: That's a good idea. Are you sure we included every graph we made?
포함하다
W: Yes, they are all there in the report. They clearly show the causes of climate change that we've researched.
원인 / 연구[조사]하다
M: Good to hear that. How about the pictures? We've chosen the five best pictures.
W: They look very convincing. What do you think about the part
설득력이 있는

discussing the students' awareness? Many of our friends
인식, 의식
participated in our survey.
(설문)조사
M: The survey results show that many students know how serious it is. How about the action plans?
실천 계획
W: We have two action plans here, but I think we need more. Could you send me the data from our research?
연구, 조사
M: Sure. I'll send the data this afternoon.

해석

여: 우리 기후 변화에 관한 보고서가 거의 다 끝났어. 함께 확인하면서 모든 게 괜찮은지 보는 게 어때?
남: 좋은 생각이야. 우리가 제작한 모든 그래프를 포함한 거 확실해?
여: 응, 보고서에 모두 있어. 우리가 조사한 기후 변화의 원인을 명확히 보여줘.
남: 그거 듣기 좋네. 사진들은 어때? 우리가 가장 훌륭한 사진 다섯 장을 골랐잖아.
여: 그것들은 아주 설득력 있어 보여. 학생들의 인식에 대해 논의하는 부분은 어떻게 생각해? 많은 친구들이 우리 설문조사에 참여했잖아.
남: 많은 학생들이 그게 얼마나 심각한지 알고 있다는 걸 설문조사 결과가 보여주지. 실천 계획은 어때?
여: 여기 두 가지 실천 계획이 있는데, 더 필요할 것 같아. 우리 조사에서 나온 데이터를 나한테 전송해 줄 수 있어?
남: 물론이지. 오늘 오후에 데이터를 전송할게.

문제 풀이

여자가 남자에게 조사에서 나온 데이터를 전송해 달라고 부탁했다.

6. ① | 금액

선택지 선택비율	① 72%	② 5%	③ 11%	④ 11%	⑤ 1%

M: Welcome to the World History Museum. How may I help you?
W: Hi, I'd like to purchase three admission tickets. What's the fee for
구매하다 입장권 요금
an adult?
M: ⓐAn adult ticket is $10.
W: What about for seniors?
노인, 어르신
M: If you look at the price board, ⓑpeople over 65 years of age are
가격표
charged $8.
W: Okay, then ⓒI'll buy one senior ticket, and two adult tickets.
M: May I see an identification card for the senior?
신분증
W: Yeah, just a moment. Here it is.
M: Thank you. And today is National Museum Day, so ⓓyou can get 50% off the total price.
W: Wow, that's amazing!
M: ⓔIf you need audio guides, they're $5 each.
W: ⓕNo, thanks. Only the tickets, please. Here's my credit card.

해석

남: 세계 역사 박물관에 오신 것을 환영합니다. 어떻게 도와드릴까요?
여: 안녕하세요, 입장권 세 장을 사고 싶어요. 성인 요금은 얼마인가요?
남: ⓐ성인 입장권은 10달러입니다.
여: 노인 입장권은요?
남: 가격판을 보시면, ⓑ65세 이상 노인은 8달러입니다.
여: 알겠습니다, 그럼 ⓒ노인 입장권 한 장과 성인 입장권 두 장 구매할게요.
남: 어르신의 신분증을 볼 수 있을까요?
여: 네, 잠시만요. 여기 있습니다.
남: 감사합니다. 그리고 오늘이 국립 박물관의 날이어서, ⓓ총 금액의 50%를 할인받으실 수 있습니다.
여: 와, 굉장해요!
남: ⓔ오디오 가이드가 필요하시면, 그건 각각 5달러입니다.
여: ⓕ아니요, 괜찮습니다. 입장권만 주세요. 제 신용카드 여기 있습니다.

문제 풀이

ⓐⓒ10달러짜리 성인 입장권 두 장과 ⓑⓒ8달러짜리 노인 입장권 한 장을 구매했는데 ⓓ50프로 할인을 받았고, ⓔ5달러짜리 오디오 가이드는 ⓕ필요하지 않다고 했으므로, 여자가 지불할 총 금액은 14달러이다.

7. ⑤ | 이유

선택지 선택비율	① 2%	② 1%	③ 1%	④ 3%	⑤ 91%

W: I'm so happy our exams are over.
M: Me, too. They were really tough this time.
힘든, 어려운
W: I know. Getting a cold made me even more stressed.
M: Are you still sick?
W: No, I feel all right now. What are you doing after school today?
M: Some of our classmates are going to play board games to celebrate
기념하다, 축하하다
the end of exams. Do you want to come?
W: I'd love to go, but I can't.
M: Why not?
W: Did I tell you my family is going on a ski trip this weekend?
M: No, you didn't. Why are you going skiing?
W: It's my dad's birthday, so we planned this trip for him.
M: That sounds like a perfect gift for your dad.
W: I hope so. I need to go shopping for goggles and a ski suit for myself
고글 스키복
today.
M: Oh, I see. Have a nice trip.

해석

여: 우리 시험이 끝나서 너무 기뻐.
남: 나도 그래. 이번에는 정말 어려웠어.
여: 맞아. 감기에 걸린 게 나를 훨씬 더 스트레스를 받게 했어.
남: 너 아직도 아프니?
여: 아니, 지금은 괜찮아. 오늘 방과 후에 뭐해?
남: 몇몇 우리 반 친구들이 시험 끝난 걸 기념하기 위해 보드게임을 할 거야. 너도 올래?
여: 나도 가고 싶지만, 그럴 수 없어.
남: 왜?
여: 내가 우리 가족이 이번 주말에 스키 여행을 간다고 말했었나?
남: 아니, 말 안 했어. 왜 스키 타러 가니?
여: 우리 아빠 생신이셔서, 아빠를 위해 이 여행을 계획했어.
남: 너희 아빠에게 딱 알맞은 선물인 것 같아.
여: 그러면 좋겠어. 오늘은 내 고글과 스키복을 사러 가야 해.
남: 아, 그렇구나. 즐거운 여행 되렴.

문제 풀이

여자는 오늘 고글과 스키복을 사러 가야 하기 때문에 보드게임을 하러 갈 수 없다고 했다.

코드 +α 계획을 나타내는 표현

I'm **going to** move to a city. (난 도시로 이사할 거야.)
I'm **planning to** learn a new language. (난 새로운 언어를 배울 계획이야.)
I'm **thinking of** rearranging my room. (난 방을 재배치할 생각이야.)

8. ④ | 언급

선택지 선택비율	① 6%	② 2%	③ 3%	④ 84%	⑤ 4%

M: Hello, Dr. Peterson. How are you doing these days?
W: Hello, Dr. Collins. Good, I'm working on the Dream Bio Research Project.

M: You mean the medical research project sponsored by the
의학의 후원하다
government?
W: That's right. ⓐMore than 20 researchers are involved in the project
참여시키다
and I'm the head researcher.
수석 연구원
M: Wow, you're in charge of a really big job. How big is the budget for
be in charge of: ~을 담당하다 예산
the project?
W: ⓑWe're allowed to spend one million dollars on the project.
M: That's a really huge amount. ⓒIt's a project to develop a new drug
양, 액수 개발하다
for lung cancer, isn't it?
폐암
W: That's right.
M: How long will the research project last?
지속되다
W: ⓓIt's a 5-year project. I hope we can develop the drug within this period.
M: I wish you success, Dr. Peterson.
W: Thank you, Dr. Collins.

해석

남: 안녕하세요, Peterson 박사님. 요즘 어떻게 지내세요?
여: 안녕하세요, Collins 박사님. 잘 지내고 있습니다, 드림 바이오 연구 프로젝트를 하고 있어요.
남: 정부가 후원하는 의학 연구 프로젝트를 말씀하시는 건가요?
여: 맞아요. ⓐ20명 이상의 연구원들이 프로젝트에 참여하고 있고, 제가 수석 연구원입니다.
남: 와, 정말 큰 일을 담당하고 계시네요. 프로젝트의 예산은 얼마나 큰가요?
여: ⓑ저희는 프로젝트에 백만 달러의 지출을 허가받았어요.
남: 정말 엄청난 액수네요. ⓒ그건 폐암 신약을 개발하기 위한 프로젝트죠, 그렇지 않나요?
여: 맞아요.
남: 연구 프로젝트가 얼마나 오래 지속될까요?
여: ⓓ5년짜리 프로젝트입니다. 이 기간 내에 저희가 약을 개발할 수 있기를 바라고 있어요.
남: 성공을 기원합니다, Peterson 박사님.
여: 감사합니다, Collins 박사님.

문제 풀이

Dream Bio Research Project의 ⓐ연구원 수, ⓑ예산 규모, ⓒ연구 목적, ⓓ연구 기간은 언급되었지만, 연구 장소는 언급되지 않았다.

9. ④ | 내용 일치

선택지 선택비율	① 1%	② 1%	③ 1%	④ 96%	⑤ 1%

W: Good morning, everyone. I'm Olivia Benson, the president of Golden
회장, -장
Star Observatory. We'll be hosting Space Science Camp for
관측소, 천문대 주최하다
teenagers this summer vacation. ⓐIt's a 3-day camp which goes
십 대
from August 21st to August 23rd. Our programs will help you learn more about space. A former astronaut, Dr. Michael Russell, ⓑwill
예전의, 이전의 우주비행사
give a special lecture about space travel. Participants ⓒwill even
참가자
have a chance to look at stars through our telescopes. If you want
망원경
to join this camp, you should sign up at our website. ⓓThe
신청하다
reservation page will open two weeks before the camp. ⓔThe participation fee is $50 per person. We hope to see you then. Thank you.

해석

여: 안녕하세요, 여러분. 저는 Golden Star 관측소 소장 Olivia Benson입니다. 저희는 이번 여름 방학에 십 대들을 위한 우주 과학 캠프를 주최할 것입니다. ⓐ8월 21일부터 8월 23일까지 진행되는 3일간의 캠프입니다. 저희의 프로그램은 여러분이 우주에 대해 더 많이 배우도록 도울 것입니다. 전직 우주비행사인 Michael Russell 박사님이 ⓑ우주 여행에 관한 특별 강연을 할 예정입니다. 참가자들은 저희의 망원경을 통해 ⓒ별을 관측할 기회도 가질 것입니다. 이 캠프에 참가를 원하시면, 저희 웹사이트에서 신청하셔야 합니다. ⓓ예약 페이지는 캠프 2주 전에 열릴 것입니다. ⓔ참가비는 1인당 50달러입니다. 그때 뵙기를 바랍니다. 감사합니다.

문제 풀이

ⓓ예약 페이지는 캠프 2주 전에 열릴 것이라고 했다.

10. ① | 도표

선택지 선택비율	① 82%	② 11%	③ 1%	④ 6%	⑤ 1%

W: Hey Adam, Mom's birthday is coming up. Why don't we buy a gold ring for her present?
M: Good idea. I heard that jewelry online is cheaper than in stores. So
보석, 장신구
let's buy one online.
W: Okay. Let me see... Rings are pretty expensive. What's our budget?
M: We spent a lot for Mother's Day last month, so ⓐI don't think we can spend more than $400 on her present this time.
W: You're right. Let's decide on a color now. ⓑWe have three options:
~을 정하다
white, yellow, and rose.
M: Mom already has several yellow gold rings. ⓒWe shouldn't choose yellow.
W: Good point. Both the white and rose ones look better anyway.
M: That's true. What about a stone for the ring?
보석
W: ⓓHow about a ruby? It would go well with Mom's red earrings.
M: I agree. Oh, this one provides a gift-wrapping service.
제공하다 선물 포장
W: ⓔWe don't need that. I'd rather wrap it myself.
M: Okay, then let's order this one.

해석

여: Adam, 엄마 생신이 다가오고 있어. 엄마 선물로 금반지를 사는 게 어때?
남: 좋은 생각이야. 온라인에서 파는 보석이 가게에서 파는 것보다 더 저렴하다고 들었어. 그러니까 온라인으로 사자.
여: 그래. 한번 보자… 반지가 꽤 비싸네. 우리 예산이 얼마야?
남: 우리가 지난달 어머니의 날에 돈을 많이 썼으니까, ⓐ이번에는 엄마 선물로 400달러 넘게 쓸 수 없을 것 같아.
여: 맞아. 이제 색을 정하자. ⓑ우리에겐 세 가지 선택 사항이 있어: 흰색, 노란색, 그리고 로즈골드.
남: 엄마는 이미 노란 금반지를 몇 개 가지고 계셔. ⓒ노란색은 선택하지 말자.
여: 좋은 지적이야. 어차피 흰색이랑 로즈골드가 더 좋아 보이네.
남: 맞아. 반지에 들어갈 보석은?
여: ⓓ루비는 어때? 엄마의 빨간 귀걸이랑 잘 어울릴 거야.
남: 나도 동의해. 오, 이건 선물 포장 서비스를 제공하네.
여: ⓔ그건 필요 없어. 내가 직접 포장하고 싶어.
남: 알겠어, 그럼 이걸 주문하자.

문제 풀이

ⓐ가격이 400달러를 넘지 않으며 ⓑⓒ흰색이나 로즈골드 색의 ⓓ루비 보석이 있는 반지를 선택했고 ⓔ선물 포장 서비스는 필요 없다고 했다.

11. ② | 짧은 대화 응답

선택지 선택비율	① 7%	② 78%	③ 5%	④ 2%	⑤ 8%

W: Richard, have you chosen a place for Mom's birthday party? It's already next week!
M: ⓐI've been trying to make a reservation at Palace Bistro, but the restaurant never answers my calls.
예약하다
W: Haven't you heard? ⓑIt's closed for repairs until next month!
수리
M: Oh, no. I must find another place as soon as possible.

해석

여: Richard, 엄마 생신 파티 장소 정했니? 벌써 다음 주야!
남: ⓐPalace Bistro에 예약하려고 하는데, 식당에서 전화를 안 받아.
여: 너 못 들었니? ⓑ거기 수리하느라 다음 달까지 문을 닫아!
남: 아, 이런. 가능한 한 빨리 다른 장소를 찾아야겠다.

문제 풀이

엄마 생신 파티를 위해 ⓐ한 식당에 예약하려 했지만 전화를 받지 않는다고 말하는 남자에게 여자가 ⓑ그 식당은 다음 달까지 문을 닫는다고 말했으므로, 가능한 한 빨리 다른 장소를 찾아야겠다는 ②가 남자의 응답으로 가장 적절하다.
① 미안해. 나는 이미 그 식당에 예약했어.
③ 좋아. 지금 당장 전화기를 고치자.
④ 말도 안 돼! 그곳은 너무 멀어서 갈 수 없어.
⑤ 고마워. 네 파티에 꼭 갈게.

12. ① | 짧은 대화 응답

선택지 선택비율	① 80%	② 2%	③ 1%	④ 2%	⑤ 15%

M: Olivia, did you hear the news about the music festival this weekend?
W: No, I didn't. Is there anything special about it?
M: Actually, I heard your favorite band will be playing music live at the festival on Sunday. I thought you might like it.
라이브로
W: Thanks. I've always wanted to see their live performance.
라이브의 공연

해석

남: Olivia, 이번 주말 음악 축제에 대한 소식 들었어?
여: 아니, 못 들었어. 특별한 거라도 있어?
남: 실은, 네가 좋아하는 밴드가 일요일에 축제에서 라이브로 음악을 연주할 거라고 들었어. 네가 좋아할 것 같았지.
여: 고마워. 나 그들의 라이브 공연을 항상 보고 싶었거든.

문제 풀이

남자는 여자가 좋아하는 밴드의 축제에서의 라이브 연주 소식을 말해주고 있으므로, 고마움을 표현하며 공연에 대한 기대감을 드러내는 ①이 여자의 응답으로 가장 적절하다.
② 네 말이 맞아. 어쨌든 그 콘서트는 취소될 거야.
③ 미안해. 나는 그 밴드와의 라이브 채팅에 참여할 수 없어.
④ 오, 안 돼. 너는 이 특별한 기회를 놓치지 말았어야 했어.
⑤ 멋지다! 축제에서 네 연주 보는 게 기대돼.

13. ④ | 긴 대화 응답

선택지 선택비율	① 7%	② 2%	③ 2%	④ 87%	⑤ 2%

M: Hi, Sandra. You look excited.
W: Yeah, I just got my driver's license.
운전면허
M: Congratulations! Are you planning to buy a car?
W: Actually, I've been browsing cars online. But they're more expensive than I expected.
browse: (정보를 찾아) 인터넷을 돌아다니다 / 예상하다
M: Then, ⓐwhat about a used car? My brother happens to be selling his car.
중고의
W: ⓑI was considering buying a used car, too. Can I see some pictures of his car?
생각하다, 고려하다
M: Let me check... Here you go. He's had it for about three years.
W: Wow, it looks as shiny as new. Also, it's in my favorite color and design.
빛나는, 반짝거리는
M: I'm glad you like it. You'll be even more satisfied when you see it in person.
만족하는 / 직접
W: I hope so! Do you know how much he's selling it for?
M: He wants $10,000 for it.
W: That's within my budget. But ⓒI'd need to test-drive it first.
시승하다
M: No problem. We can schedule a time with my brother.

해석

남: 안녕, Sandra. 신나 보이네.
여: 응, 나 방금 운전면허를 땄거든.
남: 축하해! 차를 살 계획이야?
여: 사실, 온라인으로 차 정보를 찾고 있어. 근데 내가 예상한 것보다 더 비싸네.
남: 그럼, ⓐ중고차는 어때? 우리 형이 마침 차를 팔게 됐거든.
여: ⓑ나도 중고차를 살까 생각하고 있었어. 너희 형 차 사진 좀 볼 수 있을까?
남: 확인해볼게··· 여기 있어. 형은 이 차를 3년 정도 탔어.
여: 와, 새 차처럼 반짝이네. 게다가 내가 좋아하는 색과 디자인이야.
남: 네 마음에 든다니 기뻐. 네가 직접 보면 훨씬 더 만족할 거야.
여: 그러면 좋겠다! 형이 얼마에 팔고 있는지 알아?
남: 형은 10,000달러를 원해.
여: 내 예산 안에 있네. 그런데 ⓒ먼저 시승을 해야 할 것 같아.
남: 물론이지. 형이랑 일정을 잡으면 돼.

문제 풀이

여자에게 남자가 ⓐ자신의 형이 차를 팔고 있다며 중고차를 살 생각이 있는지 묻자 여자도 ⓑ중고차를 살까 생각 중이라며 ⓒ먼저 시승을 해야 할 것 같다고 했으므로, 이에 대한 남자의 응답으로는 형과 일정을 잡으면 된다고 말하는 ④가 가장 적절하다.
① 걱정 마. 그는 곧 운전면허를 딸 거야.
② 정말? 네가 내 차에 관심 있는지 몰랐어.
③ 아, 이런. 그럼 내 차를 정비소에 맡겨야겠네.
⑤ 신경 쓰지 마. 나는 내일 다른 걸 살 거야.

14. ① | 긴 대화 응답

선택지 선택비율	① 80%	② 3%	③ 6%	④ 5%	⑤ 3%

W: Jay, why do you look so annoyed?
짜증이 난
M: ⓐI've been surfing the Internet, but there are so many ads.
광고 (=advertisement)
W: What kinds of ads?
M: Pop-up advertisements. Whenever I open a new website, ads pop up. It takes a lot of time for me to close all of them.
튀어 오르다
W: That used to happen to me, too. Maybe I can help you.
used to-v: ~하곤 했다
M: Is there a way to stop them?
W: ⓑI'm using a program that blocks pop-up advertisements.
차단하다
M: Is it difficult to use?
W: It's very simple and easy. Just install a pop-up blocker on your computer, and it'll prevent ads from popping up.
설치하다 / prevent A from v-ing: A가 ~하는 것을 막다

M: That sounds good. But ⓒwhat if I can't see important pop-up messages that are not advertisements?
W: Don't worry. It'll only filter out the ads.
~을 걸러 내다

해석

여: Jay, 너 왜 그렇게 짜증 나 보이니?
남: ⓐ인터넷 서핑을 하고 있는데, 광고가 너무 많아.
여: 어떤 광고?
남: 팝업 광고. 새로운 웹사이트를 열 때마다, 광고가 튀어나와. 그것들을 모두 닫느라 시간이 많이 걸려.
여: 내게도 그런 일이 있곤 했지. 아마 내가 네게 도움이 될 수 있을 거야.
남: 팝업 광고를 막는 방법이 있니?
여: ⓑ나는 팝업 광고를 차단하는 프로그램을 사용하고 있어.
남: 사용하기 어렵니?
여: 아주 간단하고 쉬워. 팝업 차단 장치를 컴퓨터에 설치하기만 하면, 광고가 튀어나오는 걸 막아 줄 거야.
남: 그거 좋겠다. 그런데 ⓒ광고가 아닌 중요한 팝업 메시지를 못 보면 어떻게 하니?
여: 걱정하지 마. 광고만 걸러 낼 거야.

문제 풀이

ⓐ인터넷 서핑 중에 팝업 광고로 불편함을 호소하는 남자에게 여자는 ⓑ팝업 광고 차단 프로그램을 소개하고 있다. 이어 ⓒ중요한 팝업 메시지를 못 보는 일이 생길 것을 우려하는 남자의 마지막 말에 대한 응답으로 가장 적절한 것은 ①이다.
② 조심해. 온라인 광고를 너무 많이 믿지 마.
③ 맞아. 그 프로그램을 사용할 것을 생각해 볼게.
④ 그건 네 개인 정보를 위험에 빠뜨릴 수 있어.
⑤ 그 프로그램을 다운로드하면 컴퓨터가 느려질 거야.

15. ③ | 상황에 적절한 말

선택지 선택비율	① 2%	② 6%	③ 80%	④ 6%	⑤ 4%

M: Emma is the captain of her school badminton team. Her team is planning to participate in the upcoming tournament, but one of the team members recently got injured. Emma feels a strong responsibility to find a replacement as the team leader. Then she thinks of Anthony, who used to be a badminton team member. So ⓐshe asks Anthony to join the team once again. However, Anthony is very busy preparing for an important presentation next week. ⓑHe thinks he cannot accept Emma's request and thinks of another way to help her. He decides to recommend one of his close friends instead. His friend is not only good at badminton, but has always wanted to join the badminton team. In this situation, what would Anthony most likely say to Emma?
Anthony: I'm afraid I can't. But I'll recommend a close friend instead.

(주장 / ~에 참가하다 / 다가오는, 곧 있을 / 최근에 / get injured: 부상을 당하다 / 책임(감) / 대신할 사람 / used to-v: ~였다 / be busy v-ing: ~하느라 바쁘다 / 받아들이다 / 요청, 요구 / not only A but (also) B: A뿐만 아니라 B도)

해석

남: Emma는 학교 배드민턴 팀의 주장이다. 그녀의 팀은 다가오는 토너먼트에 참가할 계획인데, 팀원 중 한 명이 최근에 부상을 당했다. Emma는 주장으로서 대체 선수를 찾아야 한다는 강한 책임감을 느낀다. 그때 그녀는 예전에 배드민턴 팀의 팀원이었던 Anthony를 생각한다. 그래서 ⓐ그녀는 Anthony에게 다시 한번 팀에 들어올 것을 부탁한다. 하지만 Anthony는 다음 주에 있을 중요한 발표를 준비하느라 매우 바쁘다. ⓑ그는 Emma의 요청을 받아들일 수 없다고 생각하고 그녀를 도울 다른 방법을 생각한다. 그는 자신의 친한 친구들 중 한 명을 대신 추천하기로 결심한다. 그의 친구는 배드민턴을 잘 칠 뿐만 아니라, 늘 배드민턴 팀에 들어가고 싶어 했다. 이 상황에서, Anthony는 Emma에게 뭐라고 말하겠는가?
Anthony: 미안하지만 나는 할 수 없을 것 같아. 하지만 대신 내 친한 친구를 추천할게.

문제 풀이

Anthony는 ⓐ배드민턴 팀에 다시 들어와 달라는 Emma의 요청을 ⓑ받아들일 수 없지만 친한 친구를 추천하려고 하므로, ③이 가장 적절하다.
① 나는 잘 모르겠어. 나는 너처럼 책임감 있는 리더가 되지 못할 거야.
② 나는 도와줄 수 없을 것 같아. 이미 다른 팀에 들어갔어.
④ 기꺼이! 다시 팀에 들어갈 수 있어서 영광이야.
⑤ 맞아. 나는 부상 때문에 배드민턴 팀을 그만둬야 했어.

16~17. | 세트 문항

16. ② 17. ③

선택지 선택비율					
16	① 8%	② 84%	③ 2%	④ 1%	⑤ 5%
17	① 1%	② 1%	③ 95%	④ 1%	⑤ 1%

M: Hello, students. Last time, we talked about the problem of wasting materials. Today, ⓐwe're going to discuss how used materials are recycled and turned into new products. Used ⓑpaper is usually cut down into small pieces and sent into a machine to remove any ink or glue on it. Then it can be used for making things such as toilet paper and paper bags. ⓒMetals like steel and iron are also valuable as recyclable materials. They are melted down and easily transformed into car parts, frames, foils, and other things. ⓓGlass is another special material that can be recycled endlessly. Like metals, glass is also melted down after being crushed, and then it is made into new bottles and jars. ⓔPlastics are complicated to recycle because there are so many types. After sorting and melting the plastics, they can be turned into new products like bottles and toys through a special process. Now, let's take a look at some video clips and then we'll discuss them in detail.

(재료, 소재 / 논의하다 / 제거하다 / (화장실용) 화장지 / 강철 / 철, 쇠 / ~을 녹이다 / 변형시키다 / 끝없이 / 눌러 부수다 / 병, 단지 / 복잡한 / 분류하다 / 과정, 공정)

해석

남: 안녕하세요, 학생 여러분. 지난 시간에 우리는 소재 낭비 문제에 대해 이야기했습니다. 오늘은 ⓐ어떻게 중고 소재가 재활용되어 새로운 제품으로 변하는지에 대해 논의해 보겠습니다. 사용된 ⓑ종이는 보통 작은 조각으로 잘리고 거기 묻은 잉크나 접착제를 제거하기 위해 기계로 보내집니다. 그러고 나면 그것은 화장실용 화장지와 종이봉투 같은 것들을 만드는 데 사용될 수 있습니다. 강철과 쇠 같은 ⓒ금속들도 재활용 가능한 소재로서 가치가 있습니다. 그것들은 녹아서 자동차 부품, 틀, 포일, 그리고 그밖의 것들로 쉽게 변형됩니다. ⓓ유리는 끝없이 재활용될 수 있는 또 다른 특별한 소재입니다. 금속처럼, 유리는 부순 후에 녹이고 나면, 새로운 병과 단지로 만들어집니다. ⓔ플라스틱은 종류가 너무 많아서 재활용하기에 복잡합니다. 플라스틱을 분류해서 녹인 후에, 그것들은 특별한 공정을 통해 병과 장난감 같은 새로운 제품으로 바뀔 수 있습니다. 이제 몇 가지 동영상을 보고 자세히 논의해 보겠습니다.

문제 풀이

16. ⓐ중고 소재가 재활용되어 새로운 제품으로 변하는 방법에 대해 논의해 보겠다고 했으므로, 남자가 하는 말의 주제로 ② '재활용의 과정 및 결과'가 가장 적절하다.
① 재활용 제품에 대한 오해
③ 폐기물 오염으로 야기된 문제들
④ 재활용 시스템의 역사
⑤ 쓰레기를 줄이기 위한 조언
17. ⓑ종이, ⓒ금속, ⓓ유리, ⓔ플라스틱은 언급되었지만, 섬유(fabrics)는 언급되지 않았다.

[코드 공략하기]

제3회 중급 모의고사

1	⑤	2	②	3	①	4	⑤	5	⑤	6	②
7	①	8	③	9	③	10	④	11	①	12	②
13	②	14	①	15	⑤	16	④	17	③		

1. ⑤ | 목적

선택지 선택비율	① 1%	② 2%	③ 1%	④ 2%	⑤ 93%

M: Good afternoon. I'm Tom Anderson, the student council president.
학생회장
I'm glad to announce that the student council is recruiting
알리다 / 모집하다
volunteers for our campus tour event. Next Saturday, our school
자원봉사자
will be welcoming middle schoolers who are interested in attending
welcome: 맞이하다 / 다니다
our school. Student volunteers will show the middle schoolers around our campus, and provide them with useful information about our school's extracurricular activities and traditions. To sign
정규 과목 이외의 / 전통
up to volunteer, please visit our school website. Your participation
sign up to-v: ~하려고 신청하다 / 참여
will be a great help to those who wish to attend our school.

해석

남: 안녕하십니까. 학생회장 Tom Anderson입니다. 학생회가 우리 캠퍼스 투어 행사에 자원봉사자를 모집하고 있다는 것을 알리게 되어 기쁩니다. 다음 주 토요일에, 우리 학교는 우리 학교에 다니는 데 관심이 있는 중학생들을 맞이할 예정입니다. 학생 자원봉사자는 중학생들에게 우리 캠퍼스를 둘러보도록 안내하고, 우리 학교의 정규 과목 이외의 활동과 전통에 관한 유용한 정보를 주게 됩니다. 자원봉사하려고 신청하려면, 우리 학교 웹사이트를 방문해 주세요. 여러분의 참여는 우리 학교에 다니길 희망하는 사람들에게 큰 도움이 될 것입니다.

문제 풀이

남자는 학생회에서 캠퍼스 투어 행사 자원봉사자를 모집하고 있음을 알리고 있다.

2. ② | 의견

선택지 선택비율	① 4%	② 87%	③ 3%	④ 2%	⑤ 1%

M: Hi, Monica. I haven't seen you at the gym in a while.
체육관
W: Yes. I've been out of town on business.
볼일이 있어, 업무로
M: Glad to see you again. I saw you running very quickly on the treadmill.
러닝 머신
W: Right. These days I'm gaining weight. So, I decided to work out
운동하다
more intensely.
강렬하게, 격하게
M: Hmm.... ⓐThat's not a good idea this late at night.
W: Well, I heard that running fast helps burn calories.
칼로리를 소모하다
M: That's right. But ⓑintense evening exercise is not good for sleep.
W: Oh, it's not? I thought exercising before bedtime could make me exhausted and help me sleep.
기진맥진한
M: I'm afraid you're mistaken. ⓒHeavy exercise in the evening raises your heart rate and body temperature, so it prevents you from
체온 / prevent A from v-ing: A가 ~하는 것을 막다
falling into a deep sleep.
W: I see. Now I know why people say, "Evening walk, morning run."

해석

남: 안녕하세요, Monica. 당신을 한동안 체육관에서 못 본 것 같아요.
여: 네. 업무차 도시를 떠나 있었어요.
남: 다시 보니 기쁘네요. 당신이 러닝 머신 위에서 매우 빠르게 뛰고 있는 걸 봤어요.
여: 맞아요. 요즘 살이 찌고 있어서요. 그래서 더 격렬하게 운동하기로 결심했어요.
남: 음…. ⓐ이렇게 밤늦게는 좋은 생각이 아니에요.
여: 음, 전 빨리 뛰는 것이 칼로리를 소모하는 걸 돕는다고 들었어요.
남: 맞아요. 하지만 ⓑ격렬한 저녁 운동은 수면에 좋지 않아요.
여: 아, 좋지 않나요? 전 잠자리에 들기 전 운동이 기진맥진하게 만들어서 잠자는 걸 도울 것이라 생각했어요.
남: 오해한 것 같아요. ⓒ저녁 시간의 심한 운동은 심박수와 체온을 올려서, 깊은 잠을 자는 걸 막아요.
여: 알겠어요. 이제 왜 사람들이 "저녁엔 걷고, 아침엔 달리기"라고 말하는지 알겠네요.

문제 풀이

ⓐⓑⓒ남자는 저녁 시간의 격렬한 운동이 숙면을 취하는 데 좋지 않다고 말하고 있다.

3. ① | 요지

선택지 선택비율	① 95%	② 1%	③ 3%	④ 1%	⑤ 0%

W: Good afternoon, listeners! Do you have a hard time figuring
figure out: ~을 이해하다
out your emotions? Have you suddenly gotten really angry but
감정
didn't know exactly what made you feel that way? If so, keeping an emotion diary can be a powerful tool for understanding your
강력한
feelings. In an emotion diary, you write down in detail how you feel
상세하게
in each situation. This will give you an opportunity to understand
기회
why you're feeling a certain way. Writing an emotion diary won't be
특정한
easy at first, but you'll soon get used to it. After the break, I'll tell
~에 익숙해지다
you how to keep an emotion diary effectively. Stay tuned!
효과적으로

해석

여: 안녕하세요, 청취자 여러분! 여러분의 감정을 이해하는 데 어려움을 겪고 있나요? 갑자기 매우 화가 난 적이 있는데 왜 그런 기분이 드는지 정확히 알지 못했나요? 그렇다면, 감정 일기를 쓰는 것이 여러분의 감정을 이해하는 데 강력한 도구가 될 수 있습니다. 감정 일기에, 각 상황에서 여러분이 어떻게 느끼는지 상세하게 적습니다. 이것은 여러분이 왜 특정 방식으로 느끼고 있는지 이해할 수 있는 기회를 줄 것입니다. 감정 일기를 쓰는 것이 처음에는 쉽지 않겠지만, 여러분은 곧 그것에 익숙해질 겁니다. 잠시 후에, 효과적으로 감정 일기를 쓰는 방법에 대해 알려드리겠습니다. 채널 고정하세요!

문제 풀이

감정 일기를 쓰는 것이 자신의 감정을 이해하는 데 강력한 도구가 될 수 있다고 말하고 있다.

4. ⑤ | 그림 일치

선택지 선택비율	① 7%	② 5%	③ 4%	④ 3%	⑤ 78%

W: How was the magic show last night?
M: Fantastic! Let me show you a picture.
W: ⓐThe man wearing the hat must be the magician.
마술사
M: Right. Look at ⓑthe bird sitting on the branch. At the start of the
나뭇가지

show, the bird came out of the magician's hat.
W: Wonderful! And who is ⓒthe lady with glasses on next to the magician?
M: She was a member of the audience.
청중, 관객
W: What did she do?
M: She made sure that the box was empty and put it on the table.
make sure: 확인하다
W: ⓓThat box on the table?
M: Yes, unbelievably, the magician pulled flowers out of the box. That's
믿을 수 없게도
why ⓔthe flowers are on the floor.
W: Wow, it must have been awesome!
M: Absolutely! I couldn't take my eyes off of the stage.
take one's eyes off of: ~에서 눈을 떼다

해석

여: 지난밤 마술쇼는 어땠어?
남: 기막히게 좋았어! 사진 한 장을 보여 줄게.
여: ⓐ모자를 쓰고 있는 남자가 마술사겠구나.
남: 맞아. ⓑ나뭇가지에 앉아 있는 새 좀 봐. 쇼 시작 때, 마술사의 모자에서 새가 나왔어.
여: 멋지다! 그리고 ⓒ마술사 옆에 안경 쓴 여자분은 누구니?
남: 관객 중 한 사람이었어.
여: 그녀가 뭘 했니?
남: 상자가 비었는지 확인하고 그것을 테이블 위에 올려놨어.
여: ⓓ테이블 위에 있는 저 상자?
남: 응, 믿을 수 없게도, 마술사가 상자에서 꽃을 꺼냈어. 그래서 ⓔ꽃이 바닥에 있는 거야.
여: 와, 어마어마했겠다!
남: 물론이지! 무대에서 눈을 뗄 수가 없었어.

문제 풀이

ⓔ바닥에 꽃이 있다고 했으므로 그림의 ⑤는 대화 내용과 일치하지 않는다.

5. ⑤ | 할 일

선택지 선택비율	① 1%	② 1%	③ 2%	④ 2%	⑤ 93%

W: Billy, I'm so excited about our first trip to Jeju Island next week.
M: Indeed, honey. We've been waiting so long for it.
정말, 사실
W: Yeah. I checked the weather forecast, and it says it will be nice.
일기 예보
M: Good. Is there anything we're forgetting to do before going?
W: Hmm... Oh! I forgot to make a reservation for a rental car.
렌터카
M: Don't worry. I've already made one at a reasonable price.
(가격이) 적정한
W: What a relief! How about our plan to change our room from a city
안도
view to an ocean view?
M: I've already called the hotel and changed it to have an ocean view.
W: Great. I heard that the Jeju Tourism Organization is having a special event. They provide discount coupons to fancy restaurants.
값비싼[고급의]
M: Really? How can we get some?
W: ⓐWe can download them from their website.
M: Okay, ⓑI'll do that right away.

해석

여: Billy, 다음 주 우리의 첫 제주도 여행이 너무 기대돼요.
남: 정말이에요, 여보. 우린 정말 오래 기다렸잖아요.
여: 네. 일기 예보를 확인하니, 날씨가 좋을 거라고 하네요.
남: 좋아요. 가기 전에 해야 하는데 잊어버린 게 있을까요?
여: 음… 아! 렌터카 예약하는 걸 잊었어요.
남: 걱정하지 마요. 내가 이미 적정 가격으로 예약을 했어요.
여: 정말 다행이네요! 우리 방을 도시 전망에서 바다 전망으로 변경하는 계획은요?
남: 이미 호텔에 전화해서 바다 전망으로 변경했어요.
여: 좋아요. 제주관광공사가 특별한 행사를 한다고 들었어요. 고급 식당들의 할인 쿠폰을 제공해요.
남: 그래요? 어떻게 구할 수 있죠?
여: ⓐ웹사이트에서 그것들을 다운받을 수 있어요.
남: 알았어요, ⓑ내가 지금 바로 할게요.

문제 풀이

여자가 ⓐ고급 식당 할인 쿠폰을 웹사이트에서 다운받을 수 있다고 하자, 남자가 ⓑ자신이 지금 바로 하겠다고 했다.

6. ② | 금액

선택지 선택비율	① 13%	② 70%	③ 7%	④ 8%	⑤ 3%

M: Honey, we need four extra cups for our housewarming party.
집들이
W: Okay. Let's buy them online. *[Typing Sound]* Look, I love this floral
꽃무늬의
tea cup.
M: I like it too, and ⓐit only costs $8.
W: Hold on. The store's promotion says, "Buy one cup, get one cup
판촉, 광고
free."
M: Fantastic! We only have to pay for two cups. Then, we can afford to
can afford to-v: ~할 여유가 있다
buy a new teapot as well.
찻주전자 역시, 또한
W: That's a good idea. Let's buy one that matches the tea cups.
어울리다
M: ⓑI like the white one that costs $20.
W: Okay. ⓒLet's pay for two tea cups and one teapot. Do we also have to pay for shipping?
운송, 배송
M: Yes. ⓓThe total shipping fee is $3. Do we need anything else?
운송료
W: Not really. Let me pay with my credit card.

해석

남: 여보, 우리 집들이를 위해 컵 네 잔이 더 필요해요.
여: 알았어요. 온라인으로 사요. [타이핑하는 소리] 봐요, 이 꽃무늬 찻잔이 정말 마음에 들어요.
남: 나도 좋아요, 그리고 ⓐ가격이 8달러밖에 안 하네요.
여: 잠시만요. 가게 광고에 "한 잔 사면, 다른 한 잔은 무료"라고 쓰여 있어요.
남: 환상적이네요! 우리는 컵 두 잔 값만 지불하면 돼요. 그러면 새로운 찻주전자도 살 여유가 있어요.
여: 좋은 생각이에요. 찻잔이랑 어울리는 거로 사요.
남: ⓑ나는 20달러짜리 흰색 찻주전자가 마음에 들어요.
여: 좋아요. ⓒ찻잔 두 잔과 찻주전자 한 개를 결제해요. 배송비도 내야 해요?
남: 네. ⓓ총 배송비는 3달러예요. 더 필요한 건 없나요?
여: 없어요. 내 신용카드로 결제할게요.

문제 풀이

ⓐ8달러짜리 ⓒ찻잔 두 개와 ⓑ20달러짜리 ⓒ찻주전자 한 개를 구매하기로 했는데 (8X2+20), ⓓ배송비가 3달러라고 했으므로 총 39달러를 지불해야 한다.

7. ① | 이유

선택지 선택비율	① 92%	② 2%	③ 1%	④ 1%	⑤ 1%

W: What a cute dog! Is it yours?
M: Yes. I adopted him from an animal rescue center.
입양하다 동물 구조 센터
W: I've always wanted a dog. But I can't have one.
M: Why? Are you allergic to animal hair?
~에 알레르기가 있는

W: I'm only allergic to cat hair. Dogs are totally fine.
M: What's the problem, then? Your house has a big backyard, so I think
뒷마당
it's a perfect place for dogs.
W: I think so, too. It's a really dog-friendly environment.
환경
M: Do your parents not like dogs?
W: No, they love dogs. But ⓐI'm worried about a dog being alone during the day.
M: Is there nobody who can look after a dog?
~을 돌보다
W: ⓑThere is no one at home during the day. My parents work, and my brother and I go to school.
M: Oh, I see. That's why you can't get a dog.

해석

여: 개 정말 귀엽다! 너희 개니?
남: 응. 동물 구조 센터에서 입양했어.
여: 나도 늘 개를 원했는데. 하지만 키울 수가 없어.
남: 왜? 동물 털에 알레르기가 있니?
여: 나는 고양이 털에만 알레르기가 있어. 개는 완전히 괜찮아.
남: 그럼 뭐가 문제니? 너희 집은 큰 뒷마당이 있어서, 개에게 완벽한 곳 같은데.
여: 나도 그렇게 생각해. 정말 개에게 친화적인 환경이지.
남: 부모님이 개를 안 좋아하시니?
여: 아니, 개를 무척 좋아하셔. 하지만 ⓐ나는 개가 낮 동안 혼자 있는 게 걱정이야.
남: 개를 돌볼 수 있는 사람이 아무도 없니?
여: ⓑ낮 동안 집에 아무도 없어. 부모님은 일하시고, 오빠랑 나는 학교에 가잖아.
남: 아, 그렇구나. 그래서 개를 키울 수가 없구나.

문제 풀이

ⓐⓑ낮에 집에 아무도 없어서 개가 혼자 있는 게 걱정이라고 했다.

8. ③ | 언급

선택지 선택비율	① 2%	② 2%	③ 91%	④ 1%	⑤ 3%

M: Amy, what are you reading?
W: Our school newsletter. It says our school is holding the West Lake Fun Run.
M: Sounds interesting. When is it?
W: ⓐIt'll be held on April 17th.
M: I see. ⓑHow long is the course?
W: ⓒIt's 5km long. Starting at the school, participants will run through Vincent Park and Central Stadium, and finish at West Lake.
M: Cool!
W: Why don't we sign up together?
등록하다
M: Good idea. ⓓHow much is the entry fee?
참가비
W: ⓔIt's $5 per person. ⓕThe money raised will be used to renovate
개조[보수]하다
the school gym.
M: Great. It's so old. It'll be wonderful to have a new gym.
W: I agree.

해석

남: Amy, 뭘 읽고 있니?
여: 학교 신문. 학교에서 West Lake Fun Run을 개최할 거래.
남: 재미있겠다. 그게 언제니?
여: ⓐ4월 17일에 열릴 거야.
남: 그렇구나. ⓑ코스 길이가 어떻게 되니?
여: ⓒ5km 길이야. 참가자들은 학교에서 시작해서 Vincent 공원과 중앙 경기장을 지나 West 호수에서 마쳐.
남: 멋지다!
여: 같이 등록하는 게 어때?
남: 좋은 생각이야. ⓓ참가비가 얼마니?
여: ⓔ인당 5달러야. ⓕ모금액은 학교 체육관을 개조하는 데 사용될 거야.
남: 잘됐네. 너무 낡았잖아. 새 체육관이 생기면 멋질 거야.
여: 동의해.

문제 풀이

ⓐ개최 날짜, ⓑⓒ코스 길이, ⓓⓔ참가비, ⓕ모금액 용도는 언급되었으나, 출발 시간은 언급되지 않았다. 출발 위치와 혼동해서는 안 된다.

9. ③ | 내용 일치

선택지 선택비율	① 1%	② 3%	③ 90%	④ 5%	⑤ 1%

M: Good morning, math lovers of Hamington High School. I'm your math teacher, Allen Steward. We have a special announcement
발표
for you. ⓐThe Afterschool Math Festival will be held for three days starting next Monday. ⓑNine activities are planned, and you may participate in up to three different activities. Keep in mind that
~에 참여하다
ⓒactivities such as the Math Escape Room and the Math Quiz Show will take longer than other activities. This year, we are also offering a guest lecture. Our lecturer, Dr. Hilbert will tell us the
제공하다 강연자
stories behind famous mathematicians. ⓓStudents who attend this
수학자 참석하다
special lecture will get a copy of his book for free. Lastly, during the festival, ⓔspecial snacks and drinks will be served at the cafeteria.
구내식당
See you there.

해석

남: 좋은 아침입니다, 수학을 사랑하는 Hamington 고등학교 학생 여러분. 저는 수학 교사 Allen Steward입니다. 여러분들을 위한 특별 발표가 있습니다. ⓐ다음 주 월요일에 시작해서 3일간 방과후 수학 축제가 열릴 것입니다. ⓑ9개 활동이 계획되어 있으며, 각기 다른 3개 활동까지 참여할 수 있습니다. ⓒ수학 방탈출과 수학 퀴즈쇼 같은 활동은 다른 활동들보다 시간이 더 오래 걸린다는 것을 명심하십시오. 올해는 게스트 강의도 제공합니다. 강연자인 Hilbert 박사님이 유명 수학자들의 비하인드 스토리를 우리에게 들려주실 것입니다. ⓓ이 특별 강연에 참석하는 학생들은 박사님의 책 한 부를 무료로 받게 될 것입니다. 마지막으로, 축제 동안, ⓔ특별한 간식과 음료가 구내식당에서 제공될 것입니다. 그곳에서 만나요.

문제 풀이

ⓒ수학 방탈출과 수학 퀴즈쇼 같은 활동은 다른 활동들보다 시간이 더 오래 걸린다고 했다.

10. ④ | 도표

선택지 선택비율	① 1%	② 5%	③ 1%	④ 89%	⑤ 3%

W: Tom, we have so many dishes to wash after every meal.
M: You're right. Let's buy a dishwasher from this online mall.
식기세척기
W: Well, what's our budget for that?
예산
M: ⓐWe can't spend more than $800. We've already spent too much this month.
W: I agree. Well, dishwashers get dirty easily, so white is not a good choice for the color.
M: Right. Plus, ⓑsilver or black would match our kitchen cabinets.
어울리다 부엌 찬장
W: Okay. Which would you prefer, a portable or a built-in type?
이동가능한 붙박이의
M: ⓒI'd prefer a built-in. We would have more space with a built-in.
공간
W: Besides, it would look more stylish.
게다가

M: Good point. Then, there are two options left. Which one would be better?
W: Definitely this one. ⓓWhen it comes to warranty periods, the longer, the better.
분명히, 절대로 / ~에 관한 한 / 보증 기간
M: Perfect! Then let's order this one.

해석

여: Tom, 우리는 매 식사 후에 설거지할 접시들이 너무 많아요.
남: 맞아요. 이 온라인 쇼핑몰에서 식기세척기를 사요.
여: 음, 그에 대한 우리 예산은 얼마죠?
남: ⓐ800달러 넘게는 못 써요. 우리는 이번 달에 이미 너무 많이 썼어요.
여: 동의해요. 음, 식기세척기는 쉽게 더러워지니까, 흰색은 좋은 색상 선택이 아니에요.
남: 맞아요. 그리고 ⓑ은색이나 검은색이 우리 부엌 찬장과 어울릴 거예요.
여: 좋아요. 이동 가능한 것과 붙박이 타입 중 어느 것이 더 좋아요?
남: ⓒ붙박이가 더 좋아요. 붙박이로 하면 공간이 더 넓어질 거예요.
여: 게다가, 더 멋져 보일 거예요.
남: 좋은 지적이에요. 그러면 두 가지 선택지가 남았네요. 어떤 게 더 좋을까요?
여: 당연히 이거죠. ⓓ보증 기간에 관한 한, 길수록 더 좋으니까요.
남: 완벽해요! 그럼 이걸로 주문해요.

문제 풀이

두 사람은 ⓐ800달러가 넘지 않고 ⓑ은색이나 검은색인 ⓒ붙박이 타입 식기세척기 중 ⓓ보증 기간이 더 긴 것을 주문하기로 했다.

11. ① | 짧은 대화 응답

선택지 선택비율	① 80%	② 4%	③ 2%	④ 4%	⑤ 7%

[Cell phone rings.]
W: Hi, David. I'm almost halfway to the restaurant. Where are you?
중간[가운데쯤]에
M: Hi, Amy. I just finished work and got in my car. ⓐI'll take the highway, so I'll arrive on time.
get in: ~에 타다 / 고속도로 / 제시간에
W: I heard on the radio that ⓑthere has been a car accident on the highway. So ⓒyou're going to get stuck.
꼼짝 못하다
M: I see. I'll take another road then.

해석

[휴대전화가 울린다.]
여: 안녕, David. 난 식당에 거의 가운데쯤 왔어. 넌 어디니?
남: 안녕, Amy. 난 이제 막 일이 끝나서 차에 탔어. ⓐ고속도로를 탈 테니, 제시간에 도착할 거야.
여: ⓑ고속도로에서 사고가 있었다고 라디오에서 들었어. 그래서 ⓒ꼼짝 못할 거야.
남: 알았어. 그러면 다른 길을 탈게.

문제 풀이

ⓐ고속도로를 탈 거라는 남자의 말에 여자는 ⓑ고속도로에 사고가 있었어서 ⓒ밀릴 거라고 말하고 있다. 따라서 남자의 응답으로 가장 적절한 것은 다른 길을 이용하겠다는 내용의 ①이 가장 적절하다.
② 정말? 지금 당장 병원에 가 봐.
③ 정말 유감이야. 넌 더 일찍 출발했어야 해.
④ 미안해. 고속도로에서 속도 위반 딱지를 떼었어.
⑤ 알았어. 내가 식당을 예약할게.

12. ② | 짧은 대화 응답

선택지 선택비율	① 4%	② 70%	③ 18%	④ 2%	⑤ 6%

M: Ouch! I got a paper cut.
종이에 베인 상처
W: Are you okay? I know how painful paper cuts are.
아픈, 괴로운
M: This is the third time this week. Maybe my hands are so dry that I get paper cuts too easily.
W: If so, applying hand cream might help.
(페인트·크림 등을) 바르다

해석

남: 아야! 종이에 베였어.
여: 괜찮아? 종이에 베이면 얼마나 아픈지 알아.
남: 이번 주에 벌써 세 번째야. 아마 내 손이 너무 건조해서 아주 쉽게 종이에 베이는 것 같아.
여: 그렇다면, 핸드크림을 바르는 것이 도움이 될지도 몰라.

문제 풀이

남자가 자신의 손이 너무 건조해서 종이에 쉽게 베이는 것 같다고 했으므로, 핸드크림을 바르는 것이 도움이 될지도 모른다고 조언하는 ②가 응답으로 가장 적절하다.
① 내가 논문을 늦게 제출한 것 같아.
③ 재단 가위 사용할 때 조심해.
④ 음, 그 장갑은 제 아들에게 너무 크네요.
⑤ 이번에는 종이 장바구니를 가져 가자.

13. ② | 긴 대화 응답

선택지 선택비율	① 4%	② 82%	③ 9%	④ 3%	⑤ 1%

M: Sandy, what are you doing with your bike?
W: Oh, hi, Jack. I'm checking it out. It makes strange sounds when I ride it.
M: Let me take a look. *[Pause]* Hmm.... I think the brakes are not working properly.
제대로
W: Oh, no. I should get them fixed at the bike shop. It'll cost too much.
M: ⓐWhy don't you try a repair cafe? You can save money.
W: A repair cafe? What's that?
M: It's a place where you can fix your broken stuff on your own. The cafe provides tools and materials.
물건 / 도구 / 재료
W: Well, I don't think I can fix my bike by myself.
M: Don't worry. Expert volunteers will be around to help you out there. There are many repair cafes around town.
전문가 / 자원봉사자
W: That's great. I'll give it a try. ⓑDo you know where the nearest place is?
시도하다, 한번 해 보다
M: Well, I saw a repair cafe next to the post office.

해석

남: Sandy, 네 자전거로 뭘 하고 있니?
여: 아, 안녕, Jack. 난 그걸 확인하고 있어. 내가 자전거를 탈 때 이상한 소리가 나서.
남: 내가 좀 볼게. [잠시 후] 음…. 브레이크가 제대로 작동하지 않는 것 같아.
여: 아, 이런. 자전거 가게에서 고쳐달라고 해야겠네. 비용이 너무 많이 들 거야.
남: ⓐ수리 카페를 이용해 보는 게 어때? 돈을 절약할 수 있어.
여: 수리 카페? 그게 뭐야?
남: 네가 고장 난 물건을 스스로 고칠 수 있는 곳이야. 카페에서 도구와 재료를 제공해.
여: 글쎄, 내가 혼자서 자전거를 고칠 수 없을 것 같아.
남: 걱정하지 마. 거기에 전문 자원봉사자들이 널 도와주려고 주위에 있을 거야. 시내 주변에 수리 카페가 많이 있어.
여: 잘됐네. 한번 해 볼게. ⓑ가장 가까운 곳이 어딘지 아니?
남: 음, 우체국 옆에서 수리 카페를 하나 봤어.

문제 풀이

자전거 수리가 필요한 여자에게 남자가 ⓐ수리 카페를 이용해 볼 것을 권유했고, 여자는 ⓑ가장 가까운 곳이 어디인지 물었으므로, 가장 가까운 수리 카페의 위치를 말하는 ②가 응답으로 가장 적절하다.

① 좋아, 네가 전에 추천해 준 수리 카페를 방문해 볼게.
③ 물론이지, 자원봉사할 곳을 쉽게 찾을 수 있어.
④ 응, 새로운 자전거 가게는 저렴하게 제공해.
⑤ 미안하지만, 난 너무 바빠서 네 자전거를 고칠 수가 없어.

14. ① | 긴 대화 응답

선택지 선택비율	① 85%	② 2%	③ 10%	④ 3%	⑤ 1%

W: Dad, did you throw away all the empty plastic bottles?
~을 버리다 빈
M: Yes. Why?
W: ⓐI need plastic bottle caps for our school's zero waste challenge.
챌린지, 도전
M: Interesting. So what are you doing with the caps?
W: We'll send them to an upcycling company, and they make products
제품
like chairs and hairpins from the caps.
M: That's cool.
W: Yeah, and the teacher said if we bring in more than 20 bottle caps, she'll give us a bamboo toothbrush as a prize.
M: Great. How many bottle caps have you collected so far?
지금까지
W: I've collected only eight bottle caps. I need some more.
M: Hmm, ⓑI threw the plastic bottles away just an hour ago, so they should be in the recycling area.
재활용 구역
W: Okay. I'll go there to check if I can find more caps.

해석

여: 아빠, 빈 플라스틱병 다 버리셨어요?
남: 응. 왜?
여: 학교 제로 웨이스트 챌린지에 ⓐ플라스틱병 뚜껑이 필요해요.
남: 흥미롭구나. 그래서 뚜껑으로 뭘 할 거니?
여: 업사이클링 회사에 보내면, 뚜껑으로 의자나 머리핀 같은 제품을 만들어요.
남: 멋지구나.
여: 네, 그리고 병뚜껑을 20개 넘게 가져오면, 상으로 대나무 칫솔을 주신다고 선생님께서 말씀하셨어요.
남: 좋구나. 지금까지 병뚜껑을 몇 개나 모았니?
여: 겨우 병뚜껑 여덟 개 모았어요. 더 필요해요.
남: 음, ⓑ겨우 한 시간 전에 플라스틱병을 버렸으니, 재활용장에 있을 거야.
여: 알겠어요. 뚜껑을 더 찾을 수 있는지 거기 가서 확인해볼게요.

문제 풀이

ⓐ플라스틱병 뚜껑이 필요하다는 여자의 말에 남자가 ⓑ한 시간 전에 플라스틱병을 버렸으니 재활용장에 있을 거라고 말했다. 따라서 가서 병뚜껑이 있는지 확인해보겠다는 내용의 ①이 응답으로 가장 적절하다.
② 잠깐만요. 병에서 뚜껑을 분리하는 걸 깜빡했어요.
③ 잘됐네요. 우리 미술품에 병뚜껑을 사용할 수 있어요.
④ 걱정하지 마세요. 이미 쓰레기를 내놓았어요.
⑤ 아니요, 괜찮아요. 칫솔은 충분해요.

15. ⑤ | 상황에 적절한 말

선택지 선택비율	① 3%	② 2%	③ 6%	④ 3%	⑤ 87%

W: Bill and Susan are second-grade high school students and friends. They are preparing for their final exams at the library after school. It used to be easy for Susan to focus on studying. However, these
~였었다 ~에 집중하다
days she's noticing that she gets distracted easily at the library
notice: 알아채다 산만해진
and doesn't know why she cannot maintain her attention. So, she
유지하다 주의, 집중
decides to get some advice from Bill, who gets high scores in school. When Bill hears her problem, he's suddenly reminded of
remind of: ~을 생각나게 하다
his own experience of losing focus. He recalls that he changed his
경험 집중(력) 기억해 내다
study location and that really helped him get back his
장소
concentration. Therefore, he wants to suggest that Susan try
집중(력)
studying in a different place to find her focus again. In this situation, what would Bill most likely say to Susan?
Bill: How about changing where you study to regain your focus?
되찾다

해석

여: Bill과 Susan은 고등학교 2학년 학생이자 친구이다. 그들은 방과 후에 도서관에서 기말고사를 준비하고 있다. Susan은 공부에 집중하는 것이 쉬웠다. 하지만 요즘 그녀는 도서관에서 쉽게 산만해진다는 것을 알아채고 있는데, 왜 집중을 유지할 수 없는지 모른다. 그래서 그녀는 학교에서 좋은 성적을 받는 Bill에게 조언을 얻기로 결심한다. Bill은 그녀의 문제를 듣자, 자신도 집중력을 잃었던 경험이 갑자기 생각난다. 그는 공부 장소를 바꾸었고 그것이 집중력을 되찾는 데 정말 도움이 되었다는 것을 기억해 낸다. 그래서 그는 Susan에게 집중력을 다시 찾기 위해 다른 장소에서 공부해 보라고 제안하고 싶다. 이 상황에서, Bill은 Susan에게 뭐라고 말하겠는가?
Bill: 집중력을 되찾기 위해 공부하는 장소를 바꿔보는 게 어때?

문제 풀이

Bill은 Susan이 집중력을 다시 찾을 수 있도록 다른 장소에서 공부해 볼 것을 제안하고 싶어 한다고 했으므로, Bill이 Susan에게 할 말로는 ⑤가 가장 적절하다.
① 너는 휴식을 취할 알맞은 때를 찾아야 할 것 같아.
② 좋은 성적을 받는 게 가장 중요한 게 아니야.
③ 도서관에서 공부하는 데는 많은 이점이 있는 게 틀림없어.
④ 시험을 준비하기 위해 공부 계획을 세우는 게 어때?

16~17. | 세트 문항

16. ④ 17. ③

선택지 선택비율	① 6%	② 2%	③ 3%	④ 85%	⑤ 1%
	① 4%	② 2%	③ 89%	④ 1%	⑤ 1%

W: Welcome back, students. Last time we talked about your favorite numbers. They might come from your birth date or the date of a special occasion in your life. Interestingly, some beliefs about
때, 경우 믿음
numbers seem to depend on one's culture. Today, ⓐwe're talking
~에 달려 있다, ~에 좌우되다
about what numbers symbolize in different parts of the world.
상징하다
In Asia, ⓑthe number four is considered extremely unlucky, but
생각하다, 여기다 극도로
Western people think it is promising. In Islam, ⓒthe number seven
조짐이 좋은
is important. "Seven heavens" is one example of this number's importance. ⓓTen is considered a good number in Japan because it is pronounced "joo", like the Japanese word for "enough." In
발음하다
the Western world, ⓔthe number thirteen is believed to be the unluckiest by millions of people. So, to satisfy anxious customers,
만족시키다 불안해하는
airlines and hotels often don't use the number thirteen. Numbers
항공사
can be captivating and mystical. Numbers are also just fun to play
매혹적인 신비(주의)적인
around with. Let's enjoy learning more about numbers together.

해석

여: 돌아온 것을 환영합니다, 학생 여러분. 지난 시간에 우리는 여러분이 가장 좋아하는 숫자들에 대해 얘기했어요. 그것들은 여러분의 생년월일이나 여러분 인생의 특별한 때가 있는 날에서 기인할지도 모릅니다. 흥미롭게도, 숫자에 대한 어떤 믿음은 그 사람의

문화에 좌우되는 것처럼 보입니다. 오늘, ⓐ우리는 세계 각지에서 숫자들이 무엇을 상징하는지에 대해 이야기하려고 합니다. 아시아에서는 ⓑ숫자 4가 극도로 불길한 것으로 여겨지지만, 서양 사람들은 그것이 조짐이 좋다고 생각합니다. 이슬람에서는 ⓒ숫자 7이 중요합니다. '일곱 개의 천국'은 이 숫자의 중요성의 한 예입니다. ⓓ10은 일본어의 '충분한'이란 단어처럼 'joo'로 발음되기 때문에 일본에서 좋은 숫자로 여겨집니다. 서양에서는 ⓔ숫자 13이 수백만 명의 사람들에게 가장 불길하다고 여겨집니다. 그래서 불안해하는 고객들을 만족시키기 위해, 항공사와 호텔은 흔히 숫자 13을 사용하지 않습니다. 숫자들은 매혹적이고 신비로운 것일 수 있습니다. 숫자들은 또한 그저 가지고 노는 재미일 뿐입니다. 우리 함께 숫자들에 대해 더 많이 배우는 것을 즐겨봅시다.

문제 풀이

16. ⓐ세계 각지에서 숫자들이 무엇을 상징하는지에 대해 이야기하겠다고 했으므로, 여자가 하는 말의 주제로는 ④ '각 문화에 따른 숫자의 상징적 의미들'이 가장 적절하다.
   ① 고대의 행운의 숫자들
   ② 사람들에게 부를 가져다주는 숫자
   ③ 숫자와 종교의 관계
   ⑤ 비밀번호에 좋아하는 숫자들을 사용하는 것의 위험성
17. 숫자 ⓑ4, ⓒ7, ⓓ10, ⓔ13은 언급되었으나, 9(nine)는 언급되지 않았다.

[코드 공략하기]

제4회 중급 모의고사

1	⑤	2	①	3	①	4	⑤	5	④	6	③
7	⑤	8	④	9	⑤	10	①	11	①	12	②
13	②	14	⑤	15	⑤	16	①	17	⑤		

1. ⑤ | 목적

선택지 선택비율	① 2%	② 1%	③ 3%	④ 3%	⑤ 91%

M: Good morning, students. This is the head of the student council and I have an important announcement today. Recently, our school has installed vending machines in the dormitory. But many students have complained that the items in the vending machines do not fully meet their tastes. To address this, ⓐwe are conducting an online survey to gather your suggestions on what products you'd like to see in the vending machines. The survey link will be sent to you in a text message after this announcement. ⓑPlease take a few minutes to answer the survey by this Friday. Your opinion is important, and we're looking forward to receiving your ideas. Thank you!

head 우두머리, (회)장 / student council 학생회 / announcement 발표, 공지 / installed 설치하다 / vending machines 자판기 / dormitory 기숙사 / complained 불평하다 / meet one's taste: ~의 취향을 만족시키다, ~의 취향에 맞다 / address 처리하다 / conducting 실시하다 / survey 설문 조사 / suggestions 제안, 의견 / products 제품 / opinion 의견 / receive: 받다

해석

남: 좋은 아침입니다, 학생 여러분. 저는 학생회 회장이고 오늘 중요한 공지가 있습니다. 최근 우리 학교는 기숙사에 자판기를 설치했습니다. 하지만 많은 학생들이 자판기의 품목이 자신의 취향에 잘 맞지 않는다고 불평해왔습니다. 이를 해결하기 위해, ⓐ여러분이 자판기에서 어떤 제품을 보고 싶어 하는지에 대한 의견을 수집하는 온라인 설문 조사를 실시합니다. 이 공지 후 여러분께 문자 메시지로 설문 조사 링크가 전송될 예정입니다. ⓑ이번 주 금요일까지 몇 분만 시간을 내셔서 설문 조사에 응해 주시기 바랍니다. 여러분의 의견은 중요하며, 좋은 아이디어를 받길 기대하고 있습니다. 감사합니다!

문제 풀이

남자는 ⓐ기숙사 자판기에서 판매되길 원하는 제품에 대한 의견을 모으기 위해 온라인 설문 조사를 실시하니 ⓑ설문 조사에 응해 줄 것을 요청하고 있다.

2. ① | 의견

선택지 선택비율	① 94%	② 1%	③ 2%	④ 0%	⑤ 3%

M: Jane, are you feeling okay?
W: Well, I exercised at the gym and my muscles are hurting a bit now, Dad.
M: Did you stretch after exercising?
W: No. I only stretched before.
M: Oh. ⓐYou should definitely stretch after you finish exercising.
W: Really? I thought stretching after working out would put more pressure on my muscles.
M: That's not true. ⓑStretching afterward helps to loosen your tight muscles and reduce injuries.

muscles 근육 / definitely 확실히 / put pressure on ~에 압력[압박]을 가하다 / afterward 나중에 / loosen 느슨하게 하다, 풀다 / tight 단단한 / injury: 부상

W: That makes sense. Are there any other benefits?
이점
M: Absolutely. ⓒIt allows both your body and mind to slow down and helps you feel relaxed.
W: All right. I'll give it a try. Thanks for your tip, Dad.

해석

남: Jane, 괜찮니?
여: 음, 체육관에서 운동했더니 지금 근육이 조금 아파요, 아빠.
남: 운동 후에 스트레칭을 했니?
여: 아니요. (운동) 전에만 스트레칭을 했어요.
남: 아, ⓐ운동을 마치고 스트레칭을 꼭 해야 한단다.
여: 정말요? 저는 운동 후에 스트레칭을 하면 근육을 더 압박할 거라고 생각했어요.
남: 그건 사실이 아니야. ⓑ나중에 스트레칭을 하면 단단한 근육을 풀어주고 부상을 줄이는 데 도움이 돼.
여: 그렇군요. 다른 이점들도 있나요?
남: 물론이지. ⓒ몸과 마음을 진정하게 하고, 편안해지도록 도움을 주지.
여: 알겠어요. 한번 해볼게요. 조언 고맙습니다, 아빠.

문제 풀이

ⓑ운동 후에 스트레칭을 하면 단단한 근육을 풀어주고 부상을 줄이는 데 도움이 될 뿐 아니라, ⓒ몸과 마음을 진정하게 하고 편안해지도록 도움을 주기 때문에 ⓐ운동 후에 반드시 스트레칭을 해야 한다고 말하고 있다.

3. ① | 관계

선택지 선택비율	① 88%	② 2%	③ 4%	④ 2%	⑤ 2%

W: Hello, what can I do for you?
M: ⓐI went to the literature section, but I couldn't find *Romeo and Juliet* by Shakespeare.
문학 구획
W: Let me check.... *[Typing sound]* Oh, ⓑsomeone just borrowed it.
M: Oh, no. ⓒI really need it for my school assignment. When can I borrow the book, then?
과제
W: I'm not sure, but it is supposed to be returned in a week.
be supposed to-v: ~하기로 되어 있다 반납하다
M: Then, are there any other books by Shakespeare? My teacher wants me to write a book review on a work by Shakespeare.
W: Okay. *[Typing sound]* We have several books by Shakespeare. How about *Hamlet*?
M: Oh, I've heard about that story. I'll read that book instead, then.
W: ⓓ*Hamlet* is in literature section H. I can show you where it is if you want.
M: No, that's okay. I can go get it. Thank you so much.
W: You're welcome.

해석

여: 안녕하세요, 뭘 도와드릴까요?
남: ⓐ문학 구획에 갔는데, 셰익스피어의 〈로미오와 줄리엣〉을 못 찾았어요.
여: 확인해 보겠습니다…. [타이핑하는 소리] 아, ⓑ누군가 방금 빌려가셨네요.
남: 이런. ⓒ학교 과제에 정말 필요해서요. 그럼 언제 그 책을 빌릴 수 있나요?
여: 확실하지는 않지만, 일주일 안에 반납하기로 되어 있어요.
남: 그럼 셰익스피어의 다른 책 있나요? 선생님은 제가 셰익스피어 작품에 관한 서평을 쓰길 원하시거든요.
여: 그렇군요. [타이핑하는 소리] 셰익스피어 책이 몇 권 있네요. 〈햄릿〉은 어떠세요?
남: 아, 그 이야기에 대해 들은 적 있어요. 그럼 대신에 그 책을 읽을래요.
여: ⓓ〈햄릿〉은 문학 H 구획에 있어요. 원하시면 어디에 있는지 알려드릴게요.
남: 아니에요, 괜찮아요. 제가 가서 찾을게요. 고맙습니다.
여: 천만에요.

문제 풀이

남자는 ⓐⓒ학교 과제에 필요한 문학 서적을 찾으며 빌리길 원하고 있고, 여자는 ⓑⓓ서적의 대여 상태와 위치 등을 알려주는 것으로 보아, 도서관 사서와 학생의 대화임을 알 수 있다.

4. ⑤ | 그림 일치

선택지 선택비율	① 2%	② 3%	③ 2%	④ 5%	⑤ 88%

M: Hi, Julia. You were amazing in the play yesterday.
연극
W: Thanks, Mason! Here's a picture from the dressing room after the play. Do you want to take a look?
M: Sure. *[Pause]* I see ⓐyou're holding the flowers I gave you.
W: They're so beautiful. Thanks again.
M: My pleasure. What are ⓑthose two boxes on the floor?
W: I stored some items for the play in them. I needed many items because I played both a prisoner and the queen.
저장하다, 보관하다 죄수
M: You wore ⓒthat striped T-shirt on the hanger as a prisoner, right?
W: Yes. Do you remember ⓓthat crown on the table?
왕관
M: I remember! You wore that as the queen. Wasn't it difficult to change your costume during the play?
의상
W: Not really. But it was hard to see my entire outfit in ⓔthat star-shaped mirror on the wall.
전체의 옷, 복장 거울
M: I understand. Anyway, you did a great job.

해석

남: 안녕, Julia. 너 어제 연극에서 놀라웠어.
여: 고마워, Mason! 여기 연극 끝나고 분장실에서 찍은 사진이야. 한번 볼래?
남: 응. [잠시 후] 내가 너에게 준 ⓐ꽃을 들고 있네.
여: 정말 아름다워. 다시 한번 고마워.
남: 천만에. ⓑ바닥에 있는 저 상자 두 개는 뭐야?
여: 연극에 필요한 물품을 그 안에 보관해뒀어. 죄수와 여왕 역 둘 다 맡았기 때문에 물품이 많이 필요했거든.
남: 네가 죄수 역일 때 ⓒ옷걸이에 있는 저 티셔츠를 입었어, 맞지?
여: 응. ⓓ탁자 위에 있는 저 왕관 기억해?
남: 기억해! 여왕 역일 때 저걸 썼잖아. 연극 도중에 의상을 갈아입는 게 어렵지 않았니?
여: 그다지. 하지만 ⓔ벽에 있는 저 별 모양 거울로 내 옷 전체를 보는 게 어려웠어.
남: 이해된다. 어쨌든 너 정말 잘했어.

문제 풀이

ⓔ벽에 별 모양 거울이 있다고 했으므로, 그림 ⑤의 하트 모양 거울은 대화 내용과 일치하지 않는다.

5. ④ | 할 일

선택지 선택비율	① 4%	② 4%	③ 5%	④ 82%	⑤ 2%

[Phone rings.]
W: Hey, honey. What's going on?
M: I got a call from Jeff's soccer coach. He said they rescheduled their practice match to next Thursday.
일정을 변경하다 연습 경기
W: Oh, Jeff must be disappointed.
실망한
M: Yeah. And since there's no game today, we need to pick Jeff up right after school.
~을 (차에) 태우러 가다
W: His school ends at three, right? Can you go and pick him up when he finishes?
M: I'm afraid I can't. Work is really busy today.
W: I see. But, aren't you meeting with his homeroom teacher at 4:30?
M: That's why I called you. ⓐCan you pick Jeff up at 3:00 instead of me? Otherwise, he'll wait for over an hour and a half.
그렇지 않으면

W: No worries. ⓑI'll leave work early and drive him home.
M: Thank you, honey.

해석

[전화벨이 울린다.]
여: 네, 여보. 무슨 일이에요?
남: Jeff의 축구 코치로부터 전화를 받았어요. 그가 말하길 그들의 연습 경기 일정을 다음 주 목요일로 변경했대요.
여: 이런, Jeff가 분명 실망할 거예요.
남: 그러게요. 그리고 오늘 경기가 없기 때문에, 우리는 학교 끝나고 바로 Jeff를 데리러 가야 해요.
여: 그 애 학교는 세 시에 끝나요, 그렇죠? 아이가 끝나면 당신이 가서 데리고 올 수 있나요?
남: 안 될 것 같아요. 오늘 일이 정말로 바빠요.
여: 알겠어요. 그런데, 당신 4시 30분에 아이 담임 선생님을 뵙지 않나요?
남: 그래서 내가 당신에게 전화한 거예요. ⓐ나 대신 Jeff를 3시에 데리러 갈 수 있나요? 그렇지 않으면, 아이는 한 시간 반 넘게 기다릴 거예요.
여: 걱정 마요. ⓑ내가 일찍 퇴근해서 아이를 집에 태워 갈게요.
남: 고마워요, 여보.

문제 풀이

ⓐ아들 Jeff를 3시에 데리러 갈 수 있는지 남자가 묻자 여자는 ⓑ일찍 퇴근해서 학교에서 아들을 데려오겠다고 했다.

6. ③ | 금액

선택지 선택비율	① 2%	② 8%	③ 86%	④ 3%	⑤ 1%

M: Hello! Welcome to Tom's Party Supplies. How can I help you?
용품
W: Hi. I want to get something for my grandma's birthday party.
M: You've come to the right place. What do you have in mind?
W: I'm looking for some balloons and gift bags.
M: I see. ⓐThis set of birthday balloons is very popular, and it's only $20 per set.
W: Excellent. ⓑI'll take two sets. Can you show me some gift bags?
M: Certainly. These are our gift bags. We can also make special ones for you, if you'd like.
W: Awesome. Is it possible to put my grandma's picture on this bag?
굉장한
M: Sure. ⓒThat would be $2 for each bag with a picture.
W: Great. Then, ⓓI'll take 30.
M: So two sets of balloons and 30 special gift bags, right?
W: Yes. I have this discount coupon. Can I use it now?
M: Of course. ⓔThat'll give you 10% off the total.
W: Good. Here's my credit card.

해석

남: 안녕하세요! Tom's Party Supplies에 오신 것을 환영합니다. 무엇을 도와드릴까요?
여: 안녕하세요. 할머니의 생신 파티를 위해 뭔가를 사고 싶어요.
남: 잘 찾아오셨네요. 어떤 걸 생각하고 계신가요?
여: 풍선과 선물 봉투를 찾고 있어요.
남: 알겠습니다. ⓐ이 생일 풍선 세트가 아주 인기 있고, 세트당 20달러밖에 하지 않습니다.
여: 아주 좋네요. ⓑ두 세트 주세요. 선물 봉투도 좀 보여주실 수 있나요?
남: 물론이죠. 이것들이 저희 선물 봉투입니다. 원하시면 고객님을 위한 특별 봉투를 제작해드릴 수 있습니다.
여: 굉장하네요. 이 봉투에 할머니 사진을 넣을 수 있나요?
남: 물론이죠. ⓒ사진이 들어간 봉투는 개당 2달러입니다.
여: 좋아요. 그럼 ⓓ30개 주세요.
남: 그러면 풍선 두 세트와 특별 선물 봉투 30개, 맞나요?
여: 네. 이 할인 쿠폰이 있어요. 이걸 지금 사용할 수 있을까요?
남: 물론입니다. ⓔ총 금액에서 10% 할인해 드립니다.
여: 좋아요. 여기 제 신용카드예요.

문제 풀이

여자는 ⓐ세트당 20달러인 풍선 ⓑ두 세트(20x2)와 ⓒ개당 2달러인 사진 들어간 선물 봉투 ⓓ30개(2x30)를 구입하고 ⓔ총 금액에서 10% 할인을 받으므로, 여자가 지불할 금액은 90달러이다.

7. ⑤ | 이유

선택지 선택비율	① 1%	② 8%	③ 3%	④ 5%	⑤ 83%

W: Hey, Mike. How was dinner at the French restaurant downtown last weekend? I heard it was recently renovated.
개조하다
M: Well, I went there, but I didn't get to eat anything.
W: Why? Were there too many people waiting in line?
줄 서서 기다리다
M: Not really. There were tables available.
W: Did you bring your dog and the restaurant said no?
M: No, I checked their website and it said I could sit with my dog at an outdoor table.
W: Okay, so then ⓐwhy couldn't you eat anything?
M: ⓑThe restaurant said they ran out of ingredients, so I left.
run out of: ~를 다 써버리다 재료
W: Oh, you must have been disappointed. How about we go there for lunch this Saturday?
실망한
M: Sounds great! They don't take reservations on weekends, so we should get there early.
예약을 받다
W: Good idea. I look forward to it.

해석

여: 안녕, Mike. 지난 주말 시내 프랑스 음식점에서의 저녁은 어땠어? 최근에 개조했다고 들었는데.
남: 음, 거기 갔었는데, 아무것도 먹지 못했어.
여: 왜? 줄 서서 기다리는 사람이 너무 많았어?
남: 아니 그다지. 이용 가능한 테이블이 있었어.
여: 개를 데려가서 식당에서 안 된다고 했어?
남: 아니, 웹사이트를 확인했는데 실외 테이블에서는 개랑 같이 앉을 수 있다고 되어 있었어.
여: 좋네, 그럼 ⓐ왜 아무것도 못 먹었어?
남: ⓑ식당에서 그러는데 재료가 다 떨어졌대, 그래서 나왔지.
여: 아, 실망했겠네. 우리 이번 주 토요일 점심에 거기 가는 건 어때?
남: 좋아! 주말에는 예약을 받지 않아서, 일찍 가야 해.
여: 좋은 생각이야. 기대된다.

문제 풀이

ⓐⓑ남자는 여자의 질문에 재료가 다 떨어져서 아무것도 먹지 못했다고 답했다.

8. ④ | 언급

선택지 선택비율	① 1%	② 0%	③ 2%	④ 94%	⑤ 0%

M: Honey, check out this poster. Friday Night Walk is going to be held this month.
W: Friday Night Walk? Is it walking through the city at night?
M: Well, yes. But ⓐits purpose is to raise money for children's hospitals.
목적 모금하다
W: That's meaningful. And we can enjoy the beautiful city views at night. Why don't we join it?
의미 있는
M: All right. Let's do it.
W: Great. Look. ⓑThere are two walking courses we can choose from, a 5km course and a 10km one.

M: Hmm... How about the 10km one? It would be a lot more exercise.
W: Good idea. ⓒThe participation fee (참가비) is $20 for the 10km course.
M: I see. How can we sign up for (~에 등록하다) the event?
W: It says ⓓwe must register (등록하다) on their website.
M: Okay. Let's register right away.

해석

남: 여보, 이 포스터 좀 확인해 봐요. 이번 달에 Friday Night Walk가 개최될 거예요.
여: Friday Night Walk요? 밤에 도시를 걷는 건가요?
남: 음, 맞아요. 그런데 ⓐ아동 병원을 위해 모금하는 게 목적이에요.
여: 의미 있네요. 그리고 우리는 밤에 아름다운 도시 풍경을 즐길 수 있고요. 참여하는 게 어때요?
남: 좋아요. 그럽시다.
여: 좋아요. 봐요. ⓑ5km 코스와 10km 코스, 고를 수 있는 두 개 코스가 있어요.
남: 음… 10km 코스 어때요? 훨씬 더 운동이 될 거예요.
여: 좋은 생각이에요. ⓒ10km 코스 참가비는 20달러에요.
남: 그렇군요. 어떻게 행사에 등록할 수 있죠?
여: ⓓ웹사이트에서 등록해야 한다고 되어 있어요.
남: 알겠어요. 지금 바로 등록합시다.

문제 풀이

ⓐ행사 목적, ⓑ코스 종류, ⓒ참가비, ⓓ신청 방법은 언급되었으나, 기념품은 언급되지 않았다.

9. ⑤ | 내용 일치

선택지 선택비율	① 2%	② 10%	③ 1%	④ 4%	⑤ 83%

M: Hello, I'm Tony Jones, a librarian at Greenfield Library. We're thrilled (아주 흥분한, 신이 난) to tell you about a brand-new service called Library Plus. ⓐOur library volunteers will deliver (배달하다) books straight (곧장) to your home. Our book delivery service is here to provide (제공하다) more people with the opportunity (기회) to read. ⓑAll library members can use this service free of charge (무료로). In order to get started, use the library's mobile application on your phone. ⓒYou can borrow a maximum (최대) of five books at a time (한 번에). Books may be borrowed for two weeks, but ⓓyou can extend (연장하다) the borrowing period (기간) simply by giving us a call. ⓔYou don't even need to come to the library to return your books. We'll pick up the books at your place. For more information, visit our website. Thank you.

해석

남: 안녕하세요, 저는 Greenfield 도서관의 사서 Tony Jones입니다. 저희는 Library Plus라는 새로운 서비스에 대해 알려드리게 되어 기쁩니다. ⓐ저희 도서관 자원봉사자들이 책을 여러분의 집으로 곧장 배달해 드릴 예정입니다. 저희 책 배달 서비스는 더 많은 분들께 독서할 기회를 제공하기 위해 마련되었습니다. ⓑ모든 도서관 회원이 이 서비스를 무료로 이용할 수 있습니다. (서비스를) 시작하려면, 휴대전화에서 도서관 모바일 애플리케이션을 사용하세요. ⓒ한 번에 최대 다섯 권까지 대출할 수 있습니다. 책은 2주간 빌릴 수 있지만, ⓓ저희에게 전화 한 통으로 간단히 대출 기간을 연장할 수 있습니다. ⓔ도서 반납을 위해 도서관에 올 필요조차 없습니다. 저희가 여러분의 집에서 책을 회수할 것입니다. 더 자세한 정보는 저희 웹사이트를 방문해 주세요. 감사합니다.

문제 풀이

ⓔ도서 반납을 위해 도서관에 올 필요 없이, 도서관 측에서 집으로 와서 책을 회수할 것이라고 했다.

10. ① | 도표

선택지 선택비율	① 80%	② 5%	③ 3%	④ 6%	⑤ 3%

M: Anna, what are you looking at?
W: It's a list of the five best mini projectors of 2017. I'm looking for one I could use for camping.
M: Do you have anything specific (구체적인) in mind?
W: ⓐI'd like one with a battery that lasts ((기능이) 지속되다) at least two hours after it's charged (충전하다).
M: Okay. Do you need wireless (무선 (시스템)) support for your projector?
W: Sure, ⓑI want to connect (연결하다) the projector to my smartphone without using a cord (전기코드).
M: I see. What about the weight (무게)? If you're going to carry it around (가지고 다니다) a lot, I guess ⓒthe lighter the better.
W: I agree. Then this leaves me with these two models.
M: How much are you willing to pay for your projector? (be willing to-v: 기꺼이 ~하다)
W: ⓓI don't want to spend more than 600 dollars.
M: Then you have only one choice.
W: Right, I'll buy that one.

해석

남: Anna, 뭘 보고 있니?
여: 그건 2017년 가장 잘 팔리는 5개 소형 프로젝터의 목록이야. 내가 캠핑에서 사용할 수 있는 걸 찾고 있어.
남: 마음속에 구체적인 걸 생각한 게 있니?
여: ⓐ난 충전 후에 최소한 2시간 이상 지속되는 배터리가 있는 게 좋아.
남: 알겠어. 프로젝터에 무선 시스템 지원이 필요하니?
여: 물론이지, ⓑ전기코드를 사용하지 않고 그 프로젝터를 내 스마트폰에 연결하고 싶어.
남: 알겠어. 무게는 어때? 만약 네가 그것을 많이 가지고 다닐 거라면, ⓒ가벼울수록 더 좋을 것 같아.
여: 동의해. 그러면 이것이 나에게 이 두 가지 모델을 남기네.
남: 넌 네 프로젝트에 얼마를 쓸 의향이 있어?
여: ⓓ난 600달러 이상은 쓰고 싶지 않아.
남: 그러면 넌 딱 한 가지 선택만이 남네.
여: 맞아. 난 그걸 살 거야.

문제 풀이

ⓐ충전 후 2시간 이상을 사용할 수 있는 배터리를 가지고 있고, ⓑ무선 지원을 하며, ⓒ가볍고, ⓓ600달러가 넘지 않는 소형 프로젝터를 사기로 했다.

11. ① | 짧은 대화 응답

선택지 선택비율	① 84%	② 5%	③ 2%	④ 5%	⑤ 1%

W: Honey, what a beautiful Sunday! I don't want to stay home all day.
M: Neither do I. ⓐWhy don't we take a walk (산책하다) in a park or go to watch a movie?
W: We went to the movies last weekend. ⓑLet's enjoy the nice weather this time!
M: All right! It's perfect for walking outside.

해석

여: 여보, 정말 아름다운 일요일이에요! 하루 종일 집에 있고 싶진 않아요.
남: 나도 그래요. ⓐ공원에서 산책하거나 영화를 보러 가는 게 어때요?
여: 우리 지난 주말에 영화 보러 갔잖아요. ⓑ이번에는 멋진 날씨를 즐기자고요!
남: 알겠어요! 밖에서 산책하기 딱 좋은 날이에요.

문제 풀이

ⓐ공원에서 산책하거나 영화를 보러 가자는 남자의 제안에, 여자가 ⓑ멋진 날씨를 즐기자고 말했으므로, 이에 동의하며 밖에서 산책하기 딱 좋은 날이라는 내용의 ①이 응답으로 가장 적절하다.
② 좋아요! 그 영화는 꼭 봐야 할 영화예요.
③ 고마워요. 내가 혼자 주차할게요.
④ 미안해요. 내가 날씨를 확인하지 않았어요.
⑤ 휴! 난 더 이상 걸을 수가 없어요.

12. ② | 짧은 대화 응답

선택지 선택비율	① 3%	② 87%	③ 2%	④ 5%	⑤ 2%

M: Cassie, I think ⓐyou'll have to find another way to get to school tomorrow instead of taking the bus.
W: Why, Dad? The bus is the fastest way to school.
M: I know. But ⓑthe road on your bus route will be under construction
도로 / 노선 / 공사 중인
tomorrow, so traffic will be heavy.
교통(량) / 많은, 심한
W: I see. I'll take the subway tomorrow instead.

해석

남: Cassie, ⓐ내일은 버스 타는 대신 학교에 갈 다른 방법을 찾아야 할 것 같구나.
여: 왜요, 아빠? 버스가 학교 가는 가장 빠른 방법인데요.
남: 알고 있단다. 하지만 ⓑ네가 타는 버스 노선의 도로가 내일 공사 중이라서 교통량이 많을 거야.
여: 알겠어요. 내일은 대신 지하철을 탈게요.

문제 풀이

남자는 ⓑ여자가 학교 갈 때 타는 버스 노선의 도로가 내일 공사 중이어서 교통량이 많을 것이니 ⓐ버스 대신 다른 방법을 찾아야 한다고 말했으므로, 대신 지하철을 타겠다고 말하는 ②가 여자의 응답으로 가장 적절하다.
① 맞는 말씀이에요. 공사가 지금은 끝났어요.
③ 말도 안 돼요. 학교 가는 버스를 막 놓쳤어요.
④ 문제없어요. 내가 차로 출근시켜 줄 수 있어요.
⑤ 물론이에요. 집에 일찍 올게요.

13. ② | 긴 대화 응답

선택지 선택비율	① 3%	② 85%	③ 5%	④ 2%	⑤ 2%

W: Honey, ⓐwould you stop letting Kevin use your smartphone?
M: Why? He's just playing a game. He looks so happy.
W: It's been an hour. That's too long for a 6-year-old boy.
M: It's natural for him to be interested in digital devices.
당연한 / 장치, 기구
W: ⓑThe problem is when he plays with your phone, he rubs his eyes
문지르다[비비다]
a lot.
M: Well, could it be a problem?
W: Come on, honey! ⓒKevin might have poor eyesight later on.
시력 / 나중에
M: Hmm.... Now I see what you mean.
W: Honey, I can't fix this problem without your help.
바로잡다
M: All right. I won't let him use my phone too long.

해석

여: 여보, ⓐKevin이 당신 스마트폰을 그만 사용하게 해줄래요?
남: 왜요? 아이는 게임을 하고 있는 것뿐이에요. 정말 행복해 보이잖아요.
여: 한 시간 됐어요. 6살 남자아이에게는 너무 긴 시간이에요.
남: 아이가 디지털 기기에 관심을 갖는 것은 당연한 거예요.
여: ⓑ문제는 아이가 당신의 전화기를 가지고 놀 때, 눈을 많이 비빈다는 거예요.
남: 음, 그게 문제가 될 수 있나요?
여: 이런, 여보! ⓒKevin이 나중에 나쁜 시력을 갖게 될지도 몰라요.
남: 음…. 당신이 무슨 말을 하는지 이제 알겠어요.
여: 여보, 당신 도움 없이는 내가 이 문제를 바로잡을 수 없어요.
남: 알겠어요. 아이가 내 전화기를 너무 오래 사용하게 하지 않을게요.

문제 풀이

여자가 남자에게 ⓐKevin이 남자의 스마트폰을 그만 사용하게 하라고 요청하며, 그 이유로 ⓑ아이가 전화기를 가지고 놀 때 눈을 많이 비벼서 ⓒ나중에 나쁜 시력을 갖게 될지도 모른다고 말하고 있으므로, Kevin이 전화기를 너무 오래 사용하지 못하도록 하겠다는 ②가 남자의 응답으로 가장 적절하다.
① 괜찮아요. 당신이 내게 게임하는 방법을 가르쳐 주면 돼요.
③ 알겠어요. 내 전화기로 사진을 더 찍읍시다.
④ 음, 수면 부족이 나쁜 시력을 유발할 수 있어요.
⑤ 물론이죠. 난 이미 시력 검사를 했어요.

14. ⑤ | 긴 대화 응답

선택지 선택비율	① 11%	② 9%	③ 3%	④ 4%	⑤ 73%

M: Jenny, ⓐI'm having trouble sticking to my study plans these days.
have trouble v-ing: ~하는 데 어려움을 겪다 / stick to: ~을 굳게 지키다
How do you handle it?
다루다
W: ⓑFor me, things have improved a lot since I started using
개선되다, 나아지다
a scheduling app.
M: Really? I'd love to hear more.
W: It's called "Study Detector," and it has several useful features that
특징
help me stay on track.
계획대로 나아가다
M: What features does it have?
W: First of all, it tracks how much time I study each day, week, and
추적하다
month, and then provides me with a report of my progress.
provide A with B: A에게 B를 제공하다 / 진척, 진행
M: That's amazing!
W: It is! It also sends me reminders that help me stay focused on my
생각나게 하는 것, 알림
schedule.
M: That sounds great! Are there any other features?
W: Yes. It even sends me famous quotes that motivate me to study.
인용구 / 동기를 부여하다
M: Oh, I think I really need to try that app. ⓒDo you think it will help me too?
W: Absolutely! This app will help you solve your problem.

해석

남: Jenny, ⓐ나는 요즘 공부 계획을 잘 지키는 데 어려움을 겪고 있어. 너는 그걸 어떻게 해?
여: ⓑ내 경우에, 일정 관리 앱을 사용하기 시작한 이후로 많이 나아졌어.
남: 정말? 자세히 듣고 싶어.
여: 그건 'Study Detector'라고 하는데, 내가 계획대로 할 수 있도록 도와주는 유용한 특징들이 몇 가지 있어.
남: 어떤 특징들이 있어?
여: 우선, 내가 매일, 매주, 매달 얼마나 많은 시간을 공부했는지 추적하고, 그런 다음에 진행 상황을 내게 보고서로 제공해.
남: 그거 놀랍다!
여: 그렇지! 또 내가 일정에 집중 상태를 유지하도록 돕는 알림도 보내줘.
남: 정말 좋다! 다른 특징도 있어?
여: 응. 심지어 내가 공부하도록 동기 부여하는 유명한 인용구들도 내게 보내줘.
남: 오, 나도 꼭 그 앱을 써 봐야 할 것 같아. ⓒ넌 그게 나한테도 도움이 될 거라고 생각해?
여: 물론이지! 이 앱은 네가 문제를 해결하도록 도와줄 거야.

문제 풀이

ⓐ공부 계획을 지키는 것이 어렵다는 남자의 말에, 여자는 ⓑ자신이 사용하는 일정 관리 앱

의 특징들을 소개하고 있다. 이에 남자가 마지막에 ⓒ그 앱이 자신에게도 도움이 될지 물었으므로, 도움이 될 것이라고 답하는 ⑤가 여자의 응답으로 가장 적절하다.
① 응. 내 일정 계획표에 동기 부여가 되는 인용구를 옮겨 적을래.
② 물론이야. 나한테 이미 알림이 왔어.
③ 그럴 것 같아. 앱을 사용하면 때때로 집중이 흐트러질 수 있어.
④ 바로 그거야! 너 스스로 보고서를 제출해야 해.

15. ⑤ | 상황에 적절한 말

선택지 선택비율	① 2%	② 3%	③ 2%	④ 1%	⑤ 91%

M: Jack and Emma are close friends. Emma invites Jack to join her at a local charity flea market this upcoming weekend. While Emma
자선 벼룩시장
has participated in flea markets several times before, Jack is
~에 참여하다
new to this kind of event. He's looking forward to it, and excitedly
look forward to+명사: ~을 기대하다 신이 나서
searches for items to sell. But he wonders what kinds of things
~을 찾다 팔다 궁금하다
attract more customers at flea markets. He thinks Emma can help
끌어 모으다
him choose the right items to sell. So, Jack wants to ask Emma about what kinds of items would be popular at flea markets. In this situation, what would Jack most likely say to Emma?
Jack: Can you tell me what items sell well at flea markets?
팔리다

해석

남: Jack과 Emma는 친한 친구이다. Emma는 다가오는 이번 주말에 지역 자선 벼룩시장에 자신과 함께 하자고 Jack을 초대한다. Emma는 전에 여러 번 벼룩시장에 참여했던 반면, Jack은 이런 종류의 행사에 처음이다. 그는 이를 기대하며, 판매할 물건들을 신이 나서 찾는다. 하지만 그는 어떤 종류의 물건들이 벼룩시장에서 더 많은 손님을 끌어 모을지 궁금하다. 그는 Emma가 자신이 판매할 적절한 물건을 고르는 데 도움을 줄 수 있다고 생각한다. 그래서 Jack은 Emma에게 벼룩시장에서 어떤 종류의 물건들이 인기가 있을지 묻고 싶어 한다. 이 상황에서, Jack은 Emma에게 뭐라고 말하겠는가?
Jack: 벼룩시장에서 어떤 물건들이 잘 팔리는지 내게 말해 줄 수 있어?

문제 풀이

Jack은 벼룩시장에서 어떤 물건이 인기가 있을지 Emma에게 묻고 싶어 한다고 했으므로, 이 상황에서 가장 적절한 말은 ⑤이다.
① 어떻게 내 부스를 장식할 수 있을지 궁금해.
② 벼룩시장을 위한 물건들을 기부해 줘.
③ 너는 손님에게 늘 친절해야 해.
④ 누가 우리와 함께 자선 행사에 참여할 거야?

16~17. | 세트 문항

16. ① 17. ⑤

선택지 선택비율	① 89%	② 3%	③ 2%	④ 3%	⑤ 3%
	① 1%	② 1%	③ 1%	④ 2%	⑤ 95%

W: Hello, students! In our last lesson, we learned how animals use their senses to find food. Today, ⓐwe'll talk about ways some
감각
animals defend themselves from enemies. First, one of the most
방어하다 enemy: 적
well-known of these animals is the ⓑskunk. Skunks spray a bad-smelling liquid to keep enemies away. Skunk spray does
액체
not cause any lasting damage, though its smell is hard to remove.
유발하다 영속적인, 지속적인 피해 없애다
Second, ⓒchameleons change the color of their skin to match
맞추다
their surroundings, making them hard to spot. That's one clever
주위 환경 발견하다 영리한
way to hide from their enemies! Next, we have ⓓfrogs. By making
숨다
themselves look bigger, they appear more threatening. Another
~하게 보이다 위협적인
animal that uses its body for survival is the ⓔlizard. Interestingly,
생존 도마뱀
lizards can cut off their own tails to escape. But don't worry—the
꼬리
tail eventually grows back! So far, we've looked at animals' defense
결국 방어
strategies. In our next lesson, we'll cover plants that have similar
strategy: 전략 다루다, 포함하다
ways to protect themselves.
보호하다

해석

여: 안녕하세요, 학생 여러분! 지난 수업에서 우리는 동물들이 먹이를 찾기 위해 감각을 어떻게 사용하는지 배웠습니다. 오늘은 ⓐ일부 동물들이 적으로부터 자신을 방어하는 방법에 대해 이야기해 보겠습니다. 첫째로, 이런 가장 잘 알려진 동물들 중 하나는 ⓑ스컹크입니다. 스컹크는 적을 쫓기 위해 냄새가 고약한 액체를 분사합니다. 스컹크의 분사물 냄새는 없애기 어렵지만, 지속적인 피해를 유발하진 않습니다. 둘째로, ⓒ카멜레온은 주위 환경에 맞춰 피부 색깔을 바꿔, 그것들을 발견하기 어렵게 합니다. 적들로부터 숨는 한 가지 영리한 방법이지요! 다음으로는, ⓓ개구리가 있습니다. 그것들은 자신을 더 크게 보이게 만듦으로써, 더 위협적으로 보입니다. 생존을 위해 몸을 사용하는 또 다른 동물은 ⓔ도마뱀입니다. 흥미롭게도, 도마뱀은 도망치기 위해 자신의 꼬리를 끊을 수 있습니다. 하지만 걱정하지 마세요—꼬리는 결국 다시 자랍니다! 지금까지, 우리는 동물들의 방어 전략을 살펴보았습니다. 다음 수업에서는, 자신을 보호하는 비슷한 방식을 가진 식물들에 대해 다루겠습니다.

문제 풀이

16. 여자는 ⓐ동물들이 적으로부터 자신을 방어하는 방법에 대해 이야기하고 있으므로, 여자가 하는 말의 주제로 가장 적절한 것은 ① '동물들이 자신을 보호하기 위해 사용하는 전략들'이다.
② 동물들의 독특한 모습의 이점
③ 멸종 위기에 처한 야생 동물들을 구하는 것의 중요성
④ 동물들이 먹이를 찾을 때 직면하는 어려움
⑤ 동물들이 새끼를 지키기 위해 개발하는 능력
17. ⓑ스컹크, ⓒ카멜레온, ⓓ개구리, ⓔ도마뱀은 언급되었지만, 얼룩말(zebra)은 언급되지 않았다.

[코드 공략하기]

제5회 중급 모의고사

1	⑤	2	①	3	①	4	④	5	②	6	③
7	⑤	8	③	9	⑤	10	②	11	④	12	①
13	①	14	④	15	①	16	②	17	③		

1. ⑤ | 목적

선택지 선택비율	① 6%	② 5%	③ 4%	④ 5%	⑤ 78%

M: May I have your attention, please? This is from the management (관리실) office of Vincent Hospital. ⓐThe west entrance (출)입구, 문 facing (face: ~을 마주보다[향하다]) Main Street is being repaired (수리하다), so it cannot be used. We'd like to remind (상기시키다, 다시 한 번 말해 주다) you all to use the east entrance today. ⓑThe east entrance is on Wilson Street, and it is open during regular (정규의, 정식의) visiting hours ((병원 등의) 면회 시간) from 8 a.m. to 6 p.m. And during non-visiting hours, please use the north entrance facing Hyde Street. The west entrance will be in use from tomorrow. We're sorry for any inconvenience (불편) this might cause.

Thank you for your cooperation (협조).

해석

남: 주목해 주시기 바랍니다. Vincent 병원 관리실에서 알려드립니다. ⓐMain 가를 향해 있는 서쪽 출입구는 수리 중이라 사용이 불가합니다. 오늘은 여러분 모두 동쪽 출입구를 사용하실 것을 다시 한 번 말씀드리고 싶습니다. ⓑ동쪽 출입구는 Wilson 가에 있으며, 오전 8시부터 오후 6시까지 정규 면회 시간 동안 개방됩니다. 그리고 면회 시간이 아닌 때에는 Hyde 가를 향해 있는 북쪽 출입구를 사용해 주시기 바랍니다. 서쪽 출입구는 내일부터 사용될 예정입니다. 이로 인해 불편을 끼쳐 죄송합니다. 협조해 주셔서 감사합니다.

문제 풀이

남자는 병원의 ⓐ서쪽 출입구가 수리 중이어서 오늘 사용이 불가능하므로, ⓑ정규 면회 시간에는 동쪽 출입구를, 그 외 시간에는 북쪽 출입구를 사용할 것을 안내하고 있다.

2. ① | 의견

선택지 선택비율	① 85%	② 4%	③ 2%	④ 2%	⑤ 6%

M: Kate, you don't look good. Are you okay?
W: Yes, I'm fine. It's nothing.
M: Are you sure? You seem really stressed.
W: Well, I'm having a hard time being the leader of a team project.
M: What's the problem?
W: It's hard handling (handle: 다루다, 처리하다) different opinions (의견) because my teammates get (~을 (시작)하게 되다) into arguments (논쟁) easily.
M: I understand, however, ⓐarguments can lead (이끌다) people to make better decisions (결정).
W: Do you really think so?
M: Absolutely! Arguments happen all the time (늘, 항상). ⓑTry to think of arguments as a way to reach (~에 이르다[도달하다]) a better decision.
W: That's good advice. I'll try to remember that.

해석

남: Kate, 너 안 좋아 보여. 괜찮니?
여: 응, 괜찮아. 아무것도 아니야.
남: 정말이야? 너 정말 스트레스받는 것처럼 보여.
여: 그게, 팀 프로젝트의 리더로 힘든 시간을 보내고 있어.
남: 뭐가 문제인데?
여: 팀원들이 쉽게 논쟁을 벌이게 돼서 각기 다른 의견들을 처리하는 게 어려워.
남: 이해해, 하지만 ⓐ논쟁은 사람들이 더 나은 결정을 내리도록 이끌 수 있어.
여: 정말 그렇게 생각하니?
남: 물론이지! 논쟁은 항상 생겨. ⓑ논쟁을 더 나은 결정에 도달하기 위한 방법으로 생각하도록 노력해 봐.
여: 좋은 충고야. 기억하도록 노력할게.

문제 풀이

남자는 ⓐⓑ논쟁을 더 나은 결정에 도달하기 위한 방법으로 여기라고 여자에게 충고하고 있다.

3. ① | 요지

선택지 선택비율	① 92%	② 2%	③ 1%	④ 2%	⑤ 3%

M: Hello, everyone. Today, I am going to talk about how we can support (지원하다) senior citizens (노인, 어르신) in the digital age (시대). You may have heard that many seniors are struggling with (struggle with: ~로 고군분투하다) digital technologies in their daily lives, such as ordering food at kiosks or using mobile banking apps. Because they are not familiar with (be familiar with: ~에 친숙[익숙]하다) these digital services, seniors may find it difficult to keep up with ((~의 진도·증가 속도 등을) 따라가다) all the changes in today's world. That's why ⓐwe need to provide them with (provide A with B: A에게 B를 제공하다) digital education. ⓑBy teaching seniors how to utilize (활용하다) digital skills, we can help them navigate (항해하다) modern life smoothly (부드럽게, 순조롭게) and they won't feel left behind (leave behind: ~을 뒤로 하다).

해석

남: 안녕하세요, 여러분. 오늘 저는 디지털 시대에 어떻게 우리가 어르신들을 지원할 수 있는지에 대해 이야기하려고 합니다. 여러분은 아마 많은 어르신들이 키오스크에서의 음식 주문이나 모바일 뱅킹 앱 사용처럼 일상 생활의 디지털 기술로 애를 먹고 있다는 것을 들어보셨을 겁니다. 어르신들은 이러한 디지털 서비스에 익숙하지 않기 때문에, 오늘날의 세상의 그 모든 변화를 따라가기 힘들다고 생각할 수 있습니다. 그것이 바로 ⓐ우리가 어르신들에게 디지털 교육을 제공해야 하는 이유입니다. ⓑ어르신들에게 디지털 기술을 활용하는 방법을 가르쳐 드림으로써, 우리는 그들이 현대 생활을 순조롭게 해 나가도록 도울 수 있고, 그들은 뒤처진다고 느끼지 않을 것입니다.

문제 풀이

ⓐⓑ어르신들에게 디지털 교육을 제공함으로써 디지털 시대에 그들의 생활을 도울 수 있다고 말하고 있다.

4. ④ | 그림 일치

선택지 선택비율	① 1%	② 1%	③ 1%	④ 93%	⑤ 4%

M: Rebecca, look at this picture.
W: Sure. What is it?
M: This is the garage (차고) in my new house. I finally have one.
W: Great. It was your dream to have your own garage, right?
M: Right. ⓐLook at this tool (도구) board (판) on the wall. It's very convenient (편리한) for

hanging tools.
걸다
W: Good. And ⓑyou put a table below the board.
~ 아래에
M: Yes, I use it for repairing broken things. ⓒCan you see the skateboard in the box? I changed its wheels all by myself.
W: Awesome. But isn't it boring to work alone?
M: Yes, that's why I ⓓput a big speaker in the corner to listen to music.
W: Cool. ⓔIs that your new bicycle near the door?
M: Yes, now I can safely store it inside the garage.
저장[보관]하다
W: That's good. You were always worried about your bicycle when it rained. Congratulations.

해석

남: Rebecca, 이 사진을 봐.
여: 응. 그게 뭐니?
남: 이건 우리 새집에 있는 차고야. 드디어 하나 생겼어.
여: 잘됐다. 너만의 차고를 갖는 것이 네 꿈이었잖아, 그렇지?
남: 맞아. ⓐ벽에 있는 이 도구판을 봐. 도구를 걸기 아주 편리해.
여: 좋네. 그리고 ⓑ판 아래에 테이블을 놨구나.
남: 응, 고장 난 물건들을 수리하는 데 그걸 사용하거든. ⓒ상자 안에 있는 스케이트보드 보이니? 내가 오로지 혼자 바퀴를 바꿨어.
여: 멋지다. 하지만 혼자 작업하는 게 심심하지 않니?
남: 응, 그래서 음악을 들으려고 ⓓ모퉁이에 큰 스피커를 둔 거야.
여: 멋지다. ⓔ문 근처에 있는 저게 네 새 자전거니?
남: 응, 이제 그걸 차고 안에 안전하게 보관할 수 있어.
여: 그거 잘됐다. 너 비가 올 때 항상 자전거에 대해 걱정했잖아. 축하해.

문제 풀이

ⓓ모퉁이에 큰 스피커를 두었다고 했으므로, ④의 사다리는 대화 내용과 일치하지 않는다.

5. ② ㅣ 할 일

선택지 선택비율	① 4%	② 86%	③ 2%	④ 4%	⑤ 1%

M: Reina, what are you reading?
W: Hi, Peter. This is a book that introduces simple yoga poses.
소개하다 자세
M: I didn't know you're interested in yoga.
W: I became interested in it recently since I heard yoga could help to relieve my back pain.
요통 최근에
(불쾌감 · 고통 등을) 없애 주다, 덜어 주다
M: Well, why don't you go to see a doctor first?
W: Actually I did, and the doctor recommended yoga for me.
추천하다
M: I see. Then how about taking a yoga class at the community center?
W: When I checked, the class hours didn't fit my schedule. So, I'm looking for some simple yoga poses I can do every day from this book.
맞다
M: Then I'll send you some yoga video clips through email. You can follow the poses while watching them.
W: Oh, that would be great. Thanks a lot.

해석

남: Reina, 너 무엇을 읽고 있니?
여: 안녕, Peter. 이건 간단한 요가 자세들을 소개하고 있는 책이야.
남: 난 네가 요가에 관심이 있는 줄 몰랐어.
여: 요가가 요통을 덜어 주는 걸 도울 수 있다는 걸 들은 이후 최근에 그것에 관심이 생겼어.
남: 음, 먼저 병원에 가 보는 게 어때?
여: 사실 갔었는데, 의사 선생님께서 내게 요가를 추천하셨어.
남: 그렇구나. 그러면 주민 센터에서 요가 수업을 듣는 건 어때?
여: 내가 확인했을 때, 수업 시간들이 내 스케줄과 맞지 않았어. 그래서 이 책에서 내가 매일 할 수 있는 몇몇 간단한 요가 자세들을 찾고 있어.
남: 그러면 내가 이메일로 요가 동영상들을 좀 보내 줄게. 그것들을 보면서 자세들을 따라 할 수 있어.
여: 오, 그거 좋겠다. 정말 고마워.

문제 풀이

남자가 여자에게 이메일로 요가 동영상을 보내기로 했다.

6. ③ ㅣ 금액

선택지 선택비율	① 1%	② 5%	③ 77%	④ 6%	⑤ 12%

W: Honey, how about getting a pizza from Toby's Place for dinner?
M: Sounds great! Let's try the new delivery app that I downloaded recently. *[Pause]* Hmm... How about a potato pizza?
배달
W: I like that idea. How much is one large potato pizza?
M: ⓐIt's $25. Oh, we have to order a minimum of $30 for delivery.
최소한
W: Then we can add some drinks. How much is a cola?
더하다, 추가하다
M: One small can is $2, and ⓑa large one is $3.
W: Then let's order two large cans.
M: Great, ⓒone large potato pizza and two large cans of cola. Now we can place the order.
주문하다
W: Is there a delivery fee?
배달료
M: Normally we have to pay $5, but ⓓit's free now because of the app promotion. So I'll pay using the app.
보통은, 정상적으로
W: Thank you. I'm starving. I hope it gets here quickly.
배가 고파 죽을 지경인

해석

여: 여보, 저녁으로 Toby's Place에서 피자를 시키는 게 어때요?
남: 좋아요! 내가 최근에 다운로드한 새 배달 앱을 한번 써 봐요. [잠시 후] 음… 포테이토 피자는 어때요?
여: 좋은 생각이에요. 라지 포테이토 피자 한 판이 얼마예요?
남: ⓐ25달러예요. 아, 배달하려면 최소 30달러를 주문해야 해요.
여: 그럼 음료수를 추가하면 되겠네요. 콜라는 얼마예요?
남: 작은 캔은 2달러, ⓑ큰 캔은 3달러예요.
여: 그럼 큰 캔 두 개 주문해요.
남: 좋아요, ⓒ라지 포테이토 피자 한 판과 큰 콜라 두 캔. 이제 주문할 수 있어요.
여: 배달료가 있나요?
남: 보통은 5달러를 내야 하는데, 앱 프로모션 때문에 ⓓ지금은 무료예요. 그러니까 앱으로 지불할게요.
여: 고마워요. 배고파 죽겠어요. 빨리 도착하면 좋겠어요.

문제 풀이

ⓐⓒ25달러인 피자 한 판과 ⓑⓒ3달러인 콜라 두 캔을 주문하기로 했고, ⓓ현재 배달료는 무료라고 했으므로, 남자가 지불할 총액은 31달러이다.

7. ⑤ ㅣ 이유

선택지 선택비율	① 3%	② 2%	③ 6%	④ 2%	⑤ 84%

W: Hey, Mark! You look serious. What's up?
M: ⓐI'm thinking of leaving my job.
W: Why? Did you get a job offer from another company?
일자리 제의
M: Not yet, but I've submitted applications to some other companies.
제출하다 지원서
W: I thought you were satisfied with your work and salary.
be satisfied with: ~에 만족하다 급여

M: Well, the pay is good and I'm comfortable with this job.
급여
W: Then, ⓑwhy do you want to leave?
M: ⓒIf I don't look for a new challenge, I will get used to doing the same easy job and I won't develop.
도전 get used to v-ing: ~에 익숙해지다 발전하다
W: You mean ⓓyou want to develop your abilities by challenging yourself with different work, don't you?
개발하다 ability: 능력 challenge: 도전하다
M: Exactly. I would be happier with a job that can help me improve my career.
향상시키다 경력
W: I understand, but you'd better make the decision after considering the matter carefully.
결정하다 생각하다, 고려하다
M: Thank you for your advice.

해석

여: 얘, Mark! 너 심각해 보여. 무슨 일이니?
남: ⓐ일을 그만둘까 생각 중이야.
여: 왜? 다른 회사에서 일자리 제의를 받았니?
남: 아직 아닌데, 다른 회사 몇 군데에 지원서를 제출했어.
여: 난 네가 일이랑 급여에 만족한다고 생각했어.
남: 음, 급여도 좋고 이 일이 편해.
여: 그럼 ⓑ왜 그만두고 싶은 거니?
남: ⓒ새로운 도전을 찾지 않으면, 똑같은 쉬운 일을 하는 데 익숙해질 것이고 발전하지 않을 거야.
여: ⓓ다른 일에 도전해서 네 능력을 개발하고 싶다는 뜻이구나, 그렇지?
남: 바로 그거야. 내 경력을 향상시키는 데 도움이 될 수 있는 일을 하면 더 행복할 것 같아.
여: 이해는 하지만, 이 문제에 대해 깊이 생각한 후에 결정하는 게 좋겠어.
남: 충고 고마워.

문제 풀이

ⓐ일을 그만둘 생각을 하는 남자에게 ⓑ이유를 묻자, ⓒⓓ새로운 도전을 통해 능력을 개발하고 싶다고 했다.

8. ③ | 언급

선택지 선택비율	① 1%	② 3%	③ 91%	④ 5%	⑤ 1%

M: Hi, Jessica. Are you ready for the trip to Nari Island?
W: Not yet. I've been too busy to make a detailed plan.
상세한
M: Then, how about booking a package tour? There should be some package tours on the island.
W: Really? Let me check online. *[Typing Sound]* ⓐThis one runs for 5 days, from April 3 to April 7. It matches my holiday schedule.
맞다 휴가
M: It provides a guided tour ⓑto beautiful caves and cliffs.
제공하다 동굴 (특히 해안의) 낭떠러지, 절벽
W: I think I'd enjoy it. I like to explore geological sites.
탐험하다 지질학상의 장소
M: And ⓒa minivan will be offered for transportation.
이동 수단
W: It sounds convenient. What do you think of the price?
편리한
M: I think ⓓ$600 for each person is quite reasonable.
(가격이) 적당한
W: Perfect. I'll book it right away.

해석

남: 안녕, Jessica. 나리섬 여행은 준비됐니?
여: 아니 아직. 너무 바빠서 상세한 계획을 못 짰어.
남: 그렇다면 패키지여행을 예약하는 건 어때? 섬에 패키지여행이 좀 있을 거야.
여: 정말? 온라인에서 확인해 볼게. [타이핑하는 소리] ⓐ이건 4월 3일부터 7일까지 5일간이네. 이게 내 휴가 일정이랑 맞아.
남: ⓑ아름다운 동굴과 절벽으로 가이드 투어도 제공하네.
여: 재미있을 것 같아. 난 지질학적인 장소를 탐험하는 걸 좋아하거든.
남: 그리고 ⓒ이동 수단으로 미니밴이 제공되네.
여: 편리하겠다. 가격은 어떤 것 같아?
남: ⓓ1인당 600달러면 상당히 합리적이지.
여: 완벽해. 당장 그걸 예약할래.

문제 풀이

ⓐ여행 기간, ⓑ방문 장소, ⓒ이동 수단, ⓓ가격은 언급되었으나, 최소 출발 인원은 언급되지 않았다.

코드+α 가격과 관련된 표현

I can't afford it. It's too expensive. (난 그걸 살 형편이 안 돼. 너무 비싸.)
That's over my budget. (그건 내 예산을 초과해.)
This restaurant sells food at reasonable prices. (이 식당은 음식을 합리적인 가격에 판매해.)

9. ⑤ | 내용 일치

선택지 선택비율	① 3%	② 1%	③ 3%	④ 4%	⑤ 89%

W: Hello, listeners. Have you ever thought about boosting your business with short-form videos? Then how about joining our Short-form Video Course? ⓐIt's a free online course that is open to everyone interested in using social media for their business. The course ⓑis made up of three stages that will teach you the art of planning, shooting, and editing videos like a professional. Please ⓒvisit our website at www.shortformclass.com to sign up. The best part of this course is that ⓓyou can take it at any time, over and over again. And guess what? ⓔWe'll randomly pick some of the participants and give feedback on their work. Don't miss this chance to level up your business!
신장시키다, 북돋우다 be made up of: ~로 구성되다 기술 촬영하다 편집하다 전문가 무작위로

해석

여: 안녕하세요, 청취자 여러분. 숏폼 동영상으로 여러분의 사업을 성장시킬 생각을 해 보신 적 있나요? 그렇다면 저희의 숏폼 동영상 강좌에 참여해 보시는 게 어떨까요? 이것은 소셜 미디어를 사업에 활용하는 데 관심 있는 모든 분에게 열려 있는 ⓐ무료 온라인 강좌입니다. 이 강좌는 전문가처럼 동영상을 기획하고, 촬영하고, 편집하는 기술을 여러분에게 가르쳐 드리는 ⓑ세 단계로 구성되어 있습니다. ⓒ저희 웹사이트 www.shortformclass.com에 방문하여 등록해 주세요. 이 강좌의 가장 좋은 점은 ⓓ언제든지 반복해서 수강할 수 있다는 것입니다. 그리고 또 놀라운 게 뭘까요? ⓔ참가자 중 일부를 무작위로 선정하여 그분들의 작품에 대해 피드백을 드릴 겁니다. 여러분의 사업을 한 단계 높일 이 기회를 놓치지 마세요!

문제 풀이

ⓔ참가자 중 일부를 무작위로 선정하여 그 사람들의 작품에 대해 피드백을 제공할 것이라고 했다.

10. ② | 도표

선택지 선택비율	① 1%	② 81%	③ 1%	④ 16%	⑤ 1%

W: Sean, look what I found for mom for her birthday.
M: Oh, an electric mug warmer set? What is it?
전기의
W: It's a set that includes a mug and a warmer, and the warmer keeps
포함하다

beverages warm.
음료

M: Cool! How much can we spend on this?

W: Well, we didn't buy a cake yet, so ⓐwe'd better not spend more than $50.
had better not+동사원형: ~하지 않는 게 낫다

M: I see. The mugs come in three different materials. Which one would she like?
소재

W: ⓑShe already has glass mugs, so let's choose from the other materials.

M: Good idea. How about the capacity of the mug?
용량

W: ⓒI think less than 500ml will be appropriate.
적절한

M: Yeah, that makes sense. ⓓDo you think it's better to buy a set with the LED display?
make sense: 일리가 있다
디스플레이, 화면 표시 장치

W: Yes. ⓔI think it's better because it allows you to check the temperature.
온도

M: I like it, too. Let's order this one.

해석

여: Sean, 엄마 생신을 위해 내가 찾은 걸 봐.
남: 아, 전기 머그 워머 세트? 그게 뭐야?
여: 머그와 워머를 포함한 세트인데, 워머가 음료를 따뜻하게 유지하는 거지.
남: 멋지다! 우리가 이거에 얼마를 쓸 수 있지?
여: 음, 케이크를 아직 안 샀으니까, ⓐ50달러 넘게 쓰지 않는 게 좋아.
남: 알겠어. 머그가 세 가지 소재로 나오네. 어떤 걸 좋아하실까?
여: ⓑ유리 머그를 이미 가지고 계시니까, 다른 소재 중에서 고르자.
남: 좋은 생각이야. 머그 용량은?
여: ⓒ500ml보다 작은 게 적절할 것 같아.
남: 응, 일리가 있네. ⓓLED 화면 표시 장치가 있는 세트를 사는 게 나을 것 같아?
여: 응. ⓔ온도를 확인할 수 있게 해 주니까 더 좋은 것 같아.
남: 나도 그 점이 마음에 들어. 이걸 주문하자.

문제 풀이

두 사람은 ⓐ50달러를 넘지 않고, ⓑ유리 이외의 소재이고, ⓒ500ml보다 용량이 작고, ⓓⓔLED 화면 표시 장치가 있는 전기 머그 워머 세트를 주문하기로 했다.

11. ④ | 짧은 대화 응답

선택지 선택비율	① 5%	② 2%	③ 2%	④ 77%	⑤ 14%

M: Katie, we have to go to the Modern Art Center sometime this month for our art class project. ⓐHow about this Sunday?

W: ⓑI have plans with my mom that day. Let's go another day.

M: But ⓒthey have a special artist lecture only this Sunday. Would you consider changing your plans?
강연

W: Yeah, just let me make sure it's okay with my mom first.

해석

남: Katie, 우리 이번 달 언젠가 미술 수업 프로젝트 때문에 현대미술관에 가야 하잖아. ⓐ이번 주 일요일 어때?
여: ⓑ나 그날 엄마랑 계획이 있어. 다른 날 가자.
남: 그런데 ⓒ이번 일요일에만 특별 화가 강연이 있어. 계획을 바꾸는 걸 고려할 수 있어?
여: 응, 우선 괜찮은지 엄마에게 확인해 볼게.

문제 풀이

남자가 ⓐ이번 주 일요일에 미술관에 가자고 제안하자 여자는 ⓑ그날 엄마와 계획이 있다고 했다. 이에 남자가 ⓒ이번 주 일요일에 특별 강연이 있으니 계획을 바꿀 수 있는지 물었으므로, 이에 대한 여자의 응답으로 ④가 가장 적절하다.
① 미안해. 우리 오늘 미술 수업 프로젝트를 끝낼 수 없어.
② 아, 네가 그 기회를 놓쳤다니 아쉽다.
③ 난 그렇게 생각하지 않아. 티켓이 그렇게 비싸지 않아.
⑤ 왜 안 돼? 엄마랑 나는 일요일에 아무 계획 없어.

12. ① | 짧은 대화 응답

선택지 선택비율	① 82%	② 2%	③ 5%	④ 5%	⑤ 6%

W: Harry, have you decided what school club you will join?

M: Not yet. ⓐI'm thinking of joining either the poetry club or the history club.

W: I've heard ⓑthe history club is already full, so they're not accepting any more new members.
(구성원으로) 받아들이다

M: Then, I'll apply for the poetry club.
~에 지원하다 / 시

해석

여: Harry, 어떤 학교 동아리에 가입할지 정했니?
남: 아니 아직. ⓐ시 동아리나 역사 동아리 둘 중에 가입할까 생각 중이야.
여: ⓑ역사 동아리는 이미 꽉 차서, 새 회원을 더 이상 받지 않는다고 들었어.
남: 그럼, 시 동아리에 지원해야지.

문제 풀이

ⓐ시 동아리나 역사 동아리 둘 중에 가입할 생각이라는 남자에게 여자가 ⓑ역사 동아리는 꽉 차서 새 회원을 받지 않는다고 말해주었으므로, 시 동아리에 지원해야겠다는 응답이 가장 적절하다.
② 응, 내가 너에게 좋은 동아리를 추천해줄 수 있어.
③ 안 될 일이야. 우리는 새 회원을 받을 수 없어.
④ 잘됐다! 방과후에 역사 동아리에서 보자.
⑤ 정말? 내가 이 동아리에 가입할 수 있게 허락해줘서 고마워.

13. ① | 긴 대화 응답

선택지 선택비율	① 55%	② 15%	③ 12%	④ 5%	⑤ 11%

M: Daisy, how was your school trip to the War Memorial Museum?
수학여행 / 전쟁기념관

W: The museum was much more impressive than I expected, Dad.
인상적인

M: Great! Tell me about it.

W: It's huge! There were lots of collections and displays about the Korean War.
수집품, 소장품 / 전시품 / 한국 전쟁

M: Then you saw many things about the war.

W: Absolutely. The museum gave me a feeling for what the Korean War was like.

M: Hmm, I've actually never thought about the war that seriously.
심각하게

W: Me, either. ⓐBut the countless names of dead people on a memorial stone there made my heart feel heavy.
무수한 / 추모비

M: I didn't know the war was such a tragedy.
비극

W: And, you know what? ⓑPeople from other countries were listed among the soldiers on the stone.
명단에 언급하다[포함하다] / 군인

M: Right. So, I wonder what you learned from your visit.

W: We got peace, but the cost was big.
희생, 손실

해석

남: Daisy, 전쟁기념관으로 갔던 수학여행은 어땠니?

여: 아빠, 그 박물관은 제가 기대했던 것보다 훨씬 더 인상적이었어요.
남: 잘됐구나! 그곳에 대해 내게 말해 주렴.
여: 그곳은 정말 커요! 한국 전쟁에 대한 많은 소장품들과 전시품들이 있었어요.
남: 그럼 전쟁에 관한 많은 것들을 봤겠구나.
여: 물론이죠. 그 박물관은 제게 한국 전쟁이 어땠을지에 대한 느낌을 주었어요.
남: 음, 난 사실 한 번도 전쟁에 대해 그렇게 심각하게 생각해 본 적이 없구나.
여: 저도요. ⓐ하지만 그곳의 추모비에 있는 죽은 사람들의 무수한 이름이 제 마음을 무겁게 했어요.
남: 난 전쟁이 그토록 비극이었는지는 몰랐구나.
여: 그리고, 그거 아세요? ⓑ다른 나라 사람들도 추모비에 적힌 군인들의 명단 중에 있었어요.
남: 그렇구나. 그래서, 난 네가 (그곳의) 방문으로 무엇을 배웠는지 궁금하구나.
여: 우리는 평화를 얻었지만, 희생이 컸다는 거예요.

문제 풀이

여자는 전쟁기념관의 추모비에서 ⓐ많은 죽은 이들과 ⓑ외국인 군인들의 이름을 보고 마음이 무겁다고 했으므로, 전쟁기념관을 다녀와서 무엇을 배웠는지 궁금하다는 남자의 말에 대한 응답으로 우리는 평화를 얻었지만 희생이 컸다는 ①이 가장 적절하다.
② 자신감을 향상시키는 것이 최고의 교육이에요.
③ 저는 아빠가 군대에 가셔야 한다고 생각했어요.
④ 그 박물관이 문을 닫았는데, 그것이 저희를 속상하게 했어요.
⑤ 군인들은 그들의 봉급이 인상되어야 한다고 주장해요.

14. ④ | 긴 대화 응답

선택지 선택비율	① 6%	② 3%	③ 2%	④ 87%	⑤ 2%

W: I've been feeling down lately about my art.
기분이 우울하다 요즘, 최근에
M: Really? What's wrong?
W: ⓐI keep posting my drawings online, but only a few people view my
게시하다
blog to look at them. It's so disappointing.
실망스러운
M: I understand how you feel, but isn't it great to create something
meaningful for yourself?
의미 있는
W: Of course it is. But I'd like to share my art with other people and
공유하다
hear from them about my work.
M: Then how about finding another way to connect with people and
이어지다, 연결되다
share your work?
W: Another way? Like what?
M: ⓑYou can join an art community or local art club and discuss your
논의하다
work with others at offline meetings.
W: ⓒThat's a good idea. I've never thought about connecting with
people in person. I think I'll look into it.
대면하여 ~을 주의 깊게 살피다
M: Good for you! You might have a more meaningful experience.

해석

여: 요즘 제 미술 활동 때문에 기분이 우울해요.
남: 정말요? 뭐가 문제예요?
여: ⓐ계속 제 그림들을 온라인에 게시하고 있는데, 그걸 보러 제 블로그를 보러 오는 사람이 극소수예요. 정말 실망스러워요.
남: 당신이 어떤 기분일지 이해하지만, 스스로를 위해 의미 있는 걸 만든다는 게 멋지지 않나요?
여: 물론 그렇죠. 하지만 제 미술 작품을 다른 사람들과 공유하고 제 작품에 대해 그들에게 듣고 싶어요.
남: 그렇다면 사람들과 연결되고 당신의 작품을 공유할 수 있는 다른 방법을 찾아보는 건 어때요?
여: 다른 방법이요? 예를 들면요?
남: ⓑ미술 커뮤니티나 지역 미술 동호회에 가입해서 오프라인 모임에서 다른 사람들과 당신의 작품에 대해 이야기해 볼 수 있어요.
여: ⓒ그거 좋은 생각이에요. 저는 사람들과 대면하여 연결되는 것에 대해서는 전혀 생각해 보지 않았었거든요. 한번 살펴봐야겠네요.
남: 잘됐네요! 더 의미 있는 경험을 할 수도 있어요.

문제 풀이

ⓐ블로그에 자신의 그림을 게시하지만 방문자가 별로 없어 실망하는 여자에게 남자는 ⓑ오프라인 모임을 통해 다른 사람들과 작품에 대해 이야기해 볼 것을 제안하고 있고, 여자는 ⓒ이에 수긍하며 살펴보겠다고 했으므로, 여자의 시도에 긍정적으로 반응하는 ④가 남자의 응답으로 가장 적절하다.
① 기운 내요! 당신은 다음에 대회에서 우승할 수 있어요.
② 동의해요. 현대 미술에 집중하는 게 중요해요.
③ 그다지요. 도움이 되는 그리기 수업을 전혀 못 찾고 있어요.
⑤ 신경 쓰지 마요. 저는 새로운 소셜 미디어 플랫폼에서 새 출발을 할 수 있어요.

15. ① | 상황에 적절한 말

선택지 선택비율	① 82%	② 4%	③ 7%	④ 2%	⑤ 5%

W: Jane and David are both violinists in the school orchestra. They have been practicing together for a month for the Spring Concert. Just three days before the concert, Jane sprains her wrist and
(손목·발목 등을) 삐다 손목
her doctor recommends taking a rest for at least a week. Since Jane cannot play at the concert, David should take her solo part.
솔로 연주[공연]의, 단독의
They have been practicing together and David knows Jane's part. However, ⓐDavid says that he is too nervous to play the solo part.
긴장한
Jane knows that David is a skilled violinist. So, ⓑJane wants to
숙련된, 노련한
encourage David to be more confident. In this situation, what would
격려하다 자신감 있는
Jane most likely say to David?
Jane: I'm sure you can play the solo part beautifully.

해석

여: Jane과 David 둘 다 학교 오케스트라에서 바이올린을 연주한다. 그들은 봄 연주회를 위해 한 달 동안 함께 연습해 오고 있다. 연주회 겨우 3일 전에, Jane은 손목을 삐어서, 의사가 최소한 일주일 동안 쉴 것을 권했다. Jane은 연주회에서 연주할 수 없기 때문에, David가 그녀의 솔로 파트를 맡아야 한다. 그들은 함께 연습해왔고 David는 Jane의 파트를 알고 있다. 하지만, ⓐDavid는 너무 긴장돼서 솔로 파트를 연주할 수 없다고 말한다. Jane은 David가 노련하게 바이올린을 연주한다는 것을 안다. 그래서 ⓑJane은 David가 더 자신감을 갖도록 격려하고 싶다. 이 상황에서, Jane은 David에게 뭐라고 말하겠는가?
Jane: 넌 분명 솔로 파트를 아름답게 연주할 수 있어.

문제 풀이

ⓐ긴장돼서 솔로 파트를 연주할 수 없다고 말하는 David에게 ⓑJane은 자신감을 갖도록 격려하고 싶다고 했으므로, ①이 가장 적절하다.
② 그건 전부 내 잘못이야. 내가 더 신중했어야 했어.
③ 네 솔로 파트를 다른 누군가에게 주는 게 어때?
④ 안됐다. 우리는 연주회를 일주일 연기해야 해.
⑤ 나는 봄 연주회에 참여하기 위해 최선을 다할 거야.

16~17. | 세트 문항

16. ② 17. ③

선택지 선택비율	① 4%	② 92%	④ 1%	④ 1%	⑤ 1%
	① 1%	② 1%	④ 95%	④ 3%	⑤ 0%

M: Good evening, viewers. Last time, I introduced some paintings by well-known Western artists. Today, ⓐI'd like to talk about objects
잘 알려진, 유명한 서양의 물건, 물체

that have symbolic meanings in Western art. Let's begin with
상징적인
ⓑmirrors. The reflection seen in mirrors can reveal a hidden truth
(거울 등에 비친) 상[모습] 드러내다
or expose a lie. As you might imagine, a broken mirror generally
폭로하다 일반적으로
represents bad luck. Second, ⓒcandles. They can symbolize the
나타내다, 상징하다 상징하다
passing of time or show a timeline. This is seen in how much of the candles have burned. Third, let's talk about ⓓbooks. Books often represent a higher educational status. They're also a symbol of
교육의 신분, 지위
learning or of giving knowledge. Lastly, ⓔflowers can be a symbol
지식
of life. Blooming flowers are used to show power and growth. In
꽃을 피우다
a moment, I'll present some paintings with these symbols.
보여 주다

해석

남: 안녕하세요, 시청자 여러분. 지난 시간에는 유명한 서양 화가들의 그림을 몇 점 소개해 드렸습니다. 오늘은 ⓐ서양 미술에서 상징적인 의미를 가진 물건들에 대해 이야기하려고 합니다. ⓑ거울부터 시작하겠습니다. 거울에 보이는 모습은 숨겨진 진실을 드러내거나 거짓을 폭로할 수 있습니다. 어쩌면 짐작하시는 것처럼, 깨진 거울은 일반적으로 불운을 상징합니다. 두 번째로, ⓒ양초입니다. 그것들은 시간의 흐름을 상징하거나 시간의 경과를 보여줄 수 있습니다. 이는 양초가 얼마나 타들어갔는지로 보여집니다. 세 번째로, ⓓ책에 대해 이야기해 봅시다. 책은 종종 더 높은 교육적 지위를 나타냅니다. 그것들은 또한 학습이나 지식 전달의 상징이기도 합니다. 마지막으로, ⓔ꽃은 생명의 상징이 될 수 있습니다. 피어나는 꽃은 권력과 성장을 나타내는 데 사용됩니다. 잠시 후, 이러한 상징들이 담긴 몇몇 그림들을 보여드리겠습니다.

문제 풀이

16. ⓐ서양 미술에서 상징적인 의미를 가진 물건들에 대해 이야기하고 있으므로, 주제로는 ② '서양 미술에서 상징으로 사용되는 물건들'이 가장 적절하다.
① 예술가들이 사용한 다양한 그림 스타일
③ 서양 문화에 미친 종교적 물건들의 영향
④ 역사 속에서 그림 도구들의 변화
⑤ 물체를 사실적으로 색칠하는 방법

17. ⓑ거울, ⓒ양초, ⓓ책, ⓔ꽃은 언급되었으나, 껍질(shells)은 언급되지 않았다.

[코드 공략하기]

제6회 중급 모의고사

1	①	2	⑤	3	②	4	④	5	②	6	②
7	②	8	②	9	⑤	10	④	11	⑤	12	④
13	⑤	14	②	15	②	16	②	17	④		

1. ① | 목적

선택지 선택비율	① 94%	② 2%	③ 1%	④ 2%	⑤ 1%

W: Good morning, students! This is your school nurse, Emma Lee. What do you think of high school life so far? Since this is your first
지금까지
semester, I'm going to give you some guidelines for visiting our
학기 지침
school clinic. First, the clinic is located on the third floor next to the
보건실 be located: 위치해 있다
school cafeteria. And it's open Monday through Friday, from 9 a.m. to 4 p.m. I'll be there to help you with anything you need like medicine or some treatment. Lastly, when you are in the clinic,
약 치료
please be careful not to disturb the other students. I hope you have
방해하다
a safe and healthy school life. Thank you.

해석

여: 좋은 아침입니다, 학생 여러분! 저는 여러분의 보건 교사, Emma Lee입니다. 고등학교 생활은 지금까지 어떤가요? 이번이 여러분의 첫 학기이니, 보건실 방문에 대한 몇 가지 지침을 드리려고 합니다. 먼저, 보건실은 3층 학교 식당 옆에 위치하고 있습니다. 그리고 월요일부터 금요일까지 오전 9시부터 오후 4시까지 열려 있습니다. 저는 거기서 약이나 치료와 같이 여러분이 필요로 하는 것을 도와드릴 것입니다. 마지막으로, 보건실에 있을 때는, 다른 학생들을 방해하지 않도록 조심해 주세요. 여러분이 안전하고 건강한 학교생활을 하기를 바랍니다. 감사합니다.

문제 풀이

보건실 이용에 관한 지침 사항을 안내하고 있다.

2. ⑤ | 의견

선택지 선택비율	① 1%	② 2%	③ 2%	④ 2%	⑤ 93%

W: Honey, how about having beef for dinner tonight? We have some in the freezer.
냉동실
M: Great idea, but that beef has been in the freezer for so long. We'd better not eat it.
had better not + 동사원형: ~하지 않는 게 낫다
W: Well, it's been frozen this whole time, so it should be fine.
M: Not really. ⓐEating food that's been kept frozen for a long time can be harmful.
해로운
W: Really? I thought it would be alright.
M: Well, ⓑwhile freezing can slow bacteria growth in food, it cannot completely stop them from growing.
완전히 stop A from v-ing: A가 ~하는 것을 막다
W: Hmm, that makes sense.
M: Besides, if we open the freezer often, the temperature inside
게다가 온도
doesn't stay constant.
일정한
W: Oh. That might also encourage bacteria growth.
조장하다, 촉진하다

M: Correct! That's why ⓒit can be harmful to eat food that's been stored frozen for a long time.
저장[보관]하다
W: I see. Let's go grocery shopping for some beef then.
장보러 가다

해석

여: 여보, 오늘 저녁으로 소고기를 먹는 게 어때요? 냉동실에 좀 있잖아요.
남: 좋은 생각이긴 한데요, 그 소고기는 냉동실에 아주 오랫동안 있었어요. 그건 먹지 않는 게 낫겠어요.
여: 음, 계속 냉동 상태였으니 괜찮을 것 같은데요.
남: 꼭 그렇진 않아요. ⓐ오랫동안 냉동 보관된 음식을 먹으면 해로울 수 있어요.
여: 정말요? 괜찮을 거라고 생각했어요.
남: 음, ⓑ냉동은 음식 속 세균 증식을 늦출 수는 있지만, 그것들이 증식하는 걸 완전히 막을 수는 없어요.
여: 흠, 맞는 말이에요.
남: 게다가 냉동실을 자주 열면, 안의 온도가 일정하게 유지되지 않아요.
여: 아. 그게 세균 증식을 촉진하기도 하겠네요.
남: 맞아요! 그래서 ⓒ오랫동안 냉동 보관된 음식을 먹는 게 해로울 수 있는 거예요.
여: 알겠어요. 그럼 소고기를 좀 사러 장보러 가요.

문제 풀이

남자는 ⓑ냉동이 음식 속 세균 증식을 완전히 막지 못하기 때문에 ⓐⓒ오랫동안 냉동 보관된 음식을 먹으면 해로울 수 있다고 말하고 있다.

코드 +α 조언·경고를 나타내는 표현 had better

You look tired. You **had better get** some rest.
(너 피곤해 보여. 좀 쉬는 게 좋겠어.)
You **had better not eat** too much before swimming.
(수영하기 전에 너무 많이 먹지 않는 게 좋겠어.)

3. ② | 관계

선택지 선택비율	① 5%	② 83%	③ 3%	④ 3%	⑤ 3%

W: Hello, Mr. Smith.
M: Oh, Mrs. Roberts, I'm glad to work with you again.
W: Me, too. ⓐIt was a pleasure to draw pictures for your last book.
가장 최근의
M: ⓑYour pictures made my book more attractive to children. The little bear was especially cute.
매력적인 / 특히
W: Thank you. Is there anything you want to emphasize on the cover of your new book?
강조하다
M: Yes. The story is about a father and his daughter. So, I want to show the father's love clearly.
분명히
W: Then, I'll draw the father putting his arms around his daughter.
M: That's great. How about drawing her with a big smiling face?
W: Then the daughter will look more cheerful.
발랄한, 쾌활한
M: That's exactly what I want.
W: Okay. ⓒAfter finishing the book cover design, I will e-mail my first draft to you.
초고, 초안
M: Alright. I look forward to seeing your work soon.
look forward to v-ing: ~하는 것을 기대하다

해석

여: 안녕하세요, Smith 씨.
남: 오, Roberts 씨, 당신과 다시 함께 일하게 되어 기쁩니다.
여: 저도요. ⓐ당신의 가장 최근 책을 위한 그림을 그리게 되어 기뻤어요.
남: ⓑ당신의 그림들이 제 책을 아이들에게 더 매력적이게 만들었어요. 작은 곰이 특히 귀여웠어요.
여: 고맙습니다. 당신의 새로운 책 표지에 강조하고 싶으신 것이 있나요?
남: 네. 이야기가 아버지와 딸에 관한 것이에요. 그래서, 아버지의 사랑을 분명하게 보여 주고 싶어요.
여: 그렇다면, 딸에게 팔을 두르고 있는 아버지를 그릴게요.
남: 그거 좋네요. 딸을 크게 미소 짓는 얼굴로 그리는 것은 어떨까요?
여: 그러면 딸이 더 쾌활해 보이겠네요.
남: 그게 바로 제가 원하는 거예요.
여: 좋습니다. ⓒ책 표지 디자인을 마친 후, 제 초안을 당신에게 이메일로 보낼게요.
남: 알겠습니다. 곧 당신의 작품을 보기를 기대합니다.

문제 풀이

여자가 ⓐ남자의 가장 최근 책을 위한 그림을 그리게 되어 기뻤다고 하며, ⓒ책 표지 디자인을 마친 후 초안을 보내겠다고 하고, 남자는 ⓑ여자의 그림이 자신의 책을 아이들에게 더 매력적이게 했다고 말하는 것으로 보아, 두 사람은 삽화가와 동화 작가의 관계임을 알 수 있다.

4. ④ | 그림 일치

선택지 선택비율	① 1%	② 1%	③ 1%	④ 96%	⑤ 2%

M: Hello, Cindy. What are you looking at on your phone?
W: Hi, Tom. This is my own space in the metaverse.
M: Wow, it's amazing. Oh, there's ⓐa heart-shaped door in your house. That's unique.
W: Yes. I can enter my home through the door like a real house.
M: Fantastic! Is it possible to ride ⓑthe bicycle next to the tree?
W: Of course. We can do everything in virtual reality.
가상 현실
M: Awesome. I love ⓒthe two dogs looking at each other.
W: Yeah, they make my place so lovely.
M: I agree. I also like ⓓthat striped-patterned mat on the ground.
땅바닥
W: Thanks.
M: Oh, there's ⓔa girl sitting on the bench. She looks a lot like you.
W: Yes, she's my avatar in the metaverse.
M: That's so cool. I also want to design my own space like yours.

해석

남: 안녕, Cindy. 전화기로 뭘 보고 있니?
여: 안녕, Tom. 이건 메타버스의 내 공간이야.
남: 와, 놀랍다. 아, ⓐ집에 하트 모양 문이 있네. 독특해.
여: 응. 이 문을 통해 진짜 집처럼 우리 집에 들어갈 수 있어.
남: 굉장하다! ⓑ나무 옆에 있는 자전거를 탈 수 있어?
여: 물론이지. 우린 가상 현실에서 모든 걸 할 수 있어.
남: 엄청나다. ⓒ서로를 쳐다보고 있는 개 두 마리가 정말 좋아.
여: 응, 그들이 우리 집을 아주 사랑스럽게 만들지.
남: 동의해. ⓓ땅바닥에 있는 저 줄무늬 매트도 마음에 들어.
여: 고마워.
남: 아, ⓔ벤치에 앉아 있는 여자아이가 있네. 너랑 많이 닮았어.
여: 응, 메타버스에서의 내 아바타야.
남: 그거 정말 멋지다. 나도 네 것처럼 나만의 공간을 디자인하고 싶어.

문제 풀이

ⓓ땅바닥에 줄무늬 매트가 있다고 했으므로, 그림 ④의 물방울무늬 매트는 대화 내용과 일치하지 않는다.

5. ② | 부탁한 일

선택지 선택비율	① 1%	② 80%	③ 14%	④ 1%	⑤ 3%

W: Henry, the weather's so nice today. We should do some of the outdoor activities Los Angeles has.

M: I agree. Because it's been so hot, we've been going to museums to enjoy the air conditioning.
에어컨
W: I'm ready to enjoy the real Los Angeles. How should we spend the day?
M: We could go to the beach for lunch first, and I think there's a baseball game that we can go to in the evening.
W: That sounds great. I've always wanted to see the local team play.
M: Should we prepare a lunch to take to the beach? The restaurants there might be crowded.
붐비는
W: I think it would be better to pick up something to eat on the way there.
~을 사다
M: Okay. ⓐWhat about tickets to the baseball game? They might sell out.
다 팔리다, 매진되다
W: Oh, you're right. ⓑWill you buy the tickets? I'll search for a place where we can pick up food for our lunch.
~을 찾다
M: All right. I'll take care of that now.

해석

여: Henry, 오늘 날씨가 정말 좋아요. Los Angeles의 야외 활동을 좀 해야겠어요.
남: 그래요. 무척 더웠어서, 에어컨을 누리려고 박물관을 다니고 있었잖아요.
여: 난 진정한 Los Angeles를 즐길 준비가 됐어요. 하루를 어떻게 보내야 할까요?
남: 우선 점심 먹으러 해변에 갈 수 있고, 저녁에 갈 수 있는 야구 경기가 있을 거예요.
여: 그거 좋겠어요. 늘 현지 팀이 경기하는 걸 보고 싶었어요.
남: 해변에 가져갈 점심을 준비해야 할까요? 그곳 식당들은 붐빌 수 있어요.
여: 거기 가는 길에 먹을 것을 사는 게 더 좋을 것 같아요.
남: 좋아요. ⓐ야구 경기 티켓은요? 매진될지도 몰라요.
여: 아, 당신 말이 맞아요. ⓑ당신이 티켓을 구매할래요? 난 점심으로 먹을 음식을 살 수 있는 곳을 찾아볼게요.
남: 그래요. 그건 지금 내가 할게요.

문제 풀이

ⓐ야구 경기 티켓이 매진될지 모른다는 남자의 말에, 여자는 ⓑ남자에게 야구 경기 티켓을 사 달라고 했다.

6. ② | 금액

선택지 선택비율	① 1%	② 88%	③ 4%	④ 5%	⑤ 1%

W: Welcome to Gardener's! How can I help you?
M: Hi! I'd like to add some new flowers to my garden.
W: That's wonderful! What flowers do you have in mind?
have ~ in mind: ~을 염두에 두다
M: I like lilies. How much are they?
lily: 백합
W: ⓐThey're $4 each.
M: ⓑI'll take five lilies. Can you recommend any other flowers? I was thinking of mixing a few different types.
섞다
W: In that case, how about pairing them with some tulips?
짝을 짓다
M: Oh, that sounds great. How much are the tulips?
W: They're half the price of lilies — ⓒjust $2 each.
M: Great. ⓓI'll take five tulips, then.
W: Five lilies and five tulips, right? ⓔWhen you buy 10 flowers or more, we offer a 10% discount.
제공하다
M: Thank you. Here's my credit card.

해석

여: Gardener's에 오신 걸 환영합니다! 무엇을 도와드릴까요?
남: 안녕하세요! 제 정원에 새 꽃을 좀 추가하고 싶어서요.
여: 멋지네요! 어떤 꽃을 염두에 두고 계신가요?
남: 백합이 좋아요. 얼마예요?
여: ⓐ한 송이에 4달러입니다.
남: ⓑ백합 다섯 송이 주세요. 다른 꽃도 추천해 주실 수 있나요? 몇 가지 다른 종류를 섞을 생각이었거든요.
여: 그렇다면 그것들을 튤립과 조합하시는 건 어때요?
남: 오, 좋아요. 튤립은 얼마예요?
여: 백합 가격의 절반이에요. ⓒ한 송이에 단돈 2달러예요.
남: 좋아요. 그럼 ⓓ튤립 다섯 송이 주세요.
여: 백합 다섯 송이랑 튤립 다섯 송이 맞으시죠? ⓔ꽃을 열 송이 이상 사시면, 10% 할인해 드려요.
남: 감사합니다. 여기 제 신용카드요.

문제 풀이

ⓐ한 송이에 4달러인 ⓑ백합 다섯 송이(4x5)와 ⓒ한 송이에 2달러인 ⓓ튤립 다섯 송이(2x5)를 구매하고 ⓔ열 송이 이상 구매 혜택으로 10% 할인을 받으므로, 남자가 지불할 금액은 27달러이다.

7. ② | 이유

선택지 선택비율	① 2%	② 79%	③ 4%	④ 14%	⑤ 1%

W: Michael, what do you think about doing some volunteer work tomorrow?
M: Well, I thought we're going to join a sports program tomorrow.
W: You haven't heard? It's been cancelled.
M: Oh. Then, tell me more about the volunteer work.
W: We'll pick up meals at the community center and then deliver them to the elderly in the neighborhood.
근처, 이웃
M: Hmm.... When does it end? I'm having a family dinner.
W: Before noon. We'll be working for three hours in the morning.
M: Sounds good. Are there any restrictions for applicants?
제한 지원자
W: Yes. You have to be 16 or older to participate.
M: Then, I'm qualified. I just turned 16 last February.
자격이 있는
W: Oh, I almost forgot. ⓐYou also need a flu vaccination record since you'll meet the elderly in person.
백신[예방] 접종
M: ⓑI haven't got a flu shot yet. I'm afraid I can't come.
독감 예방 주사
W: Too bad. Maybe next time then.

해석

여: Michael, 내일 봉사 활동을 하는 거 어때?
남: 음, 난 우리가 내일 스포츠 프로그램에 참가할 거라고 생각했어.
여: 너 못 들었니? 그거 취소됐어.
남: 아. 그럼 봉사 활동에 대해 더 말해줘.
여: 우리는 주민센터에서 식사를 받아서 동네 어르신들께 전달할 거야.
남: 음… 언제 끝나? 난 가족 저녁 식사가 있거든.
여: 정오 전에. 오전에 3시간 동안 일할 예정이야.
남: 좋아. 지원자에 대한 제한이 있니?
여: 응. 참가하려면 16세 이상이어야 해.
남: 그럼, 나는 자격이 있네. 지난 2월에 딱 16살이 되었거든.
여: 아, 깜빡 잊을 뻔했네. ⓐ어르신들을 직접 뵙기 때문에 독감 예방 접종 기록도 필요해.
남: ⓑ아직 독감 예방 주사를 맞지 않았어. 안타깝지만 나는 못 가겠다.
여: 너무 아쉽네. 그럼 다음에 함께 하자.

문제 풀이

ⓐ봉사 활동을 하려면 독감 예방 접종 기록이 필요한데, ⓑ남자는 아직 예방 주사를 맞지 않아서 봉사 활동에 같이 갈 수 없다고 했다.

8. ② | 언급

선택지 선택비율	① 2%	② 79%	③ 3%	④ 3%	⑤ 14%

M: Emily, come have a look at this leaflet(전단 광고). It's about the Modern(현대의) Architecture(건축) Expo.

W: Oh, it looks interesting.

M: We both have an interest in architecture. Why don't we go there together?

W: Good idea. ⓐIt'll be held at the Grand Convention Center. It's close to our school.

M: Great! When should we go?

W: ⓑIt starts on April 1 and ends on April 15. Can you make it on Saturday, April 9?

M: Yes, I can. Look here. ⓒAdmission(입장료) is $20 for students.

W: Oh, that's quite expensive.

M: I'm sure it'll be worth it(~의 가치가 있는). ⓓTen great architects(건축가) will be giving lectures on their best architectural(건축의) works. We can attend(참석하다) as many of them as we want.

W: Cool! It'll be great to see them in person(직접).

해석

남: Emily, 와서 이 전단 광고를 봐봐. 현대 건축 엑스포에 관한 거야.

여: 오, 재미있을 것 같아.

남: 우리 둘 다 건축에 관심이 있잖아. 거기 함께 가는 게 어때?

여: 좋은 생각이다. ⓐGrand Convention Center에서 개최될 거야. 우리 학교랑 가까워.

남: 잘됐다! 언제 갈까?

여: ⓑ4월 1일에 시작해서 4월 15일에 끝나. 4월 9일 토요일에 갈 수 있니?

남: 응, 갈 수 있어. 여기 봐. ⓒ학생 입장료는 20달러야.

여: 아, 꽤 비싸네.

남: 그럴 가치가 있을 거라고 확신해. ⓓ훌륭한 건축가 10명이 자신의 최고의 건축 작품에 대해 강연을 할 거야. 우리는 원하는 만큼 거기 다 참석할 수 있어.

여: 멋지다! 그들을 직접 보면 정말 좋을 거야.

문제 풀이

ⓐ개최 장소, ⓑ개최 기간, ⓒ입장료, ⓓ강연자 수는 언급되었지만, 주최 기관은 언급되지 않았다.

9. ⑤ | 내용 일치

선택지 선택비율	① 1%	② 2%	③ 3%	④ 4%	⑤ 90%

W: Hello, I'm Grace, a manager of Dream Marine(바다의, 해양의) Museum. This year, our museum has a special program, called Ocean World. ⓐThe topic(주제) of the program is deep-sea exploration(탐사, 탐험). Through this program, children will become interested in the plants and fish living deep in the ocean. ⓑIt runs(운영하다) from 10 a.m. to 6 p.m. this Saturday, October 28. This event will be held on the first floor. ⓒYou can watch videos of deep-sea exploration on a huge screen in the central hall. There will be a photo booth where you can take selfies(셀피(스마트폰 등으로 찍은 자신의 사진)) wearing various masks of ocean creatures(생물). In addition, ⓓyou can make fish-shaped cookies with a chef. Anyone can participate in(~에 참가하다) Ocean World for free ⓔwithout having to make a reservation(예약하다). I hope to see you all there.

해석

여: 안녕하세요, 저는 Dream 해양 박물관의 매니저인 Grace입니다. 올해, 저희 박물관에는 Ocean World라는 특별한 프로그램이 있습니다. ⓐ프로그램의 주제는 심해 탐험입니다. 이 프로그램을 통해, 어린이들은 바다 깊은 곳에 사는 식물과 물고기에 관심을 갖게 될 것입니다. 10월 28일 이번 토요일 ⓑ오전 10시부터 오후 6시까지 운영됩니다. 이 행사는 1층에서 열릴 예정입니다. ⓒ여러분은 중앙 홀에 있는 거대한 스크린에서 심해 탐험 영상을 시청할 수 있습니다. 다양한 해양 생물의 가면을 쓰고 셀카를 찍을 수 있는 포토 부스가 있을 것입니다. 뿐만 아니라, 요리사와 함께 ⓓ물고기 모양의 쿠키도 만들 수 있습니다. ⓔ예약할 필요 없이 누구나 무료로 Ocean World에 참여할 수 있습니다. 여러분 모두 그곳에서 보기를 바랍니다.

문제 풀이

ⓔ예약할 필요 없이 Ocean World에 참여할 수 있다고 했다.

10. ④ | 도표

선택지 선택비율	① 2%	② 6%	③ 6%	④ 82%	⑤ 1%

M: Honey, what are you looking at?

W: A website that sells air fryers. I want one so we can cook more healthily.

M: Good idea. We can fry foods using less oil if we buy one. How much do you think we should spend?

W: Well, ⓐI don't want to spend more than 100 dollars.

M: Okay. Then how about these models?

W: Hmm... ⓑit's safer to buy one that will turn off(꺼지다) if it gets too hot.

M: You're right. ⓒLet's choose one with the automatic(자동의) switch off function(기능).

W: What about capacity(용량)? My friend bought one that could only hold(수용하다, 담다) two liters. She regretted not buying(regret not v-ing: ~하지 않은 것을 후회하다) a bigger one.

M: In that case, ⓓwe should get one with a capacity of at least four liters. Now we have these two to choose from.

W: They both look good. But I think ⓔthe one with the longer warranty(보증 기간) is better.

M: I agree. Let's order this one.

해석

남: 여보, 뭘 보고 있어요?

여: 에어프라이어를 파는 웹사이트요. 더 건강하게 요리할 수 있게 하나 갖고 싶어요.

남: 좋은 생각이에요. 사게 되면 기름을 더 적게 사용해서 음식을 튀길 수 있죠. 얼마나 쓸 생각이에요?

여: 음, ⓐ100달러 이상은 쓰고 싶지 않아요.

남: 좋아요. 그럼 이 모델들은 어때요?

여: 음… ⓑ너무 뜨거워지면 꺼지는 걸로 사는 게 더 안전해요.

남: 맞는 말이에요. ⓒ자동 꺼짐 기능이 있는 걸로 선택합시다.

여: 용량은요? 친구는 겨우 2리터 수용할 수 있는 걸 샀는데요. 더 큰 걸 사지 않은 걸 후회했어요.

남: 그렇다면 ⓓ우리는 최소 4리터 용량인 걸 사야겠어요. 이제 고를 수 있는 이 두 가지 선택권이 있네요.

여: 그것들 둘 다 좋아 보여요. 하지만 ⓔ보증 기간이 더 긴 것이 더 좋다고 생각해요.

남: 동의해요. 이걸로 주문합시다.

문제 풀이

ⓐ100달러가 넘지 않고, ⓑⓒ과열되면 자동으로 꺼지는 기능이 있고, ⓓ용량은 최소 4리터이고, ⓔ보증 기간이 더 긴 에어프라이어를 고르기로 했다.

코드+α 동의를 나타내는 표현

I agree. / I couldn't agree more. / You can say that again. / I'm with you. / Absolutely. (전적으로 동의해.)

11. ⑤ | 짧은 대화 응답

선택지 선택비율	① 2%	② 4%	③ 4%	④ 3%	⑤ 87%

W: Jake, are we going to drive to the restaurant for the dinner meeting with our client?
고객
M: Yes. It would be best to go by car. ⓐThe problem is the place doesn't have a parking lot.
주차장
W: ⓑI'm sure we can find a place for the car around the restaurant.
M: Right. I'll check if there's any public parking nearby.
공공의, 공영의

해석

여: Jake, 우리 고객과의 저녁 만남에 차를 가지고 식당에 갈 건가요?
남: 네. 차로 가는 게 가장 좋을 거예요. ⓐ문제는 그곳에 주차장이 없다는 거죠.
여: ⓑ분명히 식당 주변에 주차할 곳을 찾을 수 있을 거예요.
남: 맞아요. 제가 근처에 공영 주차장이 있는지 확인해 볼게요.

문제 풀이

남자가 ⓐ가려는 식당에 주차장이 없다고 하자 여자는 ⓑ식당 주변에 주차할 곳을 찾을 수 있을 것이라고 했으므로, 이에 대한 남자의 응답으로는 근처에 공영 주차장이 있는지 확인해 보겠다고 말하는 ⑤가 가장 적절하다.
① 좋은 생각이에요. 제 대신 당신이 요리하면 돼요.
② 제 잘못이에요! 제가 저녁 값을 냈어야 했어요.
③ 아쉽게도, 그 식당은 오늘 밤 문을 닫아요.
④ 알겠어요, 그럼 우리 계획을 취소해야 할 것 같아요.

12. ④ | 짧은 대화 응답

선택지 선택비율	① 5%	② 3%	③ 2%	④ 86%	⑤ 3%

M: Mom, our school is having a flea market for charity this weekend.
자선
So I'm thinking of donating my old stuff.
donate: 기부하다 물건
W: Oh, that sounds like a great idea! It'll really help others.
M: Yes, but I'm not sure what to give. Could you help me with selecting the things for donation?
고르다 기부
W: Sure. Let's first pick out some items in good condition.
상태

해석

남: 엄마, 이번 주말에 우리 학교에서 자선 바자회를 해요. 그래서 제 오래된 물건들을 기부할까 생각 중이에요.
여: 오, 아주 좋은 생각이네! 다른 사람들에게 정말 도움이 될 거야.
남: 네, 그런데 뭘 낼지 잘 모르겠어요. 기부할 물건들 고르는 걸 좀 도와주실 수 있어요?
여: 물론이지. 먼저 상태가 좋은 물건들을 골라보자.

문제 풀이

남자는 학교 자선 바자회에 기부할 물건 고르는 것을 도와달라고 했으므로, 상태 좋은 물건을 골라보자는 내용의 ④가 여자의 응답으로 가장 적절하다.
① 물론이지. 대신 다음에 그것들을 기부하면 돼.
② 걱정 마. 지금 바로 슈퍼마켓에 가는 길이야.
③ 신경 쓰지 마. 우리는 이미 써야 할 물건들을 가지고 있어.
⑤ 미안해. 아이들에게 장난감을 사줄 돈이 충분하지 않았어.

13. ⑤ | 긴 대화 응답

선택지 선택비율	① 5%	② 6%	③ 9%	④ 5%	⑤ 72%

W: Harry, you look angry. What's wrong?
M: My tablet PC is out of order.
고장 난
W: That's too bad. Have you been to customer service to repair it?
수리하다
M: Yes, I have, but I was shocked at the cost.
W: How much would it cost to get your tablet fixed?
M: ⓐIt's as much as the cost of a new one!
~만큼
W: You bought that one last year. Isn't it still under warranty?
(상품이) 보증 기간 중인
M: ⓑI had a one-year warranty, and the tablet died when it was one year and one week old.
W: How about asking the staff to be flexible about the warranty period?
직원 융통성 있는 기간, 시기
It was just one week!
M: Actually, I did, but ⓒthe staff said the company is very strict regarding their warranty policies.
엄격한 ~에 관하여
W: I'm sorry for that. So, what do you think you'll do?
M: I think I'll buy a new one of a different brand.

해석

여: Harry, 너 화나 보여. 무슨 일이니?
남: 내 태블릿 PC가 고장 났어.
여: 정말 안됐다. 그것을 수리하러 고객 서비스 센터에 가 봤니?
남: 응, 가 봤는데, 비용에 충격을 받았어.
여: 네 태블릿을 고치는 데 비용이 얼마나 많이 들어?
남: ⓐ새것(을 살) 만큼의 비용이야!
여: 너 그거 작년에 샀잖아. 아직 보증 기간 중 아니니?
남: ⓑ난 1년 보증이었는데, 태블릿이 1년하고 1주일이 지났을 때 고장 났어.
여: 직원에게 보증 기간에 대해 융통성 있게 해 달라고 요청하는 게 어때? 겨우 일주일이었잖아!
남: 사실, 요청했는데, ⓒ직원이 말하길 회사가 보증 정책에 관해 굉장히 엄격하대.
여: 그거 유감이다. 그래서, 어떻게 할 생각이야?
남: 나는 다른 브랜드의 새것을 살 생각이야.

문제 풀이

ⓑ보증 기간이 1년이었던 남자의 태블릿 PC가 1년 1주일 된 시점에 고장 났는데 ⓒ태블릿 회사가 보증 정책에 엄격하여 ⓐ수리 비용이 새것을 살 만큼이라고 했으므로, 어떻게 할 생각인지를 묻는 여자의 말에 대한 남자의 응답으로 다른 브랜드의 새것을 사겠다는 ⑤가 가장 적절하다.
① 나는 온라인 수업에 내 태블릿을 사용할 거야.
② 나는 그것을 고쳐준 그들의 도움에 정말로 감사해.
③ 나는 이 제품의 보증 기간을 확인할 거야.
④ 나는 내 휴대전화 없이 살 수 없을 것 같아.

14. ② | 긴 대화 응답

선택지 선택비율	① 4%	② 86%	③ 2%	④ 4%	⑤ 4%

M: Sarah, where did you get those bananas?
W: I just took them out of the parcel box in front of the door.
소포
M: What box? I haven't ordered anything recently.
최근에
W: Really? ⓐI thought you ordered them, so I ate some.
M: Let's check the address on the box.

W: Oh no! The package was misdelivered. This is not our address.
잘못 배달하다
M: Umm... ⓑThe bananas were supposed to be delivered to our
be supposed to-v: ~하기로 되어 있다, ~해야 한다
next-door neighbor, Mr. Jones.
W: What should I do?
M: I think it would be good to explain to him why you took them. And
설명하다
we should buy him some new bananas.
W: Okay. ⓒI'll tell him what happened right away.
일어나다, 발생하다
M: Wait! ⓓIt's too late. Mr. Jones usually goes to bed really early, so I don't think it's a good idea to wake him up now.
W: You're right. I'll take care of it tomorrow.

해석

남: Sarah, 그 바나나는 어디서 났어요?
여: 방금 문 앞에 있는 소포 상자에서 꺼냈어요.
남: 무슨 상자요? 난 최근에 아무것도 주문하지 않았어요.
여: 그래요? ⓐ당신이 주문했다고 생각해서, 내가 조금 먹었어요.
남: 상자에 있는 주소를 확인해 보죠.
여: 아 이런! 소포가 잘못 배달되었네요. 이건 우리 주소가 아니에요.
남: 음… ⓑ바나나는 우리 옆집 이웃 Jones 씨에게 배달되어야 했어요.
여: 어떻게 해야 하죠?
남: 당신이 왜 그걸 가져갔는지 그분께 설명하는 게 좋을 것 같아요. 그리고 우리가 그분께 새 바나나를 사드려야 해요.
여: 알겠어요. ⓒ그분께 무슨 일이 있었는지 지금 바로 말씀드릴게요.
남: 잠깐만요! ⓓ너무 늦었어요. Jones 씨는 대게 아주 일찍 주무시니까, 지금 깨우는 건 좋은 생각이 아닌 것 같아요.
여: 당신 말이 맞아요. 내가 내일 해결할게요.

문제 풀이

여자는 ⓐⓑ잘못 배달된 이웃의 바나나를 먹은 상황을 ⓒ이웃에게 말하려고 하는데, 남자가 ⓓ너무 늦은 시간이라고 말했으므로, 내일 해결하겠다고 말하는 ②가 응답으로 가장 적절하다.
① 걱정하지 마요. 내가 이미 주문했어요.
③ 내 잘못이에요! 내가 거기에 주소를 잘못 적었어요.
④ 미안해요. 다음에는 내가 일찍 깨울게요.
⑤ 그럼요. 빌린 물건을 지금 돌려주는 게 좋겠어요.

15. ② | 상황에 적절한 말

선택지 선택비율	① 4%	② 79%	③ 7%	④ 5%	⑤ 5%

M: Sandra is the president of the student council of her school. Today the student council is having their regular meeting. One of the
규칙적인, 정기적인
issues at today's meeting is about how to improve students' mental
주제[안건], 쟁점 / 향상시키다 / 정신의
and physical health. These days, many students have health
육체[신체]의
problems because they don't get much exercise. The student council agrees that it'd be good to hold a sports competition to improve the students' health. After the meeting, Sandra goes to the principal's office and tells Mr. Wilson about what they discussed.
논의하다
Now she wants to ask him for permission to host the sports event
승인, 허가 / 주최하다
for the sake of the students. In this situation, what would Sandra
~을 위해
most likely say to Mr. Wilson?
Sandra: Can we hold a sports competition for student health?

해석

남: Sandra는 학교 학생회 회장이다. 오늘 학생회가 정기 회의를 한다. 오늘 회의의 안건 중 하나는 학생들의 심신 건강을 향상시키는 방법에 관한 것이다. 요즘, 많은 학생들이 운동을 많이 하지 않기 때문에 건강 문제가 있다. 학생회는 학생들의 건강을 향상시키기 위해 체육대회를 개최하는 것이 좋을 것이라는 데 동의한다. 회의 후에, Sandra는 교장실로 가서 Wilson 선생님에게 그들이 논의한 것에 대해 이야기한다. 지금 그녀는 학생들을 위해 체육대회를 주최할 수 있는 허가를 구하고 싶어 한다. 이 상황에서, Sandra는 Wilson 씨에게 뭐라고 말하겠는가?
Sandra: 학생들의 건강을 위해 체육대회를 개최해도 되나요?

문제 풀이

Sandra는 학생들을 위해 체육대회를 주최할 수 있는지 허가를 받고 싶어 한다고 했다.
① 학생회 회의를 어떻게 운영하는지 알려주시겠어요?
③ 학생들에게 새로운 운동 장비를 제공해 주세요.
④ 저희 정기 회의에 참석하실 수 있나요?
⑤ 우리 학교를 대표해서 저희가 스포츠 리그에 참가하게 해 주세요.

16~17. | 세트 문항

16. ② 17. ④

선택지 선택비율	① 6%	② 76%	③ 3%	④ 8%	⑤ 4%
	① 2%	② 2%	③ 3%	④ 87%	⑤ 3%

W: Hello, students. ⓐAs you all know, heavy traffic is a major source
차량들, 교통(량) / 근원
of air pollution. To tackle this problem, many European cities are
~와 맞싸우다
taking various actions. For instance, in Copenhagen, the capital of
take actions: 조치를 취하다
ⓑDenmark, large parts of the city have been closed to vehicles for
차량
decades, and the city plans to become carbon neutral by 2025. Also, Paris, in ⓒFrance, bans cars in many historic districts on weekends
금지하다
and encourages car-and bike-sharing programs. In ⓓBelgium, the
장려하다
city of Brussels operates "Mobility Week" to encourage public over
운용하다
private transportation. And for one day every September, all cars
개인의 / 교통수단
are banned from the entire city center. Lastly, cities in ⓔGermany
전체의
are establishing "green zones" in city centers. If vehicles don't have
설립하다
a sticker showing they have an acceptable emission level, they can't
허용할 수 있는 / 배기가스
enter those places. Now, I'll show you some pictures that illustrate
분명히 보여 주다
this.

해석

여: 안녕하세요, 학생 여러분. ⓐ알다시피, 많은 차량은 대기 오염의 주된 근원입니다. 이 문제와 맞싸우기 위해 많은 유럽 도시들이 다양한 조치를 취하고 있습니다. 예를 들면, ⓑ덴마크의 수도 코펜하겐에서는 도시의 상당 부분이 수십 년간 차량을 막았고, 그 도시는 2025년까지 탄소 중립이 될 계획입니다. 또한 ⓒ프랑스 파리는 많은 역사지구에서 주말마다 차량을 금지하고, 차량 및 자전거 공유 프로그램을 장려합니다. ⓓ벨기에 브뤼셀 시는 대중들에게 개인 교통수단보다 대중교통을 장려하기 위해 '교통 주간'을 운용합니다. 그리고 매년 9월 하루 동안 도시 중심부 전체에서 차량이 금지되지요. 마지막으로, ⓔ독일의 도시들은 도시 중심에 '친환경 지역'을 만들고 있습니다. 배기가스가 허용 수위임을 보여 주는 스티커가 차량에 없으면, 그 장소에는 들어갈 수 없지요. 이제, 이를 보여 주는 사진을 보여드리겠습니다.

문제 풀이

16. 대기 오염 문제와 싸우기 위해 유럽 도시들이 취하고 있는 조치에 관해 이야기하고 있으므로, 주제로는 ② '차량으로 인한 대기 오염을 해결하기 위한 유럽에서의 노력'이 가장 적절하다.
① 도시에서 주차 공간을 빠르게 찾는 유용한 정보
③ 온실가스가 환경에 미치는 영향

④ 유럽 수도에서의 교통 체증의 원인
⑤ 유럽의 다양한 재생 가능 에너지 원천

17. ⓑ덴마크, ⓒ프랑스, ⓓ벨기에, ⓔ독일은 언급되었으나, 스위스(Switzerland)는 언급되지 않았다.

코드 +α 탄소 중립(carbon neutral)

이산화탄소를 배출한 만큼 이산화탄소 흡수량을 늘려 이산화탄소의 실제 배출량을 제로(0)로 만든다는 뜻이다. 이산화탄소 배출에 대한 책임감을 갖고 이산화탄소 배출을 줄이려는 노력이다.

[코드 공략하기]

제7회 중급 모의고사

1	③	2	①	3	④	4	⑤	5	①	6	②
7	③	8	④	9	④	10	①	11	①	12	④
13	②	14	④	15	①	16	②	17	④		

1. ③ | 목적

선택지 선택비율	① 2%	② 3%	③ 91%	④ 1%	⑤ 4%

M: Good morning, students. This is your vice principal (교감), Mr. Gunning. I have an announcement regarding (~에 관한) our 'Spring Flower Photo Day' event this afternoon. As you know, we planned to take pictures of beautiful spring flowers as we walk around our neighborhood (인근). I regret (유감스럽게 생각하다) to inform (알리다) you that the event is canceled due to heavy rain. I understand you've been looking forward to it, but unfortunately (유감스럽게도) it appears (~인 것 같다) we won't be able to get the best photos today. We will reschedule (일정을 변경하다) the event for a sunny day in the near future. Please understand that this decision (결정) was made to ensure (반드시 ~하게 하다) that the event will be a success.

해석

남: 안녕하세요, 학생 여러분. 저는 여러분의 교감 선생님인 Gunning입니다. 오늘 오후에 예정된 '봄꽃 사진 촬영의 날' 행사에 관한 공지가 있습니다. 알다시피, 우리는 인근을 걸어다니며 아름다운 봄꽃 사진을 찍을 계획이었습니다. 폭우로 인해 행사가 취소됨을 알려드리게 되어 유감입니다. 여러분이 이 행사를 고대하고 있다는 것을 알지만, 유감스럽게도 오늘은 좋은 사진을 찍을 수 없을 것 같습니다. 가까운 시일 내에 맑은 날로 행사 일정을 변경할 것입니다. 이 결정은 행사가 반드시 성공하기 위해 내린 것이니 양해 부탁드립니다.

문제 풀이

폭우로 인해 행사가 취소됨을 알리고 있다.

2. ① | 의견

선택지 선택비율	① 94%	② 2%	③ 0%	④ 0%	⑤ 1%

W: Hi, Chris. Where are you going?
M: I'm going to the library to check out ((책을) 빌리다) some books. Do you want to come along (함께 가다)?
W: Well, I don't often read books these days. I'm busy helping (be busy v-ing: ~하느라 바쁘다) with housework, exercising, and so on.
M: ⓐWhy don't you try audio books then? They're convenient (편리한) to listen to while you're doing other things.
W: I've never tried it. Do you think it'll work for me?
M: Sure. It's an easy way to enjoy books even if you have a busy schedule. I always listen to a short story when I take a walk.
W: Cool! I guess I could try listening to audio books while I do chores (일).
M: ⓑI'm sure you'll enjoy listening to books while dealing with other stuff.

W: Can you recommend some audio books to me?
M: I have a few in mind. I'll text you a list later.

해석

여: 안녕, Chris. 어디 가니?
남: 책을 좀 빌리려고 도서관에 가는 중이야. 함께 갈래?
여: 음, 난 요즘 책을 자주 읽지 않아. 집안일 돕고, 운동하고, 등등으로 바빠.
남: ⓐ그러면 오디오 북을 시도해 보지 그래? 다른 일을 하면서 듣기 편리해.
여: 그걸 시도해 본 적 없어. 나한테 효과가 있을 거라고 생각하니?
남: 물론이지. 바쁜 일정일 때도 책을 즐길 수 있는 쉬운 방법이야. 난 산책할 때 늘 짧은 이야기를 들어.
여: 멋지다! 일을 하는 동안 오디오 북을 들어볼 수 있겠어.
남: ⓑ분명 다른 일들을 처리하면서 책을 듣는 걸 즐기게 될 거야.
여: 나에게 오디오 북을 좀 추천해 줄 수 있니?
남: 염두에 둔 게 몇 개 있어. 나중에 목록을 문자로 보낼게.

문제 풀이

남자는 여자에게 ⓐⓑ오디오 북 듣기를 추천하며 다른 일을 하면서 책을 즐길 수 있는 편리한 방법이라고 말하고 있다.

3. ④ | 관계

선택지 선택비율	① 1%	② 4%	③ 4%	④ 90%	⑤ 1%

W: Hello, Mr. Baker. Thank you for doing this interview.
M: My pleasure. ⓐI really like reading your articles(기사) on modern painting in your newspaper.
W: Thank you so much. ⓑI'm honored to be interviewing the person who organized(준비하다, 개최하다) the Modern Asia exhibition(전시회) at the National Art Museum.
M: Thank you. I'm very surprised it has gotten so much attention(주의, 주목, 관심).
W: It certainly has. Our readers have expressed(표현하다) interest(관심) in it, too. What was the idea behind it?
M: The idea was to show contemporary(동시대의, 현대의) Asia to the public(대중).
W: I see. Are you planning to do any other exhibitions?
M: Yes. I'm planning to do one about contemporary Africa. It will contain(포함하다) paintings featuring(feature: 특징으로 삼다) people, cities, and homes from around the continent(대륙).
W: That sounds great. I look forward to checking it out.
M: You won't be disappointed.
W: Thanks again for your time, Mr. Baker.

해석

여: 안녕하세요, Baker 씨. 이 인터뷰를 해 주셔서 감사합니다.
남: 천만에요. ⓐ저는 신문에서 현대 그림에 관한 당신의 기사를 읽는 것을 매우 좋아해요.
여: 정말 감사해요. ⓑ국립미술관에서 현대 아시아 전시회를 준비하신 분을 인터뷰하게 되어 영광입니다.
남: 감사합니다. 이렇게 많은 관심을 받다니 정말 놀라워요.
여: 확실히 그래요. 저희 독자들도 그것에 관심을 표명했습니다. 그 이면의 발상은 무엇이었나요?
남: 그 발상은 대중에게 현대 아시아를 보여주는 것이었습니다.
여: 그렇군요. 다른 전시회들도 할 계획이신가요?
남: 네. 저는 현대 아프리카에 대해 전시회를 하려고 계획하고 있습니다. 그것은 그 대륙의 사람, 도시, 그리고 집을 특징으로 하는 그림들을 포함할 것입니다.
여: 멋지네요. 그걸 살펴보게 되길 고대합니다.
남: 실망하시지 않을 거예요.
여: 시간을 내 주셔서 다시 한번 감사드립니다, Baker 씨.

문제 풀이

남자는 여자에게 ⓐ신문에서 현대 미술에 관해 여자가 쓴 기사를 읽는 것을 좋아한다고 했고, 여자는 남자에게 ⓑ현대 아시아 전시회를 준비한 분을 인터뷰하게 되어 영광이라고 말하는 것으로 보아, 신문 기자와 전시 기획자의 관계임을 알 수 있다.

4. ⑤ | 그림 일치

선택지 선택비율	① 3%	② 1%	③ 3%	④ 2%	⑤ 90%

W: Hi, David. You look happy.
M: I won a prize at the science fair(박람회). Look at this photo from the fair.
W: Wow! Congratulations. Oh, ⓐthe prize ribbon is on the wall above the board(게시판). Cool!
M: Yeah, I'm so proud.
W: ⓑYou set up your board on the round table. I see your topic was 'Lemon Battery.' What did you do?
M: I showed how to make a battery using lemons.
W: Interesting. So that's why ⓒthere is a basket of lemons next to the battery.
M: That's right.
W: Who is ⓓthis woman wearing a flower-patterned dress?
M: That's my grandmother. She came to congratulate me.
W: How nice! Oh, ⓔyou're holding(들다) flowers in your hand. They're so beautiful.
M: Thanks. It was a great day.

해석

여: 안녕, David. 너 행복해 보여.
남: 과학 박람회에서 상을 탔거든. 박람회에서 찍은 이 사진을 봐.
여: 와! 축하해. 오, ⓐ상품 리본이 게시판 위 벽에 있구나. 멋지다!
남: 응, 정말 자랑스러워.
여: ⓑ원탁 위에 게시판을 설치했네. 네 주제는 '레몬 배터리'였구나. 뭘 했니?
남: 레몬을 사용해서 배터리를 만드는 방법을 보여주었어.
여: 흥미로워. 그래서 ⓒ배터리 옆에 레몬 바구니가 있는 거구나.
남: 맞아.
여: ⓓ꽃무늬 드레스를 입고 있는 이 여성분은 누구셔?
남: 우리 할머니셔. 나를 축하해 주러 오셨어.
여: 정말 좋으시다! 아, ⓔ너는 손에 꽃을 들고 있네. 정말 아름다워.
남: 고마워. 참 멋진 하루였어.

문제 풀이

ⓔ손에 꽃을 들고 있다고 했으므로, ⑤의 트로피는 대화 내용과 일치하지 않는다.

5. ① | 할 일

선택지 선택비율	① 86%	② 3%	③ 2%	④ 4%	⑤ 2%

W: Tom, did you pack everything for tomorrow's backpacking trip(배낭여행)?
M: I'm almost done, Mom. I just need a few more things.
W: Good! Don't forget to pack(싸다, 꾸리다) some extra(여분의) clothes!
M: Sure, I did. Just in case!
W: Well done! What about hiking boots? Didn't you say you were going to borrow Jake's?
M: Yes, he told me to pick them up in the afternoon.
W: That's so sweet of him. Anything else?
M: There is just one more important thing left. ⓐI have to go to the grocery store(식료품점) to buy some snacks!

W: Snacks are important. ⓑI'm going to the grocery store right now. I could buy them for you if you want.
M: ⓒCould you? That would be great!
W: Sure, sweetie. No problem.
M: Then all I have to do is get the boots from Jake!

해석

여: Tom, 내일 배낭여행 갈 짐 다 쌌니?
남: 거의 다 쌌어요, 엄마. 몇 가지만 더 있으면 돼요.
여: 잘했구나! 여분 옷 싸는 거 잊지 마렴!
남: 네, 쌌어요. 만약을 위해서요!
여: 잘했구나! 등산화는? Jake 것을 빌릴 거라고 하지 않았니?
남: 네, 내일 오후에 가져가라고 했어요.
여: 참 다정하구나. 다른 것들은?
남: 중요한 것 한 가지만 더 남았어요. ⓐ간식 사러 식료품점에 가야 해요!
여: 간식 중요하지. ⓑ지금 식료품점에 갈 건데. 원한다면 너 대신 사다 줄 수 있어.
남: ⓒ그래 주실래요? 그게 좋겠어요!
여: 물론이지, 얘야. 문제없지.
남: 그럼 Jake한테 등산화를 받기만 하면 되겠네요!

문제 풀이

ⓐ식료품점에 가서 간식을 사야 한다는 남자에게 여자는 ⓑ대신 사다 줄 것을 제안했고 남자는 ⓒ그래 줄 것을 부탁했다.

6. ② | 금액

선택지 선택비율	① 2%	② 81%	③ 5%	④ 11%	⑤ 1%

W: Good afternoon, sir. May I help you?
M: Yes, please. ⓐI'm looking for swimming goggles for my kids.
W: We have several kinds. Take a look at this display.
M: All right, thank you. *[Pause]* Oh, how much are these? These would be perfect for my children.
W: They're 50 dollars each. They're anti-fog(흐림 방지, 김 서림 방지), which guarantees(보장하다) clear vision(시야) for fast swimming.
M: I see. They're a little bit expensive, though.
W: In that case, there are cheaper ones with basically(기본적으로) the same function(기능). How about these? ⓑThey cost 40 dollars each.
M: Sounds better. ⓒI'll buy two pairs of these. ⓓI also need a swimming cap for myself.
W: I recommend this new cap. It uses high-quality(고품질의, 고급의) materials(소재) and ⓔcosts only 20 dollars.
M: Okay. Then ⓕI'll buy two pairs of swimming goggles and one swimming cap.
W: We also have brand-new(아주 새로운, 금방 들여온) swimsuits(수영복) in our store. Are you interested?
M: No, thanks. These are enough.
W: Sounds good. We have a promotion(판촉 행사) this week, so ⓖyou can get a 10% discount on the total amount.
M: That's great. Here's my credit card.

해석

여: 안녕하세요, 고객님. 도와드릴까요?
남: 네. ⓐ아이들을 위한 수경을 찾고 있어요.
여: 몇 가지 종류가 있어요. 여기 전시된 것을 한 번 보세요.
남: 알겠습니다, 고맙습니다. [잠시 후] 아, 이건 얼마인가요? 이게 저희 아이들에게 딱 좋을 것 같아요.
여: 개당 50달러예요. 김 서림 방지가 돼서, 빠른 수영에도 선명한 시야가 보장돼요.
남: 그렇군요. 하지만 조금 비싸네요.
여: 그렇다면 기본적으로 같은 기능이 있는 더 저렴한 게 있어요. 이건 어떠세요? ⓑ개당 40달러예요.
남: 더 좋네요. ⓒ이거 두 개 살게요. ⓓ제가 쓸 수영모도 필요해요.
여: 이 새 모자를 추천드려요. 고급 소재를 사용한 것이고 ⓔ20달러밖에 안 해요.
남: 알겠습니다. 그럼 ⓕ수경 두 개랑 수영모 한 개 살게요.
여: 저희 가게에 금방 들어온 수영복도 있어요. 관심 있으세요?
남: 아니요, 괜찮습니다. 이거면 충분해요.
여: 좋아요. 이번 주에 판촉 행사가 있어서, ⓖ총액에서 10% 할인받으실 수 있어요.
남: 그거 좋네요. 여기 제 신용카드요.

문제 풀이

ⓐⓑⓒⓕ40달러짜리 수경 2개와 ⓓⓔⓕ20달러짜리 수영모 1개를 사고, ⓖ총액에서 10% 할인받으므로, 남자가 지불할 금액은 {(40x2)+20}x0.9=90달러이다.

7. ③ | 이유

선택지 선택비율	① 3%	② 2%	③ 89%	④ 2%	⑤ 1%

W: Jake. There's going to be a Vincent van Gogh exhibition in the Art Center.
M: Really? He's my favorite artist.
W: Mine, too. How about going to the exhibition together this Sunday?
M: This Sunday? I'd really love to, but I'm afraid I can't go.
W: Come on. Do you have to do volunteer work(자원봉사) on that day?
M: No, I usually volunteer on Saturdays.
W: Oh, I remember. You said you're going to play soccer?
M: I did, but our game was delayed(미루다, 연기하다) because of weather.
W: Then, do you have another appointment(약속)?
M: Actually, I have to work on a science assignment(과제). It's due next Monday.
W: You must be busy then.
M: Yeah. I hope you have a good time.

해석

여: Jake. 아트 센터에서 빈센트 반 고흐 전시회가 있을 예정이야.
남: 정말? 그는 내가 가장 좋아하는 화가야.
여: 나도 그래. 이번 주 일요일에 전시회에 같이 가는 게 어때?
남: 이번 주 일요일? 나도 정말 가고 싶지만, 갈 수 없을 것 같아.
여: 이런. 넌 그날 봉사활동을 해야 하니?
남: 아니, 난 보통 토요일에 자원봉사를 해.
여: 아, 기억나. 너 축구할 거라고 했지?
남: 그랬는데, 날씨 때문에 우리 경기가 연기됐어.
여: 그럼, 다른 약속이 있니?
남: 사실, 난 과학 과제를 해야 해. 다음 주 월요일까지거든.
여: 그럼 바쁘겠구나.
남: 응. 좋은 시간 보내길 바라.

문제 풀이

남자는 과학 과제를 해야 해서 고흐 전시회에 갈 수 없다고 했다.

8. ④ | 언급

선택지 선택비율	① 1%	② 1%	③ 3%	④ 93%	⑤ 1%

M: How was your visit to the Electronics Fair(박람회), Christine?
W: It was spectacular(구경거리인). You should check it out if you have time.
M: I might. What was there to do at the fair?

W: There were displays for the latest models of electronic devices and
전시 최신의 전자 장비
new technology.
M: Wow! You must have seen a lot of brand-new electronic devices!
Did you participate in any hands-on activities there?
hands-on activity: 체험 활동
W: Of course I did. ⓐVarious programs were available including 3-D printing, VR games, and chatting with AI.
~와 이야기하다
M: I want to try talking with AI. Where is the fair held?
W: ⓑIt takes place at Dream Expo Center.
개최되다, 열리다
M: That's near here! When does the fair end?
W: ⓒIt ends on November 30th.
M: ⓓCan you tell me what the price of a ticket is?
W: ⓔIt's 5 dollars. But if you purchase it online, you can buy it for
구입하다
3 dollars.
M: Great! I'll order my ticket now.

해석

남: Electronics Fair에 갔던 건 어땠어요, Christine?
여: 구경거리가 많았어요. 시간 있으면 당신도 가 봐야 해요.
남: 갈지도 모르겠어요. 박람회에서 할 게 뭐가 있었나요?
여: 전자 장비 최신 모델과 신기술 전시가 있었어요.
남: 와! 아주 새로운 전자 장비를 많이 봤겠네요! 거기서 체험 활동에 참여했나요?
여: 물론 했죠. ⓐ3-D 인쇄, 가상현실 게임, 인공지능과 이야기하기를 포함한 다양한 프로그램을 이용할 수 있었어요.
남: 인공지능과 이야기해 보고 싶네요. 박람회가 어디서 열리죠?
여: ⓑDream Expo Center에서 열려요.
남: 여기 근처네요! 박람회가 언제 끝나나요?
여: ⓒ11월 30일에 끝나요.
남: ⓓ티켓 가격이 얼마인지 말해 줄 수 있나요?
여: ⓔ5달러에요. 하지만 온라인에서 구입하면, 3달러에 살 수 있어요.
남: 잘됐네요! 지금 티켓을 주문할래요.

문제 풀이

ⓐ프로그램, ⓑ장소, ⓒ종료일, ⓓⓔ티켓 가격은 언급되었으나, 참가 업체는 언급되지 않았다.

9. ④ | 내용 일치

선택지 선택비율	① 1%	② 3%	③ 3%	④ 83%	⑤ 10%

W: Hello, students. This is Ms. Miller, your music teacher. Are you interested in operas? Then, we invite you to 2022 Opera in School. Five professional opera singers will come to our school and
직업의, 전문적인
ⓐpresent *Romeo and Juliet* to you. They'll bring the classic story to
공연하다 bring ~ to life: ~에 활기를 불어넣다
life with opera costumes and sets. The show ⓑwill be held at the
의상 세팅, 무대 장치
school auditorium on March 25, starting at 6 p.m. ⓒIt'll last for 45
강당
minutes and be followed by a question and answer session. ⓓYou
시간
can take photos with the singers after the question and answer session is finished. There's no admission fee, but ⓔto attend, you
입장료 참석하다
must register in advance. I hope to see you there.
등록하다 사전에, 미리

해석

여: 안녕하세요, 학생 여러분. 여러분의 음악 교사 Miller입니다. 여러분은 오페라에 관심이 있나요? 그렇다면 여러분을 2022 Opera in School에 초대합니다. 5명의 전문 오페라 가수들이 우리 학교에 와서 여러분에게 ⓐ<로미오와 줄리엣>을 공연할 것입니다. 그들은 오페라 의상과 무대 장치로 고전 이야기에 활기를 불어넣을 것입니다. 공연은 ⓑ3월 25일 오후 6시에 시작하며, 학교 강당에서 열릴 예정입니다. ⓒ공연은 45분간 진행되고 질의응답 시간이 이어질 것입니다. ⓓ질의응답 시간이 끝나고 나서 여러분은 가수들과 사진을 찍을 수 있습니다. 입장료는 없지만, ⓔ참석하려면 사전에 등록해야 합니다. 거기서 만나기를 바랍니다.

문제 풀이

ⓓ질의응답 시간이 끝나고 나서 가수들과 사진을 찍을 수 있다고 했다.

10. ① | 도표

선택지 선택비율	① 93%	② 1%	③ 5%	④ 1%	⑤ 0%

W: Dad, I found a website that provides a service to make photo albums. How about creating one with the photos from our winter
create: 만들다
holiday?
M: Great! Let me see. *[Pause]* Oh, it says all we need to do is choose a few options and upload our photos.
W: Right. First, let's choose the cover material.
M: Umm... Leather might be too heavy.
가죽
W: You're right. ⓐLet's choose either paper or fabric.
천
M: Okay. For the number of pages, is 40 too many?
W: Yes. ⓑLet's just go for 20 or 30 pages. What color would be good for the cover?
M: I want it to reflect our winter holiday. ⓒHow about white?
반영하다
W: Perfect. That leaves us with two options.
M: Then, ⓓlet's choose the cheaper one.
W: Sounds great. I'll choose the best pictures and upload them.

해석

여: 아빠, 제가 사진첩 만들기 서비스를 제공하는 웹사이트를 찾았어요. 겨울 휴가 사진들로 하나 만드는 게 어때요?
남: 좋아! 어디 보자. [잠시 후] 오, 우리가 해야 할 일은 몇 가지 선택 사항을 고르고 사진을 업로드하는 것뿐이라고 하는구나.
여: 맞아요. 먼저 표지 소재를 선택해요.
남: 음… 가죽은 너무 무거울 것 같아.
여: 맞아요. ⓐ종이나 천 중에서 골라요.
남: 좋아. 페이지 수는, 40장은 너무 많으려나?
여: 네. ⓑ그냥 20장이나 30장으로 해요. 어떤 색이 표지로 좋을까요?
남: 그 색이 겨울 휴가를 반영하면 좋겠어. ⓒ흰색 어떠니?
여: 완벽해요. 이제 두 가지 선택 사항이 남았어요.
남: 그럼, ⓓ더 저렴한 걸 고르자.
여: 좋아요. 제가 가장 좋은 사진들을 골라서 업로드할게요.

문제 풀이

ⓐ종이나 천 소재의 표지이고 ⓑ20장 또는 30장인 ⓒ흰색 표지 사진첩 중에 ⓓ더 저렴한 것을 고르기로 했다.

11. ① | 짧은 대화 응답

선택지 선택비율	① 88%	② 2%	③ 4%	④ 0%	⑤ 3%

M: Mom, ⓐI have to borrow some books from the library today. But it's
빌리다
raining outside.
W: Don't worry. ⓑI'll give you a ride. Do you want to leave now?
give ~ a ride: ~을 태워주다
M: Yes. But I need to look for my library card first. ⓒCould you wait for a second?
잠시

W: No problem. Just let me know when you're ready.

해석

남: 엄마, ⓐ오늘 도서관에서 책을 좀 빌려야 해요. 하지만 밖에 비가 내리고 있어요.
여: 걱정하지 마. ⓑ내가 태워줄게. 지금 출발하길 원하니?
남: 네. 그런데 도서관 카드를 먼저 찾아야 해요. ⓒ잠시 기다려 주실 수 있나요?
여: 되고 말고. 준비되면 알려주기만 해.

문제 풀이

ⓐ도서관에 가야 한다는 남자에게 여자는 ⓑ태워주겠다고 했고, 남자는 ⓒ잠시 기다려 달라고 했으므로, 이에 대한 여자의 응답으로 준비되면 알려 달라는 내용의 ①이 가장 적절하다.
② 안 될 것 같아. 어제 도서관 카드를 잃어버렸어.
③ 그럼. 네가 원할 때 언제든 내 책을 빌리면 돼.
④ 미안하구나. 햇살이 너무 강해서 외출할 수가 없네.
⑤ 물론이지. 난 도서관까지 걸어갈 거야.

12. ④ | 짧은 대화 응답

선택지 선택비율	① 4%	② 1%	③ 1%	④ 69%	⑤ 22%

W: Excuse me. ⓐDo you have Gilbert Norton's new novel, *Space War*?
M: ⓑYes, we do. It just came in yesterday.
come in: (상품 등이) 들어오다
W: Great. I've been waiting for it. ⓒWhere can I find it?
M: It's in the new-release section over there.
신간 구역

해석

여: 실례합니다. ⓐGilbert Norton의 새 소설인 〈우주 전쟁〉 있나요?
남: ⓑ네, 있습니다. 어제 막 들어왔어요.
여: 잘됐네요. 그것을 기다리고 있었거든요. ⓒ제가 그걸 어디서 찾을 수 있죠?
남: 그것은 저쪽 신간 구역에 있습니다.

문제 풀이

ⓐ자신이 원하는 책이 있는지 묻는 여자에게 남자는 ⓑ어제 들어와서 있다고 답했고, 여자가 ⓒ그것을 어디서 찾을 수 있는지 물었으므로, 책의 위치를 알려주는 ④가 남자의 응답으로 가장 적절하다.
① 그는 새 소설을 쓰는 중입니다.
② 뉴욕에서 책 사인회가 있을 예정입니다.
③ 그의 새 소설은 4월에 출간될 예정입니다.
⑤ 길 아래에서 더 큰 서점을 찾으실 수 있습니다.

13. ② | 긴 대화 응답

선택지 선택비율	① 3%	② 78%	③ 11%	④ 6%	⑤ 2%

M: Ms. Williams! Do you have a minute?
W: Sure. What is it?
M: I have to write an essay to get a scholarship, but I don't know what to write about.
장학금
W: Maybe you can start by expressing your passion for learning and school life.
표현하다 열정
M: I already wrote about that, but it doesn't seem good enough.
W: Umm... How about mentioning a weakness you've worked on?
언급하다 약점
M: Weakness? Wouldn't that be a bad idea for an essay?
W: Not necessarily. If you describe how you've been trying to deal with it, your story will show your potential.
잠재력
M: Well, I used to put my work off until the last minute. But ⓐby using a planner, I make my schedule on an hourly basis. Now I no longer have any trouble finishing my work on time.
used to-v: ~하곤 했다 put off: ~을 미루다 한 시간마다 기반 have trouble v-ing: ~하는 데 어려움을 겪다 제때
W: That's perfect! ⓑThat will be a great story to include in your essay for the scholarship.
M: ⓒThank you for your help! That actually makes me feel a lot more confident.
자신감 있는
W: Good luck. Show them who you are, and you'll make it.

해석

남: Williams 선생님! 잠깐 시간 있으세요?
여: 물론이지. 무슨 일이니?
남: 제가 장학금을 받기 위해 에세이를 써야 하는데, 무엇에 대해 써야 할지 모르겠어요.
여: 아마도 학업과 학교 생활에 대한 네 열정을 표현하는 것으로 시작할 수 있겠지.
남: 그것에 대해 이미 썼는데 만족스럽지 않은 것 같아요.
여: 음… 네가 극복해 온 약점을 언급하는 건 어떠니?
남: 약점이요? 그건 에세이에는 안 좋은 생각 아닐까요?
여: 꼭 그렇진 않아. 네가 그걸 해결하려고 어떻게 노력해 왔는지 기술하면, 네 이야기는 네 잠재력을 보여줄 거야.
남: 음, 저는 일을 마지막 순간까지 미루곤 했어요. 하지만 ⓐ플래너를 사용해서 시간 단위로 제 일정을 짜요. 이제는 제때 일을 끝내는 데 더 이상 어려움을 겪지 않아요.
여: 그거 완벽하구나! ⓑ그게 장학금을 위한 에세이에 포함시키기에 훌륭한 이야기가 될 거야.
남: ⓒ도와주셔서 감사합니다! 그게 정말 훨씬 더 자신감이 생기게 해요.
여: 행운을 빌어. 그들에게 네가 어떤 사람인지 보여 줘, 그러면 해낼 수 있을 거야.

문제 풀이

남자가 ⓐ일을 미루던 약점을 플래너를 사용해서 극복하고 제때 일을 끝내는 데 어려움이 없게 되었다고 말하자, 여자는 ⓑ이 이야기가 장학금을 위한 에세이에 포함되면 좋을 것이라 격려한다. 남자가 ⓒ이에 대해 여자에게 감사를 표하며 더 자신감을 가지게 되었다고 말하고 있으므로, 이에 대한 여자의 응답으로 남자에게 행운을 빌며 격려하는 ②가 가장 적절하다.
① 맞아. 가능한 한 약점을 숨기는 게 더 좋아.
③ 물론이지. 너는 숙제를 효과적으로 해낼 수 있어.
④ 동의해. 넌 플래너를 사용해서 일정을 짤 수 있어.
⑤ 조심해! 약점은 네가 성장하는 것을 방해해.

14. ④ | 긴 대화 응답

선택지 선택비율	① 2%	② 0%	③ 22%	④ 72%	⑤ 1%

W: Hi, Steve. I have something to tell you.
M: Hi. What is it, Sophie?
W: ⓐWe need to decide on a research topic for our science club.
~을 결정하다
M: Yeah. What topic do you have in mind?
~을 염두에 두다
W: I don't have any specific idea. Why don't we ask the other members for their opinions?
특정한, 구체적인 의견
M: I'm not sure about that. I think it's our job to determine a research topic as club leaders.
결정하다
W: But do you remember last semester? ⓑWe chose the research topic ourselves, and some members didn't like it.
학기
M: You're right. Then, how can we hear everyone's opinion?
W: Well, ⓒwe'll have time to discuss with all of our club members next week.
논의하다
M: That sounds good. But what if they have too many different ideas?
W: Then ⓓwe can put the research topic to the vote and choose what
put ~ to the vote: ~을 표결에 부치다

most members want for the topic.
M: All right. That way we'll satisfy more members than last time.
만족시키다

해석

여: 안녕, Steve. 너한테 말할 게 있어.
남: 안녕. 뭔데, Sophie?
여: ⓐ우리는 과학 동아리 연구 주제를 결정해야 해.
남: 응. 무슨 주제를 염두에 두고 있니?
여: 구체적인 생각은 전혀 없어. 다른 회원들에게 의견을 구하는 게 어때?
남: 그건 잘 모르겠어. 동아리 대표로서 연구 주제를 결정하는 게 우리의 일이라고 생각해.
여: 하지만 지난 학기 기억해? ⓑ우리가 직접 연구 주제를 골랐는데, 몇몇 회원들이 그걸 마음에 들어 하지 않았잖아.
남: 네 말이 맞네. 그럼, 모든 사람의 의견을 어떻게 들어볼 수 있을까?
여: 음, ⓒ다음 주에 모든 회원들과 논의할 시간이 있을 거야.
남: 그게 좋겠어. 그런데 서로 다른 생각이 너무 많으면 어쩌지?
여: 그러면 ⓓ연구 주제를 표결에 부쳐서 가장 많은 회원들이 주제로 원하는 것을 선택하면 돼.
남: 그래. 그 방법이 지난번보다 더 많은 회원들을 만족시킬 거야.

문제 풀이

두 사람은 ⓐ과학 동아리 연구 주제를 결정해야 하는 상황인데, ⓑ자신들이 고른 연구 주제를 다른 회원들이 마음에 들어 하지 않은 과거 경험에 비추어, 여자는 ⓒ모든 회원들과 논의하고 ⓓ표결에 부쳐 가장 많은 회원들이 원하는 주제를 선택하는 방법을 제안했으므로, 이에 대한 응답으로 가장 적절한 것은 ④이다.
① 걱정하지 마. 그들은 분명 네 의견을 지지할 거야.
② 물론 아니지. 우리가 지금 동아리 대표를 바꿀 수는 없어.
③ 이해해. 그러면 다른 연구 주제를 찾아볼게.
⑤ 신경 쓰지 마. 동아리 논의 시간 일정을 변경하면 돼.

15. ① | 상황에 적절한 말

선택지 선택비율	① 77%	② 4%	③ 12%	④ 2%	⑤ 4%

M: Ben and Amy are in the same environmental club in high school. They are doing an environmental campaign project and discussing ideas together. Ben sees that students sometimes throw away trash without recycling. So he wants to encourage them to recycle all the time. Meanwhile, Amy feels that asking students to reduce food waste is also a good idea because she notices a lot of leftovers in the school cafeteria. Ben thinks that both ideas will certainly help students to think more about the environment. So he wants to suggest that they include both ideas in their project. In this situation, what would Ben most likely say to Amy?
Ben: How about putting our ideas together for the project?

환경의 / 논의하다 / ~을 버리다 / 쓰레기 / 재활용 / encourage A to-v: A가 ~하도록 격려하다 / 항상 / 한편 / 줄이다 / 음식물 쓰레기 / 알아채다, 인지하다 / 남은 음식 / 분명히 / 포함하다

해석

남: Ben과 Amy는 고등학교의 같은 환경 동아리에 있다. 그들은 환경 캠페인 프로젝트를 하며 함께 아이디어를 논의하고 있다. Ben은 학생들이 때때로 쓰레기를 재활용하지 않고 버리는 것을 본다. 그래서 그는 그들이 항상 재활용하도록 격려하고 싶어 한다. 한편, Amy는 학교 식당에서 남은 음식이 많은 것을 알아채고는 학생들에게 음식물 쓰레기를 줄이라고 당부하는 것도 좋은 아이디어라고 생각한다. Ben은 두 아이디어 모두 분명 학생들이 환경에 대해 더 많이 생각하도록 도울 것이라고 생각한다. 그래서 그는 그들의 프로젝트에 두 아이디어 모두 포함하자고 제안하고 싶어 한다. 이 상황에서, Ben은 Amy에게 뭐라고 말하겠는가?
Ben: 우리의 아이디어를 함께 프로젝트에 넣는 게 어때?

문제 풀이

Ben은 프로젝트에 두 아이디어 모두 포함하자고 제안하고 싶어 한다고 했으므로, Ben이 Amy에게 할 말로는 ①이 가장 적절하다.
② 학교에서 음식물 쓰레기를 줄이는 방법을 알려줄게.
③ 우리 재활용에 관한 캠페인을 하는 게 어때?
④ 너는 지금 바로 선생님의 허락을 받아야 해.
⑤ 나는 우리가 그의 아이디어를 반 친구들과 공유해야 한다고 생각해.

16~17. | 세트 문항

16. ② 17. ④

선택지 선택비율	① 2%	② 91%	③ 3%	④ 2%	⑤ 1%
	① 1%	② 4%	③ 2%	④ 90%	⑤ 3%

W: Hello, students. As you know, ⓐanimals build many different structures in the natural world. Today, we'll talk about the different functions that these structures have. First, an important function of animal-built structures is to provide protection from predators. For example, ⓑbeavers build dams to create ponds where they can construct their homes. These structures provide a shelter from predators. Next, animal structures can also play a role in transportation. Some species of ⓒants use their own bodies to create bridges. These bridges provide a path over obstacles and allow them to search for food at an increased speed. In addition, animal structures can serve as traps. This can be observed in web-building ⓓspiders, who weave elaborate webs of sticky spider silk that capture prey. Finally, animal structures can serve as a means of attracting mates. During mating season, some species of ⓔbirds collect small branches, leaves, and colorful objects to create structures that attract the attention of females. Now, let's watch a short video about these incredible animal structures.

구조물 / 기능 / 제공하다 / 보호 / 포식자 / 댐 / 연못 / 짓다 / 은신처 / ~에서 역할을 하다 / 이동 수단 / 종 / 다리 / 길 / 장애물 / allow A to-v: A가 ~하게 해 주다 / 증가된 / 역할을 하다 / 덫 / 관찰하다 / 짜다, 엮다 / 정교한 / 끈끈한 / 잡다, 포획하다 / 먹이 / ~의 수단으로써 / 유인하다 / 짝 / 짝짓기 / 나뭇가지 / 물건 / 주의, 관심 / 암컷 / 놀라운

해석

여: 안녕하세요, 학생 여러분. 알다시피, ⓐ동물은 자연 세계에서 다양한 구조물을 만듭니다. 오늘은 이러한 구조물이 갖는 각기 다른 기능에 대해 이야기해 보겠습니다. 첫째로, 동물이 만든 구조물의 중요한 기능은 포식자로부터 보호를 제공하는 것입니다. 예를 들어, ⓑ비버는 댐을 지어 연못을 만들고 그곳에 집을 짓습니다. 이 구조물은 포식자로부터의 은신처를 제공합니다. 다음으로, 동물의 구조물은 이동 수단에서도 역할을 할 수 있습니다. 어떤 ⓒ개미 종들은 자기 몸을 이용해서 다리를 만듭니다. 이 다리는 장애물을 넘는 길을 제공하고 그것들이 증가된 속도로 먹이를 찾게 해 줍니다. 게다가, 동물의 구조물은 덫으로써의 역할을 할 수 있습니다. 이는 거미줄을 치는 ⓓ거미에게서 관찰될 수 있는데요, 거미는 먹이를 잡는 끈끈한 거미실로 정교한 거미줄을 엮습니다. 마지막으로, 동물의 구조물은 짝을 유인하는 수단으로써 역할을 할 수 있습니다. 짝짓기 철 동안 어떤 ⓔ새 종들은 작은 나뭇가지, 잎사귀, 색깔 있는 물건을 모아 암컷의 관심을 끄는 구조물을 만듭니다. 이제, 이런 놀라운 동물 구조물에 관한 짧은 영상을 봅시다.

문제 풀이

16. ⓐ동물이 자연에서 만드는 구조물의 여러 기능에 대해 이야기하고 있으므로, 주제로

가장 적절한 것은 ② '동물이 지은 구조물의 다양한 기능'이다.
① 건물에 피해를 야기할 수 있는 동물들
③ 사람이 동물로부터 배울 수 있는 건축 기술
④ 동물이 위험에서 벗어나는 효과적인 방법
⑤ 여러 동물의 창의적인 사냥 전략

17. ⓑ비버, ⓒ개미, ⓓ거미, ⓔ새는 언급되었지만, 벌(bees)은 언급되지 않았다.

[코드 공략하기]

제8회 중급 모의고사

1	①	2	③	3	④	4	⑤	5	⑤	6	②
7	①	8	③	9	⑤	10	②	11	②	12	①
13	④	14	①	15	②	16	②	17	②		

1. ① ㅣ 목적

선택지 선택비율	① 86%	② 1%	③ 8%	④ 5%	⑤ 1%

W: Good morning, students. This is your principal, Ms. Perez. I have an
교장
important announcement about our indoor gym. Since its opening,
알림 실내의 체육관
it has been a popular destination for students who'd like to stay fit.
목적지 건강을 유지하다
However, the gym has been in use for more than 10 years and most sports equipment is now outdated. So, our school has decided to
설비, 장비 구식인
renovate the gym. This means the gym will be temporarily closed
개조하다 일시적으로
until further notice. We apologize for any inconvenience this
추가의 공지 불편
may cause. Please check our school website for updates on the
최신 소식
reopening of the gym. Thank you for your understanding.
재개관

해석

여: 안녕하세요, 학생 여러분. Perez 교장입니다. 실내 체육관에 관한 중요한 알림이 있습니다. 체육관은 개관 이래로, 건강하고자 하는 학생들이 찾는 인기 장소였지요. 그런데 체육관을 사용한 지 10년이 넘어서, 대부분의 운동 장비들이 지금은 구식이 되었습니다. 그래서 우리 학교는 체육관을 개조하기로 결정했습니다. 이는 추후 공지까지 일시적으로 폐쇄될 것이라는 의미입니다. 이 때문에 야기될 불편에 사과드립니다. 체육관의 재개관에 관한 최신 소식을 위해 학교 웹사이트를 확인해 주세요. 양해 고맙습니다.

문제 풀이

여자는 학교 체육관 개조를 위한 체육관 임시 폐쇄를 알리고 있다.

2. ③ ㅣ 의견

선택지 선택비율	① 1%	② 1%	③ 95%	④ 1%	⑤ 0%

W: Dylan, what are you doing?
M: I'm learning about the history of Rome.
W: Hmm... But you are reading a comic book, aren't you?
M: Yes, ⓐit's a comic book about history. It's very helpful.
W: I think reading a general history book would be more helpful.
일반적인
M: Maybe. But ⓑlearning history through comic books has many good points.
W: Why do you think so?
M: ⓒComic books use pictures to convey information, so you can
전달하다
understand historical events more easily and remember them for
역사적인, 역사상의
a long time.
W: That makes sense. Anything else?
M: Most importantly, ⓓcomic books are interesting to read.
W: I see. Then I'll give it a try.

해석

여: Dylan, 뭐 하고 있니?

남: 로마 역사에 대해 학습하고 있어.
여: 음… 하지만 만화책을 읽고 있잖아, 그렇지 않니?
남: 응, ⓐ역사에 관한 만화책이야. 아주 도움이 돼.
여: 일반적인 역사책을 읽는 게 더 도움이 될 것 같은데.
남: 그럴지도. 하지만 ⓑ만화책을 통해 역사를 배우는 건 좋은 점이 많아.
여: 왜 그렇게 생각해?
남: ⓒ만화책은 정보를 전달하기 위해 그림을 이용하기 때문에, 역사적인 사건을 더 쉽게 이해할 수 있고 그것들을 오랫동안 기억할 수 있어.
여: 일리가 있네. 그밖에는?
남: 가장 중요하게는, ⓓ만화책은 읽는 게 재미있잖아.
여: 그래. 그럼 나도 시도해 볼게.

문제 풀이

남자는 ⓑⓒⓓ만화책을 통한 역사 공부의 장점을 말하며, ⓐ역사 만화책이 역사 공부에 도움이 된다고 말하고 있다.

3. ④ | 관계

선택지 선택비율	① 2%	② 2%	③ 2%	④ 91%	⑤ 1%

W: Hello, Mr. Stevenson. ⓐI'm Rachel Adams from *Entertainment Monthly*. Thank you for meeting with me today.
M: Hello, Ms. Adams. It's my pleasure.
W: Congratulations on gaining(얻다) more than one million subscribers(구독자) on your work, *The Invisible*. ⓑWhy do you think so many people read your webcomic?
M: I think many people enjoy the comic because my style of drawing really makes the story come alive((생기·감정·활기 등이) 넘치는).
W: I agree. I especially love Jimmy, the character who wants to be a fashion model.
M: Yes, many of my subscribers like him.
W: I heard you'll finish it soon. ⓒThe readers(독자) of our magazine have been asking if you have any plans to publish(출판[발행]하다) your work as a book or make it into a movie.
M: If there's a chance(기회), I'd love to.
W: You'll have to let our readers be the first to know if you do.
M: Of course! I hope I can bring you good news soon.

해석

여: 안녕하세요, Stevenson 선생님. ⓐ저는 〈Entertainment Monthly〉의 Rachel Adams입니다. 오늘 저를 만나 주셔서 감사합니다.
남: 안녕하세요, Adams 씨. 저도 기쁩니다.
여: 선생님의 작품인 〈보이지 않는 사람들〉로 100만 명이 넘는 구독자들을 얻게 되신 것을 축하드립니다. ⓑ왜 그렇게 많은 사람들이 선생님의 웹툰을 본다고 생각하세요?
남: 제 그림 스타일이 정말 이야기를 생생하게 만들어 주기 때문에 많은 사람들이 이 만화를 좋아하는 것 같습니다.
여: 저도 동의합니다. 저는 특히 패션 모델이 되고 싶어 하는 캐릭터 Jimmy를 아주 좋아합니다.
남: 네, 많은 제 구독자들이 그를 좋아해요.
여: 곧 완결을 내실 거라고 들었습니다. ⓒ저희 잡지 독자들이 선생님의 작품을 책으로 출판하거나 영화로 만들 계획이 있는지 묻고 있습니다.
남: 기회가 된다면, 그러고 싶어요.
여: 그렇게 하신다면 저희 독자들이 가장 먼저 알게 해 주셔야 합니다.
남: 물론이죠! 조만간 좋은 소식 전해드릴 수 있기를 바랍니다.

문제 풀이

여자가 ⓐ월간지 소속이라고 자신을 소개하며 ⓒ잡지 독자들의 질문을 전했으며, 남자에게 ⓑ왜 많은 사람들이 그의 웹툰을 본다고 생각하는지 질문하는 것으로 보아, 여자는 잡지사 기자이고 남자는 웹툰 작가임을 알 수 있다.

4. ⑤ | 그림 일치

선택지 선택비율	① 1%	② 6%	③ 1%	④ 7%	⑤ 85%

M: Look at this photo from our family camping trip last year.
W: I remember that trip. ⓐWe parked our camping van between the two trees.
M: Right. You guys really loved the camping van.
W: Yes, we did. And ⓑyou set up that square(정사각형 모양의) table for us.
M: That's right. You guys enjoyed playing board games on that table.
W: Yeah, that was so fun! And do you remember ⓒthe guitar next to the table?
M: Yes. I played the guitar and we sang songs together while we sat on the blanket.
W: ⓓThat star-patterned blanket was our dogs' favorite.
M: ⓔLook at our two dogs, Rex and Rover. They look really happy in the picture.
W: Yeah. They started to run around and bark(짖다) while we were singing. That was so funny.
M: Yeah, that was hilarious(아주 재미있는)! We had such a good time.

해석

남: 작년에 우리 가족 캠핑 여행에서 찍은 이 사진을 봐요.
여: 그 여행이 기억나요. ⓐ우리는 캠핑카를 두 나무 사이에 주차했잖아요.
남: 맞아요. 캠핑카를 정말 좋아했죠.
여: 네, 그랬어요. 그리고 ⓑ당신이 우리를 위해 네모난 테이블을 설치했죠.
남: 맞아요. 그 테이블에서 보드게임을 하면서 즐거워했잖아요.
여: 네, 정말 재미있었어요! 그리고 ⓒ테이블 옆에 있는 기타 기억해요?
남: 네. 내가 기타를 치고 우리는 담요 위에 앉아 함께 노래를 불렀죠.
여: ⓓ저 별무늬 담요는 우리 개들이 가장 좋아하는 거였어요.
남: ⓔ우리 개 두 마리 Rex와 Rover를 봐요. 그들은 사진 속에서 정말 행복해 보이네요.
여: 네. 우리가 노래하는 동안 뛰어다니며 짖기 시작했잖아요. 정말 재미있었어요.
남: 네, 정말 재미있었죠! 우리는 정말 좋은 시간을 보냈어요.

문제 풀이

ⓔ사진에 개 두 마리가 있다고 했으므로, ⑤는 대화 내용과 일치하지 않는다.

5. ⑤ | 할 일

선택지 선택비율	① 2%	② 1%	③ 4%	④ 8%	⑤ 86%

M: Hey, Sarah, the school's sports day is just a week away. Let's go over(~을 점검하다) our plan for the event.
W: Definitely, Alex. We're doing relays(계주), a tug-of-war(줄다리기), and soccer, right?
M: Yes. I'll manage(관리하다) the equipment, including(~을 포함하여) whistles(호루라기) and the ropes(밧줄).
W: Thanks. Can you also check our stock(재고) for soccer balls?
M: Sure. I'll look into it. And, Sarah, I think we need some volunteers to assist(돕다) with the event as staff.
W: I already recruited(모집하다) some from the school's sports clubs.
M: Perfect. I think we should make sure they know the basic rules of the games.
W: I agree. Let's have a meeting with the volunteers tomorrow. I'll give them a phone call about the meeting.
M: Good idea. Then, I'll make the handout(유인물) for the games' rules.
W: Deal. Let's make this sports day a success!

해석

남: Sarah, 학교 운동회가 이제 딱 일주일 남았어요. 행사 계획을 점검합시다.
여: 물론이죠, Alex. 우린 계주, 줄다리기, 축구를 할 거예요, 그렇죠?
남: 네. 내가 호루라기랑 밧줄을 포함한 장비를 관리할게요.
여: 고마워요. 축구공 재고도 확인해 줄 수 있어요?
남: 물론이죠. 내가 알아볼게요. 그리고, Sarah, 스태프로 행사를 도울 자원봉사자들이 좀 필요할 것 같아요.
여: 내가 이미 학교 스포츠 클럽에서 몇 명 모집했어요.
남: 완벽해요. 그들에게 경기의 기본 규칙을 확실히 알려줘야 할 것 같아요.
여: 동의해요. 내일 자원봉사자들과 회의를 합시다. 내가 회의에 대해 그들에게 전화할게요.
남: 좋은 생각이에요. 그럼, 내가 경기 규칙에 관한 유인물을 만들게요.
여: 좋아요. 이번 운동회를 성공적으로 치르자고요!

문제 풀이

여자가 자원봉사자들에게 회의에 대해 전화하겠다고 했다.

6. ② | 금액

선택지 선택비율	① 7%	② 64%	③ 25%	④ 8%	⑤ 4%

W: Honey, we're running out of fine dust masks. Don't we need to order some more?
(running out of: ~이 바닥나다 / fine dust: 미세먼지)
M: Oh, right. *[Typing sound]* Let's order them on this website. The masks are $2 each and ⓐa pack of 10 masks is $15.
(pack: 묶음, 꾸러미)
W: Then it's cheaper to buy them in packs. ⓑLet's get four packs.
M: Okay. We also need some hand wash, right?
W: Yes. Is there any special promotion going on?
(promotion: 판촉)
M: Let me see. *[Pause]* Oh, there is. ⓒWe can buy three bottles of hand wash for $10. It was originally $5 per bottle.
W: That's a good deal. ⓓLet's buy three bottles then.
M: All right. Do we need anything else?
W: No, that's all. Oh, hang on. Look here. ⓔIf we spend more than $50, we can get a 5-dollar discount.
M: Great. I'll place the order now with my credit card.
(place an order: 주문하다)

해석

여: 여보, 우리 미세먼지 마스크가 바닥나고 있어요. 좀 더 주문해야 하지 않을까요?
남: 아, 그래요. [타이핑하는 소리] 이 웹사이트에서 주문합시다. 마스크는 하나에 2달러이고 ⓐ마스크 10개 묶음은 15달러에요.
여: 그러면 묶음으로 사는 게 더 저렴하네요. ⓑ네 묶음을 삽시다.
남: 좋아요. 손 세척제도 필요해요, 맞죠?
여: 네. 특별 판촉 중인 게 있나요?
남: 볼게요. [잠시 후] 아, 있네요. ⓒ손 세척제 세 병을 10달러에 살 수 있어요. 원래 한 병에 5달러였어요.
여: 괜찮은 가격이네요. 그러면 ⓓ세 병 삽시다.
남: 그래요. 그밖에 다른 게 필요한가요?
여: 아니요, 그게 다예요. 아, 잠깐요. 여기 봐요. ⓔ50달러 이상 사면, 5달러를 할인받을 수 있어요.
남: 잘됐네요. 내 신용 카드로 지금 주문할게요.

문제 풀이

남자는 ⓐ10개 묶음에 15달러인 미세먼지 마스크 ⓑ네 묶음(60달러), ⓒ세 병에 10달러인 손 세척제 ⓓ세 병(10달러) 구입하여 총 70달러를 지불해야 하는데, ⓔ50달러 이상 구매로 5달러를 할인받으므로 65달러를 지불하면 된다.

7. ① | 이유

선택지 선택비율	① 84%	② 4%	③ 5%	④ 3%	⑤ 2%

M: Hi, Emily. How was your family trip last weekend?
W: It was fantastic! Did you have a nice weekend, too?
M: It was fine, but Jenny had an accident yesterday, so she is absent from school today.
(accident: 사고 / absent: 결석한)
W: Oh, what happened to her?
M: She broke her leg at a ski camp.
W: That's too bad. Is she in a hospital now?
M: Yeah, so tomorrow some of her friends and I will visit her after school. Can you join us?
W: I'm afraid I can't. I have other plans for tomorrow.
M: Are you still learning Taekwondo every afternoon?
W: No, my lessons ended last week. We're having a birthday party for my mom.
M: Oh, I see. You can't miss that.
(miss: 놓치다)
W: Thanks for understanding. Anyway, I'll give Jenny a call later.
(give ~ a call: ~에게 전화하다)

해석

남: 안녕, Emily. 지난 주말 가족 여행은 어땠니?
여: 환상적이었어! 너도 즐거운 주말 보냈니?
남: 좋았어, 그런데 Jenny가 어제 사고가 나서 오늘 학교에 결석했어.
여: 이런, 그 애에게 무슨 일이 있었니?
남: 스키 캠프에서 다리가 부러졌대.
여: 정말 안됐다. 그 애는 지금 병원에 있니?
남: 응, 그래서 내일 방과 후에 그 애의 친구들 몇 명과 내가 그 애를 찾아가려 해. 너도 우리와 함께할 수 있니?
여: 미안하지만 난 안 돼. 내일 다른 계획들이 있거든.
남: 너 아직 매일 오후에 태권도를 배우고 있니?
여: 아니, 수업은 지난주에 끝났어. 우리는 엄마 생신 파티를 할 거야.
남: 아, 그렇구나. 그걸 빠지면 안 되지.
여: 이해해 줘서 고마워. 어쨌든, 내가 나중에 Jenny에게 전화할게.

문제 풀이

여자는 어머니의 생신 파티 때문에 친구의 병문안을 함께 가지 못한다고 했다.

8. ③ | 언급

선택지 선택비율	① 3%	② 3%	③ 86%	④ 4%	⑤ 2%

M: Maria, what are you watching?
W: I'm watching the preview of the new TV drama, *Romance City*.
(preview: 예고)
M: *Romance City*? When does it start?
W: ⓐThe first episode will be aired on March 9th.
(first episode: 1회 방송분 / air: 방송하다)
M: Oh, it's this Saturday!
W: Yes, my favorite actor, ⓑLiam Collins, is the main character.
(main character: 주인공)
M: Oh, he is? I like him, too.
W: ⓒThe director is Sam Adams. He also directed *Dreamcatcher*.
(director: 감독 / direct: 감독하다)
M: Really? I loved that drama.
W: You know what? ⓓ*Romance City* is based on the best-selling novel of the same title.
(be based on: ~을 바탕으로 하다)
M: Have you read the novel?
W: Of course. I enjoyed it very much.

해석

남: Maria, 뭘 보고 있니?

여: 새로운 TV 드라마 〈연애 도시〉 예고를 보고 있어.
남: 〈연애 도시〉? 언제 시작하는데?
여: ⓐ첫 회가 3월 9일에 방송될 예정이야.
남: 아, 이번 주 토요일이네!
여: 응, 내가 제일 좋아하는 배우 ⓑLiam Collins가 주인공이야.
남: 아, 그 사람이? 나도 그 사람 좋아해.
여: ⓒ감독은 Sam Adams야. 그 사람이 〈드림캐쳐〉도 감독했어.
남: 정말? 그 드라마 정말 좋아했는데.
여: 그거 아니? ⓓ〈연애 도시〉는 동일 제목의 베스트 셀러 소설을 바탕으로 한 거야.
남: 그 소설 읽어 봤니?
여: 물론이지. 아주 재미있었어.

문제 풀이

ⓐ첫 방영 날짜, ⓑ주연 배우, ⓒ감독, ⓓ원작 소설은 언급되었으나, 줄거리는 언급되지 않았다.

9. ⑤ | 내용 일치

선택지 선택비율	① 5%	② 3%	③ 1%	④ 4%	⑤ 84%

W: Hello, Highland residents. I'm Jenny Walker, the community center
거주자, 주민
manager. ⓐWe host the Highland Movie Night every month. This
(행사를) 주최하다
event gives you a chance to enjoy classic movies. ⓑIt is free for all Highland residents. This month, we will show *The Amazing Wizard Harry*. The movie will start at seven p.m. this Saturday. As usual, ⓒit'll be held at the Lincoln Library. Due to the limited space, ⓓyou
제한된, 한정된
should register in advance. You can reserve seats on our website
등록하다 예약하다
until Friday. To keep the library clean, ⓔyou are not allowed to bring any food. For more information, feel free to call us. Thank you.

해석

여: 안녕하세요, Highland 주민 여러분. 저는 주민센터 관리자 Jenny Walker입니다. ⓐ저희는 Highland Movie Night을 매달 개최합니다. 이 행사는 여러분께 고전 영화들을 즐길 수 있는 기회를 드립니다. Highland 주민 모두에게 무료입니다. 이번 달에, 저희는 〈놀라운 마법사 해리〉를 상영할 예정입니다. 영화는 이번 주 토요일 저녁 7시에 시작할 겁니다. 언제나처럼, ⓒLincoln 도서관에서 개최될 예정입니다. 한정된 공간으로 인해 ⓓ사전에 등록하셔야 합니다. 저희 홈페이지에서 금요일까지 좌석을 예약하실 수 있습니다. 도서관을 청결하게 유지하기 위해, ⓔ어떤 음식도 가지고 오실 수 없습니다. 더 많은 정보를 원하시면 언제든지 저희에게 전화 주세요. 감사합니다.

문제 풀이

ⓔ어떤 음식도 가지고 올 수 없다고 했다.

10. ② | 도표

선택지 선택비율	① 2%	② 93%	③ 1%	④ 3%	⑤ 1%

M: Honey, why don't we buy a UV toothbrush sanitizer? This online
자외선(ultraviolet) 살균제, 소독제
store is offering a good deal.
W: That's great. How about choosing one from these five models?
M: Fine. First, we need to consider the number of slots.
고려하다 (무엇을 집어넣도록 만든 가느다란) 구멍
W: For our family, ⓐwe need four or more slots.
M: Right. Do you think ⓑwe need one with a built-in battery?
붙박이의, 내장된
W: Yes. It'd be easier to install.
설치하다
M: Okay. And I think it's important to keep the brushes dry.
W: I agree. It prevents bacteria from growing on the brushes. ⓒWe
박테리아, 세균
should definitely go with one that has a drying function.
M: That leaves us with these two models.
W: ⓓHow about staying under 50 dollars?
M: Good. ⓔLet's order the cheaper one.

해석

남: 여보, 우리 자외선 칫솔 소독기를 사는 게 어때요? 이 온라인 스토어에서 할인해 주고 있어요.
여: 잘됐네요. 이 다섯 가지 모델 중에서 하나 고르는 게 어때요?
남: 좋아요. 먼저 (칫솔 넣을) 구멍 수를 고려해야 해요.
여: 우리 가족을 위해서는 ⓐ4개 이상의 칸이 필요해요.
남: 맞아요. ⓑ배터리가 내장된 게 필요할까요?
여: 네. 그게 설치하기가 더 편할 거예요.
남: 좋아요. 그리고 칫솔을 건조하게 유지하는 것이 중요한 것 같아요.
여: 동의해요. 그래야 칫솔에서 세균이 번식하는 것을 막죠. ⓒ반드시 건조 기능이 있는 걸로 해야 해요.
남: 그러면 이 두 가지 모델이 남네요.
여: ⓓ50달러 미만으로 하는 게 어때요?
남: 좋아요. ⓔ더 저렴한 걸로 주문합시다.

문제 풀이

두 사람은 ⓐ칫솔 넣을 칸이 4개 이상이면서 ⓑ배터리가 내장되어 있고, ⓒ건조 기능이 있는 것 중에서 ⓓⓔ50달러 미만의 더 저렴한 것으로 구입하기로 했다.

11. ② | 짧은 대화 응답

선택지 선택비율	① 4%	② 84%	③ 5%	④ 2%	⑤ 4%

M: Emily, the plants you gave me are dying.
W: When taking care of plants, giving them enough sunlight and water
충분한
is very important.
M: I think there's enough sunlight. But how often should I water the
물을 주다
plants?
W: You need to water them once every three days.

해석

남: Emily, 네가 준 식물들이 죽어가고 있어.
여: 식물을 돌볼 때, 충분한 햇빛과 물을 주는 게 매우 중요해.
남: 햇빛은 충분한 것 같아. 그런데 얼마나 자주 식물에 물을 줘야 할까?
여: 3일에 한 번 물을 줘야 해.

문제 풀이

얼마나 자주 식물에 물을 줘야 하는지 물었으므로, 물 주는 횟수를 말하는 ②가 응답으로 가장 적절하다.
① 지구를 위해 많은 식물을 기르는 게 중요해.
③ 너무 많은 햇빛은 식물에 나쁠 수 있어.
④ 나는 환경을 위해 물을 절약하는 게 좋겠어.
⑤ 우리는 하루에 1리터의 물을 마셔야 해.

12. ① | 짧은 대화 응답

선택지 선택비율	① 60%	② 2%	③ 5%	④ 9%	⑤ 22%

W: Mr. Johnson, do you have a minute? ⓐI need your opinion on the
의견
project I'm doing.
M: I'd love to discuss that with you, but ⓑI'm expecting a visitor in
논의하다 (오기로 되어 있는 대상을) 기다리다
10 minutes. Is 10 minutes enough?
W: I'm afraid it'll take longer than that. ⓒShall I come back later?
M: Yes. I'll give you a call when I'm available.
시간이 되는

해석

여: Johnson 씨, 시간 좀 있나요? ⓐ제가 하고 있는 프로젝트에 관한 의견이 필요해요.
남: 함께 그걸 논의하고 싶지만, ⓑ10분 후에 올 손님을 기다리고 있어요. 10분이면 충분한가요?
여: 그보다는 더 오래 걸릴 것 같아요. ⓒ나중에 다시 올까요?
남: 네. 시간 될 때 전화할게요.

문제 풀이

ⓐ의견을 구하려는 여자에게 남자는 ⓑ손님을 기다리고 있다고 했고, 여자는 ⓒ나중에 다시 올지 물었으므로, 시간이 될 때 전화하겠다는 ①이 남자의 응답으로 가장 적절하다.
② 글쎄요, 당신은 지금 아무 프로젝트도 하고 있지 않잖아요.
③ 그래요. 손님이 방금 가셔서 지금 이야기할 수 있어요.
④ 왜 안 되겠어요? 언제든 프로젝트에 함께하면 돼요.
⑤ 물론이에요. 지금 당신을 위해 30분을 낼 수 있어요.

13. ④ | 긴 대화 응답

선택지 선택비율	① 2%	② 2%	③ 1%	④ 92%	⑤ 1%

W: Dad, I'm home. Where's Max?
M: He's sleeping in his house. I took him to the vet (수의사) this morning. He hasn't been eating well lately.
W: What did the vet say?
M: She said there's nothing wrong with him. He just needs more exercise.
W: More exercise? We take him out for a walk regularly (정기적으로).
M: That's true, but we don't walk him every day. The vet said he needs at least an hour of exercise every day.
W: Oh, I didn't know that.
M: ⓐI think we should exercise him every day from now on (이제부터).
W: I agree. ⓑWhat if we all take turns doing it? (take turns v-ing: ~을 교대로 하다)
M: ⓒGood idea. Your mom and I will do it on weekdays (평일). You're busy with your schoolwork (학업, 학교 공부) during the weekdays.
W: Okay. I'll take him out for a walk on weekends then.

해석

여: 아빠, 저 왔어요. Max는 어디 있어요?
남: 집에서 자고 있단다. 오늘 아침에 수의사에게 데려갔었거든. 최근에 잘 먹지 않았잖아.
여: 수의사가 뭐라고 했나요?
남: 아무 문제는 없다는구나. 단지 운동을 더 해야 한단다.
여: 운동을 더요? 정기적으로 산책하러 나가잖아요.
남: 그게 사실이지만, 매일 산책시키지는 않지. 수의사가 말하기를 매일 최소 한 시간 운동이 필요하다는구나.
여: 아, 그건 몰랐어요.
남: ⓐ이제부터 매일 산책시켜야 할 것 같구나.
여: 그래요. ⓑ우리 모두 그걸 교대로 하면 어떨까요?
남: ⓒ좋은 생각이야. 너희 엄마와 내가 평일에 할게. 넌 평일에 학교 공부로 바쁘잖니.
여: 좋아요. 그러면 저는 주말마다 산책시키러 나갈게요.

문제 풀이

ⓐMax를 매일 산책시켜야 하는 상황에서, ⓑ교대로 하자는 여자의 제안에 남자가 ⓒ동의하며 자신과 여자의 엄마는 평일에 하겠다고 했으므로, 주말에는 자신이 산책시키겠다는 ④가 여자의 응답으로 가장 적절하다.
① 맞는 말씀이에요. 최근에 너무 많이 먹고 있어요.
② 그건 공평하지 않아요. 제가 일주일 내내 산책시키고 싶진 않아요.
③ 죄송해요. 지금 수의사에게 데려갈 시간이 없어요.
⑤ 꼭 그렇지는 않아요. 너무 많은 운동은 건강에 좋지 않아요.

14. ① | 긴 대화 응답

선택지 선택비율	① 90%	② 2%	③ 2%	④ 1%	⑤ 5%

W: Hi, Matt. Have you finished your science club experiment (실험)?
M: Yeah, I just wrapped it up (~을 마무리하다). How's your magic club's show coming along (come along: 되어가다, 나아가다)?
W: It's going well. But I still have one thing left to do.
M: What do you have to do?
W: I need to set up (~을 설치하다) the stage (무대) in the hall, but I've run into ((곤경 등을) 만나다, 겪다) a problem.
M: What's wrong?
W: ⓐI need some dry ice for my performance (공연), but I don't have any.
M: Why do you need dry ice?
W: I need it to create special effects (특수 효과). It's really important.
M: Actually, ⓑour science club used dry ice yesterday. There might be some left in the storage room (저장고, 창고).
W: Really? ⓒCould you go and check? It'd be great if I could use some.
M: Okay. I'll let you know if I find any.

해석

여: 안녕, Matt. 과학 동아리 실험은 끝냈어?
남: 응, 방금 마무리했어. 너희 마술 동아리 공연 준비는 어떻게 돼 가?
여: 잘 되고 있어. 그런데 아직 할 일이 하나 남아 있어.
남: 뭐 해야 하는데?
여: 강당에 무대를 설치해야 하는데, 문제가 생겼어.
남: 무슨 문제야?
여: ⓐ공연에 쓸 드라이아이스가 필요한데, 내가 가지고 있는 게 없어.
남: 드라이아이스가 왜 필요해?
여: 특수 효과를 만들기 위해 그게 필요해. 정말 중요하거든.
남: 사실 ⓑ우리 과학 동아리가 어제 드라이아이스를 썼거든. 창고에 남은 게 조금 있을지도 몰라.
여: 정말? ⓒ가서 확인해 줄 수 있어? 내가 조금 쓸 수 있다면 좋겠다.
남: 알겠어. 내가 찾으면 알려줄게.

문제 풀이

ⓐ마술 동아리 공연에 쓸 드라이아이스가 필요하다는 여자의 말에 남자는 ⓑ자신의 과학 동아리에서 쓰고 남은 드라이아이스가 있을지 모른다고 했고, 이에 여자는 ⓒ가서 확인해 달라고 했으므로, 찾으면 알려주겠다는 내용의 ①이 남자의 응답으로 가장 적절하다.
② 맞아. 나는 실험을 끝내야 해.
③ 괜찮아. 나는 아까 이미 조금 썼어.
④ 꼭 그렇진 않아. 나는 특수 효과가 전혀 필요하지 않아.
⑤ 신경 쓰지 마. 그건 네 공연 끝나고 내가 처리할게.

15. ② | 상황에 적절한 말

선택지 선택비율	① 6%	② 69%	③ 4%	④ 10%	⑤ 16%

W: Katie and Jeff have been working on an important presentation (발표). They are supposed to (be supposed to-v: ~하기로 되어 있다) give the presentation together tomorrow afternoon. Unfortunately (불행하게도, 유감스럽게도), this morning, Katie fell down the stairs and broke her leg. She is in the hospital now and has to stay there for at least a week. Now she is very much worried about the presentation. Jeff hears the news and calls Katie to tell her he can take care of (~을 처리하다) everything about the presentation himself. Katie thinks that she has no other choice and feels grateful (감사하고 있는) toward him. In this situation, what would Katie most likely say to Jeff?

Katie: I appreciate your kind offer.

해석

여: Katie와 Jeff는 중요한 발표를 위한 작업을 해 오고 있었다. 그들은 내일 오후에 함께 그 발표를 하기로 되어 있다. 안타깝게도, 오늘 아침 Katie는 계단에서 떨어져서 다리가 부러졌다. 그녀는 지금 병원에 있고 최소한 일주일 동안 그곳에 있어야 한다. 지금 그녀는 발표에 대해 굉장히 걱정이 된다. Jeff가 그 소식을 듣고 Katie에게 전화를 해서 그가 혼자서 발표에 관한 모든 것을 처리할 수 있다고 그녀에게 말한다. Katie는 다른 대안은 없다고 생각하고 그에게 고마움을 느낀다. 이 상황에서, Katie는 Jeff에게 뭐라고 말하겠는가?

Katie: 네가 친절하게 제안해 줘서 고마워.

문제 풀이

Jeff가 원래는 Katie와 함께 하기로 되어 있던 발표를 혼자 맡아서 다 할 수 있다고 전화를 주자, 다른 대안이 없는 Katie가 Jeff에게 고마워하고 있다. 따라서 Jeff에게 친절한 제안을 해 줘서 고맙다는 ②가 가장 적절하다.

① 네가 곧 회복하기를 바랄게.
③ 내일 오후에 너를 방문할게.
④ 내가 직접 그 발표를 할게.
⑤ 네 도움으로 발표를 끝냈어.

16~17. ㅣ 세트 문항

16. ② 17. ②

선택지 선택비율					
	① 3%	② 85%	③ 3%	④ 4%	⑤ 5%
	① 1%	② 93%	③ 1%	④ 4%	⑤ 1%

W: Hello, students. Have any of you visited a museum recently? If so, you may have noticed some remarkable changes taking place. Today, ⓐI'd like to share some insights about the changes happening in museums. Now, traditional museums are being transformed by modern technologies. The first technology I want to introduce is ⓑvirtual reality. Museums around the world are adopting virtual reality to change how visitors interact with historical objects. For instance, visitors can now explore ancient buildings as if they were real. Another technology being used in museums is ⓒ3D animation. This brings historical scenes to life, showing how people lived in the past. Animated displays allow visitors to experience historical events in a more engaging way. Also, ⓓlaser projection creates dynamic effects on gallery walls. Using this technology, museums can highlight specific artworks and create fascinating environments that enhance the viewing experience. Finally, ⓔ3D printing has opened up new possibilities for museums. This technology makes it possible to display accurate copies of delicate or rare items that cannot be exposed to the public. These technological innovations are making museum collections more accessible, interactive, and engaging than ever before.

recently 최근에 / notice 알아차리다, (보거나 듣고) 알다 / remarkable 주목할 만한, 놀라운 / take place: 일어나다, 발생하다 / insight 통찰 / traditional 전통적인 / transform 변모시키다 / virtual reality 가상현실 / adopt 도입하다 / interact with ~와 상호 작용하다 / historical 역사적인 / object 물건, 물체 / explore 탐험하다 / ancient 고대의 / as if 마치 ~처럼 / animated 활기찬, 살아 있는 것 같은 / display 전시 / engaging 호감이 가는, 매력적인 / dynamic 역동적인 / effect 효과 / highlight 강조하다 / specific 특정한 / artwork 예술 작품 / fascinating 매혹적인 / enhance 질을 높이다 / possibility: 가능성 / accurate 정확한, 정밀한 / delicate 연약한, 부서지기 쉬운 / rare 진귀한 / be exposed to ~에 드러내다 / public 대중 / innovation 혁신 / accessible 접근하기 쉬운 / interactive 상호 작용을 하는

해석

여: 안녕하세요, 학생 여러분. 여러분 중 누구라도 최근에 박물관에 가본 적 있나요? 만약 그렇다면, (박물관에서) 일어나고 있는 놀라운 변화들을 알아차렸을지도 모릅니다. 오늘은 ⓐ박물관에서 일어나고 있는 변화에 대한 몇 가지 통찰을 나누고자 합니다. 지금 전통적인 박물관은 현대 기술에 의해 변모되고 있습니다. 제가 소개하고 싶은 첫 번째 기술은 ⓑ가상현실입니다. 전 세계의 박물관들이 가상현실을 도입해 관람객이 역사적 물건과 상호 작용하는 방식을 바꾸고 있습니다. 예를 들어, 관람객은 이제 고대 건축물을 마치 실제처럼 탐험할 수 있습니다. 박물관에서 사용되고 있는 또 다른 기술은 ⓒ3D 애니메이션입니다. 이는 역사적인 장면에 생기를 불어넣어 과거에 사람들이 어떻게 살았는지를 보여줍니다. 살아 있는 듯한 전시는 관람객이 역사적인 사건을 보다 매력적인 방식으로 경험하게 해 줍니다. 또한, ⓓ레이저 프로젝션은 전시관 벽에 역동적인 효과를 만들어 냅니다. 이 기술을 사용하여 박물관은 특정 예술 작품을 강조하고 관람 경험의 질을 높이는 매혹적인 환경을 조성할 수 있습니다. 마지막으로, ⓔ3D 프린팅은 박물관의 새로운 가능성을 열었습니다. 이 기술은 대중에게 공개할 수 없는 부서지기 쉽거나 진귀한 유물의 정밀한 복제품 전시를 가능하게 합니다. 이러한 기술 혁신들은 박물관 소장품들을 그 어느 때보다 더 접근하기 쉽고, 더 상호 작용적이며, 더 매력적이게 만들고 있습니다.

문제 풀이

16. ⓐ박물관에서 일어나고 있는 변화에 대한 통찰을 나누겠다고 말하며 전통적인 박물관이 현대 기술에 의해 변모하는 것에 대해 이야기하고 있으므로, 여자가 하는 말의 주제로 가장 적절한 것은 ② '박물관 경험을 변화시키는 현대 기술'이다.
① 박물관에서 디지털 기기를 사용할 때의 예절
③ 급격한 기술 변화로 인해 박물관에서 생긴 문제
④ 박물관 전시에서의 기술 통합의 장애물
⑤ 박물관 건축에 사용된 건축 기술

17. ⓑ가상현실, ⓒ3D 애니메이션, ⓓ레이저 프로젝션, ⓔ3D 프린팅은 언급되었지만, 모션 트래킹(motion tracking)은 언급되지 않았다.

[코드 공략하기]

제9회 중급 모의고사

1	①	2	②	3	②	4	⑤	5	②	6	④
7	②	8	③	9	④	10	④	11	③	12	②
13	①	14	②	15	⑤	16	③	17	④		

1. ① | 목적

선택지 선택비율	① 91%	② 2%	③ 2%	④ 1%	⑤ 2%

M: Hello, everyone. This is Ted Williams, the drama teacher. As you know, there's a musical in the school festival every year. And ⓐthe auditions for actors are going to be held soon. Even if you don't think you're talented, that's okay. Most importantly, I'm looking
재능[재주]이 있는
for students with passion. All interested students should submit
열정 관심 있는 제출하다
an application to me no later than June 23rd. ⓑThe auditions are
신청서 늦어도 ~까지는
going to be held on June 24th from three to five p.m. in the school auditorium. If you need more information, please check the poster
객석, 강당
on the bulletin board. I'm looking forward to seeing you at the
게시판
auditions. Thank you.

해석

남: 안녕하세요, 여러분. 저는 연극 교사인 Ted Williams입니다. 알다시피, 매년 학교 축제에는 뮤지컬이 있습니다. 그리고 ⓐ배우 오디션이 곧 개최될 예정입니다. 본인이 재능이 없다고 생각하더라도 괜찮습니다. 가장 중요한 것은, 열정을 가진 학생들을 찾고 있다는 것입니다. 관심 있는 모든 학생들은 늦어도 6월 23일까지는 제게 신청서를 제출해야 합니다. ⓑ오디션은 6월 24일 오후 3시부터 5시까지 학교 강당에서 개최될 예정입니다. 더 많은 정보가 필요하면, 게시판에 있는 포스터를 확인해 주세요. 오디션에서 여러분을 만나기를 고대하고 있습니다. 고맙습니다.

문제 풀이

ⓐⓑ오디션이 6월 24일 오후 학교 강당에서 개최될 것임을 공지하고 있다.

2. ② | 의견

선택지 선택비율	① 2%	② 90%	③ 2%	④ 3%	⑤ 1%

W: Hi, Mike. You look distracted. Is something bothering you?
(정신이) 산만해진
M: Well, my son's preschool teacher told me he's having trouble
유치원
focusing while reading and during conversations. I don't know what
집중하다 대화
I should do.
W: Oh, I see. *[Pause]* ⓐMaybe drawing classes could help.
M: How could they help with his concentration?
집중
W: ⓑChildren develop their ability to focus as they pay attention to
발달시키다 능력 ~에 주목하다
small details while drawing.
세부 사항
M: That's reasonable. Is that why your daughter takes drawing
타당한, 합리적인
classes?
W: Exactly. When my daughter was 8 years old, she had a similar
비슷한
problem to your son.
M: Did you notice a big change when she started drawing?
W: Sure. She concentrates better on reading and conversations now. It
~에 집중하다
might help your son, too.
M: Okay, I'll look for a class right away.

해석

여: 안녕하세요, Mike. 정신이 없어 보이시네요. 무슨 걱정거리라도 있으신가요?
남: 음, 제 아들의 유치원 선생님께서 제게 아들이 책을 읽는 동안이나 대화 중에 집중하는 데 어려움을 겪고 있다고 말씀하셨어요. 제가 어떻게 해야 할지 모르겠어요.
여: 아, 그렇군요. [잠시 후] ⓐ어쩌면 그림 그리기 수업이 도움이 될 수도 있겠네요.
남: 어떻게 그게 아들의 집중력에 도움이 될 수 있을까요?
여: ⓑ아이들은 그림을 그리는 동안 작은 세부 사항에 주목하면서 집중하는 능력을 발달시켜요.
남: 타당한 말씀이세요. 그래서 따님이 그림 그리기 수업을 듣는 건가요?
여: 맞아요. 제 딸이 8살이었을 때, 아드님과 비슷한 문제가 있었거든요.
남: 따님이 그림을 그리기 시작했을 때 큰 변화를 알아차리셨나요?
여: 물론이죠. 딸은 지금 독서와 대화에 더 잘 집중합니다. 아드님에게도 도움이 될지도 몰라요.
남: 네, 지금 바로 수업을 찾아볼게요.

문제 풀이

여자는 ⓑ아이들이 그림을 그리는 동안 세부 사항에 주목함으로써 집중력을 발달시키기 때문에 ⓐ그림 그리기 수업이 도움이 될 수 있다고 말하고 있다.

3. ② | 관계

선택지 선택비율	① 4%	② 86%	③ 1%	④ 1%	⑤ 5%

M: Excuse me, are you Anna Zimmerman? I can't believe I'm seeing you here!
W: Oh, hello. Have we met before?
M: No, but ⓐI'm a big fan of yours.
열렬한 팬
W: Thank you. I love meeting my fans.
M: ⓑI just finished your latest book, *The Beautiful Days*. I read the whole thing in a day.
W: I'm flattered. What did you like most?
으쓱한
M: I really liked the part where Emma and Jason first dance.
W: That's my favorite moment, too. It took me more than two weeks to write that chapter.
M: Wow! It was worth it. It was so beautifully described. I hope this
~할 가치가 있는 묘사하다
book will be made into a movie.
W: I'm so glad you like it that much.
M: ⓒI think you're one of the best novelists in the world. Can I get your
소설가
autograph, please?
사인
W: Sure.

해석

남: 실례합니다만, Anna Zimmerman 선생님이신가요? 여기서 선생님을 뵙다니 믿기지 않아요!
여: 아, 안녕하세요. 저희가 전에 만난 적이 있나요?
남: 아니요, 하지만 ⓐ선생님의 열렬한 팬이에요.
여: 감사해요. 팬을 만나는 건 아주 좋죠.
남: ⓑ이제 막 선생님의 최신 책 〈아름다운 날들〉을 읽었어요. 하루만에 전부 읽었죠.
여: 으쓱해지네요. 어떤 점이 가장 마음에 드셨나요?
남: Emma와 Jason이 처음 춤추는 부분이 정말 마음에 들었어요.
여: 제가 가장 좋아하는 순간이기도 해요. 그 챕터를 쓰는 데 두 주 넘게 걸렸답니다.
남: 우와! 그럴 만한 가치가 있었네요. 정말 아름답게 묘사됐어요. 이 책이 영화로 만들어지면 좋겠어요.
여: 그렇게 많이 좋아해 주시니 정말 기뻐요.

남: ⓒ제 생각에 선생님은 세계 최고 소설가 중 한 분이세요. 사인을 받을 수 있을까요?
여: 물론이죠.

문제 풀이

남자는 ⓐ자신을 여자의 팬이라고 소개했으며, ⓑ여자의 최신작을 읽었으며 ⓒ여자가 세계 최고 소설가라고 생각한다고 말한 것으로 보아, 독자와 소설가의 대화임을 알 수 있다.

4. ⑤ | 그림 일치

선택지 선택비율	① 3%	② 2%	③ 2%	④ 20%	⑤ 73%

M: Honey, I've finished decorating the living room for Halloween. Can you come here and take a look?
W: Sure. *[Pause]* Is ⓐthe carpet on the floor the one you ordered last week?
M: Yeah. ⓑI chose the round one because it looks cute. What do you think?
W: It looks really good there. I also love ⓒthe spider web decoration that you put on the wall above the piano.
M: Thanks. I thought it would help create the Halloween mood. (mood: 분위기)
W: It definitely does. *[Pause]* Oh! ⓓThe two carved pumpkins on the bookshelf are so cool. (carved: 조각하다, 새기다)
M: Totally. The faces we carved into the pumpkins look excellent.
W: ⓔDidn't you say you were planning to put flying ghost stickers under the window? Did you change your mind?
M: ⓕI did. I think the bat sticker looks better under the window.
W: Good choice. I prefer the bat, too. What's ⓖthat empty basket on the table for? Is it for trick-or-treating?
M: Right. We can use it when trick-or-treaters visit our house on Halloween.
W: That's a great plan. You did a terrific job decorating the room. (terrific: 아주 좋은, 멋진)

해석

남: 여보, 핼러윈 거실 장식을 마쳤어요. 이리 와서 한 번 볼래요?
여: 그래요. [잠시 후] ⓐ바닥에 있는 카펫은 당신이 지난주에 주문한 건가요?
남: 네. 귀여워 보여서 ⓑ둥근 것으로 골랐어요. 어떻게 생각해요?
여: 그곳에 정말 좋아 보여요. ⓒ피아노 위 벽에 한 거미줄 장식도 아주 마음에 들어요.
남: 고마워요. 핼러윈 분위기를 만드는 데 도움이 될 것 같았어요.
여: 분명 그렇네요. [잠시 후] 오! ⓓ책장 위에 조각된 호박 두 개가 아주 멋져요.
남: 완전히 그렇죠. 호박에 판 얼굴이 훌륭해 보이죠.
여: ⓔ창문 아래에 날아다니는 유령 스티커를 붙일 계획이라고 말하지 않았나요? 마음이 바뀐 거예요?
남: ⓕ그래요. 창문 아래에는 박쥐 스티커가 더 나아 보일 것 같아서요.
여: 좋은 선택이에요. 나도 박쥐가 더 좋아요. ⓖ탁자 위에 저 빈 바구니는 뭘 위한 거예요? 간식을 위한 건가요?
남: 맞아요. 핼러윈에 사람들이 간식을 받으러 우리 집을 방문할 때 사용하면 돼요.
여: 훌륭한 계획이에요. 방 장식 일을 멋지게 해냈네요.

문제 풀이

여자는 ⓖ탁자 위에 빈 바구니라고 말했다. 창문 아래에 날아다니는 유령 스티커 대신 박쥐 스티커를 선택했다는 내용을 놓쳐서는 안 된다.

5. ② | 할 일

선택지 선택비율	① 3%	② 90%	③ 1%	④ 1%	⑤ 2%

[Cell phone rings.]
W: Hello, Brian. Are you coming?
M: Yes, I'm on my way. Are you at the movie theater? (on one's way: ~하는 중에)
W: Yeah, I'm waiting for you. Where are you?
M: I've just arrived at Lincoln Square Station.
W: Don't rush. We still have 20 minutes before the movie starts. (rush: 서두르다)
M: Okay. I'll meet you in front of the box office. (box office: 매표소)
W: You bought tickets in advance on the website, didn't you? (in advance: 미리)
M: I did, but I have to get the tickets from the machine.
W: I see. You can use the one in the lobby.
M: Okay. I will. ⓐWhy don't we get some drinks?
W: Sure. ⓑI'll buy some at the snack bar. (snack bar: 스낵바, 간이식당)
M: Thanks. I'm almost there.

해석

[휴대전화가 울린다.]
여: 안녕, Brian. 너 오고 있니?
남: 응, 가는 길이야. 너는 영화관에 있니?
여: 응, 너를 기다리는 중이야. 너 어디야?
남: Lincoln Square 역에 막 도착했어.
여: 서두르지 마. 우리는 영화 시작하기 전까지 아직 20분 있어.
남: 알겠어. 매표소 앞에서 만나.
여: 너 미리 웹사이트에서 표를 샀지, 그렇지 않니?
남: 샀어, 하지만 기계에서 표를 받아야 해.
여: 알겠어. 너는 로비에 있는 것을 사용하면 돼.
남: 응. 그럴게. ⓐ우리 음료를 좀 사는 것이 어때?
여: 좋아. ⓑ내가 스낵바에서 좀 살게.
남: 고마워. 나 거의 다 왔어.

문제 풀이

남자가 ⓐ음료를 사는 것이 어떻겠냐고 제안하자 여자가 ⓑ스낵바에서 사겠다고 했다.

6. ④ | 금액

선택지 선택비율	① 3%	② 11%	③ 4%	④ 80%	⑤ 1%

M: Welcome to Sky Cable Car. How may I help you?
W: Hi. I want to buy tickets. I see two types of cable cars. What's the difference between the Regular and the Crystal Cable Car?
M: The Crystal Cable Car has a glass floor, so you can see below you. (floor: 바닥, below: 아래에)
W: That must be thrilling! How much is it for an adult? (thrilling: 아주 신나는, 짜릿한)
M: ⓐAn adult ticket is $20.
W: Is that round-trip? (round-trip: 왕복의)
M: No, this is a one-way ticket. ⓑYou need to pay an additional $5 each for round-trip tickets. (additional: 추가의)
W: Then I'll buy round-trip tickets for two adults.
M: So ⓒround-trip Crystal Cable Car tickets for two adults, right?
W: Yes, and I have a discount coupon for local residents. Can I use it? (residents: 주민)
M: Let me take a look. *[Pause]* Yes. ⓓYou can get a $5 discount off the total.
W: Very good. Here's my credit card.

해석

남: Sky 케이블카에 오신 것을 환영합니다. 어떻게 도와드릴까요?
여: 안녕하세요. 표를 사고 싶은데요. 두 종류의 케이블카가 보여요. 일반 케이블카와 크리스털 케이블카의 차이점은 무엇인가요?
남: 크리스털 케이블카는 유리 바닥이라서, 아래를 볼 수 있어요.
여: 짜릿하겠네요! 성인은 얼마예요?
남: ⓐ성인 표는 20달러입니다.
여: 왕복인가요?
남: 아니요, 이건 편도표입니다. ⓑ왕복표는 각각 추가 5달러를 내셔야 해요.

여: 그럼 성인 2명 왕복표를 살게요.
남: 그럼 ⓒ성인 2명 크리스털 케이블카 왕복표인 거죠, 그렇죠?
여: 네, 그리고 지역 주민들을 위한 할인 쿠폰이 있어요. 쓸 수 있나요?
남: 제가 한번 볼게요. [잠시 후] 네. ⓓ총액에서 5달러를 할인받으실 수 있어요.
여: 아주 좋아요. 여기 제 신용카드입니다.

문제 풀이

ⓐⓑⓒ크리스털 케이블카 성인 왕복표 2장(25달러x2)을 구입하려고 하는데, ⓓ총액에서 5달러를 할인 받을 수 있는 쿠폰이 있으므로, 여자가 지불할 금액은 45달러이다.

7. ② | 이유

선택지 선택비율	① 1%	② 96%	③ 1%	④ 1%	⑤ 1%

M: Sarah, have you heard about the special lecture at the community center this Saturday?
W: Yeah, Brian. It's a lecture on how to design (설계하다) effective (효과적인) presentation (발표) materials (재료, 자료), right?
M: Exactly! It'll help you create impressive (인상적인) presentations. Do you want to sign up for (~을 신청하다) it with me?
W: I'd love to, but I can't attend (참석하다).
M: Oh. Is it because you have a part-time job on weekends?
W: No. I don't work on weekends anymore.
M: Hmm. Then, do you have to work on your physics (물리(학)) assignment (과제)?
W: I already finished it. Actually, I'm participating in (participate in: ~에 참가하다) a volleyball match (경기, 시합).
M: Really? You told me that you wouldn't play this time, didn't you?
W: I'm filling in for (~을 대신하다) Judy. She injured (부상을 입히다) her knee (무릎) last week.
M: I see. Good luck!

해석

남: Sarah, 이번 토요일에 주민 센터에서 열리는 특강에 대해 들었어?
여: 응, Brian. 효과적인 발표 자료를 설계하는 방법에 관한 강연 말이지?
남: 맞아! 네가 인상적인 발표를 만드는 데 도움이 될 거야. 나랑 같이 신청할래?
여: 정말 가고 싶지만, 난 참석할 수 없어.
남: 아. 주말마다 아르바이트가 있어서?
여: 아니. 이제 주말에는 일하지 않아.
남: 흠. 그러면 물리 과제를 해야 하는 거야?
여: 그건 이미 끝냈어. 사실은, 배구 경기에 참가해.
남: 정말? 너 이번에는 경기를 안 할 거라고 했잖아, 그렇지 않니?
여: Judy를 대신하는 거야. 그녀가 지난주에 무릎을 부상당했거든.
남: 그렇구나. 잘해!

문제 풀이

여자는 무릎을 다친 Judy를 대신해서 배구 경기에 참가해야 해서 특강에 참석할 수 없다고 했다.

8. ③ | 언급

선택지 선택비율	① 2%	② 1%	③ 76%	④ 1%	⑤ 19%

W: Honey, I picked up a flyer (전단지) about the Noodle Cooking Contest.
M: What is it about?
W: It's a competition to cook the most creative (창의적인) dish using noodles.
M: Sounds interesting. Who can participate?
W: ⓐAny city resident can participate. Why don't you give it a try?
M: Let me take a look at the flyer. I should check the date first.
W: Here. ⓑIt's on the 20th of June. Are you free then?
M: Luckily, I don't have any plans that day. Maybe I can apply for (~에 지원하다) the contest.
W: You should! ⓒThe winner will receive $500.
M: Great! It says ⓓI have to send a recipe by email to apply for the contest. Any suggestions (제안)?
W: Well, do you remember the cold noodle salad you made for my birthday? It was so good. You should use that recipe.
M: That's a great idea. I'll do it.

해석

여: 여보, 내가 면 요리 대회에 관한 전단지를 가져왔어요.
남: 그게 어떤 건가요?
여: 면을 사용해서 가장 창의적인 요리를 만드는 대회예요.
남: 재미있겠네요. 누가 참가할 수 있나요?
여: ⓐ시 거주자라면 누구나 참가할 수 있어요. 당신이 한번 도전해보는 게 어때요?
남: 전단지 좀 볼게요. 먼저 날짜를 확인해야겠어요.
여: 여기 있어요. ⓑ6월 20일에 열려요. 그날 시간 괜찮아요?
남: 다행히도 그날은 아무 계획이 없어요. 아마 대회에 지원할 수 있겠어요.
여: 그렇게 해요! ⓒ우승자는 500달러를 받을 거예요.
남: 좋아요! ⓓ대회에 지원하려면 이메일로 레시피를 보내야 한다고 해요. 추천해 줄만한 거 있어요?
여: 음, 당신이 내 생일에 만들어준 냉국수 샐러드 기억나요? 정말 맛있었거든요. 그 레시피를 사용하는 게 좋겠어요.
남: 좋은 생각이에요. 그렇게 할게요.

문제 풀이

ⓐ참가 대상, ⓑ대회 날짜, ⓒ우승 상금, ⓓ지원 방법은 언급되었으나, 대회 장소는 언급되지 않았다.

9. ④ | 내용 일치

선택지 선택비율	① 5%	② 5%	③ 7%	④ 78%	⑤ 2%

M: Hello, listeners and viewers! Are you tired of only getting a few television channels? Then it's time to switch to (전환하다, 바꾸다) ABC Cable Network. ⓐWith 150 channels, ABC Network is one of the leading (선두의) cable providers (제공자) in the country. For a small monthly service fee, ⓑyou can enjoy a wide variety of (매우 다양한) entertainment programs, local and international news, and a good selection of movies. ⓒThis year, we were recognized (인정하다) as the most watched cable network. To celebrate (기념하다, 축하하다) this achievement (성취, 달성), ⓓnew customers can have a one-month free trial ((특히 최종 결정을 내리기 전의) 시험, 실험) for our network channels, excluding (~을 제외하고) movie channels. ⓔIf you want more specific information on our service plans, visit our website at www.ABCNet.co.ca.

해석

남: 안녕하세요, 청취자 그리고 시청자 여러분! 적은 텔레비전 채널만 보시게 되어 싫증이 나시나요? 그러면 ABC Cable Network로 바꾸실 시간입니다. ⓐ150개의 채널을 가진 ABC Network는 우리나라 선두의 케이블 방송 제공 업체 중 하나입니다. 적은 월 서비스 요금으로, ⓑ여러분은 매우 다양한 연예 프로그램, 지역 및 국제 뉴스, 그리고 좋은 영화들을 즐길 수 있습니다. ⓒ올해, 저희는 가장 많은 사람들이 시청한 케이블 방송사로 인정받았습니다. 이러한 성취를 기념하기 위해, ⓓ신규 고객들은 영화 채널들을 제외한 저희 방송 채널들을 한 달간 무료로 체험하실 수 있습니다. ⓔ저희 서비스 계획에 대한 더 구체적인 정보를 원하시면, 저희 웹 사이트인 www.ABCNet.co.ca를 방문해 주세요.

문제 풀이

ⓓ신규 고객은 영화 채널을 제외한 방송 채널들을 무료로 한 달간 볼 수 있다고 했다.

10. ④ | 도표

선택지 선택비율	① 2%	② 3%	③ 3%	④ 89%	⑤ 1%

M: Hey, Tiffany. What are you doing?
W: I'm thinking of buying some wireless earbuds. Do you want to help
(초소형) 이어폰
me choose from these five options?
M: Sure. How much can you spend?
W: ⓐI don't want to spend more than 200 dollars.
M: These models are within your budget.
예산
W: What do you think would be a good play time from a single charge?
충전
M: Hmm.... I think ⓑit should be longer than six hours so you don't have to charge them very often.
충전하다
W: That's a good point. I'll cross out this one. What is noise canceling?
(선을 그어) 지우다
M: It reduces unwanted sound using active noise control.
줄이다 고성능의
W: Does that make a big difference?
M: It can really improve the sound quality of what you listen to.
향상시키다 음질
W: I see. Then, ⓒI'll go with ones with noise canceling.
M: Good choice. There are only two models left. Which color do you prefer?
선호하다
W: ⓓI don't want white ones because they'll get dirty too easily. So, I'll buy this model.

해석

남: 얘, Tiffany. 너 뭐 하고 있니?
여: 무선 이어폰을 살까 생각 중이야. 내가 이 다섯 가지 선택 사항 중에서 고르는 걸 도와줄래?
남: 물론이지. 얼마 정도 쓸 수 있는데?
여: ⓐ난 200달러 이상은 쓰고 싶지 않아.
남: 이 모델들은 네 예산 안에 있어.
여: 한 번의 충전으로 얼마간의 재생 시간이 좋을 것 같아?
남: 음…. 내 생각에는 ⓑ6시간 이상은 되어야 네가 너무 자주 충전을 안 해도 될 것 같아.
여: 좋은 지적이야. 이건 지울게. 소음 제거가 뭐야?
남: 그건 고성능의 소음 제어를 사용해서 원치 않는 소리를 줄여 줘.
여: 그게 큰 차이를 만들까?
남: 그건 네가 듣는 것의 음질을 매우 향상시킬 수 있어.
여: 그렇구나. 그럼, ⓒ소음 제거가 있는 것으로 할게.
남: 좋은 선택이야. 두 모델밖에 안 남았네. 너는 어떤 색을 선호하니?
여: 너무 쉽게 더러워질 거라 ⓓ난 흰색은 원하지 않아. 그래서 난 이 모델을 살 거야.

문제 풀이

여자는 ⓐ200달러가 넘지 않고, ⓑ한 번 충전해서 6시간 이상 사용할 수 있으며, ⓒ소음 제거 기능이 있는, ⓓ흰색이 아닌 다른 색상의 무선 이어폰을 사기로 했다.

11. ③ | 짧은 대화 응답

선택지 선택비율	① 6%	② 5%	③ 79%	④ 6%	⑤ 2%

M: Good afternoon. ⓐI'd like to donate these old clothes to this charity.
기부하다 자선 단체
W: Thank you. ⓑAre they all in good condition?
상태
M: Yes, but ⓒthe colors of some shirts have changed a bit.
W: Let me check if we can accept them.

해석

남: 안녕하세요. ⓐ이 헌 옷들을 이 자선 단체에 기부하고 싶습니다.
여: 감사합니다. ⓑ모두 상태가 좋은가요?
남: 네, 하지만 ⓒ몇몇 셔츠의 색이 조금 변했어요.
여: 저희가 그것들을 받을 수 있는지 살펴볼게요.

문제 풀이

여자가 ⓐ옷을 기부하고 싶다는 남자에게 ⓑ옷의 상태가 좋은지 물었는데 남자가 ⓒ몇몇 셔츠의 색이 변했다고 대답했으므로, 그 옷들을 받을 수 있는지 살펴보겠다는 내용의 ③이 여자의 응답으로 가장 적절하다.
① 저는 더 이상 기부할 옷이 없어요.
② 오늘 오후에 그것들을 찾아가시면 됩니다.
④ 흰색과 색 있는 것들을 분리하는 것을 잊었어요.
⑤ 환불을 받으시려면 영수증을 가져와 주세요.

12. ② | 짧은 대화 응답

선택지 선택비율	① 6%	② 80%	③ 3%	④ 4%	⑤ 6%

W: ⓐI can't find my science textbook anywhere! I really need it now for my science project.
M: That sounds frustrating. Maybe you left it in your desk drawer or in
실망하게[답답하게] 하는 서랍
your school locker.
사물함
W: I already checked both places, but I couldn't find it. ⓑWhat should I do?
M: You can borrow an extra copy from our school library.

해석

여: ⓐ내 과학 교과서를 어디에서도 못 찾겠어! 과학 프로젝트 때문에 지금 꼭 필요한데.
남: 답답하겠다. 아마 네 책상 서랍이나 학교 사물함에 그걸 두고 왔을 거야.
여: 두 곳 모두 이미 확인했는데, 못 찾았어. ⓑ어떻게 해야 할까?
남: 우리 학교 도서관에서 여분의 책을 빌릴 수 있어.

문제 풀이

여자가 ⓐ교과서를 잃어버렸다고 말하며 ⓑ어떻게 하면 좋을지 조언을 구하고 있으므로, 학교 도서관에서 빌릴 수 있다고 해결책을 제시하는 내용의 ②가 남자의 응답으로 가장 적절하다.
① 네 사물함 열쇠를 잃어버리지 않도록 조심해야 해.
③ 네 책을 중고 서점에 팔지 말았어야 했어.
④ 네 과학 교과서에 필기하는 건 허용돼.
⑤ 네가 다른 프로젝트 주제를 고를 수도 있었어.

13. ① | 긴 대화 응답

선택지 선택비율	① 73%	② 13%	③ 3%	④ 8%	⑤ 2%

M: Hello, is there anything I can do for you?
W: ⓐMy umbrella is missing. I thought I might have left it in the
없어진
restroom, but when I checked, it wasn't there.
화장실
M: Which restroom did you use?
W: The one on the third floor.
M: What does your umbrella look like? Could you describe it?
묘사하다, 말로 설명하다
W: It's yellow and it has a wooden handle. There's a big picture of
나무로 된 손잡이
a flower on it.
M: Okay, I'll check if it's in the Lost and Found box right now... *[Pause]* Oh! ⓑWe have an umbrella that looks like yours. Is this it?

W: Wow, that's mine!
M: Wait. ⓒHere's a note that says a lady found it and brought it to us.
메모, 쪽지
W: How kind of her! I was worried that I wouldn't find it.

해석

남: 안녕하세요, 제가 도와드릴 일이 있나요?
여: ⓐ제 우산이 없어졌어요. 화장실에 두고 온 게 아닐까 생각했는데, 확인해보니 우산이 거기에 없었어요.
남: 어느 화장실을 이용하셨나요?
여: 3층에 있는 거요.
남: 우산이 어떻게 생겼나요? 설명해 주시겠어요?
여: 노란색이고 나무로 된 손잡이가 있어요. 큰 꽃 그림이 그려져 있고요.
남: 네, 지금 분실물 보관함에 있는지 확인해 보겠습니다… [잠시 후] 아! ⓑ선생님 우산처럼 생긴 우산이 있네요. 이건가요?
여: 와, 제 거예요!
남: 잠시만요. ⓒ여기 어떤 여성분께서 그걸 발견해서 저희에게 가져다주셨다고 쓰여 있는 쪽지가 있네요.
여: 정말 친절한 분이시네요! 못 찾을까 봐 걱정했거든요.

문제 풀이

남자가 ⓑ분실물 보관소에서 여자에게 ⓐ잃어버린 우산을 찾아주며 ⓒ어떤 사람이 우산을 발견해서 가져다주었다는 내용의 쪽지가 있다고 했으므로, 우산을 가져다준 사람에게 고마움을 표하며 우산을 못 찾을까 봐 걱정했다고 말하는 ①이 응답으로 가장 적절하다.
② 그럼, 그녀에게 당신 잘못이 아니라 제 잘못이라고 말씀드릴게요.
③ 비가 올 때 다시 들러 주시겠어요?
④ 당신의 새 우산을 빌려주셔서 감사합니다.
⑤ 그녀에게 다음에 무엇을 하고 싶은지 물어보는 게 어때요?

14. ② | 긴 대화 응답

선택지 선택비율	① 2%	② 92%	③ 2%	④ 2%	⑤ 2%

M: Hello, welcome to Glow Cosmetics Shop. How can I help you?
화장품
W: Hi, I'm looking for sunscreen.
자외선차단제
M: Certainly. Is it for you, or someone else?
W: It's for my husband. He asked me to buy one for him.
M: Okay, does your husband spend much time outdoors, playing sports, or working outside?
야외에서
W: No, not really. He works in an office and usually stays at home after work.
M: In that case, he might not need one with strong sun protection. A mild one is probably best for him.
보호, 차단 / 순한
W: Okay. I'll go with that.
M: ⓐWe have two types of sunscreen, spray and cream type. Which one would he prefer?
W: ⓑI'm not sure but I guess he is used to cream type.
be used to: ~에 익숙하다
M: I see. Then this one is a perfect choice for him.

해석

남: 안녕하세요, Glow 화장품 가게에 오신 것을 환영합니다. 어떻게 도와드릴까요?
여: 안녕하세요, 자외선차단제를 찾고 있어요.
남: 알겠습니다. 본인이 쓰실 건가요, 아니면 다른 분을 위한 건가요?
여: 제 남편을 위한 거예요. 남편이 저에게 하나 사달라고 했거든요.
남: 그러시군요, 남편분이 운동을 하시거나 밖에서 일하셔서 야외에서 보내시는 시간이 많은가요?
여: 아니요, 그렇진 않아요. 사무실에서 일하고 퇴근 후에는 주로 집에 있어요.
남: 그렇다면 강한 자외선 차단이 있는 게 필요하신 건 아니겠네요. 아마도 남편분에게는 순한 제품이 가장 좋을 것 같습니다.
여: 네. 그걸로 할게요.
남: ⓐ저희는 스프레이형과 크림형 두 가지 타입의 자외선차단제가 있어요. 남편분이 어느 것을 선호하실까요?
여: ⓑ확실히는 모르겠지만 남편은 크림형에 익숙한 것 같아요.
남: 알겠습니다. 그럼 이 제품이 남편분에게 딱 맞는 선택이네요.

문제 풀이

남자가 ⓐ스프레이형과 크림형 두 가지 자외선차단제 중에서 어떤 것이 남편에게 더 좋을지 묻자 여자가 ⓑ크림형이 더 좋겠다고 대답했으므로, 그에 알맞은 제품을 추천하는 ②가 남자의 응답으로 가장 적절하다.
① 걱정하지 마세요. 신용카드로 지불하시면 됩니다.
③ 괜찮을 거예요. 남편분이 들러서 가져가시면 됩니다.
④ 정말요? 외출 전에 자외선차단제를 바르시는 게 좋아요.
⑤ 맞아요. 강력한 자외선 차단이 되는 제품이 더 좋아요.

15. ⑤ | 상황에 적절한 말

선택지 선택비율	① 2%	② 7%	③ 2%	④ 2%	⑤ 85%

W: Brian and Jennifer are good friends who go to the gym together almost every day. When they're working out, they drink a lot of water. Brian always brings his own tumbler with him while Jennifer always buys a bottle of water at the convenience store before going to the gym. Brian thinks that buying a bottle of water every day is not only a waste of money but is also harmful to the environment. One day at the gym, ⓐJennifer makes a comment about how much she likes Brian's tumbler. ⓑBrian thinks this is a good chance to suggest that she bring her own reusable bottle to the gym. In this situation, what would Brian most likely say to Jennifer?
운동하다 / 편의점 / 해로운 / 환경 / 논평하다, 발언하다 / 재사용할 수 있는
Brian: Why don't you get a tumbler and bring it to the gym?

해석

여: Brian과 Jennifer는 거의 매일 체육관에 같이 가는 좋은 친구다. 그들은 운동할 때 물을 많이 마신다. Brian은 항상 자신의 텀블러를 가지고 다니는 반면 Jennifer는 체육관에 가기 전에 항상 편의점에서 물 한 병을 산다. Brian은 매일 물 한 병을 사는 것은 돈 낭비일 뿐만 아니라 환경에 해롭다고 생각한다. 어느 날 체육관에서, ⓐJennifer는 Brian의 텀블러가 얼마나 마음에 드는지에 대해 말한다. ⓑBrian은 이것이 그녀에게 체육관에 재사용이 가능한 그녀 자신의 병을 가지고 오라고 제안할 좋은 기회라고 생각한다. 이 상황에서, Brian은 Jennifer에게 뭐라고 말하겠는가?
Brian: 텀블러를 하나 사서 체육관에 그걸 가져오는 것이 어때?

문제 풀이

ⓐJennifer가 Brian의 텀블러가 마음에 든다고 말하자 Brian은 ⓑJennifer에게 체육관에 재사용 가능한 병을 가지고 오라고 제안할 좋은 기회라 생각했으므로, Brian이 할 말로는 ⑤가 가장 적절하다.
① 우리는 더 자주 같이 운동해야 해.
② 그렇게 많은 텀블러를 사는 데 돈을 낭비하지 마.
③ 우리는 운동하는 동안 물을 더 많이 마시는 것이 좋겠어.
④ 체육관 근처 편의점은 언제 문을 닫니?

16~17. | 세트 문항

16. ③ 17. ④

선택지 선택비율	① 3%	② 1%	③ 89%	④ 6%	⑤ 1%
	① 2%	② 1%	③ 2%	④ 95%	⑤ 1%

M: Good afternoon, students. ⓐToday we are going to talk about different national flags. There are some colors commonly used in
국기 / 일반적으로

national flags. The most common color is ⓑred, which makes up (~을 차지하다) about 30 percent of all colors used in national flags. Usually red means life, courage(용기), and revolution(혁명). For example, the red stripes(줄무늬) of the United State's national flag symbolize(상징하다) the struggle(노력, 분투) for independence(독립). The next is ⓒblue, with about a 20 percent share(몫). The color often symbolizes the natural(자연의) element(요소) of water or sky. For example, the blue in Greece's national flag means the seas surrounding(둘러싸다) the country. The next two most common(흔한) colors are ⓓwhite and ⓔgreen. In some countries' flags, white means peace(평화) and honesty(정직), such as in the United Kingdom's flag. Green is often related to(be related to: ~와 관계가 있다) nature, such as grasslands(풀밭, 초원) and forests(삼림). Can you guess what the green in Brazil's national flag means? Of course, it's the Amazon Rainforest(\(열대\)우림). Now, let's look at the shapes of national flags.

해석

남: 안녕하세요, 학생 여러분. ⓐ오늘 우리는 여러 국기에 대해 이야기할 겁니다. 국기에 일반적으로 사용되는 몇몇 색이 있답니다. 가장 일반적인 색은 ⓑ빨간색인데요, 국기에 사용되는 전체 색 중 30퍼센트 정도를 차지합니다. 보통 빨간색은 생명, 용기, 혁명을 의미하지요. 예를 들어, 미국 국기의 빨간 줄무늬는 독립을 위한 노력을 상징합니다. 다음은 ⓒ파란색인데요, 20퍼센트의 몫이 있답니다. 이 색은 흔히 물이나 하늘의 자연의 요소를 상징합니다. 예를 들어, 그리스 국기의 파란색은 나라를 둘러싸고 있는 바다를 의미합니다. 다음으로 가장 흔한 색 두 가지는 ⓓ흰색과 ⓔ초록색입니다. 영국 국기에서처럼 어떤 나라의 국기에서, 흰색은 평화와 정직을 의미합니다. 초록색은 흔히 초원과 삼림과 같은 자연과 관계가 있습니다. 브라질 국기의 초록색이 뭘 의미하는지 추측해볼 수 있겠어요? 물론, 그건 아마존 열대우림이지요. 이제, 국기의 모양을 봅시다.

문제 풀이

16. ⓐ국기에 대해 이야기할 거라며, 국기에 일반적으로 사용되는 몇 가지 색이 있다고 말하고 있으므로, 남자가 하는 말의 주제로는 ③ '국기의 일반적인 색과 그 의미'가 가장 적절하다.
① 국기가 디자인과 색이 단순한 이유
② 국가 정체성에 영향을 미치는 지리학적 특성
④ 국기에서 가장 빈번히 사용되는 상징
⑤ 문화마다 선호하는 색에 있어서의 차이
17. ⓑ빨간색, ⓒ파란색, ⓓ흰색, ⓔ초록색은 언급되었지만, 검은색(black)은 언급되지 않았다.

[코드 공략하기]

제1회 고급 모의고사

1	①	2	②	3	④	4	④	5	①	6	④
7	⑤	8	④	9	③	10	④	11	②	12	①
13	⑤	14	③	15	⑤	16	②	17	⑤		

1. ① ㅣ 목적

선택지 선택비율	① 96%	② 0%	③ 1%	④ 0%	⑤ 0%

M: Attention, Whittenberg Dragons and Westbrook Whales fans. This is an announcement about today's game at Estana Stadium.
공고, 공지
Today's baseball game was supposed to begin in twenty minutes.
be supposed to-v: ~하기로 되어 있다
ⓐBut it started raining one hour ago, and has not stopped. According to the forecast, the weather will only get worse. Because of this, we have decided to cancel today's game.
(날씨의) 예보
Tickets you purchased for today's event will be fully refunded. And information about the make-up game will be updated on our website soon.
구입하다 환불하다
ⓑOnce again, today's game has been canceled due to heavy rain. Thank you for visiting our stadium, and we hope to see you again at our next game.

해석

남: Whittenberg Dragons와 Westbrook Whales 팬 여러분께 알립니다. Estana 경기장에서 열리는 오늘 경기에 대한 공지입니다. 오늘 야구 경기는 20분 후에 시작하기로 되어 있었습니다. ⓐ하지만 한 시간 전에 비가 내리기 시작했고 멈추지 않고 있습니다. 예보에 따르면 날씨가 더 나빠질 뿐이라고 합니다. 이 때문에 저희는 오늘 경기를 취소하기로 결정했습니다. 오늘 경기를 위해 여러분이 구입한 표는 전액 환불될 것입니다. 그리고 재경기에 대한 정보는 곧 저희 웹사이트에서 알려드릴 것입니다. ⓑ다시 한 번 말씀드리지만 오늘 경기는 폭우로 인해 취소되었습니다. 저희 경기장을 방문해 주셔서 감사드리며 다음 경기에서 다시 뵙기를 바랍니다.

문제 풀이

ⓐⓑ비가 계속 내리고 있고 날씨가 더욱 안 좋아질 것이므로 경기를 취소하기로 결정했다고 알리고 있다.

2. ② ㅣ 의견

선택지 선택비율	① 1%	② 99%	③ 0%	④ 0%	⑤ 0%

M: Honey, do you want some apples with breakfast?
W: Sounds great. Can you save the apple peels for me?
남겨 두다 껍질
M: Why? What do you want them for?
W: I'm going to use them to make a face pack. ⓐApple peels are effective for improving skin condition.
효과적인
M: Where did you hear about that?
W: I recently read an article about their benefits for our skin.
이득, 이로움
M: Interesting. What's in them?
W: It said apple peels are rich in vitamins and minerals, so they moisturize our skin and enhance skin glow.
~이 풍부한
촉촉하게 하다, 수분을 제공하다 높이다, 강화하다 (빰의) 홍조, (피부의) 윤기
M: That's good to know.
W: Also, they remove oil from our skin and have a cooling effect.
냉각 효과
M: Wow! Then I shouldn't throw them away.
~을 버리다
W: Right. ⓑApple peels can help improve our skin condition.
M: I see. I'll save them for you.

해석

남: 여보, 아침으로 사과 좀 먹을래요?
여: 좋아요. 사과 껍질 좀 내게 남겨 줄래요?
남: 왜요? 뭐에 필요한데요?
여: 얼굴 팩을 만드는 데 그것들을 사용할 거예요. ⓐ사과 껍질은 피부 상태를 개선하는 데 효과적이거든요.
남: 어디서 그것에 관해 들었어요?
여: 그것이 피부에 이로운 점에 관한 기사를 최근에 읽었어요.
남: 흥미롭군요. 그 안에 뭐가 있죠?
여: 사과 껍질은 비타민과 미네랄이 풍부해서, 피부에 수분을 공급하고 피부 윤기를 강화시킨다고 했어요.
남: 알게 돼서 좋네요.
여: 또 그것은 피부에서 유분을 제거하고 냉각 효과가 있어요.
남: 와! 그럼 그걸 버리면 안 되겠네요.
여: 맞아요. ⓑ사과 껍질은 우리의 피부 상태를 개선하는 데 도움을 줄 수 있어요.
남: 알겠어요. 당신을 위해 남겨 둘게요.

문제 풀이

여자가 남자에게 ⓐⓑ사과 껍질이 피부 상태 개선에 도움이 된다고 말하고 있다.

3. ④ ㅣ 요지

선택지 선택비율	① 0%	② 6%	③ 4%	④ 89%	⑤ 0%

W: Hello, listeners. This is Dr. Graham's One-minute Health Tips. Getting a good night's sleep is important for your health. But recently, more and more people are experiencing trouble falling asleep.
최근에 잠들다
If that's your case, wearing an eye mask for sleeping can help you fall asleep.
안대
If your room doesn't get dark enough, it'll be difficult to fall asleep. This is because light interferes with the release of the hormone that makes you sleepy.
~을 방해하다 방출 호르몬
An eye mask can block the light, which makes it easier for you to fall asleep.
차단하다
Why not try one tonight? I'll be back with more tips next time!

해석

여: 안녕하세요, 청취자 여러분. 의사 Graham의 1분 건강 팁입니다. 숙면을 취하는 것은 건강에 중요합니다. 하지만 최근 들어 점점 더 많은 사람들이 잠드는 데 문제를 겪고 있습니다. 만약 여러분이 이런 경우라면, 수면 안대를 착용하는 것이 여러분이 잠드는 데 도움이 될 수 있습니다. 만약 여러분의 방이 충분히 어두워지지 않으면, 잠드는 것이 어려울 것입니다. 이는 빛이 여러분을 졸리게 만드는 호르몬의 분비를 방해하기 때문입니다. 안대는 빛을 차단할 수 있기 때문에, 여러분이 잠드는 것을 더 쉽게 만듭니다. 오늘 밤 한번 시도해 보는 것은 어떨까요? 다음 번에 더 많은 팁을 가지고 돌아오겠습니다!

문제 풀이

여자는 수면 안대를 착용하는 것이 잠드는 데 도움이 될 수 있다고 말하고 있다.

4. ④ ㅣ 그림 일치

선택지 선택비율	① 0%	② 0%	③ 0%	④ 98%	⑤ 0%

M: Wow, Ms. Peters! It looks like everything is ready for the exchange student welcoming ceremony.
교환학생 환영식

W: Almost, Mr. Smith. What do you think?
M: It looks great. There's ⓐa basket beside the stairs. What is it for?
W: We're going to put flowers in it for the exchange students.
M: That'll be nice. I like ⓑthe striped tablecloth on the table. It makes
줄무늬가 있는 식탁보
the table look fancy.
화려한
W: Yeah, I'm going to put water bottles there. What do you think about ⓒthe balloons next to the welcome banner?
M: They really brighten up the stage. Oh, look at ⓓthe bear on the flag.
밝히다
It's cute.
W: Yes. It's the symbol of the exchange students' school.
상징
M: I see. And you set up ⓔtwo microphones.
W: It's because there'll be two MCs.
M: Good idea. Everything looks perfect.

해석

남: 와, Peters 씨! 교환학생 환영식을 위한 모든 게 준비된 것 같아요.
여: 거의 다 됐어요, Smith 씨. 어떤 것 같아요?
남: 멋져 보여요. ⓐ계단 옆에 바구니가 있네요. 무엇에 쓰는 거죠?
여: 그 안에 교환학생들을 위한 꽃을 둘 거예요.
남: 그거 좋겠네요. ⓑ테이블 위 줄무늬 식탁보가 마음에 들어요. 그게 테이블을 화려하게 보이게 하거든요.
여: 네, 거기에 물병들을 놓을 거예요. ⓒ환영 현수막 옆에 있는 풍선들에 대해 어떻게 생각하세요?
남: 그것들은 정말 무대를 밝게 해줘요. 오, ⓓ깃발에 있는 곰을 보세요. 귀여워요.
여: 네. 교환학생들 학교의 상징이에요.
남: 그렇군요. 그리고 ⓔ마이크 두 개를 설치하셨네요.
여: 왜냐하면 MC가 두 명 있을 거라서요.
남: 좋은 생각이에요. 모든 것이 완벽해 보여요.

문제 풀이

ⓓ깃발에 있는 곰을 보라고 했으므로, 돌고래 그림이 그려진 ④는 대화 내용과 일치하지 않는다.

5. ① | 할 일

선택지 선택비율	① 87%	② 1%	③ 8%	④ 4%	⑤ 1%

M: Honey, I'm excited that we're opening our homemade-pie store tomorrow.
W: Me, too. Do you think everything's ready?
M: I do. But let's go over what we've done.
W: Good idea. I completed the product list for sale. Did you take photos
완성하다 제품
of the pies?
M: I took photos of the walnut, pumpkin, blueberry, and apple pies.
W: Perfect. What about uploading information onto social media?
올리다, 게시하다 정보
M: Don't worry. I advertised our pies on social media.
광고하다
W: I hope it brings in a lot of customers. I also prepared forks and
~을 유치하다
plates for customers on our opening day.
접시
M: One more thing, ⓐdon't forget to confirm the delivery of the
확인하다
ingredients for making more pies.
재료
W: ⓑRight. I'll do that this afternoon.
M: Wonderful. See, we're ready for tomorrow.

해석

남: 여보, 내일 우리가 홈메이드 파이 가게를 연다고 생각하니까 신이 나요.
여: 나도 그래요. 모든 게 준비된 것 같아요?
남: 그런 것 같아요. 그래도 우리가 한 일들을 한번 점검해 봅시다.
여: 좋아요. 나는 판매할 제품 목록을 완성했어요. 파이 사진은 찍었어요?
남: 호두파이, 호박파이, 블루베리파이, 그리고 애플파이 사진을 찍었어요.
여: 완벽하네요. 그럼 소셜 미디어에 정보 올리는 건요?
남: 걱정하지 마요. 우리 파이를 소셜 미디어에 광고했어요.
여: 그게 많은 손님을 끌어모으면 좋겠어요. 우리 오픈 날에 손님들이 사용할 포크와 접시도 준비했어요.
남: 한 가지 더, ⓐ파이를 더 만들 재료 배송 확인하는 것 잊지 마요.
여: ⓑ알겠어요. 그건 오늘 오후에 할게요.
남: 좋아요. 자, 우리 내일을 위한 준비가 됐네요.

문제 풀이

ⓐ파이 재료 배송 확인하는 것을 잊지 말라는 남자의 말에, 여자는 ⓑ오후에 하겠다고 했다.

6. ④ | 금액

선택지 선택비율	① 1%	② 1%	③ 4%	④ 93%	⑤ 1%

M: Welcome to Camoo Traditional Village. How can I help you?
전통의
W: Hi. I'd like to buy admission tickets for my family. Is there a discount
입장권
for senior citizens?
노인, 어르신
M: Yes. ⓐRegular tickets are $30 each, and senior tickets are $20 each for people over 65 years old.
W: Good. My parents are in their 70s. So ⓑI'll take two regular tickets and two senior tickets.
M: Great. Would you also like lunch tickets? We serve traditional local
지역의
food. ⓒIt's $25 per person.
W: I'd love that. Is the lunch ticket cheaper for senior citizens?
M: No. I'm sorry. It's the same price.
W: Ah, okay. ⓓI'll buy four lunch tickets as well.
역시, 또한
M: Alright. So you want two regular tickets and two senior tickets with four lunch tickets, right?
W: That's right. Here's my credit card.

해석

남: Camoo 전통 마을에 오신 것을 환영합니다. 무엇을 도와드릴까요?
여: 안녕하세요. 저희 가족을 위한 입장권을 사고 싶은데요. 노인 할인 있나요?
남: 네. ⓐ일반 입장권은 각 30달러이고, 65세 이상 어르신 입장권은 각 20달러예요.
여: 잘됐네요. 제 부모님은 70대이시거든요. 그러면 ⓑ일반 입장권 두 장과 노인 입장권 두 장 구매할게요.
남: 알겠습니다. 점심 식사권도 원하시나요? 저희는 전통 지역 음식을 제공합니다. ⓒ인당 25달러예요.
여: 그거 좋네요. 점심 식사권이 노인의 경우 더 저렴한가요?
남: 아니요. 유감이에요. 그건 동일한 가격이에요.
여: 아, 그렇군요. ⓓ점심 식사권도 네 장 구매할게요.
남: 알겠습니다. 일반 입장권 두 장과 노인 입장권 두 장, 그리고 점심 식사권 네 장 원하시는 거죠, 맞나요?
여: 맞아요. 여기 제 신용카드요.

문제 풀이

ⓐⓑ30달러짜리 일반 입장권 두 장, 20달러짜리 노인 입장권 두 장, ⓒⓓ25달러짜리 점심 식사권 네 장을 구매하므로, 여자가 지불할 금액은 200달러이다.

7. ⑤ | 이유

선택지 선택비율	① 0%	② 0%	③ 8%	④ 6%	⑤ 84%

W: Hi, Michael.

M: Hi, Sarah. Did you apply for the cooking contest?
~에 지원하다
W: I did. I've already finished developing a recipe.
개발하다
M: That's great. Actually, I gave up participating in it.
give up: ~을 포기하다 participate in: ~에 참가하다
W: Why? Is your arm still hurt?
M: No, it's fully healed.
치유하다, 낫게 하다
W: Is your recipe not ready yet?
M: I already created a unique recipe for the contest.
W: Then, what made you give up the contest?
M: You know I've planned to study abroad. The cooking school in Italy
외국에서 공부하다
just informed me that I've been accepted. The problem is I have to
통지하다 (기관 등에서) 받아들이다
leave before the contest begins.
W: I'm sorry you'll miss the contest. But it's good for you since you've always wanted to study in Italy.
M: I think so, too. I wish you luck in the contest.
W: Thanks. I'll do my best.

해석

여: 안녕, Michael.
남: 안녕, Sarah. 요리 대회에 지원했니?
여: 했어. 이미 조리법 개발을 끝냈어.
남: 잘됐구나. 사실 나는 거기 참가하는 걸 포기했어.
여: 왜? 아직도 팔이 아프니?
남: 아니, 팔은 완전히 나았어.
여: 조리법이 아직 준비되지 않았어?
남: 대회를 위한 독특한 조리법을 이미 만들었어.
여: 그럼 왜 대회를 포기한 거니?
남: 너도 알다시피, 내가 외국에서 공부할 계획을 해 왔잖아. 이탈리아에 있는 요리 학교에서 내가 합격했다고 지금 막 통지했어. 문제는 대회가 시작하기 전에 떠나야 한다는 거야.
여: 네가 대회를 놓치다니 유감이야. 하지만 넌 늘 이탈리아에서 공부하고 싶어 했으니 네게 좋은 일이지.
남: 나도 그렇게 생각해. 대회에서 행운이 있기를 바랄게.
여: 고마워. 최선을 다할게.

문제 풀이

요리 대회 시작 전에 이탈리아 유학을 떠나야 해서 요리 대회 참가를 포기했다고 했다.

8. ④ | 언급

선택지 선택비율	① 1%	② 0%	③ 1%	④ 97%	⑤ 0%

M: Honey, I'm looking at the Natural History Museum's website. The museum's going to hold the Winter Discovery Camp.
W: What's it about?
M: It says here that the theme is dinosaurs.
공룡
W: That sounds interesting. You know our son Peter loves dinosaurs.
M: He does. ⓐThe camp is for elementary school students, so it's
초등학교
perfect for him.
W: What activities will they do?
M: The camp offers fun, hands-on activities. For example, ⓑparticipants
제공하다 (말만 하지 않고) 직접 해 보는 참가자
will look for dinosaur bones hidden in sand and then put them
뼈 (부품을) 조립하다
together.
W: I'm sure Peter will love the camp. When is it?
M: ⓒIt'll be held from January 11 to 13.
W: That's good. It won't overlap with our family trip. And how much
겹치다
does it cost?
M: ⓓThe participation fee is $20.
W: That's not bad. I'll ask Peter if he wants to go.
M: Okay.

해석

남: 여보, 난 자연사 박물관 웹사이트를 보고 있어요. 박물관에서 Winter Discovery 캠프를 개최할 예정이에요.
여: 무엇에 관한 건가요?
남: 여기 주제가 공룡이라고 쓰여 있어요.
여: 재미있게 들리네요. 당신도 알다시피 우리 아들 Peter가 공룡을 좋아하잖아요.
남: 그렇죠. ⓐ그 캠프는 초등학생을 위한 것이라고 하니, 그에게 딱 알맞네요.
여: 어떤 활동들을 하게 되나요?
남: 캠프에서는 재미있고, 직접 해 보는 활동들을 제공해요. 예를 들면, ⓑ참가자들은 모래 속에 숨겨진 공룡 뼈를 찾은 다음 그것들을 조립하게 돼요.
여: 분명 Peter가 그 캠프를 좋아하겠네요. 언제인가요?
남: ⓒ1월 11일부터 13일까지 열릴 거예요.
여: 좋아요. 우리 가족 여행과 겹치지 않겠어요. 그리고 비용이 얼마나 드나요?
남: ⓓ참가비는 20달러예요.
여: 나쁘지 않네요. Peter에게 가고 싶은지 물어볼게요.
남: 알겠어요.

문제 풀이

Winter Discovery 캠프의 ⓐ참가 대상, ⓑ활동 내용, ⓒ기간, ⓓ참가비는 언급되었지만, 기념품은 언급되지 않았다.

9. ③ | 내용 일치

선택지 선택비율	① 1%	② 1%	③ 97%	④ 0%	⑤ 0%

W: Hello, listeners. I'm Carla Jones from the National Baking Association. I'm glad to announce that we're hosting the National
협회 알리다, 발표하다 개최하다
Baking Competition on December 20th. ⓐIt's an annual event
연례의
aimed to discover people with a talent and passion for baking.
목표하다 열정
ⓑThis year, the theme of the competition is "healthy desserts."
주제
We had the most applicants in the history of this competition, and
지원자
ⓒonly 10 participants will advance to the final round. The top three
~에 진출하다 결선
will win the grand prize of $10,000 each, and ⓓthe recipes of the winners will appear in our magazine. You can enjoy watching
나오다, 발간되다
the entire competition from home. ⓔIt'll be broadcast live on our
전체의 방송하다 생방송으로, 생중계로
website starting from 9 a.m. If you're a food lover, you won't want to miss watching this event.

해석

여: 안녕하세요, 청취자 여러분. 전국 제과 협회의 Carla Jones입니다. 12월 20일 전국 제과 대회를 개최하게 됨을 알리게 되어 기쁩니다. 이는 제과에 재능과 열정을 지닌 사람들을 발굴하는 것을 목표로 하는 ⓐ연례 행사입니다. ⓑ올해 대회 주제는 '건강한 디저트'입니다. 저희는 이 대회 역사상 가장 많은 지원자를 받았으며, ⓒ오직 10명의 참가자만 결선에 진출할 것입니다. 3위까지 각각 최우수상금 10,000달러를 받게 되며, ⓓ수상자들의 조리법은 저희 잡지에 실릴 것입니다. 여러분은 댁에서 전체 대회 시청을 즐기실 수 있습니다. 오전 9시부터 시작해서 ⓔ저희 웹 사이트에서 생중계될 것입니다. 음식을 사랑하는 분이라면, 이 행사를 보는 걸 놓치고 싶지 않을 겁니다.

문제 풀이

ⓒ참가자 10명만 결선에 진출할 것이라고 했다.

10. ④ | 도표

선택지 선택비율	① 0%	② 2%	③ 1%	④ 96%	⑤ 1%

M: Hi, Nicole. What are you doing?
W: Hi, Jack. I'm trying to buy a reusable straw set on the Internet. Do
재사용 가능한 빨대
you want to see?
M: Sure. *[Pause]* ⓐThese bamboo ones seem good. They're made
대나무
from natural materials.
천연 소재
W: That's true, but I'm worried they may not dry quickly.
M: Okay. Then ⓑlet's look at straws made from other materials. How much are you willing to spend on a set of straws?
be willing to-v: 기꺼이 ~하다
W: ⓒI don't want to spend more than $10.
M: That's reasonable. How about length?
적정한, 너무 비싸지 않은
W: To use with my tumbler, ⓓeight or nine inches should be perfect.
M: Then you're down to these two. ⓔA carrying case would be very
~밖에 남지 않다
useful when going out.
W: Good point. I'll take your recommendation and order this set now.
추천

해석

남: 안녕, Nicole. 뭐 하고 있니?
여: 안녕, Jack. 인터넷에서 재사용 빨대 세트를 사려고 하고 있어. 볼래?
남: 그래. [잠시 후] ⓐ이 대나무로 된 것 좋아 보여. 천연 소재로 만들어졌네.
여: 그렇긴 한데, 빨리 건조되지 않을지 몰라서 걱정돼.
남: 응. 그러면 ⓑ다른 소재로 만든 빨대를 보자. 빨대 세트에 얼마나 쓸 요량이니?
여: ⓒ10달러보다 더 쓰고 싶지 않아.
남: 적정하네. 길이는?
여: 내 텀블러와 쓰려면, ⓓ8인치나 9인치가 딱 좋을 거야.
남: 그러면 이 두 가지밖에 남지 않아. 외출할 때 ⓔ휴대 케이스가 무척 유용할 거야.
여: 좋은 지적이야. 네 추천을 받아서 지금 이 세트를 주문할래.

문제 풀이

여자는 ⓐⓑ대나무 아닌 다른 소재로 만들어졌으며, ⓒ10달러가 넘지 않으며, ⓓ8인치나 9인치 길이이며, ⓔ휴대 케이스가 있는 빨대 세트를 주문하기로 했다.

11. ② | 짧은 대화 응답

선택지 선택비율	① 1%	② 93%	③ 1%	④ 1%	⑤ 5%

M: Jane, have you ordered a cake for our tennis coach's farewell party
송별회
next week?
W: Yes, ⓐI ordered a walnut cake with pistachio nuts on top. I'll pick it
호두 피스타치오
up next Wednesday afternoon from the bakery.
M: Oh, no. ⓑI should have told you that he's allergic to all kinds of nuts.
알레르기가 있는
W: That's okay. I'll check if I can change the order.

해석

남: Jane, 다음 주에 있을 우리 테니스 코치님 송별회 케이크 주문했나요?
여: 네, ⓐ피스타치오를 위에 올린 호두 케이크를 주문했어요. 다음 주 수요일 오후에 제과점에서 찾아올 예정이에요.
남: 아, 이런. ⓑ코치님이 모든 종류의 견과류에 알레르기가 있다는 걸 제가 말했어야 했는데요.
여: 괜찮아요. 주문을 변경할 수 있는지 확인해 볼게요.

문제 풀이

여자가 ⓐ테니스 코치 송별회 케이크로 호두 케이크를 주문했는데 ⓑ코치가 견과류 알레르기가 있음을 남자가 여자에게 미처 이야기하지 못했다고 했으므로, 주문을 변경할 수 있는지 확인해 보겠다는 ②가 여자의 응답으로 가장 적절하다.
① 좋은 생각이에요! 그를 파티에 초대해요.
③ 믿기지 않아요! 우리가 드디어 테니스 경기에서 이겼어요.
④ 괜찮아요. 저는 견과류가 올라간 케이크는 별로 안 좋아해요.
⑤ 문제없어요. 알레르기 반응을 일으키는 음식은 먹지 않을게요.

12. ① | 짧은 대화 응답

선택지 선택비율	① 89%	② 4%	③ 1%	④ 2%	⑤ 4%

W: Excuse me, sir. I'm from the management office. ⓐYou cannot park
관리사무실
here because we're about to close off this section of the parking lot.
be about to-v: 막 ~할 참이다 부분, 구획 주차장
M: Why? What's going on here?
W: We're going to paint the walls in this section. ⓑIf there are cars parked here, we cannot start our work.
M: I see. Then I'll park somewhere else.

해석

여: 실례합니다, 선생님. 관리사무실에서 나왔습니다. ⓐ주차장의 이 구획을 막 폐쇄할 참이어서 이곳에 주차하실 수 없습니다.
남: 왜요? 여기 무슨 일 있나요?
여: 이 구획의 벽을 칠할 예정입니다. ⓑ여기 주차된 차가 있으면, 저희가 작업을 시작할 수가 없답니다.
남: 알겠습니다. 그러면 어딘가 다른 곳에 주차할게요.

문제 풀이

여자는 ⓐ주차장이 폐쇄 예정이어서 ⓑ남자의 주차를 저지하고 있다. 따라서, 다른 곳에 주차하겠다는 내용의 ①이 남자의 응답으로 가장 적절하다.
② 괜찮아요. 제가 당신의 차를 이쪽으로 가져올게요.
③ 고맙지만 괜찮아요. 제 차를 칠하고 싶지 않아요.
④ 신경 쓰지 마세요. 주차요금은 나중에 낼게요.
⑤ 알겠어요. 대신 다른 차를 선택할게요.

13. ⑤ | 긴 대화 응답

선택지 선택비율	① 1%	② 1%	③ 4%	④ 0%	⑤ 94%

[Telephone rings.]
M: Front desk. How may I help you?
W: I'm in Room 201. ⓐI specifically booked a non-smoking room, but
분명히, 특별히
I smell cigarette smoke in my room.
담배
M: We're sorry about that. Let me check that for you. *[Typing sound]* You're Wendy Parker, right?
W: Yes, that's correct.
M: Hmm, the record says we assigned you a non-smoking room.
배정하다
W: Then why do I smell cigarette smoke here?
M: Well, ⓑsince your room is close to the ground level, cigarette smoke must have come in from outside. Sorry for the inconvenience.
불편
Would you like to switch rooms?
W: Yes, please. The smell is really bothering me.
M: Let me first check if there are any rooms available.
W: If it's possible, ⓒI'd like to move to a higher floor. Maybe higher than the 5th floor?
M: Okay. *[Typing sound]* Oh, we have one. ⓓRoom 908 on the 9th floor is available.
W: Perfect. That's high enough to avoid the smell.

해석

[전화벨이 울린다.]
남: 프런트 데스크입니다. 무엇을 도와드릴까요?

여: 201호에 묵고 있는 사람입니다. ⓐ제가 분명히 금연 객실을 예약했는데, 방에서 담배 냄새가 나요.
남: 죄송합니다. 제가 확인해 드릴게요. [타이핑하는 소리] Wendy Parker 맞으시죠?
여: 네, 맞습니다.
남: 흠, 기록에 따르면 저희가 금연 객실로 배정해 드렸습니다.
여: 그런데 왜 여기서 담배 냄새가 나죠?
남: 음, ⓑ고객님의 방이 지면과 가까워서, 밖에서 담배 연기가 들어왔나 봅니다. 불편을 드려 죄송합니다. 방을 바꾸고 싶으신가요?
여: 네, 그렇게 해 주세요. 냄새가 정말 신경 쓰여요.
남: 사용 가능한 방이 있는지 먼저 확인해 보겠습니다.
여: 가능하다면 ⓒ더 높은 층으로 옮기고 싶어요. 혹시 5층 이상으로요?
남: 알겠습니다. [타이핑하는 소리] 오, 하나 있네요. ⓓ9층의 908호실이 사용 가능합니다.
여: 아주 좋아요. 냄새를 피할 수 있을 만큼 충분히 높네요.

문제 풀이

ⓐ금연 객실을 예약한 여자가 방에서 담배 냄새가 난다고 항의하자 직원인 남자가 ⓑ그 방이 지면과 가까워서 담배 연기가 밖에서 들어왔을 것이라고 설명한다. 이에 여자가 ⓒ방을 높은 층으로 옮기고 싶다고 했는데 남자가 ⓓ9층에 사용 가능한 방이 있다고 했으므로, 이에 대한 여자의 응답으로는 냄새가 들어오지 않을 정도로 충분히 높아서 좋다고 말하는 ⑤가 적절하다.
① 다시 확인해 주세요. 그 호텔이 예약이 꽉 차 있을 리가 없어요.
② 정말 안타깝네요. 제가 가능한 한 일찍 체크아웃을 했어야 했어요.
③ 물론이죠. 청소 서비스에 매우 만족합니다.
④ 죄송합니다. 당신의 방을 제 방과 바꿀 수 없어요.

14. ③ | 긴 대화 응답

선택지 선택비율	① 4%	② 2%	③ 92%	④ 1%	⑤ 1%

M: Alice, why didn't you come to the music festival yesterday?
음악제
W: I was busy doing my homework. I wish I could've gone. How was it?
M: It was great! My favorite band signed my ticket.
서명하다, 사인하다
W: Wow! Can I see it?
M: Sure. It's in my wallet. *[Pause]* Wait! ⓐMy wallet! It's gone!
지갑
W: Really? Look in your coat pockets. Maybe it's there.
주머니
M: It's not here. Oh, no! What should I do?
W: When was the last time you saw your wallet?
M: Umm... ⓑI remember having it at the subway station. Did I leave it there?
W: ⓒYou should contact the station's lost and found right away.
연락하다 / 분실물 센터 / 즉시, 곧바로
M: ⓓBut what if someone already took it?
~라면 어떨까
W: Don't worry. ⓔSomeone with a good heart might have turned it in.
~을 돌려주다
M: I hope you're right. I'll check with them.

해석

남: Alice, 왜 어제 음악제에 안 왔어?
여: 숙제하느라 바빴어. 갈 수 있었으면 좋았을 텐데. 축제는 어땠어?
남: 아주 좋았어! 내가 가장 좋아하는 밴드가 입장권에 사인을 해 줬어.
여: 우와! 보여 줄 수 있어?
남: 물론이지. 지갑 안에 있어. [잠시 후] 잠깐! ⓐ내 지갑! 내 지갑이 사라졌어!
여: 정말이야? 코트 주머니를 봐. 아마 거기 있을 거야.
남: 여기 없어. 아, 이런! 어떻게 해야 하지?
여: 지갑을 마지막으로 본 게 언제였어?
남: 음… ⓑ지하철역에서 가지고 있었던 건 기억나. 거기에 두고 왔나?
여: ⓒ지금 곧바로 역 분실물 센터에 연락해 봐야겠다.
남: ⓓ그런데 누군가가 벌써 가져갔으면 어떻게 하지?
여: 걱정하지 마. ⓔ마음씨 좋은 누군가가 돌려줬을지도 몰라.
남: 네 말이 맞으면 좋겠어. 확인해 볼게.

문제 풀이

ⓐ지갑을 잃어버린 남자가 여자의 제안대로 ⓑⓒ마지막으로 지갑을 본 지하철역의 분실물 센터에 연락을 하려고 하면서 ⓓ다른 사람이 가져갔을 것을 걱정하자 여자는 ⓔ돌려준 사람이 있을지도 모른다고 안심시키고 있다. 따라서 이어질 남자의 말로 가장 적절한 것은 ③이다.
① 좋은 생각이야. 즉시 없앨게.
② 닫았을 것 같아. 책은 내일 반납하렴.
④ 너무 늦었어. 표가 매진됐어.
⑤ 지갑 여기 있어. 이걸 역으로 가져가렴.

15. ⑤ | 상황에 적절한 말

선택지 선택비율	① 10%	② 3%	③ 2%	④ 8%	⑤ 77%

W: Jason is a sculptor and Sarah is the head of a local library. A few
조각가
days ago, Sarah hired Jason to create a sculpture for the library's
고용하다 / 조각품
reopening by the end of next month. This morning, Sarah received the final design of the sculpture from Jason. She likes his design, but it looks quite complicated to her. She's worried whether he can
복잡한
finish in time, so she calls him to express her concern. However,
~에 시간 맞춰[늦지 않게] / 표(현)하다 / 우려, 걱정
Jason thinks that he has enough time to make it since he has worked on these types of sculptures before. So Jason wants to tell Sarah that he can finish it in time and that she doesn't have to be concerned. In this situation, what would Jason most likely say to
걱정스럽게 만들다
Sarah?
Jason: Don't worry. I can get the job done before the deadline.

해석

여: Jason은 조각가이고 Sarah는 지역 도서관장이다. 며칠 전, Sarah는 다음 달 말까지 도서관의 재개관을 위한 조각품을 만들기 위해 Jason을 고용했다. 오늘 아침, Sarah는 Jason으로부터 조각품의 최종 디자인을 받았다. 그녀는 그의 디자인이 마음에 들지만, 그녀에게는 그것이 꽤 복잡해 보인다. 그녀는 그가 제시간에 끝낼 수 있을지 걱정이 되어, 그에게 전화를 걸어 우려를 표한다. 하지만, Jason은 이전에 이런 종류의 조각품들을 작업했기 때문에 그것을 만들 충분한 시간이 있다고 생각한다. 그래서 Jason은 Sarah에게 제시간에 끝낼 수 있으니 걱정할 필요가 없다고 말하고 싶어 한다. 이 상황에서, Jason은 Sarah에게 뭐라고 말하겠는가?
Jason: 걱정하지 마세요. 저는 마감일 전에 그 일을 끝낼 수 있습니다.

문제 풀이

Jason은 Sarah에게 제시간에 일을 끝낼 수 있으니 걱정할 필요 없다고 말하고 싶어 하므로, 정답으로는 ⑤가 가장 적절하다.
① 행운을 빕니다. 당신이 제시간에 일을 끝내길 바랍니다.
② 좋습니다. 만나서 조각품의 변경 사항을 의논합시다.
③ 끔찍하네요. 재개관이 연기되어 유감입니다.
④ 서두르세요. 최종 디자인을 즉시 보내 주셔야 합니다.

16~17. | 세트 문항

16. ② 17. ⑤

선택지 선택비율					
16	① 3%	② 95%	③ 1%	④ 1%	⑤ 1%
17	① 1%	② 1%	③ 1%	④ 2%	⑤ 97%

M: Good morning, everyone. Last class, we learned about different kinds of musical instruments around the world. Today, ⓐwe'll talk
악기
about a variety of materials used to make them. One common
다양한 / 재료

source of materials is different parts of animals. For example, in ⓑChina, a wing bone from a large bird was made into a flute about 8,000 years ago. Another example of making musical instruments from animals comes from ⓒMongolia. There, people made a stringed instrument(현악기) using animal skin around a frame(틀) and horsehair(말 털) for the strings(현). In another part of the world, people in ⓓNigeria dig out(~을 파내다) clay(점토) from the ground to make a traditional drum. The entire(전체의) process(과정, 절차) of making this musical instrument takes around a month. Lastly, in ⓔAustralia, the material of choice is hardwood(견목) from local trees. It's made into a type of wind instrument(관악기) by the native people there. Now let's take a look at(~을 보다) some photos, and then we'll discuss(논의하다) them in detail.

해석

남: 안녕하세요, 여러분. 지난 수업에서, 우리는 전 세계의 다른 종류의 악기에 대해 배웠습니다. 오늘, ⓐ우리는 그것들을 만드는 데 사용되는 다양한 재료들에 대해 이야기할 것입니다. 재료들의 흔한 원천 중 하나는 동물의 일부입니다. 예를 들어, ⓑ중국에서는, 8000여 년 전에 큰 새의 날개 뼈가 피리로 만들어졌습니다. 동물로부터 악기를 만든 또 다른 예는 ⓒ몽골에서 온 것입니다. 그곳에서, 사람들은 틀 주변에 동물 가죽을 사용하고 현으로 말 털을 사용해서 현악기를 만들었습니다. 세계의 또 다른 지역에서, ⓓ나이지리아 사람들은 전통 북을 만들기 위해 땅에서 점토를 파냅니다. 이 악기를 만드는 전체 과정은 한 달 정도가 걸립니다. 마지막으로, ⓔ호주에서, 선택된 재료는 지역 나무의 견목입니다. 그것은 그곳의 원주민들에 의해 관악기 종류로 만들어집니다. 이제 사진 몇 장을 본 다음, 그것들에 대해 자세히 논의하도록 하겠습니다.

문제 풀이

16. ⓐ남자는 악기들을 만드는 데 사용되는 다양한 재료들에 대해 말하고 있으므로 이 글의 주제로는 ② '악기를 만드는 데 사용되는 재료들'이 가장 적절하다.
    ① 음악과 문명의 관계
    ③ 전 세계 현대 미술의 경향
    ④ 고대 악기를 보존하는 방법
    ⑤ 휴식과 위안을 위한 음악의 사용
17. ⓑ중국, ⓒ몽골, ⓓ나이지리아, ⓔ호주는 언급되었지만, 콜롬비아(Colombia)는 언급되지 않았다.

[코드 공략하기]

제2회 고급 모의고사

1	②	2	②	3	③	4	⑤	5	①	6	③
7	③	8	③	9	⑤	10	②	11	①	12	⑤
13	④	14	②	15	②	16	③	17	⑤		

1. ② | 목적

선택지 선택비율	① 2%	② 95%	③ 2%	④ 1%	⑤ 0%

W: Good morning, students. This is your vice principal(교감), Ms. Morris. ⓐI want to inform(알리다) you that each class period(수업 시간) will be reduced(줄이다) from 50 minutes to 40 minutes next Tuesday. Due to the parent-teacher conferences(회의, 상담) that will be held on that day, school will end one hour earlier than usual. You'll still take the same classes that you normally(보통) would on that day. The starting and ending bells will ring according to(~에 따라) the reduced class time schedule. Once again, ⓑplease keep in mind that next Tuesday's class periods will be shortened(단축하다) by 10 minutes each. Thank you.

해석

여: 안녕하세요, 학생 여러분. 저는 교감 Morris입니다. ⓐ다음 주 화요일에 각 수업 시간이 50분에서 40분으로 단축될 것임을 알리려고 합니다. 그날 열릴 학부모 상담 때문에, 학교는 평소보다 한 시간 더 일찍 끝날 것입니다. 여러분은 그날 보통 때와 같은 수업을 할 것입니다. 시작 종과 종료 종은 단축된 수업 시간표에 따라 울릴 것입니다. 다시 한번, ⓑ다음 주 화요일 수업 시간이 각 교시마다 10분씩 단축될 것임을 명심하길 바랍니다. 감사합니다.

문제 풀이

ⓐⓑ다음주 화요일 수업 시간이 교시마다 10분씩 단축될 것임을 알리고 있다.

2. ② | 의견

선택지 선택비율	① 1%	② 95%	③ 1%	④ 1%	⑤ 1%

M: Ji-na, what are you reading?
W: Hi, Mr. Brown. It's an English book titled(제목을 붙이다) *The Global Economy*.
M: That sounds difficult.
W: It is. I spend so much time looking up(~을 찾아보다) new words in the dictionary.
M: Hmm. ⓐYou should choose a more level-appropriate(적절한, 어울리는) English book. You'll be able to read faster without distractions(집중을 방해하는 것).
W: That makes sense. But I thought I would learn English better if I read difficult things.
M: Well, ⓑwhen learners read English books that are too hard, they get exhausted(지치다) and give up(~을 포기하다) their studies easily.
W: So, do you mean I need to read something that's not so hard?
M: Yes. ⓒReading at an appropriate level is more enjoyable(즐거운) and motivates(동기를 부여하다) learners to keep going.
W: I see what you mean.

M: ⓓWhy don't you drop by the library and choose an English book that's appropriate for your level?
~에 들르다
W: I think that's a good idea. Thank you, Mr. Brown.

해석

남: 지나야, 뭘 읽고 있니?
여: 안녕하세요, Brown 선생님. 〈세계 경제〉라는 제목의 영어 도서예요.
남: 어려워 보이는구나.
여: 그래요. 사전에서 새로운 단어를 찾느라 시간을 아주 많이 소비해요.
남: 음. ⓐ더 수준에 적합한 영어 도서를 골라야 한단다. 집중을 방해하는 것 없이 더 빨리 읽을 수 있을 거야.
여: 일리 있는 말씀이세요. 하지만 저는 어려운 것을 읽으면 영어를 더 잘 배울 거라고 생각했어요.
남: 음, ⓑ학습자가 너무 어려운 책을 읽으면, 지쳐서 공부를 쉽게 포기한단다.
여: 그러면 그리 어렵지 않은 것을 읽어야 한다는 뜻이세요?
남: 그렇단다. ⓒ적절한 수준으로 읽는 것이 더 즐겁고 학습자들이 계속할 수 있게 동기를 부여한단다.
여: 무슨 뜻인지 알겠어요.
남: ⓓ도서관에 들러서 네 수준에 적절한 영어책 한 권을 고르는 게 어떻겠니?
여: 좋은 생각인 것 같아요. 감사합니다, Brown 선생님.

문제 풀이

남자는 ⓑ학습자가 너무 어려운 책을 읽으면 지쳐서 포기하기 쉬우므로 ⓒ즐겁게 읽을 수 있도록 ⓐⓓ수준에 맞는 맞는 영어 도서를 읽어야 한다고 말하고 있다.

3. ③ | 관계

선택지 선택비율	① 1%	② 1%	③ 97%	④ 0%	⑤ 0%

W: Mr. Thomson. Thank you for your demonstration. I learned a lot today.
(시범) 설명
M: Glad to hear that. Everyone should know what to do in emergencies.
emergency: 비상 사태
W: Right. Can I ask you some questions? I'm thinking of getting a job in your field after graduation.
분야 졸업
M: Sure. Go ahead.
W: ⓐFighting fires is your main duty. But what other things do you do?
의무
M: One thing we do is search for and rescue people during natural disasters like floods.
구조하다 자연 재해 홍수
W: Wonderful. I'd love to learn more.
M: Well, ⓑwe provide a job experience program for high schoolers on weekday afternoons at our fire station.
평일
W: Really? I think I have time after school. What would I do there?
M: You'll practice how to use various equipment for extinguishing fires. You can also check out the fire trucks.
장비 (불을) 끄다
W: Sounds great. How do I sign up?
신청하다
M: Your teacher has some pamphlets, so you can ask her.

해석

여: Thomson 선생님. 시범 설명 감사해요. 오늘 많이 배웠어요.
남: 그 말을 들으니 기쁘구나. 모두가 비상시에 무엇을 해야 하는지 알아야 한단다.
여: 맞아요. 제가 질문을 좀 드려도 되나요? 전 졸업 후에 선생님 분야에서 일자리를 얻으려고 생각 중이거든요.
남: 물론이지. 어서 하렴.
여: ⓐ불과 싸우는 것이 선생님의 주된 의무죠. 그런데 어떤 다른 일을 하시나요?
남: 우리가 하는 한 가지 일은 홍수와 같은 자연 재해 동안 사람들을 찾고 구조하는 거야.
여: 멋져요. 더 알고 싶어요.
남: 음, ⓑ우리는 평일 오후에 소방서에서 고등학생들을 위한 직업 체험 프로그램을 제공한단다.
여: 정말이요? 방과 후에 시간이 있을 것 같아요. 거기서 제가 뭘 하게 되나요?
남: 불을 끄기 위한 다양한 장비를 어떻게 사용하는지 연습할 거야. 소방차도 볼 수 있단다.
여: 좋네요. 어떻게 신청하나요?
남: 선생님께서 팸플릿을 가지고 계시니, 선생님께 여쭈어 보렴.

문제 풀이

여자가 남자에게 ⓐ불과 싸우는 것이 남자의 주된 의무라고 했고, 남자는 여자에게 ⓑ평일 오후에 소방서에서 고등학생들을 위한 직업 체험 프로그램이 있다고 말해주는 것으로 보아 여자는 학생이고 남자는 소방관임을 알 수 있다.

4. ⑤ | 그림 일치

선택지 선택비율	① 0%	② 0%	③ 0%	④ 1%	⑤ 97%

W: Wow, Sam. You turned the student council room into a hot chocolate booth.
M: Yes, Ms. Thompson. We're ready to sell hot chocolate to raise money for children in need.
어려움에 처한
W: Excellent. What are you going to put on the ⓐbulletin board under the clock?
게시판
M: I'll post information letting people know where the profits will go.
게시하다 수익금
W: Good. I like ⓑthe banner on the wall.
M: Thanks. I designed it myself.
W: Awesome. Oh, I'm glad you put ⓒmy stripe-patterned tablecloth on the table.
식탁보
M: Thanks for letting us use it. Did you notice ⓓthe snowman drawing that's hanging on the tree?
W: Yeah. I remember it was drawn by the child you helped last year. By the way, there are ⓔthree boxes on the floor. What are they for?
M: We're going to fill those up with donations of toys and books.
fill A up with B: A를 B로 가득 채우다 기부, 기부물품
W: Sounds great. Good luck.

해석

여: 와, Sam. 네가 학생회실을 핫초코 부스로 만들었구나.
남: 네, Thompson 선생님. 저희는 어려움에 처한 아이들을 위한 돈을 모으기 위해 핫초코를 팔 준비가 되어 있어요.
여: 훌륭하구나. ⓐ시계 밑에 있는 게시판에 뭘 붙일 거니?
남: 수익금이 어디에 쓰일지 사람들에게 알려주는 정보를 게시할 거예요.
여: 좋구나. ⓑ벽에 있는 현수막이 마음에 드는구나.
남: 감사합니다. 제가 직접 디자인했어요.
여: 멋지다. 오, ⓒ탁자 위에 내 줄무늬 식탁보를 올려놓으니 기쁘구나.
남: 저희가 그걸 사용하게 해 주셔서 감사해요. ⓓ나무에 걸려 있는 눈사람 그림 보셨어요?
여: 그래. 작년에 네가 도와준 아이가 그린 것으로 기억나는구나. 그런데 ⓔ바닥에 상자가 세 개 있네. 무엇에 쓰는 거니?
남: 그것들을 장난감과 책 기부물품으로 가득 채울 거예요.
여: 좋은 생각이구나. 행운을 빈다.

문제 풀이

여자는 ⓔ바닥에 상자가 세 개 있다고 했다.

5. ① | 할 일

선택지 선택비율	① 92%	② 1%	③ 3%	④ 2%	⑤ 1%

W: Hey, Brian. The Playful Cat Photo Contest is only two days away.
장난기 많은

M: That's right, Lisa. Many students are excited about our club's contest.
W: Yeah. Let's check the preparations we've done so far.
준비 사항
M: Alright. I checked our email and confirmed that all the participants
확인하다
had submitted their photos.
제출하다
W: Great. I'll print them out tomorrow.
M: Okay. What about the bulletin board in the school lobby? We'll need
게시판
it to post the photos on.
W: Don't worry. I already got permission to use it. Have you ordered
허락, 승인
stickers yet?
M: Yes, I ordered enough for everyone to use when voting for their
vote: 투표하다
favorite photos.
W: Good. ⓐWhat about the trophy for the winner?
M: It's at my house. ⓑI'll bring it tomorrow.
W: Thanks. I think we're all set.
be all set: 만반의 준비를 하다

해석

여: 안녕, Brian. Playful Cat 사진 대회가 겨우 이틀 남았어.
남: 맞아, Lisa. 많은 학생들이 우리 동아리의 대회를 기대하고 있어.
여: 응. 우리가 지금까지 준비한 것들을 점검해 보자.
남: 좋아. 내가 이메일을 확인했는데, 참가자들 모두 사진을 제출한 걸 확인했어.
여: 잘됐네. 내가 내일 그것들을 출력할게.
남: 알겠어. 학교 로비에 있는 게시판은? 거기에 사진들을 게시해야 할 거야.
여: 걱정 마. 내가 이미 사용 허락을 받았어. 스티커는 이미 주문했니?
남: 응, 모두가 좋아하는 사진에 투표할 때 사용할 만큼 충분히 주문했어.
여: 좋아. ⓐ우승자 트로피는?
남: 우리 집에 있어. ⓑ내일 가져올게.
여: 고마워. 우리 만반의 준비를 한 것 같아.

문제 풀이

여자가 ⓐ우승자 트로피에 대해 묻자 남자가 ⓑ내일 가져오겠다고 대답했다.

6. ③ | 금액

선택지 선택비율	① 1%	② 1%	③ 96%	④ 1%	⑤ 1%

W: Welcome to Jamie's Gift Shop! What can I do for you?
M: Hi. I need to get Christmas gifts for my friends. Is there anything you can recommend?
W: Sure. How about this photo tumbler? You can insert a picture of
끼우다, 넣다
your friends into the tumbler to decorate it.
장식하다
M: Ooh, my friends will love it. How much is it?
W: ⓐIt's $30.
M: It seems a bit pricey, but I like it. ⓑI'll take two of them.
값비싼
W: Okay. Anything else?
M: These Christmas key chains look cute. Oh, ⓒthey're $5 each.
열쇠고리
W: Yes. They're only available this month.
M: Are they? ⓓI'll take four then. I think that's all.
W: So, that's ⓔtwo tumblers and four key chains.
M: That's right.
W: And ⓕyou get 10% off the total cost for our Christmas promotion.
판촉
M: Great. Here's my credit card.

해석

여: Jamie의 선물 가게입니다! 무엇을 도와드릴까요?
남: 안녕하세요. 친구들을 위한 크리스마스 선물을 사야 해서요. 추천해 주실 만한 게 있나요?
여: 물론이죠. 이 포토 텀블러는 어떠세요? 텀블러에 친구들 사진을 넣어서 장식하실 수 있어요.
남: 오, 제 친구들이 무척 좋아하겠어요. 얼마예요?
여: ⓐ30달러입니다.
남: 좀 비싼 것 같지만, 마음에 들어요. ⓑ두 개 주세요.
여: 알겠습니다. 다른 것은요?
남: 이 크리스마스 열쇠고리가 귀여워 보여요. 아, ⓒ개당 5달러네요.
여: 네. 그것들은 이번 달에만 사실 수 있어요.
남: 그런가요? 그럼 ⓓ4개 주세요. 그게 다인 것 같아요.
여: 그럼 ⓔ텀블러 2개와 열쇠고리 4개네요.
남: 맞습니다.
여: 그리고 ⓕ크리스마스 판촉으로 총 값에서 10% 할인받으십니다.
남: 잘됐네요. 여기 제 신용카드 있습니다.

문제 풀이

남자는 ⓐⓑⓔ30달러짜리 텀블러 2개와 ⓒⓓⓔ5달러짜리 열쇠고리 4개를 구매하기로 했는데(30x2+5x4=80) ⓕ총 값에서 10퍼센트 할인받을 수 있다고 했으므로, 지불할 금액은 72달러이다.

7. ③ | 이유

선택지 선택비율	① 1%	② 0%	③ 98%	④ 0%	⑤ 0%

W: Honey, I'm home.
M: How was your day?
W: Alright. Hey, did you order something? There's a large box outside the door.
M: It's the tent we bought online for our camping trip. I'm returning it.
반품하다
W: Is it because of the size? I remember you said it might be a little small to fit all of us.
(어느 장소에 들어가기에) 맞다
M: Actually, when I set up the tent, it seemed big enough to hold us all.
~을 설치하다 수용하다
W: Then, did you find a cheaper one on another website?
M: No, price is not the issue.
W: Then, ⓐwhy are you returning the tent?
M: ⓑIt's too heavy to carry around. We usually have to walk a bit to get to the campsite.
야영지
W: I see. Is someone coming to pick up the box?
M: Yes. I already scheduled a pickup.
일정을 잡다 찾으러 오기

해석

여: 여보, 나 왔어요.
남: 오늘 어땠어요?
여: 괜찮았어요. 저기, 당신이 뭔가 주문했어요? 문 밖에 커다란 상자가 있네요.
남: 우리가 캠핑 여행 때문에 온라인에서 산 텐트예요. 반품할 거예요.
여: 크기 때문이에요? 우리 모두가 들어가기에 조금 작을 수 있다고 당신이 말한 게 기억나요.
남: 실은, 텐트를 설치할 때, 우리 모두를 수용하기에 충분히 커 보였어요.
여: 그럼 다른 웹 사이트에서 더 저렴한 것을 찾았나요?
남: 아니요, 가격이 문제는 아니에요.
여: 그러면 ⓐ왜 텐트를 반품하려고요?
남: ⓑ갖고 다니기에 너무 무거워요. 우리가 보통 야영지까지 가려면 조금 걸어야 하잖아요.
여: 알겠어요. 저 상자를 가지러 누군가가 올 건가요?
남: 네. 이미 찾으러 오는 일정을 잡았어요.

문제 풀이

ⓐ텐트 반품 이유를 묻는 여자의 말에 남자는 ⓑ갖고 다니기 너무 무거워서라고 답했다.

8. ③ | 언급

선택지 선택비율	① 1%	② 1%	③ 91%	④ 0%	⑤ 5%

W: Hi, Ross. How's everything going for our Ten Year Class Reunion (동창회) Party?
M: I think we're done, Jennifer.
W: Then let's go over (~을 점검하다) what we've prepared.
M: I ⓐalready booked the Silver Corral Restaurant for the party.
W: Good. It must have been very difficult to get a reservation because ⓑour party is on December 24th.
M: Yeah, we were lucky.
W: What food will they serve (음식을 제공하다)?
M: ⓒTheir steak, spaghetti, and pizza are famous, so that's what I ordered.
W: Sounds delicious. And the souvenirs (기념품) for the party are ready, too.
M: ⓓYou ordered mugs for souvenirs, right?
W: Yes, I did. I'll bring them that day.
M: Perfect. It's going to be a great party.

해석

여: 안녕, Ross. 우리 10회 동창회 파티는 잘 되어 가니?
남: 다 된 것 같아, Jennifer.
여: 그러면 우리가 준비한 것들을 점검해 보자.
남: ⓐ내가 파티를 위해 Silver Corral 식당을 이미 예약했어.
여: 좋아. ⓑ우리 파티가 12월 24일이라 예약하기 무척 어려웠을 텐데.
남: 응, 운이 좋았어.
여: 어떤 음식을 낼 거지?
남: ⓒ그곳의 스테이크, 스파게티, 피자가 유명해서, 그걸 주문했어.
여: 맛있겠다. 그리고 파티 기념품도 준비됐지.
남: ⓓ네가 기념품으로 머그잔을 주문했지, 그렇지?
여: 응. 그날 가져올게.
남: 완벽해. 멋진 파티가 될 거야.

문제 풀이

Ten Year Class Reunion Party의 ⓐ장소, ⓑ날짜, ⓒ음식, ⓓ기념품은 언급되었으나, 회비는 언급되지 않았다.

9. ⑤ | 내용 일치

선택지 선택비율	① 0%	② 0%	③ 0%	④ 1%	⑤ 96%

W: Attention, please. I'm Jenny Stone, the manager of the community center. I'm going to tell you about the 2018 Upcycling (upcycle: (재활용품을) 더 나은 것으로 만들다) Workshop. Upcycling is creative (창의적인) reuse (재사용). It gives new life to old objects (물건). ⓐThe workshop will last three days, from November 23rd to 25th. It'll run from 1 to 4 p.m. ⓑThe workshop will be held in the seminar room. And we have a special treat (특별한 것) this time. ⓒThe famous fashion designer, Elizabeth Thompson, will teach you in the workshop. You'll learn many upcycling methods (방법) from her. For example, you'll remake (바꾸다) plastic bags into rugs (깔개) and old shirts into hats. ⓓAll materials (재료) are provided. And there's no participation (참가) fee (요금). ⓔThe workshop is open to people 18 and older. We're looking forward to seeing you.

해석

여: 안내 말씀 드립니다. 저는 주민 센터 관리자인 Jenny Stone입니다. 2018년 Upcycling 워크숍에 대해 말씀 드리겠습니다. 업사이클링은 창의적인 재사용입니다. 그것은 오래된 물건에 새 생명을 줍니다. ⓐ워크숍은 11월 23일부터 25일까지 3일간 이어질 것입니다. 오후 1시부터 4시까지 진행될 것입니다. ⓑ워크숍은 세미나실에서 열릴 것입니다. 그리고 저희는 이번에 특별한 행사를 마련했습니다. ⓒ유명한 패션 디자이너인 Elizabeth Thompson이 워크숍에서 여러분을 가르칠 것입니다. 여러분은 그녀로부터 많은 업사이클링 방법을 배울 것입니다. 예를 들어, 여러분은 비닐봉지를 깔개로, 그리고 오래된 셔츠를 모자로 바꿀 것입니다. ⓓ모든 재료는 제공됩니다. 그리고 참가비는 없습니다. ⓔ워크숍은 18세 이상이 참가할 수 있습니다. 여러분을 뵙기를 고대합니다.

문제 풀이

ⓔ워크숍은 18세 이상이 참가할 수 있다고 했다.

10. ② | 도표

선택지 선택비율	① 1%	② 95%	③ 2%	④ 0%	⑤ 0%

M: Alice, Blackhills Hiking Jackets is having a big sale this weekend.
W: Nice. I need a jacket for the hiking trip next week, Jason.
M: Here. Have a look at their online catalog.
W: Wow! They all look nice. But ⓐI don't want to spend more than $80.
M: Then you should choose from these four. How many pockets (주머니) do you want?
W: The more the better. ⓑThree pockets are not enough.
M: ⓒDoes it need to be waterproof (방수의)?
W: ⓓOf course. It's really important because it often rains in the mountains.
M: Then there're two options left.
W: I like this yellow one.
M: It looks nice, but ⓔyellow can get dirty easily.
W: That's true. Then ⓕI'll buy the other one.
M: I think that's a good choice.

해석

남: Alice, Blackhills Hiking Jackets에서 이번 주말에 대대적인 할인을 할 거야.
여: 잘됐다. Jason, 난 다음 주 등산 때문에 재킷이 하나 필요하거든.
남: 여기야. 온라인 카탈로그를 좀 봐.
여: 와! 모두 좋아 보여. 하지만 ⓐ난 80달러 이상을 쓰고 싶지는 않아.
남: 그러면 이 네 가지에서 골라야 해. 주머니 몇 개를 원해?
여: 많을수록 더 좋아. ⓑ주머니 세 개는 충분하지 않아.
남: ⓒ방수일 필요가 있니?
여: ⓓ물론이지. 산에서는 비가 자주 오기 때문에 그건 정말 중요해.
남: 그러면 두 가지 선택 사항이 남았네.
여: 난 이 노란색이 좋아.
남: 좋아 보이긴 하지만, ⓔ노란색은 쉽게 더러워질 수 있어.
여: 맞아. 그러면 ⓕ나머지 다른 걸 사야겠다.
남: 좋은 선택인 것 같아.

문제 풀이

ⓐ80달러가 넘지 않고, ⓑ주머니가 3개보다 많으며, ⓒⓓ방수가 되고, ⓔⓕ노란색이 아닌 재킷을 사기로 했다.

11. ① | 짧은 대화 응답

선택지 선택비율	① 85%	② 3%	③ 4%	④ 4%	⑤ 4%

M: Hey, Tina. I have something to tell you about your birthday party this Saturday.

W: Oh, Clark. You're coming, right? ⓐI'd really love it if you could come. All our friends will be there.
M: ⓑI'm afraid I can't make it this time. I have to go on a business trip with my boss this weekend.
(모임 등에) 참석하다 / 출장

W: That's too bad. I was looking forward to seeing you there.
look forward to v-ing: ~하기를 고대하다

해석

남: 안녕, Tina. 이번 주 토요일 네 생일 파티에 대해 말할 게 있어.
여: 오, Clark. 너 오는 거지, 그렇지? ⓐ네가 오면 정말 좋을 거야. 우리 친구들이 모두 거기에 올 거거든.
남: ⓑ안타깝지만 이번에는 참석하지 못할 것 같아. 이번 주말에 상사랑 출장을 가야 하거든.
여: 정말 안됐다. 거기서 너를 보기를 고대하고 있었는데.

문제 풀이

여자는 ⓐ남자가 자신의 생일 파티에 오기를 바라지만 남자는 ⓑ출장 때문에 참석하지 못할 것 같다고 말하고 있으므로, 안타까움을 표현하는 ①이 여자의 응답으로 가장 적절하다.
② 고마워. 네가 파티에 올 수 있어서 정말 기뻐.
③ 괜찮아. 생일 파티는 벌써 끝났어.
④ 물론이죠. 당신과 팀의 출장 일정을 제가 잡아 드릴게요.
⑤ 걱정 마. 내 상사는 이번 주 월요일에 출장에서 돌아올 거야.

12. ⑤ | 짧은 대화 응답

선택지 선택비율	① 4%	② 11%	③ 15%	④ 1%	⑤ 69%

W: Dad, we should leave soon to watch the fireworks in the park. Shall we bring something to eat?
불꽃놀이
M: Yeah, we might get hungry. Oh, we also need the picnic mat to sit on. I think I put it on one of the shelves in the storage room, but I'm not sure.
shelf: 선반 / 저장소, 창고
W: Then, could you find the mat while I pack some snacks and soft drinks?
싸다, 챙기다 / 청량음료
M: No problem. I'll take care of it.

해석

여: 아빠, 공원에서 불꽃놀이를 보러 곧 출발해야 해요. 먹을 걸 가지고 갈까요?
남: 그래, 배고파질 수 있으니까. 아, 우리가 앉을 소풍 매트도 필요하구나. 내가 창고 선반들 중 하나에 올려놓은 것 같은데, 확실치 않네.
여: 그럼 제가 간식과 음료를 챙기는 동안 매트를 찾아주실 수 있나요?
남: 그러마. 내가 처리할게.

문제 풀이

여자가 자신이 간식과 음료를 챙기는 동안 남자에게 매트를 찾아달라고 부탁했으므로, 그 일을 처리하겠다는 ⑤가 응답으로 가장 적절하다.
① 맞아. 우리가 그걸 봤어야 했어.
② 왜 안 돼? 그냥 매트를 선반 위에 올려두렴.
③ 좋아. 집에 간식을 좀 보관할 수 있어.
④ 미안해. 주차장을 못 찾겠어.

13. ④ | 긴 대화 응답

선택지 선택비율	① 2%	② 6%	③ 11%	④ 80%	⑤ 1%

M: Can I come in, Professor Rossini?
교수

W: Of course. Come on in, Ben. What brings you here?
M: ⓐI came to ask for advice on studying Italian.
조언 / 이탈리아어
W: Is there anything specific you're having trouble with?
특정한, 특별한 / have trouble with: ~에 어려움을 겪다
M: Yes. I'm experiencing difficulty using words properly. Could I get some tips?
experience: 경험하다, 겪다 / 제대로, 적절히
W: Sure. First, let me ask how you use your dictionary.
사전
M: Well, I use it to look up words that I don't know the meanings of.
~을 찾아보다 / 뜻, 의미
W: ⓑDictionaries provide example sentences for most words. Do you read them, too?
제공하다
M: No, I don't pay attention to the example sentences.
~에 유의하다[신경 쓰다]
W: Knowing the meaning of words is important, but ⓒyou should also understand the context in which the words are properly used.
맥락, 문맥
M: I see. ⓓSo you're suggesting that I study the example sentences as well, right?
제안하다, 완곡하게 말하다
W: Exactly. That way you can use the proper words in context.

해석

남: 들어가도 될까요, Rossini 교수님?
여: 물론이지. 들어오렴, Ben. 무슨 일로 왔니?
남: ⓐ이탈리아어 공부에 대한 조언을 구하려고 왔어요.
여: 특별히 어려움을 겪고 있는 부분이 있니?
남: 네. 단어를 제대로 사용하는 데 어려움을 겪고 있어요. 조언 좀 얻을 수 있을까요?
여: 물론이지. 우선, 네가 사전을 어떻게 사용하는지 물어봐야겠구나.
남: 음, 뜻을 모르는 단어를 찾기 위해 그걸 사용해요.
여: ⓑ사전은 대부분의 단어에 대한 예문들을 제공하잖니. 그것들도 읽니?
남: 아니요, 저는 예문은 신경 쓰지 않아요.
여: 단어의 의미를 아는 것도 중요하지만, ⓒ단어가 적절히 쓰이는 문맥 또한 이해해야 한단다.
남: 알겠습니다. ⓓ그러니까 제가 예문도 공부해야 한다는 말씀이시죠?
여: 맞아. 그래야 문맥에 맞는 적절한 단어를 사용할 수 있어.

문제 풀이

남자가 ⓐ이탈리아어 공부에 대한 조언을 구하자, 여자는 ⓑ사전의 예문을 통해 ⓒ단어가 쓰이는 문맥을 이해하라고 조언한다. 이에 남자가 ⓓ예문도 공부하라는 의미가 맞는지 확인차 물어보고 있으므로, 그래야 문맥에 맞는 적절한 단어를 사용할 수 있다고 답하는 ④가 응답으로 가장 적절하다.
① 꼭 그렇진 않아. 간단한 문장으로 말하는 게 더 좋아.
② 맞아. 단어의 어근을 익혀서 단어를 암기하도록 하렴.
③ 맞아. 네가 제대로 된 예문을 공부했다니 기쁘구나.
⑤ 나는 그렇게 생각하지 않아. 항상 이탈리아어-이탈리아어 사전을 사용하렴.

14. ② | 긴 대화 응답

선택지 선택비율	① 1%	② 95%	③ 1%	④ 1%	⑤ 0%

W: Hi, Justin. I heard you're going to be the MC at the school festival.
사회자(= master of ceremonies)
M: Yes, I am, Cindy.
W: Do you have everything ready?
M: Mostly. I have all the introductions ready and I've practiced a lot.
머리말, 인사말
W: I'm sure you'll do a great job.
M: I hope so, too. But there's one thing I'm worried about.
W: What is it?
M: I need a suit, so I'm thinking of buying one. But it's expensive, and I don't think I'll wear it after the festival.
정장

W: Well, if you want, ⓐI can ask my older brother to lend you one of his suits. He has a lot of them.
빌려주다
M: ⓑCould you please?
W: I'd be happy to.
M: Thanks. But ⓒwill his suit be my size?
W: ⓓIt will. You and my brother pretty much have the same build.
사람의 체구
M: It would be awesome to borrow your brother's.

해석

여: 안녕, Justin. 네가 학교 축제에서 사회자가 될 거라고 들었어.
남: 응, 그럴 거야, Cindy.
여: 모든 게 준비됐니?
남: 거의. 인사말은 다 준비했고 많이 연습했어.
여: 틀림없이 너는 잘할 거야.
남: 나 역시 그러길 바라고 있어. 하지만 걱정되는 한 가지가 있어.
여: 그게 뭔데?
남: 정장이 필요해서, 한 벌을 살 생각 중이야. 하지만 정장이 비싸기도 하고, 내가 축제 이후에 그걸 입을 것 같지 않아.
여: 음, 네가 원한다면, ⓐ우리 오빠에게 정장 한 벌을 네게 빌려주라고 부탁할 수 있어. 정장이 여러 벌 있거든.
남: ⓑ그렇게 해 줄래?
여: 기꺼이.
남: 고마워. 하지만 ⓒ너희 오빠의 정장이 내 사이즈에 맞을까?
여: ⓓ맞을 거야. 너와 우리 오빠는 아주 비슷한 체구야.
남: 너희 오빠의 정장을 빌린다면 정말 좋겠구나.

문제 풀이

ⓐⓑ여자의 오빠의 옷을 빌리길 원하는 남자가 ⓒ사이즈를 걱정하자 여자는 ⓓ두 사람의 체구가 비슷해서 사이즈가 맞을 거라고 안심시켰다. 따라서 남자의 응답으로 가장 적절한 것은 ②이다.
① 정장에 돈을 쓰는 것은 가치 있는 일이야.
③ 너희 오빠는 축제에서 재미있는 시간을 보낼 거야.
④ 새 정장을 입은 네 모습을 정말 보고 싶어.
⑤ 너는 사회자로서 대단한 명성을 쌓을 거야.

15. ② | 상황에 적절한 말

선택지 선택비율	① 5%	② 52%	③ 4%	④ 2%	⑤ 38%

M: Sophia and Jack are sister and brother. They're going to their favorite singer's concert tonight. The concert starts at 7 p.m., and since it takes an hour to get to the concert, Jack proposes that they leave their house at 6 p.m. While this is Jack's first time going to a concert, Sophia has been to several concerts. She knows that even after they arrive at the concert site, it takes a long time to go through the security line and get to their seats. Also, she wants to take pictures and stop by the gift shops before the concert. So, Sophia wants to suggest to Jack that they should leave for the concert much earlier than he proposed. In this situation, what would Sophia most likely say to Jack?
제안하다 / ~을 통과하다 / 보안 / ~에 들르다
Sophia: Let's head out for the concert far in advance.
~로 출발하다 / 미리

해석

남: Sophia와 Jack은 남매이다. 그들은 오늘 저녁에 좋아하는 가수의 콘서트에 갈 예정이다. 콘서트가 오후 7시에 시작하고 콘서트에 가는 데 한 시간이 걸리기 때문에, Jack은 집에서 오후 6시에 출발하자고 제안한다. Jack이 콘서트에 가는 것은 이번이 처음인 데 반해, Sophia는 여러 콘서트에 가 봤다. 그녀는 콘서트장에 도착한 후에도 보안 검사를 통과하여 좌석까지 가는 데 시간이 오래 걸린다는 것을 알고 있다. 또한, 그녀는 콘서트 전에 사진을 찍고 기념품 가게에 들르고 싶다. 그래서 Sophia는 Jack에게 그가 제안한 것보다 훨씬 더 일찍 콘서트장으로 출발하자고 제안하고 싶다. 이 상황에서, Sophia는 Jack에게 뭐라고 말하겠는가?
Sophia: 콘서트장으로 훨씬 미리 출발하자.

문제 풀이

Sophia는 Jack에게 그가 제안한 것보다 훨씬 더 일찍 콘서트장으로 출발하자고 제안하고 싶다고 했으므로, Sophia가 Jack에게 할 말로는 ②가 가장 적절하다.
① 네 계획을 고수하는 게 나을 것 같아.
③ 우리가 함께 앉을 수 있도록 자리 변경을 요청하면 돼.
④ 우리가 리허설을 한 번 더 해야 한다고 생각하지 않아?
⑤ 교통 혼잡을 피하기 위해 콘서트장에서 일찍 나서는 게 어때?

16~17. | 세트 문항

16. ③ 17. ⑤

선택지 선택비율	① 1%	② 3%	③ 90%	④ 1%	⑤ 5%
	① 0%	② 0%	③ 0%	④ 1%	⑤ 98%

M: Good morning, students. You might think that math is all about boring formulas, but actually it involves much more. Today, ⓐwe'll learn how mathematics is used in the arts. First, let's take ⓑmusic. Early mathematicians found that dividing or multiplying sound frequencies created different musical notes. Many musicians started applying this mathematical concept to make harmonized sounds. Second, ⓒpainting frequently uses math concepts, particularly the "Golden Ratio." Using this, great painters created masterpieces that display accurate proportions. The *Mona Lisa* is well-known for its accurate proportionality. ⓓPhotography is another example of using mathematical ideas. Photographers divide their frames into 3 by 3 sections and place their subjects along the lines. By doing so, the photo becomes balanced, thus more pleasing. Lastly, ⓔdance applies mathematics to position dancers on the stage. In ballet, dancers calculate distances between themselves and other dancers, and adjust to the size of the stage. This gives the impression of harmonious movement. I hope you've gained a new perspective on mathematics.
공식 / 수반[포함]하다 / 수학자 / 곱하다 / frequency: 진동수, 주파수 / 음, 음표 / 적용하다 / 조화를 이루다, 화음을 넣다 / 황금비 / 걸작, 명작 / 정확한 / 비율 / 비례, 균형 / divide A into B: A를 B로 나누다 / (그림, 사진 등의) 대상[소재], 피사체 / 계산하다 / 조정[조절]하다 / 느낌, 인상 / 얻다 / 관점, 시각

해석

남: 좋은 아침입니다, 학생 여러분. 여러분은 수학이 지루한 공식에 관한 것이 전부라고 생각할지도 모르지만, 사실 수학은 훨씬 더 많은 것을 포함합니다. 오늘은 ⓐ수학이 예술에서 어떻게 사용되는지 배워보겠습니다. 첫째로, ⓑ음악을 살펴보겠습니다. 초기 수학자들은 소리의 주파수를 나누거나 곱하는 것이 다른 음을 만든다는 것을 발견했습니다. 많은 음악가들이 조화로운 소리를 만들기 위해 이 수학적 개념을 적용하기 시작했습니다. 둘째로, ⓒ그림은 특히 '황금비'라는 수학 개념을 자주 사용합니다. 이를 사용하여, 위대한 화가들은 정확한 비율을 보여주는 걸작을 만들었습니다. 〈모나리자〉는 정확한 비례로 잘 알려져 있습니다. ⓓ사진은 수학적 아이디어를 사용하는 또 다른 예입니다. 사진작가들은 테두리를 3x3 구획으로 나누고 그 선들을 따라 피사체를 배치합니다. 그렇게 함으로써, 사진의 균형이 잡혀서 더 만족스럽습니다. 마지막으로, ⓔ무용은 무대 위의 무용수들을 배치하는 데 수학을 적용합니다. 발레에서, 무용수들은 자신과 다른 무용수들 사이의 거리를 계산하고, 무대의 크기에 맞춰 조절합니다. 이는 조화로운 움직임의 느낌을 줍니다. 저는 여러분이 수학에 대한 새로운 관점을 얻었기를 바랍니다.

문제 풀이

16. ⓐ수학이 예술에서 어떻게 사용되는지 배워보겠다며 뒤에서 다양한 예를 들어 설명하고 있으므로, 이 글의 주제로는 ③ '다양한 예술 분야에서의 수학의 적용'이 가장 적절하다.
   ① 수학 교육에 그림을 접목한 효과
   ② 예술 산업 성장에 대한 수학적 분석
   ④ 예술의 중요한 개념에 대한 역사적 고찰
   ⑤ 수학과 예술을 조화시키는 과제
17. ⓑ음악, ⓒ그림, ⓓ사진, ⓔ무용은 언급되었으나, 영화(cinema)는 언급되지 않았다.

[코드 공략하기]

제3회 고급 모의고사

1	⑤	2	②	3	①	4	④	5	②	6	②
7	①	8	④	9	⑤	10	②	11	②	12	③
13	④	14	⑤	15	①	16	①	17	③		

1. ⑤ | 목적

선택지 선택비율	① 1%	② 0%	③ 1%	④ 1%	⑤ 97%

W: Hello, Timberglade High School students. This is your P.E. teacher, Ms. Larsen. I'd like to announce(알리다) that we're looking for volunteers(자원봉사자) to help with the charity(자선) soccer match next month. As you know, our best players will compete against(~와 경쟁하다) our graduates(졸업자) at Ebanwood Stadium. Volunteers will show the audience(관중) to their seats and tidy up(깨끗하게 정리하다) after the match. All the money from the ticket sales will get donated(기부하다) to the local(지역의) children's hospital. This will be a great opportunity(기회) to get involved in(~에 참여하다) helping children. Please don't hesitate(망설이다) to apply for(~에 지원하다) this volunteer work at our charity soccer match. For more information, you can check the school website. Thank you.

해석

여: 안녕하세요, Timberglade 고등학교 학생 여러분. 체육 교사 Ms. Larsen입니다. 다음 달에 있을 자선 축구 경기를 도울 자원봉사자를 찾고 있다는 것을 알리고자 합니다. 여러분도 알다시피, 우리의 최고 선수들이 Ebanwood 경기장에서 우리 졸업생들과 경쟁할 것입니다. 자원봉사자들은 관중들을 자리로 안내하고 경기 후에 깨끗하게 정리할 것입니다. 티켓 판매로 얻은 모든 돈은 지역 어린이 병원에 기부될 예정입니다. 이는 어린이들을 돕는 데 참여할 수 있는 아주 좋은 기회일 것입니다. 자선 축구 경기의 이 자원봉사 활동에 주저하지 말고 지원하세요. 더 많은 정보는 학교 웹사이트를 확인하시면 됩니다. 고맙습니다.

문제 풀이

다음 달에 있을 자선 축구 경기를 도울 자원봉사자 모집을 안내하고 있다.

2. ② | 의견

선택지 선택비율	① 1%	② 95%	③ 1%	④ 2%	⑤ 0%

M: Honey, I heard the Smith family moved out to the countryside(시골[전원] 지역). I really envy(부러워하다) them.
W: Really? Why is that?
M: ⓐI think we can stay healthy if we live in the country(시골, 전원).
W: Hmm, can you be more specific(구체적인)?
M: Here in the city the air is polluted(오염된), but ⓑit's cleaner in the country.
W: That makes sense(일리가 있다) because there're fewer cars.
M: Right. And ⓒit's less noisy in the country, too. We'll be less stressed(스트레스받다).
W: I guess we could also sleep better since there isn't constant(끊임없는) noise at night.

M: Plus, ⓓwe can even grow our own fruits and vegetables.
W: That'd be nice. We can have a healthier diet.
식사
M: Definitely. ⓔI'm sure country living will help us enjoy a healthy life.
W: I agree.

해석

남: 여보. Smith 씨 가족이 시골 지역으로 이사를 갔다고 들었어요. 정말 그들이 부러워요.
여: 정말이요? 왜요?
남: ⓐ우리가 시골에 산다면 더 건강하게 지낼 수 있을 것 같아요.
여: 음, 더 구체적으로 말해 줄 수 있나요?
남: 여기 도시에는 공기가 오염되었지만, ⓑ시골에는 더 깨끗하잖아요.
여: 차가 더 적으니 일리가 있네요.
남: 맞아요. 그리고 또 ⓒ시골은 덜 시끄럽잖아요. 우리는 스트레스를 덜 받을 거예요.
여: 밤에 끊임없는 소음이 없으니 더 잘 잘 수도 있겠네요.
남: 게다가, ⓓ우리는 심지어 우리 자신의 과일과 채소도 재배할 수 있어요.
여: 그거 좋겠네요. 우리는 더 건강한 식사를 할 수 있어요.
남: 그렇고말고요. ⓔ난 시골 생활이 우리가 건강한 삶을 누리는 데 도움이 될 거라고 확신해요.
여: 동의해요.

문제 풀이

남자는 ⓐ시골에 살면 더 건강하게 지낼 수 있다고 말하며, 그 이유로 ⓑ시골의 공기가 더 깨끗하고 ⓒ소음이 적으며 ⓓ과일과 채소를 재배할 수 있다는 점을 말하고 있다. 마지막으로 ⓔ시골 생활이 건강한 삶에 도움이 될 것임을 다시 한번 강조하고 있다.

3. ① | 관계

선택지 선택비율	① 97%	② 2%	③ 1%	④ 0%	⑤ 0%

W: Hello, Mr. Newton. Welcome to the *Delicacies Show*.
M: Thanks for inviting me.
invite: 초대하다
W: I want to first start talking about your famous apple bread. ⓐCan you briefly introduce it to our radio show listeners?
간단히 소개하다
M: Sure. ⓑInstead of sugar, I use home-made apple sauce when I bake bread.
W: That's interesting. What inspired the recipe?
영감을 주다
M: Well, one day, I saw a news report about local apple farmers. They were experiencing difficulty due to decreasing apple consumption.
~ 때문에 감소하는, 점점 줄어드는 소비
W: So you created this new recipe to help the local economy.
경제
M: Yes. I also thought that the apple's sweetness could add a special flavor.
달콤함, 단맛
맛, 풍미
W: Sounds delicious. ⓒI'll definitely go to your bakery and try some of your bread.
M: Actually, I brought some for you and your radio show staff.
W: Oh, thank you. We'll be back after a commercial break.
(텔레비전·라디오의) 광고 (방송)

해석

여: 안녕하세요, Newton 선생님. 'Delicacies Show'에 오신 걸 환영합니다.
남: 초대해 주셔서 감사합니다.
여: 먼저 선생님의 유명한 사과빵에 대해 이야기해 보고 싶어요. ⓐ저희 라디오 쇼 청취자분들께 그것을 간단히 소개해 주시겠어요?
남: 물론이죠. ⓑ저는 빵을 구울 때 설탕 대신 수제 사과 소스를 사용합니다.
여: 흥미롭네요. 무엇이 그 레시피에 영감을 주었나요?
남: 음, 어느 날 지역 사과 농부들에 대한 뉴스 보도를 봤습니다. 감소하는 사과 소비 때문에 그분들이 어려움을 겪고 있더라고요.
여: 그래서 지역 경제를 돕기 위해 새로운 레시피를 만드신 거군요.
남: 네. 또한 사과의 단맛이 특별한 맛을 더할 수 있다고 생각했습니다.
여: 맛있을 것 같아요. ⓒ꼭 선생님의 제과점에 가서 빵을 먹어 봐야겠어요.
남: 사실, 진행자님과 라디오 쇼 직원들을 위해 빵을 좀 가져왔습니다.
여: 오, 감사합니다. 잠시 광고 후에 돌아오겠습니다.

문제 풀이

여자가 남자에게 ⓐ라디오 쇼 청취자들을 위해 남자가 만든 유명한 사과빵을 소개해 달라는 것으로 보아 여자는 라디오 쇼 진행자이며, 남자가 ⓑ자신이 빵을 굽는 방법을 설명하고 여자는 ⓒ남자의 제과점에 가봐야겠다고 말하는 것으로 보아 남자는 제빵사임을 알 수 있다.

4. ④ | 그림 일치

선택지 선택비율	① 1%	② 0%	③ 0%	④ 97%	⑤ 0%

M: Hello, Ms. Miller. I'm Joshua's father.
W: Hi, Mr. Smith. Thanks for coming to our parent-teacher meeting.
M: It's nice to meet you. This room looks great. Wow! Look at the wall.
W: You know, Joshua loves ⓐthe elephant between the lion and the panda.
M: Does he like ⓑthe mobile hanging from the ceiling, too?
매달리다
W: He does. The children made it together.
M: They did a wonderful job. ⓒThat toy dinosaur next to the bookshelf looks good.
W: Oh, I put it there because the children have been learning about dinosaurs.
M: That sounds fun. There are ⓓtwo boxes under the Christmas tree. What are they for?
W: They're presents for the class. We've got some candies for the kids.
M: Aha. The Christmas tree is decorated so nicely. ⓔThe star on top of the tree looks very pretty.
장식하다
W: Thanks. The meeting will start soon. Let's go upstairs, Mr. Smith.
위층[2층]으로

해석

남: 안녕하세요, Miller 선생님. 저는 Joshua의 아빠입니다.
여: 안녕하세요, Smith 씨. 학부모 교사 모임에 와 주셔서 감사합니다.
남: 만나서 반갑습니다. 이 방은 아주 좋아 보이네요. 우와! 벽을 보세요.
여: 아시다시피, Joshua가 ⓐ사자와 팬더 사이에 있는 코끼리를 아주 좋아한답니다.
남: ⓑ천정에 매달려 있는 모빌도 좋아하나요?
여: 좋아해요. 아이들이 함께 만든 거예요.
남: 아주 잘했네요. ⓒ책장 옆에 있는 저 공룡 장난감이 좋아 보이네요.
여: 아, 아이들이 공룡에 대해 배우는 중이라 그걸 그곳에 두었죠.
남: 재미있겠네요. ⓓ크리스마스트리 아래 상자 두 개가 있네요. 뭘 위한 거죠?
여: 반 아이들을 위한 선물이에요. 아이들을 위해 사탕을 좀 준비했거든요.
남: 아하. 크리스마스트리가 굉장히 멋지게 장식되었네요. ⓔ트리 꼭대기에 있는 별이 무척 예뻐 보여요.
여: 고맙습니다. 모임이 곧 시작할 거예요. 위층으로 가시죠, Smith 씨.

문제 풀이

ⓓ크리스마스트리 아래 상자 두 개가 있다고 했다.

5. ② | 할 일

선택지 선택비율	① 1%	② 98%	③ 1%	④ 0%	⑤ 0%

W: Brian. I'm so excited about our school club photo this Friday.
M: Me, too. The photo will be included in our graduation album. Let's check our preparations for it.
졸업, 졸업식
준비
W: All right. I'm going to decorate our club's room with ribbons.

M: You said you'll bring some from home, right?
W: Yes. When is the photographer coming?
사진작가, 사진사
M: The photographer is coming after lunch.
W: Great. That gives us time to get ready. You know I surveyed our club
(설문) 조사하다
members about what to wear for the photo.
M: Right. What were the results?
W: Most of our members wanted to wear heart-shaped sunglasses. Now all that's left is to buy them for our members.
M: I know a good online store. ⓐI can order the sunglasses.
W: Could you? That'll be great.
M: No problem. ⓑI'll take care of that.

해석

여: Brian, 난 이번 주 금요일에 우리 학교 동아리 사진 찍는 것이 너무 기대돼.
남: 나도 그래. 그 사진은 우리 졸업 앨범에 실릴 거야. 그것에 대한 우리의 준비를 점검해 보자.
여: 좋아. 나는 우리 동아리 방을 리본으로 장식할 거야.
남: 네가 집에서 좀 가져온다고 했지, 그렇지?
여: 응. 사진사는 언제 오지?
남: 사진사는 점심 식사 후에 올 거야.
여: 잘됐다. 우리가 준비할 시간이 있겠어. 너도 알다시피 내가 우리 동아리 회원들에게 사진 찍을 때 뭘 입을지 설문 조사를 했잖아.
남: 맞다. 결과가 뭐였어?
여: 대부분의 회원들이 하트 모양의 선글라스를 쓰고 싶어 했어. 이제 회원들한테 선글라스를 사 주는 일만 남았네.
남: 내가 좋은 온라인 상점을 하나 알고 있어. ⓐ내가 선글라스를 주문할 수 있어.
여: 그렇게 해 줄 수 있겠니? 그럼 정말 좋지.
남: 문제없어. ⓑ그건 내가 맡을게.

문제 풀이

남자는 동아리 사진 촬영 때 쓸 ⓐ선글라스를 주문할 수 있다며 ⓑ자신이 그 일을 맡겠다고 했다.

6. ② | 금액

선택지 선택비율	① 5%	② 85%	③ 5%	④ 1%	⑤ 1%

M: Welcome to the Science and Technology Museum. How can I help you?
W: Hi. I want to buy admission tickets.
입장권
M: Okay. ⓐThey're $20 for adults and $10 for children.
W: Good. ⓑTwo adult tickets and two child tickets, please. ⓒAnd I'm a member of the National Robot Club. Do I get a discount?
할인을 받다
M: Yes. ⓓYou get 10 percent off all of those admission tickets with your membership.
W: Excellent.
M: We also have the AI Robot program. You can play games with the robots and take pictures with them.
W: That sounds interesting. How much is it?
M: ⓔIt's just $5 per person. But the membership discount does not apply to this program.
~에 적용되다
W: Okay. ⓕI'll take four tickets.
M: So ⓖtwo adult and two child admission tickets, and four AI Robot program tickets, right?
W: Yes. Here are my credit card and membership card.

해석

남: 과학기술 박물관에 오신 것을 환영합니다. 어떻게 도와드릴까요?
여: 안녕하세요. 입장권을 사고 싶어요.
남: 알겠습니다. ⓐ어른은 20달러이고 아이는 10달러입니다.
여: 좋네요. ⓑ어른 입장권 두 장과 아이 입장권 두 장 주세요. ⓒ그리고 저는 국립 로봇 클럽 회원이에요. 할인을 받나요?
남: 네. ⓓ회원이시면 모든 입장권에 10퍼센트 할인을 받습니다.
여: 정말 잘됐네요.
남: 저희는 AI 로봇 프로그램도 있습니다. 로봇과 게임을 하고 같이 사진을 찍으실 수 있습니다.
여: 그거 재미있겠네요. 얼마인가요?
남: ⓔ인당 5달러밖에 안 합니다. 하지만 회원 할인이 이 프로그램에는 적용되지 않습니다.
여: 알겠습니다. ⓕ표 네 장 살게요.
남: 그러면 ⓖ어른 입장권 두 장과 아이 입장권 두 장, 그리고 AI 로봇 프로그램 표 네 장이지요, 맞나요?
여: 네. 여기 제 신용 카드와 회원증입니다.

문제 풀이

ⓐ어른은 20달러이고 아이는 10달러인 입장권을 ⓑⓖ두 장씩 구매하면서 ⓒⓓ10퍼센트 회원 할인을 받으며, ⓔ회원 할인이 적용되지 않고 한 장에 5달러인 AI 로봇 프로그램 표 ⓕⓖ네 장을 구입한다. 따라서 지불할 금액은 74달러이다.

7. ① | 이유

선택지 선택비율	① 98%	③ 1%	③ 0%	④ 0%	⑤ 0%

M: Good morning, Ms. Lee. Are you heading to Morning Tea Club?
~로 향하다
W: Not today, Mr. Thomson. I can't attend it this time.
참석하다
M: Really? But you enjoy starting the workday by drinking tea with
근무일, 평일
co-workers. Did you forget to bring your tea?
동료
W: No, I always keep it in my bag.
M: Are you just too tired this morning because you worked late last night?
W: Not at all. I feel fine, just like usual.
M: Then, has your doctor told you not to drink too much tea?
W: No, my doctor actually encourages me to drink tea. He says it's
권장[장려]하다
good for my health.
M: Oh, I see. Something else must have come up then.
발생하다
W: Yes. I have an early business meeting that overlaps with the tea
겹치다
club.
M: That's too bad. I hope your meeting goes well.

해석

남: 안녕하세요, 이 선생님. Morning Tea Club에 가시는 건가요?
여: 오늘은 아니에요, Thomson 선생님. 이번에는 거기에 참석할 수 없어요.
남: 정말요? 하지만 동료들과 함께 차를 마시면서 근무일을 시작하는 걸 좋아하시잖아요. 차를 가져오는 걸 잊으셨나요?
여: 아니요, 저는 그걸 항상 제 가방 안에 넣어 놔요.
남: 어젯밤에 늦게까지 일해서 오늘 아침에 너무 피곤하신 건가요?
여: 전혀요. 평소처럼 괜찮아요.
남: 그럼, 의사 선생님이 차를 너무 많이 마시지 말라고 하신 건가요?
여: 아니요, 의사 선생님은 오히려 제게 차를 마시라고 권장해요. 그게 제 건강에 좋다고 말씀하시거든요.
남: 아, 그렇군요. 그럼 다른 일이 생긴 거겠네요.
여: 네. 차 모임 시간이랑 겹치는 이른 비지니스 미팅이 있어서요.
남: 아쉽네요. 미팅 잘 하시길 바랍니다.

문제 풀이

아침 일찍 비지니스 미팅 시간과 겹쳐 차 모임에 참석할 수 없다고 말하고 있다.

8. ④ | 언급

선택지 선택비율	① 0%	② 0%	③ 1%	④ 98%	⑤ 0%

M: Honey, did you hear that the local aquarium is holding an event called Outstanding [뛰어난] Octopuses?

W: Outstanding Octopuses? What's it for?

M: ⓐThe purpose [목적] of the event is to promote [홍보하다] World Octopus Day.

W: Sounds interesting. What programs does the event have?

M: There are several programs. ⓑThey include [포함하다] exhibiting [전시하다] various octopuses from the Pacific [태평양] Ocean and showing a documentary about how to protect them.

W: Really? Let me search for more information on my phone. *[Pause]* Oh, ⓒit's sponsored [후원하다] by the Aqua Life Council [의회, 협회].

M: I'm glad that they're helping people realize how remarkable [놀라운] these creatures [생물] are.

W: I agree. ⓓThe event started on October 4th and will end on December 8th.

M: Good. We still have a lot of time to visit.

W: You're right. Let's make plans to go soon.

해석

남: 여보, 지역 수족관에서 Outstanding Octopuses라고 하는 행사가 열리고 있다는 거 들었어요?
여: Outstanding Octopuses? 그게 무슨 행사예요?
남: ⓐ그 행사의 목적은 세계 문어의 날을 홍보하는 거예요.
여: 흥미롭네요. 행사에 어떤 프로그램들이 있나요?
남: 여러 프로그램이 있어요. ⓑ태평양에서 온 다양한 문어 전시와 그들을 보호하는 방법에 관한 다큐멘터리 상영을 포함하고 있어요.
여: 그래요? 내 휴대전화로 정보를 더 찾아볼게요. [잠시 후] 아, ⓒ해양 생물 협회의 후원을 받네요.
남: 그들이 사람들로 하여금 이 생물이 얼마나 놀라운지 깨닫도록 돕고 있어서 기뻐요.
여: 동의해요. ⓓ행사는 10월 4일에 시작했고 12월 8일에 끝날 거예요.
남: 좋아요. 방문할 시간이 아직 많이 있네요.
여: 맞아요. 조만간 갈 계획을 세워요.

문제 풀이

ⓐ목적, ⓑ프로그램, ⓒ후원 기관, ⓓ기간은 언급되었으나, 입장료는 언급되지 않았다.

9. ⑤ | 내용 일치

선택지 선택비율	① 1%	② 1%	③ 0%	④ 1%	⑤ 96%

W: Welcome back to Design Talk. Today I have exciting news for you. One of the world's largest design conferences [회의, 학회] is coming soon. It's the Global Design Conference. ⓐThe conference is held every year in Chicago. It aims to [~을 목표로 하다] keep people informed [알려주다] about the current [현재의] trends in design. This year ⓑthere'll be lectures by famous designers and practical [실용적인] workshops. In addition, ⓒthe works made by 100 designers will be displayed [전시하다]. These selected [선택된, 엄선된] works will change the way you look at design. ⓓThe conference begins on June 20 and ends on the 22. Registration is only available on the conference website. The registration fee is $30, and ⓔit's non-refundable [환불이 안 되는]. If design is important to you, mark [표시하다] your calendar now!

해석

여: Design Talk에 돌아오신 걸 환영합니다. 오늘은 여러분을 위한 흥미로운 소식이 있습니다. 세계에서 가장 큰 디자인 학회들 중 하나가 곧 찾아옵니다. 그 학회는 세계 디자인 학회입니다. ⓐ그 학회는 매년 시카고에서 개최됩니다. 그 학회는 사람들에게 현재의 디자인 추세에 대해 알려주는 것을 목표로 합니다. 올해에는 ⓑ유명 디자이너들의 강연과 실용적인 워크숍이 있을 예정입니다. 게다가, ⓒ100명의 디자이너들이 만든 작품들이 전시될 것입니다. 이 엄선된 작품들은 여러분이 디자인을 보는 방식을 바꿀 것입니다. ⓓ학회는 6월 20일에 시작해서 22일에 끝납니다. 등록은 오직 학회 웹사이트에서만 가능합니다. 등록비는 30달러이고, ⓔ환불이 불가능합니다. 디자인이 여러분에게 중요하다면, 지금 달력에 표시하세요!

문제 풀이

ⓔ등록비는 환불이 불가능하다고 했다.

10. ② | 도표

선택지 선택비율	① 1%	② 93%	③ 2%	④ 2%	⑤ 1%

W: Jason, what's that in your hand?

M: It's a flyer [전단지] from the neighborhood flower shop, Mom.

W: Oh, they're selling plant seed [씨] kits! I want one. Can you help me choose?

M: Sure. ⓐI don't think you need the most expensive kit since it's your first try.

W: Right. But I'd like some variety [여러 가지, 다양성]. So, ⓑat least four kinds of plants would be nice.

M: Okay. What about the pots [화분]? They come in different materials [재질].

W: ⓒI don't want the ceramic [도자기] one. It'll be too heavy for me.

M: Good point. ⓓI think the one that comes with a plant growing guide would be helpful for you.

W: Yes, I can easily find out how to grow plants.

M: Then this seed kit is perfect for you.

W: Thanks for helping me. I'll buy that one.

해석

여: Jason, 네 손에 있는 그거 뭐니?
남: 동네 꽃가게에서 받은 전단지예요, 엄마.
여: 오, 식물 씨앗 키트를 파는구나! 하나 사고 싶네. 선택하는 거 도와줄래?
남: 물론이죠. ⓐ처음 해보시는 거니까 제일 비싼 키트는 필요하시지 않을 것 같아요.
여: 맞아. 하지만 좀 다양하면 좋겠구나. 그러니까 ⓑ적어도 네 가지 식물이 좋을 것 같아.
남: 알겠어요. 화분은요? 재질이 여러 가지로 나와요.
여: ⓒ도자기 화분은 원하지 않아. 나한테는 너무 무거울 것 같아.
남: 맞아요. ⓓ제 생각에는 식물 재배 설명서가 함께 나오는 것이 엄마에게 도움이 될 것 같아요.
여: 응, 식물 키우는 방법을 쉽게 알 수 있겠네.
남: 그러면 이 씨앗 키트가 엄마에게 딱이에요.
여: 도와줘서 고마워. 그걸로 살게.

문제 풀이

ⓐ가격이 가장 비싼 것은 제외하고 ⓑ네 가지 이상의 식물이 있으며 ⓒ도자기 화분이 아닌 ⓓ식물 재배 설명서가 포함된 식물 씨앗 키트를 사기로 했다.

11. ② | 짧은 대화 응답

선택지 선택비율	① 1%	② 97%	③ 0%	④ 1%	⑤ 0%

W: Dad, I want to send this book to Grandma. Do you have a box?

M: Yeah. I've got this one to put photo albums in, but it's a bit [조금, 다소, 약간] small.

W: The box looks big enough for the book. Can I use it?
M: Of course. You can have it.

해석

여: 아빠, 이 책을 할머니께 보내 드리고 싶어요. 상자 가지고 계세요?
남: 응. 사진첩을 넣을 이 상자가 있는데, 조금 작구나.
여: 상자가 책을 넣기엔 충분히 커 보여요. 제가 써도 될까요?
남: 물론이지. 네가 써도 된단다.

문제 풀이

여자가 상자가 책을 넣기에 충분히 커 보인다며 그 상자를 써도 되는지 물었으므로, 써도 된다는 ②가 응답으로 가장 적절하다.
① 아직. 그것을 보내는 걸 잊어버렸단다.
③ 미안해. 사진이 다 팔렸단다.
④ 맞아. 넌 책을 사면 안 돼.
⑤ 고맙지만 괜찮아. 난 앨범을 원치 않아.

12. ③ | 짧은 대화 응답

선택지 선택비율	① 1%	② 2%	③ 92%	④ 2%	⑤ 0%

M: Amy, you said you're going to study at Donna's house tonight, right?
W: Yes, Dad. We have to submit our team report online by midnight.
제출하다
M: I think you'll be quite late. Should I pick you up?
~을 데리러 가다
W: Sure. I'll call you when I'm done.

해석

남: Amy, 너 오늘 밤 Donna의 집에서 공부할 거라고 했지, 그렇지?
여: 네, 아빠. 저희는 자정까지 팀 보고서를 온라인으로 제출해야 해요.
남: 네가 꽤 늦을 것 같구나. 내가 널 데리러 가야 할까?
여: 좋아요. 제가 끝나면 전화할게요.

문제 풀이

여자가 늦게 올 것 같아서 남자가 데리러 가야 할지 물었으므로, 끝나고 전화하겠다는 ③이 응답으로 가장 적절하다.
① 아니에요. 아빠는 저희와 함께 공부할 수 없어요.
② 알겠어요. 제가 보고서를 혼자 쓸게요.
④ 네. 저는 아빠 팀에 들어와서 기뻐요.
⑤ 죄송해요. 아빠는 내일까지 마쳐야 해요.

13. ④ | 긴 대화 응답

선택지 선택비율	① 2%	② 3%	③ 3%	④ 79%	⑤ 13%

[Cell phone rings.]
M: Hello, Joe Burrow speaking.
W: Hello. This is Officer Blake from the Roselyn Police Station.
M: Oh, it's good to speak to you again.
W: Nice to speak to you, too. ⓐDo you remember the boy who found your briefcase and brought it here?
서류 가방
M: Sure. I wanted to give him a reward. But he wouldn't accept it.
보상, 사례금 / 받다, 받아들이다
W: I remember you saying that before.
M: Yeah. I'd still like to somehow express my thanks in person.
어떻게든 / 표현하다 / 직접
W: Good. ⓑThat's why I'm calling you. Are you available next Friday at 10 a.m.?
M: Yes. I'm free at that time. Why?
W: The boy will receive the Junior Citizen Award for what he's done for you.
받다 / 시민
M: That's great news!
W: ⓒThere'll be a ceremony for him at the police station, and he invited you as his guest. I was wondering if you can make it.
기념식 / 가다, 참석하다
M: Definitely. I want to go to congratulate him myself.
축하하다

해석

[휴대전화가 울린다.]
남: 여보세요, Joe Burrow입니다.
여: 여보세요. Roselyn 경찰서의 Blake 경찰관이에요.
남: 아, 다시 통화하게 되니 반갑네요.
여: 저도 반갑습니다. ⓐ선생님의 서류 가방을 찾아서 여기로 가져왔던 소년 기억하세요?
남: 물론이죠. 사례금을 주고 싶었죠. 하지만 받으려고 하지를 않았어요.
여: 전에 그렇게 말씀하신 게 기억나요.
남: 네. 여전히 어떻게든 직접 감사를 표하고 싶어요.
여: 잘됐네요. ⓑ그래서 제가 전화드리는 거예요. 다음 주 금요일 오전 10시에 시간 되세요?
남: 네. 그때 한가해요. 왜요?
여: 그 소년이 선생님을 위해 한 일로 청소년 시민상을 받게 돼요.
남: 좋은 소식이네요!
여: ⓒ경찰서에서 그를 위한 의식이 있을 거고, 그가 선생님을 손님으로 초대했어요. 참석하실 수 있는지 궁금했어요.
남: 되고 말고요. 제가 직접 가서 그를 축하해 주고 싶어요.

문제 풀이

여자는 남자에게 전화해서 ⓐ남자의 서류 가방을 찾아준 ⓒ소년을 위한 의식이 경찰서에서 있을 예정임을 알리며 ⓑ참석 여부를 물었으므로, 참석 여부를 말하며 가서 축하해 주겠다는 내용의 ④가 응답으로 가장 적절하다.
① 걱정하지 마세요. 이미 그의 서류 가방을 찾았어요.
② 물론이에요. 당신은 그 상을 받을 만해요.
③ 천만에요. 저는 그저 시민으로서의 의무를 했을 뿐인걸요.
⑤ 멋져요. 제가 갔던 최고의 의식이었어요.

14. ⑤ | 긴 대화 응답

선택지 선택비율	① 1%	② 1%	③ 2%	③ 1%	⑤ 93%

M: Hey, Jessica. You got here early.
W: You too, Mike. What are you reading?
M: I'm reading a magazine article about the musical *Spring Empire*.
기사 / 제국, 왕국
W: Oh, *Spring Empire*? I'm going to see it next week. What does the article say?
M: It mentions that the leading actors are geniuses and that the musical is going to be so popular.
말하다, 언급하다 / 주연 배우
W: Wow, I really can't wait to see it.
can't wait to-v: 빨리 ~하고 싶다
M: Actually, I've seen it already. ⓐSince you haven't watched the musical, I recommend you read the original novel first.
추천하다, 권하다
W: Why do you say that?
M: The storyline is complicated. In my case, reading the novel first helped me fully understand and better enjoy the musical.
줄거리 / 복잡한
W: ⓑThen, I need to get a copy of the book.
(책의) 한 부, 한 권
M: ⓒI have one. I can lend it to you if you want.
W: Thanks. Then, I'll read the novel before I watch the musical.

해석

남: 안녕, Jessica. 여기 일찍 왔구나.
여: 너도네, Mike. 뭘 읽고 있어?
남: 뮤지컬 〈봄의 제국〉에 관한 잡지 기사를 읽는 중이야.
여: 아, 〈봄의 제국〉? 나 그거 다음 주에 보러 갈 거야. 기사에서 뭐라고 하니?

남: 주연 배우가 천재들이며 그 뮤지컬이 인기가 아주 많을 거라고 하네.
여: 와, 정말로 그걸 빨리 보고 싶다.
남: 실은, 난 이미 그거 봤어. ⓐ네가 그 뮤지컬을 보지 않았으니 너에게 원작 소설을 먼저 읽어보는 것을 추천해.
여: 왜 그런 말을 하니?
남: 줄거리가 복잡하거든. 내 경우에는 소설을 먼저 읽는 게 뮤지컬을 완전히 이해하고 더 즐기는 데 도움이 됐어.
여: ⓑ그럼 그 책을 한 권 구해야겠다.
남: ⓒ내가 가지고 있어. 네가 원하면 빌려줄 수 있어.
여: 고마워. 그럼 나는 뮤지컬 보기 전에 그 소설을 읽을래.

문제 풀이

ⓐ뮤지컬을 보기 전에 원작 소설을 먼저 읽어볼 것을 권하는 남자의 말을 듣고 여자가 ⓑ책을 구해야겠다고 하자, 남자는 ⓒ여자가 원한다면 자신의 책을 빌려줄 수 있다고 했으므로 고마움을 표하는 ⑤가 응답으로 가장 적절하다.
① 동감이야. 그 배우들은 뮤지컬에서 연기를 잘했어.
② 맞아. 뮤지컬에 대한 평을 기다려 보자.
③ 좋아. 이제 우리는 뮤지컬 대본을 다시 써야 해.
④ 아주 좋아. 나는 우리 공연을 위해 새 악기가 필요해.

15. ① | 상황에 적절한 말

선택지 선택비율	① 87%	② 1%	③ 3%	④ 6%	⑤ 1%

M: Jake and Yuna are members of a climbing club. Today, they're visiting a national park (국립 공원) with other club members. At the top of the mountain, Jake sees a beautiful rock. He starts taking selfies (셀피) with it. When Yuna sees Jake, she offers (제안하다) to take photos for him. Jake finds a great spot (자리) to take a photo with the rock and gives Yuna his smartphone. ⓐAfter Yuna takes some photos of him, Jake looks at the photos and notices (알게 되다) that the rock is not in them. So ⓑJake wants to ask Yuna to get another shot of him and this time include (포함하다) the rock. In this situation, what would Jake most likely say to Yuna?
Jake: Could you please take my picture again with the rock in it?

해석

남: Jake와 Yuna는 등산 동아리 회원이다. 오늘, 그들은 동아리 다른 회원들과 함께 국립 공원을 방문한다. 산 정상에서, Jake는 아름다운 바위를 본다. 그는 그것과 함께 셀피를 찍기 시작한다. Yuna가 Jake를 보고, 그를 위해 사진을 찍어주겠다고 제안한다. Jake는 바위와 함께 사진을 찍을 좋은 자리를 찾아 Yuna에게 자신의 스마트폰을 준다. ⓐYuna가 그의 사진들을 찍은 후, Jake는 사진들을 보고 그 바위가 그 안에 없다는 것을 알게 된다. 그래서 ⓑJake는 Yuna에게 자신의 사진을 한 장 더 찍는데 이번에는 그 바위를 포함시켜 달라고 부탁하고 싶다. 이 상황에서, Jake는 Yuna에게 뭐라고 말하겠는가?
Jake: 바위가 나오도록 내 사진을 다시 한번 찍어줄 수 있니?

문제 풀이

ⓐJake는 Yuna가 자신을 찍어준 사진에 바위가 나오지 않았다는 사실을 알게 되고, ⓑYuna에게 그 바위를 포함해서 다시 한번 사진을 찍어달라고 부탁하고 싶어 하므로, ①이 가장 적절하다.
② 나와 함께 산에 가준다면 고맙겠어.
③ 바위에 오르는 동안에는 사진을 찍으면 안 돼.
④ 바위 앞에서 포즈를 취할 수 있는지 궁금해.
⑤ 국립 공원에서 셀피를 찍는 게 어때?

16~17. | 세트 문항

16. ① 17. ③

선택지 선택비율	① 92%	② 1%	③ 1%	④ 1%	⑤ 3%
	① 0%	② 0%	③ 94%	④ 3%	⑤ 0%

M: ⓐHow did people send mail before they had access to (have access to: ~을 이용할 수 있다) cars and trains? There were simple options out there, like delivery by animal. ⓑHorses were frequently utilized (이용하다) in delivery of letters and messages. In the 19th century, a mail express system that used horses serviced a large area of the United States. ⓒPigeons may be seen as a problem by many people today. However, in ancient Greece, they were used to mail people the results of the Olympics between cities. Alaska and Canada are known for their cold winters. In their early days, ⓓdogs were utilized to deliver mail because they've adapted (적응하다) to run over ice and snow. Maybe the most fascinating (대단히 흥미로운) of all delivery animals is the camel. Australia imported (수입하다) ⓕcamels from the Middle East and utilized them to transfer (수송하다) mail across vast deserts. They were ideally (이상적으로) suited (적합한) to this job because they can go without water for quite a while. Fortunately, we've developed faster and more reliable (신뢰할 수 있는) delivery systems, but we should not ignore the important roles these animals played in the past.

해석

남: ⓐ사람들은 자동차와 기차를 이용할 수 있기 전에 어떻게 우편물을 보냈을까요? 동물에 의한 배달과 같은 간단한 선택이 있었답니다. ⓑ말이 편지와 메시지 전달에 자주 이용되었죠. 19세기에 말을 이용한 우편물 급행 시스템이 미국의 넓은 지역에서 서비스를 했습니다. ⓒ비둘기는 오늘날 많은 사람들에게 문제로 여겨질 수도 있습니다. 하지만 고대 그리스에서, 비둘기는 도시들 사이에서 사람들에게 올림픽 경기의 결과를 전하는 데 이용되었습니다. 알래스카와 캐나다는 추운 겨울로 알려져 있는데요. 초기에는 ⓓ개가 우편물을 배달하는 데 이용되었는데요, 얼음과 눈 위에서 달리도록 적응했기 때문입니다. 아마도 모든 배달 동물 중에서 가장 흥미로운 동물은 낙타일 것입니다. 호주는 중동에서 ⓕ낙타를 수입해서 광활한 사막을 건너 우편물을 수송하는 데 이들을 이용했습니다. 낙타는 물 없이 상당히 오랫동안 지낼 수 있기 때문에 이 일에 이상적으로 적합했지요. 다행히, 우리는 더 빠르고 더 신뢰할 수 있는 배달 시스템을 개발했지만, 이 동물들이 과거에 담당했던 중요한 역할을 무시하면 안 됩니다.

문제 풀이

16. ⓐ교통수단이 발달하기 전에 우편물을 전달하기 위해 어떤 동물이 이용되었는지에 관해 말하고 있으므로, 남자가 하는 말의 주제로 가장 적절한 것은 ① '역사상 우편 배달에 이용된 동물들'이다.
② 야생 동물 훈련의 어려움
③ 환경 변화에 대한 동물의 적응
④ 여러 나라의 멸종 위기 동물
⑤ 동물들이 서로에게 메시지를 전달한 방법들
17. ⓑ말, ⓒ비둘기, ⓓ개, ⓕ낙타는 언급되었으나, 독수리(eagles)는 언급되지 않았다.

[코드 공략하기]

제4회 고급 모의고사

1	③	2	①	3	③	4	④	5	②	6	②
7	③	8	⑤	9	②	10	③	11	③	12	①
13	②	14	④	15	⑤	16	①	17	⑤		

1. ③ | 목적

선택지 선택비율	① 1%	② 2%	③ 97%	④ 0%	⑤ 0%

M: Hello, Lockwood High School students. This is your school librarian, Mr. Wilkins. I'm sure you're aware that our school library
(도서관의) 사서 be aware that: ~을 알다
is hosting a bookmark design competition. I encourage students
주최하다 책갈피 권장[장려]하다
of all grades to participate in the competition. The winning designs
당선된
will be made into bookmarks, which will be distributed to library
나누어 주다, 배포하다
visitors. We're also giving out a variety of other prizes. So don't let
다양한
this great opportunity slip away. Since the registration period for
기회 사라지다 등록 기간
the bookmark design competition ends this Friday, make sure you visit our school library to submit your application. Come and
제출하다 지원[신청]서
participate to display your creativity and talents.
드러내다, 발휘하다 창의력, 창조성

해석

남: 안녕하세요, Lockwood 고등학교 학생 여러분. 학교 사서 Wilkins입니다. 우리 학교 도서관이 책갈피 디자인 대회를 개최한다는 것을 여러분이 알고 있으리라 확신합니다. 모든 학년의 학생들이 대회에 참가할 것을 장려합니다. 당선된 디자인은 책갈피로 제작되어 도서관 방문자들에게 배포될 것입니다. 다른 다양한 상품도 드릴 예정입니다. 그러니 이 좋은 기회가 사라지게 하지 마세요. 책갈피 디자인 대회 등록 기간이 이번 주 금요일에 끝나니, 꼭 우리 학교 도서관에 방문해서 신청서를 제출하세요. 여러분의 창의력과 재능을 발휘하기 위해 와서 참가하세요.

문제 풀이

학교 도서관에서 책갈피 디자인 대회를 개최함을 알리며 참가할 것을 장려하고 있다.

2. ① | 의견

선택지 선택비율	① 94%	② 1%	③ 0%	④ 1%	⑤ 0%

W: Andrew, you look unhappy. What's wrong?
M: Hi, Ms. Benson. I've been trying this chemical reaction experiment
화학 반응 실험
again and again, but it's not working.
되풀이해서
W: Why isn't it working?
M: I don't know. Maybe I don't have much talent for chemistry.
재능 화학
W: Don't be so hard on yourself.
~을 심하게 대하다[나무라다]
M: So what should I do?
W: ⓐI believe that the path to success is through analyzing failure.
길 analyze: 분석하다 실패
M: Analyzing failure? What do you mean?
W: By examining what went wrong in your experiment, you can do it
examine: 검토하다 go wrong: 잘못되다
right.
M: Hmm. You mean that even though my experiment didn't work, I can learn something from failure?
W: Exactly. ⓑIf you figure out how and why it didn't work, you can
~을 이해하다[알아내다]
succeed at your experiment.
성공하다
M: Now I understand. I'll review my experiment. Thanks.
재검토하다

해석

여: Andrew, 기분이 안 좋아 보이네. 무슨 일이니?
남: 안녕하세요, Benson 선생님. 이 화학 반응 실험을 되풀이해서 해보고 있는데 제대로 되지 않아요.
여: 왜 잘 안 되는 걸까?
남: 모르겠어요. 아마 제가 화학에 그다지 재능이 없나 봐요.
여: 네 자신을 너무 심하게 나무라지 마라.
남: 그럼 제가 어떻게 해야 하죠?
여: ⓐ나는 실패를 분석하는 것을 통한 성공의 길이 있다고 생각한단다.
남: 실패를 분석한다고요? 무슨 말씀이세요?
여: 네 실험에서 무엇이 잘못되었는지 검토함으로써, 네가 그것을 제대로 할 수 있다는 거야.
남: 음. 선생님은 제 실험이 제대로 되지 않았더라도 제가 실패로부터 무언가를 배울 수 있다는 말씀이신가요?
여: 그렇지. ⓑ네가 실험이 어떻게, 그리고 왜 잘 되지 않았는지 이해한다면 실험에서 성공할 수 있단다.
남: 이제 알겠어요. 제 실험을 다시 검토할게요. 감사합니다.

문제 풀이

화학 반응 실험이 제대로 되지 않는다는 남자에게 여자는 ⓐ실패를 분석하는 것을 통한 성공의 길이 있다고 생각한다며 ⓑ실험이 어떻게, 그리고 왜 실패했는지 이해한다면 실험에서 성공할 수 있다고 말하고 있다.

3. ③ | 관계

선택지 선택비율	① 1%	② 0%	③ 95%	④ 1%	⑤ 0%

M: Hello, I'm Ted Benson. You must be Ms. Brown.
W: Hi, Mr. Benson. ⓐThank you for sparing time for this interview. I've
spare: (시간이나 돈 등을) 할애하다, 내어 주다
wanted to meet you since you won the "Best Rice Award."
M: I'm honored. I'm a regular reader of your magazine. The articles
영광으로 생각하는 정기 구독자
are very informative.
유용한 정보를 주는, 유익한
W: Thank you. Can you tell me the secret to your success?
M: ⓑI grow rice without using any chemicals to kill harmful insects.
화학 물질
It's organic.
유기농의
W: How do you do that?
M: I put ducks into my fields, and they eat the insects.
W: So that's how you grew the best rice in the country. What a great idea!
M: Yeah, ⓒthat's the know-how I've got from my 30 years of farming
노하우(실질적인 지식과 경험)
life.
W: Well, it's amazing. ⓓMay I take a picture of you in front of your rice
논
fields for my magazine article?
M: Go ahead.

해석

남: 안녕하세요, 저는 Ted Benson입니다. Brown 씨이시죠.
여: 안녕하세요, Benson 씨. ⓐ이 인터뷰를 위해 시간을 내 주셔서 감사합니다. '최고의 쌀 상'을 수상하시고 뵙고 싶었습니다.
남: 영광입니다. 저는 귀 잡지의 정기 구독자예요. 기사가 매우 유익하더라고요.
여: 감사합니다. 제게 성공 비결을 말씀해 주실 수 있나요?

남: ⓑ저는 해충을 죽이는 어떤 화학 물질도 사용하지 않고 쌀을 재배합니다. 유기농이지요.
여: 어떻게 그렇게 하시나요?
남: 논에 오리를 넣으면, 오리가 해충을 먹습니다.
여: 그럼 그게 국내 최고의 쌀을 재배하신 방법이군요. 정말 좋은 생각이에요!
남: 그래요, ⓒ그게 제 30년의 농경 생활에서 얻은 노하우예요.
여: 음, 놀라워요. ⓓ저희 잡지 기사에 쓰도록 논 앞에서 선생님 사진을 찍어도 될까요?
남: 그렇게 하세요.

문제 풀이

여자는 ⓐ남자를 인터뷰하고 있고 ⓓ잡지에 쓸 사진을 찍는 것으로 보아, 잡지기자임을 알 수 있다. 남자는 ⓑ자신의 쌀 재배 방법이 ⓒ30년의 농경 생활을 통한 노하우라고 말하는 것으로 보아, 농부임을 알 수 있다.

4. ④ | 그림 일치

선택지 선택비율	① 0%	② 0%	③ 0%	④ 96%	⑤ 1%

W: What are you looking at, honey?
M: Aunt Mary sent me a picture. She's already set up a room for Peter. (~을 준비하다[설치하다])
W: Wow! She's excited for him to stay during the winter vacation, isn't she?
M: Yes, she is. I like ⓐthe blanket with the checkered pattern on the bed.
W: I'm sure it must be very warm. Look at ⓑthe chair below the window.
M: It looks comfortable. He could sit there and read.
W: Right. I guess that's why Aunt Mary put ⓒthe bookcase next to it. (책장)
M: That makes sense. Oh, there's ⓓa toy horse in the corner.
W: It looks real. I think it's a gift for Peter.
M: Yeah, I remember she mentioned it. And do you see ⓔthe round mirror on the wall? (말하다, 언급하다)
W: It's nice. It looks like the one Peter has here at home.
M: It does. Let's show him this picture.

해석

여: 뭘 보고 있어요, 여보?
남: Mary 이모님이 사진 한 장을 보내오셨어요. Peter를 위한 방을 이미 준비하셨네요.
여: 우와! 이모님이 겨울 방학 동안 그 애가 머무는 것에 들떠 계신 것 같아요, 그렇지 않아요?
남: 그래요. ⓐ침대 위에 체크 무늬 담요가 마음에 드네요.
여: 분명 무척 따뜻할 거예요. ⓑ창문 아래 의자를 봐요.
남: 편안해 보이네요. 그 애가 거기 앉아서 책을 읽을 수 있겠어요.
여: 맞아요. 그래서 Mary 이모님이 ⓒ그 옆에 책장을 두신 것 같아요.
남: 일리가 있네요. 아, ⓓ모퉁이에 말 장난감이 있네요.
여: 진짜처럼 보여요. Peter를 위한 선물 같아요.
남: 네, 이모님이 그렇게 말씀하신 게 기억나요. 그리고 ⓔ벽에 둥근 거울 보여요?
여: 멋져요. Peter가 여기 집에 갖고 있는 것과 비슷해 보이네요.
남: 그렇네요. 그 애에게 이 사진을 보여줍시다.

문제 풀이

여자는 ⓓ모퉁이에 말 장난감이 있다고 했다.

코드+α 동의를 구하는 표현

- **Don't you think so?** (그렇게 생각하지 않니?)
- This rose is beautiful, **isn't it?** (이 장미가 아름답네, 그렇지 않니?)

5. ② | 할 일

선택지 선택비율	① 1%	② 95%	③ 2%	④ 1%	⑤ 1%

W: Oliver, I'm so excited about the party for the new members of our tennis club this Friday.
M: Me, too. Let's go through the to-do list. I want it to be perfect. (~을 살펴보다)
W: Agreed. Did you reserve the Mexican restaurant downtown for the party? (예약하다 / 시내에)
M: Yes, I did. The restaurant is spacious, so it's perfect for a party like ours. (넓은)
W: Plus, the food there is terrific. And you prepared gifts for the new members, right? (아주 좋은, 훌륭한)
M: Yeah, they're in my car. Did you remind the members about the party? (상기시키다)
W: I've just sent a text message to everyone.
M: Great. ⓐWhat about the tennis competition schedule? Have you printed it out?
W: Oh, I almost forgot. ⓑI'll do it tonight. Um, is the music ready?
M: Uh-huh. I made a playlist last night. (곡목표, 재생 목록)
W: That's great. I think we're good to go!

해석

여: Oliver, 이번 주 금요일에 우리 테니스 동아리 신입 회원들을 위한 파티가 정말 기대돼.
남: 나도. 우리 할 일 목록을 살펴보자. 완벽했으면 좋겠거든.
여: 동의해. 파티를 위해 시내에 있는 멕시코 음식 식당을 예약했니?
남: 응, 했어. 식당이 넓어서 우리 같은 동아리 파티에 제격이야.
여: 게다가 거기 음식도 훌륭해. 그리고 신입 회원들을 위한 선물도 준비했지?
남: 응, 내 차 안에 있어. 파티에 대해 회원들에게 상기시켰니?
여: 방금 모두에게 문자 메시지를 보냈어.
남: 좋아. ⓐ테니스 대회 일정은? 그거 인쇄했니?
여: 아, 깜빡할 뻔했네. ⓑ오늘 밤에 할게. 음, 음악은 준비됐니?
남: 응. 어젯밤에 재생 목록을 만들었어.
여: 잘했네. 우린 준비가 잘 된 것 같아!

문제 풀이

남자가 ⓐ테니스 대회 일정을 인쇄했냐고 묻자, 여자가 ⓑ오늘 밤에 하겠다고 대답했다.

코드+α 일의 진행 상황에 관한 표현

- Good to go. (준비 다 됐어.)
- I'm all good to go. (나는 준비 다 됐어.)
- How is it going with your project? (프로젝트는 어떻게 되고 있어?)
- Everything is working out so well. (모든 게 아주 잘 풀리고 있어.)

6. ② | 금액

선택지 선택비율	① 2%	② 95%	③ 2%	④ 1%	⑤ 0%

M: Welcome to the Chestfield Hotel. How may I help you?
W: Hi, I'm Alice Milford. I made a reservation for me and my husband.
M: *[Typing sound]* Here it is. ⓐYou reserved one room for one night at the regular rate of $100. (정상 요금)
W: ⓑCan I use this 10% discount coupon?
M: ⓒSure, you can.
W: Fantastic. And ⓓis it possible to stay one more night? (머물다, 묵다)

M: Let me check. *[Mouse clicking sound]* Yes, the same room is available for tomorrow.
W: Good. ⓔDo I get a discount for the second night, too?
M: Sorry. ⓕThe coupon doesn't apply to the second night. It'll be $100.
~에 적용되다
Do you still want to stay an extra night?
추가의
W: Yes, I do.
M: Great. ⓖWill you and your husband have breakfast? It's $10 per person for each day.
W: ⓗNo thanks. We'll be going out early to go shopping. Here's my credit card.

해석

남: Chestfield 호텔에 오신 걸 환영합니다. 어떻게 도와드릴까요?
여: 네, 저는 Alice Milford에요. 저와 제 남편으로 예약했어요.
남: [타이핑하는 소리] 여기 있네요. ⓐ100달러 정상 요금으로 객실을 하룻밤 예약하셨네요.
여: ⓑ이 10% 할인 쿠폰을 사용할 수 있나요?
남: ⓒ그럼요, 사용하실 수 있습니다.
여: 아주 좋네요. 그리고 ⓓ하룻밤 더 묵는 게 가능한가요?
남: 확인해 보겠습니다. [마우스 클릭하는 소리] 네, 같은 객실이 내일 이용 가능합니다.
여: 좋아요. ⓔ두 번째 밤도 할인받나요?
남: 죄송합니다. ⓕ이 쿠폰은 두 번째 밤에는 적용되지 않습니다. 100달러입니다. 그래도 추가 하룻밤 묵길 원하시나요?
여: 네.
남: 좋습니다. ⓖ고객님과 남편분은 아침식사를 하실 건가요? 하루에 1인당 10달러입니다.
여: ⓗ괜찮아요. 쇼핑하러 일찍 나갈 거예요. 여기 제 신용 카드요.

문제 풀이

ⓐ정상 요금이 1박에 100달러인 객실을 ⓑⓒ10% 할인받으며, ⓓ추가하는 1박은 ⓔⓕ할인이 적용되지 않아 100달러이다. ⓖⓗ아침식사는 하지 않으므로, 여자가 지불할 금액은 100(1−0.1)+100=190달러이다.

7. ③ | 이유

선택지 선택비율	① 0%	② 1%	③ 98%	④ 0%	⑤ 0%

W: Hey, John. Come and look at this poster.
M: Hi, Sharon. The Streamline Broadcasting Workshop? What's that?
방송
W: It's a student workshop that offers an opportunity to connect with
제공하다 기회 가까워지다
experts in broadcasting. How about going together?
전문가
M: Oh, it's on Friday. I wish I could, but I can't.
W: Why not? Is your dance club's performance on that day?
공연
M: No, the performance is next month.
W: Then, is your little brother's birthday party on Friday?
M: No, it was last week. I got him a hat as a present.
W: So why can't you go to the workshop?
M: Actually, I'm going to see a baseball game on that day. I have tickets for that game.
W: Oh, I see. I hope your team wins.

해석

여: 안녕, John. 와서 이 포스터 봐.
남: 안녕, Sharon. Streamline 방송 워크숍? 그게 뭐야?
여: 방송 전문가들과 가까워질 기회를 제공하는 학생 워크숍이야. 같이 가는 게 어때?
남: 아, 금요일에 하네. 가고 싶지만, 못 가.
여: 왜 못 가? 너희 댄스 동아리 공연이 그날에 있니?
남: 아니, 공연은 다음 달이야.
여: 그럼 네 남동생 생일 파티가 금요일에 있어?
남: 아니, 그건 지난주였어. 그애에게 모자를 선물로 줬지.
여: 그럼 왜 워크숍에 못 가?
남: 사실, 그날 야구 경기를 볼 거야. 그 경기 티켓을 가지고 있거든.
여: 아, 그렇구나. 너희 팀이 이기길 바랄게.

문제 풀이

금요일에 야구 경기를 볼 거라 워크숍에 갈 수 없다고 말하고 있다.

8. ⑤ | 언급

선택지 선택비율	① 1%	② 0%	③ 0%	④ 0%	⑤ 99%

W: Hey, Nathan. Have you heard of the Autumn Treasure Hunt event
가을 보물찾기
that is coming soon?
M: Autumn Treasure Hunt? That's interesting. Where will it take place?
개최되다
W: ⓐIt'll be held in Pinenut Park. Participants can search for hidden
~을 찾다
treasure there.
M: Sounds fun. You know I'm a great treasure hunter. When is it?
W: It's this Saturday, ⓑNovember 22nd.
M: Perfect. I'm free that day. There must be a big prize for the winner. Do you know what it is?
W: Yeah. If you collect the most treasure, ⓒyou'll get a gift card worth
모으다
$100 as a reward.
보상, 상
M: Wow, that's a big prize. How can I sign up for the Autumn Treasure Hunt event?
W: ⓓYou can visit its website and register online.
등록하다
M: Awesome! Let's go there together.
W: That'd be great.

해석

여: 얘, Nathan. 곧 열릴 '가을 보물찾기' 행사 들어봤어?
남: '가을 보물찾기'? 그거 흥미로운데. 어디서 열릴 예정이야?
여: ⓐPinenut 공원에서 열릴 거야. 참가자들이 그곳에서 숨겨진 보물을 찾을 수 있어.
남: 재밌겠다. 알다시피 나 보물찾기 잘하거든. 언제 하는 거야?
여: 이번 주 토요일, ⓑ11월 22일이야.
남: 잘됐다. 나 그날 시간 있어. 우승자한테는 분명 큰 상이 있을 거야. 뭔지 알아?
여: 응. 가장 많은 보물을 모으면, ⓒ100달러짜리 기프트 카드를 상으로 받게 될 거야.
남: 와, 그거 큰 상이네. '가을 보물찾기' 행사에 어떻게 신청할 수 있어?
여: ⓓ웹사이트에 방문해서 온라인으로 등록하면 돼.
남: 좋아! 우리 거기에 같이 가자.
여: 그거 좋겠다.

문제 풀이

ⓐ장소, ⓑ날짜, ⓒ상품, ⓓ신청 방법은 언급되었지만, 후원 기관은 언급되지 않았다.

9. ② | 내용 일치

선택지 선택비율	① 1%	② 76%	③ 15%	④ 4%	⑤ 3%

W: Hello, listeners. I'm Melinda Jones from the organizing committee
창립[조직] 위원회
of the Greenville Houseplant Expo. I'm here to announce that ⓐthe
실내용 화초
expo will run for three days starting on March 17th, 2023. ⓑJust on the opening day, there'll be a lecture on plant care methods. This
강의 방법
lecture will be given by Dr. Evans, host of the TV show *Plants Love You*. Most importantly, ⓒyou can buy a variety of plants, including rare species, exhibited in the expo. Due to its popularity, you'd
희귀종 인기
better get your tickets early. ⓓTickets are available through online

purchase only. If you're a plant lover, come to the expo, which
구매
ⓔwill take place at the Emerald Convention Center, and refresh
새롭게 하다, 새로 공급하다
your houseplant collection.
소장품

해석

여: 안녕하세요, 청취자 여러분. Greenville 실내용 화초 엑스포 조직 위원회의 Melinda Jones입니다. 2023년 3월 17일부터 ⓐ3일간 엑스포가 진행될 것임을 알려 드리기 위해 이 자리에 섰습니다. ⓑ개막일에만 식물 관리 방법에 관한 강의가 있을 예정입니다. 이 강의는 TV 쇼 〈Plants Love You〉의 진행자인 Evans 박사가 할 것입니다. 가장 중요한 것은, 여러분이 엑스포에 전시된 ⓒ희귀종을 포함한 다양한 식물들을 구매할 수 있다는 것입니다. 인기 때문에, 일찍 티켓을 구하는 것이 좋을 것입니다. ⓓ티켓은 온라인 구매를 통해서만 이용 가능합니다. 여러분이 식물 애호가라면, ⓔ에메랄드 컨벤션 센터에서 열릴 엑스포에 오셔서 여러분의 실내용 소장 화초를 새롭게 해 보세요.

문제 풀이

ⓑ개막일에만 식물 관리 방법에 관한 강의가 있을 것이라고 했다.

10. ③ ㅣ 도표

선택지 선택비율	① 0%	② 1%	③ 96%	④ 0%	⑤ 0%

M: Welcome to Jay's Lighting Store. How may I help you?
조명
W: I'm here to look for a floor lamp for my living room.
M: Here, take a look at this catalog. We have five models you can choose from. Are you looking for anything specific?
구체적인
W: Yes. It shouldn't be too short. ⓐI'd like to get one that's taller than one hundred and thirty centimeters.
M: Then how about these four models? ⓑWould you like LED bulbs?
W: ⓒYes, I would. They last longer than standard bulbs.
일반적인
M: And they save energy. I definitely recommend LEDs. What's your
분명히, 확실히
price range?
범위
W: Well, ⓓI don't want to spend more than fifty dollars.
M: Then you have two options left. Which color do you like better?
W: Hmm..., ⓔI'll go with the white one.
M: Good choice. Would you like to pay in cash or by credit card?
W: I'll pay in cash.

해석

남: Jay의 조명가게에 오신 것을 환영합니다. 무엇을 도와드릴까요?
여: 저는 거실에 놓을 바닥 램프를 구하러 왔어요.
남: 여기 이 카탈로그를 보세요. 고객님이 고를 수 있는 다섯 개의 모델이 있습니다. 구체적으로 찾는 것이 있으신가요?
여: 네. 높이가 너무 낮으면 안 돼요. ⓐ저는 130cm보다 높은 것을 사고 싶어요.
남: 그렇다면 이 네 개의 모델들은 어떤가요? ⓑLED 전구로 하시겠어요?
여: ⓒ네, 그러고 싶어요. 그것들이 일반 전구보다 오래가니까요.
남: 그리고 에너지도 절약되죠. 저는 단연코 LED 전구를 추천해 드립니다. 가격 범위는 얼마인가요?
여: 음, ⓓ저는 50달러 이상은 쓰고 싶지 않아요.
남: 그렇다면 두 개의 선택 사항이 남았네요. 어떤 색이 더 좋으신가요?
여: 음…, ⓔ흰색으로 할게요.
남: 잘 선택하셨어요. 현금으로 계산하시겠어요, 아니면 신용카드로 하시겠어요?
여: 현금으로 계산할게요.

문제 풀이

ⓐ높이가 130cm보다 높고, ⓑⓒLED 전구로 되어 있고, ⓓ가격이 50달러 이하이며, ⓔ흰색인 램프는 ③이다.

11. ③ ㅣ 짧은 대화 응답

선택지 선택비율	① 3%	② 1%	③ 93%	④ 1%	⑤ 0%

M: Lisa, are you okay from all the walking we did today?
W: Actually, Dad, ⓐmy feet are tired from all the sightseeing. Also,
관광
ⓑI'm thirsty because the weather is so hot out here.
목마른
M: ⓒOh, then let's go somewhere inside and get something to drink. Where should we go?
W: How about going to the cafe over there?

해석

남: Lisa, 오늘 우리가 여기저기를 걸어 다녔는데 괜찮니?
여: 사실, 아빠, ⓐ여기저기 관광하느라 발이 피곤해요. 게다가, ⓑ여기 밖에 날씨가 너무 더워서 목이 말라요.
남: ⓒ아, 그럼 안에 어디 들어가서 마실 것을 좀 사자. 어디로 갈까?
여: 저기 카페로 가는 게 어때요?

문제 풀이

ⓐ발도 피곤하고 ⓑ날씨가 더워 목이 마르다는 여자의 말에, 남자가 ⓒ마실 것을 사러 안에 들어가자고 하며 어디로 갈지 물었으므로, 가고 싶은 곳을 말하는 ③이 여자의 응답으로 가장 적절하다.
① 오늘은 나가고 싶지 않아요.
② 공항에 빨리 도착하셔야 해요.
④ 관광하러 가고 싶어 하시는지 몰랐어요.
⑤ 더 편한 신발을 신지 그러셨어요?

12. ① ㅣ 짧은 대화 응답

선택지 선택비율	① 80%	② 1%	③ 14%	④ 5%	⑤ 0%

W: Honey, the hotel offers a free yoga class on the beach to the guests.
손님, 투숙객
Do you want to go with me tomorrow morning?
M: Oh, really? ⓐI definitely want to try yoga, but I'm afraid we might be
반드시, 꼭
the only beginners.
초보자
W: Don't worry. ⓑThis class is for true beginners who have never done yoga before. So why don't we take it?
M: In that case, let's give it a try.

해석

여: 여보, 호텔에서 투숙객들에게 해변에서 무료 요가 수업을 제공해요. 내일 아침에 나랑 같이 갈래요?
남: 오, 정말요? ⓐ요가를 꼭 해보고 싶긴 한데, 우리만 초보자일까 봐 걱정이네요.
여: 걱정 말아요. ⓑ이 수업은 요가를 전에 전혀 해본 적 없는 진짜 초보자를 위한 거예요. 그러니까 우리 수업을 듣는 게 어때요?
남: 그렇다면, 한번 해보죠.

문제 풀이

ⓐ요가를 해보고 싶지만 자신들만 초보자일까 봐 걱정하는 남자에게 여자는 ⓑ초보자를 위한 수업이라며 함께 들을 것을 재차 권유하고 있으므로, 그렇다면 한번 해보자는 ①이 남자의 응답으로 가장 적절하다.
② 잘 모르겠어요. 약간 비싸네요.
③ 우리가 들어본 수업 중 최고예요.
④ 초보자들에게 요가를 가르쳐 주게 되어 기뻐요.
⑤ 당신 말이 맞아요. 호텔의 전망이 정말 멋져요.

13. ② | 긴 대화 응답

선택지 선택비율	① 1%	② 87%	③ 1%	④ 5%	⑤ 6%

W: Hi. Can I get some help over here?
M: Sure. What can I help you with?
W: ⓐI'm thinking of buying this washing machine.
M: Good choice. It's our best-selling model.
W: I really like its design and it has a lot of useful features. I'll take it.
특징
M: Great. ⓑHowever, you'll have to wait for two weeks. We're out of this model right now.
be out of: ~이 떨어지다[바닥나다]
W: Oh, no. ⓒI need it today. My washing machine broke down yesterday.
break down: 고장 나다
M: Then ⓓhow about buying the one on display?
전시[진열]된
W: Oh, I didn't know I could buy the displayed one.
전시[진열]하다
M: Sure, you can. ⓔWe can deliver and install it today.
W: That's just what I need, but it's not a new one.
M: Not to worry. It's never been used. Also, like with the new ones, ⓕyou can get it repaired for free for up to three years.
~을 수리하다
W: That's good.
M: ⓖWe can also give you a 20% discount on it. It's a pretty good deal.
W: I agree. The displayed one may be the best option for me.

해석

여: 안녕하세요. 여기 좀 도와주시겠어요?
남: 네. 뭘 도와드릴까요?
여: ⓐ이 세탁기를 살까 생각 중이에요.
남: 잘 고르셨네요. 가장 잘 팔리는 모델이에요.
여: 디자인이 정말 마음에 들고 유용한 특징이 많네요. 이걸로 할게요.
남: 좋아요. ⓑ하지만 2주를 기다리셔야 할 거예요. 지금 당장 이 모델은 다 떨어졌거든요.
여: 이런. ⓒ오늘 필요한데요. 제 세탁기가 어제 고장 났거든요.
남: 그러면 ⓓ전시된 것을 구매하시는 건 어떨까요?
여: 아, 전시된 것을 살 수 있는지 몰랐어요.
남: 물론 구입하실 수 있답니다. ⓔ오늘 배송해서 설치해 드릴 수 있어요.
여: 딱 제가 필요한 바이긴 하지만, 새 제품이 아니잖아요.
남: 걱정하실 것 없어요. 사용한 적은 결코 없어요. 그리고 새 제품과 마찬가지로 ⓕ3년까지 동안은 무료로 수리받으실 수 있어요.
여: 좋네요.
남: ⓖ그것에 20% 할인도 해 드릴 수 있습니다. 꽤 괜찮은 가격이죠.
여: 그렇네요. 저한테는 전시 제품이 가장 좋은 선택일지 모르겠네요.

문제 풀이

ⓐ여자가 구입하려는 세탁기의 ⓑ재고가 없어서 기다려야 하는데 ⓒ여자는 당장 필요한 상황에서, 남자는 ⓓ전시 제품 구입을 권하며 ⓔⓕⓖ좋은 점을 말하고 있으므로, 여자의 응답으로 가장 적절한 것은 ②이다.
① 죄송해요. 이걸 내일까지 기다릴 수는 없을 것 같아요.
③ 이런. 전시 모델을 판매하지 않으신다니 정말 안타깝네요.
④ 좋아요. 세탁기가 수리되면 전화 주세요.
⑤ 바로 그거예요. 당신이 전시 제품을 샀다니 기쁘네요.

코드 +α 제품의 기능에 관한 표현

- This device has brand-new **features**. (이 기기는 최신 기능이 있어.)
- This product has the basic **function** of remote control. (이 제품은 원격 제어의 기본 기능이 있어.)

14. ④ | 긴 대화 응답

선택지 선택비율	① 0%	② 1%	③ 2%	④ 93%	⑤ 1%

W: Honey, what did the doctor say about your neck?
M: She said that it's not too bad. I just need to take these pills and get enough rest.
알약
W: I'm relieved that it's not so serious.
안심한, 안도한
M: But there's a problem. ⓐThe doctor said I shouldn't drive after taking the medicine. It can make me very sleepy.
졸리는, 졸음이 오는
W: Oh, no. What about your business trip on Monday?
M: Exactly. ⓑI'm supposed to drive my team members since I know the area.
be supposed to-v: ~하기로 되어 있다
W: You cannot drive. It would be very dangerous.
M: Maybe I'll skip the medicine before I drive.
거르다[빼먹다]
W: Wouldn't it delay your recovery and even make your neck pain worse?
(건강) 회복
M: Yeah. I do need to take the medicine regularly.
규칙적으로
W: ⓒThen one solution would be to see if somebody else in your team can drive instead of you.
해결책 / ~ 대신에
M: Okay. I'll ask my team so I can take the medicine.

해석

여: 여보, 의사가 당신 목에 대해 뭐라고 했나요?
남: 그다지 심하지는 않다고 했어요. 그냥 이 알약을 먹고 충분히 쉬면 돼요.
여: 그리 심각하지 않다니 안심이 되네요.
남: 그런데 문제가 있어요. ⓐ의사가 말하기를 약을 먹은 후에 운전을 하면 안 된대요. 심한 졸음이 올 수 있대요.
여: 아, 저런. 월요일에 있는 당신 출장은 어쩌죠?
남: 그러니까요. 내가 그 지역을 알고 있기 때문에 ⓑ팀원들을 태워서 가기로 되어 있어요.
여: 당신은 운전할 수 없어요. 정말 위험할 거예요.
남: 아마 운전하기 전에 약 먹는 걸 거를 수 있을 거예요.
여: 그러면 회복이 늦어지고 목 통증도 더 심해지지 않을까요?
남: 맞아요. 약을 정말 규칙적으로 먹어야 해요.
여: ⓒ그렇다면 한 가지 해결책은 당신 팀에 있는 다른 누군가가 당신 대신 운전을 할 수 있는지 확인해 보는 것이겠네요.
남: 알겠어요. 내가 약을 먹을 수 있도록 팀원들에게 물어볼게요.

문제 풀이

남자는 ⓑ팀원들을 태우고 출장지까지 직접 운전을 하기로 예정되어 있는데 ⓐ복용해야 하는 약이 졸음을 유발할 수 있어 염려하는 상황이다. 이에 여자가 ⓒ남자를 대신하여 운전할 수 있는 팀원이 있는지 확인해 보는 것이 하나의 해결책이라고 했으므로, 팀원들에게 물어보겠다는 ④가 남자의 응답으로 가장 적절하다.
① 물론이죠! 당신은 가서 진찰을 받아야 해요.
② 문제없어요. 출장 중에 당신을 찾아갈게요.
③ 물론이에요. 당신은 운전하기 전에 길 안내를 확인해 볼 수 있어요.
⑤ 맞아요. 여행하는 것은 스트레스를 푸는 아주 좋은 방법이에요.

15. ⑤ | 상황에 적절한 말

선택지 선택비율	① 2%	② 4%	③ 3%	④ 4%	⑤ 86%

W: David and Julia are teachers working at the same high school. This year, they have to develop an after-school program for first-year students. Before they get to work, they look at the last year's program, which was very successful. Julia thinks the program
개발하다 / 일에 착수하다

looks quite good and wants to do it again. However, David is unsure.
확신하지 못하는
He thinks that the students may want to do different things from what last year's students did. And he wants to first find out what
~을 알아내다
this year's students would like to do. Therefore, he wants to suggest to Julia that they should hear from the students about their preferences. In this situation, what would David most likely say to
선호하는 것
Julia?
David: Let's ask the students what they prefer to do.

해석

여: David와 Julia는 같은 고등학교에서 근무하는 교사이다. 올해 그들은 1학년 학생들을 위한 방과 후 프로그램을 개발해야 한다. 그들은 일에 착수하기 전에 작년 프로그램을 보았는데, 그것은 매우 성공적이었다. Julia는 그 프로그램이 꽤 괜찮아 보인다고 생각해서 그것을 다시 하기를 원한다. 하지만 David는 확신하지 못한다. 그는 학생들이 지난해 학생들이 했던 것과 다른 것을 하고 싶어 할지 모른다고 생각한다. 그리고 그는 먼저 올해의 학생들이 무엇을 하고 싶어 하는지 알아내길 원한다. 따라서 그는 그들이 학생들로부터 선호하는 것에 대해 들어봐야 한다고 Julia에게 제안하고 싶다. 이 상황에서, David는 Julia에게 뭐라고 말하겠는가?
David: 학생들에게 뭐 하는 걸 선호하는지 물어봅시다.

문제 풀이

Julia에게 그들이 학생들로부터 선호하는 것에 대해 들어봐야 한다고 제안하고 싶다고 했으므로, 정답으로는 학생들에게 뭐 하는 걸 선호하는지 물어보자는 ⑤가 가장 적절하다.
① 우리는 작년에 우리가 무엇을 했는지 확인할 필요가 있어요.
② 올해 프로그램을 취소하는 게 어떨까요?
③ 제가 이 일을 다른 선생님들께 맡길게요.
④ 방과 후에 그 프로그램에 참여하는 게 어떨까요?

16~17. | 세트 문항

16. ① 17. ⑤

선택지 선택비율	① 94%	② 2%	③ 1%	④ 2%	⑤ 2%
	① 0%	② 0%	③ 0%	④ 1%	⑤ 98%

W: Hello, students. Do you know that plants often help scientists understand the wonders of nature? ⓐLet's look at some plants
경이, 놀라움 자연
that are perfect for science experiments because they grow
실험
quickly. First, ⓑbamboo is known for quick growth, with some
대나무 be known for: ~로 알려져 있다, ~로 유명하다
varieties growing inches per day. Therefore, it absorbs
variety: 품종, 종류 흡수하다
a large amount of CO_2, so it's often used in studies about how to
많은 양의
reduce climate change. Second, ⓒlettuce grows quickly and is
줄이다 기후 변화 상추
sensitive to environmental conditions. So, scientists grow it to
민감한 환경의 조건
see the effects of various chemicals on plant growth. Third,
영향 화학 물질
ⓓsunflowers are known for their remarkable growth rate,
놀라운 속도
sometimes reaching several feet in just a few months. That's why
~에 이르다
scientists use them to learn about the effects of soils on plant height.
토양
Finally, ⓔpeas are classic plants for experiments about genetics
완두콩 전형적인 유전학
as they grow quickly and have easily observable characteristics
~ 때문에 식별[관찰]할 수 있는 특성, 특징
like seed color and shape. For these reasons, the famous scientist, Mendel, studied them. After a short break, we'll look at other plants that are good for science experiments.

해석

여: 안녕하세요, 학생 여러분. 여러분은 식물이 종종 과학자들이 자연의 경이로움을 이해하는 데 도움을 준다는 걸 알고 있나요? ⓐ빠르게 자라기 때문에 과학 실험에 아주 적합한 몇 가지 식물들을 살펴봅시다. 첫째로, ⓑ대나무는 빠른 성장으로 유명한데, 어떤 품종은 하루에 몇 인치씩 자라기도 합니다. 그래서 그것은 많은 양의 이산화탄소를 흡수하기 때문에, 기후 변화를 줄이는 방법에 관한 연구에 자주 사용됩니다. 둘째로, ⓒ상추는 빠르게 자라고 환경 조건에 민감합니다. 그래서 과학자들은 여러 가지 화학 물질이 식물의 성장에 미치는 영향을 알아보기 위해 그것을 재배합니다. 셋째로, ⓓ해바라기는 놀라운 성장 속도로 유명한데, 때때로 몇 달 만에 몇 피트까지 자라기도 합니다. 이 때문에 과학자들은 토양이 식물의 키에 미치는 영향을 연구하기 위해 그것을 이용합니다. 마지막으로, ⓔ완두콩은 빠르게 자라고 씨앗의 색깔과 모양 같은 특성을 쉽게 관찰할 수 있기 때문에 유전학에 관한 실험을 위한 전형적인 식물입니다. 이런 이유로, 유명한 과학자인 멘델도 그것을 연구했습니다. 잠깐 휴식을 가진 뒤, 과학 실험에 좋은 다른 식물들도 살펴보도록 하겠습니다.

문제 풀이

16. ⓐ빠른 성장 속도 때문에 과학 실험에 적합한 식물들에 대해 이야기하고 있으므로, 주제로는 ① '과학 실험에 사용되는 빠르게 자라는 식물들'이 가장 적절하다.
② 과학자들이 다양한 식물 종을 보존하는 방법
③ 식물을 구매할 때 고려할 요소들
④ 식물을 빠르게 자라게 만드는 결정적인 조건들
⑤ 특정 식물들이 다른 것들보다 더 빨리 자라는 이유
17. ⓑ대나무, ⓒ상추, ⓓ해바라기, ⓔ완두콩은 언급되었으나, 옥수수(corn)는 언급되지 않았다.

[코드 공략하기]

제5회 고급 모의고사

1	①	2	③	3	②	4	④	5	②	6	④
7	①	8	③	9	④	10	④	11	①	12	②
13	①	14	④	15	①	16	⑤	17	⑤		

1. ① ㅣ 목적

선택지 선택비율	① 97%	② 1%	③ 0%	④ 0%	⑤ 0%

M: Shoppers, may I have your attention please? Thank you for visiting Miracle Department Store. We'd like to inform you of the special
알리다
events going on through this weekend. First, we're offering a 50
제공하다
percent discount on certain electronics and sporting goods on the
전자제품 상품, 물품
seventh floor. Second, we're providing a free beverage at our coffee
음료
shop on the first floor to shoppers who spend over $50. Third, we're also giving away $10 gift certificates to all shoppers who spend
give away: ~을 선물로 주다 상품권
over $100. Last but not least, you don't have to worry about
마지막으로
parking fees this weekend. Parking is free. We hope you enjoy this
주차 요금
weekend's special events at our department store.

해석

남: 쇼핑객 여러분, 주의를 기울여 주시겠습니까? Miracle 백화점을 찾아주셔서 감사합니다. 이번 주말 동안 진행되는 특별 행사를 알려드리고자 합니다. 첫째, 7층에서 특정 전자제품과 스포츠 상품에 대해 50퍼센트 할인을 제공하고 있습니다. 둘째, 50달러 넘게 지출하시는 고객님께 1층에 있는 저희 커피숍에서 무료 음료를 제공하고 있습니다. 셋째, 100달러 넘게 지출하시는 모든 고객님께 10달러 상품권을 또한 선물로 드리고 있습니다. 마지막으로, 이번 주말에는 주차 요금을 걱정하실 필요가 없습니다. 주차는 무료입니다. 저희 백화점에서 이번 주말의 특별 행사를 즐기시길 바랍니다.

문제 풀이

남자는 백화점에서 주말에 진행하는 특별 행사에 관해 안내하고 있다. 따라서 남자가 하는 말의 목적으로 가장 적절한 것은 ①이다.

2. ③ ㅣ 의견

선택지 선택비율	① 0%	② 0%	③ 97%	④ 0%	⑤ 0%

W: Hi, Sam. How are you?
M: Fine. How about you, Christine?
W: I feel really good.
M: Wow! What happened to you? You usually say you're tired.
W: Well, I changed how I sleep. ⓐI started sleeping on my left side, and it has improved my health.
개선하다
M: Really?
W: Yeah. I've done it for a week, and my digestion has got better.
소화 get better: 좋아지다
M: I didn't know how we sleep has something to do with digestion.
have something to do with: ~와 뭔가 관련이 있다
W: It does. ⓑSleeping on your left side helps the digestive process
소화 과정
because your stomach is on the left.
위
M: I can see that. But does improving digestion make you that much healthier?
W: Sleeping on the left side does more than that. ⓒI think it's good for health because it also helps blood circulation to the heart.
혈액 순환
M: That makes sense. I guess I should try it.

해석

여: 안녕, Sam. 어떻게 지내?
남: 잘 지내. 너는 어때, Christine?
여: 정말 기분 좋아.
남: 와! 어쩐 일이니? 대개는 피곤하다고 말하잖아.
여: 음, 잠자는 방식을 바꿨어. ⓐ왼쪽으로 누워 자기 시작했는데, 그게 내 건강을 개선해 줬어.
남: 정말이야?
여: 응. 일주일 동안 그렇게 했더니, 소화가 더 좋아졌어.
남: 잠자는 방식이 소화와 뭔가 관련이 있는 줄은 몰랐네.
여: 관련이 있어. ⓑ위가 왼쪽에 있기 때문에 왼쪽으로 누워 자는 것은 소화 과정에 도움이 돼.
남: 이해할 수 있겠어. 그런데 소화를 개선하는 것이 그렇게까지 훨씬 더 건강하게 해 주니?
여: 왼쪽으로 누워 자는 것은 그 이상의 효과가 있어. ⓒ나는 그게 심장으로의 혈액 순환도 돕기 때문에 건강에 좋다고 생각해.
남: 일리가 있네. 나도 시도해 봐야겠다.

문제 풀이

여자는 ⓐⓑⓒ왼쪽으로 누워 자는 것이 건강에 좋다는 것을 자신의 경험을 들어 말하고 있다.

3. ② ㅣ 관계

선택지 선택비율	① 1%	② 96%	③ 0%	④ 0%	⑤ 0%

[Cell phone rings.]
W: Hello.
M: Hello, Ms. Monroe. This is John Brown. I'm calling to invite you to a special event.
W: Oh, thank you for calling. What's the event?
M: Our museum will hold an exhibition of antique items, including
전시회 골동품 ~을 포함하여
the old pictures and tools you donated, under the theme *Life in the*
기부[기증]하다 주제
1800s.
W: That's wonderful. When is it?
M: It'll be from December 3rd to 7th. And it's all thanks to generous
~의 덕분인 관대한
people like you.
W: It's my pleasure. I want my donation to help people learn about the
기증품
past.
M: Thank you. The antique items you donated have really improved our collection.
소장품
W: I'm glad to hear that. I'm looking forward to visiting the exhibition.
M: I'll send you the invitation letter soon.
초대장
W: Great. I'll be waiting for it.
M: Again, on behalf of our museum, we appreciate your donation.
~을 대표하여 감사하다

해석

[휴대전화가 울린다.]
여: 여보세요.
남: 안녕하세요, Monroe 선생님. 저는 John Brown입니다. 선생님을 특별한 행사에 초대하고자 전화 드렸습니다.
여: 아, 전화해 주셔서 감사합니다. 행사가 뭔가요?
남: 저희 박물관에서 선생님께서 기증해 주신 오래된 그림과 도구를 포함하여 '1800년대의 삶'이라는 주제로 골동품 전시회를 개최할 예정입니다.

여: 멋지네요. 언제인가요?
남: 12월 3일부터 7일까지입니다. 그리고 이 모든 것이 선생님처럼 관대한 분들 덕분입니다.
여: 별말씀을요. 저는 사람들이 과거에 대하여 아는 데 제 기증품이 도움이 되면 좋겠어요.
남: 감사합니다. 선생님께서 기증해 주신 골동품들 덕에 저희 소장품이 정말로 훌륭해졌습니다.
여: 그 말씀을 들으니 기쁘군요. 그 전시회에 가는 게 기대되네요.
남: 곧 초대장을 보내드리겠습니다.
여: 좋습니다. 기다리고 있겠습니다.
남: 다시 한 번 저희 박물관을 대표하여 선생님의 기증에 감사드립니다.

문제 풀이

남자가 자신의 박물관에서 여자의 기증품을 포함하여 골동품 전시회를 개최할 예정이라고 말하는 것으로 보아, 기증자와 박물관 직원의 대화임을 알 수 있다.

4. ④ | 그림 일치

선택지 선택비율	① 1%	② 0%	③ 0%	④ 96%	⑤ 1%

M: Mom, I think the backyard is ready for Dad's birthday party.
뒷마당
W: Really? Let's see.
M: *[Pause]* I hung ⓐa screen between the trees.
hang: 걸다
W: That's nice.
M: I think he'll enjoy watching our old family videos there.
W: I'm sure he will. Oh, did you buy ⓑthe heart-shaped cake on the table?
M: Yes. I got it from Dad's favorite bakery.
W: He'll love it. What are ⓒthe two boxes under the chair?
M: They're gifts from Grandma and Grandpa.
W: How nice of them. Hmm. I think ⓓthe striped mat on the grass is too small. We cannot all sit there.
줄무늬가 있는
M: You're right. I'll bring more chairs.
W: Good idea. And you put ⓔthe grill next to the garden lamp.
M: Yeah. As you know, Dad loves barbecue.
W: Right. We're almost ready for the party.

해석

남: 엄마, 뒷마당에서 아빠 생신 파티를 할 준비가 된 것 같아요.
여: 그래? 어디 보자.
남: [잠시 후] 제가 ⓐ나무 사이에 스크린을 걸었어요.
여: 그거 좋구나.
남: 아빠가 그곳에서 우리의 오래된 가족 비디오를 보는 것을 좋아하실 것 같아요.
여: 분명 그러실 거야. 오, 네가 ⓑ테이블 위에 있는 하트 모양 케이크를 샀니?
남: 네. 아빠가 가장 좋아하시는 빵집에서 샀어요.
여: 정말 좋아하실 거야. ⓒ의자 밑에 있는 상자 두 개는 뭐니?
남: 할머니와 할아버지께서 주신 선물이에요.
여: 정말 다정하시다. 음. 내 생각에는 ⓓ잔디 위에 있는 줄무늬 매트가 너무 작은 것 같구나. 우리 모두가 거기에 앉을 수 없어.
남: 맞아요. 제가 의자를 더 가져올게요.
여: 좋은 생각이야. 그리고 ⓔ정원 전등 옆에 그릴을 놨구나.
남: 네. 아시다시피, 아빠는 바비큐를 정말 좋아하시잖아요.
여: 맞아. 우리 파티가 거의 다 준비됐구나.

문제 풀이

ⓓ잔디 위에 있는 줄무늬 매트라고 했으므로, 별 모양 매트인 그림의 ④는 대화 내용과 일치하지 않는다.

5. ② | 할 일

선택지 선택비율	① 1%	② 89%	③ 1%	④ 2%	⑤ 8%

W: Honey, I'm so excited for our restaurant's reopening event tomorrow.
M: So am I. Let's see. We've ordered enough ingredients, right?
재료
W: I think so. We need to remind our loyal customers of the event.
상기시키다 단골 고객
M: I already sent text messages.
W: Good. I hope people like the new menu items that we added.
M: Don't worry. We have a great chef. So I'm sure the new dishes will be a hit.
W: What about the live music? Did you confirm the song list with the band?
확정하다, 확인하다
M: Not yet. And ⓐwe also need to wrap wine glasses to give as gifts for the customers.
싸다
W: Okay. ⓑCould you wrap them?
M: Sure. ⓒI'll do it now.
W: Great! Then I'll contact the band.
연락하다

해석

여: 여보, 내일 우리 식당 재개장 행사에 너무 신나요.
남: 나도 그래요. 어디 봐요. 우리는 재료를 충분히 주문했죠, 그렇죠?
여: 그런 것 같아요. 우리는 단골 고객들에게 행사를 상기시켜야 해요.
남: 내가 이미 문자를 보냈어요.
여: 좋아요. 우리가 추가한 새 메뉴들을 사람들이 좋아하면 좋겠어요.
남: 걱정하지 마요. 우리에게 훌륭한 요리사가 있잖아요. 그래서 난 새로운 요리가 아주 잘 될 거라고 확신해요.
여: 라이브 음악은요? 밴드와 노래 목록을 확정했나요?
남: 아직이요. 그리고 ⓐ우리는 손님들에게 선물로 줄 와인 잔들 포장도 해야 해요.
여: 알았어요. ⓑ당신이 포장해 줄래요?
남: 물론이죠. ⓒ지금 할게요.
여: 좋아요! 그럼 내가 밴드와 연락해 볼게요.

문제 풀이

ⓐ고객들에게 선물로 줄 와인 잔들을 포장해야 한다고 하자, 여자가 남자에게 ⓑ포장해 주겠냐고 물었고 남자는 ⓒ지금 하겠다고 했다.

6. ④ | 금액

선택지 선택비율	① 2%	② 1%	③ 1%	④ 95%	⑤ 1%

M: Welcome to Daisy Valley Restaurant.
W: Hi. I'd like to order some food to go. How much is the shrimp pasta and the chicken salad?
M: ⓐThe shrimp pasta is $20, and the chicken salad is $10.
W: I'll take ⓑtwo shrimp pastas and ⓒone chicken salad, please.
M: Sure. Would you like some dessert, too?
W: Yes. What do you recommend?
추천하다
M: The mini cheese cake is one of the best sellers in our restaurant. ⓓIt's $5 each.
W: Great! ⓔI'll order two of them.
M: Okay. Let me confirm your order. Two shrimp pastas, one chicken salad, and two mini cheese cakes. Is that correct?
맞는
W: Yes. And I have a birthday coupon here. Can I use it?
M: Let me see. *[Pause]* Yes. ⓕYou can get a 10% discount off the total.
W: Terrific. I'll use this coupon. Here's my credit card.
아주 좋은, 훌륭한

해석

남: Daisy Valley 식당에 오신 걸 환영합니다.
여: 안녕하세요. 포장해서 가져갈 음식을 주문하고 싶은데요. 새우 파스타랑 치킨 샐러드는 얼마인가요?
남: ⓐ새우 파스타는 20달러이고, 치킨 샐러드는 10달러입니다.
여: ⓑ새우 파스타 두 개랑 ⓒ치킨 샐러드 하나 주세요.
남: 알겠습니다. 디저트도 드시겠어요?
여: 네. 무엇을 추천하시나요?
남: 미니 치즈케이크가 저희 가게에서 가장 잘 팔리는 것 중 하나입니다. ⓓ개당 5달러예요.
여: 좋아요! ⓔ두 개 주문할게요.
남: 네. 주문 확인하겠습니다. 새우 파스타 두 개, 치킨 샐러드 하나, 그리고 미니 치즈케이크 두 개 맞나요?
여: 네. 그리고 여기 생일 쿠폰이 있어요. 그걸 사용할 수 있나요?
남: 한 번 볼게요. [잠시 후] 네. ⓕ총액에서 10% 할인받으실 수 있습니다.
여: 잘됐네요. 이 쿠폰 쓸게요. 여기 제 신용카드예요.

문제 풀이

여자는 ⓐ20달러인 새우 파스타 ⓑ두 개, ⓐ10달러인 치킨 샐러드 ⓒ한 개, ⓓ5달러인 미니 치즈케이크를 ⓔ두 개 주문했는데, ⓕ총액에서 10% 할인받으므로, 여자가 지불할 금액은 (40+10+10)−6=54달러이다.

7. ① | 이유

선택지 선택비율	① 97%	② 1%	③ 1%	④ 0%	⑤ 1%

M: Ellen, what are you looking at on your smart phone?
W: Hey, John. I'm watching the movie *Romeo and Juliet*.
M: I didn't know you're interested in romantic movies.
W: To be honest, I like action movies.
솔직히 말해서
M: Then, is it for your writing assignment? You said you needed to write a paper on Shakespeare.
과제
W: No, I've already finished it.
M: Well, do you like the actors in the movie?
W: Not really. Actually, I'm going to play Juliet in the school play. And I'm watching this because I want to better understand my role.
연기하다 / 연극 / (배우의) 배역
M: Oh, that's a good idea. I'm sure it'll help you.
W: I hope so. I really want to do well.
M: Don't worry. You'll do great.
W: Thanks. You should come and watch the play.

해석

남: Ellen, 네 스마트폰으로 뭘 보고 있니?
여: 안녕, John. 나는 영화 〈로미오와 줄리엣〉을 보고 있어.
남: 네가 멜로 영화에 관심이 있는 줄 몰랐어.
여: 솔직히 말해서, 난 액션 영화를 좋아해.
남: 그러면, 작문 과제 때문이니? 네가 셰익스피어에 대한 보고서를 써야 한다고 말했잖아.
여: 아니, 벌써 그건 끝냈어.
남: 음, 영화 속 배우를 좋아하니?
여: 그렇진 않아. 사실, 난 학교 연극에서 줄리엣을 연기할 예정이야. 그리고 내 배역을 더 잘 이해하고 싶어서 이걸 보고 있는 거야.
남: 오, 좋은 생각이야. 분명 그게 널 도와줄 거야.
여: 그러길 바라. 난 정말로 잘하고 싶어.
남: 걱정하지 마. 넌 잘할 거야.
여: 고마워. 너 연극 보러 와야 해.

문제 풀이

여자는 학교 연극에서 자신의 배역을 더 잘 이해하기 위해 영화를 보고 있다고 말했다.

8. ③ | 언급

선택지 선택비율	① 1%	② 2%	③ 97%	④ 1%	⑤ 0%

[Telephone rings.]
W: Hello, Jennifer Porter speaking.
M: Hi, Ms. Porter. This is Steve Jackson from Lifetime Photo Studio.
W: Oh, how are you?
M: Good. I'm scheduled to shoot your school's graduation photos ⓐon Wednesday, November 23rd. So, I'm calling to confirm the details.
예정된 / 촬영하다 / 졸업
W: Sure. As we previously discussed, ⓑthe place will be Lily Pond Park.
이전에
M: Okay. Could you tell me the exact number of students taking part in the photo session?
정확한 / take part in: ~에 참여하다
W: Let me check. *[Pause]* Well, ⓒit'll be 180 students.
M: I see. The same as you said before.
W: That's right. How long will it take to shoot the photos?
M: ⓓIt'll take almost three hours. We should finish by noon.
W: Great. Is there any other information you need?
M: No, I'm all set. Bye.
be all set: 준비가 되어 있다

해석

[전화벨이 울린다.]
여: 여보세요, Jennifer Porter입니다.
남: 안녕하세요, Porter 씨. Lifetime 사진관의 Steve Jackson입니다.
여: 아, 어떻게 지내세요?
남: 잘 지내고 있습니다. 제가 ⓐ11월 23일 수요일에 선생님 학교의 졸업사진을 촬영할 예정이잖아요. 그래서 세부 사항들을 확인하려고 전화했습니다.
여: 네. 저희가 이전에 논의했던 것처럼, ⓑ장소는 Lily Pond 공원일 예정이에요.
남: 알겠습니다. 사진 촬영에 참여하는 학생들의 정확한 수를 제게 말씀해 주실 수 있나요?
여: 확인해 볼게요. [잠시 후] 음, ⓒ학생 180명일 거예요.
남: 그렇군요. 전에 말씀하신 것과 같네요.
여: 맞아요. 사진을 촬영하는 데 얼마나 걸릴까요?
남: ⓓ거의 세 시간 걸릴 거예요. 정오까지는 끝날 겁니다.
여: 좋아요. 다른 필요하신 정보가 있나요?
남: 아니요, 다 됐습니다. 안녕히 계세요.

문제 풀이

ⓐ날짜, ⓑ장소, ⓒ참여 학생 수, ⓓ소요 시간은 언급되었지만, 복장은 언급되지 않았다.

9. ④ | 내용 일치

선택지 선택비율	① 0%	② 0%	③ 0%	④ 96%	⑤ 1%

W: Hello, listeners. Welcome to *Good Day Movie*. We'd like to let you know about a great chance to see the preview of the movie *Green Ocean* by Feather Pictures. ⓐOne hundred people will be invited to the event. ⓑIt'll begin at the Glory Theater at 4 p.m. next Saturday. After watching the movie, ⓒyou can meet and take pictures with the actors of the movie. If you're interested, apply for admission tickets on the *Green Ocean* homepage, and ⓓthe tickets will be sent by text message to the first 100 people who apply. ⓔThose who are invited will be given a poster at the theater. Hurry up and don't miss this chance to watch *Green Ocean* in advance. Now we'll be back after the commercial break. So stay tuned.
시사회 / ~을 신청하다 / 미리 / 광고 시간 / 채널을 고정하다

해석

여: 안녕하세요, 청취자 여러분. 〈Good Day Movie〉에 오신 것을 환영합니다. 저희는

Feather Pictures가 제작한 영화 〈Green Ocean〉의 시사회를 볼 멋진 기회에 관해 알려드리고 싶습니다. ⓐ백 분이 행사에 초대받으실 겁니다. ⓑ행사는 다음 주 토요일 오후 4시에 Glory 극장에서 시작될 겁니다. 영화 관람 후에 ⓒ영화의 출연 배우를 만나 함께 사진을 찍으실 수 있습니다. 관심 있으시면 〈Green Ocean〉 홈페이지에서 입장권을 신청하세요. 그러면 ⓓ입장권은 먼저 신청하시는 100분께 문자 메시지로 발송될 겁니다. ⓔ초대받으신 분들은 극장에서 포스터를 받으실 겁니다. 서두르셔서 〈Green Ocean〉을 미리 볼 수 있는 이 기회를 놓치지 마세요. 자, 저희는 광고 시간 후에 돌아오겠습니다. 그러니 채널 고정하세요.

문제 풀이

ⓓ입장권은 문자 메시지로 발송될 것이라고 했다.

10. ④ | 도표

선택지 선택비율	① 0%	② 3%	③ 0%	④ 95%	⑤ 0%

M: Ms. Roberts, we're going on a business trip to New York City next week. Why don't we book the flight on this website?
(going on a business trip: 출장을 가다 / book: 예약하다)

W: Okay, Mr. White. Let's take a look at the flight schedule.
(flight schedule: 비행기 시간표)

M: Sure. How much can we spend on the flight?

W: ⓐOur company policy doesn't allow us to spend more than $800 per ticket.
(policy: 정책)

M: I see. And ⓑwhat about the departure time? I have to take my daughter to daycare early in the morning that day.
(departure: 출발)

W: Then ⓒhow about choosing a flight after 9 a.m.?

M: That'll be great. ⓓWhich airport should we arrive at?

W: ⓔJFK is closer to the company we're visiting.

M: Oh, you're right. Let's go there.

W: Then we have two options left, nonstop or one stop.

M: I don't want to spend hours waiting for a connecting flight.
(connecting flight: 연결 항공편)

W: Me, neither. ⓕWe should choose the nonstop flight.
(nonstop flight: 직항편)

M: Okay. Let's book the flight now.

해석

남: Roberts 씨, 우리는 다음 주에 뉴욕으로 출장을 갈 겁니다. 우리 이 웹사이트에서 항공편을 예약하는 게 어때요?
여: 알겠어요, White 씨. 비행기 시간표를 보죠.
남: 네. 항공편에 얼마를 쓸 수 있죠?
여: ⓐ회사 정책상 티켓당 800달러 넘게 쓸 수는 없어요.
남: 그렇군요. 그리고 ⓑ출발 시간은요? 저는 그날 아침 일찍 딸을 어린이집에 데려다줘야 하거든요.
여: 그렇다면 ⓒ오전 9시 이후의 항공편을 선택하는 게 어떤가요?
남: 그게 아주 좋겠어요. ⓓ어느 공항에 도착해야 하지요?
여: ⓔJFK가 우리가 방문할 회사에 더 가까워요.
남: 오, 당신 말이 맞네요. 거기로 가죠.
여: 그럼 우리에게는 직항편이나 한 번 환승하는 항공편 이렇게 두 가지 선택이 남아요.
남: 연결 항공편을 기다리며 몇 시간을 보내고 싶진 않아요.
여: 저도 그래요. ⓕ직항편을 선택해야겠어요.
남: 좋아요. 지금 그 항공편을 예약합시다.

문제 풀이

두 사람은 ⓐ티켓당 800달러가 넘지 않고, ⓑⓒ오전 9시 이후에 출발하고, ⓓⓔJFK공항에 도착하는 ⓕ직항편을 예약하기로 했다.

11. ① | 짧은 대화 응답

선택지 선택비율	① 96%	② 1%	③ 1%	④ 0%	⑤ 0%

[Cell phone rings.]

M: Honey, I've just left work. I'll be home in half an hour.

W: Good. ⓐIs it possible for you to stop by the dry cleaner's shop and pick up my dress?
(stop by: ~에 들르다 / dry cleaner's shop: 세탁소)

M: Sure. ⓑCan you tell me where the shop is located?
(be located: 위치해 있다)

W: Okay. I'll send the address to your phone.

해석

[휴대전화가 울린다.]
남: 여보, 저 방금 퇴근했어요. 30분 후에 집에 도착할 거예요.
여: 잘됐네요. ⓐ세탁소에 들러 내 옷을 찾아올 수 있어요?
남: 그럼요. ⓑ세탁소가 어디에 있는지 알려줄 수 있어요?
여: 알겠어요. 당신 휴대전화로 주소를 보낼게요.

문제 풀이

ⓐ세탁소에 들러 옷을 찾아달라는 여자의 부탁에 남자가 ⓑ세탁소 위치를 물었으므로, 주소를 휴대전화로 보내겠다는 ①이 응답으로 가장 적절하다.
② 네. 정오까지 손님의 옷을 세탁해 놓겠습니다.
③ 물론이지요. 내일 가게를 열 예정입니다.
④ 아니요. 저는 새로운 곳으로 이사하지 않을 겁니다.
⑤ 너무 늦었어요. 저는 이미 집에 와 있어요.

12. ② | 짧은 대화 응답

선택지 선택비율	① 2%	② 85%	③ 1%	④ 7%	⑤ 2%

W: David, look at this advertisement! ⓐJason Stevens is going to sing at the opening of City Concert Hall next Saturday.
(opening: 개막식)

M: Wow! You know I'm a big fan of him, Mom. Luckily, I don't have anything scheduled that day.

W: Great. ⓑMark the date on your calendar, so you don't miss his performance.
(Mark: 표시하다)

M: Absolutely. I'm so eager to see him sing in person.
(be eager to-v: 간절히 ~하고 싶어 하다 / in person: 직접)

해석

여: David, 이 광고를 봐! ⓐJason Stevens가 다음 주 토요일에 City Concert Hall 개막 행사에서 노래를 부를 예정이란다.
남: 와! 엄마, 아시다시피 제가 그 사람의 엄청난 팬이잖아요. 다행히 제가 그날 아무 계획이 없어요.
여: 잘됐구나. ⓑ달력에 날짜를 표시해 두렴, 그래야 공연을 놓치지 않지.
남: 당연하지요. 그가 노래 부르는 것을 직접 보고 싶은 마음이 너무나 간절해요.

문제 풀이

여자는 남자에게 ⓐJason Stevens의 공연 소식을 전하며 ⓑ공연을 놓치지 않도록 달력에 날짜를 표시해 두라고 말했으므로, 남자의 응답으로 가장 적절한 것은 조언을 받아들이는 ②이다.
① 믿기지 않아요. 제가 오늘 정말 무대에 오르게 돼요.
③ 사실은 그렇지 않아요. 그는 제가 예상한 것만큼 대단하지 않았어요.
④ 물론이지요. 대신 공연할 다른 사람을 찾아보겠습니다.
⑤ 오, 저런. 그의 공연을 놓치지 않으셨어야 했어요.

13. ① | 긴 대화 응답

선택지 선택비율	① 86%	② 8%	③ 2%	④ 2%	⑤ 2%

W: Excuse me. Can you tell me where the non-fiction books are?
M: Sure. They're right over here. Are you looking for anything in particular?
특히, 특별히
W: I want to buy the latest book by Harriot Braun.
최신의
M: You mean *Follow Your Own Trail*?
W: Yes, that's the book.
M: Sorry. We don't have any copies left at the moment.
copy: (책·신문 등의) 한 부 (바로) 지금
W: I can't believe it. It just came out three weeks ago.
M: ⓐThe book is so popular that it sold out very quickly. Do you want
인기 있는 sell out: 다 팔리다
me to find out if any of our other stores has a copy?
W: Yes, please. I really need to buy one for my book club meeting tomorrow. ⓑCould you check the store downtown? It's on my way
시내에
home.
M: Certainly. Let me look it up in our system. *[Typing sound]* ⓒOh,
~을 찾아보다
there's one copy left there, but unfortunately we can't hold it for
불행하게도, 유감스럽게도
you.
W: No worries. I can go pick it up now.

해석

여: 실례합니다. 논픽션 책들이 어디에 있는지 알려 주실 수 있나요?
남: 물론이죠. 바로 여기 있습니다. 특별히 찾으시는 것이 있으신가요?
여: Harriot Braun의 최신 책을 사고 싶어요.
남: 〈Follow Your Own Trail〉 말씀이신가요?
여: 네, 그 책이에요.
남: 죄송합니다. 지금은 재고가 없습니다.
여: 믿기지 않네요. 겨우 3주 전에 나온 책인데요.
남: ⓐ그 책이 굉장히 인기 있어서 정말 빨리 다 팔렸어요. 다른 지점에 재고가 있는지 알아봐 드릴까요?
여: 네, 부탁드려요. 내일 북클럽 모임 때문에 꼭 사야 하거든요. ⓑ시내 지점 좀 확인해 주시겠어요? 집에 가는 길에 있거든요.
남: 알겠습니다. 시스템에서 찾아볼게요. [타이핑하는 소리] ⓒ아, 거기에 한 권 남아 있는데, 안타깝게도 저희가 예약은 해드릴 수 없습니다.
여: 괜찮아요. 지금 가서 사면 되니까요.

문제 풀이

ⓐ여자가 구매하고 싶은 책이 품절되었고, ⓑⓒ다른 시내 지점에는 재고가 한 권 있지만 예약해 줄 수는 없다고 말한 상황이므로, 괜찮다며 지금 가서 사면 된다고 말하는 ①이 여자의 응답으로 가장 적절하다.
② 알겠어요. 내일 꼭 그것을 돌려주도록 하세요.
③ 괜찮아요. 저희가 다음 주에 시스템을 고칠 수 있어요.
④ 유감입니다. 다음번에 그것을 구매하실 수 있어요.
⑤ 신경 쓰지 마세요. 제가 새 책을 가져다 드릴게요.

14. ④ | 긴 대화 응답

선택지 선택비율	① 1%	② 1%	③ 4%	④ 93%	⑤ 1%

W: Dad, I found these old photos of our camping trip from 25 years ago.
M: Oh, I remember this trip. You were about the same age as your son, Peter.
W: Right. It was a really fun trip.
M: Yeah. I still go camping often, but that's the most memorable one.
잊혀지지 않는
W: I agree. ⓐI want Peter to have that experience, too. But he always
경험
refuses to go.
거절하다, 거부하다
M: Why doesn't he want to go camping?
W: He just wants to stay home and spend all his time on his smartphone.
M: Don't worry. I'm sure Peter will like camping once he experiences
경험하다
how fun it is.
W: You're probably right. Dad, when is the next time you're going camping?
M: This weekend. ⓑWe should all go together.
W: That'd be great. ⓒPeter might come as well if his favorite grandpa invites him.
초대하다
M: Then I'll ask him to come with me on this trip.

해석

여: 아빠, 25년 전 저희가 캠핑 갔을 때 찍은 이 오래된 사진들을 발견했어요.
남: 아, 그 여행 기억난다. 네가 네 아들 Peter의 나이쯤이었을 때였지.
여: 맞아요. 정말 재미있는 여행이었어요.
남: 그래. 난 지금도 자주 캠핑을 가지만, 그게 가장 잊혀지지 않는 캠핑이야.
여: 동의해요. ⓐ저는 Peter도 그런 경험을 하면 좋겠어요. 그런데 그 애는 항상 가길 거부해요.
남: 왜 캠핑을 가기 싫어하는 거지?
여: 그냥 집에 있으면서 하루종일 스마트폰을 하며 시간을 보내고 싶어 해요.
남: 걱정 마라. Peter도 캠핑이 얼마나 재미있는지 한 번 경험해 보면 분명 캠핑을 좋아할 거야.
여: 아마 아빠 말씀이 맞을 거예요. 아빠, 다음엔 언제 캠핑 가실 거예요?
남: 이번 주말에. ⓑ우리 다 같이 가자.
여: 그거 좋겠네요. ⓒPeter도 자기가 제일 좋아하는 할아버지가 초대하면 올지도 몰라요.
남: 그럼 내가 그 애한테 이번 여행 같이 가자고 해야겠다.

문제 풀이

ⓐ아들 Peter가 캠핑하러 가기 싫어 한다는 여자의 말에 남자는 ⓑ모두 같이 가자고 말했고, 여자는 ⓒ남자가 초대하면 Peter가 올 수도 있다고 했으므로, 자신이 Peter에게 이번 여행에 같이 가자고 말하겠다는 ④가 남자의 응답으로 가장 적절하다.
① 내가 우리 여행에서 찍은 사진들을 어제 인화했어.
② 문제는 내가 이미 모닥불을 꺼 버렸다는 거야.
③ 내가 기꺼이 그의 낚시 캠프 초대를 받아들일게.
⑤ 강 근처에 텐트를 치지 않도록 기억하렴.

15. ① | 상황에 적절한 말

선택지 선택비율	① 79%	② 3%	③ 5%	④ 3%	⑤ 10%

W: Ben and Stacy are neighbors. Ben has been growing tomatoes in his backyard for several years. Ben shares his tomatoes with
공유하다, 나누다
Stacy every year because she loves his fresh tomatoes. Today, Ben notices that his tomatoes will be ready to be picked in about a
알아차리다 따다
week. However, he leaves for a month-long business trip tomorrow.
출장
He's worried that there'll be no fresh tomatoes left in his backyard by the time he comes back. He'd like Stacy to have them while they are fresh and ripe. So, Ben wants to tell Stacy that she can come
익은
and get the tomatoes from his backyard whenever she wants. In this situation, what would Ben most likely say to Stacy?
Ben: Feel free to take the tomatoes from my backyard.
feel free to-v: 마음껏[편하게] ~하다

해석

여: Ben과 Stacy는 이웃이다. Ben은 몇 년간 뒷마당에서 토마토를 기르고 있다. Ben은 Stacy가 자신의 신선한 토마토를 무척 좋아하기 때문에 매년 그녀와 자신의 토마

토를 나눈다. 오늘 Ben은 일주일 정도 후면 토마토가 딸 준비가 될 것이라는 것을 알아차린다. 하지만 그는 내일 한 달간의 출장을 떠난다. 그는 자신이 돌아올 때쯤이면 뒷마당에 남아 있는 신선한 토마토가 없을 것을 걱정한다. 그는 Stacy가 토마토가 신선하고 잘 익었을 때 토마토를 먹었으면 한다. 그래서 Ben은 Stacy에게 원할 때 언제든지 와서 뒷마당에서 토마토를 가져가도 된다고 말하고 싶다. 이 상황에서 Ben은 Stacy에게 뭐라고 말하겠는가?

Ben: 내 뒷마당에서 토마토를 마음껏 가져가요.

문제 풀이

Ben은 Stacy에게 원할 때 뒷마당에서 토마토를 가져가도 된다고 말하고 싶다고 했다.

② 토마토 심을 때 도움이 필요하면 내게 말해요.
③ 내가 어제 딴 잘 익은 토마토를 원하나요?
④ 우리 다른 곳에서 토마토를 기르면 어때요?
⑤ 당신이 없는 동안 내가 당신의 토마토를 돌볼게요.

16~17. | 세트 문항

16. ⑤ 17. ⑤

선택지 선택비율					
	① 1%	② 4%	③ 1%	④ 3%	⑤ 91%
	① 1%	② 0%	③ 0%	④ 1%	⑤ 98%

M: Hello, students. ⓐLast time, I gave you a list of English expressions
표현
containing color terms. Today, we'll learn how these expressions
포함하다
got their meanings. The first expression is "out of the ⓑblue," meaning something happens unexpectedly. It came from the
돌연, 갑자기
phrase "a lightning bolt out of the blue," which expresses the idea
어구 번개 나타내다
that it's unlikely to see lightning when there's a clear blue sky. The
be unlikely to-v: ~할 가능성이 낮다
next expression, "ⓒwhite lie," means a harmless lie to protect
악의 없는
someone from a harsh truth. This is because the color white
가혹한
traditionally symbolizes innocence. Another expression, "ⓓgreen
전통적으로 상징하다 결백
thumb," refers to a great ability to cultivate plants. Planting pots
~을 나타내다 재배해다 화분
were often covered with tiny green plants, so those who worked in gardens had green-stained hands. The last expression, "to see
얼룩지게[물들게] 하다
ⓔred," means to suddenly get very angry. Its origin possibly comes
갑자기 기원
from the belief that bulls get angry and attack when a bullfighter
믿음 황소 공격하다 투우사
waves a red cape. I hope this lesson helps you remember these
흔들다 망토
phrases better.

해석

남: 안녕하세요, 학생 여러분. ⓐ지난 시간에, 색 용어를 포함하고 있는 영어 표현 목록을 드렸죠. 오늘 우리는 이 표현이 어떻게 그 의미를 갖게 되었는지 배울 거예요. 첫 번째 표현은 '난데없이'인데요, 어떤 일이 갑자기 일어나는 것을 의미해요. 이건 '청천벽력'이라는 어구에서 왔는데요, 맑고 ⓑ파란색 하늘이 있을 때 번개를 볼 확률이 낮다는 생각을 나타내죠. 다음 표현으로, 'ⓒ흰색 거짓말'은 누군가를 가혹한 사실로부터 보호하기 위한 악의 없는 거짓말을 의미해요. 이는 흰색이 전통적으로 결백을 상징하기 때문이에요. 또 다른 표현 'ⓓ녹색 엄지손가락'은 식물을 재배하는 엄청난 능력을 나타내요. 화분이 흔히 작은 녹색 식물로 덮여 있었기 때문에 정원에서 일하는 사람들은 손이 녹색으로 물들었죠. 마지막 표현 'ⓔ빨간색을 보다'는 갑자기 굉장히 화가 나는 것을 의미해요. 그 기원은 아마도 투우사가 빨간 망토를 흔들 때 황소가 화가 나서 공격한다는 믿음에서 왔을 겁니다. 이 수업이 이 어구들을 더 잘 기억하는 데 도움이 되길 바랍니다.

문제 풀이

16. 남자는 ⓐ지난 시간에 제공한 색 용어를 포함한 영어 표현이 어떻게 그 의미를 갖게 되었는지 배울 거라고 했으므로, 남자가 하는 말의 주제로 가장 적절한 것은 ⑤ '색 관련 영어 표현이 어떻게 그 의미를 갖게 되었는가'이다.
① 연간 자연의 색 변화
② 전통적인 영국 풍습에 사용된 다양한 색
③ 문화에 따른 색 인식의 차이
④ 영어에서 색에 관련된 표현이 흔한 이유

17. ⓑ파란색, ⓒ흰색, ⓓ녹색, ⓔ빨간색은 언급되었으나, 노란색(yellow)은 언급되지 않았다.

[코드 공략하기]

제6회 고급 모의고사

1	⑤	2	①	3	③	4	⑤	5	①	6	④
7	①	8	④	9	④	10	④	11	①	12	②
13	⑤	14	②	15	⑤	16	③	17	④		

1. ⑤ | 목적

선택지 선택비율	① 1%	② 0%	③ 0%	④ 0%	⑤ 98%

M: Hello, viewers. Thank you for clicking on this video. I'm Ronnie Drain, and I've been a personal fitness trainer for over 15 years.
개인의
Today, ⓐI'd like to tell you about my channel, *Build Your Body*. On my channel, you can watch videos showing you how to do a variety
여러 가지의
of exercises that you can do at home or at your office. If you've experienced difficulty exercising regularly, my videos can provide
experience difficulty v-ing: ~하는 데 어려움을 겪다 규칙적으로
easy guidelines and useful resources on exercise routines. New
지침 일정
videos will be uploaded every Friday. ⓑVisit my channel and build a stronger, healthier body.

해석

남: 안녕하세요, 시청자 여러분. 이 동영상을 클릭해 주셔서 감사합니다. 저는 Ronnie Drain이고, 15년 이상 동안의 개인 피트니스 트레이너입니다. 오늘 ⓐ저는 제 채널 '몸을 만드세요'에 대해 말씀드리려고 합니다. 제 채널에서 여러분은 집이나 사무실에서 할 수 있는 여러 가지 운동 방법을 보여 주는 동영상을 보실 수 있습니다. 규칙적으로 운동하는 데 어려움을 겪으셨다면, 제 동영상은 운동 일정의 쉬운 지침과 유용한 자료를 제공할 수 있습니다. 매주 금요일에 새로운 동영상이 업로드될 겁니다. ⓑ제 채널을 방문하셔서 더 튼튼하고 더 건강한 몸을 만드세요.

문제 풀이

남자는 ⓐ자신의 채널 내용을 소개하며 ⓑ방문할 것을 홍보하고 있다.

2. ① | 의견

선택지 선택비율	① 96%	② 1%	③ 0%	④ 0%	⑤ 0%

W: Good morning, Chris.
M: Good morning, Julie. How was your weekend?
W: It was wonderful. I went to an event called Stargazing Night with my 7-year-old son.
M: Oh, so you went outdoors to look up at stars. Your son must have had a great time.
W: Yes. And ⓐI think it helped my son become familiar with
~에 익숙한
mathematical concepts.
수학적인
M: Interesting! How does it do that?
W: By counting the stars together, my son had a chance to practice counting to high numbers.
M: Ah, that makes sense.
W: Also, he enjoyed identifying shapes and tracing patterns that stars
식별하다 trace: 추적하다, 찾아내다
form together.
형성하다
M: Sounds like you had a magical and mathematical night!
W: Absolutely. ⓑI think looking at stars is a good way for kids to get used to mathematical concepts.
~에 익숙해지다
M: Maybe I should take my daughter to the event next time.

해석

여: 좋은 아침이에요, Chris.
남: 좋은 아침이에요, Julie. 주말은 어땠어요?
여: 정말 멋졌어요. 7살짜리 아들과 함께 Stargazing Night라는 행사에 갔어요.
남: 아, 그러니까 별을 보려고 밖에 야외로 간 거군요. 아들이 분명 즐거운 시간을 보냈겠어요.
여: 네. 그리고 ⓐ그게 아들이 수학 개념에 익숙해지도록 도와준 것 같아요.
남: 재미있네요! 그게 어떻게 그럴 수 있죠?
여: 별을 함께 세는 것으로, 아들은 높은 숫자까지 세기를 연습할 기회를 가진 거죠.
남: 아, 말이 되네요.
여: 그리고 그 애는 별들이 함께 형성하는 모양을 식별하고 패턴을 찾아내는 걸 즐겼어요.
남: 마법 같고 수학적인 밤을 보낸 것 같아요!
여: 물론이죠. ⓑ별을 보는 것이 아이들이 수학 개념에 익숙해지는 좋은 방법이라고 생각해요.
남: 아마 다음에는 내 딸을 그 행사에 데리고 가야겠어요.

문제 풀이

여자는 ⓐⓑ별 관찰이 아이들이 수학 개념에 익숙해지도록 돕는 방법이라고 직접적으로 말하고 있다.

3. ③ | 관계

선택지 선택비율	① 0%	② 0%	③ 97%	④ 2%	⑤ 0%

W: Hello, Mr. Roberts. I appreciate you taking the time to share your
고마워하다
experience and knowledge.
경험 지식
M: My pleasure, Ms. Lee. ⓐI've enjoyed all your bestselling books. So, I'm excited to help you.
W: Thanks. ⓑSince I'm writing about world-class athletes, I wanted to
세계적인 운동선수
hear how you've trained children who became Olympic swimming champions.
M: Then we should start with what I observe on the first day of my
보다, 관찰하다
swimming classes.
W: Do some children stand out right away?
눈에 띄다
M: Yes. Some kids are able to pick up my instructions quickly and
설명, 지시
easily.
W: I see. So did many of those kids go on to become Olympic champions?
M: Well, practicing is much more important. Those who consistently
지속적으로
practiced made great improvements and ultimately became
개선, 향상 궁극적으로, 결국
champions.
W: This is good insight I can use in my book.
통찰
M: I hope it helps.

해석

여: 안녕하세요, Roberts 씨. 경험과 지식을 공유해 주시기 위해 시간을 내 주셔서 감사합니다.
남: 천만에요, 이 선생님. ⓐ선생님의 베스트셀러 책들을 모두 즐겁게 읽었어요. 그래서 선생님을 도울 수 있어서 흥분됩니다.
여: 고맙습니다. ⓑ제가 세계적인 운동선수들에 대한 글을 쓰고 있어서, 올림픽 수영 챔피언이 된 아이들을 어떻게 훈련시키셨는지 듣고 싶었어요.
남: 그러면 제가 수영 수업 첫날에 보는 것부터 시작해야겠네요.
여: 일부 아이들은 바로 눈에 띄나요?
남: 네. 몇몇 아이들은 제 지시를 빠르고 쉽게 이해할 수 있어요.
여: 그렇군요. 그래서 그 아이들 중 다수가 나아가 올림픽 챔피언이 되었나요?

남: 음, 연습하는 것이 훨씬 더 중요해요. 지속적으로 연습한 사람들은 크게 향상되었고 결국 챔피언이 되었어요.
여: 이것은 제 책에서 사용할 수 있는 좋은 통찰이네요.
남: 도움이 됐으면 좋겠어요.

문제 풀이

남자가 ⓐ여자의 베스트셀러 책들을 모두 즐겁게 읽었다고 했고, 여자는 ⓑ자신이 쓰고 있는 글 때문에 남자에게 올림픽 수영 챔피언이 된 아이들을 어떻게 훈련시켰는지 듣고 싶다고 했으므로, 작가와 수영 코치의 관계임을 알 수 있다.

4. ⑤ | 그림 일치

선택지 선택비율	① 1%	② 0%	③ 1%	④ 1%	⑤ 95%

M: Honey, Aunt Sophie just called me and said we can stay at her house next weekend.
W: Wonderful. I really like the family room there.
M: She said she rearranged it and emailed me a photo. *[Clicking sound]* Here. Look.
(rearranged: 재배열[재배치]하다)
W: Wow, ⓐthe curtains on the window are pretty. I like their star pattern.
M: That's her favorite style.
W: Do you see ⓑthe chair next to the sofa? It looks comfortable.
M: Maybe we should get one like that.
W: Good idea.
M: What do you think of ⓒthe vase between the lamp and the book?
W: Oh, it's lovely. I also like ⓓthe flowers in the vase.
M: Wait. I know ⓔthose two candles on the fireplace. They were our gift for her birthday.
(fireplace: 벽난로)
W: That's right. Hey, look at ⓕthe round mirror on the wall.
M: It looks cute. I can't wait to see it all in person.
(in person: 직접)

해석

남: 여보, Sophie 고모가 지금 막 내게 전화해서 우리가 다음 주말에 고모 집에 머물러도 된다고 했어요.
여: 멋지네요. 나는 그곳 가족실이 정말 마음에 들어요.
남: 고모가 그곳을 재배치했다고 사진을 이메일로 보내왔어요. [클릭하는 소리] 여기요. 봐요.
여: 우와, ⓐ창문의 커튼이 예쁘네요. 별 무늬가 마음에 들어요.
남: 고모가 아주 좋아하는 스타일이죠.
여: ⓑ소파 옆에 의자 보여요? 편해 보여요.
남: 아마 우리도 저런 걸 사야겠어요.
여: 좋은 생각이에요.
남: ⓒ전등과 책 사이에 있는 화병은 어떻게 생각해요?
여: 아, 사랑스러워요. ⓓ화병에 있는 꽃도 마음에 들어요.
남: 잠깐요. ⓔ벽난로 위에 있는 저 양초 두 개는 내가 알아요. 우리가 고모님 생신 선물로 드린 거였죠.
여: 맞아요. 여기, ⓕ벽에 있는 둥근 거울 봐요.
남: 귀여워 보이네요. 얼른 모두 직접 보고 싶어요.

문제 풀이

여자는 ⓕ벽에 둥근 거울을 보라고 말했다.

5. ① | 할 일

선택지 선택비율	① 98%	② 1%	③ 0%	④ 1%	⑤ 1%

M: Hi, Mary. You look worried. What's the matter?
W: Hi, Steve. Remember the report about wildflowers I've been working on?
(wildflowers: 야생화)
M: Of course. That's for your biology class, right?
(biology: 생물학)
W: Yeah. I was able to get pictures of all the wildflowers in my report except for daisies.
(except for: ~을 제외하고, daisy: 데이지 꽃)
M: I see. Can't you submit your report without pictures of daisies?
(submit: 제출하다)
W: No. I really need them. I even tried to take pictures of daisies myself, but I found out that they usually bloom from spring to fall.
(bloom: 꽃이 피다)
M: You know what? This spring, I went hiking with my dad and took some pictures of wildflowers.
W: Do you have them on your phone? Can I see them?
M: Sure. Have a look.
W: ⓐOh, the flowers in the pictures are daisies! These will be great for my report.
M: Really? Then ⓑI'll send them to you.
W: Thanks. That would be very helpful.

해석

남: 안녕, Mary. 너 걱정스러워 보여. 무슨 일이니?
여: 안녕, Steve. 내가 작업하고 있는 야생화에 관한 보고서 기억해?
남: 물론이지. 생물학 수업을 위한 것이잖아, 맞지?
여: 응. 데이지 꽃을 제외하고는 보고서의 모든 야생화 사진을 구할 수 있었어.
남: 그렇구나. 데이지 사진 없이는 보고서를 제출할 수 없니?
여: 응. 그게 정말 필요해. 심지어 내가 직접 데이지 꽃 사진을 찍으려고도 해 봤지만, 데이지 꽃은 대개 봄에서 가을에 핀다는 것을 알게 됐어.
남: 있잖아. 이번 봄에 내가 아빠와 등산 가서 야생화 사진을 좀 찍었어.
여: 전화기에 사진이 있니? 봐도 될까?
남: 물론이지. 한번 봐.
여: ⓐ오, 사진의 꽃이 데이지 꽃이야! 이거면 보고서에 훌륭할 거야.
남: 정말? 그럼 ⓑ내가 사진들을 너한테 보내줄게.
여: 고마워. 그게 무척 도움이 될 거야.

문제 풀이

여자는 ⓐ남자의 전화기에 있는 데이지 꽃 사진이 보고서에 적합하다고 했고, 남자는 ⓑ사진을 여자에게 보내주겠다고 했다.

6. ④ | 금액

선택지 선택비율	① 0%	② 2%	③ 1%	④ 96%	⑤ 0%

W: Welcome to Winter Land Mart. How may I help you?
M: Hi. I'm shopping for an electric heater.
(shop for: ~을 사다, electric heater: 전기 히터)
W: How about this type? It's very popular.
M: Let me see. Oh, I like it.
W: Well, we have it in three sizes. The small one is $50, ⓐthe medium is $70, and the large is $100.
M: ⓑI'll take one medium-sized heater. Do you also have slippers?
W: Yes. We have wool and leather ones. A pair of wool slippers is $5, and ⓒa pair of leather ones is $10.
(wool: 털, 양모, leather: 가죽)
M: Hmm, ⓓI'll take two pairs of leather ones.
W: Great. So, one medium-sized electric heater and two pairs of leather slippers. Is that correct?
M: Yes, that's right. Can I use this 10% off coupon?
W: I'll check. *[Pause]* Oh, I'm sorry. ⓔYou cannot use this coupon because it isn't valid anymore.
(valid: 유효한)
M: That's okay. Here's my credit card.

해석

여: Winter Land 마트에 오신 걸 환영합니다. 무엇을 도와드릴까요?
남: 안녕하세요. 전기 히터를 하나 사려고 하는데요.
여: 이 종류는 어떠세요? 아주 인기 많아요.

남: 한번 볼게요. 오, 마음에 드네요.
여: 음, 이건 세 가지 사이즈로 나와요. 작은 것은 50달러, ⓐ중간 것은 70달러, 큰 것은 100달러예요.
남: ⓑ중간 사이즈 히터 하나 할게요. 슬리퍼도 있나요?
여: 네. 양모와 가죽 슬리퍼가 있어요. 양모 슬리퍼 한 켤레는 5달러이고, ⓒ가죽 슬리퍼 한 켤레는 10달러입니다.
남: 음, ⓓ가죽 슬리퍼 두 켤레 주세요.
여: 알겠습니다. 그럼, 중간 사이즈 전기 히터 하나와, 가죽 슬리퍼 두 켤레 맞으시죠?
남: 네, 맞아요. 이 10% 할인 쿠폰을 사용할 수 있을까요?
여: 확인해 볼게요. [잠시 후] 아, 죄송합니다. ⓔ이 쿠폰은 유효 기간이 지나서 사용하실 수 없습니다.
남: 괜찮아요. 여기 제 신용카드예요.

문제 풀이

남자는 ⓐ70달러인 ⓑ중간 사이즈 전기 히터 하나와 ⓒ한 켤레에 10달러인 가죽 슬리퍼 ⓓ두 켤레를 사려고 하는데 ⓔ할인 쿠폰은 쓸 수 없다고 했으므로, 남자가 지불할 금액은 (70+10x2)=90달러이다.

7. ① | 이유

선택지 선택비율	① 99%	② 1%	③ 0%	④ 0%	⑤ 0%

W: Hey, Mike. How's your shoulder? Are you still in pain? (아픈)
M: No, I feel totally fine, Emily. I should be ready for the table tennis tournament.
W: That's good to hear. Then do you want to practice with me now?
M: I'm sorry but I can't right now.
W: Why not? Do you have to work on your history homework?
M: No, I already submitted it to Mr. Jackson.
W: Oh, then I guess you have to study for the science quiz, right?
M: I think I'm ready for it. Actually, I'm on my way to volunteer at the school library. (volunteer: 자원하다, 자원봉사로 하다)
W: I see. Then, don't forget about our drama club meeting tomorrow. (drama: 연극)
M: Of course not. See you there.

해석

여: 얘, Mike. 어깨는 어때? 아직도 아파?
남: 아니, 정말 괜찮아, Emily. 나는 탁구 시합에 나갈 준비가 된 것 같아.
여: 잘됐다. 그럼 지금 나와 같이 연습할래?
남: 미안하지만 지금은 안 되겠어.
여: 왜 안 되는데? 너 역사 숙제 해야 하니?
남: 아니, 그건 Jackson 선생님께 이미 제출했어.
여: 아, 그럼 혹시 과학 퀴즈를 위한 공부를 해야 하는 거니, 그렇지?
남: 난 그것에 대한 준비는 된 것 같아. 사실, 나는 학교 도서관에 자원봉사를 하러 가는 길이야.
여: 그렇구나. 그럼 내일 우리 연극부 모임 잊지 마.
남: 물론 잊지 않지. 거기서 보자.

문제 풀이

남자는 지금 학교 도서관에 자원봉사를 하러 가야 해서, 탁구 연습을 할 수 없다고 말하고 있다.

8. ④ | 언급

선택지 선택비율	① 1%	② 0%	③ 1%	④ 96%	⑤ 0%

M: Hey, Kelly. Have you been to the Bradford Museum of Failure? (Failure: 실패)
W: I've never even heard of it.
M: Well, I went there yesterday and it was amazing.
W: What does the museum exhibit?
M: ⓐIt exhibits numerous failed products from the world's best-known companies. (numerous: 수많은)
W: Interesting. That makes me curious about the purpose of founding the museum. (curious: 궁금한, purpose: 목적, founding: 설립하다)
M: ⓑIt was founded to deliver the message that we need to admit our failures to truly succeed. (deliver the message: 메시지를 전달하다, admit: 인정하다)
W: That's quite a message, and it makes a lot of sense. Did it just open?
M: No, ⓒit opened in 2001.
W: How come I've never heard of it?
M: I guess many people don't know about it. But visiting the museum was an eye-opening experience.
W: Where is it?
M: ⓓIt's located in Greenfalls, Hillside.
W: That's not too far from here. I'll be sure to visit it.

해석

남: 이봐요, Kelly. Bradford 실패 박물관에 가 봤어요?
여: 그곳에 대해 들어본 적도 없어요.
남: 음, 어제 갔었는데 놀라웠어요.
여: 박물관은 뭘 전시하나요?
남: ⓐ세계의 가장 잘 알려진 회사들의 수많은 실패 제품들을 전시해요.
여: 흥미로워요. 박물관을 설립한 목적이 궁금해지게 만드네요.
남: ⓑ진정으로 성공하기 위해서는 실패를 인정해야 한다는 메시지를 전달하기 위해 설립되었어요.
여: 그건 꽤 좋은 메시지고, 많은 의미가 있네요. 그곳이 이제 막 개관했나요?
남: 아니요, ⓒ2001년에 개관했어요.
여: 어째서 난 한 번도 그곳에 대해 들어본 적이 없을까요?
남: 많은 사람들이 그곳에 대해 모르는 것 같아요. 하지만 그 박물관을 방문한 것은 눈을 뜨게 하는 경험이었어요.
여: 그게 어디 있어요?
남: ⓓHillside Greenfalls에 위치해 있어요.
여: 그곳은 여기에서 너무 멀진 않네요. 꼭 가 볼게요.

문제 풀이

Bradford 실패 박물관과 관련하여 ⓐ전시품, ⓑ설립 목적, ⓒ개관 연도, ⓓ위치는 언급되었지만, 입장료는 언급되지 않았다.

9. ④ | 내용 일치

선택지 선택비율	① 1%	② 0%	③ 1%	④ 98%	⑤ 0%

W: Hello, listeners. This is Lisa Cooperson from Leverin Radio Station. Are you considering a career related to law? ⓐThe 2025 Court Visit Program will be held on November 19th at Woodfield County Courthouse. It allows high school students to experience working in law. ⓑThis program offers an opportunity to meet with judges and lawyers and learn what happens in court. Its activities include a trial role-play. Also, ⓒthe program gives participants a certificate that shows completion of the program. To join, ⓓyou must apply as a team, not as an individual. Applications should be submitted to the courthouse by the end of this week. Lastly, ⓔthe program includes a free lunch, so you won't need to bring your own. Don't miss this wonderful opportunity!
(Station: 방송국, considering: 고려하다, career: 직업, 경력, related to: ~와 관련된, law: 법, offers: 제공하다, opportunity: 기회, judges: 판사, lawyers: 변호사, court: 법정, 법원, include: 포함하다, trial: 재판, role-play: 역할극, certificate: 수료증, completion: 완료, apply: 신청하다, individual: 개인, Applications: 지원[신청]서, submitted: 제출하다, courthouse: 법원 청사)

해석

여: 안녕하세요, 청취자 여러분. Leverin 라디오 방송국의 Lisa Coopersonㅇ입니다. 법과 관련된 진로를 생각하고 계신가요? ⓐ2025 법정 방문 프로그램이 11월 19일, Woodfield 카운티 법원에서 개최될 예정입니다. 이는 고등학생들이 법 관련 직업을 체험해볼 수 있게 해줍니다. ⓑ이 프로그램은 판사와 변호사를 만나고, 법정에서 어떤 일이 일어나는지 배우는 기회를 제공합니다. 활동에는 재판 역할극도 포함되어 있습니다. 또한, ⓒ이 프로그램은 참가자들에게 프로그램 이수 완료를 증명하는 수료증을 줍니다. 참가하려면 ⓓ개인이 아니라 팀으로 신청해야 합니다. 신청서는 이번 주말까지 법원에 제출해야 합니다. 마지막으로, ⓔ프로그램에는 무료 점심 식사가 포함되어 있어서 점심을 따로 가져올 필요는 없습니다. 이 멋진 기회를 놓치지 마세요!

문제 풀이

ⓓ개인이 아니라 팀으로 신청해야 한다고 했다.

10. ④ | 도표

선택지 선택비율	① 0%	② 4%	③ 0%	④ 93%	⑤ 0%

M: Welcome to Camilo's Kitchen.
W: Hello. I'm looking for a cutting board.
도마
M: Let me show you our five top-selling models, all at affordable prices. Do you have a preference for any material? We have plastic, maple, and walnut cutting boards.
가장 잘 팔리는 / (가격 등이) 알맞은 / 선호 / 원료, 재료 / 단풍나무
W: ⓐI don't want the plastic one because I think plastic isn't environmentally friendly.
환경 친화적인
M: I see. What's your budget range?
예산 / 범위
W: ⓑNo more than $50.
기껏해야, ~밖에
M: Okay. Do you prefer one with or without a handle?
W: I think a cutting board with a handle is easier to use. So ⓒI'll take one with a handle.
M: Then, which size do you want? You have two models left.
W: Hmm. ⓓA small-sized cutting board isn't convenient when I cut vegetables. I'll buy the other model.
편리한
M: Great. Then this is the cutting board for you.

해석

남: Camilo's Kitchen에 오신 것을 환영합니다.
여: 안녕하세요. 저는 도마를 찾고 있습니다.
남: 저희 매장에서 가장 잘 팔리는, 모두 알맞은 가격의 모델 다섯 개를 보여 드리겠습니다. 선호하시는 어떤 재질이 있나요? 플라스틱, 단풍나무, 호두나무 도마가 있습니다.
여: 저는 플라스틱이 환경 친화적이지 않다고 생각해서 ⓐ플라스틱 도마는 원치 않아요.
남: 알겠습니다. 예산 범위는 어떻게 되시나요?
여: ⓑ50달러밖에 안 돼요.
남: 알겠습니다. 손잡이가 있는 것 혹은 없는 것 중 어떤 것을 선호하시나요?
여: 손잡이가 있는 도마가 사용하기 더 쉬울 것 같아요. 그러니 ⓒ손잡이가 있는 것을 사겠습니다.
남: 그러면 어떤 크기가 좋으신가요? 두 가지 모델이 남았네요.
여: 음. ⓓ작은 크기의 도마는 채소를 썰 때 편리하지 않아요. 다른 모델을 살게요.
남: 좋습니다. 그렇다면 이게 손님을 위한 도마네요.

문제 풀이

여자는 ⓐ플라스틱 재질이 아니면서 ⓑ가격이 50달러 이하이고, ⓒ손잡이가 있으며, ⓓ작지 않은 크기의 도마를 사겠다고 했으므로, 여자가 구매할 도마는 D이다.

11. ① | 짧은 대화 응답

선택지 선택비율	① 95%	② 3%	③ 1%	④ 0%	⑤ 1%

W: Honey, I'm going out for a walk. Do you want to join me?
go out for a walk: 산책하러 나가다
M: Sure. But can you wait for a moment? ⓐI have to send an email to one of my co-workers right now.
함께 일하는 사람, 동료
W: No problem. ⓑHow long do you think it'll take?
M: Just give me about ten minutes.

해석

여: 여보, 나 산책하러 나가려고 해요. 나와 같이 갈래요?
남: 물론이죠. 근데 잠시만 기다려 줄래요? ⓐ내가 지금 바로 동료 한 명에게 이메일을 보내야 하거든요.
여: 괜찮아요. ⓑ얼마나 걸릴 것 같아요?
남: 10분 정도만 시간을 줘요.

문제 풀이

남자가 ⓐ동료에게 이메일을 보내야 한다고 하자 여자가 ⓑ얼마나 걸릴 것 같은지 물었으므로, 10분 정도만 시간을 달라는 ①이 남자의 응답으로 가장 적절하다.
② 우리가 집에 돌아가는 데 한 시간이 걸렸어요.
③ 당신은 일에 집중해야 할 것 같아요.
④ 내 동료들을 초대해 주다니 당신은 참 친절해요.
⑤ 이메일 다 보내면 나한테 전화해요.

12. ② | 짧은 대화 응답

선택지 선택비율	① 3%	② 88%	③ 6%	④ 3%	⑤ 0%

[Telephone rings.]
M: Hello, this is Bob's Camera Shop.
W: Hi, this is Clara Patterson. ⓐI'm calling to see if I can pick up my camera today.
M: Let me check. *[Clicking sound]* Yes. ⓑI've finished repairing your camera. It's ready to go.
수리하다
W: Good. I'll stop by and get it on my way home.
들르다

해석

[전화벨이 울린다.]
남: 여보세요, Bob의 카메라 가게입니다.
여: 안녕하세요, Clara Patterson입니다. ⓐ오늘 제 카메라를 찾아갈 수 있는지 확인하려고 전화 드렸어요.
남: 확인해보겠습니다. [클릭하는 소리] 네. ⓑ고객님의 카메라 수리를 마쳤습니다. 준비됐어요.
여: 좋아요. 집에 가는 길에 잠깐 들러서 가져갈게요.

문제 풀이

여자가 ⓐ오늘 자신의 카메라를 찾으러 가도 되는지 물어봤는데 남자가 ⓑ카메라 수리를 다 마쳐서 가져가도 좋다고 했으므로, 집에 가는 길에 들러서 가져가겠다는 ②가 여자의 응답으로 가장 적절하다.
① 훌륭해요. 당신이 제게 사 준 카메라가 마음에 들어요.
③ 신경 쓰지 마세요. 제가 내일 카메라를 맡길게요.
④ 알겠습니다. 제 그 사진들을 찍어 주셔서 감사합니다.
⑤ 말도 안돼요. 수리비가 너무 비싸요.

13. ⑤ | 긴 대화 응답

선택지 선택비율	① 6%	② 3%	③ 1%	④ 1%	⑤ 89%

W: Shaun, you really rocked the runway as a senior fashion model
뒤흔들다

yesterday!
M: Thanks for coming to my first show, Grace.
W: My pleasure. You'll be an inspiration to many people our age.
영감, 영감을 주는 사람
M: I'm so flattered.
be flattered: (어깨가) 으쓱해지다
W: It's amazing that you successfully switched careers.
전환하다, 바꾸다 직업, 경력
M: Thank you. My dream has finally come true.
이루어지다
W: ⓐIt couldn't have been easy to realize your dream in your 60s.
실현[달성]하다
M: It wasn't. But I've always believed in myself, and ⓑage was never an issue for me.
W: ⓒYou make me think of my old passion to be a painter, but I put it off for too long.
열정 ~을 미루다
M: Now is the time to give it a try.
시도하다
W: ⓓI think it's too late for that.
M: Be positive. You can start pursuing your dream at any time.
pursue: 뒤쫓다

해석

여: Shuan, 어제 시니어 패션모델로 런웨이를 정말 들썩이게 하셨어요!
남: 제 첫 번째 쇼에 와주셔서 감사해요, Grace.
여: 천만에요. 당신은 우리 나이대의 많은 사람들에게 영감을 주는 분이 될 거예요.
남: 정말 영광입니다.
여: 성공적으로 직업을 바꾸신 게 놀라워요.
남: 고맙습니다. 드디어 제 꿈이 이루어졌어요.
여: ⓐ60대에 꿈을 실현한다는 게 쉽지 않으셨을 텐데요.
남: 쉽지 않았죠. 하지만 저는 항상 저 자신을 믿어왔고, ⓑ나이는 제게 전혀 문제가 되지 않았어요.
여: ⓒ화가가 되고 싶다는 저의 오랜 열정에 대해 생각하게 만드시는데요, 전 그걸 너무 오래 미뤄두었어요.
남: 지금이 시도할 때네요.
여: ⓓ그러기엔 너무 늦은 것 같아요.
남: 긍정적으로 생각하세요. 언제든 꿈을 좇기 시작할 수 있어요.

문제 풀이

남자는 ⓐ60대에 패션모델이라는 꿈을 실현했고 ⓑ나이는 전혀 문제가 되지 않았다고 말하고 있다. 한편 여자는 ⓒ화가가 되고 싶다는 오랜 열정이 있지만 ⓓ너무 늦었다고 생각한다고 했으므로, 나이에 상관없이 언제든 꿈을 좇을 수 있다는 ⑤가 남자의 응답으로 가장 적절하다.
① 포기하지 마세요! 당신은 제가 화가가 되도록 영감을 주었습니다.
② 힘내세요! 패션 시장은 누구에게나 열려 있어요.
③ 일리가 있네요. 저는 패션 감각이 전혀 없어요.
④ 저도 동의합니다. 일과 삶의 균형을 맞춰야 해요.

코드+α 「조동사+have p.p.」 표현

- We **should have been** more careful. (우린 더 신중했어야 했어.)
- He **must have been** embarrassed. (그는 틀림없이 당황했을 거야.)
- She **couldn't have told** a lie. (그녀가 거짓말을 했을 리가 없어.)
- They **might** already **have left** the town. (그들은 이미 마을을 떠났을지도 몰라.)

14. ② | 긴 대화 응답

선택지 선택비율	① 2%	② 92%	③ 2%	④ 2%	⑤ 0%

[Cell phone rings.]
W: Hello.
M: Hi, Cindy. It's Danny.
W: Hey, Danny. How are you?
M: I'm fine, but a little confused. ⓐI'm in the library, but none of our group members are here.
혼란스러운
W: What? You're at the library now? We're not meeting until Thursday.
M: Really? I think there was some kind of misunderstanding. I thought we were supposed to meet here at 12:30 this afternoon.
오해, 착오
be supposed to-v: ~하기로 되어 있다
W: We were going to, but ⓑwe changed the date because we needed more time for individual work.
개인의
M: Huh? No one told me about it.
W: Don't you remember? We decided that in class last Friday.
M: I wasn't there, Cindy. I stayed home sick.
W: Oh, no! That's right. ⓒYou were absent last Friday when we changed the date! I was going to call you after school, but I forgot.
M: Oh, that explains it. Well, it's not a big deal.
W: It's my fault. I should've told you earlier.
should have p.p.: ~했어야 했다

해석

[휴대전화가 울린다.]
여: 여보세요.
남: 안녕, Cindy. 나 Danny야.
여: 안녕, Danny. 잘 있지?
남: 응, 그런데 좀 혼란스러워. ⓐ난 도서관에 있는데, 여기 우리 조원이 아무도 없어.
여: 뭐? 지금 도서관에 있다고? 우리 목요일까지 만나지 않는데.
남: 정말? 착오가 있었던 것 같아. 오늘 오후 12시 30분에 여기서 만나기로 했다고 생각했는데.
여: 그러기로 했었지만, 개인 작업에 시간이 더 필요해서 ⓑ날짜를 바꿨잖아.
남: 응? 아무도 내게 그 얘기를 안 해줬어.
여: 기억 안 나니? 지난 금요일 수업에서 그렇게 결정했잖아.
남: Cindy, 나는 거기 없었어. 아파서 집에 있었잖아.
여: 이런! 맞다. ⓒ우리가 날짜를 바꾼 지난 금요일에 넌 결석했지! 학교 끝나고 네게 전화하려고 했는데, 잊었어.
남: 아, 설명이 되네. 음, 별 문제 아니야.
여: 내 잘못이야. 내가 네게 더 일찍 말했어야 했는데.

문제 풀이

여자는 ⓑⓒ조 모임 날짜가 변경된 것을 남자에게 말해주지 않아 ⓐ남자가 곤란을 겪은 상황으로, 일찍 말하지 않은 자신의 잘못이라고 말하는 ②가 여자의 응답으로 가장 적절하다.
① 아마도 아닐 거야. 너는 진찰을 받는 게 좋겠어.
③ 정말 유감이야. 우리는 오늘 너를 기다렸어.
④ 문제없어. 내가 거기 가는 방법을 설명해 줄 수 있어.
⑤ 맞아. 우리 어제 도서관에서 만났지.

15. ⑤ | 상황에 적절한 말

선택지 선택비율	① 1%	② 3%	③ 2%	④ 12%	⑤ 80%

W: Brian is a high school student. He has only traveled with his family before. Until now his mother has always taken care of his travel bag, so he doesn't have any experience preparing it himself. This weekend, Brian is supposed to go on a school trip with his friends. He asks his mother to get his stuff ready for his trip this time, too.
물건

However, she believes Brian is old enough to prepare what he needs, and she thinks this time is a great opportunity for him to learn to be more independent. So, she wants to tell Brian that he should get his things ready and put them in his bag without her help. In this situation, what would Brian's mother most likely say to Brian?

old enough to-v: ~할 충분한 나이인 / 독립적인

Brian's mother: Why don't you pack your bag by yourself for the trip?

해석

여: Brian은 고등학생이다. 그는 이전에 오직 가족과 함께만 여행을 해 보았다. 지금까지 어머니가 항상 그의 여행 가방을 챙겨 주었기 때문에, 그는 여행 가방을 직접 준비한 경험이 없다. 이번 주말에 Brian은 친구들과 수학여행을 가기로 되어 있다. 그는 이번에도 어머니에게 여행에 필요한 물건을 준비해 달라고 부탁한다. 하지만 어머니는 Brian이 자신이 필요한 것을 준비할 충분한 나이라고 믿고, 이번이 Brian이 더 자립적이 되는 법을 배울 아주 좋은 기회라고 생각한다. 그래서 어머니는 Brian에게 자신의 도움 없이 물건을 준비해서 가방에 꾸려야 한다고 말하고 싶어 한다. 이 상황에서, Brian의 어머니는 Brian에게 뭐라고 말하겠는가?

Brian의 어머니: 여행을 위해 네 가방을 스스로 꾸리는 게 어떻겠니?

문제 풀이

어머니는 Brian에게 여행 가방을 스스로 꾸리라고 말하고 싶어 하는 상황이므로, 어머니가 Brian에게 할 말로 가장 적절한 것은 ⑤이다.

① 새로운 곳에 갈 때마다 꼭 내게 전화하렴.
② 수학여행은 친구를 사귈 좋은 기회야.
③ 나는 여행이 네 시각을 넓혀준다고 믿어.
④ 짐을 너 스스로 옮기는 게 어떻겠니?

16~17. | 세트 문항

16. ③ 17. ④

선택지 선택비율					
	① 2%	② 0%	③ 95%	④ 0%	⑤ 1%
	① 1%	② 0%	③ 2%	④ 95%	⑤ 0%

M: Hello, class. Last time we learned about insects, their life cycles and what they eat. As you know, many insects get food from flowers, but they aren't the only creatures that do. Today, ⓐwe'll learn about a variety of animals that use flowers as a food source. First are ⓑhummingbirds. These birds use their long narrow beaks to get the flower's sweet liquid called nectar. Mysteriously, they only feed from upside down flowers. We still don't know why. Next are ⓒbats. Although most bats eat insects, some get their food from flowers. These bats have a strong sense of smell and sight compared to insect-eating bats. There are also ⓓlizards that drink nectar. These lizards are found on tropical islands that have few natural enemies. Finally, there is a type of ⓔsquirrel that feeds from flowers. Most nectar-drinking animals help flowers grow in numbers, but these squirrels often harm the plant. When drinking nectar, they bite through the flower, which causes damage. Interesting, huh? What other animals use flowers in their diet? Take a minute to think, and then we'll talk about it.

생활 주기 / 원천 / 벌새 / 부리 / 도마뱀 / 열대의 / natural enemy: 천적 / 해를 끼치다 / 물다 / 피해, 손상

해석

남: 안녕하세요, 여러분. 지난 시간에 우리는 곤충, 그들의 생활 주기와 그들이 무엇을 먹는지에 대해 배웠죠. 알고 있듯이, 많은 곤충이 꽃에서 식량을 얻는데, 곤충이 그렇게 하는 유일한 생명체는 아니에요. 오늘은 ⓐ식량원으로 꽃을 이용하는 다양한 동물에 대해 배울 거예요. 첫 번째는 ⓑ벌새에요. 이 새는 길고 얇은 부리를 사용하여 과일즙이라 불리는 꽃의 달콤한 액체를 얻습니다. 이상하게도, 그들은 거꾸로 피는 꽃에서만 식량을 얻습니다. 그 이유는 여전히 모릅니다. 다음은 ⓒ박쥐입니다. 대부분의 박쥐는 곤충을 먹지만, 일부는 꽃에서 식량을 얻습니다. 이런 박쥐는 곤충을 먹는 박쥐에 비해 강력한 후각과 시각을 지니고 있습니다. 과일즙을 마시는 ⓓ도마뱀도 있습니다. 이런 도마뱀은 천적이 거의 없는 열대섬에서 발견됩니다. 마지막으로, 꽃에서 식량을 얻는 ⓔ다람쥐 종류도 있습니다. 과일즙을 먹는 대부분의 동물은 꽃이 수적으로 증가하도록 돕지만, 이 다람쥐는 종종 식물에 해를 끼칩니다. 과일즙을 마실 때, 그들은 꽃을 무는데, 이는 손상을 야기합니다. 흥미롭죠? 다른 어떤 동물이 그들의 식사에 꽃을 이용할까요? 잠시 생각해 보세요, 그러고 나서 우리는 그것에 대해 이야기해 볼 거예요.

문제 풀이

16. 남자는 ⓐ식량원으로 꽃을 이용하는 동물에 대해 배울 거라고 했으므로, 남자가 하는 말의 주제로 가장 적절한 것은 ③ '꽃에서 식량을 얻는 다양한 동물'이다.
① 꽃이 동물을 유인하는 몇 가지 방법
② 동물과 연관된 인기 직업
④ 동물에게 위협을 가하는 주된 요인
⑤ 열대섬에 살고 있는 멸종 위기 동물

17. ⓑ벌새, ⓒ박쥐, ⓓ도마뱀, ⓔ다람쥐는 언급되었으나, 앵무새(parrots)는 언급되지 않았다.

多빈출 Pattern Practice 1 p.189

STEP 2

1. What do you think of
2. I'm planning to
3. I'm thinking of buying
4. were supposed to meet
5. I'd like to
6. It looks like
7. looking forward to seeing
8. I'd like to make a reservation
9. is supposed to go
10. are going to participate

STEP 3

1	○	2	×	3	×	4	○	5	○
6	○	7	○	8	○	9	×	10	○

2. Why don't you give her something she likes when she sleeps?
▶ 왜 그녀가 잘 때 좋아하는 것을 주는지 이유를 묻는 것이 아니라, 그녀가 좋아하는 것을 주자고 제안하는 내용

3. We're going to ask people geography questions.
▶ 질문을 하고 있다는 게 아니라, 질문을 할 것이라는 미래의 일에 대한 내용

9. I'm looking forward to it.
▶ 그것을 보고 있다는 게 아니라, 고대하고 있다는 뜻

多빈출 Pattern Practice 2 p.191

STEP 2

1. What about starting
2. have a model in mind
3. Have you ever wondered
4. I'm afraid
5. Make sure you bring
6. I was wondering if
7. Would you like to
8. let me confirm
9. Did you finish preparing
10. it's time to replace

STEP 3

1	×	2	×	3	○	4	○	5	○
6	○	7	×	8	×	9	×	10	○

1. Do you have any special program in mind?
▶ 어떤 특별 프로그램이 있냐는 게 아니라, 특별한 프로그램을 염두에 두고 있냐는 질문

2. Have you heard of a silicone straw?
▶ 실리콘 빨대가 있는지 묻는 게 아니라, 들어본 적이 있는지 경험을 묻는 내용

7. Let me take a look.
▶ 보여 주겠다는 게 아니라, 보겠다는 내용

8. Make sure to visit the observation deck on the 32nd floor.
▶ 가서 확인해 보라는 뜻이 아니라, 반드시 가 보라는 뜻

9. Would you like to switch rooms?
▶ 방을 바꾸는 것을 좋아하냐는 질문이 아니라, 바꾸겠냐고 묻는 내용

多빈출 Pattern Practice 3 p.193

STEP 2

1. You'd better
2. I've been busy helping
3. What if
4. feel free to ask
5. on my way home
6. Could you give me
7. How's it going
8. they were interested in
9. was able to fix
10. I'm good at

STEP 3

1	○	2	×	3	○	4	○	5	×
6	○	7	×	8	○	9	○	10	○

2. I think we'd better decide on the topic for our presentation.
▶ had better는 '~하는 게 좋겠다'의 뜻으로 조언을 할 때 사용하는 표현

5. I've been really busy with my science assignment.
▶ 바빠서 과제를 못 한 게 아니라, 과제를 하느라 바빴다는 뜻

7. How are your preparations going?
▶ 어떻게 갈 준비를 했냐는 게 아니라, 준비가 어떻게 되어 가는지를 묻는 뜻

多빈출 Pattern Practice 4 p.195

STEP 2

1. used to sit
2. I'd rather take
3. how to use
4. must have been
5. asked me to buy
6. How long
7. seems to be
8. I'm calling to see
9. That sounds like
10. May I take a picture

STEP 3

1	×	2	×	3	○	4	×	5	○
6	×	7	×	8	○	9	×	10	○

1. It must have been awesome!
▶ 멋져야 한다는 게 아니라, 멋졌음에 틀림없다는 뜻

2. I used to have the same problem just like you.
▶ used to+동사원형은 '사용했다'는 뜻이 아니라, '~했었다'는 뜻

4. It seems like they're looking for something.
▶ 찾고 싶어 한다는 게 아니라, 찾고 있는 것 같다는 추측의 내용

6. I don't know how to make QR codes.
▶ 얼마나 많이 만들어야 할지가 아니라, 어떻게 만들어야 할지라는 뜻

7. How long do you think it'll take?
▶ 거리를 묻는 게 아니라, 소요 시간을 묻는 내용

9. That sounds quite demanding.
▶ 듣기 어렵다는 뜻이 아니라, 어렵게 들린다는 뜻

多빈출 Pattern Practice 5

p.197

STEP 2

1. I'm looking for
2. Don't forget that
3. two options left
4. Do you have to
5. is about to call
6. I prefer wireless
7. I'm looking for
8. Do you have to study
9. I'm here to purchase
10. trying to buy

STEP 3

1	○	2	×	3	○	4	×	5	○
6	○	7	○	8	×	9	×	10	○

2. That's why there're two guitars in the room.
▶ 이유를 말하는 게 아니라, 결과를 말하는 내용

4. I should've told you earlier.
▶ 더 일찍 말한 게 틀림없다는 게 아니라, 더 일찍 말했어야 했다는 뜻

8. This is because the color white traditionally symbolizes innocence.
▶ 결과를 말하는 게 아니라, 이유를 말하는 내용

9. Don't forget to take pictures when they come in.
▶ 과거에 있었던 일을 잊지 말라는 게 아니라, 앞으로 할 일을 잊지 말라는 내용

MEMO

MEMO

MEMO

독해

Reading TUTOR 리딩튜터

체계적인 초·중·고등 독해 프로그램

Starter 1 | 2 | 3
Junior 1 | 2 | 3 | 4
Challenger 1 | 2 | 3

READING EXPERT

중고등 대상 7단계 원서 독해 교재

Level 1 | Level 2 | Level 3 | Level 4 | Level 5 | Advanced 1 | Advanced 2

기강잡고

기본을 강하게 잡아주는 고등영어

독해 잡는 필수 문법 | 기초 잡는 유형 독해

빠독 바독 (빠른독해 바른독해)

빠른 독해를 위한 바른 선택

기초세우기 | 구문독해 | 유형독해 | 수능실전

The 상승

독해 기본기에서 수능 실전 대비까지

직독직해편 | 문법독해편 | 구문편 | 수능유형편 | 어법·어휘+유형편

수능

맞수

맞춤형 수능영어 단기특강 시리즈

구문독해 기본편 | 실전편
수능유형 기본편 | 실전편
수능문법어법 기본편 | 실전편
수능듣기 기본편 | 실전편
빈칸추론

pick 수능유형

핵심만 콕 찍어주는 수능유형 필독서

독해 기본 | 독해 실력 | 듣기

수능 1up

수능 영어 1등급 올려주는 상위권 수능 독해서

빈순삽함 유형편 | 간접연계 소재편

얇빠 얇고 빠른 미니 모의고사 10+2회

수능 핵심유형들만 모아 얇게! 회당 10문항으로 빠르게!

입문 | 기본 | 실전

수능만만

만만한 수능영어 모의고사

기본 영어듣기 20회 | 기본 영어듣기 35회+5회 | 기본 영어독해 10+1회 | 기본 문법·어법·어휘 150제 | 영어듣기 20회 | 영어듣기 35회 | 영어독해 20회 | 어법·어휘 228제

NE능률 영어교육연구소

NE능률 영어교육연구소는 전문성과 탁월성을 기반으로
영어 교육 트렌드를 선도합니다.

2027 수능대비 다빈출코드 듣기

펴 낸 날	2026년 1월 5일 (개정판 제1쇄)
펴 낸 이	이정진
펴 낸 곳	(주)NE능률
지 은 이	NE능률 영어교육연구소
개발책임	김지현
개 발	전성호
영문교열	Curtis Thompson
디자인책임	오영숙
디 자 인	장혜진
제작책임	한성일
등록번호	제1-68호
I S B N	979-11-253-5080-4

＊이 책의 저작권은 (주)NE능률에 있습니다.
＊본 교재의 독창적인 내용에 대한 일체의 무단 전재 모방은 법률로 금지되어 있습니다.

대표전화	02 2014 7114
홈페이지	www.neungyule.com
주 소	서울시 마포구 월드컵북로 396(상암동) 누리꿈스퀘어 비즈니스타워 10층